PENGUIN ACADEMICS

THE STRUGGLE FOR FREEDOM
A History of African Americans

Combined Volume

SECOND EDITION

CLAYBORNE CARSON
Stanford University

EMMA J. LAPSANSKY-WERNER
Haverford College

GARY B. NASH
University of California, Los Angeles

Prentice Hall

Boston   Columbus   Indianapolis   New York   San Francisco   Upper Saddle River
Amsterdam   Cape Town   Dubai   London   Madrid   Milan   Munich   Paris   Montréal   Toronto
Delhi   Mexico City   Sao Paulo   Sydney   Hong Kong   Seoul   Singapore   Taipei   Tokyo

Publisher: Charlyce Jones-Owen
Editorial Assistant: Maureen Diana
Senior Marketing Manager: Maureen Prado Roberts
Production Manager: Fran Russello
Cover Art Director: Jayne Conte
Cover Designer: Suzanne Behnke
Manager, Visual Research: Beth Brenzel
Image Cover Permission Coordinator: Karen Sanatar
Cover Art: Mark Ralston/AFP/Getty Images
Composition and Full-Service Project Management: Niraj Bhatt/Aptara®, Inc.
Printer/Binder: Courier North Chelmsford
Cover Printer: Courier North Chelmsford
Text Font: Glypha

Credits and acknowledgments borrowed from other sources and reproduced, with permission, in this textbook appear on appropriate page within text.

Library of Congress Cataloging-in-Publication Data

Carson, Clayborne,
  The struggle for freedom : a history of African Americans / Clayborne Carson, Emma J. Lapsansky-Werner, Gary B. Nash.—2nd ed.
    p. cm.
  ISBN-13: 978-0-13-405674-6 (combined volume)
  ISBN-10: 0-13-405674-4 (combined volume)
  ISBN-13: 978-0-13-405676-0 (v. 1)
  ISBN-10: 0-13-405676-0 (v. 1)
  ISBN-13: 978-0-13-405677-7 (v. 2)
  ISBN-10: 0-13-405677-9 (v. 2)
  1. African Americans—History. I. Lapsansky-Werner, Emma J. (Emma Jones), 1945- II. Nash, Gary B. III. Title.
  E185.C36 2011
  973'.0496073—dc22

2010038678

2 3 4 5 6 7 8 9 10   V092   17 16 15

www.pearsonhighered.com

ISBN 10:   0-13-405674-4
ISBN 13: 978-0-13-405674-6

Clayborne Carson

CLAYBORNE CARSON was born in Buffalo, New York. He received his BA, MA, and PhD from the University of California, Los Angeles, and has taught at Stanford University since 1974. He has also been a visiting professor or fellow at the University of California, Berkeley, Emory University, Emory University, Harvard University, and the Center for Advanced Studies in the Behavioral Sciences at Stanford. Active during his undergraduate years in the civil rights and antiwar movements, Carson has published many works on the African American protest movements of the post–World War II period. His first book, *In Struggle: SNCC and the Black Awakening of the 1960s* (1981) won the Frederick Jackson Turner Award from the Organization of American Historians. He has also edited *Malcolm X: The FBI File* (1991) and served as an advisor for the award-winning PBS series on the civil rights movement entitled *Eyes on the Prize,* as well as for other documentaries, such as *Freedom on My Mind* (1994), *Blacks and Jews* (1997), *Brother Outsider: The Life of Bayard Rustin* (2002), *Negroes with Guns: Rob Williams and Black Power* (2005), and *Have You Heard from Johannesburg?* (2010). Carson is director of the Martin Luther King, Jr., Research and Education Institute at Stanford, an outgrowth of his work since 1985 as editor of King's papers and director of the King Papers Project, which is producing a comprehensive fourteen-volume edition of *The Papers of Martin Luther King, Jr.* The biographical approach of *The Struggle for Freedom: A History of African Americans* grew out of Carson's vision. He has used it with remarkable results in his course at Stanford.

Emma J. Lapsansky-Werner

EMMA J. LAPSANSKY-WERNER received her BA, MA, and PhD from the University of Pennsylvania. From 1973 to 1990 she taught at Temple University, the University of Pennsylvania, and Princeton University. Since 1990 she has been a professor of history and curator of special collections at Haverford College. From her experience with voter registration in Mississippi in the 1960s, she became a historian to try to help correct misinformation about black Americans. Her professional, research, and teaching interests—all informed by her concern for the African American story–include family and community life, antebellum cities, Quaker history, and religion and popular culture in nineteenth-century America. Lapsansky-Werner has published on all these topics, including *Back to Africa: Benjamin Coates and the Colonization Movement in America, 1848–1880* (2005, with Margaret Hope Bacon), *Neighborhoods in Transition: William*

Penn's Dream and Urban Reality (1994), and *Quaker Aesthetics: Reflections on a Quaker Ethic in American Design and Consumption, 1720–1920* (2003). She is also a contributor to Yale University Press's *Benjamin Franklin, In Search of a Better World* (2005) and to several anthologies on the history of Pennsylvania. She hopes that *The Struggle for Freedom: A History of African Americans* will help broaden the place of African American history in the scholarly consciousness, expanding the trend toward including black Americans as not just objects of public policy, but also as leaders in the international struggle for human justice, and participants in the development of our global community. Through stories, black Americans are presented as multidimensional, alive with their own ambitions, visions, and human failings.

Gary B. Nash

GARY B. NASH was born in Philadelphia and received his BA and PhD in history from Princeton University. He taught at Princeton briefly and since 1966 has been a faculty member at the University of California, Los Angeles, where he teaches colonial American, revolutionary American, and African American history and directs the National Center for History in the Schools. He served as president of the Organization of American Historians in 1994–95. Nash's many books on early American history include *Quakers and Politics: Pennsylvania, 1681–1726* (1968); *Red, White, and Black: The Peoples of Early North America* (six editions since 1974); *The Urban Crucible: Social Change, Political Consciousness, and the Origins of the American Revolution* (1979); *Forging Freedom: The Formation of Philadelphia's Black Community, 1720–1840* (1988); *Race and Revolution* (1990); *Forbidden Love: The Secret History of Mixed-Race America* (1999; 2nd ed., 2010); *First City: Philadelphia and the Forging of History Memory* (2001); *Landmarks of the American Revolution* (2003); *The Unknown American Revolution: The Unruly Birth of Democracy and the Struggle to Create America* (2005); *The Forgotten Fifth: African Americans in the Age of Revolution* (2006); *Friends of Liberty: Thomas Jefferson, Tadeuz Kosciuszko, and Agrippa Hull* (2008); *Liberty Bell* (2010); and *The American People: Creating a Nation and a Society* (eight editions since 1981. Nash wanted to coauthor this book with two good friends and esteemed colleagues because of their common desire to bring the story of the African American people before a wide audience of students and history lovers. African American history has always had a central place in his teaching, and it has been pivotal to his efforts to bring an inclusive, multicultural American history into the K–12 classrooms in this nation and abroad.

brief contents

BRIEF CONTENTS

vi

detailed contents

CHAPTER 13   "Colored" Becomes "Negro" in the Progressive Era 320

CHAPTER 14   The Making of a "New Negro": World War I to the Great Depression 349

preface

Those who profess to favor freedom and yet depreciate agitation, are people who want crops without ploughing the ground; they want rain without thunder and lightning; they want the ocean without the roar of its many waters. The struggle may be a moral one, or it may be a physical one, or it may be both. But it must be a struggle. Power concedes nothing without a demand; it never has and it never will.

—Frederick Douglass

The Struggle for Freedom is a narrative of the black experience in America, using a distinctive biographical approach to guide the story and animate the history. This biographical approach places African American lives at the center of the narrative. In each chapter, individual African Americans are depicted initiating and responding to the historical changes of the era. Life stories capture the rush of events that envelop individuals and illuminate the momentous decisions that, collectively, shape the American past and present.

This book introduces the concepts, milestones, and significant figures of African American history. Inasmuch as that history is grounded in struggle—in the consistent and insistent call to the United States to deliver on the constitutional promises made to all its citizens—this book is also an American history text, weaving African American history into the main narrative of American history, including developments in the nation's economy, politics, religion, family, and arts and letters.

The biographical approach of *The Struggle for Freedom* uses African American lives as the basis for understanding, and analyzing not only of the black experience in America but of American history as a whole. Too often, expressions such as *the sweep of history, the transit of civilization, manifest destiny,* and *the march of progress* plant the idea that history is inexorable, unalterable, and foreordained—beyond the capacity of men and women to change. That idea has been used to justify a winner's history, an approach that diminishes the full humanness of those who were captured and traded as slaves and those who struggled for generations against entrenched prejudice. To promote the understanding that no individual is forever trapped within iron circumstances beyond his or her ability to alter, every chapter in this book is grounded in the experience of *people* as agents of their own liberation rather than simply as victims of oppression.

The human stories in *The Struggle for Freedom* illustrate the ways in which African Americans resisted slavery and became part of an international movement to eliminate the slave trade and ultimately the entire system of slavery.

These stories also depict the sustained freedom struggles of African American peasants, who were, in the period after the civil war, mostly illiterate, without land of their own, and denied basic human rights. Like peasants elsewhere in the world, they sought greater opportunities by educating themselves and their children, by migrating to urban areas, by creating their own churches and self-help organizations, and by resisting oppression in all its forms. During the twentieth century, just as peasants and the descendants of peasants in Africa and Asia were overcoming colonialism, African Americans overcame the systematic segregation and discrimination of the American Jim Crow system. Hands that once picked cotton could now pick presidents, and, early in the twenty-first century, they indeed helped elect their descendant of an African peasant as president of the United States.

Coverage and Organization

The remarkable and distinctive people and events of American history are all featured in *The Struggle for Freedom.* In these pages, readers will learn of the Europeans' first encounter with native peoples and a new environment; they will see how the American Revolution raised the ideal of human society cleansed of slavery. They will encounter other pivotal events of American history: African American responses to the Haitian Revolution; the Missouri Compromise; sectional conflicts; wars, from the Civil War through this century's war against terrorism; and the Civil Rights Movement for our times. Readers will also be able to examine cultural and economic trends throughout American history—from the resistance poetry of revolutionary-era Phillis Wheatley and nineteenth-century artists such as Henry Ossawa Tanner through the development of urban communities and technology that support such movements as modern-day hip-hop.

Chapters 1 through 7 of *The Struggle for Freedom* explore the period up to 1830, when most Africans in North America were enslaved. The book begins, as all human history begins, in Africa with ancient history and the rise of empires in West and Central Africa during the period American and western historians think of as the Middle Ages. European contact with West and Central Africa and the growth of the Atlantic slave trade are followed by an analysis of the new conditions of slavery in the Americas. Because Africans were not all enslaved in the same ways and in the same conditions, the chapters treat the formation of notions about race and how they figured in the descent into slavery in different zones of European settlement—French, Dutch, Portuguese, and Spanish as well as English—in the Americas. The galvanizing effect of the American Revolution and the decades thereafter during which free black people in the North and in the South built families, founded churches, forged friendships and communities, and struggled for autonomy and dignity are central themes.

Chapters 8 through 14 examine pivotal junctures in African American history that parallel the American focus on expansion, reform, and nationality. The 1830s marked the first years when the majority of black Americans were not forced immigrants but rather were born on American soil. Echoing the religious reawakening that undergirded both abolitionism and a vigorous defense of slavery, enslaved and free African Americans alike claimed their voice in an international antebellum debate about the future of American democracy. Then, through a long and merciless Civil War, the end of slavery, and the South's attempt to re-create the essence of slavery, black Americans persisted in holding forth, before white Americans and the world, the guarantees of equality and citizenship built into the new constitutional amendments. The post-Civil War dispersal of newly freed African Americans to every corner of North America shows how, in the face of a still-hostile white America that abandoned Reconstruction, black people built families, communities, and viable economic lives; established churches, mutual aid and literary societies, and businesses; launched schools and publishing ventures as they sought to transform themselves from slaves to soldiers and citizens and to wrest equality and justice from white America.

The last eight chapters of the book, Chapters 15 through 22, address African American life in modern America. The narrative explores the increasing diversity of African Americans and examines how—during world wars, the Great Depression, and other momentous national and international transformations—they struggled for full participation and full citizenship in a society still marred by racist attitudes and practices. Throughout twentieth-century scientific, technological, and economic changes, one theme permeates African American strategies for securing justice and equal opportunity: the ongoing struggle for a positive sense of identity amidst racism and destructive racial stereotypes. Whether in fighting the nation's wars; helping build the modern economy; adding to urban dynamics and to the explosion of cultural creativity through innovations in music, art, film, dance, and literature; inserting themselves into political leadership and rhetoric, or emerging on the political stage at the local, state, and national level, African Americans in the last century are portrayed as the principal innovators of the nation's most important liberation movement.

Special Features and Pedagogy

Complementing the multitude of stories connecting African American lives and American history, *The Struggle for Freedom* includes several features designed to increase the book's usefulness and enhance its appeal to readers.

- *Chapter-Opening Vignettes:* Each chapter begins with a personal story—such as the rebelliousness of Venture Smith (Chapter 4) or the wartime experience of First Lieutenant Thomas Edward Jones (Chapter 14)—that draws the reader into the chapter narrative, illuminates the chapter period, and heralds the chapter's events and themes.
- *Chronologies:* Chapter chronologies, placed at the beginning of each chapter following the opening vignette, alert readers to the significant developments in African American history to be covered in the chapter.

- *Conclusions:* Each chapter ends with a summary of the main ideas and events discussed in the chapter, helping the reader recall the essential points of the narrative. A look ahead to the next chapter prepares the reader for the next installment of the story.
- *Visual History:* The graphic materials and illustrations—maps, charts, photographs, lithographs, and paintings—that enrich each chapter impart an additional dimension to the narrative, allowing the reader to see history as participants saw it. Tables that summarize a sequence of events or milestones—for example, judicial decisions, legislative acts, and protest movement flashpoints—facilitate the reader's comprehension of complex or subtle concepts.

African American history has achieved breadth and depth in recent decades, indeed has become one of the most vibrant components of American history, reshaping the way we understand everything from the American economy to innovations in science, politics, and the arts. Reflecting that dynamism, *The Struggle for Freedom* is not a story set in stone. Drawing on both classic and recent historical research, it crafts a new synthesis that challenges our understandings of the past and offers new insights about differing historical possibilities. As it engages the reader in viewing history through the lens of many biographies and through the perspectives of people who lived those struggles, *The Struggle for Freedom* seeks to ensure, in the words of Langston Hughes's famous poem, that "America Will Be."

What's New in the Second Edition

The major change in this second edition is the addition of Chapter 22, Barack Obama and the Promise of Change, 2005–Present. This new chapter considers the historic campaign and election of Barack Obama as well as the key events of the time period, from the devastation of Hurricane Katrina through the end of the Bush years, up to the key events of the first year of the Obama administration. Additional changes throughout the book include

- New critical thinking questions, Questions for Review and Reflection, have been included at the end of each chapter;
- a new discussion of the *Liberator* story (1831) that presages the election of Barack Obama in 2008 (Chapter 8);
- an expanded discussion of the life story of Nancy Johnson (Chapter 10);
- new information on Colonel Charles Young to highlight African American participation in the development of early national parks and conservation (Chapter 12);
- new discussion of the rise of Barack Obama and his campaign for the presidency (Chapter 22);
- new coverage of the war on terrorism (Chapter 22).

Supplements

The following supplements are available for download on Pearson's Instructor's Resource Center. The Instructor's Resource Center is a password-protected Web site where instructors can download the online supplements for *The Struggle for Freedom* described below: (Contact your local Pearson representative for an access code, or visit www.pearsonhighered.com/irc.)

Instructor's Manual

This resource contains learning objectives, significant themes, chapter outlines, enrichment ideas, and further resources for each chapter.

Test Item File

The test bank includes multiple-choice, true/false, and essay questions for each chapter. Multiple-choice and true/false questions are referenced by topic and text page number.

PowerPoints

Presentation resources for the instructor include maps, figures, and images from the text and selected documents for use in the classroom.

mysearchlab

MySearchLab is a unique research and writing resource that offers resources for researching and writing in history, including interdisciplinary journals, writing resources, and information for writing effectively—namely, information on the writing process, the research process, and avoiding plagiarism. For more information, contact your local Pearson representative, or visit www.mysearchlab.com.

For Further Interest

African-American Biographies, Volume 1 and Volume 2

Volume 1 ISBN: 0-13-193785-5; Volume 2 ISBN: 0-13-193794-4

This collection of brief biographical sketches of the many African American figures represented in the text serves as an indispensable companion to *The Struggle for Freedom.*

Sources of the African-American Past, Second Edition

ISBN: 0-32-116216-1

This collection of primary sources covers themes in the African American experience from the West African background to the present. Balanced between political and social history, the documents offer a vivid snapshot of the lives of African Americans in different historical periods. The collection includes documents representing women and different regions of the United States.

Penguin Books

Prentice Hall has partnered with Penguin in order to offer you a comprehensive collection of seminal African-American works, both fiction and non-fiction. All of these titles are available at a reduced price when purchased in conjunction with *The Struggle for Freedom*. For more information about these and other Penguin titles, contact your local Pearson representative.

Frederick Douglass, *My Bondage and My Freedom*

Frederick Douglass, *Narrative of the Life of Frederick Douglass* (Penguin Classics Edition)

W. E. B. Du Bois, *The Souls of Black Folk*

Olaudah Equiano, *The Interesting Narrative and Other Writings*

Nelson George, *The Death of Rhythm & Blues*

John Howard Griffin, *Black Like Me* (Penguin Classics Edition)

Lorraine Hansberry, *A Raisin in the Sun: The Unfilmed Original Screenplay*

Joel Chandler Harris, *Nights with Uncle Remus*

Joseph Harris, *Africans and Their History*

Harriet Jacobs, *Incidents in the Life of a Slave Girl*

James Weldon Johnson, *The Autobiography of an Ex-Colored Man*

Martin Luther King Jr., *Why We Can't Wait*

Nella Larsen, *Passing*

Julius Lester, *From Slave Ship to Freedom Road*

Ellen Levine, *Freedom's Children*

James McBride, *The Color of Water: A Black Man's Tribute to His Mother*

Toni Morrison, *The Bluest Eye*

Rosa Parks, *Rosa Parks: My Story*

Patricia Raybon, *My First White Friend: Confessions of Love, Race, and Forgiveness*

Randall Robinson, *The Debt*

Harriet Beecher Stowe, *Uncle Tom's Cabin*

Clinton L. Taulbert, *Once Upon a Time When We Were Colored*

Sojourner Truth, *The Narrative of Sojourner Truth*

Mark Twain, *The Adventures of Huckleberry Finn*

Various, *Against Slavery*

Various, *The Classic Slave Narratives*

Various, *The Portable Harlem Renaissance Reader*

Rebecca Walker, *Black, White, and Jewish*

Booker T. Washington, *Up from Slavery*

Phillis Wheatley, *The Complete Writings*

Juan Williams, *Eyes on the Prize: America's Civil Rights Years 1954–65*

Harriet L. Wilson, *Our Nig*

August Wilson, *Fences*

August Wilson, *Joe Turner's Come and Gone*

Acknowledgments

We gratefully acknowledge Abel A. Bartley, Clemson University; Hasan Kwame Jeffries, The Ohio State University; and Derrick White, Florida Atlantic University for their insightful reviews and comments in preparation for this new edition.

The authors would like to thank the staff of Special Collections at Haverford College and the Crisis Publishing Co., Inc., the publisher of the magazine of the National Association for the Advancement of Colored People, for the use of material published in the November 1935 and June 1938 issues of *Crisis*. The project also owes a monumental debt of gratitude to Ann Grogg. Ann was by turns editor, counselor, circuit rider, diplomat, and loyal friend. Her broad and subtle knowledge of history and of those who teach and learn it were crucial to our progress. So too was her deft editing without altering the authors' voices or meaning.

Clay Carson offers particular thanks to Damani Rivers, Caitrin McKiernan, and Sarah Overton of the King Research and Education Institute at Stanford University for their exceptional research assistance. Susan A. Carson also helped with editing the manuscript. Tenisha Armstrong, Miya Woolfalk, and other King Project staff members and student researchers offered useful comments on the manuscript at various stages of its development. Emma Lapsansky-Werner extends a special thank-you to student research assistants James Chappel, Sarah Hartman, and Caroline Boyd, and to her ever-patient husband, Dickson Werner. Gary Nash thanks research assistants Grace Lu and Marian Olivas for their good cheer in carrying out many tasks.

—*The Authors*

CHAPTER 1

Ancient Africa

African Storytelling and African American History

The storytellers of the Yoruba people of West Africa, the *griots,* have a saying passed down for generations: "However far the stream flows, it never forgets its source." This wisdom is as fresh today as it was a thousand years ago.

From their first arrival in the Americas, Africans knew that without history they would be water without a source, trees without roots. Those roots derive from oral cultures in Africa, where young people heard adults tell stories about the origins of their own village-based people. Other stories taught children what it means to live properly. Still others "handed on the torch," as many Africans say, by capturing the sweep of a people's long history.

Once they were wrenched from their homelands, enslaved Africans continued to keep ancient traditions alive—passing down to their children the stories, morals, and values of their ancestors. Under slavery, the desire to preserve memory of long-ago traditions, as well as more recent experiences, intensified. As soon as they could, Africans began recounting the horrors of capture and transport to the Americas (the Middle Passage), the desperate struggle for survival under slavery, and the bravery and resolve of those who struck out for freedom. History could not ward off a brutal master's blows or break slavery's chains. Nevertheless, it sustained Africans' souls and nourished their hopes for a better life.

For many generations, Africans in America nurtured the collective memory of their history through oral storytelling. They had few opportunities to publish written accounts because most of them were in bondage to masters who forbade them to learn how to read and write. That began to change in the era of the American Revolution. Enslaved Africans such as Phillis Wheatley and free black people such as Venture Smith were the first black writers to find white patrons who helped publish their recorded thoughts and experiences. In the decades before the Civil War, a handful of black historians, such as Boston's William C. Nell and Philadelphia's William Douglass, published the first histories of black people in North America. Meanwhile, former bondsman

Chronology

(BCE means "Before Common Era"; CE means "Common Era," with years coinciding with the Christian "BC" and "AD" dates.)

3,750,000 BCE	Ancient ancestors of humans in East Africa.
1,800,000 BCE	The oldest humans, *Homo erectus,* in East Africa.
500,000 BCE	Early human ancestors learn to use fire.
160,000 BCE	*Homo sapiens* migrate out of Africa.
3100 BCE	Pharaohs unify Egypt.
1570–1085 BCE	The New Kingdom in Egypt.
750–670 BCE	The Kushites rule Egypt.
c. 450 BCE	Nok iron smelting begins.
332 BCE–c. 400 CE	Greece and then Rome control Egypt.
c. 100–200 CE	Bantu-speaking people migrate south.
c. 500–1100 CE	The rise of the kingdom of Ghana.
c. 610 CE	Muhammad founds the Islamic faith.
632–750 CE	Muslim faith spreads across North Africa.
c. 1000 CE	The kingdom of Benin takes form.
1324 CE	Mansa Musa's pilgrimage to Mecca.
c. 1460s–1590s CE	Songhai kingdom controls West African trade.
1235 CE	Mali is the major power in West Africa.
1435 CE	Songhai breaks away from the kingdom of Mali.
1591 CE	Morocco captures Timbuktu and Gao.

Frederick Douglass wrote an autobiographical account of his travails in slavery and his long walk to freedom. His story carried such power and poignancy that it made him an international figure. A people whose memory had been officially suppressed began to regain their voice.

Most nineteenth-century African American histories did not enjoy a wide readership. White Americans, in particular, ignored them. In recent years, however, these accounts have been republished and have attracted a growing audience. They have also inspired contemporary black historians to build on their work. Twentieth-century historians such as W. E. B. Du Bois, Rayford Logan, Carter Woodson, and John Hope Franklin insisted that African American history be included in the American story. A half-century ago, a young preacher named Martin Luther King, Jr., prophesied on the night of the Montgomery bus boycott in 1955, "When the history books are written in future generations, the historians will say, 'There lived a great people—a black people—who injected new meaning and dignity into the veins of civilization.'" King's prophecy has come to be.

The story of humankind began several million years ago in East Africa, where, according to archaeologists, humans first made their appearance on Earth. Egypt gave birth to the first great African civilization. That civilization, in turn, shaped ancient Greece and Rome. The spread of Islam and the emergence of West and Central African kingdoms set the stage for an era in which millions of African people were torn from their homelands and forced across the Atlantic to serve as slaves in the Americas.

This chapter looks at the cultures of these African peoples—and some of the individuals who embodied their ways of life. By understanding the societies these men and women came from, the gods they worshiped, the family traditions they cherished, and the social systems and artistic works they created, we will see them as more than faceless units of labor carried across the ocean. By seeing them as peoples with long, rich histories, we can better understand their—and our own—experiences in the Americas.

From Human Beginnings to the Rise of Egypt

For generations, Yoruba storytellers told young people how Olodumare, the god of the sky, sent two sons down to Earth with a bag, a hen, and a chameleon. The bag contained soft white sand and rich black soil. One son sprinkled the white sand on the water's surface. From the sand sprouted a palm tree. The chameleon gingerly stepped across the sand, discovering that the grains supported its weight. Seeing this, the other son spread the soil over the sand. Then the hen scratched in the dark earth, scattering it in all directions. Pleased with his sons' work, Olodumare sent Aje—goddess of prosperity—from Heaven to dwell there for the rest of her life. The sky god sent his sons additional gifts: maize to plant for food; cowrie shells for trading; and iron bars for forging hoes, knives, and other tools. In this way, Olodumare created Yorubaland.

Like the Yoruba, every human society has developed creation myths to make sense of its beginnings and to understand the mighty forces of nature. Since the emergence of humankind, a rich array of creation stories has arisen. Around the world, these stories yield many interpretations of the first stirrings of humankind. The Yoruba creation story leads us to consider the long history of ancient Africa—from human beginnings through the flourishing of Egyptian civilization to the Roman and Greek conquest of North Africa.

Human Beginnings in East Africa

Scientists offer several explanations of how the Earth was formed and how human beings came to inhabit it. Though much remains to be discovered, the common scientific understanding is that all humans descended from hominids. These humanlike primates had enlarged brains and could walk upright on two legs. Archaeologists have found the oldest fossilized remains of these hominids in eastern Africa. As early as 1871, Charles Darwin proposed in his *Descent of Man* that Africa was probably the birthplace of humankind. But this notion offended Europeans, who saw their own race as superior to that of the African. Some Europeans thus maintained that human life began not in Africa but in Europe—specifically in Germany's Neander Valley, where fossil remains of an early human species dubbed *Neanderthal man* were discovered in 1856.

Not until 1925, when an archaeologist found a child's skull in a limestone cave at Taung, in South Africa, did the European origins thesis come under scientific scrutiny. Apelike in appearance, the skull also had human characteristics in its forehead and nose structure. Examination revealed it as the most ancient example of *Australopithecine*—a creature who walked upright around three million years ago. Once again, the notion that humans emerged in Africa gained credence.

Then, in the 1950s, the British anthropologists Louis and Mary Leakey found additional fossils of the *Australopithecine* species in East Africa's Olduvai Gorge. Scholars soon felt convinced that human life indeed began in Africa. In 1961, the Leakeys found confirming evidence of the evolution from primate to human being—fossil bones resting alongside simple stone tools. Dating technology revealed that members of this first group of human ancestors were toolmakers who lived between 1.5 and 3.75 million years ago in East Africa.

More evidence came to light in 1974 in Hadar, Ethiopia. There, paleoanthropologists (who study human origins) discovered "Lucy," the first example of *Homo erectus,* or upright human. This exceptionally complete skeleton, about $3\frac{1}{2}$ feet tall, dates back about 1.8 million years. Thanks to this finding, scientists now widely accept the idea that the ancient ancestors of all humans originated in Africa about 120,000 to 160,000 years ago. These ancestors are called *Homo sapiens*—meaning "wise human."

Though a small group of dissenters argue that hominids originated in several regions of the world and evolved separately in Africa, the Middle East, Europe, and Asia, new discoveries have consolidated the "out of Africa" scenario. In 2002, for example, three fossilized *Homo sapiens* skulls excavated in Herto, Ethiopia, were dated through argon-isotope analysis to about 160,000 years ago, solidly supporting the "out of Africa" theory. Though many African Americans speak of "Mother Africa" to signify the homeland of their forebears, most modern scientists agree that Africa is the mother of *all* humans.

The Rise of Egyptian Civilization

By at least 60,000 years ago, humans began to migrate out of East Africa to what we today call the Middle East, Asia, and Australia. About 20,000 years later, they appeared in Europe. There they made spear and harpoon points for hunting large fish and big animals such as the wild ox and hippopotamus, and they crafted thin scrapers for cleaning hides. These nomadic groups discovered ways to increase their food supply by domesticating and herding animals. They also made simple clothing out of hides to protect themselves against the cold. By about 10,000 BCE, some of these groups began settling along the banks of the Jordan River in the Middle East. By 6000 BCE, they were harvesting millet and sorghum (grains used to make bread) as they settled along the Nile, the world's longest river, in today's Egypt. This area became the most densely populated part of the ancient world.

Over the next 4,000 years, Egyptian civilization flourished and spread. Learning to use the predictable flooding of the mighty Nile to irrigate crops in a land of little rainfall, early hydrology engineers transformed Egypt from a sparsely populated and forbidding desert into a thriving civilization. By about 3100 BCE, local kingdoms began to emerge throughout Egypt, led by rulers called *pharaohs*. Over many centuries, rival kingdoms set aside their differences and united along the Nile's 4,000-mile-long banks.

Strong, centralized governments evolved out of these kingdoms, headed by pharaohs who claimed godlike power. These rulers commanded the labor of a vast peasantry. They amassed enough wealth from the production of crop surpluses to erect royal tombs, temples, and pyramids that showcased their power. Pharaohs drew their strength from civil servants who collected taxes and supervised irrigation projects. These same servants also compiled and maintained tax and administrative records. To record information, they used a sophisticated system of writing that consisted of *hieroglyphs*, picture signs that represented concepts and numbers.

In the New Kingdom period (1570–1085 BCE), the pharaohs accumulated large armies and led them into wars of expansion against the peoples of Palestine, Syria, and Nubia. The massive statues and temples built by Rameses II, which visitors to Egypt can view today, testify to the power of the empire forged out of conquered lands. As the realm extended its reach, cultural change accelerated as well. Ancient Egypt became a crossroads for merchants and other enterprising men and women seeking to trade with other societies. Within this vast realm, a composite culture arose that comprised Mediterranean peoples from the west, Semitic nomads from the east, and dark-skinned traders and farmers from Kushite and Ethiopian societies to the south.

The Egyptian civilization dominated the lands bordering the Mediterranean Sea for 3,000 years—from about 3100 to roughly 332 BCE, when the Greeks invaded the kingdom. Indeed, ancient Egypt stands as the longest-lasting civilization in human history. Scholars trace about thirty dynasties during this epoch. Perhaps no dynasty has captured the imaginations of students of history more than that of the female pharaoh Hatshepsut, who reigned during the New Kingdom period. This shrewd and skillful ruler built a great temple on the banks of the Nile and restored numerous old temples that foreign invaders had destroyed. Hatshepsut's successor, Thutmose III, became one of Egypt's mightiest pharaohs. Through military expeditions into the eastern Mediterranean region, he extended his empire into Palestine and Syria. Later rulers continued to enlarge the realm while building impressive monuments at home. For example, the three pyramids at Giza still testify to Egyptian achievements in hydraulic engineering, architecture, and sculpture.

Owing to its location, Egypt played virtually no role in the forced migration of Africans to the Americas that unfolded centuries later. Rather, it became a transshipment point for West Africans slated for Muslim slave markets to the east.

Debates over Black Egypt

Since the eighteenth century, African Americans have cited Egypt's greatness as a way to counter charges that "the dark continent" was home to "savages" useful only as labor for other, more civilized peoples. Europeans had long recognized ancient Egypt as a cradle of civilization and the source of many ideas that powerfully shaped ancient Greece and Rome. In denigrating African peoples, however, these same Europeans mentally plucked Egypt out of Africa and Africans out of Egypt. Yet as any glance at a world map shows, Egypt is solidly part of the African continent.

For generations, African Americans fought the notion that Egypt was not part of Africa. They referred to Egypt as an African society, and many called the Egyptians "Ethiopians." This name was a reference to nearby Ethiopia, with which Egypt had traded extensively over many centuries. By the 1870s, the first historians who tried to write a comprehensive African American history—such as George Washington Williams and Edward Blyden—pointedly began their narratives with accounts of Egypt (see Chapter 11).

Today, scholars still argue passionately over whether the ancient Egyptians were "black," "white," or racially mixed and the degree to which Egypt influenced ancient Greece and Rome. In 1987, Martin Bernal's *Black Athena: The Afroasiatic Roots of Classical Civilization,* set off a furious controversy. Bernal claimed that dark-skinned Egyptian and Semitic peoples played a significant role in the making of Greek civilization, especially in its mathematics, philosophy, and religion. Modern Western civilization, he concluded, owes a great debt to ancient Africa.

Though many scholars dispute Bernal's findings, few deny that they have inspired much new research on the circulation of ideas throughout the Mediterranean basin. Traditional scholarship on ancient Greece now looks much more carefully at Egyptian influences and at the connections among the ancient peoples living around the Mediterranean Sea. *Black Athena* has also provoked discussions about whether identity is determined primarily by race and whether race should be the basis of political empowerment and entitlement programs. Many scholars argue that the ancient Egyptians had no concept of "race" or even "blackness." Rather, this school of thought holds, white people invented these notions to exclude and exploit people of color.

Egypt and Nubia

Nubia, the state the Egyptians called Kush, has also caught the attention of modern-day African Americans seeking to reclaim a noble past. In ancient times, Nubia lay to the south of Egypt, along the lower Nile from the first great cataract (waterfall) to below the fifth cataract. For centuries, Egypt's rulers sent ships south along the Nile to trade with the dark-skinned Nubians living in Kush. Both societies benefited from this trade. Still, the pharaohs considered Kush part of their empire, so from time to time they sent armies into the region to maintain their control of its valuable assets.

Although Kush adopted many elements of Egyptian culture, it retained its individual character and political structures. Yet power shifted back and forth between Egypt and Kush. By about 1070 BCE, Egypt fell into decline. Emboldened, the Kushite rulers broke away from Egyptian control. By 750 BCE, the Kushite kings had conquered Upper Egypt and its capital city, Thebes, and seized Memphis, the main Egyptian capital. Later, Shabaka became the first Kushite monarch to control all of Egypt. Yet governing a vast empire is complex, difficult work. The Kushites' rule lasted for less than one hundred years. Slowly, Egypt regained its former stature. During the centuries that followed, the two civilizations—each with its own distinct legacy—remained closely connected. Intermarriage, trade, and the exchange of artistic traditions renewed the fusion of peoples living in the vast Nile River region.

Egypt after the Greek Conquest

In 332 BCE, the twenty-four-year-old Macedonian warrior Alexander the Great swept into Egypt with his armies and added the region to his rapidly expanding collection of conquests. Though the last Egyptian dynasty came to an end, Egypt continued to serve as a cultural crossroads in the ancient Middle East as its Greek rulers spread their influence. For the next three centuries, Alexander's general, Ptolemy, and his successors governed Egypt. As one of their most striking achievements, they founded the city of Alexandria, named after the conquering Macedonian king. A port city on the Mediterranean Sea, Alexandria became a vibrant trading and cultural hub. As a crossroads, the city enabled those who lived around the Mediterranean to exchange goods and ideas with people living in the mineral-rich African interior and in Alexander's conquered lands east into India.

Egypt maintained this central cultural position when, around 500 BCE, the Romans began conquering lands as far west as Spain and dominating the Mediterranean. By about 146 BCE, the Romans had supplanted Greek control in northern Africa. The Roman government made Tunisia and Egypt dependent provinces, extracting from them grain, papyrus for papermaking, and even wild animals that were pitted against one another in the vaunted Roman circus games.

In Roman Africa, trade and periodic warfare accelerated the intermingling of peoples. A new faith, Christianity, spread through the Roman Empire as a result of this intermingling. Christianity sank its roots deep into Egypt in the first century CE. Alexandria, Egypt's commercial center, became one of the most vital hubs of early Christendom. Gradually, Christianity spread west across North Africa among Berber-speaking peoples. It also moved south from Egypt into Nubia where today, in Ethiopia, it still flourishes.

The Spread of Islam

"The seat of Mansa Sulayman [the sultan] was a sprawling, unwalled town set in a 'verdant and hilly' country," wrote the seasoned traveler Abu Abdallah Ibn Battuta in 1351 CE after visiting the capital of Mali, a kingdom in northwest Africa. "The sultan had several enclosed palaces there . . . and covered [them] with colored patterns so that it turned out to be the most elegant of buildings. Surrounding the palaces and mosques were the residences of the citizenry, mud-walled houses roofed with domes of timber and reed. . . . Amongst their good qualities is the small amount of injustice amongst them, for of all people they are the furthest from it. Their sultan does not forgive anyone in any matter to do with injustice. . . . There is also the prevalence of peace in their country, the traveler is not afraid in it nor is he who lives there in fear of the thief or of the robber by violence. They do not interfere with the property of the white man who dies in their country even though it may consist of great wealth, but rather they entrust it to the hand of someone dependable among the white men until it is taken by the rightful claimant."

This vivid excerpt from one of the greatest travelers of premodern times opens a window onto the theme of this section: the spread of Islam in Africa, beginning in the seventh century. Enslaved Africans later carried this faith to North America. The excerpt's author, Ibn Battuta, embodied the rise of Islam. Born in 1304 CE into a family of Muslim legal scholars in Tangier, Morocco (on the southern shore of the Mediterranean Sea), he came of age as Islam was connecting Europe, Asia, and Africa by dint of religious, cultural, and military force. At age twenty-one, Ibn Battuta made a pilgrimage along well-beaten trading routes to the sacred Muslim city of Mecca in Arabia. For more than twenty years he traveled through much of the eastern hemisphere. He visited territories equivalent to forty-four present-day countries and covered about 73,000 miles—three times the distance covered by the legendary Marco Polo. He recorded the words in the excerpt above as he journeyed in 1351 from Fez across the Atlas Mountains to Sijilmasa, a bustling trade center in southern Morocco. Ibn Battuta's careful recordkeeping provides a rare glimpse into a vibrant era in African history.

The Origins of Islam

Islam, meaning "submission to Allah," was born in 610 CE. That year, a young warrior named Muhammad began preaching in his Arabian village after he saw a vision of the angel Gabriel. The angel, Muhammad claimed, had commanded him to spread messages from God to peoples throughout the land. A gifted orator, Muhammad attracted numerous followers and became the founder of the new faith. Like Christianity, Islam is monotheistic; it recognizes only one god. Muhammad preached that he was God's final prophet. The Qur'an, he avowed, was God's word revealed to him. According to Muhammad, the messages he received from God completed the earlier revelations of the Hebrew prophets and Jesus.

Muhammad won many converts because his message had great appeal. The theological foundation of the faith he advocated was easily understood; it did not require an exclusive, elite class of priests. All believers, Muhammad preached, were equal in the eyes of Allah. Through private prayer, kindness and generosity, and fasting before the holy feast of Ramadan, anyone could embrace the will of the One True God. Islam also provided a code for right living. For example, the rich must demonstrate compassion, share their wealth with the poor, and contribute to public charities such as hospitals. Every Muslim (follower of Islam) must forswear drinking alcohol and gambling. Adherents to the faith must struggle to resist temptation and overcome evil. Muslims also held scholarship in high regard and established strict rules governing commercial activities such as bookkeeping, credit arrangements, and dispute resolution.

Islam's Great Reach

Like Christians, Muslims believed they had a mandate from God to convert all people to their faith. Within a century of Muhammad's death in 632, his followers had reached out aggressively, often militarily, and established control over regions larger than those making up the Roman Empire. Spreading rapidly in Arabia, the new faith soon extended into Syria and Mesopotamia. It then moved east all the way to China, west across Mediterranean North Africa to Spain, and south along the Red Sea coast of East Africa. Invaded by Arab Muslims in 639 CE, Egypt became Islamized, just as it had earlier been Christianized under Roman influence. By the tenth century CE, Egypt had a predominantly Muslim population. Islam then spread south from Mediterranean North Africa across the Sahara Desert into the savannah region of western Africa, then called the Sudan. (The word *sudan* is Arabic for "black people." Today's Sudan is an East African nation bordering the Red Sea.)

Islam initially made little headway among villagers in the Sudanese countryside because these men and women lived far from the trading routes that accelerated the spread of ideas. But Islam began to build momentum, first along trading routes and in urban commercial centers and then deeper into the countryside. Five centuries later, when Portuguese traders initiated the slave traffic in West Africa, they found that many of the Africans they packed into Atlantic slave ships were devout Muslims.

Along with Muslim conquering armies, relying heavily on camels, came the exchange of Muslim goods, ideas, technologies, and religious belief. With its emphasis on scholarship, the religion fostered the spread of literacy and book-learning throughout West Africa. African rulers began embracing the Muslim faith.

Islam spread much faster in East Africa, the region south of Egypt and bordering the Red Sea and Indian Ocean. From its origins in Arabia, it spread through India, Ceylon, the East Indies, and China. As trading flourished in this region during the tenth century, Arab traders settled in the ports along Africa's east coast and intermarried with native people. A blended culture emerged. Muslim city-states arose across the continent, with Kilwa and Sofala, the southernmost ports on the Indian Ocean trade route, controlling the export of gold and ivory to the east. Visiting the immense palace, vast irrigated gardens, and imposing Muslim mosque in Kilwa in 1331, that avid traveler Ibn Battuta described the city as "one of the most beautiful and well-constructed towns in the world. . . . The whole of it is elegantly built."

The Kingdoms of West and Central Africa

In 951, a Muslim traveler and geographer named Ibn Hawkal journeyed from Baghdad (in modern-day Iraq) to Sijilmasa, the Moroccan trade center that lay north of the Sahara. There he heard reports that the king of Ghana was the wealthiest of all monarchs on Earth. Traveling south, Ibn Hawkal entered the Ghanaian city of Awdaghost, where he observed a brisk trade in gold. He also learned that the Ghana king's title was *Kaya-Maghan*—Lord of the Gold.

Ibn Hawkal's *Opus Geographicum,* written more than a millennium ago, sheds light on why West African kingdoms proliferated with such energy during the tenth century. The gold trade—and the control of the cross-Sahara traffic it required—united peoples of many cultures living in the grasslands of western Africa. Societies built on the wealth made possible by the gold trade developed along the trading routes. Over time, ambitious local rulers expanded their control to create centralized kingdoms.

By the tenth century, Islam had spread across the Sahara Desert to West Africa, a vast region encompassing desert, grasslands, forests, and woodlands. Like Europeans, most West Africans tilled the soil, developing sophisticated agricultural and livestock management practices. The West Africans' iron-making skills enabled them to make tools that improved their agricultural production.

Iron production began among the Nok, in present-day Nigeria, about 450 BCE, long before peoples on the European continent mastered this technology. By crushing iron ore and smelting it in a forced-air blast furnace, these early Iron Age Africans produced molten metal that they forged into finely crafted tools for cultivating and harvesting crops. Their agricultural productivity soared, igniting a population boom. With larger populations came greater specialization of tasks. Some workers became experts in toolmaking, some in leatherworking. Specialization, in turn, catalyzed greater efficiency and additional technical improvements. This pattern resembled that of the so-called agricultural revolution that independently transformed the Americas, Europe, the Middle East, and elsewhere.

West African societies evolved on the southern flank of the Sahara at different rates. Villages and towns in regions blessed by fertile soil, adequate rainfall, and abundant minerals, as in coastal West Africa, grew rapidly, especially with the advent of interregional trade. Meanwhile, groups living in inhospitable deserts or impenetrable forests remained small and changed slowly.

People tend to migrate when their natural environment changes for the worse. For example, the vast Sahara, once a land of flowing rivers and lush pastures and forests, became uninhabitable to humans owing to climate changes that raised temperatures and lowered rainfall. As the region dried up between about 4000 and 2500 BCE, Saharan peoples moved south in search of more fertile land. First they migrated to oases situated along a strip of grassland, or savannah, on the desert's southern border. Then they headed farther south to the fertile rainforests of the Niger River basin. In these forests, they built some of Africa's greatest kingdoms, all inland civilizations whose trading routes ran overland rather than by sea.

The Kingdom of Ghana

The first of these inland civilizations was the kingdom of Ghana. Developing between the fifth and eleventh centuries CE (after the Roman Empire collapsed

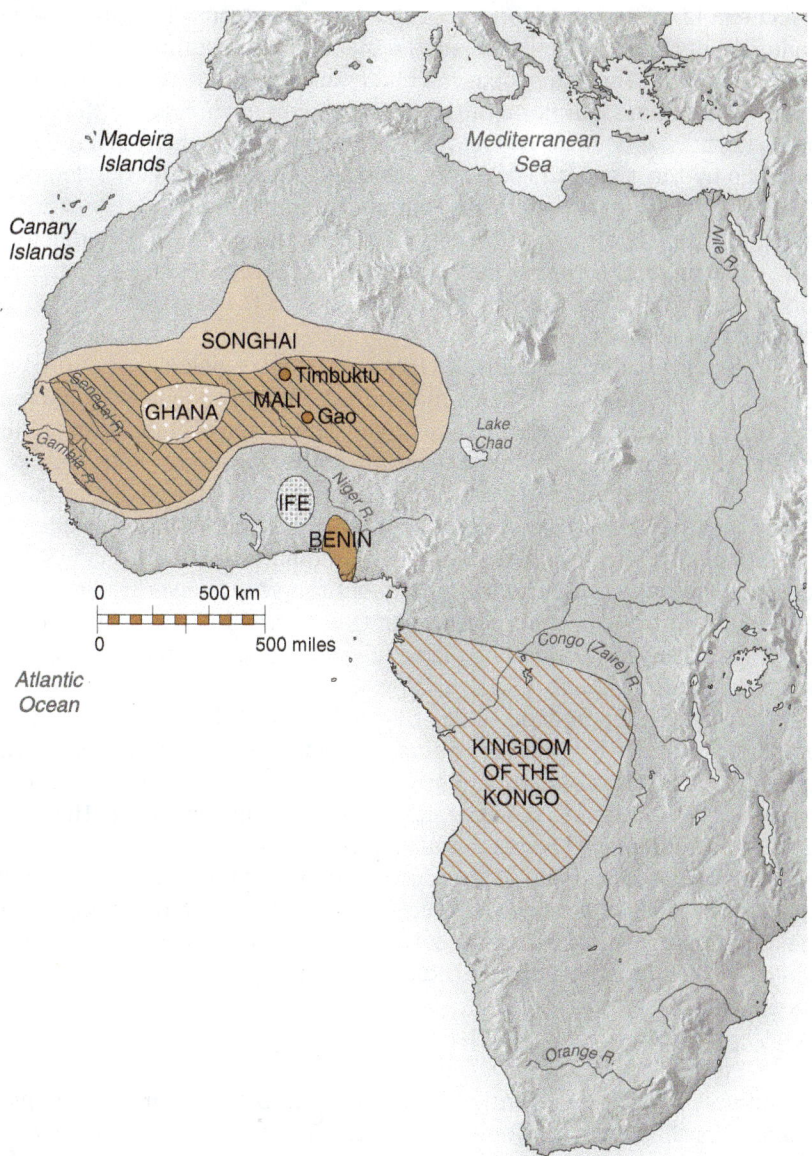

MAP 1.1 West African Kingdoms, 700–1600

Through archaeological research, scholars have learned a great deal about the empires of Ghana, Mali, and Songhai in recent years. Still, their main sources consist of the writings of contemporary Arabic historians such as Leo Africanus. This celebrated Moroccan traveled through Songhai in 1510 and 1513 and left a vivid account of the empire at its peak under Muhammad Ture.

and medieval Europe fell into decline), Ghana occupied a huge territory from the Sahara Desert to the Gulf of Guinea, from the Niger River to the Atlantic Ocean. Ghana evolved from a collection of small villages into a major kingdom noted for its extensive urban settlements, skillfully designed buildings, elaborate sculpture, and effective political and military structure.

The gold trade fueled Ghana's growth and success. The precious metal made Kumbi-Saleh, Ghana's capital, the busiest and wealthiest marketplace in West Africa. The Soninke people of Ghana took advantage of their location just south of the Sahara and north of the Senegal River goldfields to establish trading contacts with Muslim Arabs, who had crossed the Sahara Desert in camel caravans by the eleventh century. In this cross-desert trade, the Soninke exchanged gold for ceramics, glass, oil lamps, and salt from Saharan mines— essential for preserving and flavoring food. From the south, they traded for kola nuts, palm oil, and copper. Their customers carried gold back to Europe, the Middle East, and North Africa, where people used the precious metal to make coins and jewelry.

Gold proved so plentiful that Ghanaian kings devised ways to keep its value high. For example, they maintained a royal monopoly over gold bars, allowing traders to deal only in gold dust. The exhaustion of gold mines in Europe and the Middle East helped boost the value of Ghanaian gold. Even so, salt was so equally coveted that it carried the same value, pound for pound, as gold.

By the time of the western Middle Ages, two-thirds of the gold circulating in the Christian Mediterranean region had originated in Ghana, and Ghanaian gold was the preferred currency throughout the vast Muslim trading network centered in Cairo. The thriving caravan trade spread Muslim influence deep into West Africa, and enterprising Arab merchants came to settle in the empire, especially in Kumbi-Saleh.

With the trading of goods came the exchange of ideas. Arabs brought the first system of writing and numbers to West Africa. The Ghanaian kings adopted Arabic script and appointed Arabs to government positions in charge of trade and taxation. As these Arabs gained influence in Ghana, they spread the Islamic faith. Many Ghanaian rulers kept their traditional religion, however, which emphasized worship of the natural world, and rejected the Muslim principle of patriarchy, whereby royal succession followed the ruling father's lineage. But numerous Ghanaians, especially those living in the cities, converted to Islam. By 1050, Kumbi-Saleh boasted twelve Muslim mosques.

The Kingdom of Mali

Beginning in the late eleventh century, Muslim Berber warriors swept into Ghana from the north, weakening the realm and sowing religious and political strife. The resulting instability emboldened a ruler of Mali, a state within Ghana, to make war against his overlords. The troops of the Mali king Sundiata crushed Ghanaian warriors in 1235 at the Battle of Kirina, dealing the deathblow to the crippled realm. The Islamic kingdom of Mali, populated primarily by Mandingo people, rose in Ghana's place. The Mandingo quickly mastered agricultural production and seized control of the gold trade. They also cultivated rice and harvested inland deltas for fish, augmenting trade in salt, gold, and copper. Like Ghana before it, Mali grew wealthy from long-distance trade.

Under Sundiata's grandson Mansa Musa, a devout Muslim who assumed the throne in 1307, Mali came to control territory three times as great as Ghana.

Young Mansa Musa won fame when in 1324 he began a 3,500-mile pilgrimage across the Sahara, through Cairo, and all the way to Mecca, accompanied by an entourage of 50,000. Dispensing lavish gifts of gold, he made Mali gold legendary. His image on maps of the world for centuries thereafter testified to his importance in promoting West Africa's treasures.

Returning home after several years of pilgrimage, Mansa Musa brought Muslim scholars and artisans with him who helped establish the inland city of Timbuktu, a gateway to the Sahara in the Sudanese region of Songhai. Traveling to Timbuktu in the 1330s, the Arab geographer Ibn Battuta wrote admiringly of "the discipline of [the city's] officials and provincial governors, the excellent condition of public finance, and . . . the respect accorded to the decisions of justice and to the authority of the sovereign."

Noted for its extensive wealth, Timbuktu was also home to an Islamic university with a distinguished faculty who wrote on legal, historical, geographical, and moral topics. Two of the first histories of the western Sudan, both completed in 1665, were written by Timbuktu scholars, Mahmud Kati and Abd al-Rahman as-Sadi. North Africans and southern Europeans flocked to the university to study.

The Kingdom of Songhai

After Mansa Musa died in 1332, his successors could not maintain Mali's dominance in West Africa. The Songhai, a subject people living along the Niger River, saw an opportunity to regain their freedom from the Mandingo. They broke away from Mali in 1435 and began to conquer new territories. Just as Mali had grown out of a state within the empire of Ghana, the new Songhai Empire grew out of a region that had once been part of Mali.

In the late 1400s, when Portuguese traders began establishing commercial links with the Kongo kingdom to the south, the Songhai Empire reached its peak under the Muslim rulers Sonni Ali (1468–1492) and Askia Muhammad (1493–1528). Yet Songhai, too, collapsed, as some tribes, resentful of Muslim kings, began to break away. But the worst threat came from Morocco, in North Africa. There, rulers coveted Songhai's control of salt and gold—the two critical commodities of African trade. Armed with guns procured in the Middle East, Morocco's ruler captured the major Songhai towns of Timbuktu and Gao in 1591. The North Africans maintained loose control of western Sudan for more than a century as the last great trading empire of West Africa faded into history.

During an era when centralized kingdoms began emerging in Europe, West Africa devolved into smaller states. By the time Europeans reached the continent's Atlantic coast, most Africans resided in states no larger than Switzerland or Denmark. As the next chapter shows, conflicts among these small states enabled European slave traders to gain a foothold in the region, persuading tribal leaders to send out warrior parties to capture slaves.

The Forest Kingdoms of Ife and Benin

To the south of Songhai, Yoruba-speaking peoples lived in villages and towns of considerable size. Their territory stretched from the inland savannah woodlands to the long Gulf of Guinea on the Atlantic coast. These peoples—hunters, farmers, and craftsmen—began to cluster in states during the eleventh and twelfth centuries. The kingdoms of Ife and Benin were among the most influential. Here inland cities developed, their rulers governing surrounding peoples. Ife's settlement dates to about the eighth century. It became a religious and cultural center of the Yoruba people.

To the south of Ife stood Benin, which arose about 1000 CE west of the Niger Delta. About 50 miles from the Gulf of Guinea lay Benin City, a major West African center of metalworking and ceramic production. When the Portuguese arrived in Benin in 1485, they found a highly organized society governed by an absolute monarch with an elaborate court of aristocrats, an efficient bureaucracy, and a powerful military force. Benin City was a walled urban complex with broad streets and hundreds of buildings. In 1602, when a Dutch artist visited the city, he compared it favorably to Amsterdam.

Owing to their location on the African coast and their military might, the leaders of the Yoruba-speaking peoples became powerful slave traders. They captured thousands from the African interior and sold them in Benin City as slaves to the Portuguese. Later, they sold bondspeople (as slaves were also known) to the English at the coastal city of Calabar, the site of a major slave fort.

Both Ife and Benin enjoyed fertile soil and plentiful rainfall. These advantages, along with knowledge of ironworking, enabled the two kingdoms to cultivate surplus cereal and root crops as well as raise domestic animals. This

In this view of Benin, a Dutch artist shows the procession of the oba ("king") through the city.

bounty, in turn, supported trade with outside states. The wealth pouring in from trade freed enough leisure time for some people to explore artistic endeavors such as making jewelry and decorative ceramics.

The Kingdoms of Kongo and Ndongo

West Africa became the biggest source of slaves shipped across the Atlantic, but an area farther south along the Atlantic coast, in Central Africa, ultimately became another major source. Hundreds of thousands of modern-day African Americans trace their ancestry to this region, which included the vast kingdoms of Kongo and Ndongo (Angola). The religious, musical, medical, and burial traditions that first emerged in Central Africa still find expression in the United States today.

Kongo, which Europeans first encountered in 1482, was home to the Bakongo people, some two million strong by the 1400s. Their origins trace to Bantu-speaking farmers who began a great migration out of Central Africa in the first few centuries CE. Some traveled east, all the way to the Indian Ocean, while others made their way south to the Kongo Basin. Among those migrating south, the Nok carried with them the knowledge of smelting iron ore and fashioning the metal into spears, axes, fishhooks, and hoes. Thanks to these tools, farmers and fishers could accumulate more food than they needed to survive. So renowned was the Nok's knowledge of ironmaking that one historian has called Kongo "the land of the blacksmith kings." The technology of ironmaking spread from the Kongo Basin through much of West Africa.

The combination of ironworking skills and fertile river valleys enabled the Kongo Basin settlers to flourish in the millennium after the Nok's migration. Ironworking was widespread by the eighth century. Fertile river valleys aided the spread of population. As the centuries unfolded, hunter-gatherer groups who already had been living in the region made permanent homes in agricultural villages. Gradually, strong leaders loosely united these villages into a kingdom that had its royal city at Mbanza Kongo.

Built on a fertile plateau surrounded by rainforests, Mbanza lay 100 miles east of the coast and 50 miles south of the Kongo River. In this lively trade center, artisans, craftspeople, and manufacturers conducted an energetic business. Using the fibers of the raffia palm tree, skilled weavers wove fine cloth, which they traded to merchants from the north for salt and for seashells—used as local currency. From the wheels of hundreds of potters came decorative and functional bowls for carrying water and grain. As will be discussed in Chapter 2, Mbanza also became a slave-trading center after the Portuguese arrived on the Atlantic coast of Kongo in 1482.

South of Kongo, along the Atlantic coast, arose Ndongo (modern-day Angola), which also played a central role in the slave trade after the Portuguese reached Africa. In the 1300s, the Ndongo region consisted of three main chiefdoms—the Pende, Libolo, and Ndongo—but by 1500 the Ndongo chieftains had welded these groups into a unified state. Chapter 2 shows how this centralization enabled the Portuguese to establish solid trade relationships with the kingdom as well as spread their Catholic belief among the Ndongo peoples.

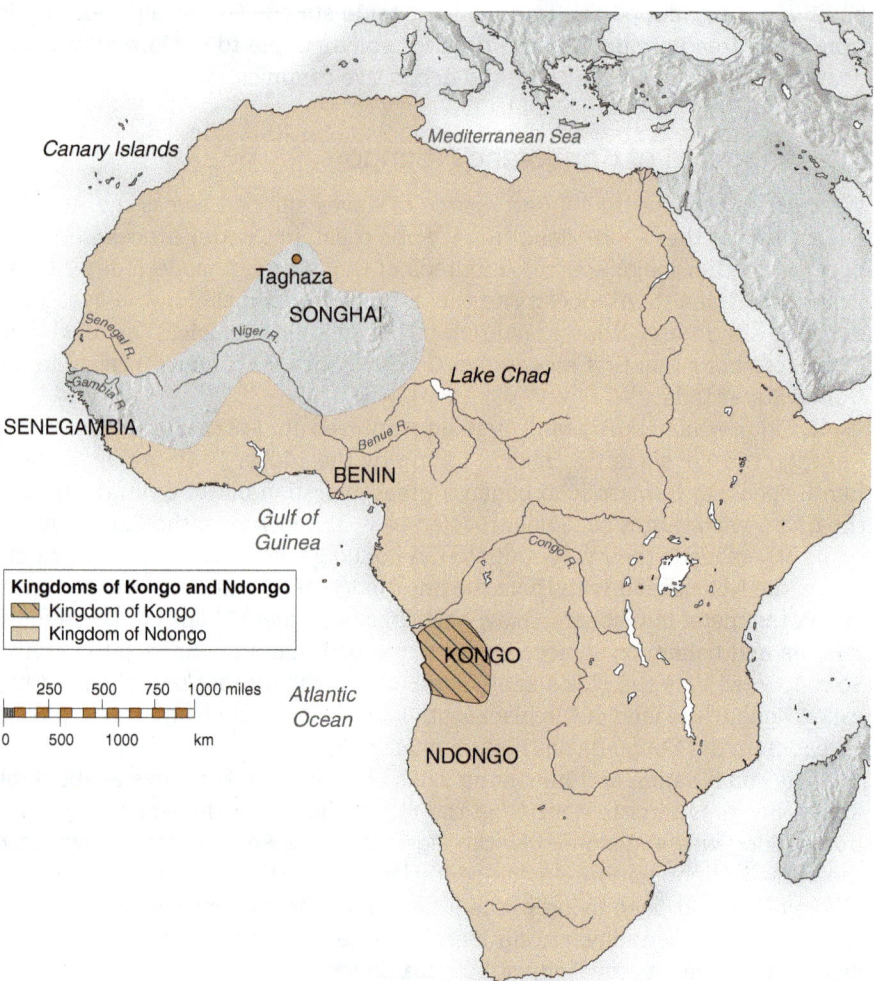

MAP 1.2 Kingdoms of Kongo and Ndongo

In 1591, the Portuguese explorers Filippo Pigafetta and Duarte Lopes provided the first European accounts of the densely populated Kongo kingdom.

African Culture

Many of the peoples of West and Central Africa—Ndongo, Mandingo, Yoruba, Fon, Hausa, Ibo, Bakongo, Whydah, Ga, and others—eventually saw some of their members sent away in slave ships. Though their societies and languages varied greatly, most shared certain ways of life that differentiated them from Europeans. By understanding these cultures, we can better appreciate how Africans refashioned themselves in the Americas and how they built defenses against the cruelties inflicted on them during four centuries of enslavement.

Family and Community

In ancient and medieval Africa, as elsewhere, the family served as the basic unit of society. Most families lived in villages, though by the 1200s, cities of many thousands dotted the continent. In most villages, people were part of a single lineage—a large, extended family claiming a common ancestor. Thus each person felt closely linked by family ties to others in the village. Individuals defined themselves in terms of their place in a constellation of fathers, mothers, aunts, uncles, brothers, sisters, and cousins. In such close-knit village life, it is not surprising that elders commanded profound respect.

Unlike Europeans, who put fathers and husbands at the center of family life and political power, Africans organized themselves according to a rich variety of kinship systems. Though some were patrilineal, most were matrilineal: property rights and political power descended through the mother rather than the father. Thus, when a chief died, his sister's son claimed the throne. After a wedding, the new husband joined his bride's people. This matrilineal tradition carried over into slavery, as African women continued to wield influence in their families in ways not typically seen in European families.

Regardless of the kinship system they lived by, all Africans emphasized the interdependencies among people over their roles as individuals. Indeed, African languages did not contain a word for *individualism.* When black slaves first encountered the notion of individualism in North America, they found it alien, distasteful, and nearly meaningless. As the historian Nathan Huggins has explained, "Alone, a person was nobody. Alone, one was helpless before all that was unknown. The smallest thing could threaten the isolated person—the elements, inanimate objects, animals, and above all, other people."

Many Africans practiced polygamy, so most adult women were co-wives. In many of these family units, one woman ranked as the senior wife and had authority over the others. Outside their dwelling, women cultivated the land and tended the family's livestock and fowls. They also did the marketing, bartering surplus produce such as yams, peppers, rice, chickens, millet, and nuts in return for other produce or household items they wanted.

Many Africans revered female deities. For example, the Yoruba worshiped the river goddess Oshun for giving them life force, fertility, family, power, and wealth. According to legend, Oshun bore twins with a fiery god of thunder, accumulated great wealth, and carried her treasures to the bottom of the Niger River, where she still reigns. Many Yoruba-speaking people today visualize Oshun as wielding a sword, always ready to slay the immoral. They thank her for protecting the people of the Niger River basin from witchcraft.

Religion

As in almost every human society, religious thought and practice in Africa made life's challenges meaningful and bearable. Across Africa, people believed that a supreme being had created the universe. They also associated a pantheon of lesser gods with phenomena they saw in nature, such as rain, animals, mountains, and the fertility of the Earth. Many people considered the Supreme Creator good and merciful. Sayings such as "Rejoice, God never does wrong to people" and epithets like the God of Pity, the Merciful One, and the Kind One reveal the belief in a kind rather than an angry and vengeful god.

Because they believed lesser deities also could intervene in human affairs, Africans honored them with elaborate rituals. West Africans maintained that spirits dwelled in the trees, rocks, and rivers around them. Thus, they exercised care in their treatment of these natural objects. For example, men who went fishing in a great river or tried to cross it in a canoe asked for the blessings of the river divinity through offerings or prayers. When drought struck their crops, they implored the rain gods to show mercy.

Africans also believed their ancestors retained a life force after death. Ancestors thus had the power to affect a village's welfare by mediating between the Supreme Creator and the living. Because the dead could exert a significant impact on the living, their surviving relatives held elaborate funeral rites to ensure a deceased person's proper entrance into the spiritual world. The more ancient an ancestor, the greater this person's power became. Therefore, villagers and townspeople invoked the "ancient ones" in prayers and honored them with shrines. Deep family loyalty and regard for family lineage flowed naturally from this reverence of ancestors.

West Africans also believed in spirit possession—gods speaking to men and women through priests, other religious figures, and natural forces and objects. Olaudah Equiano, who wrote an autobiographical account of his enslavement and his later purchase of his freedom, recalled, "Though we had no places of public worship, we had priests and magicians, or wise men . . . held in great reverence by the people. They calculated time, foretold events . . . and when they died, they were succeeded by their sons." In some African societies, evil spirits caused misfortune, sickness, and even death. People beset by an evil spirit often sought the aid of a diviner or medicine man to drive off the troublesome or malicious spirit.

Beginning in the eighth century, the spread of Islam across North Africa into the sub-Saharan Sudan and down the coast of the Red Sea through large regions of East Africa brought thousands of Africans into the Muslim faith. Islam's acceptance of polygamy, which most African societies practiced, facilitated this spread. By the late fifteenth century, as Muslim Arab traders migrated into Africa and believers launched wars of conquest and conversion, Islam had begun displacing traditional African religions in many parts of West and Central Africa, where the Atlantic slave trade began to gather momentum.

This was the complex religious heritage enslaved Africans brought to the Americas. No amount of desolation or physical abuse could wipe out these deeply rooted beliefs. In fact, it was their spiritual traditions that enabled many slaves to bear the hardships inherent in the master–slave relationship.

Yet despite many cultural differences, slaves and their Western owners also shared common ground. For example, people of both cultures recognized a physical world in which the living dwelled and an "other world" inhabited by the souls of the dead. Both believed that this "other world" could not be seen. However, people could come to know it by listening to revelations interpreted by spiritually gifted persons.

These shared foundations of religious belief enabled a hybrid African Christianity to develop in both Africa and the Americas. For example, in the kingdom of Kongo and several small realms close to the Niger Delta, extensive contact between Africans and the Portuguese interwove Christian beliefs with African religious beliefs in the seventeenth century. The worship of the Christian god did not eliminate the reverence for traditional African gods. Although enslavement suppressed some African religious customs, many spiritual beliefs and practices survived and are embraced by some African Americans today.

Social Organization

When Africans first welcomed Europeans to their lands, they were surprised to discover that Europeans had political organizations as sophisticated as their own. At the top of both European and African societies stood the king. Landowning nobles, military leaders, and priests (usually elderly men) supported the monarch. Beneath them were bureaucrats who collected taxes, kept records, and oversaw commerce. The next layer down comprised craftspeople, traders, teachers, and artists of the villages and towns. The broad base of this hierarchy consisted of the great mass of people, most of whom cultivated the soil. "Agriculture is our chief employment," recalled Olaudah Equiano, "and every one, even the children and women, are engaged in it. Thus we are habituated to labour from our earliest years." Equiano continued: "Everyone contributes something to the common stock."

A Benin sculptor created this brass bas-relief in the sixteenth or seventeenth century. The work shows a Benin oba, or king, astride a small animal. Attendants shade the royal figure with palm leaves. Such bas-reliefs provide a valuable record of court life and rituals.

Source: © President and Fellows of Harvard College, Peabody Museum, 16-43-50/B1481.

African societies also included slaves—men and the women who had the lowest status and the least freedom. Slavery was not new to Europeans or Africans—or to any other peoples. It had flourished in ancient Greece and Rome, in Russia and Eastern Europe, and in southwestern Asia. Conquering peoples everywhere sold captured enemies into slavery because they could not tolerate holding massive numbers of the enemy in their midst. Selling them to distant lands as slaves neutralized their threat, was more merciful than killing them, and generated profit.

Like peoples living almost everywhere else in the world, Africans accepted enslavement as a condition of servitude and considered slaveholding a mark of wealth. Owning slaves made a person wealthy; trading them boosted his or her wealth. The trade in other humans thus gave upper-crust men and women access to coveted European goods such as Venetian beads, fine cloth, and horses. Equiano described how his tribe traded slaves to "mahogany-coloured men from the south west" of his village: "Sometimes we sold slaves to them but they were only prisoners of war, or such among us as had been convicted of kidnapping, or adultery, and some other crimes which we esteemed heinous."

In this way, African societies conducted a small but far-reaching slave trade that carried bondspeople across the Sahara Desert to the Christian Roman Europe and the Islamic Middle East. From the tenth to fifteenth centuries, about 5,000 enslaved West Africans each year crossed the Sahara Desert to toil as sugar workers in Egypt, as domestic servants and artisans throughout the Arabic world, and as soldiers in North Africa. These slaves rarely ended up as field hands. Islam facilitated this process by establishing secure trade routes connecting West Africa with the Mediterranean world and the regions to the east. By the time Songhai rose to prominence in West Africa, that kingdom was the major supplier of enslaved captives across the Sahara to North Africa. Songhai warriors especially valued horses, which enabled them to wage war against neighboring peoples and thus capture still more slaves. Though this slave traffic was on the rise, it remained an occasional rather than a highly organized trade.

Africans' conception of slavery contrasted sharply with the notion that developed in European colonies in the Americas during the sixteenth century. Whereas most slaves in overseas European colonies engaged in field labor, generally for life, the majority of slaves within African societies supplied personal service to their masters for a limited period. "Those prisoners which were not sold or redeemed," remembered Equiano, "we kept as slaves; but how different was their condition from that of slaves in the West-Indies! With us, they do no more work than other members of the community, even their master. Their food, clothing, and lodging were nearly the same as theirs, except they were not permitted to eat with the free-born and there was scarce any other difference between them, than a superior degree of importance which the head of a family possesses in our state, and that authority which, as such, he exercises every part of his household. Some of the slaves even have slaves under them as their own property and for their own use."

The kind of slavery Equiano described was also well known in Europe. It emerged when Christians and Muslims enslaved one another during centuries

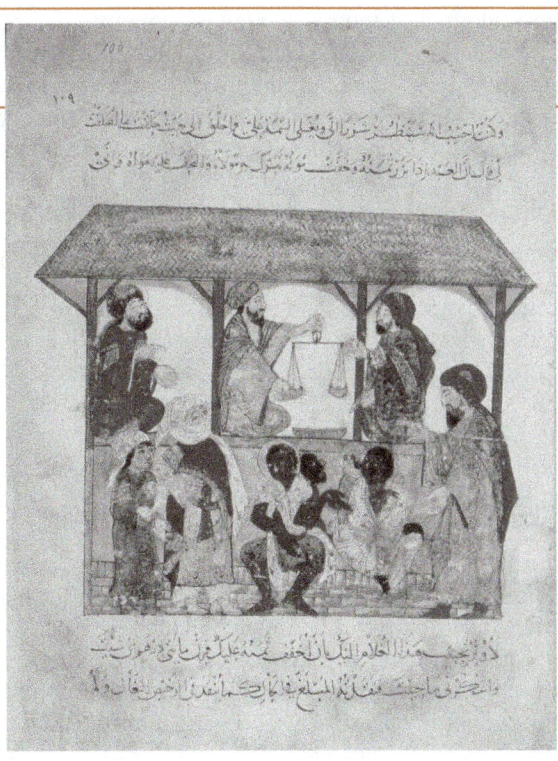

This rare image of three Africans at a Yemen slave market shows the sale price weighed in gold.

of religious wars in the Middle Ages. In these times, some people became slaves by being "outsiders" or "infidels" (nonbelievers) captured in war. Others voluntarily sold themselves into slavery to obtain money for their family. Still others were enslaved as punishment for committing a heinous crime.

Enslavement in Africa or Europe severely restricted a person's rights and prevented that individual from improving his or her lot in life. Yet these slaves still had certain protections. For example, they could obtain an education, marry and raise families, and count on decent treatment from their owners. In fact, some slaves in Africa were so highly trusted that they served as soldiers, administrators, royal advisors, and even occasionally as royal consorts.

But African slavery differed from that in North America in two important ways. First, slavery was not a lifelong condition in Africa. Second, it was not automatically passed down to the children of slaves. Because of these differences, black slaves in North America faced a far bleaker existence than slaves elsewhere.

Music, Dance, and Art

Aesthetics—what a society considers beautiful, moving, and life-sustaining—constituted a core value in traditional African society. People expressed their love of beauty through music, dance, and art as well as through body decoration, hair styling, and the concoction of elaborate, savory meals. Maintaining these expressions helped Africans endure enslavement in North America. Later chapters show how these forms of expression took deep root in African American life and embedded themselves in the larger American culture.

Africans engaged in dance and music-making to celebrate life and wove these activities into communal religious observances and festivals. Most religious gatherings involved *antiphony*—the call of a religious leader and the spoken or sung responses of the worshipers—a practice that prevails today in African American church services. Drums, rattles, flutes, bells, banjoes, other stringed instruments, and the *balafo* (similar to a xylophone) also enhanced religious rejoicing—akin to the ecstatic singing and shouting also a part of African American spiritual services. In addition, Africans engaged in singing and dancing at funeral observances.

Music and dance also served a playful purpose. Ibn Khaldun, one of the first Arab Muslim historians of Islamized Africa, observed of the Africans he encountered in the fourteenth century that "they are found eager to dance whenever they hear a melody." Dancing, singing, and playing instruments enabled Africans to celebrate life together, and entire villages participated. Individual performance for a passive audience, a practice widespread in Europe at the time, was foreign to African village life.

Often dancing and music-making bridged the sacred and the secular. From ancient times, African societies performed ceremonies honoring rain, sun, and other important natural phenomena. For instance, the Dinka people conducted rain ceremonies each year at the start of the rainy season. The purpose of these ceremonies was not to open the skies again; rather it was to celebrate rain as an indispensable force on which life depended.

African music featured antiphony, syncopation, and a percussive style characterized by multiple rhythms unfolding simultaneously. The drum, in its many forms, played an essential part. African musicians also prized improvisation—the continual changing of a piece of music. With improvisation, musicians felt they shared ownership of a musical composition rather than attributing a work to a single creator, as was the case in Europe. This sense of sharing echoed the emphasis on community and interdependence that marked African culture.

African art also involved communal expression. Most traditional African artists created functional objects rather than paintings of scenes or individuals. But some works served the same purpose as European court art. For example, Benin artists carved their kings' likenesses in stone or wood to glorify and commemorate their (kings') power.

From Ife, Benin, and other parts of West and Central Africa came a diverse array of sculptures and carvings fashioned from wood, terra cotta, ivory, copper, brass, and bronze. Inheritors of the ancient knowledge of iron production and metal casting from Nok culture, the artists of Ife and Benin were prized for their abilities. Many people believed these individuals possessed spiritual powers that found expression in their work. In other parts of West Africa, craftspeople carved elephant tusks into delicate pedestals surmounted by containers meant to hold salt, a precious commodity. When Portuguese traders first encountered the Sapis in what is now Sierra Leone, they were dazzled by such carvings.

A Benin artist carved this saltcellar from an elephant tusk in the early sixteenth century. Europeans were so struck by the virtuosity of Benin carvers that they commissioned ivory pieces, sometimes providing sketches of decorative motifs. This saltcellar features a king or warrior with a spear in one hand, a sword in the other, and a cross hanging from a beaded necklace.

Especially intriguing to Europeans was the African ability to carve ivory to a lace-like thinness. In 1520, the German artist Albrecht Dürer purchased two African saltcellars carved in ivory and transported those to the Netherlands by a slave ship captain.

African objects worked in brass, wood, and gold were equally impressive. For example, in Senegambia, European traders found elaborately carved antelope headdresses worn by young, masked Bambara men in agricultural rites. On the Gold Coast, they found carved royal stools inlaid with gold and silver. One Frenchman described "very fine gold casting that even a European artist would find difficult to imitate." In Benin, Europeans encountered impressive bronze funerary portraits depicting the mothers of Benin's kings.

Private collectors and museums around the world now eagerly bid for the art of Africa both for its beauty and sophistication and for what these objects reveal about cultural interchange. Not only were African saltcellars sold in Europe, but also Kongo craftsmen working in bronze began to fashion crosses and statues of saints after the Portuguese spread Catholicism in that kingdom.

Conclusion

In ancient and medieval times, a rich variety of African societies arose in the distinct ecological zones that made up the vast and diverse continent. By the fifteenth century, intercultural contacts within Africa—as well as trade among Mediterranean Europe, North Africa, Egypt, and parts of eastern Africa—knit an elaborate web of connections among these diverse peoples. The rise of Islam accelerated this interweaving. By the early fifteenth century, peoples previously unknown to each other began to trade, exchange ideas, and intermingle throughout various parts of the continent. Though the slave trade was a minor part of this mingling and trading, it was to become the most dominant and tragic aspect of African–European–Middle Eastern contact, as discussed in Chapter 2.

Questions for Review and Reflection

1. How can comprehending the rise of Egyptian civilization enrich our understanding of African American history?

2. What accounts for the rise of Islam and its extraordinary spread after its advent in the seventh century CE?

3. To what extent did trade shape the rise of West African kingdoms? How? What other factors influenced the emergence of such kingdoms as those in Ghana, Mali, and Songhai?

4. What were the major features of African society and culture prior to contact with European traders?

CHAPTER 2

Africa and the Atlantic World

King Nomimansa Meets Diego Gomes

In 1456, the Mandingo king Nomimansa welcomed Diego Gomes, a Portuguese ship captain and emissary, into his home. The king was curious about these light-skinned people who called themselves "Christians." A gracious host, he presented them with generous gifts of ivory and gold. Living near the mouth of the Gambia River, the Mandingo people in the Songhai kingdom were eager to establish mutually advantageous trade arrangements like those they had forged with other foreign travelers to their coast. But Nomimansa also knew that during the previous decade marauding Europeans had made war against Africans on offshore islands and seized some of them. So the king decided to step carefully in cultivating relations with these newcomers.

Nomimansa listened as Gomes explained how his sovereign, Prince Henry, had sent him to negotiate trade. True, the Portuguese had prospered by using the raid-and-trade tactic, Gomes admitted. But now, the captain reassured his host, they wanted peaceful, well-regulated trade. The Mandingo king agreed to a deal. Gomes sealed the commercial treaty by presenting Portugal's new trading partner with damask cloth from Flanders, huge brass pots from Germany, glass beads from Venice, and swords and knives from Spain. Nomimansa understood that his people were about to become participants in a trading network that could bring them valuable goods and luxuries in return for their gold, ivory, and salt.

But that night, King Nomimansa learned his guest's true intentions. As Gomes tells the story, "Twenty-two people were sleeping. I herded them as if they had been cattle towards the boats." Disobeying Henry's instructions, Gomes seized the people of the Gambia River and forced them onto his three ships. "We

Chronology

1402	Castile sponsors a permanent colony in the Canary Islands.
1417	The Portuguese seize the Madeira Islands.
1420s–1430s	Portuguese sailors explore the African coast and engage in raiding for slaves.
1427	The Portuguese seize the Azores.
1434	Gil Eannes navigates south of Cape Bojardor and returns home.
1444	The Portuguese work enslaved Africans on the Madeiras' sugar plantations.
1453	Turks' capture of Constantinople blocks access to traditional slave markets.
1456	Diego Gomes negotiates agreements with African rulers that initiate the slave trade.
1460s	Portugal colonizes Cape Verde Islands.
1492	Ferdinand and Isabella expel the Muslims from Spain and sponsor Christopher Columbus.
1496	Kongo king converts to Catholicism, which becomes the royal court's religion.
1498	Vasco da Gama sails around Africa's southern tip.
1502	The first enslaved Africans reach the Americas on the Spanish ship Hispaniola.
1518	Spain's Charles I authorizes importation of enslaved Africans to overseas colonies.
1526	Africans first settle in North America as part of Ayllón's expedition.
1530	Portugal's king John III authorizes transport of enslaved Africans to the Americas.
1534–1539	The African slave Estévan serves in Spanish exploration parties in North America.
1550	Beginning of the Catholic and Protestant Wars in Europe.
1562	John Hawkins makes first English slave voyage.

captured on that day . . . nearly 650 people, and we went back to Portugal, to Lagos in the Algarve, where the prince was, and he rejoiced with us."

Gomes's act prefigured a tragic aspect of European-African relations that would unfold for four centuries to come. From the mid-fifteenth century to the late nineteenth century, European slave traders carried off huge numbers of the most able-bodied members of African societies, especially in West and Central Africa. The Africans' fate? To toil in the new colonies European nations were founding on islands off the West African coast and in the Americas. As it turned out, ship captains who followed Gomes would not find it necessary to kidnap slaves because the Portuguese, and then other Europeans, found willing

African trading partners to supply captives. Four years after his first meeting with King Nomimahsa, Captain Gomes was trading again near the mouth of the Gambia River. But this time, he complained, "the natives used to give twelve Negroes for one horse, now they gave only six."

This chapter describes the first encounters between the Portuguese and Africans as the former worked their way down Africa's west coast. It examines the impact of the slave trade on both Europeans and Africans. The Europeans transformed an ancient, widespread practice into a harsh, lifelong bondage where skin color and African origins became the distinguishing marks of bondage. Black men, women, and children became commodities—not much different from horses or casks of tobacco. The Portuguese were the first to use slave labor to cultivate sugar on the Atlantic islands off the coast of West Africa, creating what became known as the plantation system. Understanding how this system worked reveals insights into the experience of enslaved Africans in the Americas. A closer look at "the middle passage," the waterborne journey to the Western Hemisphere that huge numbers of Africans endured, sheds additional light on African lives under slavery. Once across the Atlantic, the lives of slaves owned by Spanish explorers differed markedly from those of Africans who worked on Portuguese and English plantations. Many of the Spanish-owned slaves became part of the Spanish conquest of an immense part of the Western Hemisphere in the late fifteenth and early sixteenth centuries.

Africa and Europe: The Fateful Connection

The point of no return was Cape Bojador. Beyond it lay "the green sea of darkness." Cape Bojador, just south of the Canary Islands off West Africa's shore, struck fear into the hearts of European and Muslim sailors riding the Atlantic Ocean current along the Saharan coast from Portugal and Spain. Ship captains dared not venture south of the cape because they had no way of defying the prevailing wind and current to return to their point of origin. But all that changed in 1434, when the bold Portuguese ship captain Gil Eannes sailed south on "seas none had sailed before" and managed to make his way back home. How did Eannes accomplish this feat? He modified Moorish-designed small wooden ships with lanteen (three-cornered) sails. Now he could sail into the wind and return to Portugal.

With Eannes's successful voyage, a new era of high-seas sailing had dawned. The Atlantic basin now lay open to any sailor who had the technology and nerve to navigate it. This revolution in trans-Atlantic navigation would have profound consequences for both Europeans and Africans. Most important, it cast a dark shadow over Africa that has not altogether lifted even today.

Portugal Colonizes the Atlantic Islands

Prince Henry, son of Portugal's king João I, earned his name as Henry the Navigator. Politically ambitious, energetic, and experienced on the battlefield, the young monarch brimmed with both business and religious zeal. Henry

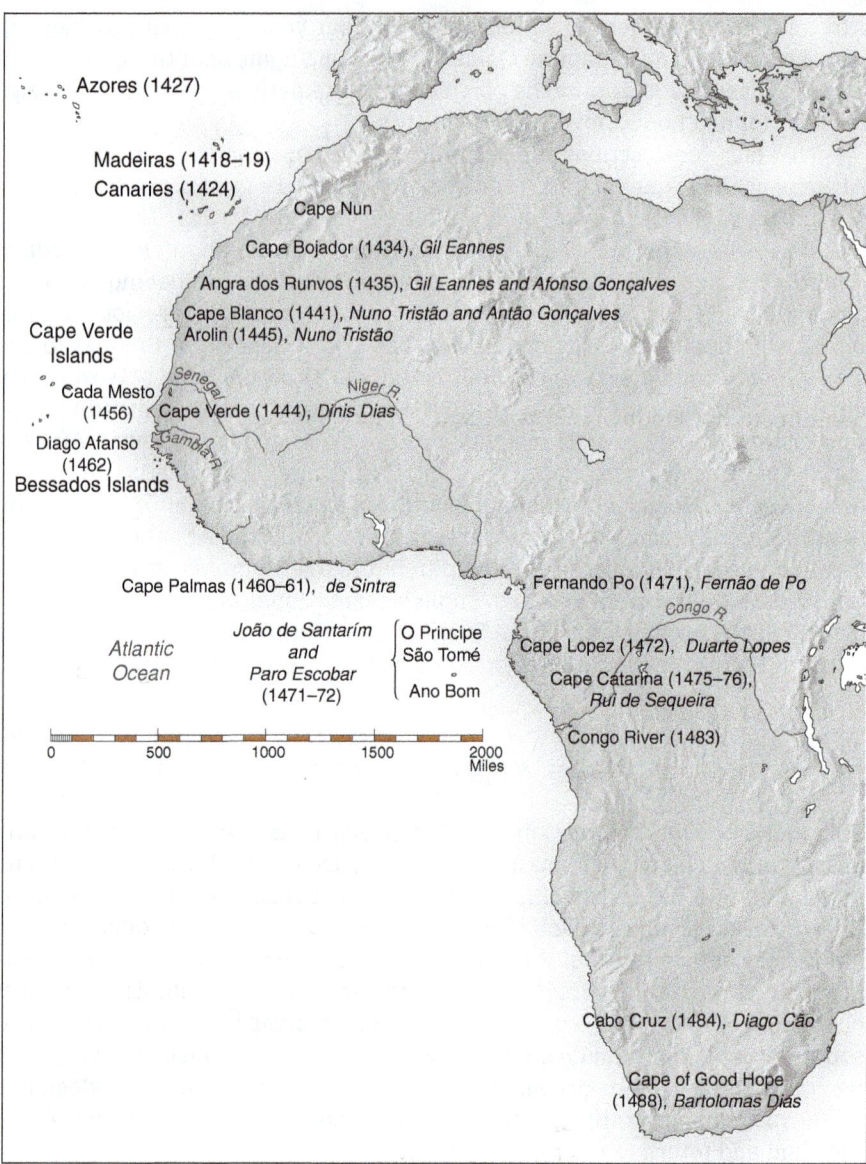

Azores (1427)

Madeiras (1418–19)
Canaries (1424)

Cape Nun

Cape Bojador (1434), *Gil Eannes*

Angra dos Runvos (1435), *Gil Eannes and Afonso Gonçalves*

Cape Blanco (1441), *Nuno Tristão and Antão Gonçalves*
Arolin (1445), *Nuno Tristão*

Cape Verde
Islands

Cada Mesto
(1456)   Cape Verde (1444), *Dinis Dias*

Diago Afanso
(1462)
Bessados Islands

Senegal

Niger R.

Gambia R.

Cape Palmas (1460–61), *de Sintra*

Fernando Po (1471), *Fernão de Po*

Congo R.

Atlantic
Ocean

João de Santarím
and
Paro Escobar
(1471–72)

O Principe
São Tomé

Ano Bom

Cape Lopez (1472), *Duarte Lopes*

Cape Catarina (1475–76),
Rui de Sequeira

Congo River (1483)

0   500   1000   1500   2000
Miles

Cabo Cruz (1484), *Diago Cão*

Cape of Good Hope
(1488), *Bartolomas Dias*

MAP 2.1   Portuguese Colonization of the Atlantic Islands

The earliest European expeditions took sailors along the eastern shores of the Atlantic and onto the islands off West Africa's coast in the mid-fifteenth century. Europeans would not venture across the Atlantic to the "strange new lands" of the Americas for a few more years.

sponsored improvements in navigation and energetically promoted his kingdom's expansion into the Atlantic Ocean. In 1417, he ordered the seizure of the unoccupied Madeira Islands off the northern part of West Africa. Subsequently, he took the Canaries and the Azores.

The Portuguese put down roots on these islands. At first they gathered treasures from the wild, such as honey and indigenous plants from which they made dyes to trade. Then they began experimenting with growing wheat and grapevines in the islands' rich volcanic soils. Around the same time, they sent infrequent raiding parties to the African coast in search of a few slaves to work the fields on these island colonies. By the 1470s, the Portuguese had sailed farther south to forge trading agreements along the coast of what is today's Ghana. They also struck deals with the African kingdom of Benin, trading in exchange for the "grains of paradise"—high-quality pepper that fetched a handsome price in Europe.

The Portuguese combined their cautious, small-scale experiments on the Atlantic islands with slave raiding on the West African coast. Initially they supplied slaves to Europe, where landowners kept up a modest demand for raw labor. But as populations on the European continent boomed in the late fifteenth century, landowners had plenty of human muscle to work the fields. Demand for slaves in Europe began to dry up, leaving the Portuguese with little reason to continue slave raiding in Africa. But all this shifted when the Portuguese began cultivating sugar on the Madeiras in the 1450s.

The Plantation System: A Model for Misery on the Atlantic Islands

Produced in the temperate Mediterranean region since the eighth century, sugar had long been an exotic and expensive luxury. Only the wealthiest families could afford to sweeten their diets with the precious flavoring. Yet by the mid-1400s, the demand for sugar spread. On islands hundreds of miles from the African coast, Portuguese settlers spotted an opportunity. They experimented with growing sugarcane first on the Madeiras. To their delight, the plant flourished. Now these entrepreneurs needed laborers—not a few, but many. The plantation system they established became the first of its kind. It comprised three interwoven components: large landholding, the forced labor of gangs of enslaved peoples, and a cash crop that commanded steep prices in distant places. The plantation system meshed perfectly with the emerging European notion of mercantilism, whereby overseas colonists combined land and labor to produce wealth for the benefit of their home countries.

On the Madeiras, enslaved Africans initially toiled alongside slaves procured from Russia and the Balkans, where slavery was common. The Portuguese had imported these light-skinned individuals because they had long experience with planting and chopping cane in the sugar fields of Cyprus and Sicily. They also knew how to extract sugar from the cane. But the Portuguese found it far cheaper to import black men and women from the nearby West African coast than from distant Mediterranean locations. Thus, the forced migration of Africans started unofficially in the 1440s, when Portuguese ship captains like Diego Gomes started kidnapping them for lifelong labor on the Atlantic islands.

Soon the Portuguese were cultivating sugar on other islands they had claimed, especially São Tomé, off Angola's coast. By 1500, they were importing about five thousand African slaves annually. As sugar production increased, it became more affordable, increasing demand. Soon the Portuguese were using the islands as slave-trading centers. Slave trading became increasingly lucrative after the Turks conquered Constantinople in 1453, closing European access to the slave markets in Russia and the Balkans. For generations, Europeans had relied on these sources for domestic and agricultural laborers. It was precisely for these reasons that Prince Henry had sent Diego Gomes to negotiate treaties with African rulers. Though Gomes betrayed his charge—stealing rather than bartering for slaves—the Portuguese entrepreneurs who followed him established a mutually beneficial reciprocal trade with African coastal rulers.

Africa and the Rising Atlantic World

In 1486, the Spanish king put his seal on a grant to Fernão Dulmo, a military commander with a taste for exploration. The grant entitled Dulmo to all lands he could discover in the vast Atlantic Ocean—including "a great island or islands, or coastal parts of a mainland." European adventurers had no idea where they might find such islands. Moreover, they assumed that the "mainland" referred to in the grant was faraway China, then known as Cathay. Despite his determined forays throughout the Atlantic, Dulmo found nothing. But six years later, in 1492, Christopher Columbus reached what he believed were parts of Asia. Continued improvements in European navigation that for half a century had allowed colonization and trade along the African coast enabled the intrepid Genoese sailor to make his way across the entire Atlantic, an expedition chartered by the king and queen of Spain. In an instant, the momentum of European overseas colonization shifted from the Portuguese to the Spanish. This change would redirect the entire course of African history.

Initiating the Atlantic Slave Trade

After 1492, Europeans began settling in the Americas (including the Caribbean), where they cultivated valuable cash crops such as sugar, coffee, tobacco, and rice. Sensing new opportunities, European merchants and investors turned their attention from the Mediterranean Sea in Old World Europe to the Atlantic Ocean in the New World. As investment capital began flowing into the plantations dotting the Americas, a far-reaching new trade network took shape and expanded throughout the Atlantic basin. The continent of Africa provided this network with the labor and agricultural expertise plantation owners in the Americas needed to sell their bounty to the merchant houses of England, France, Spain, Portugal, and the Netherlands. Individuals fortunate enough to hold favored positions in this network—slave traders, shipbuilders, land speculators, and plantation owners—amassed great wealth. Almost every European nation sent ships to trade in Africa for slaves in addition to the usual gold, ivory, and other luxuries.

As Europeans launched themselves across the Atlantic, conquering and colonizing vast territories, their nearly insatiable demand for labor transformed the entire calculus of African trade. Plantations on large tracts of land could be productive only with mass human labor. Soon Europeans began referring to

African slaves as "black gold." For almost four centuries after Columbus's voyages to the Americas, European colonizers transported Africans out of their homeland in the largest forced migration in human history. Estimates vary widely, but the number of Africans who survived the trip across the Atlantic to labor in the Americas probably reached about twelve million. Several million more perished during the forced marches from the African interior to coastal trading forts or during the ocean voyage west to the Americas.

In Angola, beginning in 1491 the Portuguese used their considerable military might to capture and enslave Africans—a change from earlier policy. Elsewhere in Africa, local rulers controlled the raiding of slaves, marching captives to the coast and selling them to European merchants and ship captains. Coastal political authorities extracted taxes and tolls from the Europeans according to African law and custom. Not every African ruler engaged in the Atlantic slave trade, but over four centuries, the leaders of some two hundred African societies participated.

Why did some African leaders engage in slave raiding and selling? In part, the answer lies in the long history of slave trading among a variety of peoples in West and Central Africa. The tendency of human beings to mistreat those perceived as different from themselves also offers insight. Black rulers and their agents did not think of themselves as Africans capturing and selling other Africans. Rather, they viewed themselves as raiding enemies and members of outside—and thus inferior—societies. There was no unified African identity. The people of Mali or Benin did not identify themselves as Africans any more than the people of France or Portugal identified themselves as Europeans.

Thus Africans felt no moral distaste for the practice of capturing and selling slaves. Indeed, as early as the 1650s, they had been selling captives to Muslim slave traders, who transported them in caravans across the Sahara to slave markets around the Red Sea and Indian Ocean. Estimates suggest that as many enslaved Africans went east by land between the 1650s and 1800 as went west by water from the 1490s to 1800.

The living conditions of slaves sold in Muslim lands differed markedly from those sold in the New World. Because most Muslim societies had large peasant populations, they did not need agricultural laborers. Rather, they needed porters, soldiers, concubines (mistresses), cooks, and personal attendants. Muslim masters did not exploit their slaves but valued them for their personal services. For this reason, slave traders sent roughly two captured African women east for every man—the reverse of the gender ratio for slaves sent across the Atlantic for male-dominated field labor in the plantation system.

Other differences distinguished slavery in Muslim lands from that in European colonies. Whereas their masters in the Americas viewed slaves as nonhuman possessions, Muslim masters saw bondsmen and bondswomen as people, though to be sure, they treated them harshly. In the east, slaves had more rights than in the Americas. Some had the right to embrace the religion of their captors, while others were obligated to convert on pain of death. Muslim masters freed more of their slaves than owners in the Americas did. Once they gained their freedom, many Africans living in Muslim societies had the same rights as non-Africans and blended into the general population—seldom the case in the Americas. A final difference is that Islam emphasized a universal community that transcended race, so former African slaves who had embraced the faith found it easier to feel united spiritually with other Muslims. This was not so in the Americas.

The African rulers who negotiated the first trade treaties with Europeans could not have predicted the damage these new partnerships would ultimately do to their own kingdoms. One example of the slave trade reveals its dire consequences. By the early 1500s, when the Portuguese began pressing their Kongo trading partners for slaves, missionaries had also reached the Kongo court. King Mani-Kongo was receptive to the Catholic religious message, even allowing his son to be baptized with the Christian name Alfonso I. In a spirit of cordiality, the king agreed to an exchange of gold, ivory, and slaves for Portuguese guns, knives, and trade goods. But soon Kongo was engulfed in conflict. By 1526, Portuguese merchants from São Tomé were urging village chiefs to wage war against each other to increase the slave catch, and supplying guns for the task. When Alfonso succeeded his father as monarch, he asked the Portuguese king to ban slave trading in Kongo. "Merchants are taking every day our natives, sons of the land and sons of our noblemen," he wrote. "So great is the corruption and licentiousness that our country is becoming completely depopulated." But Alfonso's request fell on deaf ears. Trapped in a web of guns, slaves, and power, the beleaguered ruler could not find a way out. As slave raiding devastated Africa's heartlands, rebels in Kongo's provinces ignited a civil war.

Sugar and Slavery

The African slave trade would never have become more than a minor commerce without the burgeoning labor shortage created by Europe's overseas expansion and the intensifying hunger for sugar. Were it not for Europe's colonization of the Americas, the early slave trade that brought limited numbers of African slaves to southern Europe and the Atlantic islands might have ceased and been remembered simply as a short-lived phenomenon stemming from early European contacts with Africa. Sugar changed all that. When the Spanish and Portuguese stepped up their colonizing in the Caribbean and South America during the sixteenth century, they quickly learned that sugarcane grew just as easily in these lands as it did in the Atlantic islands off the west coast of Africa. Once the newcomers had subdued the native peoples they encountered, they replicated the plantation system they had developed on the Atlantic islands. Now increased demand for slaves came from the Caribbean and South America.

At first, the Spanish and Portuguese looked to the native peoples of the Americas as an obvious source of forced gang labor. In some areas, such as Mexico and Brazil, the newcomers coerced local men and women into working on plantations and in mines. But diseases to which native Americans were not immune—such as smallpox, influenza, and scarlet fever—soon devastated the local populations. Far more familiar with their surroundings than their white captors, slaves who survived these plagues often escaped back to their villages.

Now in need of a new source of labor, the Europeans turned their attention to the huge supply of labor available in Africa. Whereas they previously traded *with* Africans, they now began trading *in* Africans. By the mid-1600s in Portuguese Brazil, and by the early 1600s on islands throughout the Caribbean, enslaved Africans were hacking out sugar plantations from tropical forest. By the mid-eighteenth century, about nine out of every ten West Africans captured for export across the Atlantic went to labor in New World sugarcane fields. After finding gold and silver mines in Mexico and Peru, the Spanish stepped up their purchase of African laborers. After successfully introducing additional cash crops—coffee, tobacco, rice, and indigo—the Spanish and Portuguese sent thousands of ships to the West African coast and packed them with slaves. Dutch, French, and English vessels followed. Hardly anyone would have disagreed with one seventeenth-century Englishman who called African slaves "the strength and the sinews of this western world."

Once established on a large scale, the Atlantic slave trade transformed slave recruitment in Africa. At first, African leaders had sold criminals or prisoners of war. But the intensifying demand for workers in the New World presented irresistible new opportunities. Now African kings waged war against their neighbors to secure sufficient quantities of the black gold for which the Europeans paid so handsomely. European guns perpetuated this shift. By 1730, Europeans were providing about 180,000 arms a year to African slave traders. The availability of guns enabled unscrupulous traders to kidnap slaves and set up paramilitary organizations throughout Africa. Eager to maintain their lucrative commercial relations with European powers, some African rulers declined to stop the kidnapping and organized violence. In several cases, their decision cost them their kingdoms. Others used the situation to strengthen their own militaries.

As the demand for African slaves multiplied in the eighteenth century, the armies and agents of coastal and interior kings repeatedly invaded the hinterlands of western and Central Africa. At least half of the slaves transported to English North America came from the part of western Africa that lies

Sugar production in Brazil. The demand for sugar led to the cultivation of the crop in the Atlantic islands and in the Americas.

between the Senegal and Niger Rivers and the Gulf of Biafra. Most of the others were enslaved in Angola, on the west coast of Central Africa. By the end of the eighteenth century, slaving had devastated these regions' populations.

European Competition for the Slave Trade

For Europeans, the slave trade generated immense profits. As early as 1550, one chronicler asserted that slaves "will triple your investment." During the sixteenth and seventeenth centuries, European nations warred incessantly for trading advantages and coastal forts on the West African coast. For example, the major Portuguese slaving fort at Elmina on the Gold Coast, constructed by the Portuguese in 1481, was captured by the Dutch and then by the English. By the end of the seventeenth century, European nations were negotiating for the sole right to supply slaves to the plantations in the Americas.

The English came late to the slave trade, which was long dominated by the Portuguese. But in 1562, Englishman John Hawkins seized a slave ship, sold the slaves to the Spanish, and returned with a fat profit for Queen Elizabeth I. After this, the English gave priority to supplying the Spanish colonies with slaves. It would be another century before their dominance was secure. Meanwhile, the

In 1624, Queen Njinga took the throne of Ndongo (present-day Angola), defying a custom that prohibited women from ruling. She quickly solidified her rule by contesting Portuguese incursions into her domain. When the Portuguese went on the offensive in a series of wars to secure territory as well as access to the slave trade, Queen Njinga led the resistance. Her fierce battle cry, which reportedly could be heard from miles away, established her as a heroic figure who has become an enduring legend. Here, the kneeling Queen Njinga receives a blessing from the standing Portuguese governor with African and Portuguese attendants looking on. Three hundred years after her death in 1663, Angolans fighting for independence from Portugal went into battle inspired by the woman who had come to symbolize resistance to European imperialism in Africa.

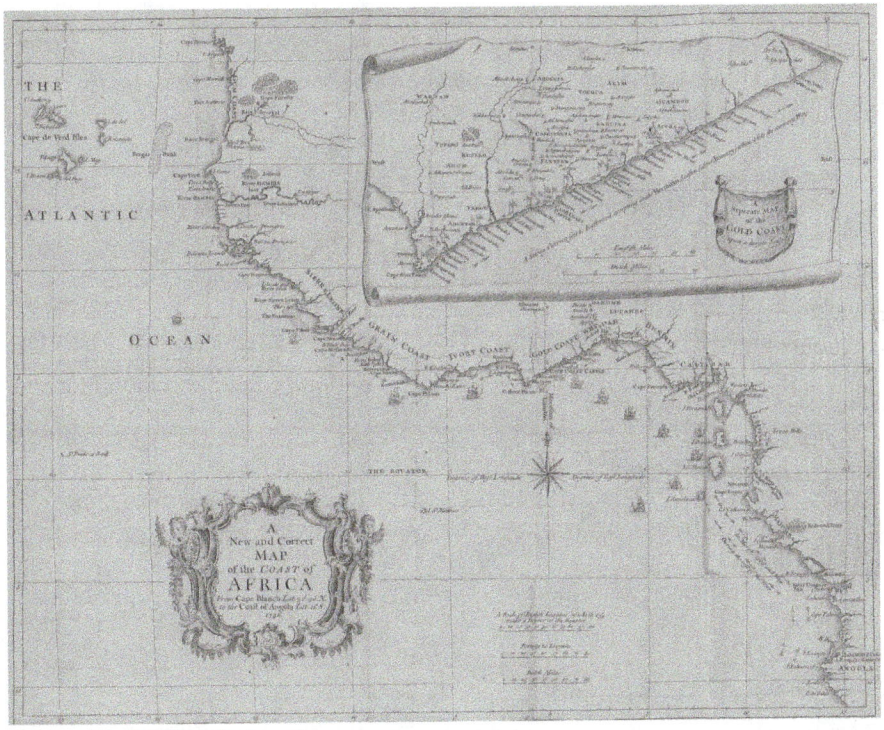

MAP 2.2 · English Slave Trade

This map appeared in a pamphlet promoting the English slave trade. The pamphlet author described the British Empire in gushing terms as "a magnificent superstructure of American commerce and naval power on an African foundation." The Gold Coast, the Bight of Biafra, and the Bight of Benin—all on West Africa's coast— became major slave-trading centers for English traders.

English king Charles II granted a charter to the Royal Adventurers to Africa—a joint-stock company headed by his brother, the Duke of York—giving it the exclusive right to carry slaves to England's overseas colonies. For thirty-four years after 1663, each slave transported across the Atlantic bore the brand "DY" for the Duke of York. Eventually, merchants pressured Parliament to end slave trade monopolies. Then the English slave trade boomed—from some 10,000 slaves carried out of Africa per year in the 1680s to more than 20,000 per year by the early 1720s. By the 1690s, England was the foremost slave-trading nation in Europe.

Though the motive for the slave trade was profit, racist sentiment began to build. Regarding black Africans as an inferior species enabled the Europeans to rationalize their brutal traffic in human beings. Almost from the start the Europeans had thought of their captives as heathen, savage, and deserving of their fate. Notions of African "backwardness" and cultural impoverishment strengthened European justifications. These ignorant heathens, thought the Europeans, were better off toiling in the sugar, rice, and tobacco fields of the Americas than living where they were born. In the Americas, the Europeans believed that the black "savages" could be "civilized" through exposure to Christianity and European culture.

The Trauma of Enslavement

"The first object which saluted my eyes when I arrived on the coast [in about 1755]," wrote Olaudah Equiano, "was the sea, and a slave-ship, which was then riding at anchor, and waiting for its cargo." The eleven-year-old had arrived at the old slave fort at Calabar, which still stands, and was about to endure the so-called Middle Passage across the Atlantic. This journey constituted the second leg of the three-part transit that for captives began in the African interior and concluded with the march to a final destination in the Americas, where they were purchased as slaves.

Equiano's account is the most vivid of the few to survive Africans' centuries-long diaspora. Many enslaved Africans would have told stories different from Equiano's, for each experience was unique. But most who reached the shores of the Americas did not live long enough to record their experiences. On average, they died in just seven years. So Equiano's story, covering fifty-three years, has assumed a place in historical literature far greater than he could have hoped for. Yet even his account cannot fully convey the agony and demoralization of the forced march to the west coast of Africa, the loading of captives onto wooden-hulled ships, the miserable journey across the ocean, and the sale, as chattel, in a new land.

Capture and Sale in Africa

Born in a village in a "charming fruitful vale," Equiano regarded his homeland as "the most considerable" of a variety of kingdoms in the "part of Africa known by the name of Guinea." European slave traders preferred young men, like Equiano, over women because they knew that buyers on the other side of

Nobody has discovered who painted this handsome picture of Olaudah Equiano, completed probably when he was in his forties. Equiano saw nine editions of his *Interesting Narrative of the Life of Olaudah Equiano* published in London, Dublin, Edinburgh, and Norwich before he died in March 1797. After his death, enterprising printers republished his *Narrative* in many cities. Today, Equiano's *Narrative* is republished every several years, is read by thousands of people, and has won widespread recognition as the most compelling first-person story of enslavement and liberation from the pen of an African American or Afro-Briton. Equiano was enslaved a few decades after the map shown on page 35 was drawn, but this map accurately depicts the region where he first saw the slave ship that took him to Barbados and then Virginia.

the Atlantic valued physical strength over everything else. Most captives were in their teens, twenties, and thirties. Only about 10 percent were under ten or elderly.

Once captured, slaves were marched to the sea in "coffles," or trains, or brought by large canoes down the rivers that emptied into the Atlantic. A Scotsman, Mungo Park, described the coffle he marched with for 550 miles through Gambia in the 1790s. In this coffle, seventy-three men, women, and children were tied together by the neck with leather thongs. Several captives attempted to commit suicide by eating clay. Another was abandoned after being badly stung by bees. Still others died of exhaustion and starvation. After two months, depleted by thirst, hunger, and exposure, the prisoners reached the coast. There their captors herded them into fortified enclosures called barracoons.

The forced march was just the first leg of the 5,000-mile journey. On the coast, the captives were brought forth from the enclosures for purchase. Ship surgeons, wrote one slave trader, "examine every part of every one of them, to the smallest member, men and women, being all stark naked." Then the bargaining began. Negotiating the purchase price of slaves proved a complicated, capricious affair, as African sellers were wily barterers. "The natives have a splendid mental capacity with much judgment and sharp and ready apprehension," wrote one slave ship captain. A male slave might bring thirteen bars of iron; a female, nine bars and two brass rings. Often the bargaining dragged on for days. In addition to slaves, ship captains purchased the provisions (such as yams and other foods) that the slaves and crews would consume during the fifty to eighty days it took to cross the ocean.

When the bargaining ended, the slaves were ferried in large canoes, manned by local Africans, to the ships waiting at anchor offshore. Some tried to swallow handfuls of sand in a desperate effort to maintain a link to their homeland. Often branded with a hot iron and shackled in pairs, they huddled on deck, watching other prisoners being hauled aboard. Sometimes weeks passed before the captain had packed the ship with as many slaves as possible. During those weeks, some of the captives succumbed to disease or killed themselves.

Equiano recalled, "When I was carried on board, I was immediately handled, and tossed up, to see if I were sound, by some of the crew; and I was now persuaded that I had gotten into a world of bad spirits, and that they were going to kill me." Frightened by their long hair, their strange language, and their bleached skin, the Ibo youth concluded that "if ten thousand worlds had been my own, I would have freely parted with them all to have exchanged my condition with that of the meanest slave in my own country."

On the slave ship, the bound Africans were thrust below into half-decks with little more than four feet of headroom. If the ship that carried Equiano was typical, he would have been jammed below deck among roughly three hundred other slaves. Like him, about forty-five of them would have been under fourteen years of age. "The stench of the hold while we were on the coast," Equiano recalled, "was so intolerably loathsome, that it was dangerous to remain there for any time. . . . The closeness of the place, and the heat of the climate added to the number in the ship which was so crowded that each had scarcely room to turn himself, almost suffocated us. This . . . produced copious perspirations, so that the air soon became unfit for respiration, from a variety of loathsome smells, and brought on a sickness amongst the slaves of which many died, thus falling victims to the improvident avarice, as I may call it, of their purchasers."

Confined below deck as the ship was readied for sail, the Africans lost all hope of seeing their families and homelands again. As European slave traders knew, this was the moment when the chance of suicide or an uprising was greatest. One slaver warned that "these slaves have so great a love for their country, that they despair when they see that they are leaving it forever; that makes them die of grief, and I have heard merchants . . . say that they die more often before leaving the port than during the voyage."

The Middle Passage: A Floating Hell

The fear that inspired suicide while still on African land lessened as the ship got under way and the "middle passage" began, but the chance of death by disease or privation increased. Even on the better ships, the shackled Africans found that their cramped quarters made it impossible to walk unless their captors dragged them on deck for exercise. On the worst ships, they could barely turn over in the holds. "They had not so much room as a man in his coffin," testified one ship's surgeon. "This wretched situation," Equiano wrote in his narrative, "was again aggravated by the galling of the chains, now become insupportable; and the filth of the necessary tubs, into which the children often fell, and were almost suffocated. The shrieks of the women, and the groans of the dying, rendered the whole scene of horror almost inconceivable."

European ships had transported enslaved Africans across the Atlantic for more than three centuries before any European sketched or painted a below-deck scene from such a vessel. In about 1840, an officer of the *HMS Albatross*—a British Royal Navy ship intercepting Portuguese slave ships carrying Africans to Brazil—painted this haunting scene, which he witnessed on the slave ship Albanez.

Even though it was to the advantage of the ship captains to deliver sellable slaves on the other side of the Atlantic, few stocked their ships properly. Pitiful rations led to undernourishment, confinement in leg irons spread disease, and the impossibility of basic hygiene eroded the Africans' self-respect. Equiano explained that "the loathsomeness of the stench and crying together" below decks made him unable to eat, for which he was flogged. Slaves who refused to eat were sometimes force-fed. The ship's crew applied hot coals to open captives' lips or used an instrument, the speculum oris (mouth opener), to wrench their jaws apart.

Dehydration imperiled the captives as well. On one ship, the captain provided just one coconut shell filled with water with each meal—which amounted to less than two pints of liquid a day. On many ships, the slaves had even less water. As their sodium and potassium levels dropped due to dehydration, they lost weight, grew listless, and fell into a dazed state. The slavers called this condition "melancholy" and believed it set in as slaves willed themselves to die. But some perceptive observers, such as the port physician in Charleston, South Carolina, knew otherwise. Recognizing the symptoms of malnutrition and dehydration, he wondered how any incoming Africans "escape with life."

For enslaved African women, the Middle Passage had one additional terror and humiliation: rape. Slavers of all European nations separated African men and women during the ocean crossing, in part because they feared the women would incite the men to mutiny. But the arrangement also gave sailors access to their female captives, whom they regarded as fair sexual prey. They brought women above deck often only to rape them. Equiano had "even known them [sailors] to gratify their brutal passion with females not ten years old."

Desperate for deliverance from this living hell, some enslaved Africans plotted mutiny. Rebellions on slave ships may have been as high as one in every ten. Experienced English ship captains tried to prevent conspiracy by obtaining their human cargo from different regions along the African coast so the captives could not communicate. To stifle insurrection, captains also used stark brutality. Leaders of a suspected uprising were flogged to death or dismembered in full view of the others to send a warning. John Atkins, aboard an English slave vessel in 1721, described how the captain "whipped and scarified" several plotters and sentenced others "to cruel deaths, making them first eat the Heart and Liver of one of them killed." The captain hoisted one female resistor up by the thumbs, then "whipp'd and slashed her with knives, before the other slaves, till she died."

Sale in the Americas

Probably not more than two of every three captured Africans lived to see the Americas. Those who survived were psychologically numb and physically depleted. But stumbling ashore, they had to endure yet another horror: being sold as chattel to a European master and then transported to the place of their labor. For Equiano, this final stage proved as devastating as the physical agony of the crossing. In Barbados, a slave-based English sugar colony in the West Indies, he trembled as merchants and planters clambered aboard ship. He believed that "we should be eaten by these ugly men, as they appeared to us." But the merchants informed the slaves that they "were not to be eaten, but to work, and were soon to go on land, where we should see many of our country people." Taken ashore, Equiano shrank in terror as "the buyers rush at once into the yard where the slaves are confined, and make choice of that parcel they like best. The noise and clamor with which this is attended . . . serve not a little to increase the apprehensions of the terrified Africans. . . . In this manner, without scruple, are relations and friends separated, most of them never to see each other again."

No one bought Equiano; he was too young and weak. So he was shipped to North America. Far up a river off the Chesapeake Bay, the owner of a small Virginia plantation purchased the boy. There, torn from all that was familiar, he had "now totally lost the small remains of comfort I had enjoyed in conversing with my countrymen; the women too, who used to wash and take care of me, were all gone different ways, and I never saw one of them afterwards." Isolated, Equiano remembered being "exceedingly miserable, and thought myself worse off than any of the rest of my companions; for they could talk to each other, but I had no person to speak to that I could understand. In this state I was constantly grieving and pining, and wishing for death rather than anything else."

From capture in Africa to arrival at the plantation, farm, or city home of a European master may have averaged six months. During this time the African was completely cut off from family, home, and community life. The body was tortured, the spirit shocked and seared. Now the African had to learn a new language, adjust to a new diet, adapt to a new climate and physical environment, and master new work routines. Most important, he or she had to find a way to live in bondage forever. But for many, "forever" proved short. Every fourth African arriving on American soil died within just four years.

Early Africans in North America

"We commended ourselves to God Our Lord and made our escape. . . . As we traveled that day, in considerable fear that the Indians would follow us, we saw some smoke and, toward the end of the day, reached it, where we espied an Indian who, when he saw us coming toward him, fled without waiting for our arrival. We sent the black after him, and when the Indian saw that he was alone, he waited for him." With these words, Alvar Núñez Cabeza de Vaca, a Spanish conquistador (conqueror), told the story of his epic escape from enslavement by Florida Indians in the 1530s and the start of a five-year journey through the southern reaches of North America. The "black" he referred to was Estévan, also called Estéban, Estévanico, and sometimes "the black Arabian." "The black," continued de Vaca, "told [the Indian] that we were looking for the people who were making that smoke. He replied that . . . he would guide us to them: and so we followed him and he ran to tell the people that we were coming;

at sunset . . . we reached them . . . and they indicated that they were happy to have our company; and so they took us to their houses and lodged Dorantes [de Vaca's compatriot] and the black in the house of one medicine man."

This encounter among Spanish explorers, a black Arabian, and Native Americans in the forests of Florida occurred in 1534. Fifty years later, the English would make their first attempt to plant a colony in North America. Nearly a century later, the young Equiano would labor in the fields and houses of Virginia. The incident de Vaca describes shows how cultures converged and the definitions of race blurred in this early era in North American history.

Africans and the Spanish Conquest in the Americas

Estévan was the product of three cultures coming together along the western edge of the Atlantic. His experience embodied the beginning of a long process by which the notion of race first emerged in Europe, Africa, and the Americas. The Spanish referred to him as "a black," "a Moor," or "an Arabian." But these words merely described his skin color (dark), his religion (Islam), and his homeland (Morocco). De Vaca never called him a slave—though he was owned by Andrés Dorantes. Nor did de Vaca ever suggest that Estévan was inferior, primitive, or savage. Rather, de Vaca's account described how four men—three Spanish and one African—became the first nonnatives to penetrate the vast interior of North America. What mattered in this strange and often hostile land was not Estévan's blackness or even his slave status. It was his linguistic abilities, his fortitude, and his cleverness as a go-between. Estévan was an Atlantic Creole—a person from the eastern shore of the Atlantic who acquired new cultural and linguistic attributes on the western shore. His owner and companions counted on him to help them navigate the challenges of their daunting journey.

Seventy-five years before the English first tried to establish colonies in North America, Africans had been in the Americas. By 1600, as many as 56,000 of them had arrived in the Spanish colonies in Florida and present-day New Mexico. Africans had also come to South America. By 1650 about 40,000 had been shipped to Brazil, where Portuguese entrepreneurs were setting up huge sugar and coffee plantations.

Many Spanish explorers and settlers came to the Americas with enslaved Africans whose ability to soldier and to learn native languages made them valuable negotiators with native peoples. For example, two Africans with Hispanicized names—Juan Garrido and Juan González—were on Juan Ponce de León's expedition to explore and seize Puerto Rico in 1508. By assisting the explorer, Garrido and González obtained their freedom and stayed on to mine gold. Some Africans also aided the Spanish in slaving raids against the Caribs on the islands of Guadalupe, Dominica, and Santa Cruz. In 1513, when Vasco Nuñez de Balboa became the first European to cross the Isthmus of Panama and see the Pacific Ocean, he had thirty Africans with him. Africans also accompanied Hernán Cortés during his siege of the Aztec capital of

Tenochtitlán (in modern-day Mexico) in 1521. Cortés's entourage included Garrido, who later became a gold miner, landowner, caretaker of one of the conquered city's aqueducts, and gatekeeper of its *cabildo* (city hall). Likewise, Africans participated in Francisco Pizarro's conquest of the Incas in Peru in 1532. Later, when local Indians murdered Pizarro, Africans carried his body to the Catholic cathedral that the Spanish had built in Lima. Some historians have claimed that one of Columbus's mariners, Pedro Alonso Niño, was an African, though this is disputed.

Africans in Early Spanish North America

As early as 1513, when the Spanish first set foot on what would become the United States, they had African slaves with them. As in Puerto Rico, Ponce de León included Juan Garrido and Juan González, as well as African scouts and ship handlers, in his expedition to Florida. In 1521, they returned with de León to Florida to help stake Spain's claim to the entire eastern coast of North America. To make good on this claim, 600 Spanish settlers—led by Lucas Vásquez de Ayllón and accompanied by many black slaves—tried to establish a permanent colony in La Florida (as the Spanish called it) in 1526. The group settled near present-day Sapelo Sound in Georgia. When starvation, disease, and a leadership crisis beset the expedition and Guale Indians attacked, some Africans fled and joined the Guale tribe. They married Guales, started families, and began the mixing of Africans and Native Americans that would continue in North America for centuries.

In 1528, Estévan arrived in Florida with his Spanish master as part of Pánfilo de Narváez's expedition. There, the 500 Spanish and Africans settled near the swamplands of Tampa Bay. This colony fared as poorly; only four members survived, including de Vaca and Estévan, and were shortly enslaved by nearby Native Americans. During his captivity, Estévan became a linguist, healer, guide, and negotiator.

Born in Africa, Juan Garrido accompanied Juan Ponce de León on his expeditions to Puerto Rico and Florida. This image shows Garrido with de León astride a Spanish horse as the two approach several Indian chiefs in about 1519. The picture appeared in Diego Duran's Historia de las Indias de Nueve España e Islas de la Tierra Firme, published in Spain in 1581.

Following their escape, the four fled Florida and headed west. Estévan continued to negotiate with the hostile Indians they encountered. In the course of the journey, his status as the slave of a Spanish adventurer all but dissolved. Paddling crude boats across the Gulf of Mexico, the four shipwrecked on the Texas coast, took refuge among merciful natives, and then plunged into the Texas interior. Following Indian guides for the next two years, the four came to be regarded as holy men who possessed the power to heal. Indians in Spanish New Mexico described them as "four great doctors, one of them black, the other three white, who gave blessings [and] healed the sick." On one occasion, Indians gave Estévan a sacred gourd rattle—a rare honor. Making their way southwest, the four eventually met with Spanish settlers in Mexico. Evidence suggests that they reached the Pacific Ocean in 1536.

In 1539, Estévan joined a new Spanish expedition. Departing from Mexico City and heading north into Spanish New Mexico, the group blazed a trail for Francisco Vásquez de Coronado's expedition of 1540. In what would later be Arizona, the Spanish selected Estévan to forge ahead into Zuni country with Indian guides in search of the fabled seven gold-filled cities of Cíbola. He became the first outsider to penetrate the vast Colorado Plateau. Unfortunately for him and his group, the Zuni saw him as an intruder and killed him.

In the same year that Estévan had set out, Hernando de Soto made a further attempt to settle La Florida. Like every other Spanish expedition, this one included free and enslaved Africans. But the search for silver in the country of the Creeks failed, and de Soto perished at the hands of the Indians. Half of his soldiers and the accompanying Africans died as well. Those who survived limped back to Mexico "dressed only in animal skins."

Late in the sixteenth century, the Spanish—again accompanied by free and enslaved Africans—finally established a secure presence in La Florida. When French Huguenots (Protestants) planted a small rival colony near present-day Jacksonville in 1562, the Spanish sent Pedro Menéndez de Avilés, captain general of the Spanish fleets in the West Indies, to crush them. Avilés quickly identified a talented, free mulatto (part European and part African) named Luis living with the Calusa tribe south of St. Augustine. He came to depend on Luis to negotiate with the native people to gain their support. Avilés found other Africans living with Indian tribes as well, many of whom had fled French masters. Avilés destroyed the French outpost and established a Spanish colony in Florida that lasted for two centuries.

Life in La Florida was harsh for Spaniards and Africans alike. But the scarcity of capable workers and skilled linguists gave enslaved Africans a higher status and a greater degree of freedom than they would have after the English set up colonies in North America. By the time the English had mounted their Jamestown expedition in 1606, about one hundred African slaves and a small number of free black people, many of them married to Indians or Spaniards, lived in La Florida.

The role of Africans on these grueling expeditions through mapless territory gave slavery a distinct character in the early Spanish settlements. The slaves did much of the backbreaking work in the fields, on supply trains, and in fort and church construction. But they also served as soldiers, guides, and linguists. Along the west coast, Africans were a significant fraction of settlers in Mexico's northern frontier, including what would become the American Southwest, where they also served in a variety of roles. On both the east and west coasts, Africans forged sexual unions and raised children with Native Americans and Spanish people. This genetic blending blurred the definition of slavery. Officially, the Spanish regarded purity of lineage as the entitlement to elite status and ranked people on a social scale according to their ancestry. But pure lineage meant little on the frontiers of New Spain. There, Spanish, Native Americans, and Africans intermingled so much that traditional social categories broke down. A person's value to the community mattered far more than his or her "race." By the early 1700s, one observer of New Spain's northern frontier remarked that "practically all those who wish to be considered Spaniards are people of mixed blood."

Conclusion

When Diego Gomes first reached the coast of West Africa in 1456 to arrange treaties of commerce with African rulers, he unwittingly formed links between Europeans and Africans that would lock the two in a shameful embrace. Struggling to establish plantations on the islands off Africa's coast, the Portuguese began depending on enslaved Africans to produce highly profitable sugar. By the end of the 1400s, the Portuguese had extended the plantation system to the other side of the ocean. Europe, Africa, and the Americas were now bound together in a vast, Atlantic-wide system of trade and cultural exchange. The system would exert a disastrous impact on the peoples of Africa—not only those left behind but also those who survived the brutal journey to the Americas.

From the mid-fifteenth to the late nineteenth centuries, Europeans tore millions of Africans from their ancestral homelands and shipped them to the Atlantic islands and the Americas to labor in their colonies. No account of the enslavement of Africans can quite convey the demoralization and agony that accompanied the forced march to the coast of Africa and the subsequent loading aboard of the unfortunate captives. One historian has called it "the most traumatizing mass human migration in modern history."

Africans who ended up in North America met with profoundly different experiences, depending on who owned them, when they arrived on the coast, and where they ended up living. In the 1500s, only a few thousand Africans arrived in the Americas in chains. Many of them assumed roles based on their valuable skills, not on their "race." Moreover, they raised families with Native American and Spanish partners, contributing to a blending of cultures that would powerfully shape the New World. But during the 1600s, the trickle of Africans across the Atlantic burgeoned into a steady stream. By the time Equiano arrived in the mid-eighteenth century, it was a torrent. With increasing numbers of slaves, the English entry into the Atlantic slave trade, and English challenges to Spanish, French, and Dutch footholds in North America, came changing attitudes toward Africans and changes in the practice of slavery itself.

Questions for Review and Reflection

1. Once the Portuguese found a way to navigate down the west coast of Africa, was it inevitable that a slave trade would begin? To what extent was the slave trade forced upon West Africans? What were some of the dynamics of African complicity in it?

2. Once colonizing Europeans established the plantation system on the west side of the Atlantic, what labor sources might they have drawn upon instead of enslaved Africans?

3. What strategies and resources did enslaved Africans draw on to endure the traumas of capture, the "middle passage" across the Atlantic, and sale in New World European colonies?

4. How would you characterize the first encounters between colonizing Spaniards and enslaved Africans taken to their colonies? What were some of the possibilities and limits within which African Americans negotiated the terms of their bondage?

3

CHAPTER

Africans in Early North America, 1619–1726

Anthony Johnson and His Family in the Early Chesapeake

Antonio had been in Virginia only a year before a furious assault by Powhatan Indians nearly destroyed Warresquioke, his master's tobacco plantation. The day was March 22, 1622—Good Friday. Antonio survived, along with just four others of the fifty-seven people (mostly field laborers) living on the plantation. Opechancanough, the Indian leader intent on driving the English back into the ocean after fifteen years of clashes, led the well-planned attack. Antonio was no stranger to violence, having been wrenched from his home in Africa. Now he witnessed firsthand the bitter conflicts between indigenous people and Europeans seeking to establish settlements in North America.

Antonio was almost certainly brought to the Americas on a Portuguese slave ship from the Kongo-Angolan region of Africa. Then he was likely captured by a Dutch ship and sold in Jamestown, the center of the Virginia colony the English had founded in 1607. The young African labored on the plantation for nearly twenty years after his owner recovered his losses and replenished his supply of slaves.

After the Powhatan attacks, Antonio found a wife—quite a feat in a colony that now had only a handful of women. He married Mary, an African woman who had just recently arrived in Virginia, and they started a family. The couple lived together for more than forty years. One of their grandchildren honored the family's heritage by naming his 44-acre Maryland farm Angola.

1586	Africans help defend Spanish St. Augustine against the English.
1607	The first permanent North American English colony at Jamestown, Virginia.
1613	The first Africans on Manhattan Island (later New Amsterdam).
1619	Ships deliver Africans to Virginia for sale into bondage.
1620	Pilgrims settle Plymouth Colony in Massachusetts.
1625	The Dutch in New Amsterdam begin to purchase enslaved Africans.
1630s	English planters begin importing slaves to the Caribbean.
1630	English Puritans establish colonies in New England.
1637	Puritans trade captured Pequot Indians for enslaved Africans.
1663	South Carolina settlers import slaves from the West Indies.
1664	English seize New Netherlands (now New York) and sanction slavery.
1675	Bacon's Rebellion in Virginia fuels replacement of white servants with African slaves.
1682	The French claim the vast North American interior.
1684	English settlers in Pennsylvania engage in the slave trade.
1690s	Chesapeake planters shift from white indentured labor to African slave labor.
1696	English Parliament opens slave trade to British merchants.
1702	New York passes a slave code. English marauders burn Spanish St. Augustine, a slave sanctuary.
1712	Slave revolt in New York City sparks executions and brutal punishments. South Carolina passes a comprehensive slave code.
1715	Yamasee War pits Indians and Africans against English colonists and Africans.
1718	The French build New Orleans with the labor of enslaved Africans.
1724	Louisiana's *Code Noir* regulates slavery.
1725–1726	Pennsylvania passes act "for the better regulation of Negroes."

Sometime in the 1640s, Antonio and Mary gained their freedom. They chose the names Anthony and Mary Johnson to signify their new status and made a place for themselves in Northampton County, on Virginia's eastern shore. By 1651, they had acquired 250 acres of tobacco land, built up a small herd of cattle and hogs, and had two black servants. In this corner of North

America, where slave status and racial boundaries had not yet hardened in legal terms, the Johnsons were among many small planters scrambling to improve their lot in life. They apparently enjoyed respect from the authorities; in 1653, the county court forgave their taxes after a fire destroyed their dwelling. As Anthony Johnson told the court, "[Our] hard labors and known services for obtaining [our] livelihood were well known."

Both of Anthony and Mary's sons acquired homesteads—one of 550 acres; the other, 100 acres. One of the young men married a white woman. This wasn't unusual at a time when an African man could offer a woman just as decent a life as a white man could.

However, by the 1640s slave status and racial boundaries began to harden. Virginia's planter-lawmakers moved to regulate human bondage and interracial relations. Yet because slavery did not exist in England, they had no laws to copy. They began to create laws of their own, just as English settlers had done in the West Indies. Bit by bit, court judges and legislators established precedents that assigned Africans to lifelong slavery. The newly defined institution contrasted sharply with indentured servitude, an ancient English labor contract into which master and servant entered freely. Most indentured servitude agreements specified terms of five to seven years. During that time, the servant was entirely at the master's disposal but looked forward to regaining his or her freedom at the end of the term.

In 1655, Anthony Johnson himself became involved in distinguishing between servant and slave. A neighboring white planter had taken up the case of John Casor, the Johnsons' servant. The Johnsons, the neighbor argued before the county court, had held Casor beyond the agreed-upon seven years specified in most indentured servitude terms. Johnson retorted that he and Casor had not made an indenture. In fact, he added, neither Casor nor the neighbor could produce the indenture they claimed Johnson had violated. In the end, the court accepted Johnson's argument that he had purchased the lifelong labor of Casor—that, in effect, Casor was a slave. Because Casor had been enslaved in his African homeland, the court decided that anyone who bought him—even a fellow African—could count on his service for life. Losing his case, Casor served the Johnsons for another seventeen years before they gave him his freedom. Eventually, he succeeded in his own right as a tobacco planter.

By 1664, perhaps sensing diminishing opportunities for their children and their mixed-race grandchildren in Virginia, the Johnsons and one son began selling their land to white neighbors. They then moved north to Maryland, a colony founded in 1632 as a refuge for English Catholics. Renting land there, they took up farming and cattle-raising again. Six years later, when Anthony died, Virginia's tightening restrictions on Africans thwarted the execution of his will. A jury of white men declared that because Johnson "was a Negroe and by consequence an alien," the 50 Virginia acres he had deeded to his son Richard before moving to Maryland should go to a local white planter. In a colony filled with unfree laborers of many skin hues, the legal net began tightening around the small number of free Africans and their children.

By the late seventeenth century, enslaved Africans laboring in Maryland and Virginia became trapped in a legal system designed to keep them in perpetual bondage. Those who did manage to win their freedom were forced to the margins of society by whites eager to claim the fruits of former slaves' initiative and hard work. In just this way, Anthony and Mary Johnson's family suffered a slow decline from being landowners to tenant farmers. In the early 1680s, one of the couple's sons, John, moved north into Delaware. There, one of his daughters married a local Indian and became part of a triracial community that survives to the present day. The other son, Richard, stayed behind in Virginia. Stripped of the land left him by his parents, he worked as a carpenter and had little to leave his own sons when he died in 1689. Anthony and Mary Johnson's grandchildren in Virginia worked as tenant farmers and servants, laboring on plantations owned by white people.

The Johnson family's story mirrors the plight of many African newcomers in the seventeenth and early eighteenth centuries. During the first few decades of English settlement along the Atlantic coast of North America, slave status and racial boundaries were fluid. Black people born and enslaved in Africa could marry in the young Virginia colony, earn their freedom, farm "myne owne ground," testify in court, and see a son marry a white woman. But after the mid-eighteenth century, new laws eroded Africans' standing and security and eventually defined slavery solely on the basis of race. In Virginia, Maryland, and the Carolinas, a few Africans captured as slaves initially mingled with white indentured servants and eventually obtained their freedom. Now plantation owners—increasingly dependent on the labor of captives from Africa—had a vested interest in consigning black people to lifelong slavery.

As this momentous change transformed the southern colonies, slavery began to take root in the northern colonies as well, though not on the same scale. The institution also emerged along the boundaries of English settlement, in the Spanish and French colonies of Florida and Louisiana. However, the shape and character of these Afro-Spanish and Afro-French societies contrasted sharply with those of the English settlements. Those differences exerted an impact that persists today.

The First Africans in English North America

"Your country? How came it yours? Before the Pilgrims landed we were here." Thus wrote W. E. B. Du Bois, the pioneering black historian and political leader who in 1895 became the first African American to receive a PhD in history at Harvard University. Du Bois posed this question many decades ago, prompted by history textbooks' near total silence on the subject of Africans' contributions to the building of European colonies in North America. As he rightly pointed out, Africans were present at the beginning of almost every European settlement. Probably 80 percent of all who crossed the Atlantic to take up life in the Americas from 1600 to 1820 were Africans. In North America, more than half the newcomers were Africans.

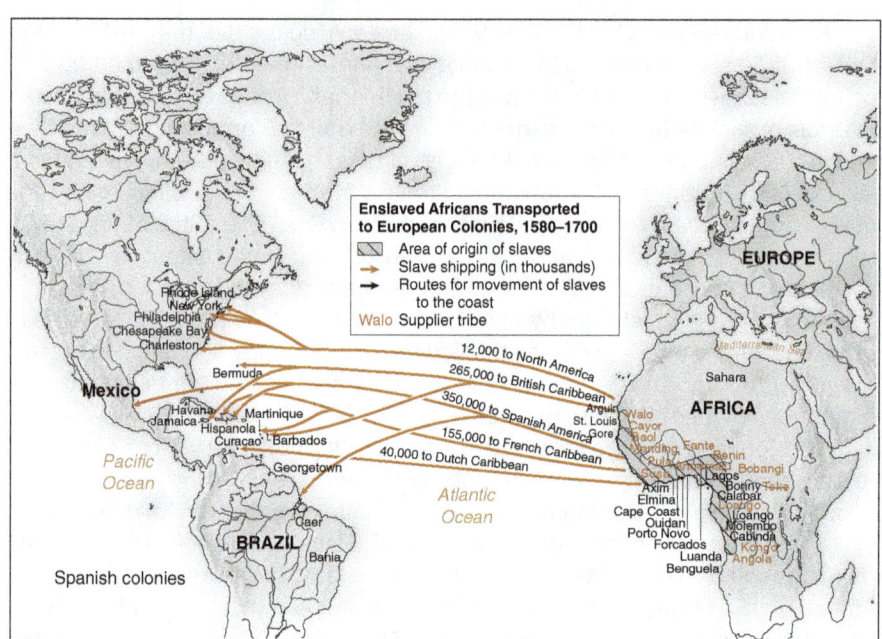

MAP 3.1 Enslaved Africans Transported to European Colonies, 1580–1700

This map contrasts the small number of enslaved Africans transported to the North American colonies in the seventeenth century with the number imported to the Caribbean and Spanish America. For example, from 1660 to 1700, about 120,000 Africans arrived in Barbados. During that same time, only about 10,000 came to Maryland and Virginia.

By the end of the 1600s, the use of African slaves had enabled plantation owners to make whopping profits. The slave trade also catalyzed exchanges of valuable crops, agricultural techniques, and medical knowledge that redefined ways of life not only in the Americas but also in Europe and Africa. During this period, white indentured labor gave way to slave labor in the English colonies, and colonial legislators created laws to sanction, justify, and administer the emerging slave system.

The Chesapeake Colonies

When Anthony Johnson reached Virginia in 1621, he probably met countrymen and women who had arrived in 1619 from the Kongo-Angola region of West Central Africa. Most had been caught in the slave network operating out of Luanda, the primary port of Angola, a Portuguese colony in Africa. Luanda shipped about 8,000 slaves across the Atlantic each year. The vast majority were sold in Spanish and Portuguese New World colonies where white settlers had established the plantation system. By 1650, the Spanish had imported at least 235,000 slaves to their colonies in the West Indies and Mexico, while the Portuguese had brought upward of 42,000 slaves to the coffee and sugar fields of Brazil. Thus, Anthony Johnson was among the handful of Africans forced into North America before the slave trade boomed there.

English plantation owners in Virginia and Maryland, along the Chesapeake Bay, needed field hands to work their tobacco fields. Because they found plenty of white indentured servants and English prisoners eager to contract their labor for passage to the Americas, they had little interest in buying black slaves from Africa. After all, it was much cheaper to transport poor English and Irish laborers in English ships than to purchase enslaved Africans from Portuguese and Dutch slave traders, whose monopoly of the African slave trade allowed them to charge high prices.

By 1650, Virginia's white settlers had weathered early conflicts with Native Americans and had grown to about 18,300 in number—including thousands of white indentured servants. Only about 400 Africans lived in Virginia—a stark contrast to European-African population ratios in the Caribbean and South American colonies. Maryland, England's Catholic colony, also had few Africans. In the Chesapeake region white indentured servants and white convicts planted, weeded, harvested, cured, and packed tobacco.

As late as 1680, when the Chesapeake colonies' populations had swelled to about 57,000 in total, only some 3,200 were slaves (about 5 percent of the population). Despite the boom in tobacco production, indentured white people still made up the majority of the people working the fields.

The Northern Colonies

Anthony and Mary Johnson were among the first of just a few Africans in the English colonies in the early 1600s. But as the century wore on, the number of Africans grew. The Puritans of Massachusetts Bay colony, founded in 1630, first imported Africans in 1637 after enslaving Pequot Indian survivors of the bloody Puritan-Pequot war. Knowing they could not hold the Pequots in slavery in an area the natives knew better than their captors, the Puritans shipped them to Providence Island, off the coast of South America, where Puritan planters had already begun using African slaves. Here, the Massachusetts planters exchanged the captive Indians for Africans.

Even though Massachusetts law books didn't specify slavery terms, buyers expected that Africans brought to the Puritan colony would serve a lifetime in bondage. So did the Rhode Islanders who purchased slaves when they could find them. However, like the Virginians, they employed mainly white indentured servants for most of the seventeenth century. The number of Africans grew slowly in New England, in part because the climate didn't support year-round farming. In addition, most white settlers prized homogeneous Christian communities and had little interest in seeing Africans "do all our business." As late as 1700, slaves made up less than 3 percent of New England's population. Most were domestic laborers in the port towns on the rocky coastline.

Nonetheless, New Englanders did have connections to the slave trade. For example, they supplied grain, flour, wood products, and salted fish to the large slave plantations in the West Indies. Moreover, they constructed and sailed ships to the English-run sugar and tobacco islands, where they dealt in slaves and rum. New Englanders also began consuming slave-produced sugar, coffee, rice, tobacco, and indigo—and prizing these luxuries. Not until the late 1690s did England allow New Englanders to enter the slave trade directly by sailing their ships to Africa's west coast. Nonetheless, New England's economy, almost as much as the Chesapeake's, came to rely on the slave system. By the eighteenth century, many upper-class officials, merchants, and ministers measured their status by the number of slaves they owned.

In the Dutch colony of New Netherlands (later renamed New York by the English), slavery eventually took root more firmly and deeply than it did in seventeenth-century Virginia and Maryland. But at first, some newly arriving Africans had opportunities to build lives based on freedom. For example, Jan Rodrigues—an African probably transported by a Portuguese slaver—was left on Manhattan Island in 1613 by a Dutch ship captain. The first non-Indian resident of the island, Rodrigues learned the Indian language, married a Rockaway woman, and fathered several children. He also initiated trade between the Indians and Europeans, which eventually formed the foundation of the colony the Dutch established eleven years later.

Interest in African slaves intensified as the agricultural families, soldiers, and officials of the Dutch West Indies Company set up farms along the Hudson River. In 1625, the Company purchased sixteen black slaves from pirates who had stolen them from Spanish vessels. Their names—including Paul D'Angola, Simon Congo, Anthony Portuguese, and Anthony Portuguis Gracia—suggest that they had either come from Angola or were captured by Portuguese slavers. The Dutch bought additional captive Africans and set them to work building forts, constructing roads, clearing land, and sawing boards out of trees.

Like Anthony and Mary Johnson, these people were slaves, but not necessarily forever. To be sure, the Europeans had begun to consider a person's skin color a mark of slave or free status. However, these Africans with Portuguese names still had opportunities to regain their freedom, accumulate land, and mix with white neighbors. They could also drill with the Dutch militia, sue and be sued in court, and trade independently. Former slave Anthony Jansen van Vaes, for example, took a Dutch wife, joined the Dutch Reformed Church, acquired farmland in Coney Island, and worked as a merchant on Manhattan Island. By 1660, free Afro-Dutch farms were sprinkled along lower Manhattan in the area known today as the Bowery, and a "negro burying ground" served this emerging free black community.

But just as the first Africans in New Netherlands were working their way out of servitude, more and more Africans slated for lifelong bondage began arriving in the colony. By 1650, New Netherlands ranked as the largest slave importation center in North America. The Dutch also moved to control the source of slaves in Africa. In 1637, they captured Castle Elmina, the Portuguese slave trading center on West Africa's Guinea coast, and in the 1640s, they seized Portuguese slaving posts along the coast of present-day Angola and Zaire. Now the Dutch monopolized the flow of slaves up and down Africa's west coast. When the English captured New Netherlands in 1664, one-tenth of the colony's population, and nearly one-quarter of its capital, was African—a far greater black presence than in the Chesapeake.

Small numbers of enslaved Africans arrived in other mid-Atlantic colonies. For example, when the Swedes and Finns established a small colony along the Delaware River in the 1630s, they imported a few Africans. The Dutch seized this colony in 1655 and brought in additional African slaves. After England captured New Netherlands in 1664, English settlers streamed into East Jersey across the Hudson River in search of good land. These settlers included planters from the West Indies island of Barbados seeking larger land holdings, and many brought dozens of slaves with them. They also brought their harsh attitudes toward slaves, viewing them as chattel no different from horses or oxen. These attitudes soon infected the thinking of European settlers in North America who had not yet seen the harsher slavery practiced in the Caribbean. While the Europeans prized the opportunity to acquire land as free men and to control their own labor, they saw no irony in using slave labor to work their land.

In the 1670s, more Europeans came to the mid-Atlantic coast. English, Irish, and German Quakers fleeing religious persecution settled East and West Jersey as well as William Penn's new colony of Pennsylvania. These newcomers found only small numbers of slaves in the Delaware River valley region. But within two years of its founding, Philadelphia became a slave trading and slaveholding hub. When the English slave ship *Isabella* arrived in 1684, 150 dazed Africans staggered ashore. Pioneering Quakers, living in riverbank caves and crude buildings at first, soon put the Africans to work clearing trees and brush, splitting wood and sawing boards, digging house foundations, and laying out streets. In a town comprising about 800 settlers, these 150 Africans nearly doubled the workforce while relieving white craftsmen of heavy labor.

As members of the Society of Friends, the Quakers followed a "peace testimony" that renounced violence in human affairs. But slave ownership put them in a dilemma: how could they administer physical punishment? One Quaker objected that "Quakers do here handle men" as people in Europe "handle their cattle." And some German Quakers lamented the very nature of slavery and refused to own slaves.

How would the Society of Friends handle an outright slave revolt—the kind that erupted periodically in the English West Indies? Word had already reached Philadelphia of the 1685–1686 revolt in Jamaica, in which slaves had murdered several dozen white people and white authorities had, in retaliation, burned slaves at the stake, had them torn apart by hunting dogs, or ordered them drawn and quartered. In Barbados, too, Quakers learned, slaves had mounted a massive uprising in 1675 and plotted further revolts in 1683 and 1686.

Most Quakers held just one or a few slaves and tried to treat them humanely. Deeply disturbed by antislavery protests, they wrestled with their consciences for many years. But less conscientious Quakers joined other colonists in exploiting black labor, trading beef, wheat, and wood products for slaves, sugar, and rum in the British islands. Gradually, they entrenched themselves in the Atlantic basin human trade network connecting West Africa with the Caribbean and the North American mainland.

TABLE 3.1 REGIONAL AFRICAN POPULATION IN ENGLISH AMERICA, 1630–1710

This table reveals that the rate of growth in African populations was four times as high in the southern colonies as in New England. It also shows that throughout the seventeenth century, slaves in the English colonies lived and worked mostly in the West Indies.

	NEW ENGLAND	MID-ATLANTIC	SOUTH	WEST INDIES	TOTAL	% OF SLAVES IN WEST INDIES
1630	—	20	50	10,000	10,070	99.3
1650	400	520	700	20,000	21,620	92.5
1670	500	800	3,400	40,000	44,700	89.5
1690	950	2,500	13,300	90,000	106,750	84.3
1710	2,600	6,200	29,000	148,000	185,800	79.6

The Fateful Transition

Anthony and Mary Johnson did not live to see what their children witnessed—the emergence of slave societies in which imported Africans performed the majority of field labor. The Johnsons had lived in a place and time in which slavery provided just one of many sources of labor. But their children experienced a pivotal changeover when slavery became the foundation of North America's southern economy—the primary means of producing goods and providing services. In Spanish Mexico, Cuba, and Peru; in Dutch Surinam; in Portuguese Brazil; and in the French Caribbean, European colonists had already seen how consigning Africans to field labor produced cash crops and handsome profits. Soon white planters in North America, inspired by this success, set out to acquire as much land and black muscle as possible.

England Captures the Slave Trade

The English were the last Europeans to engage in the slave-based plantation system, mostly because they had a late start colonizing the Caribbean. Not until the 1640s did English settlers in Barbados, Jamaica, and the Leeward Islands begin copying their European rivals by purchasing thousands of enslaved Africans, mostly from Dutch ships. Soon they embraced slavery enthusiastically, especially after England's defeat of the Dutch in the commercial wars of 1650–1674 meant that England took over the slave trade itself. As English and New England ship captains brought their human cargoes directly from Africa to British America, Britain's slave population increased exponentially. On tiny Barbados, the population was half European and half African in 1660; two generations later, Africans outnumbered Europeans three to one.

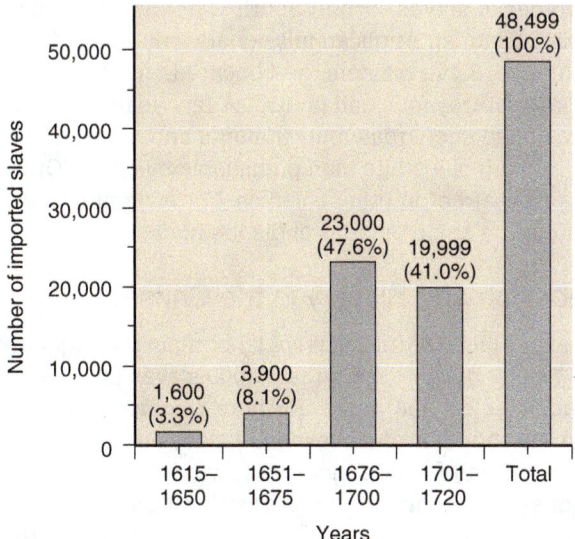

FIGURE 3.1 Number of Slaves Imported from Africa to North America, 1615–1720

This figure shows the sharp increase in the number of African slaves brought to England's North American colonies after 1675. Births to slaves added to the numbers of those brought from Africa so that by 1720, about 70,000 slaves lived in the English mainland colonies. The numbers suggest that births of slaves greatly outnumbered deaths.

South Carolina as a Slave Society

Chartered by the English king Charles II in 1663, South Carolina almost immediately (and to Charles's surprise) became the center of a thriving plantation system. Its first white settlers were well acquainted with slavery. About half came from crowded Barbados, bringing their slaves. For the next two generations, slave-owning English Barbadians controlled South Carolina's politics, commerce, and society. By the early 1700s, these planters relied almost exclusively on slaves to work their rice and indigo plantations. In the eighteenth century, more than half of all enslaved Africans brought to Britain's mainland colonies would flow through Charleston, South Carolina's capital.

Planters wanted slaves with strong backs to do the difficult work of digging ditches and draining the swampy coastal country for rice cultivation. About two-thirds of the Africans they imported were male, most in their teens or early twenties. South Carolinian planters worked these men mercilessly. On average, Africans in this colony died earlier than they did in the Chesapeake. As in the West Indies and Brazil, South Carolina planters treated slaves as replaceable commodities with little regard for how long they lived. The high death rate and need for constant replacements meant that most slaves in this colony had been born in Africa. In the Chesapeake, by contrast, more and more slaves were America born.

As the number of slaves rose in South Carolina, the slave system grew harsher. Francis Le Jau, an Anglican missionary, cringed in 1709 to see a slave woman burned alive. Slave masters, he lamented, "hamstring, maim, and un-limb those poor Creatures for small faults." A few years later, South Carolina's legislature sanctioned such grisly punishments and more. A 1714 law made a black person's striking of a white man punishable by death. Other laws permit-ted retaliations unheard of in other colonies. For example, slave owners could slit the nose or cut the ankle tendons of disobedient slaves.

Bacon's Rebellion and Slavery in the Chesapeake

In 1680, when about 65,000 Africans were laboring in the sugar and coffee fields in the English West Indies, no more than 7,000 slaves toiled in all of England's North American colonies, and in the northern colonies, except where tobacco was cultivated, the number of slaves was small. But in the Chesapeake, the number and proportion of slaves increased dramatically after 1680, especially following an uprising by angry, poor white settlers that unwittingly drew the re-gion deeper into slavery. The rebellion started in 1675, when the brash young Nathaniel Bacon, a recent immigrant from England, raised a small army of land-less but well-armed poor white people. Mostly former indentured servants, Bacon's followers chafed at their limited opportunities in Virginia's Tidewater region. They were especially enraged that Virginia's governor had closed off frontier settlement to avert conflicts with Native Americans. What began as a frontier war against Native Americans soon turned into a civil war. As free black people and runaway slaves joined the poor white rebels, Bacon's forces turned against planter aristocrats who supported the governor. By the time the violence ebbed, the rebels had burned Jamestown and forced the governor to flee.

Shaken, white planters refrained from recruiting indentured servants, who would eventually secure freedom, and began purchasing slaves, who would constitute a permanent labor force. Fear was not the only driving factor, how-ever. First, economic opportunities in England had improved, so fewer white men and women were venturing to the New World in search of a livelihood. Moreover, those who did come preferred the northern colonies, where terms of servitude were shorter and less harsh than in the Chesapeake. Second, seeking to suppress discontent, Virginia and Maryland clamped down on the shipment of white convicts to the Chesapeake. Finally, just as the supply of indentured servants and convicts in the Chesapeake dwindled, the supply of Africans boomed. England's control of the slave trade caused it to flourish, especially after 1696, when English merchants persuaded Parliament to end the royal mo-nopoly. With hundreds of new merchants now entering the trade, the flow of slaves to North America swelled. And with greater supply, the price of slaves dropped—so southern planters could purchase Africans more easily and cheaply than ever.

Africans Resist

As white colonists soon learned, dependence on black labor came at great cost. On a Monday morning in April 1712, white residents of New York awoke to a horrific sight: white bodies bleeding in the streets. Three of the dead were English, three were French, two were Dutch, one was a German, and another was a Walloon (from today's Belgium). Seven others had survived their wounds. The perpetrators were a group of more than twenty Africans who set fire to a building and then lay in wait, with knives and axes, for whites to come and extinguish the flames. Some of the attackers were newly arrived African slaves; one was a free black man who claimed mystical powers. "Had it not been for the garrison [of English soldiers] there," reported one New Yorker, "that city would have been reduced to ashes, and the greatest part of the inhabitants murdered."

After quelling the revolt, white New Yorkers took about seventy slaves into custody. They tried forty-three and convicted twenty-five, including three women and several enslaved Indians. Determined to raise the cost of rebellion, white magistrates imposed grisly death penalties: thirteen slaves died on the gallows, three were burned at the stake, one was starved to death in chains, and one was broken on the wheel. Six others killed themselves to escape this kind of retribution. Though the white leaders hoped to set an example with these punishments, neither they nor the Africans were convinced that fear would suppress revolts.

Defining Slavery, Defining Race

John Punch stood before Virginia's high court alongside his friends Victor and James Gregory in 1640. Their heads no doubt bowed, the three indentured servants waited anxiously for the judge's decision. They must have suspected that the court would punish them severely for fleeing their Welsh master, Hugh Gwyn, despite their vivid descriptions of his brutality. After escaping, they had managed to reach Maryland, but there they were captured. John Punch, an African; Victor, a Dutchman; and James Gregory, a Scot: they had joined their fates in their escape.

John Punch listened to the bewigged judge read out the sentence: Victor and James were to receive thirty lashes, serve Gwyn an extra year, and then labor three more years for the colony. Next came these astonishing words: "Being a negro . . . John Punch shall serve his said master or his assigns for the time of his natural life here or elsewhere."

John Punch left no testimony revealing his response to being singled out as "a negro." But his unique sentence revealed a profound shift in white people's attitudes toward black people. During the sixteenth and early seventeenth centuries, the English had called Africans and Native Americans "heathens," and Christian tradition had long sanctioned the enslavement of heathen peoples. Until the mid-seventeenth century in Virginia, being a heathen had defined slavery far more than being dark-skinned did.

Yet neither piety nor pigmentation had much to do with a person's ability to cultivate tobacco. So why did Virginia's high court cite John Punch's race to justify handing him a life sentence? Did simple economics lie behind the decision? Was the court acting on behalf of premier planters—seeking to secure Virginia's labor force by converting black servants' transgressions into a lifetime of hard labor? How could Punch have reasoned otherwise, if no other runaway servant had received such a sentence?

A well-known case ten years before Punch's sentencing had made clear that white Virginians viewed Africans as not just different but inferior. In 1630, the court had ordered Hugh Davis, a white man, "to be soundly whipt before an assembly of negroes & others for abusing himself to the dishonor of God and shame of Christianity by defiling his body in lying with a negro which fault he is to acknowledge next sabbath day." By shaming Davis "before negroes and others," the court hoped to stop interracial sex. Social biases were turning into unequal justice. Racial prejudice had begun paving the way for laws defining race-based slavery.

Laws Defining Social and Racial Relations

The legal decisions in the Punch and Davis cases set precedents defining how people of different races could relate. These precedents eventually influenced how white authorities defined slavery and what kinds of restrictions applied to bondspeople. As Virginia's African population grew slowly between 1640 and 1680, the legislature and courts gradually stripped away their rights and forged the fatal link between slavery and race. Step by step, the terms *English, Christian, white,* and *free* became nearly synonymous in the minds of white colonizers. Meanwhile, the words *African, heathen, black,* and *slave* became equally interchangeable. In gradually associating slavery with race, the English drew from the experience of the West Indies, where English settlers had already worked out definitions of slavery and pieced together a slave code—a comprehensive series of laws regulating the governance of bondspeople.

In Virginia, the slave code developed piecemeal. Race-based punishments and privileges first made their appearance in the 1630 Davis case. Nine years later, white fear of African rebelliousness assumed legal force when the Virginia court ruled that "all persons except Negroes" were to be provided with arms and ammunition for militia duty. Precedents in court rulings and language in legal documents distinguished between white and black, servant and slave. In 1643, the Virginia assembly levied a tax on African women, making it more expensive for Africans to marry, purchase their freedom, and establish independent households. Wills written by white colonists in the 1640s bequeathed Africans and their children "forever."

The earliest Virginian slave owners likely assumed the Africans they imported would serve them for life. But in the 1640s, such assumptions were crystallized in law. As early as 1642, county courts began recording sales of Africans and their children into lifelong bondage to their white owners. In 1660, the legislature implicitly acknowledged the lifelong servitude of Africans when it pinned extra years of indentured servitude on any white servant who ran away with an African—since "Negroes . . . are incapable of making satisfaction by addition of time."

In 1662, the ambiguous legal status of Africans ended. Virginia's House of Burgesses ruled that "all children borne in this country shall be held bond or free only according to the condition of the mother." The legislature passed this law because "some doubts have arisen whether children got by any Englishman upon a negro woman should be slave or free." Here were the two crucial distinctions that set enslavement of Africans throughout the Americas apart from slavery elsewhere in the world: Slave status was lifelong, and it was inherited through enslaved mothers.

While the 1662 law reflected a growing abhorrence of interracial sex, its primary effect was to benefit white slave owners. By declaring that an enslaved black woman's child took the mother's status (the opposite of English legal doctrine in which the child took the father's status), the law ensured that the colony's black labor force would reproduce itself.

Now African women were more vulnerable than ever to white men's sexual exploitation. Every child conceived by a white master, in either a coercive or a consensual relationship with an African woman, added to that labor force—at no extra cost to the master. By extending slave status to the womb, planter-politicians ensured that the *reproductive* as well as *productive* work of black women belonged to their master and that a child's paternity had no relevance in the eyes of the law.

Maryland law was much like Virginia's in requiring that "All Negroes" and their children must serve for life. But in 1664, to stop white women from making matches with black men, a new law required that any freeborn white wife of an

VIRGINIAN LUXURIES.

The marriage of Anthony and Mary Johnson's black son to an Englishwoman in the mid-seventeenth century occasioned little comment in the historical record. But by 1820, the approximate year this anonymous crude painting was done, interracial sex and interracial violence were seen as two sides of the same coin. Though a new Virginia law forbade interracial marriage in 1691, legal efforts could not stop such relationships.

African slave must serve her husband's master as long as her husband lived and that their children would be enslaved for life. Within decades, nearly every mainland colony had a similar law.

Restrictions on Free Black People

These noxious laws may have figured in Mary and Anthony Johnson's decision to move out of Virginia. In 1645, "Anthony the negro" (probably Anthony Johnson) had declared in a Northampton County court: "I know myne owne ground and I will worke when I please and play when I please." But by the 1660s, he would not have been so confident, as new restrictions prevented Africans from acquiring land and intruded on family relations. Mary and Anthony Johnson's new daughter-in-law, wife of their son Richard, was an Englishwoman, but evolving law set out to prohibit such unions. Though nowhere in the Dutch, Spanish, or Portuguese colonies did courts ban interracial marriage, and nowhere else in English America except in Antigua and Bermuda, now courts in Maryland and Virginia—and ultimately more than thirty states—adopted such rulings. These laws remained on the books until as late as the 1970s.

Mary and Anthony Johnson's descendants who remained in Virginia after Anthony's death in 1670 must have felt the impact of Virginia's new restrictions. After 1691, even their marriages were criminalized, as a new law, intended to prevent "that abominable mixture and spurious issue [that is, offspring] . . . by Negroes, mulattoes [mixed-race people] and Indians intermarrying with English or other white women," banished any white man or woman who married an Indian or African person—whether free or enslaved. Like other free black people, the Johnsons' children and grandchildren struggled to navigate around these hardening racial distinctions. Some joined triracial communities in southern Delaware, where Nanticoke Indian, African, and European bloodlines crisscrossed. Others, with white wives or mothers, identified loosely with full-blooded Africans but strove as free, light-skinned Negroes to maintain ties with white neighbors, patrons, and employers.

In basing the definition of slavery on race, Virginia's planters took two additional steps to seal the system. In 1667, the House of Burgesses ruled that "the conferring of baptism doth not alter the condition of the person as to his bondage or freedom." In other words, conversion to Christianity would no longer be an avenue to freedom. Like many black servants who had gained freedom before 1660, Mary and Anthony took Christian vows, baptized their children, and attended church, but now Christian faith offered no protection. The second step came in 1691, when Virginia lawmakers required masters who freed their slaves to transport them out of the colony within six months. This ruling made it clear that only enslaved Africans were welcome in Virginia.

South Carolina's Slave Code

South Carolina recognized slavery from the beginning, its Fundamental Constitutions (1669) proclaiming that "every freeman . . . shall have absolute power and authority over Negro slaves, of what opinion or religion soever."

Here white planters legislated the most complete deprivation of freedom found in the mainland colonies. South Carolina's slave laws required slaves to carry a pass when traveling on their own away from their owner's plantation. Runaways received brutal punishment—whipping for men for the first offense, branding for the second, mutilation or even castration for the third. Anyone who captured an escaped slave received a reward.

Living among legions of enslaved Africans and Indians, as well as indentured whites, Carolina lawmakers also imposed the death penalty on white servants who ran away with enslaved Africans. This unusual measure reflected planters' fear that cross-color alliances at the bottom rungs of society, such as Bacon's Rebellion in Virginia, might topple the slave system entirely. In 1712, South Carolina brought its scattered laws together in a comprehensive slave code.

Though South Carolina developed the most severe racial code in English North America, the colony displayed a remarkable tolerance for interracial sex between white men and black women specifically. Why? There were few white women in the colony. As on Caribbean islands such as Jamaica and Barbados, South Carolinians accepted sexual relations between white men and enslaved black women as a given, and the rising mulatto population testified to this attitude. But at the same time, South Carolina's lawmakers sought to prevent white women from engaging in sex with black men, consigning any white woman who delivered a child fathered by a black man to seven years' servitude. Her child, if a girl, had to serve eighteen years; if a boy, twenty-one years. To keep white women away from free black men, this 1717 law further provided that any free black father of a child born of a white woman must serve as a slave for seven years. Despite the severity of these laws, South Carolinian legislators never prohibited interracial marriages, nor did they employ the emotionally loaded language used in other colonies, where legal terminology described children of mixed parentage as "abominable mixture," "spurious issue," or "disgrace of the nation."

Slavery and Race North of the Chesapeake

Black Alice, as she was known, was born in slavery in Philadelphia, in 1686. She died in 1802—at the age of 116—and her story survived not only because of her longevity but because her remarkable character interested white Philadelphians. For forty years she was the toll keeper at Dunk's Ferry on the Delaware River. She herself was a storyteller who, in the tradition of an African griot—archivist of a tribe's collective memory—remembered the land on which Philadelphia stood "when it was a wilderness, and when the Indians hunted wild game in the woods." She remembered lighting the pipe of William Penn, a slave owner himself. Joining Christ Church, she recalled the first crude sanctuary with ceilings so low "she could reach [them] with her hands from the floor." Until age ninety-five, she rode to church on a horse. "The veneration she had for the bible," claimed one notice after her death, "induced her to lament that she was not able to read it." But when her friends read it to her, she "would listen with great attention, and often make pertinent remarks."

Lithographs, paintings, or sketches of Africans in early North America are rare because artists almost always worked by commission. Few black Americans, whether free or slave, could afford to pay for portraits. The visual record of the early black experience is even sketchier than the literary record. This engraving of Black Alice thus provides a unique glimpse into early North American life. At age ninety-six, the redoubtable Black Alice began to lose her eyesight, but her deteriorating vision hardly slowed her down. Frequently, she rowed into the middle of the Delaware River "from which she seldom returned without a handsome supply of fish for her master's table."

Black Alice's experience was far from typical, but her story reveals the flexible definitions of slavery and race in the northern colonies in this era. Gaining admission to a white Anglican church, working as toll keeper, socializing with important white figures, and winning respect and admiration for her memory of Philadelphia's earliest history, Black Alice had experiences that simply weren't possible in the southern colonies—though she was a slave her entire life.

Unlike Virginia, Maryland, and North and South Carolina, the northern colonies did not make slave labor the main prop of their economy. Nonetheless, white settlers in the North participated eagerly in the African slave trade and created slave codes that remained in force until the American Revolution and beyond.

Slave Codes in New England

During the seventeenth century, New Englanders held more enslaved Indians than imported Africans. They never specifically legislated perpetual and hereditary slavery. However, surviving legal documents such as wills show that slave owners regarded their human property as lifelong servants as early as 1641. By at least 1660, many white people living in New England also assumed that children born of slaves would be lifelong slaves themselves.

Yet Africans teetered between extended servitude and lifelong bondage while occupying an indeterminate status between that of property and that of person. Though they associated slavery with African origins, New Englanders gave their bondspeople many privileges that masters in the southern colonies denied them—for example, the right to testify and sue in court, to make contracts, and to bear arms in colonial wars with masters' consent. Northern slaves could also acquire, hold, or transfer property and even petition the legislature for their freedom. Even more significant, slaves working in New England had the right to life: Their masters could not kill them without legal repercussions, as they could in Maryland and Virginia after 1705. New Englanders never passed laws preventing masters from freeing their slaves.

Slavery and the Law in the Mid-Atlantic

The vise of slavery tightened more rapidly around black life in New Netherlands than in the New England colonies, but not nearly as quickly as in Virginia and Maryland. While the Dutch ruled New Netherlands, men who had capital to invest in imported Africans held slaves for life. They also regarded the offspring of enslaved African women as slaves at birth, though no law mandated this condition.

But the legal fog surrounding Africans evaporated when the English conquered New Netherlands in 1664 and named it New York. Within a year, the legislative assembly sanctioned lifelong servitude for black slaves. Another ruling specified that "no Negro slave who becomes a Christian after he had been bought shall be set at liberty." In 1702, after importing substantial numbers of Africans, the English in New York devised a fully developed slave code that stripped away many entitlements slaves had treasured under Dutch rule, including the right to earn money, bear arms, and secure freedom through self-purchase. The English slave code gave masters the right to inflict any punishment they wanted on a slave, short of dismemberment and death. It also outlawed the assembly of more than three slaves without their masters' consent. It prohibited slaves from buying or selling property, and it removed their right to testify in court except when providing evidence against another slave for running away, destroying his or her master's property, or conspiring to revolt.

South of New York, Quakers in Pennsylvania, New Jersey, and Delaware practiced a milder form of slavery than other white colonists did. However, Quakers still feared slave resistance and revolt. Out of this fear came slave codes meant to limit enslaved black peoples' privileges and control their activities. But discrimination was moderated. In the early years, for example, African and European servants received the same penalties for running away, and free black people had equal access to the courts. Nor was interracial sex penalized. To illustrate, Francis Johnson Anthony and Mary Johnson's grandson who moved to Delaware, married a white woman, worked as a free farmer, and, in 1687, sued a white man in court.

Yet even in William Penn's Quaker haven, a slave code slowly took shape, accompanied by discriminatory treatment of free black people. By 1693, Philadelphia forbade slaves from traveling on Sundays without passes from their owners. In 1700, the legislature authorized special courts to try, judge, and convict black persons charged with criminal offenses. Race-based justice made African Americans liable to capital punishment for burglary and to castration for the rape of a white woman—a form of retaliation reserved for them only. In 1725–1726, much later than in other colonies, Pennsylvania passed a comprehensive "act for the better regulation of Negroes." The code placed new restrictions on free African Americans. For example, any free black person convicted of fornication or adultery with a white person could be sold into servitude for seven years.

With rising numbers of Africans in all colonies came laws governing slave behavior and punishment. In general, the higher the proportion of Africans in a particular region, the harsher the code. But codes could not entirely control enslaved Africans. So long as bondsmen and bondswomen had the will to resist, slavery remained unstable. White colonists had to constantly negotiate the legal details of the institution as well as continually patrol their human holdings.

Beyond English Boundaries

Juan Fernandez, a black soldier in the Spanish garrison town of St. Augustine, Florida, awoke one morning in 1586 to see a fleet of twenty heavily armed English ships tacking along the coast. Led by England's famous explorer Francis Drake, the ships commenced a two-day bombardment of the garrison. Fernandez and other garrison soldiers fled to nearby Indian villages and tried to prevent the English from coming ashore, but in vain. The invaders looted the town, set it aflame, and departed. When the garrison's occupants returned, they found a smoking ruin where St. Augustine had once stood. Determined to persevere, the Spanish and African soldiers rebuilt this small outpost that would plague the English for more than a century, especially when it gained a reputation as a slave sanctuary.

Africans in Spanish America

By the time of Drake's attack, Africans had lived in Spanish Florida for decades, giving the early Spanish settlements a distinct character. Some Africans were royal slaves, owned by the Spanish king, who put them to work in the garrisons. Others belonged to Spanish settlers. Some had gained freedom in ways not revealed in the historical records. This mixture mirrored Africans' situation in Spain, where Muslim North Africans and black men of the African continent had mingled with the native Spaniards, known as Castilians, for centuries. In Spain, Castilian law offered many avenues out of slavery, and the Catholic church welcomed Africans.

The character of slavery in Spanish colonies such as Florida has led some historians to see a paradox: Enslaved Africans in autocratically run Spanish colonies seemed to fare better than Africans in English colonies, where white lawmakers emphasized representative government. In Spanish Florida, African slaves did the most backbreaking work—as field laborers, supply train workers, and fort and church builders. Yet they, along with free black men, also served as soldiers, guides, and linguists. Like many Spanish soldiers, black slaves mingled and started families with neighboring Indians so frequently that the Spanish didn't associate slavery with skin color or African heritage in the way that the English did. The Spanish treated slaves more humanely, gave them opportunities for freedom, and permitted freed slaves to become full citizens. Their Catholic priests viewed every slave as a potential soul to be protected and converted, and local officials enforced Catholic protections. Spanish law, inherited from the Romans, defined slaves' rights and masters' obligations. By contrast, the Church of England did not do much to Christianize slaves or demand respect for their souls, and Anglo-Saxon law said nothing on the subject of slavery. Thus, English colonists were free to establish slave codes as harsh as they wished. African slaves in England's colonies were at the complete mercy of their masters.

However, unique conditions within the Spanish colonies played just as large a role in shaping slavery as the institutions transported by European settlers from their homelands. Among these conditions, climate, crops, and the size of the slave population had the most decisive impact. In the Caribbean and Latin America, for example, slaves were driven to human limits in the difficult work of cultivating sugar and coffee, which grew only in tropical zones. Also, as slaves vastly outnumbered white settlers, masters treated bondspeople far more harshly than did owners in temperate zones where the white–black ratio was more balanced. Wherever slaves became more numerous than white people, masters' fear of a slave revolt—and their compulsion to crack down on black people—intensified.

But Florida was not quite tropical, and Spanish authorities viewed Florida as a mere outpost on the fringe of Spain's New World empire. Even though St. Augustine recovered from the English assault, its population grew only gradually, and yellow fever in 1649 and smallpox in 1654 claimed numerous African and Spanish lives. Lacking large plantations and the silver and gold mines the Spanish prized, the town was neglected by Spain. Left to their own devices, settlers in Florida established numerous cattle ranches, where some Africans became North America's first black vaqueros (cowboys).

After the 1660s, when English sugar planters from Barbados began to acquire land in South Carolina, the slaves they brought with them heard of the freedom Africans enjoyed in Spanish Florida. Catholic St. Augustine, with its massive stone fort and the promise of sanctuary, had a strong appeal. Not surprisingly, the garrison town unnerved English Protestant Carolinians.

Irritated by St. Augustine's presence, the English forged alliances with Indians and began harassing the garrison and surrounding Spanish settlements in the early 1680s. The Spanish governor retaliated in 1686, with a racially mixed militia that included free and enslaved Africans as well as Indians. His strike force even managed to steal several of the Carolina governor's slaves—a particularly humiliating blow. Border warfare between the two colonies raged for years, fueled by a constant flow of Carolinian slaves into Spanish territory. Once they had escaped their masters, many of these slaves requested baptism into the Catholic Church. They knew this sacrament would give them protections and opportunities, such as the right to marry, that the English no longer extended. When in 1693 Spain's King Charles II granted liberty to all enslaved men and women who reached Florida, he set the stage for the formation of a free black community in this Spanish outpost.

Florida grew even more turbulent in 1702, when the War of Spanish Succession (known in North America as Queen Anne's War, after the English queen) erupted in Europe. The English battered the Spanish sanctuary, and South Carolina's governor led a mixed force of Yamasee Indian allies, African

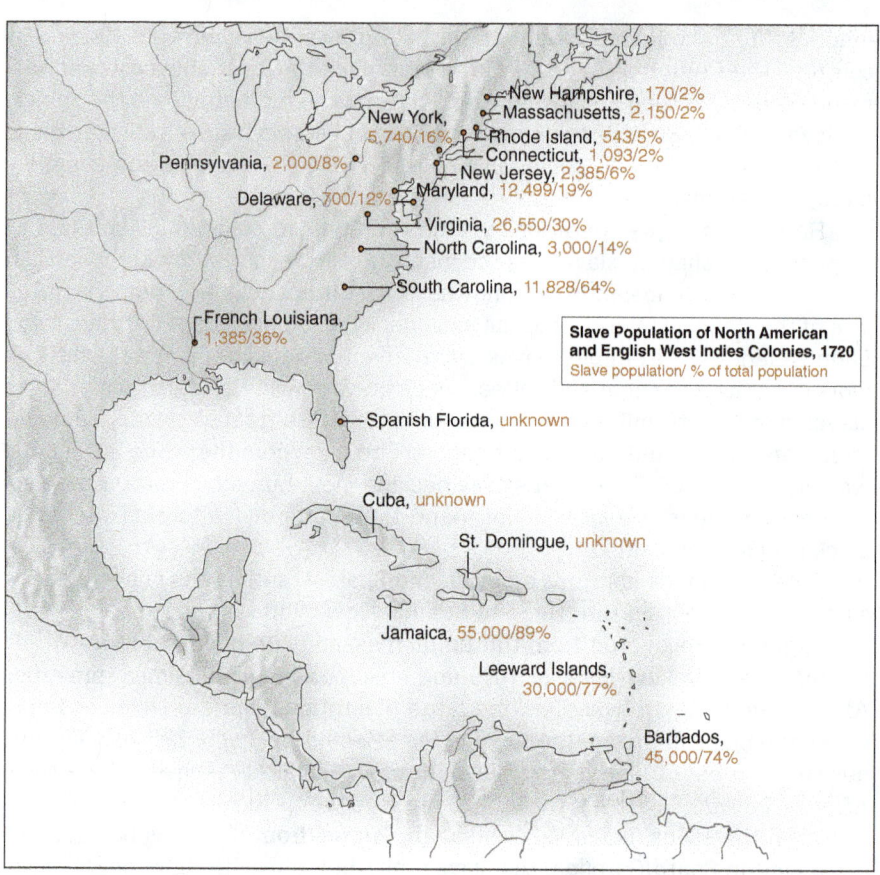

MAP 3.2 Slave Population of North American and English West Indies Colonies, 1720

In Virginia and French Louisiana, slaves composed about one-third of the entire population in 1720. In marked contrast, slaves in Jamaica, Barbados, Haiti, and most other West Indian colonies typically made up 75–90 percent of the population.

slaves, and white settlers to burn St. Augustine for the second time. Two years later, the English destroyed most of the town of Apalachee. These raids devastated the Indian villages and took the lives of many Afro-Spanish, both enslaved and free. The Carolinians also captured some 24,000–50,000 Indians, marched them north to Charleston, and sold them into slavery. Many were shipped to the West Indies and to Boston and other New England towns.

Despite the violence, Africans in English Carolina and Spanish Florida maintained communication, and South Carolina slaves increasingly associated Florida with Catholicism and the freedom and protections it offered. After a triracial Spanish force invaded Charleston in 1706, and former Carolina slaves who had escaped to Florida now attacked the men who had owned them, Carolina slaves were further encouraged to break for freedom. Though Charleston's residents repelled the Spanish assault, they lost slaves to Florida, especially in slave revolts in 1711 and 1714. The next year more slaves defected, joining the Yamasee Indians, South Carolina's former allies, in an attack on the English that united remnants of the coastal tribes and the powerful interior nations of Creeks, Choctaws, and Cherokees. Carolina's military leaders found evidence of their presence in the design of an Indian fort that incorporated African defenses. During this Yamasee War, Africans and Native Americans continued a collaboration against white masters that had gone on for years in the borderlands of Spanish Florida and Carolina.

Slavery in French Colonies

While the Spanish quickly incorporated Africans into mission and ranching life in the Southeast, the French settlers who preceded the English in Carolina hardly lasted long enough for Africans to establish a presence there. The small French settlement planted in 1562 near the mouth of St. John's River in Florida crumbled under a Spanish assault three years later. Farther north, in Canada, the French established their main North American base. Initially, they had little use for enslaved Africans because the climate did not support intensive agriculture; their interest was more in fur trading than raising cash crops. When the French explorer Robert de LaSalle canoed through the Great Lakes and down the Mississippi River to its mouth in 1682, the French king claimed for France the vast North American interior stretching from Spanish Florida to the Mississippi River. Hoping to outflank the English colonies—or at least pin them to the Atlantic coast—the French began building trading posts and garrisons in the heart of Indian America. Now they made liberal use of Indian and African slaves to establish settlements in 1699 on the Biloxi and Mobile rivers, which emptied into the Gulf of Mexico east of the Mississippi River.

In 1718, the French stepped up their effort to occupy the immense territory they had claimed, which they called Louisiana. Establishing their capital at New Orleans, members of the French Company of the Indies began building what they envisioned as a tobacco- and indigo-based bonanza port city. In time, they hoped, their presence in New Orleans would enable them to control the vast lower Mississippi Valley. They accomplished this feat of construction almost entirely with coerced labor: 1,900 Africans, some 1,200 *engagés* (criminals emptied from French jails), several thousand indentured servants, fewer than 200 adventurous French settlers, and a garrison of soldiers who held the unlikely mass together.

By 1721, nearly 2,000 black slaves—more than one-fifth of the population—formed the backbone of Louisiana's economy. These skilled rice growers, indigo processors, metalworkers, river navigators, herbalists, and cattle keepers proved indispensable to the French. Like enslaved men in Spanish Florida, African men in Louisiana mingled extensively with Indian women. These couples produced mixed-race children, born into slavery, who were known locally as *grifs*. Few French women ventured to the New World, so many French soldiers had liaisons with enslaved African women.

France's *Code Noir*, introduced in 1724 to regulate the conduct of slavery, forbade interracial marriage. But everyone in Louisiana knew that a law inscribed on the far side of the Atlantic meant little in the wilds of the lower Mississippi. To be sure, Catholic priests did not sanction interracial marriages, but a French man who took a common-law African wife raised no eyebrows in this frontier territory. Moreover, such relations often opened the door to freedom for mixed-race individuals whose white parent, usually the father, did not want his children enslaved. Many Afro-Indian, Franco-Indian, and Afro-French children born into slavery in early Louisiana won their liberty either through manumission or self-purchase. After a decade of colonization, Louisiana was still a lawless frontier zone, but it boasted a more flexible multiracial society than the English colonists had created.

Conclusion

Slavery took only shallow root in the North American English colonies for three-quarters of a century after a Dutch ship delivered a small number of Africans to Virginia in 1619. In 1637, Massachusetts Puritans traded Pequot captives for Africans enslaved in the West Indies. Because the Dutch controlled the Atlantic slave trade in North America during the mid-seventeenth century, slavery sank particularly deep roots into New Netherlands. But for most of the century, the majority of European settlers in North America satisfied their labor needs with white indentured servants and convicted felons transported from England and Ireland. In the last quarter of the seventeenth century, this pattern shifted, and the Europeans began using far more enslaved African workers than indentured white laborers. White planters made this transition in reaction to rebellions instigated by former indentured servants in the Chesapeake and to the dwindling supply of white indentured servants coming from overseas. As European planters resorted increasingly to black labor, the slave-based plantation system began to gather momentum in North America.

From English New York to Spanish Florida and French Louisiana, white people became highly dependent on black slaves by the early eighteenth century. In the northern colonies, that dependence developed more slowly. But no matter where or how quickly slavery took root, this growing dependence redefined the meaning of race. Particularly in the English colonies, skin color determined a person's status as free or slave more than ever before. Most English colonists began considering lifelong servitude the natural condition of black people. They also believed it equally natural that slaves' children should be born into perpetual slavery.

In this new color-coded social system, enslaved black people and their families faced harsh work lives, a degradation of their African heritage, and a violent system of discipline. Most died early, never having escaped bondage. The era when Anthony and Mary Johnson had been free to till their own land, testify in court, and marry as they wished—to "know myne owne ground and . . . work . . . and play when I please"—had all but ended by the 1720s. A cruel new chapter had opened for Africans in North America. As the eighteenth century wore on, blacks had to find new ways to survive and to craft lives of dignity, pride, and hope.

Questions for Review and Reflection

1. How did the experience under slavery differ in the northern and southern British colonies of North America in the seventeenth century?

2. What factors shaped resistance strategies in various regions of the North and South, and in urban and rural locations where slavery existed?

3. How did "race" and "slavery" come to be almost synonymous? Was it not possible to extend slavery to "white" persons?

4. Did geography and climate affect the development of slavery in the European colonies in North America? If so, how.

4

Africans in Bondage: Early Eighteenth Century to the American Revolution

Venture Smith Defies the Colonial Slave System

Eight-year-old Broteer was the son of a king. His world collapsed in 1736 when Bambara slave raiders captured all the members of his village in Anamaboe, Guinea. The raiders killed Broteer's father and then marched the boy, along with the other villagers, to the coast. When a slaver from Rhode Island arrived to pick up the human cargo, Broteer's captors sold him to the ship's steward for "four gallons of rum and a piece of calico." The steward renamed the boy Venture, "having purchased me with his own private venture." The steward intended to sell the youngster for a profit as soon as the ship returned to North America.

Arriving in New England by way of Barbados, Venture was purchased by a Connecticut farmer who gave him his surname—Smith. The farmer promptly set the boy to work combing sheep's wool for spinning, pounding corn for poultry feed, and carrying out household tasks. "My behavior had as yet been submissive and obedient," Smith related many years later. Then, at age nine, he reported, "I began to have hard tasks imposed on me . . . or be rigorously punished."

Smith grew tall and strong in his teens, and began chafing against slave life. He found his master's son James particularly galling. James "came up to

Chronology

1720s–1730s	The number of African slaves imported to southern colonies soars.
1720s–1740s	The Great Awakening attracts many slaves to Christianity.
1728	Runaway slaves form a community near Lexington, Virginia.
1729	Enslaved Africans join Natchez Indians in an uprising against the French in Louisiana.
1733	Founding of Georgia, which initially bans slavery but allows it after 1750.
1736	Venture Smith is captured in Guinea and sold in New England.
1738	Runaway South Carolina slaves establish a sanctuary called Fort Mose.
1739	White militia puts down the Stono Rebellion of South Carolina slaves.
1741	A slave conspiracy in New York City ends in multiple executions.
1753	John Woolman writes *Some Considerations on the Keeping of Negroes.*
1756	Olaudah Equiano reaches North America and is sold to a master in Virginia.
1756–1763	The Seven Years' War catalyzes importations of Africans to the northern colonies.
1763	Treaty of Paris ends the Seven Years' War. Francisco Menéndez leads free Spanish black people to Cuba.
1764	Venture Smith purchases his freedom.
1766	Olaudah Equiano purchases his freedom.

me . . . big with authority" and "would order me to do *this* business and *that* business different from what my master had directed me." Tempers flared. When James flew into a rage and attacked Smith with a pitchfork, the young African defended himself and pummeled the white boy until he burst into tears.

By age twenty-two, Venture Smith was a giant by eighteenth-century standards. Over six feet tall and weighing 250 pounds, he built a reputation as a prodigious worker with amazing strength. By day, he labored as a carpenter and farmhand. By night, he worked for himself, catching and selling game and fish with an eye toward purchasing his way out of slavery some day. Shortly after marrying Meg, another African slave, Smith made a break for freedom. Accompanied by three white indentured servants, he stole a boat and provisions from his master's home. The fugitives rowed across Long Island Sound for New York territory. But when one of the indentured servants ran off with the provisions, Smith returned to his master. As frequently happened with runaway slaves, his owner put him up for sale. Fortunately, his new Connecticut master, Thomas Stanton, soon purchased Smith's wife and their baby girl.

Then a battle of wills broke out between Meg and Stanton's wife. In a heated argument, Meg stood her ground and ignored her husband's pleas to apologize "for the sake of peace." When the mistress turned her whip on Smith, he hurled it into the fireplace. At first the master seemed to take no notice of the incident, but "some days after, . . . in the morning as I was putting on a log in the fireplace, not suspecting harm from anyone, I received a most violent stroke on the crown of my head with a club two feet long and as large around as a chair post." Staggering to his feet, the strapping slave threw his master to the ground and dragged him out of the house.

Smith thought himself unjustly attacked and fled to a local justice of the peace to plead his case. The justice "advised me to return to my master, and live contented with him till he abused me again, and then complain." Smith complied, but on the way home he was attacked by Stanton and his brother. The muscular Smith overpowered both men. "I became enraged," Smith recounted, "turned them both under me, laid one of them across the other, and stamped both with my feet." Soon the town constable arrived to restrain Smith, and the local blacksmith fitted the slave with ankle and wrist shackles. When his master threatened to sell Smith to the West Indies—a fate most slaves dreaded—Smith replied, "I crossed the waters to come here, and I am willing to cross them to return."

Venture Smith's owner now knew he could never break this African's will and sold him to a man who sold him again. Smith toiled for this latest master for five years, working on his own time to save money coin by coin. Finally, thirty-six years old, enslaved for twenty-eight, he purchased his freedom. But his wife, daughter, and now two sons remained in bondage, and Smith worked furiously to purchase them, too. "In four years, I cut several thousand cords of wood . . . I raised watermelons, and performed many other singular labors," he recalled. Described as a black Paul Bunyan "who swung his axe to break his chains," Smith "shunned all kind of luxuries" and "bought nothing that I absolutely did not want." By 1768, he had purchased his sons out of slavery and later managed to free his daughter. Another five years passed before he could purchase Meg.

By the eve of the American Revolution, Smith had a farm, a house, a second dwelling on Long Island, and cash savings. As the war raged around him, he owned and managed a fleet of some twenty small coastal vessels that sold cordwood, fish, and garden produce along the shores of Long Island Sound. One of Smith's sons fought the British in the American Revolution.

Venture Smith was one of about 260,000 slaves to arrive in North America's English colonies between 1700 and 1775, the year the American Revolution broke out. This influx dwarfed the 13,000 slaves who arrived in the seventeenth century. Colonial slavery had reached its peak.

The struggle to survive the system of slavery, itself still in the process of formation, was a great test of human endurance. While liberty-loving European settlers paradoxically constructed law codes, social rules, and attitudes designed to deprive Africans and their descendants of freedom, black slaves did not simply accept enslavement. They made the terms of their bondage a matter of negotiation, defying the system in a continual series of abrasive and often violent encounters with their masters and mistresses.

Slavery took many forms in different English colonies and in the Spanish- and French-controlled regions of North America. Yet no matter its shape, the interactions between masters and slaves led to a gradual merging of African and European cultures. By this process, Africans in America became African Americans, while Euro-Americans adopted elements of African culture. Embedded within their story is a subplot featuring individuals such as Venture Smith, who worked their way out of bondage and inspired hope in the hearts of those still enslaved. Only a tiny fraction of all black Americans achieved what Smith did in this era. But they had allies—a handful of white abolitionists whose voices gathered strength by the 1770s.

Colonial Slavery at High Tide

A year after reaching Virginia in 1756, Olaudah Equiano, the much-traveled slave autobiographer, had some good fortune: His Virginia master sold him to an English ship captain who later sold him to a merchant in Montserrat, English West Indies. Traveling as a shipboard slave between Caribbean ports and North American settlements, Equiano saw how slavery functioned differently in various English colonies. In the West Indies and in southern ports, he observed colonial societies that in a single generation made slavery the key to producing goods and services and measuring wealth. In Philadelphia and other northern ports, he saw societies in which slavery was one of many forms of labor and not necessarily a mark of social status for white people. Equiano thus had a broad perspective on the workings of the entire cross-Atlantic economy.

A Rising Slave Population

After Virginia and Maryland's planters replaced white indentured servants with African slave labor in the late seventeenth century, the composition of North America's population shifted dramatically. When some 75,000 slaves, almost all coming directly from Africa, reached the Chesapeake colonies between 1700 and 1750, the agricultural and domestic labor force became mostly black. In 1736, one of Virginia's largest planters already worried that his neighbors "import so many Negroes hither that I fear this colony will be confirmed by the name of New Guinea"—referring to the African region where many of Virginia's slaves originated.

In the Lower South—Georgia and South Carolina—slave importations soared after 1710. By the 1730s, field labor became overwhelmingly black in this region. Almost half of all slaves arriving in the English colonies after 1700 first saw land at Sullivan's Island, a quarantine station in Charleston harbor that has been called the Ellis Island of black America. In 1737, one Swiss newcomer traveling through South Carolina thought the colony "looks more like a negro country than like a country settled by white people."

Georgia, founded by British philanthropists in 1733, followed this pattern, though unexpectedly. Launching the colony as an experiment in settling poor English men and women on small plots of land, Georgia's founders banned slavery. But in 1750, at the insistence of the white settlers there, the colony's trustees abandoned their initial vision and permitted slavery. Now wealthy investors purchased large tracts of land and imported shiploads of Africans. By the time the American Revolution broke out, black slaves in Georgia outnumbered the white settlers.

The slaves flooding into the southern colonies originated in many parts of West and Central Africa. A small number came from Madagascar, an island off Africa's southeast coast. But southern planters were particular about the human merchandise they purchased. Moreover, they held strong—if often misinformed—opinions about which Africans were the best. Equiano claimed that West Indian planters prized "the slaves of Benin or Eboe [Ibo] to those of any other part of Guinea, for their hardiness, intelligence, integrity, and zeal." In Virginia, where Iboes like Equiano made up the largest ethnic group, slave owners echoed this sentiment. But slave buyers in South Carolina and Georgia disdained Iboes as despondent and suicidal. In the punishing climate of the Carolina low country, planters preferred Kongolese, Angolan, and Senegambian people from West Central Africa, many of whom had cultivated rice back home. These slave owners imported roughly three men for every two women, and they especially valued young, strong, and healthy males.

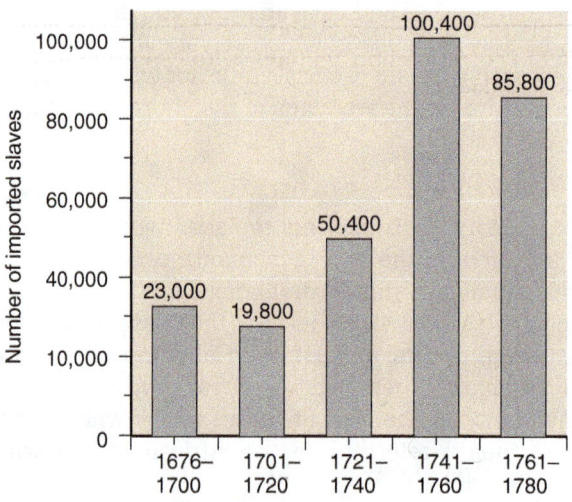

FIGURE 4.1 Importation of Slaves to North America, 1676–1780

Between 1701 and 1780, ship captains transported about 256,000 slaves directly from Africa to colonial ports, especially Savannah, Charleston, Philadelphia, New York, Newport, and Boston. After the Declaration of Independence was signed in 1776, most states banned the importation of Africans, thus lowering the number of incoming Africans in the 1770s. The disruption of seaborne traffic during the American Revolution further reduced these numbers. But after the war, slavers resumed the traffic, carrying as many as 100,000 slaves to South Carolina and Georgia between 1783 and 1808.

Slave Life in the South

By the early eighteenth century, slavery was embedded in England's southern colonies. Slave importations rivaled those in the West Indies. On South Carolina's coastal lowlands, slave importations and rice cultivation expanded together. Planters in the tidal floodplain relied on African slaves' knowledge about growing rice in such a region. Much of this "African knowledge system," as one geographer has called it, resided within women, who in Africa did most of the sowing and winnowing of rice. Though black families in Africa celebrated rice planting as a time of renewal and promise, rice cultivation in South Carolina—where the whip ruled the fields—meant just another cycle of misery and sickness.

Unlike cultivating wheat or corn in the North, growing rice demanded backbreaking, year-round labor. Slaves had to clear the swampy lowlands in winter, build dykes to keep seawater out of the fields, and plant rice in shallow trenches in the spring. In late summer, they harvested the crop. In the fall, they pounded the rice kernels with wooden mortars and pestles. Come wintertime, they turned the soil to prepare it for a new round of planting.

Rice "is the most unhealthy work in which the slaves were employed," wrote one English visitor to South Carolina, "and they sank under it in great numbers. The causes of this dreadful mortality are the constant moisture and heat of the atmosphere, together with the alternate floodings and dryings of the fields, on which the negroes are perpetually at work, often ankle deep in mud, with their bare heads exposed to the fierce rays of the sun." One-quarter of the Africans imported to the low country in the first half of the eighteenth century died within a year of their arrival—victims of overwork, inadequate nutrition, and respiratory disease. Still, their labor made their owners rich: By the late 1760s, white South Carolina planters were exporting more than 60 million pounds of rice annually.

As South Carolinian planters stepped up rice cultivation, they imported ever larger numbers of Africans. Advertisements regularly announced new arrivals: "A choice cargo of about 250 fine healthy NEGROES just arrived from the Windward & Rice Coast," proclaimed one. Owing to heavy importations, one-third of the slaves in South Carolina were African-born, and they maintained a feeling of close connection to Africa. One visitor to the Carolina low country in 1740 noticed the "many various ages, nations, [and] languages" among the "whole body of slaves"—suggesting that many still spoke their native languages.

In the Chesapeake colonies of Virginia and Maryland, as slave importations grew, Africans also retained native languages. And as masters strived for ever higher tobacco profits, the slaves' working and living conditions worsened. Their workdays were lengthened and their holidays reduced to just three (Christmas, Easter, and Pentecost—the Christian holy day commemorating the descent of the Holy Spirit on the apostles). Whereas masters had previously let slaves rest a bit during the winter, now they ordered them to grind corn, clear stumps, and chop wood in the cold months. They also imposed stricter supervision, cracking the whip and applying the branding iron with more severity than ever.

By the time Equiano arrived in 1756, Virginia had more North American-born than African-born slaves. As large plantations edged out small farms, slaves began living in larger groups, where they found marriage partners more easily, created families, and built the extended kin networks. These factors triggered a natural population increase. By the late colonial period, slaves had ties of kinship and friendship that crisscrossed the countryside, causing southern planters to complain of the "continual concourse of Negroes on Sabbath and holy days meeting in great numbers."[1]

Births in Chesapeake slave families gradually evened out the gender imbalance in slave imports. At the same time, the increase in North American-born slaves gave white planters less reason to import new captives fresh from Africa. Because a more gender-balanced population provided greater opportunity for early marriages, Virginia-born slave women bore children at younger ages than their African-born mothers had. Families thus grew larger. By the 1770s, Virginia's slave population was expanding at the rate of 5,000 per year, but only about 500 to 800 were arriving from Africa. The rest of the increase came from American-born slaves' fertility and the rising ratio of slave births over slave deaths.

In the southern colonies overall, slave fertility exceeded that in the British West Indies. White Caribbean planters imported five times as many slaves in the colonial era as white people in the mainland southern colonies did, yet on the eve of the American Revolution slave numbers in the two regions were roughly the same. In the islands, the brutal sugar work regimen extinguished lives quickly. In the southern colonies, by contrast, there were more than 400,000 slaves by 1770—a whopping increase over the 13,000 slaves in the region just eighty years earlier.

Eighteenth-century plantations were small worlds in themselves. In addition to field hands and house servants, they required the labor of carpenters, blacksmiths, bricklayers, weavers, coopers (barrelmakers), butchers, and

This depiction of conical-roofed houses at Mulberry Plantation in South Carolina shows that Africans often built their own living quarters based on designs they knew from their West African home villages. Slave housing improved during the eighteenth century, as sex-segregated barracks gave way to family cabins on many plantations.

Source: Thomas Coram, c.1668-1751. View of Mulberry. 10 × 17.6 cm. Collection of the Carolina Art Association, Gibbes Art Gallery, Charleston, South Carolina.

leatherworkers. The male slaves who acquired these artisan skills were highly valued and allowed to move around more freely—from home to workshop, plantation to town, warehouse to wharf—than field slaves could. Those who drove wagonloads of crops to river landings and piloted tobacco- and rice-laden rafts and boats through the inland waterways of the coastal South spent much of their time away from the plantation.

The experience of these slaves resembled that of urban bondspeople, many of whom were also skilled artisans and shopworkers. In visits to Charleston and Savannah, Equiano saw slave women selling goods from street carts and purchasing food for the kitchens they ran in their white masters' homes. Most urban slaves had easier lives than plantation slaves because they were spared backbreaking field labor. However, their isolation in white households made it harder for them to form families and friendships with other slaves.

Most bondsmen and bondswomen in the southern colonies labored in the fields. Nearly every black woman on a small farm or large plantation wielded a hoe and sickle as well as tended and butchered livestock, cultivated vegetable gardens, and took care of dairy cows. Slave women who worked in the houses of their masters had a more diverse work routine. They attended the births of the master's children and fed, suckled, and bathed his infants. As the children grew, slave women rocked them to sleep and supervised their play. They also washed, mended, and ironed clothes; cooked, baked, and canned; served meals and washed up afterward; and spun, wove, and stitched clothing.

Sexual Oppression

Whether in the fields or the master's household, slave women lived under the constant threat of sexual aggression by white men. The rape of an enslaved black woman probably constituted the most destructive means of control in the master's arsenal. In raping black women, white men also asserted their power over black men. Indeed, to demonstrate their dominance, some white slave owners forced black men to witness their assault on a wife, sister, or daughter. The pain stemming from these attacks disrupted black families and inflicted permanent emotional scars not only on the victims but on all who cared about them.

Interracial rape was the purview of white men. Few black men were accused of raping white women. Indeed, most sexual unions between white women and black men were consensual. Though laws forbade white–black marriages, the scores of white women dragged into court for bearing mulatto children testified to their willingness to choose a black mate.

Some sexual relationships between white men and black women were also consensual. For example, a slave woman might agree to have sex with a white man to gain advantages for herself or her children. In some cases, these relationships endured for many decades, but affection was rare. Moreover, these relationships, consensual or not, spawned excruciating tensions among both black and white people. They reinforced the dependency of black women on white men and were a painful reminder that black men had little power or worth in the society. The aggressions of white men also put their wives in a painful position, enduring silently their husbands' adulterous relations with slaves. When such unions produced children, these youngsters suffered as well. They lived in a kind of social no-man's-land. The law said they were slaves because their mothers were slaves. Yet some had the affection of their white fathers. Others received favorable work assignments and their freedom on reaching adulthood. But despite these advantages, they rarely found acceptance in white society.

Slave Life in the North

North of the Chesapeake, Africans made up only about 5 percent of the population. Still, slave importations directly from Africa continued, increasing the northern black population from 9,000 in 1710 to 32,000 in 1750. When the Seven Years' War (1756–1763) cut off the supply of white indentured servants from Ireland and Germany, it created a labor vacuum that northerners gladly filled with even more African slaves. Their numbers swelled to about 50,000 by 1770.

Like Venture Smith, most slaves in New England and the mid-Atlantic colonies had work lives characterized by variety and seasonal rhythms. Many black men and women also possessed a range of valuable skills—from farming, woodworking, and seafaring to cargo transporting, cattle tending, and cooking. Indeed, numerous slave advertisements spoke of a black man who could "turn his hand at many sorts of trades" or was "fit for town and country." A large number of black people mingled with white indentured servants and wage laborers and hired out their free time to labor for others. Many were sold from

Venture Smith died in 1805 at age seventy-nine. Four pallbearers struggled to hoist the coffin containing this giant man of more than 250 pounds. Stories about Smith's prodigious strength circulated around Connecticut for years after his death. One man recalled that "a noted wrestler tried his skill in wrestling with Venture but found he might as well try to remove a tree."

master to master, often gaining new skills. In northern cities, most wealthy households had at least one slave. By 1770, nearly one-quarter of white householders in Philadelphia and New York owned slaves—about the same proportion as in North Carolina. Even families only recently advancing to the middle class, such as Benjamin Franklin's, bought slaves to handle domestic chores.

Slaves in the North had easier work lives than those in the South, mostly because the northern climate did not permit year-round farming. But these more tolerable work lives came at the cost of family life. Like Venture Smith, most slaves ate, slept, and lived in their owner's home because slave quarters were unnecessary. Thus slaves lacked the after-sundown privacy, away from the master's watchful eye, that southern slaves prized. Northern slaves were often the only slave in a household, so they were isolated and lacked the sense of community southern slaves treasured. An excess of black men over women prevented many from forming families. Only in Rhode Island's Narragansett area and in New York's Kings and Queens Counties, where dozens of slaves worked large farms, did the black population prove dense enough for slaves to construct durable, extended kin groups. Elsewhere, slaves formed so-called abroad marriages, in which husbands and wives lived in different white households and only occasionally spent time together. The children of such marriages were often sold away from their mother at an early age.

African Americans in the North mingled more closely with white people than did slaves in the South. In streets, churches, and taverns, and along oceanside wharves and river-ferry landings, black and white peoples encountered one another every day as they went about their business. In many households, black slaves took their meals with white masters. One Englishwoman traveling in Connecticut marveled that masters allowed slaves "to sit at table with them (as they say to save time), and into the dish goes the black hoof as freely as the white hand." Yet despite these advantages, many northern slaves endured brutal treatment by masters and unequal treatment under the law.

More rapidly than in the South, black northerners became part of the wider emerging American culture. Encompassing English, Dutch, German, Scots, and Scots-Irish elements, this culture had a rich variety not seen in the South. Black people and Europeans borrowed from and adapted one another's practice of medicine and other knowledge. A notable example was the West African knowledge of smallpox inoculation, which a slave of Boston's eminent minister, Cotton Mather, demonstrated for his master. The practice spread quickly, and within a single generation, smallpox was no longer a dreaded epidemic.

Though northern colonists had relatively few slaves, they had strong ties to slavery. New England ship captains transported a large portion of the Africans brought to North America. New Englanders built and manned these ships. In them northern merchants sent fish, meat, and grain to feed the huge West Indies slave population; brought back molasses, which they distilled into rum; and shipped the rum to Africa, where they exchanged it for slaves whom they sold in the West Indies or North America. New Englanders consumed slave-produced sugar, coffee, rice, and tobacco; they dyed their clothing with slave-produced indigo. It is fair to say that most northern colonists participated in or benefited from slavery directly or indirectly.

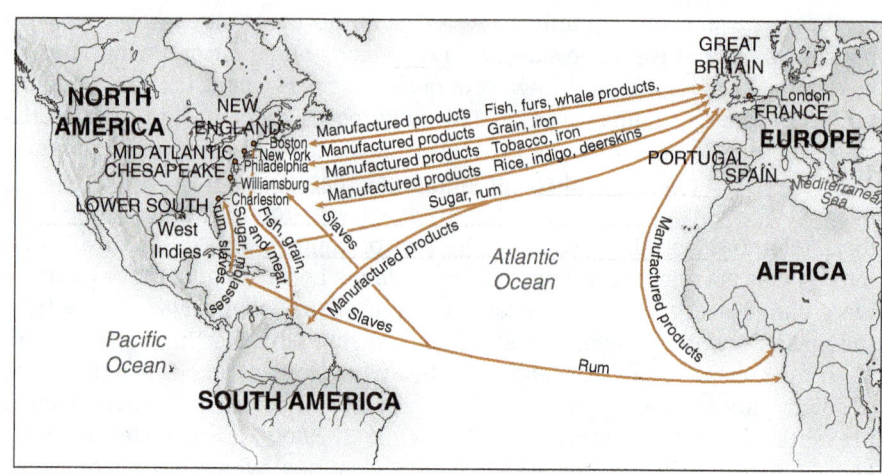

MAP 4.1 The Commercial Triangle

Southern colonists had the most extensive daily interactions with slaves, yet northern colonists acquired the most experience in doing business with slave traders in Africa and slave-owning merchants and planters in the West Indies.

Negotiated Bondage

According to white colonists' law books, Africans brought to the colonies in chains had no power. But the day-to-day realities of living with the people they enslaved forced slave owners to admit that absolute control over other humans was impossible. Of this Venture Smith's masters had no doubt. When one of his masters tried to sell Smith to William Hooker of Hartford, Smith said he would refuse to go to northern New York with his new owner. "If you will go by no other measures," Hooker warned, "I will tie you down in my sleigh." Undaunted, Smith replied "that if he carried me in that manner, no person would purchase me, for it would be thought that he had a murderer for sale." That ended the potential sale. "After this he tried no more, and said he would not have me as a gift."

The Europeans rationalized their involvement in slavery by maintaining that Africans were subhuman heathens intended to be beasts of burden. To that end, owners sought to convert slaves into mindless drudges who obeyed every command, worked efficiently for the master's profit, and accepted their lowly status. Slave owners used law, terror, torture, and, ultimately, the control of life and death over slaves to preserve this power imbalance. Yet masters never achieved absolute control. Not every slave had Smith's physical strength or defiance, but every master knew that slaves were volatile property. They always had to take into account what a slave might or might not do. Sometimes it was easier to compromise than to insist on total obedience. Slave advertisements give glimpses into this reality: "The cause of his being sold," explained one, "is that he is not inclined to farming."

Slave and master were bound in intimate interdependence. Masters could set the boundaries of the slave's existence—defining physical location, work roles, rations, and shelter. But slave owners depended on slaves to plant, tend, and harvest, to construct buildings, and to care for children. Practical owners knew that if they pushed slaves too far, the work simply would not get done, or not get done right.

In addition, masters had limited power over precisely how slaves did their work. Unless an owner wanted to monitor a slave's every action, he had to accept that the slave would make his or her own decisions about how to approach a task. Nor did masters have much say over whether and how slaves made friends, fell in love, formed kin groups, raised children, worshiped, buried their dead, and spent their scant leisure time.

Resisting Slavery

Slave owners anticipated resistance from the moment African captives stepped foot on American soil. Most white people agreed that newly imported slaves, known as saltwater Africans, were far more dangerous than "country-born" slaves. "If he must be broke, either from obstinacy, or . . . from greatness of soul, [it] will require . . . hard discipline," wrote one North Carolina planter. "You would really be surprised at their perseverance . . . they often die before they can be conquered." Many also escaped on arrival, as newspaper advertisements testify.

Resistance and the threat of violence pervaded the master-slave relationship. "When you make men slaves, you compel them to live with you in a state of war," wrote Olaudah Equiano. Every slave owner knew this. Surely all who owned Venture Smith dared not relax. One Maryland planter claimed he had "never known a single instance of a negro being contented in slavery." A German minister acknowledged that slaves were "always on the point of rebellion." In every slave-owning region of North America, some bondsmen and bondswomen murdered their masters. Such killings kept white people on edge as long as slavery existed.

Contesting Labor

Labor was the core of the slave's existence. Because their survival—as well as their dignity and self-respect—depended on work, slaves strove to perform their duties on their own terms. They controlled what they could, practicing African work habits in New World fields. For example, they preferred team to individual work and drew on homeland knowledge of rice cultivation to work in familiar ways that made their lives more bearable. All the while, they devised strategies for defying their master's authority. By shamming sickness, breaking hoes, dropping dishes, dragging out a job, pretending ignorance, uprooting freshly planted seedlings, and harvesting carelessly, they foiled their master's purpose. A Virginia planter despaired, "I find it almost impossible to make a negro do his work well. No orders can engage it, no encouragement persuade it, nor no punishment oblige it."

In this contest of wills, some masters treated their slaves leniently; others applied the lash with increasing frustration. Slave owners knew that one way to maintain discipline was through terror and torture—legalized flogging, branding, burning, amputation of limbs, and murder. But they also knew that, pushed too hard, slaves would strike back. In 1732, the *South Carolina Gazette* reported: "Mr. James Gray worked his Negroes late in his Barn at Night, and the next Morning before Day, hurried them out again, and when they came to it, found it burnt down to the Ground, and all that was in it." A decade later in Caroline County, Virginia, a slave named Phill torched his master's home, corn house, and tobacco house. Though Virginian legislators made arson a capital crime, they could not prevent it.

Savvy masters realized they could get the most out of their human chattel by sharing power. Some owners along the rice coast of South Carolina and Georgia used the tasking system, assigning slaves specific tasks—such as so many baskets of rice to thresh—and then allowing them to do what they wanted when they finished. Masters liked the tasking system because it gave slaves an incentive to get the work done. Slaves liked it because it permitted them some control over their lives.

Most slaves used any leisure to their advantage. They cultivated garden plots and kept poultry that enriched their diets. Some also traveled to towns and neighboring plantations to market their produce. Eventually, they created their own economy within the master's economy. They saved coins to buy small things or, in rare cases, to purchase their freedom. Owners recognized that slaves who had the right to produce for themselves and barter what they made were less likely to run away. From the slaves' perspective, the arrangement allowed companionship and some measure of satisfaction.

Sometimes slaves pilfered chickens, livestock, crops, or tools from their masters and sold the stolen goods in underground market systems spread over considerable distances. Domestic slaves took advantage of their station to pinch liquor and pocket household items. Most slaves saw no sin at all in taking crops they had planted, raised, and harvested, even if their master called it stealing. Most masters kept the peace by looking the other way.

Creating Family Ties

In the master's view, slave family life was theoretically impossible because allegiance was supposed to run in only one direction: from slave to master. To that end, the majority of colonies prohibited marriage contracts between slaves. Yet masters also knew that slaves who forged family ties might have children, thus increasing the owner's wealth at no additional investment. As Thomas Jefferson put it, "A woman who brings a child every two years [is] more profitable than the best man on the farm, [for] what she produces is an addition to the capital, while his labor disappears in mere consumption." (When grown, a male slave was typically worth $1,000 in today's currency.) In addition to the profitability of slave families, owners also valued the power of family ties to keep slaves from fleeing. Thus, many masters struck bargains with slaves regarding domestic life.

But such bargains always involved tension, especially when slave owners contemplated auctioning members of slave families. Often, slaves were sold after an owner's death to fulfill the terms of the deceased person's will. Aware that shattered families made for unhappy, recalcitrant slaves, a new owner might agree to let slave husbands visit "abroad" wives and children. Refusal could provoke flight, as a slave advertisement from South Carolina in 1749 reveals: Cuffee's escape, said the announcement, was "occasion'd by his Wife and Child's being sold from him." A generation later, not even a spiky iron collar could keep a slave woman named Patt from escaping to find her husband, to whom "she [was] very much attached."

Running Away

For most slaves, running away offered the best hope of resistance. Colonial newspapers recorded thousands of runaway cases, posting notices of fleeing slaves and offering rewards for their capture. Runaway-slave advertisements tell a vivid story about people who used their linguistic skills and knowledge of a region's geography to seize freedom. For example, when twenty-three-year-old Joe, a mixed-race Philadelphia slave, fled his master in 1762, he reinvented himself as Joseph Boudron—because a free black needed a full first name and a distinctive surname. He "speaks good English, French, Spanish, and Portuguese," read the advertisement announcing his escape. Boudron also knew his way around. Born in Guadalupe, a French sugar island in the West Indies, he had already lived in Charleston, South Carolina, and New York—where his Philadelphia master thought he was headed. "A good cook and much used to the Seas," Boudron could pose as a free black mariner or chef.

Many runaway slaves disguised themselves to increase their chances. Some impersonated Native Americans. In 1751, Tom, a thirty-seven-year-old mulatto in East New Jersey, cut his coat short to make Indian stockings, lopped off his hair, and searched for a blanket "to pass for an Indian." He then headed for a Susquehannah Indian village where the German Moravian sect in Pennsylvania had established a mission.

Some slaves ran away knowing they would return, often voluntarily; they just needed the comfort of a loved one, relief from a heartless overseer, or a few days in the woods on their own. But most runaways set out for permanent freedom. Men fled far more often than women, who felt tied to their places of captivity by their children. Yet many women escaped, too, sometimes while pregnant or with small children in their arms.

In the southern colonies, most runaways were recaptured and returned to their owners. A slave had to make it as far north as Philadelphia to find sanctuary in communities formed by freed slaves. A few settlements of escaped slaves survived briefly in the Carolinas and the Chesapeake. At one, near present-day Lexington, Virginia, in 1728, runaway slaves built a small village of huts resembling those they had known in Africa and formed a government under a chief whose father had been a king. But these communities did not last long, as masters were determined to root them out. In a region where there were only one or two free Africans for every hundred slaves, it was next to impossible to masquerade as a free person indefinitely.

Masters did everything they could to discourage slaves from running away. Some chopped off the toes of repeat offenders or hobbled them with heavy ankle chains and iron collars. Others branded and flogged recaptured runaways and punished their families. The first African Equiano saw in Virginia was a woman punished for running away with a lock on her mouth, "so fast that she could scarcely speak; and could not eat nor drink. I was much astonished and shocked at this contrivance, which I afterwards learned was called the iron muzzle." Though such treatment might discourage individuals, it could not vanquish the collective will for freedom.

Rebelling

For bondspeople, organized revolt was the highest form of resistance. The largest slave uprising in the colonies erupted in 1730 in Virginia's Tidewater. Some 300 slaves, after choosing "officers to command them," fled to the Dismal Swamp "where they commit[ted] many outrages against the [white] Christians." With the aid of local Pasquotank Indians, white Virginians suppressed the insurrection and hanged twenty-nine of the rebels.

Nine years later, an uprising known as the Stono Rebellion broke out in South Carolina. About twenty slaves along the Stono River southwest of Charleston—most newly arrived from Angola or Kongo—seized weapons from their masters. They killed several white people and headed for Florida, where they hoped to find refuge among the Spanish, as handfuls of slaves had done for years. Raising banners and marching to a stirring drumbeat, they burned and plundered plantations as they went. Attracting additional slaves, the small army swelled to about a hundred. But the colonial militia intercepted them and, with Indian assistance, defeated them in a pitched battle. Thirty slaves lost their lives. Shaken, South Carolina's legislature halted imports of Africans for several years and restricted slaves' use of passes. Yet punishments could not prevent slaves from organizing resistance. Southern white authorities squelched several other revolts in the making, including plots in Charleston, South Carolina, in 1730 and in Annapolis, Maryland, in 1740.

Though large-scale rebellions were rare, they occurred often enough to sustain fear. A wave of slave unrest swept the northeastern seaboard in 1740–1741, first erupting as a series of barn burnings in New Jersey. Authorities executed two slaves for the crime. The following year, New York City experienced a rash of thefts and fires. Because England and its colonies were at war with Spain and France (King George's War, 1739–1744), these fires triggered widespread concern. Then another blaze hit New York City. After authorities overheard one slave muttering "Fire, fire, scorch, scorch a little damn it," they linked the blaze to a white tavern keeper, his wife, and an indentured servant girl, a tavern prostitute. Tortured and promised immunity, the servant confessed that her master was conspiring with several slaves and a Catholic priest to burn the city to the ground, kill all its white people and free all its slaves. This confession led to the arrests and trials of the tavern keeper and his wife and two slaves, all of whom were hanged. As the dragnet pulled in more suspects, officials threatened torture and execution to extract the names of other conspirators. Eventually, 150 slaves and twenty-five white people were tried, and seventeen slaves and four white people hanged. Thirteen more slaves were burned at the stake, and seventy-two were transported out of the colony to the West Indies.

Afro-Floridians and Afro-Louisianans

Whereas England's North American colonies had an elaborate system of slavery by the mid-eighteenth century, Spain's and France's colonies had a more porous slave system, characterized by racial intermingling and communities of free Africans.

Fort Mose: The First Free Black Town

In Spanish Florida, free black people formed a fortified town—the first such community in North America. The town's founder was Francisco Menéndez. Born in a Mandingo village in Africa around 1700, Menéndez was given his Spanish name by his captors and transported to Florida in the 1720s. There his owner freed him for his bravery in a battle against the English in 1728. Menéndez rose to the rank of captain of the free black military unit charged with protecting the Spanish foothold in Florida.

Granted land two miles north of St. Augustine, Menéndez and the rest of his unit built Pueblo de Gracia Real de Santa Terese de Mose, known simply as Mose. The fort consisted of stout walls enclosing thatched huts. Mose's Afro-Spaniards swore they would be "the most cruel enemies of the English" and would spill their "last drop of blood in defense of the great Crown of Spain and the Holy Faith." Their vow reflects their adherence to Catholicism; under Spanish rule, slaves were sometimes released if willing to convert. Thoroughly intermixed with local Indians, the free Africans lived as farmers and militiamen.

In the political turmoil of the eighteenth century, Mose was hotly contested by the Spanish and English. It was also a sanctuary for Africans fleeing South Carolina slavery. Desperate to stanch the outflow of slaves, the English attacked and drove Mose's free black people from the fort several times in the early 1740s, but each time, Menéndez and his people returned to rebuild the fort. In 1763, however, when Spain ceded Florida to England, Menéndez realized that free black people had no future under English rule, and he led Mose's inhabitants to Havana, Cuba.

Now South Carolinians and Georgians took up land grants in northern Florida, and they brought enslaved Africans with them. By the onset of the American Revolution, slave labor had built profitable rice, indigo, cotton, sugar, and orange plantations along the St. Johns and St. Mary's rivers. The free black town was gone, but it remained in memory as a symbol of African freedom, and many black Floridians named their sons Mose.

French Louisiana: A Black Majority

Like the Spanish in Florida, the French in Louisiana treated their slaves differently than the English did. Louisiana was the only North American colony that started out with a black majority. By 1731, Louisiana had about 4,000 slaves—more than two Africans for every white French inhabitant. By 1746, the ratio was three to one. Most slaves were imported directly from Africa, initially from

Angola and the Gulf of Benin. By the 1730s, they came primarily from Senegambia, where the French had extensive trading contacts. The majority of these later arrivals were Malinka-speaking Bambaras.

In a raw frontier wilderness, French planters had to make concessions to enslaved Africans and militant Indians, who frequently joined forces against the French. In 1729, African slaves joined Natchez Indians in an uprising that killed more than 200 of the already disease-decimated French. The planters who survived offered freedom to those slaves who would retaliate against the rebels the next year. The French renewed the offer for slaves willing to fight against the Chickasaw Indians allied with the British in the 1730s and against the Choctaws in the 1740s. Taking advantage of black military skills, the French were able to pit Africans against hostile Indians and reduce the likelihood of a disastrous Indian-African alliance. The arrangement gave Africans more privileges, and even opportunities for authority, than slaves had in other southeastern colonies.

Samba Bambara's story provides an example. In the 1720s, Bambara worked in West Africa as a Senegal River boatman and interpreter for France's Company of the Indies. Around 1730, perhaps seeing the usefulness of Bambara's talents, the French enslaved him and shipped him to Louisiana. There, his knowledge of French and several African languages earned him a privileged position as a court translator in Louisiana's legislative and judicial body. Later, he became the overseer on the Company of the Indies' huge sugar plantation near New Orleans. But neither privilege nor position made Samba Bambara content; in 1731, he led a rebellion. The French crushed the revolt and executed Bambara and seven other conspirators.

Slave revolts in Louisiana proved rare, but the thick swamps and forests of the lower Mississippi provided cover for villages of escaped slaves. Though the French used black militiamen to ferret out the renegades, they never completely eliminated such villages from Louisiana.

Nor did the French manage to establish a thriving colony. Louisiana's rich soil, plentiful water, and year-round growing climate counted for little because the French focused their resources on the sugar islands of the West Indies. Few French settlers arrived after the frustrated Company of the Indies handed the colony back to the French king in 1731. Only a single slave ship arrived in the next thirty-five years to replenish Louisiana's African population. Consequently, planters tried to preserve what few slaves they had by moderating workloads and encouraging family formation. Catholic priests solemnized slave marriages and baptisms and permitted Africans to participate in church ceremonies. In New Orleans, where most slaves lived, white people valued their bondsmen's artisan skills highly and permitted many of them to live in their own dwellings and hire themselves out in their free time. Even more important, slaves in Louisiana slowly gained the rights to maintain their own garden plots and keep poultry and livestock. By 1763, the end of the French period in Louisiana, slaves had developed an economy of their own. They marketed poultry and produce, gained control over more of their time, and circulated with few restraints. These conditions gave them a crucial advantage—the opportunity to save for self-purchase.

Since Louisiana had never generated a profit for its investors, French diplomats happily unloaded the colony on Spain in 1763 at the end of the Seven Years' War. By that time, because there had been almost no importation of slaves, the black population stood at less than 6,000. By contrast, more than twice as many Africans lived in the New England colonies, and Maryland and Virginia's total slave population had reached 250,000. Spain controlled the territory for only twenty years; at the conclusion of the American Revolution, Louisiana returned to France. Yet during those two decades of Spanish control, Afro-Louisianans acquired unique rights. New doors opened to them when the Spanish set up a black militia to patrol French planters resistant to Spanish rule. Unheard of in any English colony, the black militia played an indispensable role in colonial defense. Its ranks swelled with former slaves who had exercised the Spanish policy of *coartación* to purchase their freedom.

The French *Code Noir* (like the English slave codes) contained no policy akin to *coartación*. Only slave owners could decide whether to free their human property. Yet in the eighteenth century, law and social custom increasingly discouraged French slave owners from taking that step. The Spanish practice of *coartación*, however, gave slaves the right to initiate self-purchase by agreement with their master. If a master resisted, slaves could petition the governor's court to gain their freedom.

Through *coartación*, hundreds of slaves in Louisiana freed themselves during the Spanish period. Those who had raised and marketed produce for years now had the means to do so. Other masters freed their slaves voluntarily, particularly their slave wives and their mixed-race children for reasons of "love and affection." By the end of the Spanish era, New Orleans had a free black population of over 900—nearly 10 percent of the city's black people, a proportion unequaled in North America.

Becoming African American

What's in a name? For Africans recently torn from their homelands, a birth name provided not just a cherished connection to family and community but a deep mark of identity. Yet even this was stripped from them. The long transition from African to African American often began when a master assigned a slave a new name. Olaudah Equiano remembered vividly how his third master named him Gustavus Vasa. "I refused to be called so," Equiano recounted, "and told him as well as I could that I would be called Jacob," the name assigned by his Virginia master. When Equiano published his autobiography, it was under his African name.

Acquiring a new name was only one part of being an African in America. The transition from African to African American unfolded gradually, influenced by factors such as the regional population density of the enslaved Africans, the ratio of imported Africans to North American-born slaves, and the type of community (town, plantation, frontier farm). Two parallel processes also shaped the transition—encounters among people from different parts of Africa, and encounters between black slaves and white European masters. The brutal

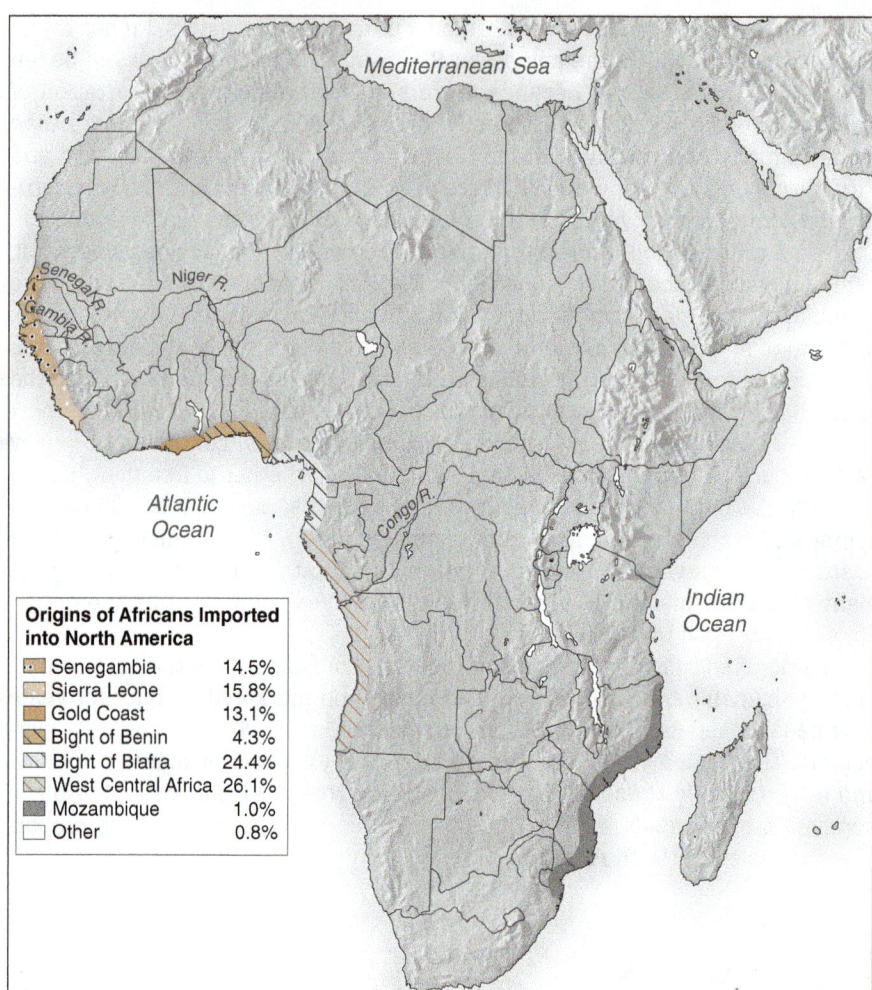

Origins of Africans Imported into North America

Senegambia	14.5%
Sierra Leone	15.8%
Gold Coast	13.1%
Bight of Benin	4.3%
Bight of Biafra	24.4%
West Central Africa	26.1%
Mozambique	1.0%
Other	0.8%

MAP 4.2 Origins of Africans Imported into North America

The origins of imported Africans changed markedly during the eighteenth and early nineteenth centuries. Slaves from West Central Africa (Kongo and Angolan peoples) predominated through the 1730s, but thereafter, Ibos from the Bight of Biafra made up the bulk of imported slaves.

circumstances of enslavement impelled peoples from different homelands to fashion a collective identity. At the same time, all slaves had to adapt to European masters whose culture differed markedly from theirs. Indeed, their lives depended on their ability to adapt. This process fueled a new African American culture that slaves expressed through religious beliefs and cultural practices.

African Christianity

In fashioning viable lives and new identities in North America, slaves struggled to clarify their place in the cosmos. Equiano was cut off from the Ibo people's

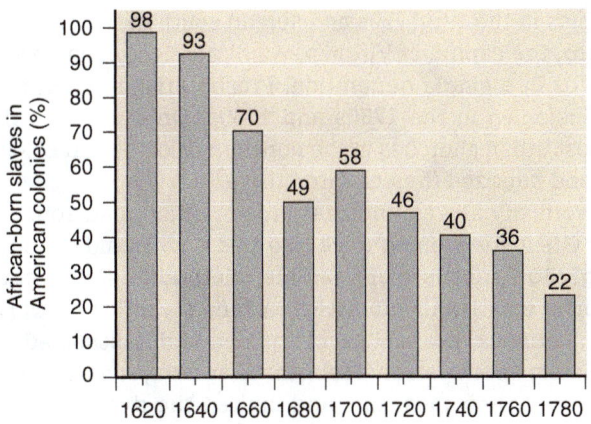

FIGURE 4.2 Percentage of African-born Slaves in American Colonies, 1620–1780
After the Seven Years' War (1756–1763) choked off slave importations and births to slave couples, the percentage of African-born slaves in the English colonies declined. However, this varied from place to place. South Carolina and Georgia had the largest ratio of African-born to North American–born slaves.

spiritual universe in 1756 when he started his long march to West Africa's coast. Like anyone plunged into harsh circumstances, he sought spiritual solace and, like most slaves, gradually embraced a religion that blended African traditions with Christian practices and beliefs. Purchasing his freedom in 1766, six years after he was baptized, he practiced a Christianity that contained traces of Ibo spirituality.

Until about the time of Equiano's conversion, most Africans in the North American colonies had known little of Christianity. Instead, they clung to the religious practices and values they remembered from their homelands. Their rituals included burying a deceased person so that the body faced east. Africans also placed coins, porcelain plates, shoes, or treasured possessions on the stomach of the deceased to ensure a journey to an afterlife of ease in the African homeland.

With most slaves following African spiritual traditions, Christianity only slowly penetrated slave life. Many bondspeople found little comfort in it. Its spirituality seemed confined to the church, and the highly intellectual Protestant message seemed cold and complex. Slave masters, moreover, did little to promote Christian thinking and practice among slaves. In their view, the religion's emphasis on equality before God and a community of all humankind threatened to undercut their own authority. In 1730, following a period of unusual missionary activity in Richmond County, Virginia, some baptized slaves claimed that their acceptance of Christ entitled them to freedom. When this claim sparked a rebellion near Norfolk, masters cracked down on slave conversions.

Then a movement known as the Great Awakening whipped up new enthusiasm for Christianizing slaves. This wave of evangelical fervor began in the northern colonies in the late 1720s and spread south in the 1740s. In the parish of Williamsburg, the capital of Virginia, Anglican clergymen baptized nearly a thousand slaves in a single generation. Presbyterians began conversions in the southern colonies in the 1750s and 1760s. On the eve of the American Revolution, most urban churches in the northern colonies had black worshipers, who married and baptized their children there.

Why did so many slaves find that Protestantism had something to offer after all? The Great Awakening gave rise to a new brand of religion that appealed strongly to Africans. For example, Methodist and Baptist preachers developed a more emotional, informal preaching style that black people appreciated. During sermons, evangelical clergymen and unschooled lay preachers spoke passionately about personal rebirth. They swayed back and forth, swept up in the power of their message, and invited the dynamic participation of worshipers. Some preachers delivered sermons spontaneously, often in fields and barns, and encouraged ecstatic dancing, chanting, shouting, rhythmic clapping, and singing. Perhaps not surprisingly, followers—black and white alike—found the experience intensely emotional compared with that of the dry sermons delivered from elevated Protestant pulpits.

For the first time in the North American colonies, slaves encountered a worship style that reminded them of African spirituality. The Awakeners stressed that Christ blessed the weak, the poor, and the humble. In the day of reckoning, "the last would be first, and the first would be last." This was a powerful, comforting message for people who had little hope of freedom in this life. Slave owners, for their part, hoped their human property would embrace the Christian values of meekness and obedience.

Once slaves had experienced Christian teaching, not even the most controlling master could suppress its uplifting message. Visiting Savannah, Georgia, in 1765, Equiano heard the spellbinding English evangelist George Whitefield preach that all souls are equal before God. The church was packed with white and black worshipers. This was a God for everyone.

Africans converted to Christianity for the comfort and hope it promised. But by interweaving their own spiritual practices into the faith, they created a unique manifestation of the religion. They found expression in slave spirituals, or songs, singing Anglo-American hymns with an African rhythm. They also created their own songs about biblical heroes who appealed to them—Daniel, Joshua, Jonah, Moses—men who had resisted persecutors to prevail in this world rather than waiting for justice in heaven. Meanwhile, "sorrow songs" both expressed and eased the pain of enslavement. "We sing," said one slave, "to take away trouble."

Other spirituals asserted individual worth and strength. Historians have no way of knowing when slaves began to sing "We Are the People of God" or "I'm Born of God, I Know I Am," but after the American Revolution slaves found these songs sustaining, suggesting that earlier generations sang songs with similar themes. Challenging white people's discredit of African culture, these songs demonstrate a sense of self-worth, a feeling of fellowship, and a commitment to life purpose.

African Muslims

While some enslaved Africans began to embrace Christianity and blend it with African religious ways, other slaves came as Muslims to North America and continued to practice Islam. The evidence of early Islam in America is fragmentary, as most descendants of Muslim slaves were reluctant to discuss it. But clearly, many slaves came from areas in West and Central Africa—especially Senegambia, Sierra Leone, the Gold Coast, and coastal Benin—where Islam had made extensive inroads. Runaway slave advertisements, especially those in South Carolina and Georgia, mention distinctly Muslim names such as Mustapha, Fatima, and Mamdo.

One such Muslim was Yarrow Mamout, who arrived aboard a slave ship around 1720. Purchased by a Maryland family, Mamout became a skilled brickmaker. He gained his freedom after making all the bricks for his master's new mansion in Georgetown, now part of the District of Columbia. For many years, Mamout lived as a free man and eventually became a property owner of modest wealth. A faithful Muslim, he often strolled Baltimore's streets singing praises to Allah.

Another Muslim, Job Ben Solomon, arrived at Annapolis, Maryland, on a slave ship in 1731. He was sold to a tobacco planter, who found him resistant to field work but of agile mind and princely demeanor. As it turned out, Solomon was the son of a king in the land of Futa, in the Senegal River region. Captured by Mandingo enemies, he had been sold as a slave to an English slave ship captain. After learning of this identity, his master sent him to England. Eventually, Solomon returned to his home in Africa, where he ascended the throne.

When the famous painter of the American Revolution, Charles Willson Peale, sought out Yarrow Mamout in Baltimore, he found the Muslim slave "healthy, active, and very full of fun." Whether Mamout was 134 years old, as he told Peale, cannot be verified. But the descendants of his first American slave master felt certain he had reached at least 100 years of age.

Source: Charles Wilson Peale, "Yarrow Mamout". Courtesy of The Historical Society of Pennsylvania Collection, Atwater Kent Museum of Philadelphia.

African American Culture: Music, Dance, and Body Adornment

Like their countrymen and women in Africa, black people in the colonies found joy in aesthetic expression. "We are almost a nation of dancers, musicians, and poets," wrote Equiano of his homeland. Music and dance played central roles in black slaves' spirituality and everyday life—in the fields where they toiled, in the quarters where they lived, and in the woods and along riverbanks where they gathered when they could. "Night is their day," one slave owner remarked. When their "day" began at sunset, slaves gathered to create a world that sustained them. Dance, rhythm, rattles, and banjoes (an instrument with direct African antecedents) all testify to Africans' ability to maintain their cherished traditions. Slaves also expressed themselves through fiddling, clapping, and drumming, though some masters forbade drums because they feared slaves used them to send coded messages to each other. Above all, slaves reveled in shout songs and singing—testaments to their African spirit.

In every one of these activities, slaves fused their inherited West African knowledge with new ideas they acquired in North America. They merged what they had experienced through encounters with Native Americans and Europeans with what they remembered from African ways—and developed innovations. How to form a pot from clay, weave a basket from sea grass, style one's hair, arrange fabric over the body, play an instrument, play with words, or

The artist of this rare watercolor of the juba, a West African dance, remains unknown. On the right, a banjo player provides music, while a cross-legged man beats a drum with two twisted leather sticks. The plantation house, outbuildings, and a row of slave cabins loom in the background.

use one's voice to sing or one's body to dance all came together in a unique culture developed by people determined to make life worth living.

Though given Western names and coarse clothes, slaves found ways to display their individuality. For example, they experimented with hairstyles. Drawing on homeland fashions and ideals of beauty, they braided their hair with beads, shells, and strips of material. They complemented these styles with turbans and bandanas, highly valued in West African societies. Eventually, they also began wearing beaver and raccoon-skin hats as well as flower-decked Scotch bonnets. Jaunty displays of hats, caps, and scarves cropped up in slave quarters throughout the colonies.

Though few slaves in North America practiced scarification, a common tradition throughout Africa, some developed other forms of body adornment. White authorities complained about slaves who dressed in apparel "quite gay and beyond their condition" or who dressed "so bold and impudent that they insult every poor white person they meet with." Slaves drew on African knowledge of natural dyes to add touches of color to their clothing. They also found ways to add bright cuffs, patches, and collars to jackets, trousers, and wraparound skirts. They fashioned brass wire earrings, beaded armbands and necklaces, and cloth bands that they draped over or wrapped around the body. These forms of personal adornment were small victories to combat the humiliation of slavery.

As another cultural defense against their plight, slaves embraced humor and playfulness. Skits mimicking masters brought the liberation of laughter, and stories from Africa kept spirits alive. The tale about the trickster spider Anansi who outwits his more powerful captors was a special favorite. In time, this story showed up in the Aunt Nancy tales recounted in Caribbean lore. It also made an appearance in the still later animal tales of Uncle Remus, collected and published in the late nineteenth century.

Slaves sought to maintain African practices even in the way they walked. Runaway slave advertisements describe "stately" or "strutting" gaits, a "proud carriage," a "swaggering knee," or a "remarkably grand and strong" walk—evidence of Africans who refused to adopt postures of defeat.

Merging Traditions

By the eve of the American Revolution, Africans had begun to shed some aspects of their individual tribal identities and develop a new, collective identity as African Americans. Slaves in the North, outnumbered twenty to one or more by white people, understandably absorbed more European ways than those in the South. We can see the merging of traditions especially in the Pinkster holiday, an adaptation of Pentecost. Introduced by the Dutch in New Amsterdam and New Jersey, Pinkster became a sacred African and Dutch holy day as well as a joyous festival. On one occasion, slave baptisms were followed by Africans "playing upon several instruments, a dancing and a shouting so loud that they might be heard half a league off." Religious services on Pentecost Monday were followed by a Tuesday holiday during which Dutch and Africans feasted, drank, and danced together.

New England's equivalent of Pinkster Day was Negro Election Day. Like Pinkster, it meshed African and Yankee traditions. These annual celebrations drew slaves from the surrounding countryside for feasting, parading, dancing, and the electing of black kings, judges, and other officials. "All the various languages of Africa, mixed with broken and ludicrous English filled the air," came one report from Newport, Rhode Island, "accompanied with the music of the fiddle, tambourine, the banjo [and] drum." In a ritualized role reversal, African Americans dressed in the clothes of their masters and rode their masters' horses. They extracted money tributes from their owners, drank wine and beer, and danced exuberantly in the streets. For a day, they symbolically ruled the town.

Why did white northerners permit such celebrations? They could afford to take the risk because they vastly outnumbered black people and, like role reversals in ancient times in other parts of the world, Negro Election Day acted as a safety valve. By offering black people a chance to let off steam, the festivals discouraged rebellion. They benefited slaves as well by providing a mechanism for them to choose and honor their own leaders, who acted throughout the year as unofficial mediators of disputes and as counselors. Such festivals did not necessarily appeal to all slaves. For example, Venture Smith shunned "superfluous finery" and "expensive gatherings" and proudly claimed that he was never "at the expense of sixpence worth" of liquor. Nor could such holidays alter the cruel fact of bondage. But they did offer momentary entertainment in an otherwise grim existence.

While Africans were becoming African American, Euro-Americans were becoming Africanized in subtle ways. For all their disparagement of African culture, white colonists knew they needed their slaves' knowledge and skills to prevail in a new environment. Only an impractical South Carolina planter would ignore the rice-growing expertise of West Africans. Similarly, New England Puritans applied African medical knowledge of inoculation for smallpox. In South Carolina, legislators granted freedom and a lifelong pension to an African who knew how to save victims of rattlesnake bites.

Apart from such sensible borrowing of African knowledge, white people became Africanized almost without realizing it. In the South, where black people outnumbered white people in many regions, masters came to appreciate foods of African origin such as barbecued pork, fried chicken, and mustard and collard greens. Black cooks working in their master's kitchen had plentiful opportunities to carry on culinary traditions brought from West and Central Africa.

A cross-pollination of languages also occurred. One commentator reflected that after generations of living in close contact with African slaves, "the language of the common people of [South Carolina] is a curious mixture of English and African." Even masters wove African phrases and tones into their speech. One wealthy plantation owner was described as speaking "like a negro." Whether influenced by African medical practices, speech patterns, music, cuisine, or even notions about death and afterlife, hardly a white colonist in the South remained untouched by African culture.

Black Americans on the Eve of the American Revolution

African-born Olaudah Equiano and Venture Smith worked their way out of slavery with extraordinary perseverance and skill. But few slaves transported directly from Africa won their freedom. Most who gained freedom were North American-born. Many were mixed-race individuals who owed their manumission to a white father.

Slaves who possessed craft skills were the best equipped to escape from bondage. Whether in towns or on farms and plantations, they had greater mobility, more thorough knowledge of the world around them, and often broader linguistic skills that served them well when they encountered patrols or constables. In making a bid for freedom, many impersonated free black sailors and hired themselves out. If they succeeded in this strategy, they hid in towns with other free black people or poor white families.

Curbing Manumission

In the early eighteenth century, white legislators turned from controlling slaves to narrowing free black people's privileges, such as the right to hold office or vote, bear arms or serve in the militia, and employ white indentured servants. In many colonies, laws slapped special taxes on free black people and defined unusually severe punishments for crimes committed by African Americans. Only by excluding "free-negros & mulattos . . . from that great privilege of a freeman," declared Virginia's governor in 1723, could whites "make the free-Negroes sensible that a distinction ought to be made between their offspring and the descendants of an Englishman, with whom they never were to be accounted equal."

Beginning in the 1690s, colonial legislators in the South erected legal roadblocks to freedom. One provision abolished slave owners' right to free their slaves without specific legislative approval. Another required slave owners to transport a newly freed man or woman out of the colony, though this ruling was not often enforced. With manumission severely curtailed, the number of free black people in the southern colonies shrank. Only a few thousand free black people lived in the southern colonies amid more than 400,000 slaves.

Beginning in the 1720s, most northern colonies also curbed manumission by requiring slave owners to post hefty bonds guaranteeing the good conduct of those they freed and to maintain those requiring public charity—a provision recognizing that most black men and women released from enforced servitude were old and sickly. Their former owners were just eager to dispose of a "burden." As in the South, lawmakers in the North barred free black people from voting, testifying in court or serving on juries, and serving in the militia.

Yet cracks were appearing in the edifice of slavery. During the Seven Years' War, the need for militia recruits convinced white northerners to set aside the ban against arming black men. Scores of slaves volunteered to fight in the war that drove France from Canada and the western frontier, thereby earning freedom. By the outbreak of the American Revolution, about 4,000 free African Americans lived in the northern colonies, a higher proportion than lived in the southern colonies.

Protesting Slavery

Even as slaves nurtured the hope of liberty and at least some of the privileges white colonists enjoyed, a few white men and women shared their vision. Every generation in North America contained a handful of white people who recognized slavery for what it was—an immoral system designed solely to enrich slave owners through the brutal use of human beings. These white people refused to be swayed by biblical sanctions of the practice or examples of the widespread use of slavery throughout human history. Though slavery may have always existed, they said, that didn't mean decent people could not—and should not—stop it now.

Back in 1688, four Quakers in Germantown, Pennsylvania, had protested slavery. In the 1730s, a new breed of antislavery advocates emerged in the same colony. Whereas earlier protesters occasionally spoke out against slavery, now white men such as Benjamin Lay, John Woolman, and Anthony Benezet dedicated themselves to eliminating it. For many such reformers, their efforts cost them their place in society.

Benjamin Lay was an outsider from the moment of his birth in England, owing to a deformity that left him a hunchback. But his twisted body did not stop his compassion and determination. Immigrating to Barbados, he witnessed the most barbaric manifestation of slavery firsthand. Arriving in Philadelphia in 1731 and seeing slavery taking hold there as well, he initiated a crusade with tactics that attracted attention. In what was later known as the *free produce strategy,* he boycotted slave-produced necessities, made his own clothes from sheep's wool and flax, and publicly smashed his wife's teacups to protest the use of slave-produced sugar. By standing with one bare foot in the snow outside a Quaker meeting, he shamed those who deprived their slaves of boots. He even kidnapped a white Quaker child to teach the Society of Friends about the grief suffered by African families when their children were sold at auctions. Once he spattered red pokeberry juice on startled Quakers, suggesting that Quakers with slaves had blood on their hands.

In the 1750s, a new wave of Quaker reformers set out to cleanse the Society's membership of slave traders and owners. John Woolman, a leader in this effort, had journeyed through the southern colonies, where he witnessed the "many vices and corruptions" created by slavery. In *Some Considerations on the Keeping of Negroes* (1753), he warned that if we "treat our inferiors with rigour, to increase our wealth and gain riches for our children, what then shall we do when God riseth up; and when he visiteth, what shall we answer him?" Like Lay, Woolman earned the resentment of his fellow Quakers who traded or owned slaves.

Another plain-spoken reformer, Anthony Benezet of Philadelphia, echoed Woolman's protests. During the day, Benezet taught poor white children; at night, he taught black children, slave and free, to read. After years of teaching, he concluded that black children were as intellectually capable as white young-sters. His published statement directly challenged the common proslavery argument that Africans were inherently inferior to Europeans, suited only for forced labor. Like Woolman, Benezet published stirring denunciations of slavery in the 1750s, inspiring a growing number of Quakers to organize anti-slavery blocs at meetings and to promote bans on the importation, sale, and ownership of slaves.

It took reformers a long time to change even Quaker minds, but Quaker leaders in Pennsylvania and New Jersey initiated a crusade that offered hope to thousands of enslaved and free African Americans and laid the foundation for a movement that, within a century, redirected the course of a fledgling nation.

Conclusion

By the eve of the American Revolution, slavery had made violence a way of life in the English colonies. Masters used violence to keep Africans under control, and slaves struck back with violence in protest. Was it true, as the Quaker John Woolman believed, that slaveholding, even among kindly masters, "depraved the mind . . . with as great certainty as prevailing cold congeals water"? If so, many people shuddered at the implications for the North American society that had begun to take shape. Did slaves' outwardly visible degradation stem directly from what Woolman called the white colonists' "inner corruption"?

Despite such anxieties, the Europeans had bound themselves to Africans in an economic system that brought wealth to the powerful and pain to the ex-ploited. That same system gradually fused elements of European, Indian, and African cultures into a unique new entity. For their part, Africans were becom-ing African American. They learned to speak their master's language, acquired knowledge of the local terrain, and even formed emotional attachments to the land. They started families, incorporated elements of Christianity into their tra-ditional religious beliefs, and devised strategies to endure the unendurable. Some ran away, lashed out at masters, or initiated slave revolts—though mas-ters countered with increasingly repressive laws and brutal punishments.

As tensions between white colonists and their British overlords mounted, few slave owners perceived the parallels between their situation and that of their slaves. If the colonists had to resort to violence to keep black people under control, what response might these same white people expect when they tried to break the shackles their British imperial masters imposed on them? Nor did white people see the bitter irony behind their own clamoring for liberty and their subjugation of black people asking for the very same thing.

Questions for Review and Reflection

1. What conclusions do you reach after reading the account of Venture Smith's struggle to escape lifelong bondage? To what extent do you imagine his experience was unique? How much of its uniqueness is a result of the fact that there is written documentation of his experience?

2. Why did slavery grow much more rapidly in the southern colonies than in the northern colonies? What were some of the benefits and disadvantages to enslaved Africans that came from living in the South or in the North.

3. What forms did resistance to slavery take? Why were slave rebellions in the North American English colonies so infrequent compared to those in Caribbean and South American colonies?

4. At what point would you say Africans became African Americans in North America? If Africans were "Europeanized," to what extent were European colonists "Africanized"?

5. The sources of abolitionism were many. Can you identify them and judge the relative importance of each?

CHAPTER 5

The Revolutionary Era: Crossroads of Freedom

Thomas Peters Seizes His Freedom

On a steamy summer day in 1775, Thomas Peters heard rumors of a slave insurrection planned for July 8. Living in the house of his master in Wilmington, North Carolina, Peters was no stranger to feverish talk of rebellion as a way to secure a person's rights. William Campbell, Peters's owner, led Wilmington's Sons of Liberty—a citizens' group protesting the British Parliament's taxation policies. The Sons of Liberty spoke avidly about the natural rights they believed belonged to everyone at birth.

Even before the colonists began grumbling about English tyranny, Peters had fought for his own freedom. He had reached North America in 1760, at about age twenty-two, after slavers snatched him from his Yoruba homeland in what is now Nigeria. Marched to the coast like Olaudah Equiano and millions of others, Peters had been sold to a French slave trader and transported to French Louisiana. Three times he tried to escape—and three times he was recaptured and punished with whipping, branding, and ankle shackling.

Sold from one owner to another, Peters acquired an array of language skills. How he came to Campbell, a Scottish immigrant in North Carolina, we do not know. But in Wilmington, a Cape Fear River town of 200 households, Peters learned his trade as a millwright, making planking and barrel staves from the pines of the coastal forests.

When Wilmington's white citizens discovered the slave plot for July 8, they quickly rounded up suspects, imposed punishments, and redoubled patrols.

1770	Crispus Attucks is killed in the Boston Massacre.
1773	Boston Tea Party inflames conflict between England and the colonies.
	Phillis Wheatley's poems are published in London.
	Slaves in Massachusetts petition for their freedom.
1775	The American Revolution opens with battles at Lexington and Concord.
	American forces, including African Americans, defend Breed's Hill.
	Quakers in Philadelphia establish the first abolition society.
	Virginia's royal governor offers freedom to slaves who join the British army.
1776	Declaration of Independence asserts "all men are created equal."
1777	Vermont towns write a constitution outlawing slavery.
1778	Americans form an alliance with the French.
1780	Pennsylvania law initiates gradual emancipation of slaves.
1781	Elizabeth Freeman sues for freedom under the new Massachusetts constitution.
	The British expel thousands of African Americans who had joined them to gain freedom.
	The British surrender at Yorktown.
1782	Laws in Maryland and Virginia repeal prohibitions on manumission.
1783	Treaty of Paris ends British rule and acknowledges U.S. independence.
	Slaves who gained freedom by serving in the British army resettle in Nova Scotia.
	Massachusetts abolishes slavery by judicial decree in Quock Walker case.
1784	Rhode Island and Connecticut begin gradual emancipation of slaves.
1786–1787	Black Bostonians offer to fight Daniel Shays; others fight with him.
1787	Northwest Ordinance bans entry of slaves into the Northwest Territory.
	The Constitutional Convention in Philadelphia writes a new constitution for the confederated colonies.
1788–1789	Ratified Constitution protects the institution of slavery.
1789	George Washington is the first president under the Constitution.
1791	A slave revolution erupts in Haiti.
1792	Former slaves in Nova Scotia return to Africa.
	Benjamin Banneker publishes his first almanac.

With American militia units and British regulars exchanging fire at Lexington and Concord in Massachusetts in the spring, the white settlers of Cape Fear worried about slave rebellions more than ever. As the Wilmington Committee of Safety warned, "There is much reason to fear, in these times of general tumult and confusion, that the slaves may be instigated, encouraged by our inveterate enemies, to an insurrection."

The Committee's warning had merit, for British military leaders were inciting black slaves to rise up against their masters. In July, the British commander of the fort at the mouth of the Cape Fear River gave "encouragement to Negroes to elope from their masters" and offered protection to those who escaped. Slaves began fleeing into the woods outside Wilmington, and word spread among them that the British had promised that "every Negro that would murder his master and family . . . should have his master's plantation." Appalled, colonial authorities imposed martial law that gave militia units wide authority to impose curfews and limit the movement of slaves.

Like enslaved Africans everywhere in the colonies, Peters had to weigh his options carefully. He had married Sally, a slave, and in 1771 she had given birth to a girl the couple named Clairy. What chance did Peters's family have of reaching the protection of British forces? If the young father fled by himself, would his wife and child suffer the retaliation white owners and colonial lawmakers threatened on kinfolk left behind? In March 1776, Peters and his family risked all. Slipping away unseen from the Campbell plantation, they headed for the British ships on Cape Fear River. There, Peters signed up with the company of Black Guides and Pioneers, led by Captain George Martin of the British army.

The Peters family had their freedom at last. But for them and half a million other African Americans, the future held opportunity and peril. Colonist rhetoric about unalienable rights and Britain's crackdown on patriots in the 1760s and 1770s suggested that slavery might come to an end. But could slaves count on that? Could they wait for that day? As the American Revolution unfolded, enslaved African Americans faced difficult choices: respond to British offers of freedom, join the white patriots' cause if given the chance, or wait out the war. As this chapter reveals, all three choices brought hope of liberation.

But unlike white colonists, black rebels lacked the luxury of town meetings, countywide gatherings, and state conventions to discuss their options. They had to make these difficult decisions individually or in small groups. All the while, newborn states created constitutions that laid out the terms of how the states would govern themselves—including what they would do about slavery. When a convention met in Philadelphia in 1787 to write a constitution for the new nation, slavery became a major point of contention.

After the Revolution, thousands of African Americans who had been promised freedom by the British had the chance to start new lives. Peters and others went to Nova Scotia, but when life there proved difficult, Peters led 1,200 former slaves back to Africa in an unprecedented return to the motherland.

British "Tyranny" and a Cry for Freedom

"In every human Breast," wrote a young New England slave named Phillis Wheatley, "God has implanted a Principle, which we call Love of Freedom." So how can the "Cry for Liberty" be reconciled with "the Exercise of oppressive Power over others"? Her question expressed the sentiments of half a million African Americans caught up in the events leading to the American Revolution. From 1764 to 1776, as white colonists proclaimed their love of freedom yet kept black people enslaved, many, like Wheatley, perceived the hypocrisy.

Born in Gambia in 1755 and abducted by slave traders as a small child, Wheatley arrived in North America in 1764. The slavers named her Phillis, after the vessel that transported her. She ended up in the household of a Boston tailor named Wheatley, who gave her his surname. Just eighteen months later, the nine-year-old girl could read the most difficult biblical passages and every piece of secular and religious literature that Boston clergymen put in her hands. At age thirteen, her first poem was published. At sixteen, she commemorated the Boston Massacre in verse. By 1773, when her poems were published in London, Wheatley created a sensation in the English-speaking world. This frail young African became the first woman in the American colonies to publish poetry

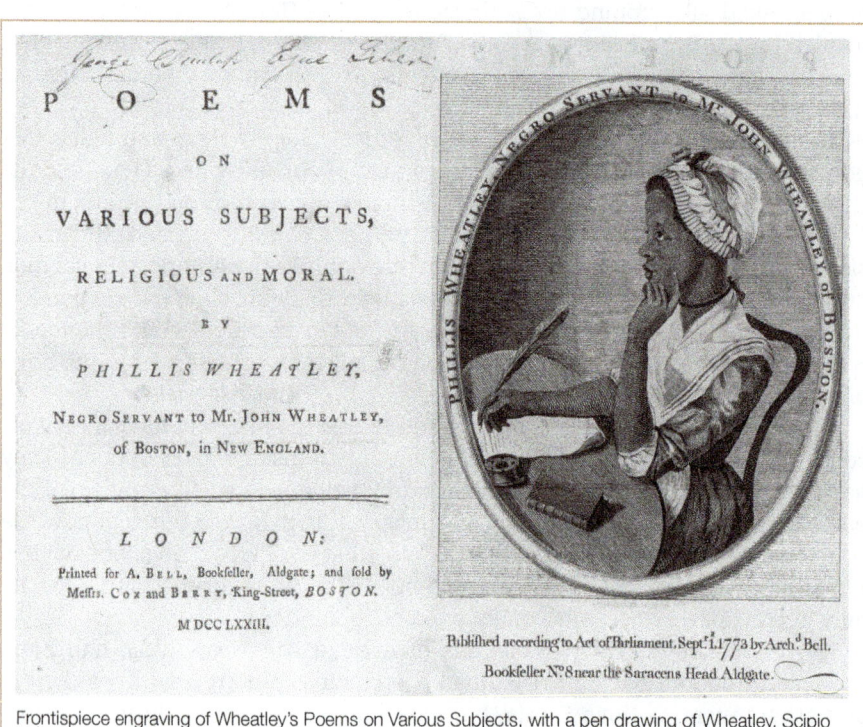

Frontispiece engraving of Wheatley's Poems on Various Subjects, with a pen drawing of Wheatley. Scipio Moorhead, a slave owned by a Boston minister, also wrote poetry and crafted this picture of Wheatley for her anthology of poems—creating the colonies' first identified African American portrait. To show her appreciation, Wheatley wrote the poem "To S. M., a young African Painter, on seeing his Works."

about political events. At that time, she was arguably read more widely than any other woman in North America.

Freedom Rhetoric Exposes Colonial Enslavement

African Americans in North America had witnessed the events that led white colonists to declare independence from England. They were aware of the riots and protests touched off by the Stamp Act of 1765 and the Townshend duties of 1767. They knew of the Boston Massacre and the Tea Act of 1773 that provoked Bostonians into dumping tea into the harbor, an event later called the Boston Tea Party. After Britain's Coercive Acts of 1774 further polarized the two sides, armed conflict broke out in April 1775 in the Massachusetts towns of Lexington and Concord.

Each step toward revolution riveted white colonists' attention on the question of Britain's rights and responsibilities regarding its colonies. But arguments about whether Britain had the right to tax colonists who had no representation in the British Parliament or whether royal governors could legally disband elected colonial legislatures mattered little to black Americans. What did capture their interest were the language and methods of protest white colonists used to resist the British government.

As the conflict between the colonies and Britain escalated, Africans in North America saw new opportunities to seize their own liberty. From the first colonial protests against British revenue policy in 1765 to the end of the Revolutionary War in 1783, black people staged the most widespread and protracted slave rebellion in American history. Their efforts exposed a lie that many white people believed—that most slaves were content with their lot. Tens of thousands of slaves fled to the British side to gain freedom. Meanwhile, other black people cast their lot with the Americans in the belief that they would be rewarded with liberation.

Thousands of black Americans overheard their masters' dinner-table conversations and debates, worked in taverns and coffeehouses where colonists argued about revolutionary politics, and listened to white patriots describing Britain's policies as tantamount to tyranny and enslavement. These Africans pondered the notion of inalienable rights—the idea that some privileges are not earned but acquired at birth. Natural rights, political theorists maintained, could not be alienated (separated) from an individual.

Black people applied the ringing phrases of the day to their own situation. And in northern towns and on some southern plantations, they had the support of a few white colonists who recognized the contradiction between natural rights and Africans' enslavement. James Otis, a fervent pamphleteer on the rights of English-born citizens, had asserted as early as 1764 that the "colonists are by the law of nature free born, as indeed all men are, white or black. . . . Does it follow that it is right to enslave a man because he is black?"

Enslaved Africans' spirits no doubt soared as white colonists' rhetoric of freedom and resistance to tyranny heated up. In 1768, the *Pennsylvania Chronicle* urged colonists to ban the African slave trade, "emancipate the whole race" of Africans, and restore "that liberty we have so long unjustly detained from them." In 1773, Nathaniel Niles wrote: "For shame, let us either cease to enslave our fellow-men or else let us cease to complain of those that would enslave us." In 1775, Thomas Paine, author of the incendiary pamphlet *Common Sense,* challenged slaveholders: "With what consistency or decency [do white colonists] complain so loudly of attempts to enslave them, while they hold so many hundred thousand in slavery?"

Such rhetoric ignited Africans' own revolutionary spirit. In northern colonies, where slaves had the right to petition, some black Americans couched pleas for freedom in ways calculated to stir the conscience of their masters. But their language grew bolder after war broke out. "We . . . ask for nothing but what we are fully persuaded is ours to claim," asserted a Connecticut slave petition in 1777, for "we are the Creatures of that God, who made of one blood, and kindred, all the nations of the earth." That same year Prince Hall, a former slave who helped found the first black Masonic lodge in North America, exclaimed that the principles on which Americans had acted "in the course of their unhappy difficulties with Great Britain pleads stronger than a thousand arguments . . . [that black people] may be restored to the enjoyments of that which is the natural right of all men." Rhetoric pressing for the end of slavery provides some of the most compelling language of the revolutionary era.

Freedom Fever in the South

In the southern colonies, laws forbade slaves from petitioning the courts. Nevertheless, black Americans stepped up demands for their liberty as revolutionary protests escalated. In Charleston, the South's largest city, enslaved Africans chanted "Liberty, liberty" as white colonists celebrated the resignation of the Stamp Act distributor in 1766. Yet the same colonists promptly cracked down on agitating black slaves. "The city was thrown under arms for a week," reported an alarmed white official, and messengers were dispatched throughout the colony to warn of possible slave uprisings.

Still, unrest among African Americans intensified. In Georgia and South Carolina in 1773, groups of slaves fled to the country's interior. The following year, rebelling slaves killed several white people. In August 1775, another slave plot percolated in South Carolina when the free black river pilot Thomas Jeremiah planned to guide the British Royal Navy into Charleston harbor and help bondspeople win their freedom. But officials discovered Jeremiah's scheme, hanged him, and set him aflame on August 18, 1775. As one historian wrote, "Behind the bewitching rhetoric of liberty was the hideous face of slavery."

African Americans and the American Revolution

By its nature, the Revolutionary War opened new doors for African Americans. With the immense movement of both civilian and military populations in and out of nearly every major seaport from Savannah to Boston between 1775 and 1783, urban slaves had unprecedented opportunities for seizing independence and destabilizing the institution of slavery. In the countryside, as British and

American forces crisscrossed the land, slaves fled to the British side by the thousands, disrupting plantation work routines. The few free African Americans faced a dilemma: Should they offer to fight with the American rebels in the hopes of improving their image in the minds of white patriots? Should they join the British as a means for overthrowing slavery? Or should they keep their heads down while waiting for the storm to pass? With war swirling around them, black Americans made their choices. For all, the hope of personal freedom guided their decisions.

Choosing the British: Black Loyalists

As Thomas Peters discovered, the British offered slaves their best chance at liberty. In November 1775, Virginia's royal governor, Lord Dunmore, issued a proclamation offering freedom for slaves and indentured servants "able and willing to bear arms" who escaped their masters and joined the British forces. Dunmore's proclamation lifted the hopes of enslaved Africans everywhere. Within just a few months, about a thousand Virginia runaway slaves reached the British lines. Many slaves who were old, infirm, very young, or pregnant decided against traveling such long distances. However, in every region, black women with children ran away from their masters in much greater proportion than they had in the colonial period. They knew that with the British offering refuge, they had a far better chance than ever before of winning—and keeping—their freedom.

Thomas Peters and his family were among those who chose the British and liberty. He fought with the Black Guides and Pioneers for eight years; others formed the Ethiopian Regiment, also led by white British officers. Some inscribed "Liberty to Slaves" across their uniforms. Peters moved north with the British forces to occupy Philadelphia in the fall of 1777 and was in New York City with the British when the war ended in 1783. Twice wounded, he received a promotion to sergeant in recognition of his leadership among his fellow escaped slaves. His family joined him in New York City by the time American and British diplomats were negotiating the peace treaty in Paris in 1782 and 1783.

Peters's wartime service brought him into contact with thousands of other black people who hoped for freedom through a similar route. It is difficult to know how many slaves allied with the British, but Thomas Jefferson acknowledged losing 10 to 20 percent of his slave labor force, and during the southern campaigns, from 1779 to 1782, plantations in South Carolina and Georgia lost thousands of slaves to occupying British forces.

Even in the North, where white masters exercised their rule less harshly than in the South, slaves opted for the British deal. When Thomas Peters was with the British regiments occupying Philadelphia, he observed slaves flocking to British ranks. Surveying Pennsylvania's losses in 1779, one white legislator lamented, "By the invasion of this state, and the possession the enemy obtain of this city and neighborhood, [a] great part of the slaves hereabouts were enticed away by the British army." New York City and its surrounding countryside offered numerous opportunities for slaves to escape because the British controlled the area during most of the war.

Yet British military leaders did not welcome all bondspeople, refusing, in particular, to accept slaves belonging to British loyalists. In 1779, Sir Henry Clinton, British commander-in-chief, issued a more restrictive version of Dunmore's proclamation; he offered freedom only to refugee slaves of rebellious Americans and warned that any African Americans captured in American uniforms would be sold back into bondage. In fact, some British officers claimed captured slaves as property rather than delivering the promised freedom.

One of the most intrepid black men enlisting with the British was the self-named Colonel Tye. A young slave in northern New Jersey, Tye fled when his master refused Quaker appeals for his freedom, and he organized a guerrilla band of other fugitive slaves and free black men. Fighting alongside New Jersey loyalists, they kidnapped farmers, seized crops and cattle, and patrolled border posts. Hiding out in familiar swamps and inlets, Tye gathered runaway slaves wherever he went. He fought many battles before dying of wounds and lockjaw in 1780. A symbol of black rebellion, he inspired awe among New Jersey patriots despite the havoc he created. The first notice of his death in local newspapers described Tye as "justly to be more feared and respected than any of his brethren of a fairer complexion."

Though thousands of black Americans saw the British as liberators, they discovered that fighting alongside them was anything but glorious. The British promise of freedom was more a military strategy, it seems, than a commitment to equality. To the British, black men and women were workers whose recruitment could disrupt the enemy's economy. Only a few, such as Peters, were soldiers; most were laborers, wagon drivers, cooks, and servants. They repaired roads, cleaned camp, hauled equipment, and built fortifications. Rations were short, clothing shabby, and barracks overcrowded. Camp fevers and contagious diseases proved more lethal than warfare, and thousands of black people who joined the British met early deaths.

Though some British royal governors and military officers genuinely believed that slaves deserved freedom, most had decidedly pragmatic interests. During the showdown at Yorktown in 1781, when British troops were surrounded and short of provisions, General Charles Cornwallis expelled thousands of African Americans from his encampments. An embarrassed Hessian officer serving with the British wrote that Cornwallis's officers "drove back to the enemy all of our black friends, whom we had taken along to despoil the countryside. . . . We had used them to good advantage and set them free, and now, with fear and trembling they had to face the reward of their cruel masters."

Fighting for Independence: Black Patriots

Choosing a different path from that of Sergeant Peters and Colonel Tye, many free African Americans and a few slaves fought for the American cause. William C. Nell, the first black American historian, honored them in the 1850s when, working to advance the abolitionist crusade, he recalled the blood shed for the "glorious cause" by black Americans in the time of the nation's birth. In his *Colored Patriots of the American Revolution* (1855), Nell cited Crispus Attucks as the first person to fall during the Boston Massacre of 1770 and thus the first to lose his life in the Americans' bid for independence.

Half Wampanoag Indian and half African, Attucks had fled slavery twenty years earlier and worked on New England whaling ships. In Boston on the night of March 5, 1770, he led an attack against a contingent of British regulars, brandishing a stout cordwood stick. When the British fired at point-blank range, five Americans perished in what was later called the Boston Massacre. "The first to defy, and the first to die," as a Boston poet wrote a century later, Attucks became a symbol of American resistance to the hated British occupation of Boston.

Salem Poor was another free black patriot. His bravery in the Battle of Charlestown in 1775 inspired fourteen Massachusetts officers to petition the Continental Congress to reward "so great and distinguished a character" and such a "brave and gallant soldier." Poor went on to fight with Washington's army at White Plains, New York, and endured the grueling winter of 1777–1778 at Valley Forge.

Some black patriots were slaves. Peter Salem, for example, a slave from Framingham, Massachusetts, served alongside his master at the Battle of Lexington. At the Battle of Bunker Hill, Salem took aim and killed Major John Pitcairn of the British Marines, the officer who led the attack on patriot fortifications. Salem later fought at Stony Point and Saratoga, New York. Prince Whipple, another slave patriot, pulled the stroke oar in the small boat that carried George Washington across the Delaware River. This crossing, amid a piercing winter storm on Christmas night in 1776, is immortalized in a painting in which Whipple is shown, that today hangs in the U.S. Capitol. The subsequent American attack, which surprised the British at Trenton, New Jersey, handed the patriots their first major victory.

One Virginia slave, James Armistead, served as a spy for the Marquis de Lafayette, the celebrated French nobleman who came to fight with the

This painting of James Armistead shows Armistead fitted out elaborately. During the war, the Marquis de Lafayette developed an antislavery stance and proposed to George Washington that the two men establish a small plantation in South America where Washington's freed slaves and Lafayette's could till the soil as tenant farmers.

Americans. Armistead's master, William Armistead, granted his desire to enlist when Lafayette called for the recruitment of black troops in March 1781. Posing as a runaway slave, Armistead infiltrated the British lines at Yorktown, observed the British formations and tactical positions, and returned with crucial information that gave the Americans the upper hand in what became the climactic battle of the war.

Just after the war, Lafayette gave Armistead a handwritten testimonial declaring, "His intelligence from the enemy's camp were industriously collected and more faithfully delivered. He perfectly acquitted himself with some important commissions I gave him and appears to me entitled to every reward his situation can admit of." In 1786, the General Assembly of Virginia responded by emancipating Armistead and appropriating money to compensate his master. Thereafter, Armistead gave up his master's surname and called himself James Lafayette. Nearly a half-century later, when the French hero returned to the United States for a triumphal tour, he visited his namesake. James Lafayette lived poor but proud on a small farm in Virginia, a pensioner of the American Revolution.

Faithful wartime service did not usually earn black Americans freedom or pensions, as William Lee, George Washington's slave, discovered. Like many revolutionary leaders, Washington professed a hatred of slavery but could not bring himself to part with his slaves. He grudgingly agreed to grant Lee's request in 1784 to transport his free black wife from Philadelphia to Mount Vernon, Washington's plantation on the Potomac River in Virginia. "I cannot refuse his request," wrote Washington, "as he has lived with me so long and followed my fortunes through the war with fidelity." The black couple lived at Mount Vernon for fifteen years—the husband a slave, the wife free—until Washington died in 1799.

In this lithograph, William Lee holds Washington's white horse while the American general accepts the surrender of General Lord Cornwallis at Yorktown.

Most patriot leaders refused to permit African Americans, whether slave or free, to fight on the American side at all. The natural rights principle, which on the eve of the revolution seemed poised to inspire a broad antislavery movement, withered once the fighting erupted. By late 1775 and early 1776, the Continental Army and most state militias had banned free blacks and slaves from military service. The idea of putting weapons in the hands of African Americans raised disturbing images of a broad black rebellion and of black men possessing inflated notions of equality.

Yet two years into the war, white patriots changed their minds once more—this time for pragmatic, not moral, reasons. Concerned about a worsening manpower shortage, the states began to accept free black men in militia units in 1777. At the same time, recruiting sergeants quietly accepted slaves in place of their masters, often privately promising them freedom at war's end. As the "spirit of '76" wore off among white people and the war dragged on, militias in the northern states and towns reached deeper and deeper into the reservoir of black manpower. Most African Americans serving in state militias fought alongside white soldiers, although Rhode Island, Connecticut, and Massachusetts created mostly black regiments led by white officers.

Some southern states also began tapping the African American population for military duty. Sorely pressed to fill the state quotas set by the Continental Congress each year, Maryland reluctantly recruited free black men into service and, after the British army came south, slaves—with their masters' consent. Not surprisingly, few slaveholders would give up able-bodied black men. Virginia permitted free black men to enlist, but not slaves.

Legislatures in South Carolina and Georgia, dominated by slave owners, banned any form of black enlistment. If the image of the revolutionary army as a refuge for runaway slaves and agitators alarmed most northerners, it terrified southerners. Especially in the Deep South and along coastal areas, where black people far outnumbered white, the thought of putting guns into the hands of any black—slave or free—struck white southerners as suicidal.

Only 1 percent of the black population was free at the outbreak of the war. Many of these African Americans viewed joining the patriots as a means to advance their place in a new republic. They believed that the patriots' rhetoric about natural rights and personal freedom foretold the end of slavery and the beginning of racial equality.

Consider James Forten of Philadelphia. His great-grandfather had been dragged to the Delaware River Valley in chains, probably by Dutch slavers, even before William Penn's Quakers arrived. His grandfather was one of the first Africans in Pennsylvania to purchase his freedom. His father became a sailmaker in Philadelphia and James was born in 1766. Enjoying the advantages of Quaker schooling and rankling at the British occupation of Philadelphia in 1777–1778, young Forten cast his lot with the Americans and signed on with a privateer—a licensed merchant ship outfitted to capture British vessels. "Scarce wafted from his native shore, and periled upon the dark blue sea," wrote William Nell, "than he found himself amid the roar of cannon, the smoke of blood, the dying, and the dead." Nell was describing a bloody engagement in 1782 in which Forten was the only survivor at his gun station.

But in the next voyage Forten was not so lucky, as his ship was captured by the British in a fierce sea battle. When the British captain's young son befriended Forten, the captain offered the black youth free passage to England and the patronage of his family. "NO, NO!" replied Forten. "I am here a prisoner for the liberties of my country; I never, NEVER, shall prove a traitor to her interests." His offer spurned, the British captain consigned Forten to the *Old Jersey*—the rotting, death-trap prison ship anchored in New York harbor. Thousands of captured Americans died on such vessels, but Forten survived even this ordeal. Released seven months later as the war drew to a close, the sixteen-year-old boy made his way barefoot from New York to Philadelphia.

Rhetoric and Reality in the New Nation

While fighting for independence from Britain, white Americans also established new governments and paved the way for expansion westward. Yet even as they argued that the British crown and Parliament had denied their inalienable rights, most white people who owned slaves exempted their human property from these very rights, and those who did not own slaves felt only a halfhearted desire to abolish the institution. The new state constitutions perpetuated this gap between rhetoric and reality by preserving slavery. Yet African Americans pushed the agenda of freedom forward—achieving success in some states.

Continued Slavery in the South

The fighting between America and England wound down at Yorktown in 1781, and the new nation's independence was guaranteed by the Treaty of Paris in 1783. During these years, enslaved Africans in the South must have hoped the discordance between slavery and a republic founded on inalienable rights would be recognized. And some white leaders did see it. For example, leaders of the fast-growing Methodists wrote in 1784 that "the practice of holding our fellow creatures in slavery . . . [is] contrary to the golden law of God on which hang all the law and the prophets and the unalienable rights of mankind." In 1788, Maryland's attorney general, Luther Martin, declared that slavery was "inconsistent with the genius of republicanism and has a tendency to destroy those principles on which it is supported, as it lessens the sense of the equal rights of mankind and habituates us to tyranny and oppression."

In 1782, lawmakers in Virginia and Maryland repealed prohibitions on masters' right to manumit, or free, their slaves. Consequently, the number of free black people in Maryland soared from about 2,000 on the eve of the revolution to 8,000 by 1790, mainly through manumission. In Virginia, where about half of all American slave owners resided, the number of free black persons expanded from about 1,800 in 1782 to more than 12,000 in 1790. By that year, about 5,000 free black persons lived in North Carolina. Enlightenment ideas about natural rights moved some white owners to release their slaves, but others were practical; by switching from tobacco production to less labor-intensive wheat production, they did not require as many slaves as before.

Despite manumissions, the vast majority of African Americans in the Upper South remained enslaved, and their numbers increased. As slave births exceeded deaths, the slave population grew, even though slave importations during the war had ceased. Virginia's slave population, for example, increased from about 200,000 to nearly 300,000 between 1776 and 1790. Maryland and North Carolina experienced similar trends.

In the Lower South, manumission was rare. While almost one out of every twenty African Americans in the Upper South had gained freedom by 1790, only one in sixty in the Lower South was free. The slave population of South Carolina and Georgia—the two states that resumed importing slaves after the revolution—continued to rise. Switching from enslaved to free labor made no economic sense to planters in these states, and the doctrine of inalienable rights had little meaning for them. Having armed themselves heavily during the war against Britain, white people in the Lower South now had the weapons to crush black rebellion and consolidate their hold on the far more numerous slaves.

Emancipation in the North

At the end of the war, only about one in ten black Americans lived in the North, and most were still in bondage. But they were encouraged when the Green Mountain towns seceded from New York in 1777 and wrote a constitution for the new state of Vermont (admitted to the Union in 1791) that outlawed slavery.

Other northern states followed suit. In 1780 Pennsylvania passed the first state law mandating the gradual abolition of slavery. Four years later, Rhode Island and Connecticut took similar steps. Yet in New Jersey and New York, where slavery played a major role in the economy, lawmakers declined to eradicate the institution. Moreover, slavery expanded steadily in these states, despite rulings that halted slave importation. Not until 1799 and 1804, respectively, would New York and New Jersey pass gradual abolition laws. Delaware never abolished slavery. White people living in that state could legally own human chattel until the Thirteenth Amendment ended slavery after the Civil War.

Though these new laws must have raised African Americans' hopes, they phased out slavery only slowly. Equally frustrating to black people, abolition laws generated such heated debate that legislators sometimes diluted them. Pennsylvania's abolition law illustrates this point. In 1775, Quakers in Philadelphia organized the Society for the Relief of Free Negroes Unlawfully Held in Bondage. Society members moved rapidly to cleanse themselves of what they saw as the sin of slaveholding. Though not explicitly an abolition society at first, the Quaker organization flowered after the revolution, attracting non-Quakers and becoming the first group in the English-speaking world dedicated to the eradication of human bondage.

The Society's strong stand against slavery influenced many of the state's political leaders. Building on this foundation, Pennsylvania lawmakers believed that the state's 1780 abolition law would gain them the respect of "all Europe, who are astonished to see a people eager for liberty holding Negroes in bondage." Yet the act sparked intense debate. Ground down by vigorous opposition from slave owners, lawmakers amended the proposed law so that it freed no slaves and postponed full emancipation for more than half a century. It specified that all children born before the day the law took effect—March 1, 1780—would remain enslaved. Children born after that date were consigned to twenty-eight years of bondage. Hence, any child born of a slave on the last day of February 1780 could live out his or her life in slavery. If an enslaved black woman bore a child in 1820, her son or daughter would not be free until 1848.

Some African Americans decided not to wait for white legislators and judges to apply the rhetoric of freedom to their own lives. In Massachusetts a slave named Elizabeth Freeman set in motion a chain of events and a judicial decision that ended slavery in her state. Her story shows that in the revolutionary era, even the humblest descendants of Africans could effect profound change.

In 1781, with the war nearing its end, Freeman and her sister served a wealthy family in Sheffield. After a blow from her mistress left Freeman with a scar that "she bore to the day of her death," Freeman stalked from the house and refused to return. When her master appealed to the court for her recovery,

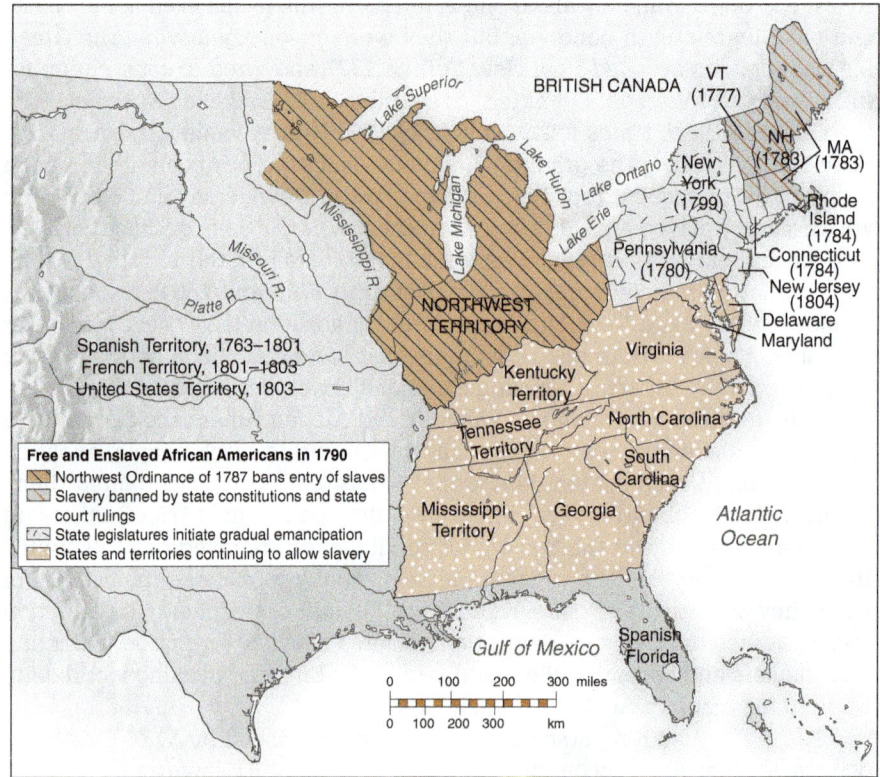

MAP 5.1 Free and Enslaved African Americans in 1790
Because many northern states abolished slavery only by degrees, a few African Americans remained in bondage until the mid-nineteenth century. For example, the federal census showed 1,129 slaves still living in the northern states in 1840; 262 in 1850; and 64 in 1860.

Susan Sedgwick, daughter of Theodore Sedgwick, painted Elizabeth Freeman's watercolor portrait in 1811 when Freeman was sixty-seven years of age. Eighteen years later, Freeman died. She left a will bequeathing to her daughter gowns belonging to Freeman's African-born parents. Freeman was buried in the Sedgwick family plot in the Stockbridge, Massachusetts, burial ground.

Freeman asked lawyer Theodore Sedgwick to test whether the language of Massachusetts's new state constitution, with its statement that "all men are born free and equal," applied to her. Arguing the case in 1781, Sedgwick convinced an all-white jury that it did, and Elizabeth Freeman was freed. Freeman then worked as a housekeeper for the Sedgwicks for many years. As a noted midwife and nurse, she was revered for her skills in curing and calming her patients. After her death in 1829, Sedgwick's son commemorated Freeman's strength: "If there could be a practical refutation of the imagined superiority of our race to hers, the life and character of this woman would afford that refutation. . . . She uniformly . . . obtained an ascendancy over all those with whom she was associated in service. . . . She claimed no distinction but it was yielded to her from her superior experience, energy, skill, and sagacity."

The Freeman decision set a precedent. In a similar case two years later, a runaway slave named Quock Walker sued for his freedom. The state supreme court upheld the county court jury decision, striking down 150 years of slavery in Massachusetts with these stirring words: "Is not a law of nature that all men are equal and free? Is not the laws of nature the laws of God? Is not the law of God then against slavery?"

The Northwest Ordinance of 1787

Four years after war's end, the Second Continental Congress passed the Northwest Ordinance to provide for the political organization of the vast region beyond the Appalachian Mountains. With land-hungry Americans heading west in droves, many accompanied by their slaves, Congress had to decide what role, if any, slavery would play. The resulting decision—the Northwest Ordinance—banned slaveholders from taking slaves north of the Ohio River but allowed slaveholders already in the region to keep their human property.

When a proposal banning slaveholders from taking slaves south of the Ohio River failed, white people in the South got what they wanted most: permission to extend slavery into a region where plantation agriculture would be profitable. This area ultimately comprised the states of Kentucky, Tennessee, Alabama, and Mississippi. But antislavery northerners also got some of what they wanted: prohibition of slavery in a specified territory, which later consisted of Ohio, Indiana, Illinois, Michigan, and Wisconsin. The Northwest Ordinance was thus the first of many compromises by which leaders of the new nation determined where slavery could spread as Americans flooded west to set up homesteads.

The Constitutional Settlement

After the revolution, some Americans viewed the emerging political landscape with deep concern. Could the newly independent republic survive, they asked, if one-fifth of its people were in chains? Though the prospect of abolition loomed large at war's end, it vanished in a few sorrowful years. Reform-minded white Americans confronted two main problems in advancing their agenda: How would the nation compensate slave owners for the immense investment they had made in their human chattel? How would free African Americans fit into the social fabric? Solutions to both problems hinged on a willingness to make economic sacrifices and to envision a biracial, republican society. To the crushing disappointment of hundreds of thousands of African Americans, white America lost its commitment to the vision. By the time members of the revolutionary generation lay in their graves, the United States had sacrificed its best opportunity to eradicate human bondage.

Roadblocks to Eradicating Slavery

Two cases illustrate the economic and social roadblocks to abolition. In 1773, Dr. Benjamin Rush of Philadelphia had predicted an end to slavery. "National crimes," he stated in his antislavery pamphlet, "require national punishment" to be imposed on high unless "God shall cease to be just or merciful." But three years later, Rush purchased a slave, showing that a public antislavery stance did not keep men from enjoying the private advantages of a household slave. Even after joining the Pennsylvania Abolition Society in 1784, Rush refused to release his slave.

Rush was aware of the hypocrisy involved in publicly attacking slavery while personally owning a human being, and his problem was a microcosm of the nation's problem. Everyone who wanted to abolish slavery knew that slave owners would have to be compensated for the loss of their human property. Some called for a compensated emancipation scheme—a plan for raising taxes with which to pay slave owners to free their slaves. But like Rush, the nation's leaders ultimately put economic interest above moral commitment and shied away from this tax burden.

Like Benjamin Rush, Thomas Jefferson knew that slavery compromised Americans' attempt to create a liberty-loving republic. Also like Rush, Jefferson could not bring himself to part with his slaves. Yet unlike Rush, Jefferson regarded black people as innately inferior to white people. Africans were "inferior to the whites in . . . mind and body," he contended in his widely read *Notes on the State of Virginia* (1782) because they were "originally a distinct race, or made distinct by time and circumstances." In particular, Jefferson wrote that an end of slavery would mean a mixing of the races that would threaten racial purity. As early as 1776, he argued that the abolition of slavery would have to be followed by the recolonization of freed slaves in Africa or some remote region of the western United States. In *Notes on the State of Virginia,* he asserted that freed Africans must be "removed beyond the reach of mixture."

Jefferson never overcame his "aversion . . . to the mixture of colour." In the early 1790s, he advocated banishing white Virginia women (but not black women) who bore "mulatto" children. The Virginia legislature defined the term as anyone "who shall have one-fourth part or more of Negro blood." Near the end of his long life, Jefferson maintained that "nothing is more certainly written in the book of fate than that the two races, equally free, cannot live in the same government." Yet Jefferson had an intimate relationship with his slave Sally Hemings. Hemings was the half-sister of Jefferson's deceased wife, and her father was Jefferson's father-in-law. Hemings bore five children whose descendants trace their lineage to Jefferson. Recent DNA analysis has confirmed Jefferson's sexual liaison with his light-skinned slave.

Black Genius and Black Activism

Jefferson's staunch view of Africans as an "inferior" and "distinct" race blinded him to the examples of black genius that surfaced in the revolutionary era. He dismissed the talent evident in Phillis Wheatley's poetry and denigrated the almanac of Benjamin Banneker, who used spheroid trigonometry to chart the heavenly bodies. The son of a freed slave from Guinea who married a mixed-race woman, Banneker grew up near Baltimore, where his English grandmother taught him to read. At age twenty-two, he used a pocketknife to carve a wooden clock that kept accurate time and struck the hours for the next half-century. In his fifties, Banneker took up astronomy. He published almanacs with calculations charting the movement of the sun, moon, and planets throughout the year. Surmising that Banneker must have received help from a white patron, Jefferson concluded that Banneker "had a mind of very common stature indeed." But Philadelphia's David Rittenhouse, the nation's foremost astronomer, thought differently, praising Banneker's first almanac, published in 1792, as a "very extraordinary performance."

In the postwar turmoil, some African Americans found themselves once again on opposing sides, much as they had been during the war. This time the issue was economic. A postwar economic downturn, combined with stiff taxes levied to pay off the revolutionary debt, drove small farmers to the brink of

Benjamin Banneker's
PENNSYLVANIA, DELAWARE, MARY-
LAND, AND VIRGINIA
ALMANAC,
FOR THE
YEAR of our LORD 1795;
Being the Third after Leap-Year.

BANNAKER.

PHILADELPHIA:
Printed for WILLIAM GIBBONS, Cherry Street

Benjamin Banneker, pictured here in a wood-cut from his Almanac, for many years kept a journal in which he recorded details about the natural world. One young white contemporary of Banneker's remembered that "he was very precise in conversation and exhibited deep reflection. . . . He seemed to be acquainted with everything of importance that was passing in the country."

bankruptcy. Deeming the taxes unfair in 1786, Daniel Shays led the farmers of western Massachusetts in armed protest against the court proceedings. Some free black farmers, also staggering under a grievous tax load, fought alongside the white rebels. Moses Sash, for example, served as an officer and was a member of Shays's council. Meanwhile, other African Americans from Boston sided with the government in this standoff. For instance, Prince Hall offered the support of Boston's black Masons, who, he wrote Governor James Bowdoin, "are willing to help and support . . . in this time of trouble and confusion, as you in your wisdom shall direct us."

Governor Bowdoin did not accept the black Masons' offer but encouraged Hall to petition the Massachusetts legislature to support a plan for their return to Africa. This ignited the first black-inspired recolonization movement in the new American republic. The movement, in turn, revealed African Americans' view of the young nation as irreparably divided by race. In a lengthy address to legislators, seventy-three "African Blacks" explained that only by finding a place of their own, beyond the reach of white power, could black people achieve dignity and fulfillment. The petitioners added that they wished "earnestly . . . to return to Africa, our native country . . . where we shall live among our equals and be more comfortable and happy, than we can be in our present situation." The state legislature refused financial support for this scheme. Nevertheless, the petition planted the seeds for a black nationalism that resurfaced again and again in later decades.

A More Perfect Union?

In the torrid summer of 1787, the revolutionary generation received another chance to turn the rhetoric of liberty and equality into reality for African Americans. Meeting in Philadelphia, fifty-five delegates representing all the states except Rhode Island wrote a new constitution designed "to create a more perfect union." What emerged, however, was a compromise between large states and small states, between North and South, and between slavery opponents and slavery advocates. Many delegates who attended the convention owned human property and considered slavery a necessary evil. But others believed the time had come to put an end to the practice. For them, the question was not whether to do so, but when and how. Gouverneur Morris, representing Pennsylvania, stated his preference for "a tax paying for all the Negroes in the United States." This plan, Morris believed, would be a far better alternative to "saddl[ing] posterity" with a constitution that preserved slavery. But northern leaders, unwilling to shoulder financial responsibility for a compensated emancipation, rejected Morris's idea. Southerners concluded that the matter merited no further discussion.

Indeed, the delegates from South Carolina and Georgia exploded at the suggestion that the nation could uproot slavery from its economy and society. The "true question," argued South Carolina's John Rutledge ominously, "is whether the southern states shall or shall not be parties to the union." Was Rutledge bluffing? Georgia and South Carolina faced a precarious situation in 1787. Their white population was just one-twentieth of the nation's total, but their black population constituted about one-third of the national number. With the powerful Creek Indian confederacy and the Spanish in Florida threatening them militarily, no two states needed a strong national government more.

But no one called Rutledge's bluff. Many years later, James Madison, principal author of the Constitution, told his friend Lafayette that to try abolishing slavery in 1787 would have been akin to setting "a spark to a mass of gunpowder." Unwilling to create a national plan for freeing slaves, northern leaders simply ducked the issue.

As a result, the delegates designed a document that never explicitly mentioned slaves or slavery. Instead, they filled the Constitution with compromises designed to satisfy southerners' desire to preserve the institution. First, to determine the number of seats each state would have in the House of Representatives (which was based on a state's population), Congress decided to count three-fifths of all slaves (called "other persons") in the population calculation. This method guaranteed southern states many more votes in the House and in the Electoral College (which elected the president) than if slaves had not been counted. Second, a fugitive slave clause forbade the states from emancipating anyone who had fled bondage. The clause also required states to return runaways to their owners. Third, another clause prohibited Congress from banning the importation of slaves (called "such persons as any of the states now existing shall think proper to admit") for twenty years. In 1807, Congress would decide whether or not to allow the slave trade to continue.

Together, these provisions protected the interests of slave owners and their allies. In the South as well as in northern states such as New York, New Jersey, and Delaware, slaveholders acquired more and more human property. North and South Carolina, along with Georgia, kept the Atlantic slave trade open. Thus, as the new nation conducted its first experiments with democracy, slave ships continued disgorging thousands of African captives on American shores.

Under the Constitution, ratified in 1788, millions of newborn Americans entered the world as lifelong chattel. Runaway slaves—even if they managed to flee to a non-slave state—were forcibly returned to their masters if captured. A half-century later, Frederick Douglass reflected, "The Constitution of the United States—What is it? Who made it? For whom and for what was it made? Liberty and Slavery—opposite as Heaven and Hell—are both in the Constitution; and the oath to support the latter is an oath to perform that which God has made impossible. . . . If we adopt the preamble, with Liberty and Justice, we must repudiate the enacting clauses, with Kidnapping and Slave holding."

Historians have used the phrase "the compromise of 1787" to justify the revolutionary generation's accommodation of slavery. In explaining the failure of the new nation to come to grips with the institution, many historians point to the vulnerability of the newly forged union. The northern and southern states, they maintain, made a compromise in order to secure the cohesion of a constellation of states that had previously been separate colonies with distinct practices and beliefs.

But some historians argue that a national abolition plan might have strengthened rather than weakened that cohesion. Ending slavery, they contend, could have helped create a truly united nation out of loosely connected regions by eliminating a rankling sore on the body politic and enabling the United States to practice the ideological principles on which its birth was founded. Any society in which a people's behavior aligns with their principles and values is far stronger than one in which practice and principle are at odds. Moreover, those who assumed the new nation could *not* have abolished slavery make the all-too-common error of inevitability. Often, people who argue that certain regrettable historical events were inevitable are the same individuals who contributed to those events—not those who suffered their consequences.

In the end, all Americans paid a high price for the compromises that sullied the Constitution. Slavery continued to pose a painful dilemma for the new nation. Both advocates and opponents of the institution continued to cast about for a solution. When the "solution" finally came, it cost 600,000 soldiers their lives—one for each of the 600,000 black Americans whose inalienable rights the Constitution had ignored to create a more "perfect union."

Long before the Civil War broke out, some Americans continued to propose ways to end slavery. Ferdinando Fairfax, a man with ties to Virginia's largest planters, published a plan in 1790 for phasing out the institution. A protégé of George Washington, Fairfax claimed that many slaveholders were ready to release their slaves voluntarily and that many others could be induced to do so with compensation. But these planters, Fairfax said, would never agree to equal rights for free black people. Therefore, newly liberated slaves would have to be repatriated to Africa.

In 1796, St. George Tucker, another prominent Virginian, laid before the state legislature a full plan for the gradual abolition of slavery. Tucker voiced alarm over the first federal census of 1790, which showed Virginia's slave population rising rapidly. He expressed fear that the massive slave revolt that erupted in Haiti in 1791 might spread to the southern states. He also quoted the French philosopher Montesquieu that "slavery not only violates the Laws of Nature and of civil Society, it also wounds the best Forms of Government; in a Democracy, where all Men are Equal." Tucker's comments fell on deaf ears. But a few months later, Jefferson prophetically wrote that "if something is not done, and done soon, we shall be the murderers of our own children . . . ; the revolutionary storm, now sweeping the globe, will be upon us."

The Resettlement of African American Loyalists

For those African Americans who had joined the British side in the revolution, the Constitution mattered little because the United States was no longer their home. In 1783, just after England and the United States signed the Treaty of Paris, the British had to resettle thousands of former slaves, refusing to return them to former masters. Yet where would England send the free black loyalists? Its West Indies sugar islands, built on slave labor, were no place for a large community of free black people. Nor was England, as officials in London and other cities were already lamenting the number of impoverished black people seeking public support. Instead black loyalists were sent to Nova Scotia, the easternmost province of Canada and, unlike all other English colonies in the Americas, a free labor agricultural society.

Black Nova Scotians

Thomas Peters and his family were among the 3,000 black persons evacuated from New York City for relocation to Nova Scotia in late 1783. The journey was grueling. Gales blew the ship off course; not until the following spring did the exiles reach their new home. Peters led his family ashore at Annapolis Royal, a small port on the east side of the Bay of Fundy, across the water from the Maine coast. In this raw, remote corner of the earth, the former American slaves sought to establish new lives based on freedom.

But their dream of life, liberty, and the pursuit of happiness soon turned into a nightmare. The refugees were segregated in impoverished villages and given scraps of rocky land impossible to till. Deprived of the rights normally extended to British subjects, they were forced to work on road construction in return for provisions. With few resources and scant support from the British, they sank into poverty. Soon British soldiers resettling in Nova Scotia attacked the black villages, burning, looting, and pulling down residents' houses.

Peters became a leader of the exiles in Digby, near Annapolis Royal, where some 500 white and 100 black families competed for land. Discouraged, he traveled across the bay to St. John, New Brunswick, in search of unallocated tracts. Working as a millwright, he struggled to feed his family and to find suitable homesteads for other black settlers. He also had to ward off so-called bodysnatchers already at work re-enslaving blacks and selling them in the United States or West Indies. To worsen matters, crop failures brought a punishing famine in 1788.

Return to Africa

By 1790, after six years of hand-to-mouth existence, Peters concluded that his people needed to move and seek true independence elsewhere. Representing more than 200 black families in St. John and Digby, he composed a petition to the Secretary of State in London. Then, despite the risk of re-enslavement that accompanied any black person who braved an ocean voyage, he sailed from Halifax to the English capital with little more in his pocket than the fragile piece of paper. In the document, the petitioners asked for fair treatment in Nova Scotia or resettlement "wherever the wisdom of government may think proper to provide for [my people] as free subjects of the British Empire."

The black leader could not have chosen a better time to head for London. English abolitionists such as Granville Sharp, Thomas Clarkson, and William Wilberforce had stepped up their activism. Though they had failed to force through Parliament a bill abolishing the English slave trade, they did win passage of a bill to charter the Sierra Leone Company for thirty-one years. The deal included a grant of trading and settlement rights on the African coast. Even better, the recruits for the new colony would consist of the former slaves from North America now living in Nova Scotia.

Peters returned to Nova Scotia a year later. There, he spread the word that the English government would provide free transport for any black exiles who wished to journey to Sierra Leone. Once on the African coast, he explained, they would receive plots of land. John Clarkson, the younger brother of one of England's best-known abolitionists, traveled with Peters to oversee the resettlement plan.

This opportunity to return to Africa excited the former slaves, but some white Nova Scotians were now reluctant to let them leave. The governor saw their emigration as an indication of his failure to provide adequately for them in Canada. Others protested that they would thus be deprived of customers. Still others had forged indentures and work contracts they claimed bound black people to them. Some even refused to settle back wages and debts in hopes of discouraging the Sierra Leone venture. "The white people . . . were very unwilling that we should go," wrote one black minister, "though they had been very cruel to us, and treated many of us as though we had been slaves."

But neither white officials nor white settlers could stem the tide of black enthusiasm for resettlement to Africa. Working through black preachers—the principal leaders in the black communities—Peters and Clarkson spread the word of the Sierra Leone plan. The telling soon took on overtones of the Old Testament story about the delivery of the Israelites from bondage in Egypt. Some 350 blacks trekked through the rain to Birchtown, a black settlement near Annapolis, to hear their blind and lame preacher, Moses Wilkinson, explain the Sierra Leone Company's terms. Ultimately, almost 1,200 black people chose to return to Africa. By the end of 1791, they had made their way to the port of Halifax, some trudging 340 miles around the Bay of Fundy through dense forest and snow-blanketed terrain.

Peters and Clarkson inspected each of the fifteen ships assigned for the return to Africa, ordering some decks removed, ventilation holes fitted, and berths constructed. Remembering the horrors of his own Middle Passage thirty-two years before, Peters resolved that the return trip would be different. As crew members prepared the fleet, the recruits talked of how they would soon "kiss their dear Malagueta," a reference to the Malagueta pepper, or "grains of paradise," that thrived in West Africa.

Setting sail on January 15, 1792, the ships held men, women, and children whose collective experiences in North America ran the gamut of slave travail. The African-born Charles Wilkinson, a former soldier in the Black Guides and Pioneers, made the trip with his mother and two small daughters. Also on board were religious leaders such as David George, founder of the first black Baptist church in North America in Silver Bluff, South Carolina, in 1773; Moses Wilkinson, who had escaped his Virginia master in 1776; and Boston King, who had converted to Methodism in New York while serving with the British. The oldest voyager was a woman whom Clarkson described in his shipboard journal as "104 years of age who had requested me to take her, that she might lay her bones in her native country." Young and old, African-born and American-born, military veterans and those too young to have seen wartime service—all shared the dream of finding a place where they could govern themselves and live in freedom. This was to be their year of jubilee.

But they had to endure additional perils before reaching Africa. Boston King recorded that the winter gales were the worst in the seasoned crew members' history. Two ship captains and sixty-five passengers died en route. Snow squalls and heavy gales scattered the small fleet, yet after two months all the vessels reached Africa. The ships had crossed an ocean that for nearly 300 years had borne Africans in the opposite direction, as shackled captives bound for the land of misery.

Legend says that Thomas Peters, sick from shipboard fever, led his shipmates ashore in Sierra Leone singing, "The day of jubilee is come; return ye ransomed sinners home." Yet despite their joy at returning to Africa, the settlers encountered difficulties. Provisions ran short. Diseases claimed lives. Land distribution proceeded slowly. British councilors sent from London to supervise the colony acted irresponsibly. Racial discord reigned. As the elected speaker-general for the black settlers in their dealings with the white governing council, Peters tried to stem the spreading frustration. Some settlers spoke of replacing the councilors appointed by the Sierra Leone Company with an elected black government. This incipient rebellion never came to pass, but

Peters remained the leader of the unofficial opposition to the white government. He died in the spring of 1792—less than four months after stepping foot on Africa's shores. His family and friends buried him in Freetown, where his descendants live today.

Conclusion

Thomas Peters lived for fifty-four years. For most of his adult life, he struggled for both survival and freedom. He crossed the Atlantic four times. He lived in Yorubaland, French Louisiana, North Carolina, New York, Nova Scotia, New Brunswick, Bermuda, London, and Sierra Leone. He worked as a field hand, millwright, ship hand, laborer, soldier, and community leader. He also struggled against slave masters, government officials, and hostile white neighbors. He worked to secure political rights, social equity, and human dignity for himself and other former slaves.

Peters's story provides a glimpse at black Americans' lives during a pivotal time in history. When war broke out between Britain and its colonies, white revolutionaries' rhetoric about British tyranny and inalienable rights spread quickly among enslaved men and women. Taking the white colonists' cries for freedom at face value, black people petitioned for the end of slavery. Many joined white colonists who themselves lamented the contradiction between white planters' freedom claims and their continued enslavement of half a million human beings.

Thousands of bondspeople who fled their masters to claim the freedom promised by the British made the American Revolution the first large-scale slave rebellion in North America. Other enslaved blacks joined the American cause, believing their decision would win them their freedom as well. Thousands of individual acts of defiance and courage created a collective legend of black struggle, testified to black strength, and set forth a black vision of a better future.

For Peters and thousands like him, war's end meant finding new homes as British subjects—first in Nova Scotia and then in Sierra Leone in what became American slaves' first return to the ancient homeland. But back in the newborn United States, a far greater number of African Americans faced a future made uncertain by the compromise-riddled Constitution of 1787. Slavery stood on the brink of extinction in the northern states but in the South, where most bondspeople lived, black people had scant hope of regaining their freedom when George Washington assumed office in 1790 as the nation's first president.

Questions for Review and Reflection

1. Which was more important in unleashing a wave of resistance to slavery: ideology about "unalienable rights" or the British offer of freedom to any slave or indentured servant reaching British lines and prepared to fight against the Americans seeking independence?

2. Why did Africans in North America fight against the British to help white colonists gain independence? What might be some examples of how different motives came into play?

3. Is it fair to call black actions in the American Revolution the greatest slave rebellion in U.S. history? As an extension activity, use Internet resources to compare the American Revolutionary case with those outside the United States, for example, in Jamaica and Brazil.

4. Despite many calls for the abolition of slavery, the founding fathers shrank from leading the antislavery cause? What were some of the political, social, and economic impediments to ending slavery in the new nation, either in writing the Constitution or by other means?

5. In what sense might Thomas Peters be considered a "founding father"? If so, in what ways? What might have been the value and/or disadvantages of his decision to encourage former enslaved Africans to return to their African homelands?

6

CHAPTER

After the Revolution: Constructing Free Life and Combating Slavery, 1787–1816

Richard Allen and Absalom Jones Lead Church Walkout

"Meeting had begun, and they were nearly done singing, and just as we got to the seats, the elder said, 'Let us pray.'" Former slave Richard Allen was remembering a momentous day in 1792 at St. George's Methodist church in Philadelphia. "We had not been long upon our knees before I heard considerable scuffling and low talking," Allen related. "I raised my head up and saw one of the [white] trustees . . . having hold of the Rev. Absalom Jones, pulling him up off of his knees, and saying, 'You must get up—you must not kneel here.' Mr. Jones replied, 'Wait until prayer is over.'" Allen was thirty-two when he witnessed this scene, and seventy when he recounted it. When prayer was over, he recalled, "we all went out of the church in a body, and they were no more plagued with us in the church."

At St. George's, white church officials had abruptly decided to relegate black worshipers to a segregated section. The incident Allen described was a defining moment in African American history because it initiated the formation of independent northern black churches. It also sounded a foreboding note for racial tensions in Philadelphia and proved a crucial moment for the nation, whose course Congress charted at Independence Hall, only a few blocks from

1787	Richard Allen and Absalom Jones establish the Free African Society of Philadelphia. The U.S. Constitution protects slavery.
1789	The French Revolution breaks out.
1791	Slaves in St. Domingue precipitate a violent revolution.
1792	Black worshipers in Philadelphia establish separate black congregations. Former American slaves settled in Sierra Leone under Britain's protection.
1793	Allen and Jones appeal for an end to slavery. The Fugitive Slave Act strengthens the Constitution's fugitive slave clause. Eli Whitney invents the cotton gin.
1794	France abolishes slavery in all its colonies.
1795	Spain cedes territory east of the Mississippi River to the United States. The slave rebellion in Pointe Coupée, Louisiana, is crushed.
1798	Congress establishes the Mississippi Territory.
1800	Gabriel's Rebellion in Richmond, Virginia, fails.
1803	The Louisiana Purchase vastly increases the size of the United States.
1804	Haiti is the first republic of African people in the Western Hemisphere.
1805	Peter Spencer establishes the Ezion Methodist Episcopal Church.
1808	Congress ends U.S. participation in the Atlantic slave trade.
1811	Paul Cuffe of Massachusetts sails for Africa to promote black emigration.
1812	The United States declares war on Britain.
1813	The Ezion Church becomes the first fully independent African American church. James Forten challenges attempts to prohibit free black people from entering Pennsylvania.
1814	The British offer freedom to slaves, some of whom participate in burning Washington, DC.
1815	The War of 1812 ends.
1816	Mother Bethel church in Philadelphia breaks from the Methodist Conference.

St. George's. Worried about a tremendous black rebellion brewing on the Caribbean island of St. Domingue (now Haiti), legislators viewed the confrontation at St. George's as ominous for similar tension in the United States.

Even before the incident at St. George's, Allen had faced a series of tests. In 1779, his Delaware master, convinced by Methodist preachers that slaveholding was a sin, offered to free him and his brother for 60 pounds of gold or silver, to be paid in installments. The brothers agreed, and Allen found work sawing cordwood and hauling salt for the patriots during the American Revolution. But already he had a different life's work in mind, inspired by Methodist meetings at a nearby farm. "One night I thought hell would be my portion," Allen remembered. "I cried unto Him who delighteth to hear the prayers of a poor sinner, and all of a sudden my dungeon shook, my chains flew off, and, glory to God, I cried. My soul was filled." From this point on, Allen later wrote, "my lot was cast."

For the duration of the war, Allen worked to pay off his purchase price. At the same time, he began to preach the Methodist faith. By 1783, when the Treaty of Paris concluded the American war for independence, the twenty-three-year-old former slave was delivering rousing sermons. Believing "it to be his Duty to Travel abroad as a Preacher of Righteousness," he traveled thousands of miles from New York to South Carolina, spending two months preaching among Native Americans. Then in the autumn of 1785, he headed north to a village west of Philadelphia, where local Methodist leaders asked him to preach to the small group of black Methodists attending services there.

Richard Allen was one of the numerous visionaries who emerged to lead the free black communities taking shape in the 1780s. The largest of these communities arose in maritime cities, from Boston to New Orleans, where free black men and women found work, companionship, and independent black churches. Most sizable towns between Maine and Louisiana also had communities of free African Americans.

In Philadelphia, Allen lifted the spirits of hundreds of black people. "I preached in the commons, in Southwark, Northern Liberties, and wherever I could find an opening," he remembered. "I frequently preached twice a day, at 5 o'clock in the morning and in the evening, and it was not uncommon for me to preach from four to five times a day." But that was before the white Methodists at St. George's demanded that Allen and other black worshipers sit in a separate section of the church.

Even as black worshipers endured this assault on their dignity, two profound transformations were overturning the Atlantic world. Both took inspiration from the American revolutionary ideology that all men are created equal and entitled by birth to certain rights. The first transformation, the French Revolution, erupted in Paris in 1789. The second, a slave rebellion in 1791 on the French sugar and coffee island of St. Domingue, compelled Americans to consider whether their experiment in democracy would include *racial* equality.

In the United States, the questions and passions stirred by these revolutions played out at the individual level. Though the Constitution preserved the institution of slavery, antislavery sentiment continued to percolate. The rebellion in St. Domingue demonstrated that slaves would not necessarily accept perpetual bondage. Though slavery was dying in the North, questions remained about how free black people would fit into the dominant white society there. Would northern states confer equal rights on black citizens—as their state constitutions implied? Could black and white people live together as fellow citizens in integrated neighborhoods, churches, workplaces, and marketplaces?

How would black Americans define themselves as a people? In the South, would slavery wither away as the slave trade ended, as many white leaders believed? Would Congress listen to petitioners urging the end of slavery? If the new nation became a republic for white men only, how would slaves and free black people respond?

Despite these questions, black Americans moved energetically to enhance the quality of their lives. In this chapter, we see how the expanding free population of African Americans constructed vital communities and churches of their own as part of their struggle for respect and equality. We also examine how the American revolutionary ideology of inalienable rights fueled revolution in France, which ignited the slave rebellion in St. Domingue and inspired similar uprisings in Virginia. Yet the twin strivings—to overthrow slavery in the South and obtain political and social equality in the North—could halt neither the expansion of slavery nor the intensifying white hostility toward dark-skinned Americans. Watching revolutionary egalitarianism fade, African Americans had little choice but to explore fresh options and forge new identities for themselves.

The Emergence of Free Black Communities

"Men are more influenced by their moral equals than by their superiors" and "are more easily governed by persons chosen by themselves for that purpose than by persons who are placed over them by accidental circumstances." Richard Allen and Absalom Jones spoke these words when they set out to establish an all-black congregation in Philadelphia shortly after the U.S. Constitution was ratified. Such democratic thoughts about self-governance strongly shaped African American community life as the ranks of free black people began to swell in the new republic. The creation of free black communities during the nation's early decades laid the foundation for the urban experience of future African Americans.

An Expanding Free Black Population

Only a few thousand African Americans had their freedom on the eve of the American Revolution. But after the war, their numbers swelled—to nearly 60,000 by 1790, to 108,000 by 1800, and to more than 233,000 by 1820. Several forces fueled this growth. Some African Americans purchased their freedom or sued for it in court, while others won freedom by escaping. Some slave owners freed their bondspeople, and several state legislatures abolished slavery. Finally, immigration of liberated people from places such as St. Domingue further expanded the ranks of free black Americans.

During the early years of the new republic, roughly 60 percent of the nation's free black people lived in the South and 40 percent in the North. However, in the South, free black people were a minority of all people of color. By contrast, freed black people in the North far exceeded the dwindling number of slaves. Free black people tended to live in the Upper South. About eight of every ten lived in Delaware, Maryland, Virginia, and Louisiana (see Figure 6.1). In 1810,

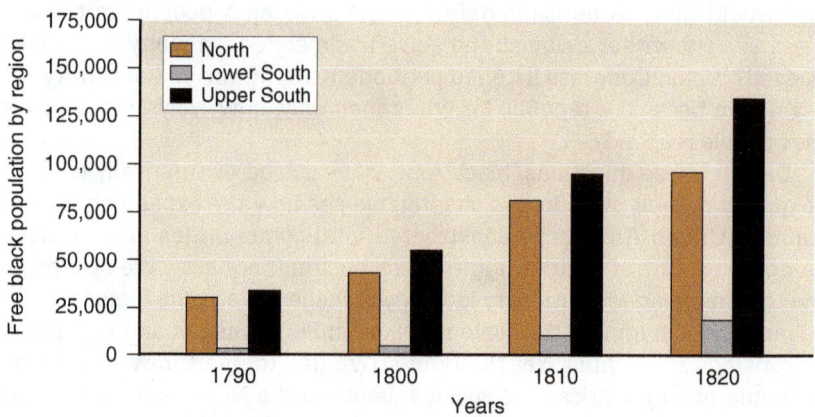

FIGURE 6.1 Free Black Population by Region, 1790–1820

The Upper South includes Delaware, Maryland, Virginia, District of Columbia, Kentucky, Missouri, Tennessee, and North Carolina. The Lower South comprises South Carolina, Georgia, Alabama, Mississippi, and Louisiana.

for example, only 14,000 free blacks lived south of Virginia (more than half of them in Louisiana). That same year, 94,000 resided in Virginia, Maryland, Delaware, and the District of Columbia. Overall, the proportion of African Americans who were free inched upward in the South—to 5 percent in 1790, 7 percent in 1800, and 8 percent in 1820.

Everywhere, free African Americans congregated in the cities, where they could find friends, marriage partners, and work. By 1820, nine cities each had more than 1,000 free African Americans, and New York, Philadelphia, Baltimore, and New Orleans each had more than 6,000.

Free Black Work Lives

Liberated African Americans took steps to establish fulfilling home and work lives in the cities. The rise of industrialization, which depended on power-driven machinery more than human labor, might have afforded them employment, but many owners of textile mills, machine foundries, and boot and shoe factories refused to hire black workers. These employers preferred native-born and immigrant whites, whom they considered as more reliable and educable. Thus, most free black people had to toil at unskilled labor. Black men typically worked as stevedores loading and unloading cargo on the wharves; as cellar-, well-, and gravediggers; as chimneysweeps and ash haulers; and as construction workers, ragpickers who collected discarded clothing, bootblacks, stablehands, and woodcutters.

Black women worked as washerwomen or domestic servants for white families. Many lived in their employers' households. But every city also had independent black seamstresses, cooks, basketmakers, confectioners, and street vendors—women who hawked pies, vegetables, fruits, fish, clothing, and handmade items from small stands. Other African American women operated small shops, boardinghouses, and oyster cellars; some worked as midwives, teachers, and nurses. Because these women's earnings were indispensable to their families' survival, their lives were different from that of white women, who increasingly withdrew from work outside the home.

Even in lowly occupations, however, free African Americans sustained independence and a sense of dignity, setting their work schedules when they could. In some occupations, such as oyster selling, carriage driving, and hairdressing, they developed near monopolies. Most opportunities for black self-employment lay in service positions or the skilled crafts. Every city had black shoemakers, tailors, and bakers. These men and women provided valued services and much-needed articles.

The free black Philadelphian James Forten, whom we met in Chapter 5, is an example of the rise of African Americans in certain industries. Forten joined the patriot cause as a teenager. After the war he took to sea as a deckhand on a merchant ship bound for London, where for a year he sewed canvas sails on the Thames River docks. He returned to Philadelphia and apprenticed himself to white sailmaker Robert Bridges. Soon he was a foreman. When Bridges retired in 1798, Forten took over the enterprise. Business proved so brisk that by 1805 he was employing a racially mixed crew of twenty-five apprentices. His workers made sails for many of the city's largest merchant ships.

Though racism kept most free blacks from the most promising occupations, it could not stifle ambition. Richard Allen exemplifies this drive. Best known as a religious leader, Allen was an entrepreneur from the day of his release

Richard Allen's earnest demeanor shows in this portrait by an unknown artist. His reputation for honesty spread just after he purchased his freedom in 1779. Finding a trunk with a small fortune in silver and gold, Allen placed newspaper notices advertising his discovery. He refused to accept a generous reward from the grateful owner who claimed the trunk. Finally, he accepted a new suit of coarse cloth.

from slavery. He took up shoemaking and wagon-driving before moving to Philadelphia, where, in 1792, he purchased his first piece of property. In the following years he bought and sold real estate frequently. His household almost always included several servants and apprentices. To supplement his minister's salary, he worked as a shoemaker, houseware dealer, shoe store proprietor, and chimneysweep supervisor. In 1794, he attempted to establish a nail factory with his friend Absalom Jones. Though the project never materialized, it reflected Allen's ambitious spirit—one shared by many free African Americans in their first generation of liberty.

Of all the black-dominated occupations, seafaring had special importance for free African Americans. From almost the moment the Atlantic slave trade brought the first Africans to the Americas, merchants and ship captains took enslaved African men and boys—such as Olaudah Equiano—to sea with them. After the revolution, black freedmen sailed before the mast in large numbers. As hard and dangerous as the work was, life at sea was more free of discrimination than life ashore, as ship captains prized any man, regardless of color, who could splice rope properly, haul down canvas in a sudden storm, or scramble aloft to handle the topsails. Though only a handful of black mariners became captains, they usually received pay equal to that of white mariners. Nearly one out of four mariners sailing out of New York, Philadelphia, Baltimore, New Orleans, and Newport, Rhode Island, was an African American. In some cases, white captains sailed with all-black crews.

As free black communities burgeoned in the North and in southern seaports such as New Orleans and Charleston, cadres of professionals and entrepreneurs created the nucleus of a black middle class. These cities had a small but influential number of landlords, doctors, ministers, musicians, and teachers. Eleanor Harris, for example, was described at her death in 1797 as a "woman of character," a "well qualified tutoress of children." James Derham, once owned by a Quaker doctor in Philadelphia, became an accomplished physician in his own right in New Orleans. Samuel Wilson was so highly regarded for his skill in treating cancers that white Philadelphians readily sought his help. In the same city Robert Bogle, a former slave, turned the idea of contracting food services at funerals, weddings, and parties into a profession, as did enterprising free black people in Charleston, South Carolina.

Family Life

In leaving slavery behind, free African Americans put a priority on reuniting families or creating new ones. Neither proved easy. The profound dislocation caused by the Revolutionary War, the migration of free black people north and west afterward, and the scourge of poverty made household formation difficult. Many black men and women postponed marriage until they could gain their financial footing; thus, black families tended to be smaller than white families in this era. Most families shared housing. In the cities they lived in narrow courts and blind alleys, the poorest in attics and cellars. Though African Americans competed with Irish and German immigrants for jobs, they often shared space with these struggling immigrants. These were "walking cities," where people lived near to their work. Neighborhoods were not segregated by race or even class, and black and white people of all backgrounds and classes interacted daily.

Accommodating themselves to stark reality, most free African Americans built their households step by step. For at least a few years after emancipation, many had little choice but to remain in white households. They saved their earnings, and many indentured their children to white masters and mistresses to save on food and clothing. Eventually, some could afford to do domestic work in white households by day and then go home to relatives, friends, and boarders by night. With some luck, they could establish individual households of their own. In Boston and New York, for example, about one-third of all free black people lived in white households in 1790, but thirty years later, only one-sixth did so. In southern cities, establishing independent black households took longer.

By 1820, three-quarters or more of the free black households in most major cities contained at least one adult male and one adult female. These numbers suggest that the female-centered form of slave family life—unavoidable owing to the sale and early death of many enslaved black men—gave way to the two-parent family form as African Americans gained freedom.

Prominent African American families emerged in every city and set standards that others sought to emulate. Again, the Forten family in Philadelphia is an example. The Fortens were unusual in many respects, especially in their success and accomplishments. But in their family life, they demonstrated widespread black values. As a young man, James Forten supported his widowed mother and the family of his sister, which had only her husband's mariner wages. His sail-loft business flourishing, Forten married in 1803 at age thirty-seven, but his wife died within the year. A few months later, when his sister was widowed, Forten opened his three-story home to her four children and put two of his nephews to work in his sail loft. A year later, Forten married Charlotte Vandine, a twenty-one-year-old woman with Indian, European, and African ancestors. Between 1808 and 1823, they raised a family of nine children.

The Forten household included an assortment of relatives, apprentices, and boarders, along with children of deceased friends for whom James Forten served as guardian. Census takers recorded that Forten presided over a household of fifteen people in 1810, eighteen in 1820, and twenty-two in 1830. Sometimes, the number decreased as a son or daughter reached marriageable age and moved out—but then it grew again if the newlyweds came back to live and work in the household. With frequent comings and goings, the Forten home bustled with activity. Its members also played music, read poetry, and received instruction in French as well as traditional subjects such as literature and mathematics. One of James Forten's daughters described the household as a "happy family circle." Of course, most free black families did not live as comfortably and graciously as the Fortens. But examples of this kind gave hope to those less fortunate.

New Orleans: A Unique City

While free black communities developed mostly in the North, one also thrived in New Orleans, at the outlet of the Mississippi River. New Orleans became a city in 1803, the year the United States purchased the immense Louisiana Territory from France. When Americans began pouring into the city to pursue new opportunities, they found a unique configuration of races. In the early nineteenth century, slaves living in Louisiana were more linguistically and culturally African than anywhere else in the United States. Yet the population of free people of color was larger, better established, and more racially mixed than in other parts of the country.

Louisiana's free black population had roots reaching back to rule by the French and the Spanish, who tolerated dark-skinned peoples more than Europeans elsewhere in North America did. Since the late seventeenth century, the French explicitly endorsed mixed-race marriages in their overseas colonies. Many French soldiers and colonists married female slaves, and the children of these liaisons often were freed. After the Spanish acquired Louisiana in 1763, the system of slave self-purchase called *coartación* ensured that the free black population would continue to grow. By 1803, New Orleans had 1,800 free black people; by 1809, 3,000, many of whom had fled revolution in Haiti. By 1810, African Americans constituted two-thirds of the city's population of 17,000, and two-thirds of them were free.

Unique among U.S. cities, New Orleans had a hierarchical society with white people at the top, free people of color in the middle, and slaves at the bottom. Over time, free people of color in Louisiana became increasingly urban,

With its large free black population, New Orleans had more black artisans, shopkeepers, and street vendors than any other U.S. city. This 1819 painting by Benjamin Latrobe portrays "market folks" in colorful headgear and garments.

lighter-skinned, and disproportionately female. Those released from slavery were mostly black women—the wives or mistresses of white masters. Their mulatto sons and daughters were also freed. By 1791, nearly two-thirds of all free black people in New Orleans were mulatto.

Independent Institutions

Finding comfort and inspiration in numbers in the cities, African Americans founded their own churches, schools, and community organizations. "We went out with our subscription paper and met with great success," wrote Richard Allen, recounting how he and Absalom Jones collected $360 on the first day of their quest to create a separate black church. This was in 1787, shortly after they launched the Free African Society of Philadelphia (FAS), a mutual aid association that used member dues to assist needy free people.

From the beginning, the FAS had religious overtones, and soon its leaders devised plans for a black church of their own. But Allen's fervent Methodism diverged from those who wanted a nondenominational "union" church. So while Jones worked to create the African Church of Philadelphia, later St. Thomas's African Episcopal Church, Allen worked to establish a black Methodist church. Yet both churches had the same guiding idea: that black Americans emerging from slavery required independent black houses of worship. As Jones and Allen

Richard Allen's first church, known as Mother Bethel, was a blacksmith's shop hauled to the lot he purchased in Philadelphia and then refurbished as a place of worship. Methodism's evangelical fervor and simplicity appealed to freed and fugitive southern slaves who reached northern cities.

explained in their subscription paper, there was a "necessity and propriety of separate and exclusive means, and opportunities, of worshiping God, or instructing their youth, and of taking care of their poor."

The Rise of Black Churches

The creation of "separate and exclusive" black churches expressed emancipated slaves' desire to stand on their own as a distinct *African* people. As one historian explains, the black church in these years became "the one impregnable corner of the world where consolation, solidarity, and mutual aid could be found and from which the master and the bossman—at least in the North—could be effectively barred." Black churches became seedbeds of black consciousness. As focal points for social and political organization, they also served as neighborhood centers where free black people could celebrate their African heritage without intrusion by white detractors.

The impulse to form all-black churches originated in the desire for self-government and self-expression. Yet often, white discrimination in interracial congregations provided just as powerful an impetus. In Wilmington, Delaware, for example, the congregation of Asbury Methodist Church was already one-third black at its founding in 1789. By 1802, it was nearly half black. The gifted young preacher Peter Spencer held separate meetings in the homes of free black worshipers or in shady groves at the city's edge, but he was not allowed to preach from the church's pulpit. Black church members were denied communion, barred from ordination, and segregated during worship services, permitted to sit only in the gallery. In 1805, when they were ordered to hold their weekday religious class meetings in the gallery rather than on the sanctuary floor, Spencer and others left to found their own church. They named their all-black church Ezion Methodist Episcopal, after the port where biblical King Solomon kept his warships.

White people often resented independent black churches and mutual aid societies. In their view, free black Americans should remain subservient instead of founding their own organizations. "Their aspiring and little vanities," sneered John Fanning Watson, Philadelphia's first historian, "have been rapidly growing since they got those separate churches. [Before], they were much humbler, more esteemed in their places, and more useful to themselves and others." Comments such as these reflect a disturbing paradox facing African Americans at the end of the eighteenth century: As they extricated themselves from white supervision and the benevolence that came with heavy obligations by founding their own religious and educational institutions, white charges about innate black inferiority intensified. According to Allen and Jones, many white people viewed African Americans as "men whose baseness is incurable." The two ministers freely admitted that "the vile habits often acquired in a state of servitude are not easily thrown off," but they thought it unrealistic to expect too much from people who had been bent and broken by slavery. "Why," they asked, "will you look for grapes from thorns, or figs from thistles?" But, they insisted, as they spoke to white audiences, that black children who were born free and enjoyed "the same privileges with your own" would flourish.

In their independent churches, black Christians heard from their preachers that God had not made them inferior, but had made them a chosen people. When Absalom Jones built his African Episcopal Church, he chose these words from St. Peter (1 Peter 2:9) to be inscribed on the side wall: "But ye are a chosen generation, a royal priesthood, and an holy nation, a peculiar people; that ye should shew forth the praise of him who hath called you out of darkness into his marvelous light; which in time past were not a people, but are now the people of God."

Free African Americans in the new territory of Louisiana tended not to form separate congregations but to stay within the interracial Catholic churches, where they married, baptized their children, and marked other turning points in their lives. Several realities prompted these differences from the experiences of African Americans in the North. First, church authorities in Louisiana never segregated black worshipers or made them feel unwelcome. Second, New Orleans was still strongly Catholic, as the Methodist and Baptist evangelical churches that thrived in the North had not yet brought diverse religious expression to this southern city.

African American Schools

After building their own churches, free African Americans felt emboldened to organize schools. In an era when public schools existed only in New England, black parents had to create educational institutions for their own youngsters. Richard Allen organized the first black Sunday school in America at Philadelphia in 1795, and five years later, Absalom Jones and others established a school for black youth. In 1807, Allen set up the Society of Free People of Color for Promoting the Instruction and School Education of Children of African Descent. Black schools also emerged alongside, or within, black churches in other parts of the country. In 1790, the Brown Fellowship Society in Charleston founded a school for black children, and in 1797, the Baltimore African Academy opened its doors.

Other emerging free black communities established separate churches and schools as well. By the early nineteenth century, black schools operated in all cities with sizeable free black populations.

Like white Americans, black Americans regarded education as the surest path to economic success, moral improvement, and personal happiness. For men and women recently released from slavery, education offered special benefits. It could restore self-confidence and undermine white claims that people of African descent were inherently inferior intellectually. But although they prized education, most black parents—like most white working-class parents—could afford little schooling for their children. Most indentured their children at an early age to reduce household expenses. Children fortunate enough to stay at home had to contribute to the family income by working instead of going to classes. Only the sons and daughters of the black middle class had the luxury of studying through their teenage years.

An Independent Black Denomination

In his attempts to build his African Methodist congregation, Richard Allen had long met with bitter resistance from white Methodist authorities. They controlled the appointment of the preacher, the licensing of lay preachers, and the administration of baptism and communion. To be sure, Allen's church's trustees were African American, and he himself occupied the pulpit at African Methodist. But he and the trustees had agreed to articles of in-corporation, necessary to receive monetary support, without realizing that this action made their church the legal property of the white Methodist Conference.

Uncomfortable with the growing independence of Allen's church, white Methodists forced the issue in 1805. Allen vividly remembered the moment when a Methodist elder "waked us up by demanding the keys and books of the church, and forbid us holding any meetings except by orders from him; these propositions we told him we could not agree to." In response, the white elder threatened to expel the entire black congregation from the Methodist Conference. "We told him the house was ours," Allen replied, for "we had bought it, and paid for it." The struggle continued for more than ten years, until the determined white Methodists laid claim to the church itself and ordered it put up for auction. Allen foiled them by outbidding white Methodists at the auction, paying more than $10,000 for the brick church he had built in 1805. Then, on New Year's Day in 1816, the Supreme Court of Pennsylvania ruled that Mother Bethel was an independent church not subject to the authority of the Methodist Conference. Black Philadelphia Methodists had finally seceded from the white Methodist church.

Allen's success in achieving full independence for the African Methodist Episcopal Church exemplified a broader rise of independent black denomina-tions in the first quarter of the nineteenth century. The movement revealed a quest for autonomy fueled by the poisonous racial relations besetting free black communities. Even before Allen's victory, the black preacher Peter Spencer in Wilmington, with forty of his parishioners, created the Union Church of Africans—the country's first fully autonomous African American church. Additional independent black denominations soon appeared in New York, Baltimore, and other cities.

After a generation of tension with white coreligionists, African Americans decided, as one historian has said, "to elect and be elected to church office, to ordain, and be ordained, to discipline as well as be disci-plined, to preach, exhort, pray, and administer sacraments—in sum, to have their gifts and graces acknowledged by the whole community." But in as-serting black autonomy, black leaders also wondered if they were thereby increasing white antagonism. Still, by the early nineteenth century, urban black leaders took that chance. Their personal emancipation from slavery had catalyzed a psychological rebirth. The collective emancipation of black worshipers from white ecclesiastical bondage enabled them to pursue their vision of a better future. By 1816, as Allen later recalled, his congregation was finally able "to sit down under our own vine and fig tree to worship, and none shall make us afraid."

Black Revolution in Haiti

In 1791, a white American writer reflecting on the astounding news of a mass slave revolt in French St. Domingue connected it to "that insurrection of Americans which secured their independence." Another urged Americans who had fought their own revolution to "justify those who in a cause like ours fight with equal bravery."

Self-Liberation in the Caribbean

The drama unfolding in the Caribbean captured the imagination of all Americans, but black Americans had particular interest in the massive uprising in St. Domingue against the most brutal slave system in the Americas. Half a million Africans toiled on the French-owned western half of this Caribbean island (Spain controlled the eastern half), a number approaching the total number of slaves in the United States. St. Domingue also had about 50,000 free people of color (mostly biracial), who occupied a middle caste. The 32,000 white French colonists—a significant minority—maintained an uncertain grip on power. Enslaved Africans outnumbered their masters fifteen to one.

When revolution broke out in France in 1789, the restive free black people on St. Domingue claimed the same "rights of man" as the French revolutionaries. Then, in 1791, a slave named Boukman led a rebellion that attracted the support of white French colonists, who now pitted themselves against French royalists. By the following year, the island was engulfed in violence. In June 1793, self-liberated slaves overran the main seaport of Le Cap Français. Panicked, thousands of French planters and merchants fled to the United States. More than 3,000 reached Philadelphia, while thousands more poured into Norfolk, Baltimore, Charleston, New Orleans, and New York.

Many Americans who initially endorsed the toppling of the brutal slave regime changed their minds when they heard firsthand stories of the bloodbath from the French refugees. Would the fever of black rebellion spread to the United States, they wondered? In 1793, newspapers reported that three slaves in Albany, New York, had set a fire that destroyed twenty-six houses. People along the eastern seaboard soon associated black arson with the overthrow of white rule on St. Domingue. A wave of fires in 1796–1797—including one that burned two-thirds of Savannah—intensified fear of a black uprising.

But black Americans had a different view, sensing a worldwide movement against slavery. They privately applauded the victories of Haitian slaves under the leadership of Toussaint L'Ouverture, formerly a trusted plantation steward.

MAP 6.1 Exodus of Haitians to U.S. Seaports, 1792–1809

French slaveholders fleeing the slave revolution in 1792 (along with small numbers of free gens de couleur) brought thousands of slaves to U.S. coastal cities. Roughly 3,000 slaves and 3,000 free mulattoes flocked to New Orleans, further enriching that city's linguistic and cultural mix.

They celebrated again when black Haitians defeated the combined French, English, and Spanish armies sent against them. On January 1, 1804, Haiti proclaimed its independence as a republic of African people. Its revolutionaries had launched the first anticolonial racial war and achieved the first mass emancipation by slaves.

Reverberations in the United States

The revolution of Haiti cast a long shadow across the United States. In Philadelphia, the latest news of Caribbean black rebellion came with yellow fever on a French ship in 1793. The virus spread, claiming 5,000 lives and turning Philadelphia into a morgue. Richard Allen and Absalom Jones mobilized

This image of Toussaint L'Ouverture appeared in *An Historical Account of the Black Empire of Hayti,* published in London in 1805. The book spoke of the black leader's "prepossessing suavity" and remarked on his "astonishing horsemanship" and ability to travel "with inconceivable rapidity."

black nurses, death-cart drivers, and gravediggers to deal with the crisis. Charged with profiteering, they produced the first African American attack on slavery after the American Revolution. *A Narrative of the Proceedings of the Black People, During the Late Awful Calamity in Philadelphia* asserted that the "dreadful insurrections" in Haiti should "convince a reasonable man, that great uneasiness and not contentment, is the inhabitant of their [the slaves'] heart." Take notice, Allen and Jones implored. "If you love your children, if you love your country, if you love the God of love, clear your hands from slaves, burden not your children or country with them."

Self-emancipation in Haiti continued to shape African American thought about a worldwide movement against slavery. In 1797, Allen, Jones, and James Forten carried a petition to Congress through the streets of Philadelphia that called for repudiation of the Fugitive Slave Act of 1793. This act, which strengthened the Constitution's fugitive slave clause, permitted southern slave owners and agents to seize free black people they suspected of being runaways. An African American seized as a fugitive slave had no right to prove his or her status as a free person. Could African Americans not expect "public justice" from the national government, the petition signers asked? When would the government end the "unconstitutional bondage" that was a "direct violation of the declared fundamental principles of the Constitution"? With a hint of irony, Jones addressed the petition to "the President, Senate, and House of Representatives of the most free and enlightened nation in the world!!!"

In 1799, Allen and Forten composed a new petition to Congress. "Though our faces are black," they wrote, "yet we are men, and . . . are as anxious to enjoy the birth-right of the human race as those who [are white]." If the Declaration of Independence and the Bill of Rights "are of any validity," then black Americans should "be admitted to partake of the Liberties and inalienable Rights therein held forth." In other cities, African Americans began using the petition and other political means to hold white legislators to the standards of their founding documents. In Boston, Prince Hall, who had led the petition-writing campaign against slavery during the American Revolution, condemned slavery again before the African Masonic Lodge in 1797. While applauding the black rebellion in St. Domingue, Hall denounced "the daily insults" suffered by black citizens on Boston's streets.

The growing self-awareness of free black people sometimes surfaced in unexpected ways. One such occasion occurred in Philadelphia on July 4, 1804, seven months after black Haitians had declared independence. For years, on the Fourth of July, Philadelphians of all classes and colors had gathered in the square facing Independence Hall, where the Declaration of Independence was signed. There they feasted, toasted, and listened to stirring speeches about the blessings of liberty and the prospects of national greatness. But in 1804, several hundred black Philadelphians also celebrated Haitian independence. Organizing themselves into military formations, electing officers, and arming themselves with bludgeons and swords, they marched through the cobblestone streets, attacking white people who crossed their path. The next night, they marched again. Venting their anger over growing white hostility, they terrorized the city, "damning the whites and saying they would shew them St. Domingo."

By 1808, when American participation in the Atlantic slave trade ended officially on January 1, black ministers in many cities turned New Year's Day into the black equivalent of the Fourth of July. African Americans needed a national day of thanksgiving and celebration that had relevance to their lives. New Year's Day served well because it marked both the legal death of the slave trade and the birth of the free black republic of Haiti. Many of the New Year's Day sermons delivered by Richard Allen and other black ministers connected religion and politics. They denounced white leaders for not extending to black people the same rights the Declaration of Independence and many state constitutions had called inalienable. Black preachers repeatedly invoked the elevated phrases of the revolutionary era, confronting white Americans with the hypocrisy of adhering to slavery when their sacred texts prohibited it. "If freedom is the right of one nation," Absalom Jones asked, "why not the right of all nations of the earth?"

The Further Spread of Slavery

The congressional prohibition of the Atlantic slave trade in 1808, accompanied by British banning of the slave trade in the same year, did not eradicate traffic in human beings. Defying the law, slave traders in the Lower South continued to import slaves while the internal slave trade—the selling of human property from region to region within the United States—intensified.

Meanwhile, Spain and especially Portugal continued and even intensified the slave trade, bringing another three million Africans in chains to Brazil and Spanish colonies. Not until the mid-nineteenth century did a decisive decline in the trans-Atlantic slave traffic occur.

In one of the greatest ironies in American history, the revolution in Haiti inadvertently aided the spread of slavery in the United States. Having lost Haiti, France's largest source of wealth in the Americas, Napoleon no longer needed the crops produced in the lower Mississippi Valley to feed the Caribbean island's slaves. Desperate for new income, he agreed to sell the Louisiana Territory (recently acquired from Spain) to the United States for $15 million. The Louisiana Purchase in 1803 doubled the size of the United States and vastly increased the area into which slavery could spread.

As we saw in Chapter 3, slavery had deep roots in Louisiana and Florida, which Spain had turned into a slave-based plantation zone. In 1795, Pinckney's Treaty settled a boundary dispute by recognizing U.S. commerce rights at the port of New Orleans and U.S. control of what later became the states of Mississippi and Alabama. With the Louisiana Purchase, the Lower South became a center of slave trading and slave-based cotton production.

After Congress established the Mississippi Territory in 1798, an immense new region opened for settlement. White Americans, with their slaves in tow, streamed into the sparsely populated but racially diverse region. To carve cotton and sugar plantations out of raw land, planters imported slaves directly from Africa. When the slave trade became illegal in 1808, they smuggled in thousands more Africans. Between 1790 and 1820, the slave population of the lower Mississippi Valley increased tenfold—from 15,000 to 146,000.

The U.S. purchase of Louisiana transformed black life in the South. Infusions of northern and southern capital and the invention of the cotton gin accelerated the transition from an economy based on tobacco, indigo, and rice to one based on sugar and cotton. These changes launched a massive transfer of slaves from the Old South to the sugar and cotton lands of the lower Mississippi Valley. With Americans taking over the Spanish legal system and abolishing slaves' right to self-purchase in 1807, the number of free black people leveled off. Now masters found it difficult to manumit slaves, and the law forbade entry of free African Americans into Louisiana from other states. Between 1810 and 1860, Louisiana changed from a territory where free black people represented 13 percent of the black population to a cluster of states in which they constituted just 1 percent. By sharply restricting opportunities for release from slavery, the laws eroded the relative freedom slaves had enjoyed under the French and Spanish.

Even so, enslaved Louisianans continued to have some advantages over slaves in other parts of the new nation. Living among large numbers of free African Americans inspired hopes of freedom. In addition, many slave masters in New Orleans permitted slaves to hire out their own time and thereby earn money. Some slaves even maintained their own quarters and cultivated close contacts with free African Americans. One observer noted just after the Louisiana Purchase that slaves and dark-skinned free black people "never approach each other without displaying signs of affection and interest, without asking each other news of their relations, their friends, or their acquaintances."

Yet not all relations between free and enslaved blacks were so positive. Light-skinned free people of color were "uncomfortably sandwiched," one historian has written, "between white free people and black slaves"—a "third caste in a social order designed for but two." Often these free people of color saw their well-being as dependent on white patronage, so they aligned themselves with white people in business transactions. Some even owned human property themselves, regarding slave ownership as proof of their social and political solidarity with whites.

Slave Resistance

While some slaves hoped to win their freedom in the new nation through self-purchase or manumission by white masters, others made their bid for liberty on their own terms. The Haitian Revolution inspired many of the rebellions that struck fear into the hearts of slave owners everywhere in the American South.

Fugitive Slave Settlements

The swamplands in the southern states were good hiding places for escaped slaves. Those who fled their masters headed for swamps, where they formed settlements that plagued slave owners and threatened the slave regime. In North Carolina and Virginia, fleeing slaves established a community in the Great Dismal Swamp in the late 1780s. There they built cabins, planted crops, and governed themselves for many years. Farther south, former slaves who called themselves the King of England's Soldiers (indicating they had gained freedom during the American Revolution by joining the British) also used swamps as staging grounds for resistance. Setting up runaway camps in the Savannah River swamplands, slaves known as Captain Cudjoe and Captain Lewis attracted new refugees in the 1780s. With weapons acquired during the Revolutionary War, they led one hundred men in plundering river plantations just before the Constitutional Convention met in Philadelphia in 1787. When Georgia militia units finally destroyed their encampment, the refugees melted into the wilderness. Similarly, in the Cypress Swamp of Louisiana, black communities in the 1780s drew runaways who fended off periodic attacks by militia units and free African Americans working as slave catchers.

In 1795, slaves organized an uprising at Pointe Coupée, Louisiana. Inspired by the success of the black revolutionaries in Haiti and hoping to ignite a general insurrection, dozens of slaves (aided by three whites, a few Indians, and several free black men) prepared their strategy. But white authorities, alerted to the plot, seized the rebels before they could strike. A white court convicted twenty-three of them and ordered them hanged, their severed heads nailed to posts along the Mississippi River from Pointe Coupée to New Orleans as a warning. But such punishments did not prevent slaves from planning another uprising a year later. Frustrated, the Spanish halted imports of West Indian slaves, whom they considered prime rebels.

Gabriel's Rebellion

No severed heads or brutal crackdowns could suppress slave insurrection. That became apparent in the summer of 1800, when a twenty-four-year-old enslaved blacksmith prepared a strike at the heart of American slavery. Gabriel's Rebellion in Virginia proved the largest slave plot in the republic's early decades.

Born in the year the Declaration of Independence was signed, Gabriel acquired his name from the slave midwife who felt the shape of the baby's head and predicted he would be bold. So the infant's parents named him Gabriel, after the angel who appeared to Old Testament prophets and to the Virgin Mary. In his youth, this choice of name seemed prophetic. Growing up among more than fifty slaves owned by Thomas Prosser, a tobacco planter and merchant in Richmond, Gabriel had the good fortune to learn to read and to master blacksmithing. By the mid-1790s, when Prosser hired him out in Richmond, Gabriel gained a measure of freedom. As his access to the wider world expanded, he learned about the Haitian Revolution. Reported in the Richmond newspapers, the uprising was also recounted by Haitian slaves brought into American port cities. Inspired by the successful slave rebellion, Gabriel developed a scheme to end slavery in the American South.

The young man planned carefully, quietly gathering recruits in Richmond and surrounding counties. Governor James Monroe—a future U.S. president—later maintained that the conspiracy included most of the slaves in the Richmond area and "pervaded other parts, if not the whole, of the State." He was probably right. Gabriel and his lieutenants found the slaves they approached willing to fight for their freedom. When asked "if he thought he could kill White people stoutly," a slave named Jacob answered: "I will fight for my freedom as long as I have breath, and that is as much as any man can do." Another said simply, "I will kill or be killed." Gabriel's brother Martin, a preacher, worked to overcome the fears of those slaves who were hesitant by quoting the Bible: "five of you shall conquer a hundred & a hundred thousand of our enemies."

Gabriel's plan centered on seizing Richmond. On August 30, 1800, 1,000 followers were to meet, divide into three columns, and enter the capital after midnight under a banner inscribed "Death or Liberty," the Haitian revolutionaries' battle cry. The first column would torch Richmond's wooden warehouse district. The second would seize 4,000 rifles from the state arsenal, and the third take Governor Monroe hostage. As white residents rushed out to fight the fires, freshly armed black insurgents would cut them down, sparing only poor women without slaves, Quakers and Methodists, and known opponents of slavery. Once in charge of Richmond, Gabriel's rebels intended to demand their freedom and the abolition of slavery. If slaves in Haiti had done so, they reasoned, why not slaves in Virginia?

But nature conspired against the rebels. As Gabriel's army gathered, a violent storm dumped torrential rain on the region, washing out the bridges by which they had planned to enter Richmond. White Virginians later regarded this downpour as providential, but authorities also knew of the plot from a few slaves who had declined to join. Twenty slaves, including Gabriel's two brothers, were quickly arrested. Gabriel himself slipped away to Norfolk, but was captured when two black sailors betrayed him for a $300 reward and their own freedom.

Using testimony from the informers, the courts tried the rebels for conspiracy and insurrection. Gabriel and his brothers were hanged in October. In all, white authorities executed twenty-six conspirators and transported dozens of others out of state, selling them into slavery in French New Orleans and the West Indies.

Still, Gabriel's Rebellion survived long in the memories of Virginians. In court testimony, one of Gabriel's associates left much to ponder: "I have nothing more to offer than what General Washington would have had to offer, had he been taken by the British and put to trial. I have adventured my life in endeavouring to obtain the liberty of my countrymen, and am a willing sacrifice in their cause." Appalled by the conspiracy and dreading a Haitian-like outbreak in the United States, white Virginians were forced to recognize, as one put it, that "there have never been slaves in any country, who have not seized the first favorable opportunity to revolt." Virginia's nervous governor, James Monroe, agreed: "Unhappily, while this class of people exists among us we can never count with certainty on its tranquil submission."

Other Uprisings

Less than a year after Gabriel's Rebellion, a slave named Sancho proved Monroe correct. A ferryman who knew upcountry Virginia well, Sancho was one of Gabriel's followers who had escaped capture. Now he plotted an "Easter rebellion"—a revolt to take place on Good Friday in 1802. By torching houses and fields, his men hoped to precipitate the collapse of slavery. They believed that a "great conflagration of houses, fodder, [hay] stacks, etc. will strike such a damp on their spirits that [white people] will be . . . willing to acknowledge liberty and equality." Word spread of an Easter uprising, even into North Carolina. But again, someone leaked news of the plan, and it quickly unraveled. White militia patrols arrested the plotters, and in 1802 thirty slaves were hanged, Sancho among them. As in Gabriel's scheme, the rebels had not managed to strike that all-important first blow.

Southern planters who hoped that hangings and deportations would end slave resistance were wrong. In 1811, a slave named Tom, arrested in Henrico County, Virginia, confessed that his murder of his master was part of a larger plan to kill slave owners. Slaves "were not made to work for the white people," asserted Tom "but [white people] are made to work for themselves; and [enslaved Africans] would have it so." Later that year, one of North America's largest slave uprisings erupted near New Orleans. Led by Charles Deslondes, a biracial slave from Haiti, about 500 escaped slaves marched on the city, "colors displayed and full of arrogance." Following a battle with white troops, in which two white people and sixty-six rebels died, twenty-one slaves were executed.

White southerners managed to avert or defeat slave revolts, but they did not consider ending slavery. Instead, slave rebellion prompted tighter restrictions on free black people. In 1806, Virginia ordered all newly freed slaves to leave the state within one year or risk re-enslavement.

Black Identity in the New Nation

In summer 1792, a procession of Philadelphians filed behind the casket of Widow Gray, wife of an African American fruit seller. What distinguished the marchers, said one newspaper, was the "pleasing indifference to complexion," for white and black people alike paid homage to the deceased. This was "a happy presage of the time, fast approaching, when the important declaration in *holy writ* will be fully verified that 'GOD hath made of one blood, all the nations of the Earth,'" the newspaper observed. But those who believed a new era of racial unity had dawned soon saw their hopes dashed.

At the end of the eighteenth century and beginning of the nineteenth, growing hostility toward free blacks led to new restrictions on people of color. Increasingly, white Americans regarded freed African Americans as more dangerous than slaves and less useful for building the new nation. Once again, black people had to rethink their options, including a return to Africa. The War of 1812 raised further questions about their place in America.

Rising Racial Hostility

George Washington had only recently become the nation's first president when Congress began restricting the rights of black people. In 1790, the Naturalization Law limited citizenship to immigrants who were "foreign whites." In 1792, enlistment in the state militias was limited to white men. In 1810, African Americans were banned from working in the U.S. postal system. States and cities added more restrictions. In the states carved out of the Northwest Territory, laws limited the entry of free black people into the region. In 1807, for example, Ohio required incoming African Americans to post a $500 bond to demonstrate their ability to support themselves. In 1815, Indiana imposed a $300 annual poll tax on all adult black and mulatto men. Even Methodists and Baptists revoked their rule prohibiting slave ownership among members in 1793.

Philadelphia, a center of humanitarian reform, also endured racial conflicts, as working-class white people resented black newcomers from the South who competed for jobs and housing. At a Fourth of July celebration in 1805, white people drove black people from the square facing Independence Hall. A few weeks later, a pamphlet described the city as overrun by black migrants "starving with hunger and destitute of employ."

Racist caricatures such as the one shown here lampooned free African Americans in the North. In this image, Governor John Hancock of Massachusetts welcomes Cuffe to "the celebrated Equality Ball given to the Negroes of Boston." In mocking free African Americans, cartoons of this kind made them seem unsuitable for citizenship rights.
Source: The Library Company of Philadelphia.

The racial fear of white Americans dovetailed with the rise of scientifically based racism. Previously, many white intellectuals believed that black people were less capable than white people owing to the degradation of slavery rather than inherent inferiority. "Nurture," not "nature," they maintained, had made black people useless. As we saw in Chapter 5, Thomas Jefferson was among the first to revive the old argument about the supposedly immutable inferiority of people of African descent. By the early nineteenth century, some of the nation's most respected thinkers agreed with Jefferson, attacking the "nurture" theory by contending that Africans had been an inferior race even *before* slavery. In 1811, Charles Caldwell, a doctor on the medical faculty at the University of Pennsylvania, argued that the social mixing of the races would lead to disaster—a mixed assortment of individuals with debased abilities who would not fit anywhere.

African American leaders tried to counter these assaults on egalitarianism. James Forten put aside his usual reserve to publish a scorching indictment of the expulsion of black Philadelphians from the July Fourth celebration at Independence Hall Square. Forten also decried proposed laws that would forbid free black people from moving into Pennsylvania.

New Organizational and Family Names

Following ratification of the Constitution, free African Americans struggled to define their identity in the expanding white nation. Were newly freed people *African* Americans? Did they have a future where they toiled if their culture remained African? Or were they Americans with dark skin who should quickly assimilate into the dominant white society? Or should they regard themselves as Africans living in a strange, hostile land—a displaced people who should return to the realms of their ancestors?

Though the rising generation of free African Americans distanced themselves from the bondage of the past, they titled their churches, schools, and social organizations in ways that suggested a shared heritage. Memories of the African homeland still stirred those who had been born there, and the idea of Africa stirred those who had never seen it. In 1903, the pioneering black historian W. E. B. Du Bois would call this phenomenon "double-consciousness." The black American, Du Bois observed, "ever feels his twoness—an American, a Negro; two souls, two thoughts, two unreconciled strivings; two warring ideals in one dark body, whose dogged strength alone keeps it from being torn asunder."

The African half of this double consciousness showed itself plainly in the way freed people named organizations and churches. The Free African Society in Philadelphia and Newport made its members' identity clear: "We, the free *Africans* and their descendants," stated their articles of incorporation. Black Philadelphians also organized under Africa-inspired names such as Daughters of Ethiopia, Angola Beneficial Society, Daughters of Samaria, Sons of Africa, Daughters of Zion Angolan Ethiopian Society, and the African Friendly Society of St. Thomas. Independent black churches were unvaryingly called "African": the African Baptist Church of Boston, the African Presbyterian Church of New York, the African Union Methodist Church of Wilmington, the First African Church of Augusta. Years later, in the face of mounting white hostility, some black leaders urged followers to remove the word *Africa* from their organizations' names, but for now, free black people embraced connections with African ancestors.

Free black people also grappled with their identity at a personal level: what to name themselves, what to name their children. Inventing a family name—a surname, which most slaves did not have—enabled them to demonstrate their independence. Just as Gustavus Vasa became Olaudah Equiano and James Armistead became James Lafayette, thousands of freed people symbolically left the slave past behind by choosing a new name. Most disposed of their slave names altogether. These names, such as classical names like Caesar and Pompey or mythological names such as Jupiter and Mars, had been conferred by slave masters. Instead, newly freed people chose plain Anglo-American names such as John or Mary or biblical names such as Isaac or Ruth. In Philadelphia, the slave Caesar became Samuel Green and Pompey became James Jones. Some freed people chose a surname that announced their new identity, for many Freemans and Newmans are found in church and census records. Others celebrated freedom with a flourish, as did Richard America in Philadelphia and Hudson Rivers in New York City. Still others took names from defining moments in their lives. A slave-born mariner who signed aboard John Paul Jones's ship *Bonhomme Richard* during the Revolution renamed himself Paul Jones. In Baltimore, John Fortune and Elisha Caution selected names that expressed their thoughts about the future. In contrast to practices farther north, freed blacks in New Orleans, Charleston, and other southern cities often tried to preserve ties with white patrons by adopting their masters' surnames.

The Back-to-Africa Movement

While most northern black leaders chose to stand and fight for their rights in the young nation, others considered a return to Africa. Feeling strong emotional ties to the homeland and desiring to carry Christianity to Africa, these people had few hopes for a decent life in the United States. As we saw in Chapter 5, the back-to-Africa impulse first welled up in Boston only a few years after the American Revolution. In the late 1780s, it surfaced in Newport, where free African Americans reported that they were "strangers and outcasts in a strange land, attended with many disadvantages and evils which are likely to continue on us and our children while we and they live in this country."

At the same time, some white leaders eagerly promoted emigration. The wealthy Quaker William Thornton, for example, garnered the support of Boston's Samuel Adams and Virginia's James Madison for a plan to resettle freed slaves on the coast of Guinea. But Thornton's plan never materialized, as he found few free African Americans willing to leave the United States.

Paul Cuffe was the strongest proponent of emigration in the early nineteenth century. Cuffe, son of an African father who had purchased his freedom and married a Wampanoag woman in Massachusetts, went to sea at age sixteen. Captured by the British in 1776, he was sent with his shipmates to a New York prison ship. Even before the war ended, Cuffe and his brothers asked why free black men—who had no vote and could not hold office—were required to pay taxes. After the war, Cuffe married a Wampanoag woman and prospered in New Bedford, Massachusetts, as a master mariner, shipowner, and merchant. He was distinctly American, even joining the New Bedford Society of Friends.

Yet disillusioned with the treatment of free black people in the North, Cuffe urged an exodus to Africa. In part, he hoped to bring Christianity to Africa, where repatriated free black people would be the principal missionaries. Supported by Philadelphia Quakers, Cuffe organized a trial voyage to West Africa in 1810 to carry out this work. He left from Philadelphia on New Year's Day in 1811 with an all-black crew. Fifty-two days later, he recorded in his ship's journal, "the dust of Africa lodged on our riggings." His voyage stirred debates about whether black Americans' best future lay in Africa, America, or both—a debate that lasted for decades.

The War of 1812

Even as Cuffe navigated his ship across the Atlantic to West Africa in early 1811, new tensions between Britain and the United States were about to break into hostilities. British cruisers had been seizing American seamen for service on British vessels in an escalation of a long dispute between the two nations. Like other seafaring captains, Cuffe hoped the United States could remain neutral while France and England clashed in the Napoleonic wars. Like other Americans, Cuffe paid the price when Congress, in 1807, passed an embargo on American shipping that threw eastern seaports into a severe depression. Two years later Congress repealed the embargo and reopened trade with all nations except Great Britain and France. But repeal did not stop British and French attacks on U.S. ships. Nor did it stop U.S. customs officials from seizing Cuffe's ship in early 1812 after he returned from West Africa. Charged with possible violations of the most recent maritime trade law, Cuffe managed to repossess his ship and its valuable cargo only by traveling to Washington. He was back in New Bedford by June 1812—the month Congress declared war on England to protect U.S. trade links to Europe. Cuffe now had to postpone his back-to-Africa movement.

The War of 1812 gave free black men and women a chance to prove their allegiance to the new nation and slaves an opportunity to shake off their shackles. Even before war was declared, African Americans had been swept up in the conflict, as black sailors had been among those seized into service by the British. Now free black men enlisted and served in both black regiments and racially mixed regiments. At least one-tenth of the sailors who fought the British on the Great Lakes were African Americans. After the Battle of Lake Erie, Captain Oliver H. Perry declared that his black sailors "seemed absolute insensible to danger." In the summer of 1814, when the British captured and burned Washington, DC, many free black men volunteered to fortify seaport defenses against the marauding British. In September, as the British moved toward Baltimore, William Burleigh of Philadelphia positioned himself in the thick of the Battle of North Point. In early 1815, at the Battle of New Orleans, several free black Louisiana militia units held a strategic position near General Andrew Jackson's main forces and played a gallant role in the U.S. victory.

Later, to promote the antislavery cause, abolitionists celebrated African American contributions to the American effort during the War of 1812. But in truth, many more African Americans served with the British than with the Americans. Just as in the American Revolution, many slaves seized the promise of unconditional freedom in return for joining Britain's cause. When the British fleet conducted hit-and-run raids in the Chesapeake Bay in 1813, Marylanders and Virginians feared a wave of slave rebellions. Rather than rising against their masters, however, slaves simply fled to British ships and bases, where many served as spies, messengers, and guides. U.S. Brigadier General John Hungerford lamented that "these refugee blacks" could "penetrate [these regions] with so much ease."

Refugee slaves' knowledge of the landscape stymied American efforts to defend the nation's capital. The British troops that sailed up the Patuxent River and debarked to march on Washington, DC, were accompanied by at least one hundred newly liberated slaves who served with the Eighty-fifth Regiment of the British Colonial Marines. These were the troops who left the capital a smoking ruin.

Before the war ended, 3,000 to 5,000 slaves of the Upper South, nearly one-third of them women, had fled to the British. Thousands more failed in the attempt. When the British invaded New Orleans in 1815, hundreds of

Louisiana slaves fled to them as well. But because the British occupied areas in the South only briefly in the War of 1812, far fewer slaves fled to them than had done so during the American Revolution. Still, the exodus represented the largest act of slave resistance between the American Revolution and the Civil War. In 1815, at war's end, the British faced the same problem they had in 1783: what to do with the escaped slaves who had gained their freedom by reaching British lines. Most went to Nova Scotia; others, to Bermuda or Sierra Leone.

Conclusion

In the late eighteenth and early nineteenth centuries, free black leaders established autonomy for African Americans by setting up independently managed black churches, schools, and other organizations. They built free black communities from Massachusetts to Louisiana, in which many black people made the transition from chattel property to propertied families. But how would black men and women translate that autonomy into equality in the workplace, in politics, and in social life?

How could African Americans continue the fight to end slavery when so many white people believed that black people should remain subordinate and deferential? Despite African American gains, slavery was still spreading geographically, and the number of slaves was soaring—even after the slave trade officially ended in 1808. The antislavery movement was losing steam. Even slave rebellions in Haiti and Virginia—the first successful, the second failed—had not persuaded southern slaveholders to phase out slavery.

Like the American Revolution, the War of 1812 gave free African Americans another chance to win white people's acceptance by showing their willingness to shed their blood for the new nation. For those still in chains, flight to the British lines offered a release from bondage. As peace returned in 1815, as Americans surged west in search of new land in recently established U.S. territories, and as tensions mounted between the North and South, what would happen to the growing population of enslaved African Americans? Bondspeople in the United States numbered about 1.3 million when James Monroe was elected president in 1816. Would they follow the examples of the Haitian black insurrectionists and black rebels in the American South such as Gabriel Prosser and Charles Deslondes? Or would they continue toiling in the fields, sorrowfully bringing children into a world of enslavement—all the while hoping that new white political leaders would finally set them free?

Questions for Review and Reflection

1. Did free African Americans in the North make a wise choice in seeking opportunities in American cities after gaining their freedom? Were there better alternatives?

2. If Richard Allen were to be seen as a character in an *American* historical narrative, rather than only in an *African*-American context, how would the stories we tell ourselves about him be different?

3. Why did the United States not recognize Haiti as an independent nation after black Haitians overthrew slavery? Do you discern any connection between Haiti's poverty and economic underdevelopment today with its history in the decades after achieving independence?

4. Was the spread of slavery in the South inevitable after the invention of the cotton gin and the acquisition of the Louisiana Territory? What arguments can you summon to support or oppose this proposition?

5. Given the rise of racial hostility to free African Americans and the exhaustion of the antislavery movement in the early nineteenth century, was the "back-to-Africa" movement the best option for free blacks?

7

CHAPTER

African Americans in the Antebellum Era

James Forten on Repatriation to Africa

On a wintry January evening in 1817, James Forten squeezed his way forward to the pulpit through nearly 3,000 black men who had thronged Philadelphia's Mother Bethel Church. They packed the main floor, overflowed the balcony, and spilled into the street in an assemblage such as the city had never seen. Representing nearly three-quarters of all African American men in Philadelphia, they had gathered to speak their minds on a hotly debated issue: a campaign initiated by white leaders to repatriate free black people to Africa.

The city's most respected black businessman, Forten opened his heart to his fellow African Americans. He recalled what recent years had been like for the nation's more than two million slaves and several hundred thousand free people of color. The antislavery movement had lost momentum since the slave trade was outlawed in 1808. In the northern cities, white hostility blocked the advancement of free black people, while the federal government restricted their job opportunities. While Forten maintained a workforce of black and white craftsmen in his thriving sail loft, most white craftsmen refused to take black apprentices and pushed skilled black artisans out of the trades. Free black Americans had struggled mightily, but the road forward seemed more difficult than ever. Earlier hopes for racial equality—and an end to slavery—were fading in what African Americans increasingly saw as a white man's country.

A year before, white political leaders had founded the American Colonization Society (ACS) in Washington, DC. Led by outgoing president James Madison and incoming president James Monroe, and including such prominent figures as Chief Justice John Marshall, Kentucky's Henry Clay, South Carolina's John C. Calhoun, and Francis Scott Key, author of "The Star Spangled Banner," ACS members aimed to resettle free African Americans on Africa's west coast.

Chronology		
	1816	Richard Allen establishes the African Methodist Church. Northern and southern political leaders establish the American Colonization Society.
	1817	Morris Brown forms a new African Methodist Episcopal congregation in Charleston.
	1820s	Newly independent republics in Central and South America abolish slavery.
	1820	Congress passes the Missouri Compromise.
	1821	The American Colonization Society establishes Liberia.
	1822	Denmark Vesey plans a slave rebellion in Charleston.
	1824	A white mob devastates the black community in Providence, Rhode Island.
	1825	Andrew Jackson assumes presidency.
	1827	Samuel Cornish and John Russwurm launch *Freedom's Journal*.
	1829	David Walker publishes *An Appeal to the Coloured Citizens of the World.* A white mob pillages a free black community in Cincinnati.
	1830	The American Society of Free People of Colour forms in Philadelphia.
	1831	William Lloyd Garrison launches *The Liberator.* Nat Turner leads a slave rebellion in Virginia.
	1832	Virginia legislators decide not to abolish slavery. A South Carolina special convention declares the 1828 tariff null and void.

White northerners endorsed the scheme for various reasons. Some believed white prejudice and the scars of slavery doomed any dream of racial equality in America. Many northern Protestant church leaders saw repatriation as a chance to Christianize the African continent. White southerners saw free African Americans as a threat to the continuation of slavery (and thus to their economy). In their view, free black people's emigration to Africa would remove this threat.

Long before the founding of the ACS, Forten and other northern black leaders had supported colonization. The notion appealed to those African Americans who doubted the United States would ever give up slaveholding. The vast new cotton lands opened to settlement in the Lower South and the Louisiana Territory had fueled the spread of slavery. In the North, white people prejudiced against free African Americans denied them citizenship and equal protection under the law. In a letter to Paul Cuffe, Forten worried that African Americans "will never become a people until they come out from amongst the white people." The idea of returning to Africa was Cuffe's dream, and he had already organized in support of it. In 1811, he had transported thirty-eight black settlers to West Africa.

Chairing the meeting at Mother Bethel, Forten asked the city's three notable black ministers—Richard Allen, Absalom Jones, and Peter Gloucester, of

This drawing of James Forten, by an unknown artist, is the only known image of the African American leader.

the African Presbyterian Church—to explain the advantages of returning to Africa. Forten added his support. Then it was time to vote. Forten called first for "ayes," those who favored colonization. Not one person spoke up or lifted a hand. Then Forten called for the "nays." The response, he recalled, was one tremendous "no" that seemed "as if it would bring down the walls of the building. . . . There was not a soul that was in favor of going to Africa."

Why did free black people oppose a plan that, on its surface, held so much promise? Ordinary black men and women understood what their leaders did not: that whatever the sincerity and goodwill of some ACS leaders, the repatriation project would almost certainly be controlled by southerners eager to deport free black people to protect the institution of slavery. Black Philadelphians, Forten reported, were "very much frightened . . . that all the free people would be compelled to go." They could not believe that whites wanted to do "a great good" for a people they hated. Rather, they were certain that "the slaveholders want to get rid of [free blacks] so as to make their [slave] property more secure."

The emotional meeting at Mother Bethel proved a defining event for black Americans. The black men who poured out of the building afterward carried with them a new commitment to the abolition of slavery and a new feeling of unity with dark-skinned peoples of different classes and religious affiliations. The resolutions they endorsed in January 1817 rejected the claim of Henry Clay that free black people were "a dangerous and useless part of the community" and expressed their determination to fight for freedom and equality on U.S. soil. "Whereas our ancestors (not of choice) were the first successful cultivators of the wilds of America," they announced, "we their descendants feel ourselves entitled to participate in the blessings of her luxuriant soil, which their blood and sweat manured; and that any measure . . . having the tendency to banish us from her bosom, would not only be cruel, but in direct violation of those principles which have been the boast of the republic. We never will separate ourselves voluntarily from the slave population of this country, . . . our brethren by the ties of consanguinity, or suffering, and of wrong."

So the old battle against prejudice was rejoined. From the founding of the ACS in 1816 to a momentous Virginia slave rebellion in 1831, black Americans across the nation waged a common struggle. Free African Americans looked to build viable communities within a white-dominated land. By establishing independent religious denominations, starting newspapers, and convening national conferences, they hoped to unite dozens of flourishing black communities to fight slavery and its expansion. For the vast majority of black Americans still trapped in slavery, life had grown more difficult than ever. The Louisiana Purchase and the Missouri Compromise triggered a massive transfer of slaves south and west.

Yet black people's dreams of freedom endured. Some African Americans in the South, both enslaved and free, challenged slavery through compelling words and deeds. Three inspirational figures—Denmark Vesey, David Walker, and Nat Turner—led attempts to end slavery, even as southerners stepped up their defense of the practice. Thomas Jefferson's 1814 letter to a friend proved predictive: "The hour of emancipation is advancing in the march of time," he wrote. Jefferson wondered if emancipation would be "brought on by the generous energy of our own minds" or perhaps would occur "by the bloody process of St. Domingo"—that is, the slave uprising in Haiti. Full of premonitions, the aging author of the Declaration of Independence could not decide. It "is a leaf of our history," he wrote, "not yet turned over."

Black Religion in the Antebellum Era

The black church was the rock on which all black struggles for freedom and equality rested. The more white hostility intensified, the more black people needed an independent church as a bastion of strength. In the early nineteenth century, separate black churches arose wherever a few hundred free black people lived. The next logical move was to connect these churches in regional networks.

The African Methodist Episcopal Church

Richard Allen had such networks in mind when he called a meeting of black Methodists in April 1816. "Taking into consideration their grievances, and in order to secure their privileges, promote union and harmony among themselves," he wrote, black ministers from Maryland, Delaware, New Jersey, and Pennsylvania resolved to "become one body under the name of the African Methodist Episcopal Church" (AME). Thus would they escape the "spiritual despotism which we have so recently experienced." The AME became the largest denomination of black Christians in the United States and spread around the world. Allen was its first bishop.

Black independence offended white Americans who wanted black subordination, not black self-assertion. Years later, one of Allen's successors as AME bishop explained the importance of separate black churches. Taking his cue from the scriptural passage "Stand up, I myself am also a man," Daniel Payne described the psychological and political transformation that came with their creation. When white religious leaders controlled black churches, said Payne, "The colored man was a mere hearer." The point of this paternalism, he believed, was "to prove that the colored man was incapable of self-government and self- support." Founding the AME was "a flat contradiction and triumphant refutation of this slander, so foul in itself and so degrading in its influence."

Charismatic Preachers

One of Allen's first challenges as bishop was to deal with a member of his church who had a mission of her own. Jarena Lee had been born free in New Jersey, but like the children of many poor free black people, she was apprenticed to a white family as a child. On coming to Philadelphia as a teenager, she was transformed by a passionate sermon Allen delivered at Mother Bethel. "That moment, though hundreds were present," she later wrote, "I did leap to my feet and declare that God, for Christ's sake, had pardoned the sins of my soul."

This image of Jarena Lee was not included in the first edition of her *Life and Religious Experience of Jarena Lee* (1836). The several editions of her book made her one of the first women of the nineteenth century to reach a wide audience through print. In 1844 and 1852, women unsuccessfully petitioned the AME General Conference to allow ordination of black women.

In 1811, seven years after joining Mother Bethel, she married Joseph Lee, a black minister. Soon she heard a voice telling her, "Go preach the Gospel! Preach the Gospel; I will put words in your mouth." Then, one night in a dream, "there stood before me a great multitude, while I expounded to them the things of religion." Startled by her ability to preach in the dream (a power few expected women to possess), Lee told Allen that God had spoken to her and had commanded her to preach. But Allen said she could not preach from Mother Bethel's pulpit because Methodism had no provision for women preachers. Lee did not back down. "If the man may preach, because the Savior died for him, why not the woman, seeing he died for her also? Is he not a whole Savior, instead of a half one?" Allen still refused, but suggested she hold prayer meetings in her home.

Eight years later, Lee arose during a Sunday service at Mother Bethel when the preacher seemed to lose the spirit. Words tumbled from her mouth, and the crowded church fell under her sway. "God made manifest His power in a manner sufficient to show the world that I was called to labor according to my ability," she recalled. Then Allen opened Mother Bethel's pulpit to her. Thereafter, Lee crisscrossed the country, turning fields, farms, and city streets into sacred spaces when she could find no consecrated church in which to preach. Convinced she had divine protection and favor, she often spoke to interracial gatherings. Traveling as far north as Canada and as far south as Maryland, she reached thousands. In one year, she journeyed more than 2,000 miles on foot and by steamboat, delivering 178 sermons.

Though never ordained, Lee served as an inspiration to AME women. Like white women in evangelical denominations, black women did the church's work: teaching in church schools, leading prayer meetings, and organizing church programs. In gaining the pulpit, Lee broke a barrier women did not surmount in other denominations, black or white, for many decades. Across the remnants of this barrier strode other spiritually gifted Methodist women, such as Rebecca Cox Jackson, sister of a lay preacher at Mother Bethel.

The Expansion of Slavery

"This man came up to me, and, seizing me by the collar, shook me violently, saying I was his property, and must go with him to Georgia. . . . [W]e must set out that very day for the south. I asked if I could not be allowed to go to see my wife and children, . . . but was told that I would be able to get another wife in Georgia." With these words, Charles Ball described the heartache he experienced when he was sold in 1805 by his Maryland master. Nearly a million slaves suffered this agony as slavery expanded to the new cotton frontiers of the South. The Missouri Compromise only worsened the plight of black Americans by facilitating the spread of southern slavery. Native Americans suffered as well. By the 1830s, land-hungry cotton planters had removed Cherokees, Creeks, Choctaws, Chickasaws, and Seminoles from their homelands to territories west of the Mississippi River.

King Cotton

The shipment of slaves from the Upper to the Lower South was triggered by the invention of a disarmingly simple machine that processed as much cotton in a single day as fifty slaves cleaned by hand. In 1793, Connecticut schoolteacher Eli Whitney had constructed an engine, or "gin"—a wooden box with a roller and wire teeth—that stripped the sticky green seeds from cotton bolls. Whitney's cotton gin was operated by hand, but when built on a large scale with a giant roller driven by horses or waterpower, the machine could be tended by a single laborer. Before 1793, the time-consuming work of cleaning cotton had limited its profitability. With the gin, cotton cultivation took off.

For landowners, Whitney's invention promised enormous benefits. In Britain and New England, new textile factories turned cotton into cloth coveted around the world. For southern planters, many chronically in debt, the invention slashed the costs of processing cotton and boosted profits to unprecedented heights. Southerners, along with some northerners, headed for the new frontier in the Old Southwest and Louisiana Territory to jump into the cotton business. After the War of 1812, the exodus of white planters from the seaboard states resembled a gold rush. By 1838, slaves in Alabama and Mississippi were producing half the nation's cotton.

But for the 800,000 slaves sold south, Whitney's invention brought heartache. Slave manumissions decreased because masters saw new ways to make slavery profitable. As in Africa centuries before, slave coffles trudged south from Virginia, Maryland, Delaware, and North Carolina. Thousands more slaves were loaded onto ships in ports such as Baltimore and Norfolk and transported to Lower South ports, especially New Orleans. There, strange new masters bought them at auction and took them even farther from family and friends.

The sharp rise in cotton production marked a turning point for the South and the nation. A minor commodity in 1790, cotton became an engine of economic development. As production of cotton soared, so did the southern slave population (see Figure 7.1). "To sell cotton in order to buy negroes—to make more cotton to buy more negroes ad infinitum is the aim and direct tendency of all the operations of the thorough-going planter," wrote one traveler in the South. "His whole soul is wrapped up in the pursuit. It is, apparently, the principle by which he lives, moves, and has his being."

The Missouri Compromise

Cotton cultivation propelled slavery west across the Mississippi River. When, in 1819, the Missouri Territory applied for statehood with explicit guarantees for slaveholding, Congress could not duck the slavery issue. Admitting Missouri as a slave state would tip the balance in the Senate—so carefully maintained to this point—to the South. For nearly three months Congress debated whether to sanction slavery in this new state. The implications for rising regional tensions filled many with foreboding. "This momentous question, like a firebell in the night," wrote Thomas Jefferson, "awakened and filled me with terror."

Both houses divided sharply on two northern proposals for the gradual abolition of slavery after Missouri gained statehood. The first proposed that slaves

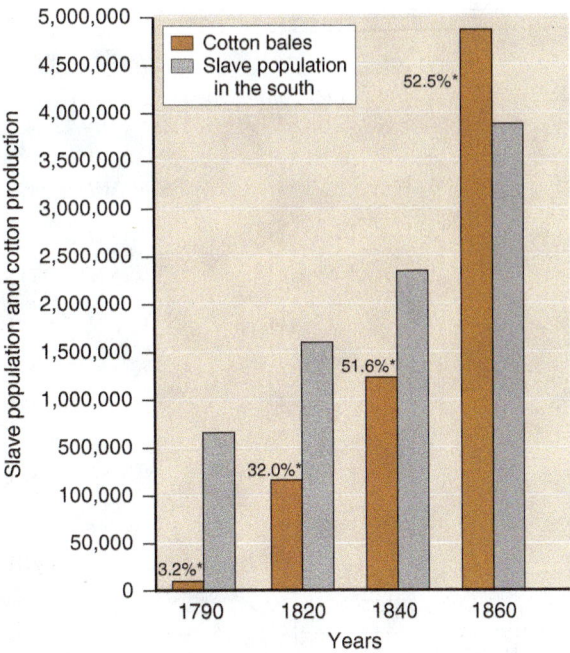

*Cotton as percentage of U.S. exports

FIGURE 7.1 Slave Population and Cotton Production, 1790–1860
This chart shows why the term "King Cotton" came into use, as it became the nation's most important export.

born in Missouri be freed at age twenty-five; the second that no new slaves be brought into the state. Both passed the House of Representatives, where free African Americans in the gallery listened with approval, but were defeated in the Senate, where northern and southern states had an even number of seats. The economic necessity and moral uncertainty of slavery was clearly a political flashpoint, preoccupying political leaders and adding fuel to regional conflicts that had been simmering for years.

By March 1820, Congress had hammered out a compromise. It admitted Maine, until now an adjunct of Massachusetts, as a free state to counterbalance the admission of Missouri as a slave state, thus maintaining the North–South balance in Senate seats. It also drew an east–west line along Missouri's southern border (lat 36° 30′) that divided the rest of the Louisiana Territory into future slave and free states.

But there was a second issue. The Missouri constitution forbade free black people from entering the new state. Were free black people not at liberty to go where they wished? Were they U.S. citizens, or not? Many northern congressmen argued that Missouri's constitution deprived free black people of constitutional rights, including the right to acquire property and the right to religious freedom. But southern congressmen defended this constitution because, in their view, free black people were *not* U.S. citizens. Southerners pointed out that many northern states denied free black people the rights to vote or hold

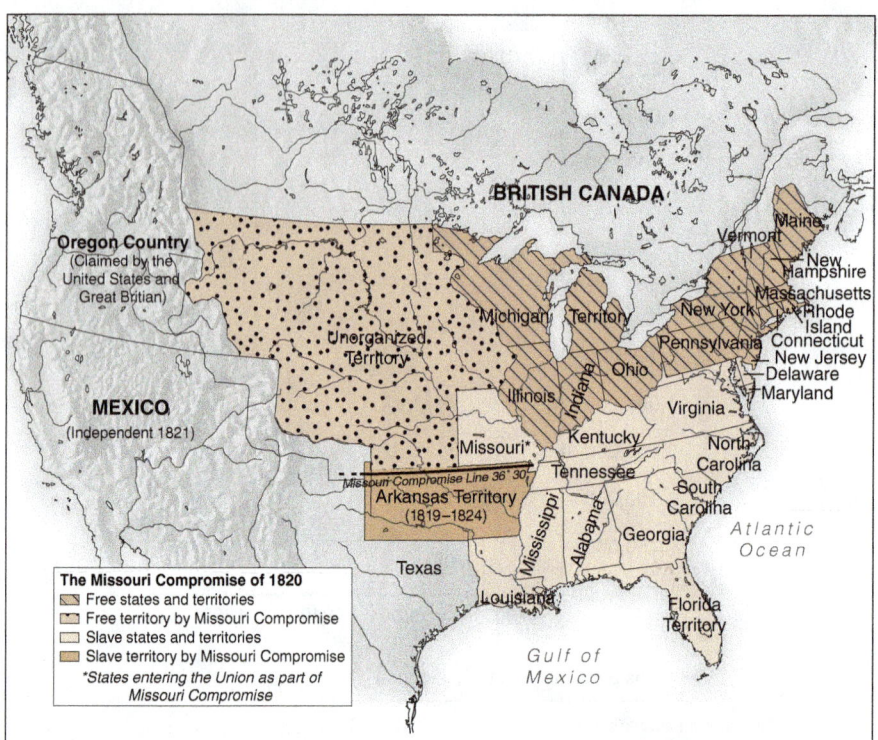

MAP 7.1 The Missouri Compromise of 1820

Most southerners were pleased with the Missouri Compromise because it sanctioned slavery in an area where slave labor was most profitable. Out of the Arkansas Territory below the 36° 30', shown on this map, the new slave state of Arkansas was admitted to the Union.

office, give evidence in court, and serve in the militia. Why should a southern state recognize the citizenship of free black people when northern states, as a Delaware congressman put it, treated African Americans as "a weaker caste" that could not "assimilate" with white Americans any more than "oil with water"?

Bringing the pivotal question of African American citizenship to a head, the debate embarrassed the North and heightened regional animosity. In the end, lawmakers added a vague clause to the Missouri constitution that left the legal status of free African Americans for local, state, and federal courts to decide. Citizenship was not defined. When the Missouri legislature later banned the entry of free black people into the state, Congress remained mute.

The Missouri Compromise temporarily shelved the issues of slavery's expansion and free black people's rights, but these would resurface and spark more violent confrontations between pro- and antislavery Americans.

The Interstate Slave Trade

The expansion of slavery across the South stimulated the interstate slave trade, which boomed between the early 1800s and the Civil War. Large slave trading firms, such as Franklin and Armfield of Virginia and Woolfolk and Slatter of Maryland made huge annual profits. Refitting stables and warehouses into slave pens, they herded bondsmen and bondswomen purchased from owners into the enclosures like cattle. From 1810 to 1860, an average of 15,000 slaves a year made the forced journey by ship or on foot through raw country to the Deep South. An estimated 300,000 Virginia slaves were sold "down the river," many from Alexandria, within view of the nation's capital, to a large depot near Natchez, Mississippi.

This vigorous commerce brought new turmoil and terror for slaves, who now faced the nightmare of being sold south. Human misery swelled in the slave pens and on the auction blocks of a country on the move. "I joined fifty-one other slaves," remembered Charles Ball, "thirty-two of these were men, and nineteen women. . . . A strong iron collar was closely fitted by means of a padlock around each of our necks. . . . We were handcuffed in pairs, with iron staples and bolts, with a short chain, about a foot long, uniting the handcuffs and their wearers in pairs. . . . The poor man to whom I was thus ironed wept like an infant when the blacksmith, with his heavy hammer, fastened the ends of the bolts that kept the staples from slipping from our arms." Such episodes reminded slaves that they were commodities to their masters and to the buyers who inspected and haggled over them, as though they were cattle.

The spread of cotton production south and west shattered slave families and separated kinfolk as never before. Enslaved families had never been secure, but in earlier decades they were usually broken up only on the death of an owner, when they were parceled out among heirs or sold to satisfy debts. Painful though the separation was, families in neighborhoods could maintain some contact. But with the rise of the interstate slave trade, husbands were now sold from wives, and children, especially boys, were torn from parents they never saw again. The records of Franklin and Armfield show that, from 1828 to 1836, three-quarters of all slaves sold south were sold as singles; four-fifths of the women sold with children were shipped off without their husbands; of the single males sold, three-quarters were under age twenty-five, and of these one-third were under seventeen. During the antebellum era, probably one-third of all Upper South young black men and boys were sold south.

Slave Life and Labor

"We were worked in all weather. It was never too hot or too cold; it could never rain, blow hail, or snow too hard for us to work in the field. Work, work, work, was scarcely more the order of the day than of the night." So remembered Frederick Douglass, the most important African American abolitionist and auto-biographer of the antebellum years. "It was—'Fred, come help me to cant this timber here,'" he continued. "'Hurra, Fred! Run and bring me a chisel.' . . . 'Come here!—Go there!—Hold on where you are! Damn you, if you move, I'll knock your brains out!' This was my school."

Douglass's words capture the essence of slave life: the expropriation of labor from all those enslaved—young as well as old, women and children as much as men. While northern free black people struggled for their place *in* the sun, a vastly larger number of slaves struggled *under* the sun in lifelong labor. During the antebellum era, the population of enslaved Americans skyrocketed, mostly through natural increase. About 697,000 in 1790, the number of slaves reached nearly 1.2 million in 1810, more than 2 million in 1830, and 3.2 million in 1850.

Sunup to Sundown: Working for the Master

Slave labor took many forms depending on the region and the crop. Slaves working in the less labor-intensive tobacco- and wheat-growing regions of the Upper South fared better than those in the snake-infested, swampy rice and indigo fields of South Carolina and Georgia. Those who worked in the city enjoyed more advantages than plantation laborers, especially slaves whose masters permitted them to hire themselves out on their own time. Yet plantation labor also varied depending on whether a person worked as a field hand, an artisan, or a domestic servant in the master's house. Men's, women's, and children's work differed markedly as well.

But despite all these differences, three-quarters of all slaves in the South cultivated cotton by the eve of the Civil War. In the cotton fields of Georgia, Alabama, and Mississippi, and even in upcountry Tennessee and Kentucky, slaves endured the harshest possible working conditions. Year-round, they hacked down trees and cleared land. During harvest time, they worked sixteen to eighteen hours a day. At any moment, a man, woman, or child could suffer the lash of the master's whip.

Solomon Northup never forgot the cruel cotton fields. During the hoeing season, "the overseer or driver follows the slaves on horseback with a whip. . . . The lash is flying from morning until night." During picking season, from "day clean to first dark," with just minutes "to swallow [an] allowance of cold bacon," slaves lived in fear that they would not meet their picking quotas. The lash came down hard on those who failed.

In part, the number of slaves living on a plantation shaped their quality of life. Where there were fewer than twenty slaves, most had to labor in the fields. But on the few plantations that had more than twenty slaves, there were more opportunities to work as craftsmen or servants in the big house. Many slaves gladly exchanged the backbreaking repetition of cotton and rice cultivation for the more creative tasks of carpentry, blacksmithing, wagoning, livestock tending, housekeeping, cooking, sewing, and childrearing. The most fortunate slaves had masters who not only trusted them but relied on them to supervise a farm or plantation, carry goods to market by wagon or boat, manage the master's affairs at the marketplace, or oversee other bondspeople's labor.

Slave women's work was sometimes distinct from men's work, but often not. On farms and plantations, as one slave remembered, "women who do outdoor work are used as bad as men." Enslaved women picked cotton, plowed with mule and ox teams, hoed endless rows of corn, dug ditches, spread manure fertilizer, and cut sugarcane. In the evenings, in the slave quarters, they prepared meals for their families, washed and sewed clothes, and cleaned the cabin. Women also worked in groups apart from men, spinning, weaving, and quilting. Elderly women had special responsibilities as nurses, midwives, and caretakers of a slave community's children.

But slavery held distinctive horrors for women. One Virginia slave remembered what thousands of others knew: that an attractive black girl or young woman could be taken into "the big house where the young masters could have the run of her." "Slavery is terrible for men," wrote Harriet Jacobs in *Incidents in the Life of a Slave Girl,* "but it is far more terrible for women." "Superadded to the burden common to all," she explained, "they have wrongs, and sufferings, and mortifications peculiarly their own." In the delicate language of the day, Jacobs tried to convey the frequent sexual abuse white masters inflicted on enslaved women. She revealed that her master, an Edenton, North Carolina, doctor who had fathered eleven children with slave women, began tormenting her as soon as she reached adolescence. "He peopled my young mind with unclean images, such as only a vile monster could think of," she explained. "I turned from him with disgust and hatred. But he was my master. . . . He told me I was his property; that I must be subject to his will in all things." Jacobs was one of the few black women in that household to fend off the master's sexual advances and escape to the North.

In southern cities, where about one-tenth of all slaves and at least one-third of free black people lived, work regimens were more varied than on the plantations, and life was more tolerable. Frederick Douglass believed that "a city slave, in Baltimore, is almost a free citizen compared with a slave on [a] plantation. He is much better fed and clothed, is less dejected in his appearance, and enjoys privileges altogether unknown to the whip-driven slave on the plantation." Slaves in cities also had greater opportunities to gather and exchange news; to participate in races, fairs, and gambling; and to find companionship with fellow African Americans, largely beyond the masters' control, on evenings, Sundays, and holidays.

Nonetheless, urban slaves worked hard: stevedoring on the docks; chopping and hauling wood; digging wells, cellars, and graves; and laboring in construction. In the 1820s, manufacturers began shifting from paid white labor to slave labor, largely to avoid the threat of strikes. In Richmond, for example, the Tredegar Iron Company shifted to slave laborers after an 1847 strike by white ironworkers. Most workers at the city's thirty tobacco-processing plants were slaves, one-third of them children. In Charleston, slaves and free African Americans were more than half the workforce, skilled and unskilled.

Central to a slave's existence, labor was the pivot point of frequent, tense negotiations between master and bondsperson. Though slaves had limited power to negotiate the terms of their lives, they demanded customs governing work hours, holidays, and the right to maintain their own gardens. A master who made no concessions on such customs risked crop sabotage, arson, and poisoning.

This tension also characterized the system of slave hiring common in southern cities. For masters, "leasing" slaves to other white people meant income. Frederick Douglass described the system and its advantages: "After learning to caulk," he wrote, "I sought my own employment, made my own contracts, and collected my own earnings, giving Master Hugh no trouble in any part of the transactions to which I was a party." Self-hiring became so prevalent by the 1840s that brokers and newspaper advertisements began managing arrangements. Long-standing experience, advised one Kentucky broker, "renders us competent of judging and picking good homes and masters for your negroes." Yet self-hiring also had disadvantages. Slaves who leased themselves out were often resented by white laborers, especially in skilled work. Douglass experienced this problem firsthand when he was beaten by a white coworker who, Douglass concluded, "was robbed by the slave system of the just results of his labor because he was flung into competition with a class of laborers who worked without wages."

Urban slaves also frequently came into contact with free African Americans, for every southern city had sizable populations of former slaves who had struggled out of bondage. By the 1830s, in Upper South cities such as Baltimore and Washington, DC, free black people outnumbered slaves. The changing ratio made bondage all the more galling even as it nourished dreams of freedom. But tensions sometimes marred relationships between enslaved and free black people. Some freedmen and women protected their legal advantages by distancing themselves from slaves. For the majority of freed people, who were mulattoes with white fathers, maintaining privileges depended on preserving white relationships.

Regardless of where they worked and what kind of work they did, slaves knew that masters held arbitrary power over most aspects of their lives. Yet the rise of evangelicalism put constraints on masters' exercise of that power. Members of evangelical churches in the South no longer advocated ending slavery, but they did urge masters to treat slaves humanely. Thrown on the defensive, many southern slave masters pointed to their paternalism, conceiving slavery as a system of mutual obligation in which masters housed, fed, and looked after their slaves, who dutifully served their masters in return. "Inspire a negro with perfect confidence in you," wrote one planter, "and learn him to look to you for support & he is your slave." Slave owners also used the idea of Christian stewardship to describe the master–slave relationship. But these concepts of mutual obligation prevailed only in settled regions like Virginia and Maryland. In raw rural states, such as Alabama and Mississippi, masters exercised their arbitrary power without qualms. Moreover, white men's sexual assaults on enslaved women belied all talk of mutual obligation.

Physical, psychological, and legal cruelty held the slave system in place. Whipping was the most common means by which masters battered slaves into compliance. Not every slave was beaten, but all knew that at any moment they *could* be beaten, and all had seen a parent, spouse, or friend subjected to the public bloodying and humiliation that was the mainstay of slave discipline. Crueler masters advocated routine flogging. "The best plan," said one from South Carolina, "would be to give them 25 or 30 lashes a piece every Saturday night anyhow, which will probably keep them straight until Monday morning." The most effective psychological weapon for controlling slaves was the threat of auction. "In Maryland," recounted Charles Ball after he escaped slavery, "it had always been the practice of masters and mistresses, who wished to terrify their slaves, to threaten to sell them to South Carolina." Every slave knew that a change in the master's moods or fortunes could mean instant—and permanent—separation from family.

In addition to the inherent cruelty of slavery, the close daily interactions of white and black people powerfully influenced the master–slave relationship. This was especially true for southern farmers with fewer than five slaves. Struggling to make a decent living, they shared their housing and meager diet of cornmeal, rice, peas, and salt pork with their slaves. On the new cotton frontiers, master and slave, side by side, put broadax and saw to timber, built log houses, slept on dirt floors, trapped and hunted, and hacked a new life out of the wilderness. But the fruits of this labor fell almost entirely into the master's hands. The "casual intimacies that had sustained them in the leaner times," one historian writes, gave way to separate slave cabins and an impressive house inhabited by only the master and his family.

Yet no matter how vast the social and psychological distance between slave and master, cultural exchange continued. The food on planters' tables blended African and European cuisines. Agricultural techniques reflected mutual knowledge of farming. Herbs and healing remedies used by black women, such as for rattlesnake bites, found their way into the world of white people. Trust and distrust, intimacy and hostility, tenderness and antagonism—these paradoxes marked the master–slave relationship. At one extreme, such relations could be cordial or even affectionate. At the other extreme, they could explode into raw hatred, violence, and murder.

Sundown to Sunup: Slaves on Their Own Time

When Frederick Douglass was just thirteen, longing "in my loneliness and destitution" for "a father and a protector," a Methodist minister "was the means of causing me to feel that in God I had such a friend." "Though I was a poor, broken-hearted mourner traveling through doubts and fears," Douglass continued, "I finally found my burden lightened, and my heart relieved. . . . I saw the world in a new light." Douglass's words affirm that the life of a slave was much more than endless travail. Though bondspeople might toil all day, they nourished their souls and maintained their dignity, creating "room for the human spirit to live." They took pleasure, as one historian explains, in "something good to eat, a splash of color to wear, the joy in one's body, the delight of dance and music, the ability to find love in another and to create space in which the personal self could exist and breathe." In this personal space, family and religion provided an indispensable sense of meaning, purpose, and joy.

In the face of huge obstacles, slave men and women made marriage commitments, brought children into the world, raised them as best they could, and maintained family connections. Men hired out or sold away from the plantation maintained "abroad" marriages, walking long distances to be with their families on holidays. Slaves authorized to travel delivered messages that kept family and friendship ties alive. In naming children, parents remembered parents and grandparents, brothers and sisters, aunts and uncles. Children sold away from parents were welcomed into new families, though no bloodline existed—gaining fictive aunts and uncles in the process.

The effort to stay in touch with family and friends was extraordinary. Lucy Tucker, born in Virginia and sold into Alabama, managed to send a letter to her mother after a separation of more than ten years. "I received a letter some year or two after I came to this country. . . . My son Burrel . . . has been absent from me nine years. He is now grown, but I have not seen him since he was a boy though I hear from him now and then."

Most slave women became mothers. Masters encouraged childbearing, whether a slave woman was married or not, because each birth constituted a capital gain. Records show that enslaved women typically had their first child at age nineteen, about two years before white women did. Most gave birth to an additional four or five babies. For slave mothers, childbearing provided emotional sustenance. "When I was most sorely oppressed," Harriet Jacobs wrote of her son, "I found solace in his smiles. I loved to watch his infant slumbers; but . . . I could never forget that he was a slave. Sometimes I wished that he might die in infancy." Despite such moments of sadness, raising a family reaffirmed slave women's life force and creative power, giving them a measure of satisfaction in a world of cruelty.

Enslaved black children's lives differed sharply from those of white youngsters. The passing down of property from parent to offspring, so vital to white families, was irrelevant for people who were themselves property. Slave parents had to raise their children under very different circumstances. At age seven or eight, typical childhood games of running and hiding and rhythm and rhyme gave way to carrying wood and water, cleaning cabins, tending gardens, and helping in the kitchen. At this early age, African American youngsters also had to learn how to survive in a white-run world. Mastering the rules governing black–white encounters counted among life's most crucial lessons. Every slave parent knew their children would soon see loved ones whipped, humiliated, maimed, killed, or sold away. Children had to be prepared for this cruel world or they could not survive it.

Survival also meant knowing how to manage white people—how to play on their vanity, feign ignorance, or talk their way out of punishment. These practices became ingrained as enslaved girls and boys grew to young adulthood. Over and over in slave cabins, children heard stories about how to outwit masters or cruel overseers. Often these stories were animal tales, such as the one featuring the trickster Brer Rabbit, who outmaneuvered his stronger foes. Meant to educate and inspire, trickster tales taught important lessons about how to survive.

Next to family, slaves found their greatest support and solace in spirituality. Afro-Christianity took many forms and expressions. In rural areas, where most slaves lived, churches and trained black ministers were rare, so slaves gathered in a forest clearing, a slave cabin, or even a cornfield to sing, pray, and worship. In the antebellum era, more and more masters instructed their slaves in Christianity, hoping to ensure compliance.

But slaves did not necessarily practice the religion their owners taught them. Many adapted Christianity to African spiritual ways that had survived passage across the Atlantic. Throughout the South, slaves believed in the supernatural, especially ghosts ("haunts")—spirits of the dead who returned to make trouble for the living. Many plantations had slave conjurors, revered for their ability to cast spells on enemies and ward off evil spirits.

Slaves and masters viewed bondage through different religious lenses. White masters used Christian teachings to encourage slaves to accept their lot. They drew from the Gospel of Matthew, in which the Sermon on the Mount promises heavenly rewards for obedience. They also emphasized Genesis, in which God makes a contract to protect the heirs of the slaveholding Abraham. African Americans, in contrast, identified with the Old Testament story of Exodus, in which Moses leads the Chosen People out of bondage in Egypt. They also identified with young David, who overcame the giant Goliath, and they longed for the new world order promised in Revelations.

As a slave in Arkansas observed after hearing a white preacher: "All he say is 'bedience to de white folks, and we hears 'nough of dat without him telling us." Most slaves believed "God never made us to be slaves for white people," as a domestic servant told her mistress. In fact, no Christian idea had more resonance for slaves than divine justice. Charles Ball, for example, believed that in the Kingdom of Heaven "all distinctions of colour, and of condition, will be abolished" and that "Heaven will be no heaven" unless "those who have tormented [slaves] here will most surely be tormented in their turn hereafter."

In southern cities, where a minority of slaves but a majority of free African Americans lived, African Baptist and African Methodist churches grew rapidly,

In this painting of an African American burial in a clearing of a Louisiana cypress forest, the black preacher, wearing a coat, conducts the service. An overseer and his horse stand at the left; white owners of the slaves watch from the right, suggesting a paternalistic plantation owner.

attracting the bondspeople living in the area. Though many urban black people maintained some West African religious practices, they tended to adopt evangelical Christianity more fully than slaves living on plantations did. In the early nineteenth century, the frequent naming of slave children after Old Testament figures—for example, Abraham and Isaac for men, Hagar and Sarah for women—reflected the spread of evangelical Christianity.

In almost all church congregations, women outnumbered men, often two to one. Male preachers played key roles in black communities. Andrew Marshall, for example, who ministered the First African Baptist Church in Savannah for more than three decades, was invited to preach in white Baptist churches and even addressed the Georgia legislature. Founding schools and mutual aid societies, he built a congregation of nearly 2,500 free black people and slaves by the mid-1830s. Like other black ministers, he had to strike a delicate balance, remembering that white people regarded church-organized education and religion as potentially subversive, while simultaneously inspiring his congregants.

Sometimes black religious and secular agendas overlapped. In one example, slaves used songs about gaining freedom in the next world to urge seizing freedom in this world. Music, like spirituality, provided crucial sustenance. Though "the songs of the slave," Douglass explained, "represent the sorrows of his heart," music also expressed faith in deliverance and triumph. The mournful tone of "Nobody knows the trouble I've seen" was balanced by a refrain about berries "sweet as de honey in de comb." The song that began

In this painting of a slave wedding in White Sulphur Springs, Virginia, in 1838, a black fiddler and a bone player provide the music for the festive nuptials of the resort's well-dressed domestic slaves.

Source: North Carolina Museum of Art.

with "Sometimes I feel like a motherless chile" ended with "Sometimes I feel like a eagle in de air, gonna spread my wings an' fly."

Spontaneity characterized slave music. Using animal hides and gourds to fashion drums and banjoes, slaves improvised tunes and created dances. They did the cakewalk or Charleston, or dances like the buzzard lope that featured moves by animals. An English musician traveling through Mississippi in the 1830s marveled at how Vicksburg slaves changed the tempo of a "fine old Psalm tune" into "a kind of negro melody." "Us old heads," a former slave explained about how to create song, "use ter make 'em up on de spurn of de moment. . . . We'd all be at the 'prayer house' de Lord's day, and de white preacher he'd splain de word and read whar Ezekial done say. . . . And, honey, de Lord would come a'shinin' thoo dem pages and revive dis ole nigger's heart, and I'd jump up dar and den and holler and shout and sing and pat, and dey would all cotch de words and I'd sing it to some ole shout song I'd heard 'em sing from Africa, and dey'd all take it up and keep at it, and keep a'addin' to it, and den it would be a spiritual."

Resistance and Rebellion

In 1822, a Charleston slave recalled a pivotal event from that year: "Denmark read at the [church] meeting different chapters from the Old Testament" and spoke of Moses' admonition that whoever steals a man "shall be put to death." White authorities later conceded that Denmark Vesey, a free black carpenter, had indeed mastered the books of the Old Testament and could "readily quote them to prove that slavery was contrary to the laws of God." Here was tangible evidence of a major new development: Black churches had become seedbeds of resistance to slavery as well as houses of spiritual solace.

During the 1820s, free and enslaved African Americans found a call to arms in religion. During this volatile decade, reformers across the nation, often inspired by the evangelicalism of the Second Great Awakening, launched a dizzying array of crusades—for temperance, free public education, and asylums for the poor. All these efforts interested African Americans, but crusades for the abolition of slavery drew their deepest commitment.

Denmark Vesey's Rebellion

Historian Vincent Harding called black Christianity a "liberation theology," one that furnished a biblical and theological justification for challenging slavery and race-based discrimination. This notion became apparent in Charleston, where black Methodists greatly outnumbered white Methodists. Here free and enslaved African Americans who had attended the white Methodist church began, by 1815, to act independently—controlling their own Sunday collections, disciplining errant members, and holding separate black conferences.

Suspecting that even a small congregation of slaves meant trouble, slave owners found this independence alarming. White religious leaders tried to curb black ministers' autonomy and restrict their conduct of services. Black Methodists responded by launching a secession movement in 1817. Led by Morris Brown, a shoemaker and minister who went to Philadelphia to meet with Richard Allen in 1816, more than 4,300 black worshipers, enslaved and free, resigned from the old Methodist church. They soon formed the new African Methodist Episcopal Church in Charleston's Hampstead district.

The leaders of this movement included a brooding free black man named Denmark Vesey. At age twenty-two, he had won $1,500 at a lottery and purchased his freedom from his ship-captain master. He was familiar with slavery in the West Indies and had witnessed the black rebellion in Haiti. Literate in French, Spanish, and English, the tall, bearded Vesey became a respected carpenter, one of the wealthiest black men in Charleston, and a leader at the Methodist church.

Following the black secession from the white Methodist church, Vesey's tolerance for racial abuse wore thin while his anger mounted. He must have fumed in 1818 when white authorities raided the black church, jailed 143 free black and slave worshipers, sentenced Brown and four other church leaders to a month's imprisonment, and ordered others to pay heavy fines or receive ten lashes each. Their crime was educating slaves and holding what white authorities saw as disorderly after-dark religious meetings. Vesey certainly bristled at new South Carolina laws in 1820 that defined teaching slaves to read or write as a crime. These laws also prohibited manumission, forbade free African Americans from entering South Carolina once they left the state, and slapped stiff special taxes on free black householders such as Vesey. This harsh treatment culminated in 1821, when white authorities shut down the AME Church altogether.

Anger turned to resolve. Vesey convinced his most trusted friends that the time was approaching when the deliverance of the children of Israel from Egyptian bondage—a story told many times among black Americans—would play out in the American South. In Charleston and the surrounding areas, Vesey and his comrades preached redemption and divine justice: "Behold the day of the Lord cometh . . . and the city shall be taken . . . and they utterly destroyed all that was in the city, both man and woman, young and old, and ox and sheep, and ass, with the edge of the sword." These Old Testament stories of deliverance inspired listeners, who connected them with the African cultural practices kept alive by "Gullah Jack" Pritchard, a Vesey lieutenant and conjuror well known among Charleston slaves.

In 1822, Vesey and his supporters developed a plan for capturing Charleston and conquering the nearby countryside. Testimony obtained after his capture suggests that he aimed to set fire to the town, seize the armory, overpower white resistance, and perhaps flee by ship to Haiti. The day chosen for the uprising was July 14, the day African Americans in Massachusetts celebrated their emancipation and French republicans celebrated the fall of the Bastille. Further, with many white people out of the city on summer retreats, its 12,000 slaves and some 3,600 free black people would outnumber white people nearly two to one. Most important, on July 14, the moon would be dark, allowing armed slaves from nearby plantations to enter Charleston unseen.

But as Vesey recruited supporters, the risk of betrayal increased. In May risk became reality, as the plan was leaked to white authorities. Rounding up suspects, officials began holding trials. In the end, thirty rebels were executed; all but Vesey were slaves. Thirty-seven others, including Brown, were condemned to die but were pardoned and transported out of state. Later, a letter found in the trunk of one slave who was executed revealed the plot's biblical inspiration: "Fear not, the Lord God that delivered Daniel is able to deliver us."

White authorities considered black rebellion suicidal. After all, white people had managed to suppress black revolts—from the Stono Rebellion of 1739 to Gabriel's conspiracy of 1800—and execute the rebels. Nor could white people understand why well-to-do free black people as well as slaves who belonged to "the most humane and indulgent owners" would conduct vicious assaults on Charleston. "It is difficult to imagine what *infatuation* could have prompted you to attempt an enterprise so wild and visionary," lectured the judge who sentenced Vesey to death. "You were a free man; were comparatively wealthy; and enjoyed every comfort, compatible with your situation. You had therefore, much to risk and little to gain. From your age and experience you *ought* to have known, that success was impracticable." Vesey remained silent, apparently seeing no need to explain why freedom did not mean turning one's back on those still enslaved.

As with earlier slave conspiracies, South Carolina's authorities cracked down on African Americans after suppressing Vesey's Rebellion. Charleston's city council stiffened patrol regulations. The legislature prohibited black crew members whose ships arrived in port from coming ashore. It also criminalized efforts to teach even free black people to sign their names and forbade slaves from hiring themselves out. Even more hurtful, authorities razed the African Church in Hampstead—the heart of black religious, social, and political life. Until the end of the Civil War, black worshipers had to conduct prayer meetings and services secretly. But in 1865, Denmark Vesey's youngest son rebuilt the church.

David Walker's *Appeal*

A thousand miles north of Charleston, another free black man insisted that the fates of enslaved and free African Americans were entwined. "They think that we do not feel for our brethren, whom they are murdering by the inches, but they are dreadfully deceived," said David Walker. Born free around 1795 in North Carolina, Walker had a white mother and enslaved black father. He traveled to Charleston in 1822, just before Vesey plotted his rebellion, but headed north. What he saw and heard along the way fortified his hatred of slavery and his anger at a republic that did not live up to its founding principles. Like other African Americans, he knew about the national tumult over the Missouri Compromise. The idea of slavery spreading across the continent further disheartened him.

Reaching Boston in 1825, Walker became a used clothing dealer, a worshiper at the black Methodist church, and an agent for the country's first black newspaper, *Freedom's Journal*. There in the shadow of Bunker Hill, where an early battle for American independence had raged, he penned one of the nineteenth century's most provocative and prophetic essays. In his *Appeal to the*

Coloured Citizens of the World, published in 1829, Walker challenged free African Americans to see themselves as part of a worldwide movement for freedom. "Your full glory and happiness," he advised, "shall never be fully consummated, but with the *entire emancipation of your enslaved brethren all over the world.* . . . There is great work for you to do" (italics in original).

Like Denmark Vesey, Walker regarded armed struggle as divinely sanctioned. The God he knew from the Bible hated injustice and oppression of the weak. To resist slavery violently demonstrated obedience to God: "The man who would not fight . . . in the glorious and heavenly cause of freedom and of God . . . ought to be kept with all of his children or family, in slavery, or in chains, to be butchered by his cruel enemies." Knowing the reprisals that followed black rebellion, Walker urged, "If you commence, make sure work—do not trifle, for they will not trifle with you—they want us for their slaves, and think nothing of murdering us in order to subject us to that wretched condition—therefore, . . . kill or be killed."

Walker also intended his *Appeal* to reach the consciences of white Americans and to demolish support for the gradualist approach, which assumed moral suasion would prompt slave owners to release their slaves. Walker also condemned the unprovoked white attacks on free black neighborhoods in Providence, Rhode Island, in 1825; in Boston in 1826; and in Cincinnati in 1829—the first wave of race-based riots in the nation. "Did not God make us all as it seemed best to himself," he asked. "What right, then, has one of us to despise another and to treat him cruel on account of his colour . . . ? Can there be a greater absurdity in nature, and particularly in a free republican country?" "I tell you Americans!" Walker warned, "that unless you speedily alter your course, *you* and your *Country are gone*!!!! For God Almighty will tear up the very face of the earth!!!!"

Grounded in Scripture, Walker's messianic advocacy of armed black resistance had never before appeared in print. White northerners who believed fervently in God and preached the glory of America's republicanism found Walker's words shocking. Black northerners found them inspiring. Christians were hypocrites, Walker insisted, when they condemned intemperance, infidelity, and even Sunday mail deliveries while shutting their eyes to slavery and confining black Christians to "nigger pews." Mocking Jefferson's belief that black people were born mentally inferior, Walker said white people were born *morally* inferior but, led by black Americans, could enter heaven by cleansing themselves of the national sin of slavery.

Appeal to the Coloured Citizens of the World affected Boston exactly as Walker had hoped. "It is evident," an evening newspaper reported, that African Americans "have read this pamphlet, nay, we know that the larger portion of them have read it, or heard it read, and that they glory in its principles, as if it were a star in the east, guiding them to freedom and emancipation." To white southerners, the *Appeal* was printed poison. Authorities tried but failed to suppress it. Some black mariners who sailed out of Boston for southern ports sewed copies inside their trousers for safekeeping. "Why do the Slave-holders or Tyrants of America and their advocates fight so hard to keep my brethren from receiving and reading my Book of Appeal to them?" asked Walker in a third edition of his treatise. "Perhaps . . . for fear they will find in it an extract which I made from their Declaration of Independence, which says, 'we hold these truths to be self-evident, that all men are created equal.'"

In July 1830, a few months after the *Appeal* was published, Walker died in Boston, probably of consumption. He was just thirty-three years old. Knowing that Georgians had put a price on his head and that friends had urged him to flee to Canada, many Bostonians believed that he had been poisoned. "I will stand my ground," he had replied to those begging him to go into hiding. *"Somebody must die in this cause."*

Five months later another Bostonian stepped forward to demand an immediate end to slavery. Twenty-six years old, William Lloyd Garrison had joined the cause in Baltimore, where he had worked with Benjamin Lundy, the Quaker publisher of the radical newspaper *Genius of Universal Emancipation,* which exposed the abominable internal slave traffic. Back in Boston, Garrison launched *The Liberator.* Its first issue hit the streets on January 1, 1831, after James Forten loaned Garrison start-up money. In the premier issue, the fiery editor promised to be "as harsh as truth, and as uncompromising as justice. On this subject [of slavery], I do not wish to think, or speak, or write, with moderation. . . . No! No! Tell a man whose house is on fire to give a moderate alarm . . . but urge me not to use moderation in a cause like the present."

Nat Turner's Insurrection

A few months after the first issue of *The Liberator* appeared, a slave in Southampton County, Virginia, witnessed an eclipse of the sun and decided that God had called him to lead a rebellion. Nat Turner may have known that slavery was collapsing in other parts of the world. Newspapers reported its abolition in the new Central and South American republics that had wrested independence from Spain. They also reported that Parliament was debating the emancipation of the millions of slaves in Britain's West Indian colonies. A Bible-conscious man and local Baptist lay preacher to fellow slaves, Turner felt certain that an avenging God would punish white oppressors and bring divine judgment to the American republic.

In his youth, Turner had taught himself to read. For years he had searched the Bible for divine inspiration. Around 1830, he had apocalyptic visions of Christ crucified against a night sky and found what he believed was Christ's blood in a cornfield the following morning. "While labouring in the field, I discovered drops of blood on the corn as though it were dew from heaven," he recounted later. Gathering a trusted group of slaves around him, Turner revealed his vision that the day of judgment was near. God had commanded him to take up the sword.

Turner first chose the Fourth of July, 1831, to launch his uprising, but postponed the date after taking ill. When an atmospheric condition caused the sun to appear bluish green, he and his followers agreed the time was near. Just before dawn on August 22, Turner put his religious mission into action. According to black oral tradition, he told his followers, "Remember, we do not go forth for the sake of blood and carnage; but it is necessary that, in the commencement of this revolution, all the whites we meet should die, until we have an army strong enough to carry out the war on a Christian basis. Remember that ours is not a war for robbery, nor to satisfy our passions; it is a *struggle for freedom*" (italics in original).

Sixty avenging slaves struck down Turner's master and his family. Then they marched toward the small town of Jerusalem, where they hoped to seize a cache of arms. Storming every house in their path, they slaughtered fifty-five men, women, and children with axes and clubs. Part prophet, part general, Turner soon came upon white militia groups who rushed to the scene as the chilling word of black rebellion spread. Heavily outgunned, the rebels scattered. Most were hunted down, captured, or killed in the woods. By the next day, only Turner and three companions remained at large. Eluding a massive manhunt, Turner was not captured until October 30. He went to the gallows a month later, the last of eighteen slaves executed. Black insurrection had again failed.

But Turner failed only in an immediate sense. Before his death he related his "confessions" to a white slave-owning lawyer. Widely circulated as a pamphlet, *The Confessions of Nat Turner* stunned white southerners. Once regarding him as a crazed fanatic, they now found him highly articulate and rational, a man who felt no guilt for pursuing the retributive justice of a Christian God. "Do you not find yourself mistaken now?" asked the white lawyer in Turner's jail cell where he was shackled. "Was not Christ crucified?" replied Turner. Like David Walker and Denmark Vesey, Turner had embraced Christianity and then used it to challenge white America's Christian conduct. Claiming himself a messenger of God, he warned Americans that slavery would destroy their empire of liberty. Slave owners who read Turner's *Confessions* saw that kindness was no protection; Turner himself had a "kind master." Though in no mood to appreciate Turner's messianic message, white southerners feared "that the same bloody deed could be acted out at any time in any place, that the materials for it were spread through the land and always ready for a like explosion." After the carnage, one Virginia legislator suspected there was "a Nat Turner . . . in every family."

Thus Virginia's legislature debated abolishing slavery, but when motions for ending it failed, punishing reprisals were passed instead. To prevent black slaves from hearing the radical message of literate black preachers, enslaved and free African Americans were forbidden to spread the Christian word. Other mandates prohibited the teaching of slaves to read and forbade them to assemble in groups of more than two or three.

Yet beyond the reach of law was memory. A new generation of black leaders knew of Turner. Growing up free in Pittsburgh, Martin Delany drew inspiration from him. Harriet Tubman, a Maryland slave, asked herself how she might continue his legacy. In 1833, white men broke up the black Sunday school class that the eighteen-year-old slave Frederick Douglass was organizing. If he "wanted to be another Nat Turner," they warned, he would suffer Turner's fate. In every place where slaves toiled, Turner's visionary quest for liberation lived on.

HORRID MASSACRE IN VIRGINIA.

Abolitionists tried to use Turner's Rebellion to tell southerners what they could expect if they did not end slavery. In this sketch, Turner attacks a white mother and her children (#1); other slaves attack Turner's master (#2); Captain John T. Barrow, a militia captain, defends himself while his wife and child retreat (#3); and the uniformed militia track down the rebels (#4).

Free Black Organizing

"Ought we not to form ourselves into a general body, to protect, aid, and assist each other to the utmost of our power?" asked David Walker four years before Nat Turner's insurrection. Black leaders in the northern cities knew they faced an urgent task in coordinating resistance to colonization, the expansion of slavery, and discriminatory treatment and laws. In their view, organizing nationally offered the best hope of achieving these goals. By the late 1820s, an urban-based network of educated and accomplished black leaders had taken steps to unite black leaders across the nation so all could speak with one voice.

The printed word became a powerful tool in this effort. The first black newspaper, *Freedom's Journal,* was printed in New York City in 1827. Edited by Samuel Cornish, a black Presbyterian minister, and John Russwurm, a recent graduate of Bowdoin College, the publication attacked the American Colonization Society (ACS). It attracted writers and subscribers from all over the North, the Upper South, and the Midwest, including James Forten and Richard Allen from Philadelphia, and David Walker from Boston. The journal became a clearinghouse for black people's exchange of news about the founding of new churches, schools, Masonic lodges, and mutual aid societies. Most important, it served as a forum for discussing the major problems facing African Americans. After Russwurm began promoting emigration and took a post in the new country of Liberia on Africa's west coast, founded by the ACS, *Freedom's Journal* stopped publication. But it was soon replaced by *Rights for All* and later by other newspapers. Clearly, African Americans could now count on a vigorous press aimed at solidifying black opinion while tying communities together in a national network.

As black leaders stepped up organizing efforts, they envisioned a national meeting of free African Americans. In 1829, a vicious attack by white people on black neighborhoods in Cincinnati accelerated plans for the national gathering. Meeting in Philadelphia in 1830, delegates from Pennsylvania, New York, Delaware, Maryland, and Virginia formed the American Society of Free People of Colour. They shared ideas and strategies for fending off white violence, for building educational and vocational institutions, for nurturing moral uplift and self-reliance, and—most essential—for confronting slavery. Seventy-year-old Richard Allen held forth as the patriarch of the 1830 gathering. Drawing on a lifetime of experience as the founder and leader of the AME Church, Allen worried about the personal and regional tensions he observed among African Americans. But he recognized that disputes and competing agendas signaled the coming of age of a new generation. Dozens of black communities were blossoming, he noted, each with its own experiences, accomplishments, problems, and leaders.

Under Allen's leadership, the delegates decried the repatriation of free black Americans to Africa but endorsed emigration to Canada. African Americans, they reasoned, shared a common language with the Canadians, and British authorities in Canada had promised "all the rights, privileges and immunities of other citizens"—exactly what African Americans sought but could not acquire in the United States. Encouraged, many free African Americans began immigrating to Ontario, where they formed new communities.

By the time black delegates arrived in Philadelphia for a second convention in 1831, slaveholders had a strong grip on the nation's economy and political system. Congress routinely rejected antislavery petitions. White southerners advocated seizing Mexican Texas—where lawmakers had abolished slavery—and adding it to the American republic as a slave state. Andrew Jackson was the fifth slaveholder president of seven, and his vice president, John C. Calhoun, was crafting doctrines that recognized state legislatures' right to void federal laws believed adverse to a state's vital interests.

In 1828, matters had come to a head with a new tariff that imposed heavier duties on manufactured goods imported from abroad. Southerners called this the Tariff of Abominations, believing that it enhanced the North's economic power and hurt their own ability to export slave-produced tobacco and cotton. Animosity between northern and southern congressmen escalated into a fiery debate in the summer of 1830. Calhoun's doctrine that states could nullify national action only intensified the conflict, as everyone knew Calhoun had more than tariffs in mind. The doctrine sent the ominous signal that if the national government ever tampered with slavery, southern states could act to protect slavery.

Amid these gathering storm clouds, black leaders accused the American Colonization Society of "pursuing the direct road to perpetuate slavery." Leading African Americans recalled that "many of our fathers, and some of us, have fought and bled for the liberty, independence, and peace which you now enjoy and, surely, it would be ungenerous and unfeeling in you to deny us a humble and quiet grave in that country which gave us birth!"

Members of the American Society of the Free People of Colour sensed that worldwide sentiment was turning sharply against slavery. Delegates to its convention pointed to Denmark's recent abolition of slavery in its West Indies colonies and Britain's plans for a general emancipation in its Caribbean colonies. Encouraged, they called for the removal of the foul "stain upon . . . this great Republic." For many years, the Society met annually to debate strategies for reforming the North and ending slavery in the South.

Conclusion

As the delegates of the American Society of Free People of Colour left Philadelphia in 1831, they knew the generation that had come of age in the republic's early years—most of them born into slavery—was passing on. Many of the founding black ministers were dead or frail, including New York's Peter Williams, Philadelphia's Absalom Jones and Richard Allen, Wilmington's Peter Spencer, and Charleston's Morris Brown. Of the three great secular leaders—Prince Hall in Boston, Paul Cuffe in New Bedford, and James Forten in Philadelphia—the first two had died and the third struggled with ill health. The three great rebels—Gabriel, Denmark Vesey, and Nat Turner—had all been executed. The mightiest pen of the era, held by David Walker, would write no more.

But in many ways, these leaders had already passed the torch to the free black men and women spread across the expanding nation. These African Americans—many born into freedom—were better educated and connected than the previous generation, thanks to the printed word and national networks. These advantages enabled them to resist the ACS's back-to-Africa movement.

As free black communities proliferated during this era, slavery also expanded—as measured by the number of bondspeople and the number of states and territories whose economies depended on slavery. Earlier hopes that slaveholding would wither away with the halt of the slave trade faded. In fact, as cotton slavery spread throughout the Lower South and west into Texas, white slave owners subjected their human chattel to more brutal treatment than before. At the same time, free African Americans were finding white abolitionist allies who yearned to end slavery. This development heightened tensions between northerners and southerners. The work of dismantling slavery and discrimination now lay in the hands of a new generation of black leaders who faced mounting challenges in an increasingly divided nation.

Questions for Review and Reflection

1. Was W. E. B. DuBois correct in saying that the independent black church was "the alpha and omega" of African American life? Do you see the black church as a progressive institution?

2. By what means did the rapidly growing enslaved Americans cope with and survive life in bondage? What do you find admirable about the antebellum slave that should make him or her worthy of studying today?

3. Some say that Nat Turner and Denmark Vesey should be honored in the nation's capitol today? Is there merit in this position?

4. In the struggle against slavery in the antebellum era, how important was it for black Americans to become literate? Of what importance was the advent of black newspapers?

CHAPTER 8

African Americans in the Reform Era, 1831–1850

James Forten Advocates an Immediate End to Slavery

"The spirit of freedom is marching with rapid strides, and causing tyrants to tremble," wrote James Forten in December 1830 to his friend, fellow abolitionist William Lloyd Garrison. Forten, a free black Philadelphian, was among many reformers exhorting Americans to renew their religious faith and moral leadership. Such efforts, these reformers felt, were necessary to topple the slave regime and end racial hostility.

Like many abolitionists during this era of reform, Forten believed the movement required new goals and strategies. Northern states had all but eradicated slavery. However, a half-century of abolitionist efforts had yielded scant returns in the South, where the slave population was continually expanding. Moreover, the growing number of free African Americans, mostly in northern cities, faced increasing oppression. "That we are not treated as freemen, in any part of the United States, is certain," Forten wrote to Garrison. "This usage . . . is in direct opposition to the Constitution; which positively declares that all men are born equal and endowed with certain inalienable rights."

Although some African Americans over the years promoted colonization in Africa as the only chance for black people to find freedom, Forten opposed this strategy. In the mid-1820s, he had considered a plan to help free black people resettle in the black republic of Haiti. But Forten—whose children counted among the first generation of African Americans born after the American slave

Chronology

1831	William Lloyd Garrison establishes *The Liberator.*
1832	New England Anti-Slavery Society forms in Boston. Maria Miller Stewart's public lecture is the first published speech by an American woman. Philadelphia experiences the first in a series of race riots. Florida's Seminole Indians and black comrades begin resettling west of the Mississippi.
1833	Abolitionists establish the American Anti-Slavery Society.
1836	Gag Rule allows U.S. Congress to ignore antislavery petitions. Americans in Texas secede from Mexico to declare an independent republic.
1837	*The Colored American* publishes Lewis Woodson's blueprint for progress.
1838	Philadelphia mob destroys abolitionists' Pennsylvania Hall.
1839	Antislavery groups organize the Liberty Party.
1840	White abolitionist James G. Birney runs for president.
1842	Second Seminole War erupts in Florida. *Prigg* v. *Pennsylvania* rules state officials are not required to capture fugitive slaves. Second Seminole War ends.
1843	Martin Delany begins publishing *The Mystery.*
1844	In a second presidential campaign, Birney receives 60,000 votes.
1845	United States annexes Texas, including more than 50,000 slaves.
1846	Mexican-American War erupts. Wilmot's Proviso that slavery be prohibited in territory acquired from Mexico is defeated.
1847	Frederick Douglass, Martin Delany, and William C. Nell establish *The North Star.*
1848	Mexico cedes a large expanse of territory to the United States. Gold is discovered in California. Frederick Douglass speaks at the Women's Rights Convention at Seneca Falls, New York.
1850	In the Compromise of 1850, Congress admits California to the Union as a free state, allows slavery in other parts of the Southwest, outlaws the slave trade in the District of Columbia, and tightens fugitive slave laws.

trade ended in 1808—soon realized he was American to the core. "To separate the blacks from the whites is as impossible as to bale out the Delaware [River] with a bucket," he wrote Garrison. He would remain in America, Forten assured Garrison, and struggle in the country where his family had toiled for more than a century.

As Garrison prepared to publish the first issue of a radical newspaper entitled *The Liberator* on January 1, 1831, Forten purchased subscriptions for

Garrison's *Liberator* Dreams America's Future?

In the Spring of 1831, Garrison's *Liberator* published an editorial that was labeled "a dream." In the dream, a fictional character identified only as "T.T." envisioned a future in which Americans had "completely united into one people . . . [with] as little thought of separate interests and feelings between blacks and whites, as between tall and short, or dark eyes and blue, or between men and women." The "dream" editorial described an elegant reception where a crowd awaited the introduction of the newly elected president.

T. T. was fascinated by the composition of the guest list: "nearly half the company were of the negro race, and blacks and whites were mingling with perfect ease in social intercourse." T. T. was even more surprised when the president-elect who arrived was himself African American. Tall, urbane—a product of "a national character improved by the union of the two races"—T. T.'s imagined brown-skinned president was now the chosen leader of "whites who had gained a certain ease and dignity" from their "intercourse with the milder [black] race." T. T.'s dream, shaped in a world of ever deeply entrenched slavery and racial hostility, nevertheless, foretold an audaciously hopeful future.

Published just as Nat Turner was shaping his slave rebellion in Virginia, T.T.'s optimistic dream was printed alongside a more ominous version of the dream. In this alternative version slave insurrectionists, aided by Cherokee rebels and northern free black people had turned the tables on white Americans, forcing them to work "incessantly in the broiling sun."

Toiling away at his Boston printing press, publisher William Lloyd Garrison seems to almost have seen that nearly eighteen decades later, after publishing a treatise titled *The Audacity of Hope,* a tall, urbane, African American president-elect named Barack Obama would *in reality* host that reception described T. T.'s dream. However, the alternative version of T. T.'s dream would be equally prophetic. In 2008, the same year that Obama was elected America's first African American president, an embittered 88-year-old white supremacist, James von Brunn, opened fire upon visitors to the museum built by Americans to memorialize the genocide of European Jews. In the twenty-first century, the *Liberator*'s prediction of two competing forces—"a union of races" and the lingering racial hatred and violence would continue to coexist.

his like-minded Pennsylvania friends. He believed strongly in the *Liberator*'s mission: an immediate end to slavery. *The Liberator* spoke for reform and for abolitionists who would not equivocate. The time of reasoning with slaveholders had ended, abolitionists agreed; the moment for direct confrontation, perhaps even violence, had arrived.

Through the 1830s, the *Liberator* remained a powerful antislavery voice. In August 1831, the paper published a piece by James Forten entitled "Men Must Be Free." Forten wrote that a recent outbreak of mysterious fires in Fayetteville, North Carolina, represented a "visitation from God"—a divine warning to slaveholders. "When we . . . hear of almost every nation fighting for its liberty, is it to be expected that the African race will continue always in the degraded state they are in?" Forten asked. "No," he answered. "The time is fast approaching when the words 'Fight for liberty, or die in the attempt' will be sounded in every African ear." Shortly after these words were published, Nat Turner led Virginia slaves in a bloody rampage to gain their liberty. Clearly, some were willing to affirm that the moment had already arrived.

In the mid-nineteenth century, two currents were indeed sweeping the nation. One carried Americans, in day-to-day mingling of peoples and cultures, toward a racially blended melting pot. As white immigrants—especially from Ireland and Germany—settled in the urban North, they toiled alongside free black people in factories and shipyards and lived in the same neighborhoods. In the rural South, slaves continued to live in intimate circumstances with their masters, serving as housekeepers, valets, and nursemaids. The second current involved intense fear and hatred, as immigrants and free African Americans swelled urban populations and caused native-born white Americans to feel overwhelmed.

Both currents reflected the new nation's complex and dynamic economic and geographic expansion. By the mid-1840s, a New York journalist declared that Americans had a "manifest destiny to overspread the continent." Americans of all backgrounds responded to the lure of the West, encountering new peoples and developing new ways of life.

In this era of expansion and reform, black leaders looked to strengthen free African American communities in order to demonstrate their right to full citizenship. They preached self-improvement and education as the best means of building their communities, finding work, and proving their worthiness. Nationwide, the African American population jumped from 2.3 million in 1830 to 3.6 million in 1850. Within this population, however, the percentage of free African Americans dropped from 15.9 to 13.6 percent. The resulting demographics meant 1.3 million more slaves and fewer than 120,000 additional free black people.

The question of citizenship, then, concerned only the shrinking proportion of black Americans who were free. The plight of the ever-increasing slave population was of far greater concern. Among the manifold reforms under public discussion—temperance, woman suffrage, religious ferment, legal punishment, and public education—African Americans focused most strongly on abolition. Always a small minority, outspoken abolitionists faced scorn, violence, and the suppression of their literature. They also struggled with dissension deep within their ranks that splintered friendships and alliances. Yet for all of this, free African Americans continued the struggle.

Black Americans in an Expanding Nation

Martin Delany, a black leader in the generation before the Civil War, had always been restless. Born in 1812 in Charles Town, Virginia, Delany grew up in Pennsylvania. After studying at a black church school, he worked as a barber and a cupper and leecher—a medical practitioner who treated illness by drawing blood from the patient. In 1843, he married free-born Catherine Richards, who was from a family of well-to-do Pittsburgh cattle farmers. She shared her husband's hatred of racial injustice, for she had seen her family cheated out of land by white neighbors.

A curious man, Delany traversed the country in 1839. In Philadelphia, he visited the Quaker-run Institute for Colored Youth (ICY). Established as an agricultural training school with white teachers, the ICY soon developed an academic curriculum and hired some black teachers at the insistence of black parents. In New York City, Delany encountered James McCune Smith, a black doctor who provided much-needed services to the city's free black community. Smith had earned a medical degree in Scotland because medical schools in the United States refused to accept him. In Boston, Delany met black abolitionist Charles Remond, whose home was a popular destination for abolitionists of all skin colors.

Delany then turned south. Earning his passage by stoking fires on Mississippi River steamboats, he traveled through Mississippi and witnessed slaves' backbreaking labor. Journeying into Louisiana, where earlier French masters had introduced the tradition of black mistresses, he found many mixed-race people, some of whom were free owners of businesses and property.

Next, Delany visited Texas, where a local slave warned him that white Texans would "as like kill you as not, and they feel the same way about Mexicans and Indians." An independent republic, Texas had recently seceded from Mexico and was attracting new slave-owning planters from the tobacco-worn soil of Virginia and North Carolina who now turned to cotton. Texas also had free black people, whom white Texans had invited there to help outnumber Mexicans and Indians. Delany continued into Arkansas and the Indian Territory of Oklahoma, where Indians and black refugees had settled in the 1830s.

Black Population Growth

In his lifetime, Delany witnessed an explosion in the nation's black population. The southern slave population grew by about 25 percent every decade from 1820 to 1860. The number of free African Americans grew more slowly; thus, while the *number* of free black people increased somewhat, the *proportion* of free black people dropped dramatically after 1830. Why were slaves an ever larger proportion of the African American population? The decrease in manumissions is a key reason. The freeing of slaves had nearly ceased across most of the South. Only in the border states of Delaware, Maryland, and Kentucky could slaves gain liberty after 1820. Also, high fertility rates of enslaved women swelled the slave population; the average black woman bore seven children. Although infant mortality rate was high (27 percent of black children died in the first year of life) and life expectancy was low (in 1840, life expectancy was only thirty-three years for black males and thirty-five for black females), the high birthrate helped overcome these factors. Also, illegal importation of slaves continued.

In both the South and North, Delany saw that free African Americans preferred cities. More plentiful jobs and established black communities made

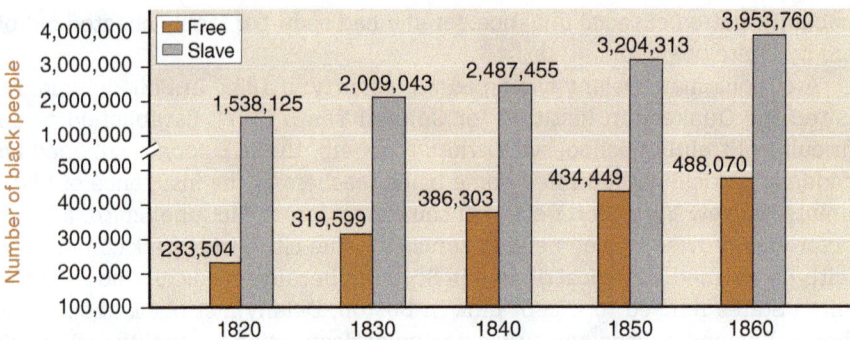

FIGURE 8.1 Free and Enslaved Black People, 1820–1860

Though the free black population more than doubled in four decades, the number of slaves, six times greater than the free population in 1820, also more than doubled, dwarfing the growth in free black communities.

urban centers attractive. Southern black people, drawn to cities like Charleston and New Orleans, were more than twice as likely as white Southerners to live in urban areas. By mid-century, Baltimore had the nation's largest black community—over 20,000 free African Americans. Black Northerners were even more urbanized. Philadelphia and New York, for example, with about 14,000 and 16,000 free black people, respectively, became thriving centers of black religious and intellectual life.

In the cities, especially in the South, both enslaved and free women outnumbered men. This imbalance resulted from urban employers' and slave owners' greater reliance on women for domestic labor, while in the rural areas black men shouldered most of the farm labor. This gender imbalance made it difficult for black women and men to find partners or sustain families.

Meanwhile, during the 1830s and 1840s, slavery spread west of the Appalachians. In 1825, the majority of black Americans lived within a hundred miles of the ocean their ancestors had crossed on slave ships. But thirty years later, most slaves lived deep in the southern interior, thousands of miles from free-state borders, far from easy contact with abolitionists and with the network of reformers known as the Underground Railroad, which helped slaves escape north to freedom. Mild climate and the labor-intensive cotton crop meant a longer and more brutal work schedule. A few of the boldest slaves escaped into Mexico, and there were rumors of aborted slave revolts, but for most, slavery in the Lower South was relentless.

Racial Separation

Although free black Americans were decreasing as a proportion of the total population of African Americans, free black people maintained tightly knit communities where they owned land and businesses and learned practical skills. Pittsburgh's Lewis Woodson embodied this community spirit. A slave until purchased by his father at age nineteen, Woodson helped form the

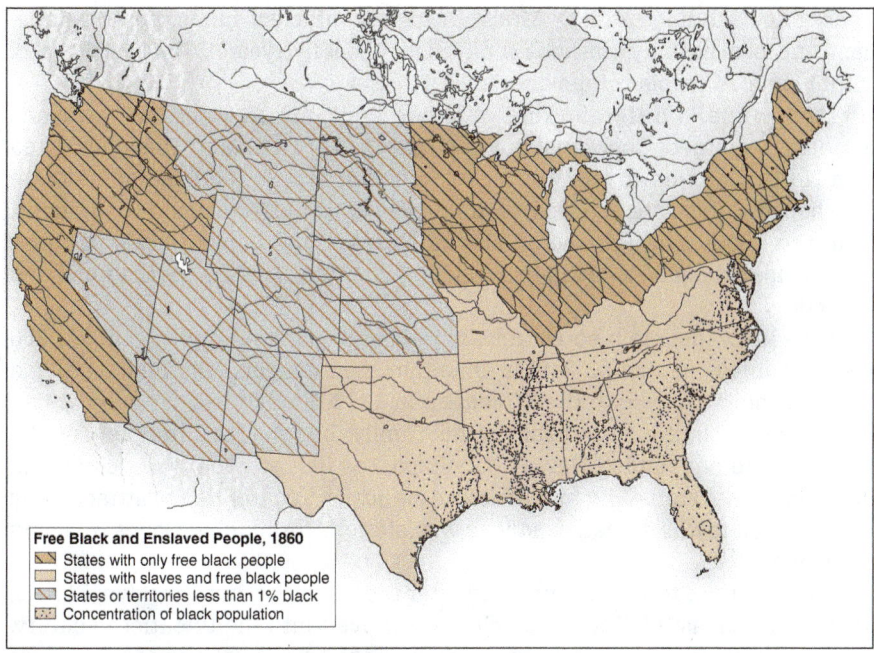

MAP 8.1   Free Black and Enslaved People, 1860

By 1860, the presence or absence of slaves defined not only the labor force but also the politics of a given region. The North and Northwest, with few slaves, harbored abolitionists. The Upper South, phasing out slavery, had mixed loyalties to the institution, while the states of the Lower South, where cotton demanded large field crews, based much of their public policy on bound labor.

Pittsburgh African Education and Benevolent Society, which aimed to educate young black people. Woodson used the classroom to preach religion, industry, thrift, and temperance. The Society assembled a library and subscribed to abolitionist newspapers like Garrison's *Liberator* and *The Colored American,* which, in 1837, published some of Woodson's prescriptions for black progress. Woodson urged free black men and women to learn artisan and farming skills, purchase land and tools, and get involved in the political process. He also urged them to establish their own settlements in sparsely populated areas where, he believed, they could build safe communities and offer sanctuary to fugitive slaves. He resisted arguments that free black people should settle in Africa, for he thought they would thereby be abandoning slaves who needed their help and protection. Black Americans need "a colony in a place of our choice," insisted Woodson, and that place should be in the United States.

Some separate black communities arose in the South, under white patronage. One was Nashoba, established in 1826 near Memphis, Tennessee. Inspired by European idealists who promoted communal living, British actress and reformer Frances (Fanny) Wright purchased 300 acres for a cooperative farming community that hosted manumitted slaves whose masters hoped to educate them before sending them to Africa. Despite insufficient funds, poor management, and local hostility, Nashoba survived for about five years. When it collapsed, Wright shipped its black members to Haiti.

Meanwhile, a different kind of experiment, aimed at promoting black autonomy, emerged. Congregations of white Quakers and Methodists relocated from North Carolina to the free states of Ohio, Illinois, and Indiana, where they hoped to insulate themselves from slavery and offer asylum to fugitives. From the 1820s through the 1850s, individuals and communities in these states helped thousands of fugitives and manumitted slaves make the transition to freedom.

Free black people also established separate communities. In 1832, 300 black Virginians settled on land in Ohio that their master, John Randolph, had willed to them along with their freedom. In 1836, Frank McWhorter, who had purchased his freedom and that of his family, bought land in Pike County, Illinois. There he founded New Philadelphia, the first of twenty settlements in Illinois and Ohio started by free African Americans. Too isolated to attract many settlers, such towns served mostly as way stations for fugitive slaves traveling to Canada.

Most of these towns disappeared after the Civil War, but Brooklyn, Illinois, 20 miles southeast of New Philadelphia, survived into the twentieth century. Brooklyn grew out of a settlement started about 1830 by eleven families from Missouri. By 1840 it had an African Methodist Episcopal church, a Baptist church, and a railroad connection. In 1873, Brooklyn's few hundred black residents incorporated to become America's first majority-black town.

Between Slave and Free

Martin Delany's national tour introduced him to people of both African and Native American heritage. John Horse, sometimes known as John Caballo (Spanish for "horse"), was one individual who combined both heritages. He was about five years old when Andrew Jackson's troops tried to seize sections of Spanish Florida where fugitive slaves found sanctuary among Seminole Indians. The Seminoles themselves owned black slaves, and John Horse was probably the son of a black slave woman and her Seminole master. However, the Seminoles allowed their slaves to form their own villages, armed them as warriors, and prized them as translators. As black fighters joined the Seminole warriors in resisting U.S. troops, Jackson's officers described the battles as waged "by the negroes."

Despite Jackson's determination, Seminole communities in east Florida survived. When, as president, Jackson signed the Indian Removal Act, some Seminoles agreed to move west to Indian territory in regions that are now Louisiana and Oklahoma. But others resisted, in the First Seminole War in 1835. For more than five years they held off American soldiers. Resistance later continued in a Second Seminole War. When it was over, all the Florida Seminoles had been removed or subdued.

Through these years, John Horse shifted his loyalties. Sometimes he helped the Seminoles battle white soldiers. Other times he aided the U.S. army, serving as a well-paid guide, interpreter, and soldier. By 1840, he had married Susan, a Seminole woman, and soon the couple started a family. As the child of a slave mother, John Horse was not free, but as a slave in the Seminole community he straddled the lines between black and Indian, and between slave and free. His participation in the U.S. army's campaign against the Indians indicates the instability of such things as racial loyalty.

Meanwhile, deep in the South, some slaves managed to carve out a degree of freedom. Benjamin Thornton Montgomery exemplified this situation. Though never free, he enjoyed many privileges usually reserved for white Americans. In 1836, Montgomery was purchased from Virginia by Joseph Davis, owner of Hurricane Plantation near Vicksburg, Mississippi. Davis, a southern reformer experimenting with crop rotation and labor management, believed that treating workers with dignity and offering them skills and responsibility would prove more profitable than harsh discipline. No Hurricane slave was ever punished without a hearing before a jury of peers. Davis fired overseers who violated this policy.

Soon after arriving at Hurricane, Ben Montgomery ran away. When he was captured, he negotiated an agreement that made staying more palatable. The literate Montgomery persuaded Davis to lend him books and, eventually, to give him control of the plantation store—including part of the profits. Encouraging Montgomery to master surveying, drafting, and mechanical skills, Davis put him in charge of Hurricane's construction projects and machinery, including several steam engines.

With thrift, discipline, and his master's indulgence, Montgomery amassed broad knowledge and considerable savings. Married in 1840 to another slave, Mary Lewis, he fathered four children. He bought books, paid tutors to educate his children, and purchased his wife's time so she could stay at home to care for their family. Montgomery's family life, with his wife and children sheltered from a bruising work regimen, mirrored the middle-class white ideal. His relationship with his white owner may have come as close to friendship as was possible within slavery. Indeed, Montgomery's children recalled that whenever their father entered a room, Davis pulled a chair up to the table and invited his slave to sit.

Apparently, Montgomery never sought legal freedom, and Davis never offered it. Montgomery's situation was enviable compared to the other 100,000 Mississippi slaves. Still, Montgomery was constrained by a society where white people controlled black people's opportunities, and Davis's blueprint for human dignity and an efficient workplace did not include black liberation.

Black Americans and Reform

"As Christ died in vain for those who will not accept his offered mercy, so will it be vain for the advocates of freedom to spend their breath in our behalf, unless [African Americans] make some mighty efforts to raise your sons and daughters from the horrible state of degradation in which they are placed." Speaking in Boston in 1832, African American Maria Miller Stewart displayed the religious, intellectual, and political energy that made her one of the era's most dedicated reformers. Though her public speaking was short-lived, she was influential, using religion to inspire broad political and social action.

Building on the reform spirit, free African Americans sought to gain skills and resources to shield themselves from racism and exploitation. They established schools and literary societies for both children and adults. They boycotted slave-produced goods. Black ministers preached about humility and patience. Some also taught rebellion.

Religion and Reform

Maria Miller Stewart's early experiences helped mold her ideas. Born to free black parents in Connecticut in 1803 but orphaned by age five, she became a servant to a white minister who taught her to read. Through this early training, she was introduced to the Second Great Awakening, a wave of religious energy that swept America in the 1820s, inspiring leaders to try to cleanse the country of sin.

In 1818 Stewart moved to Boston, working as a domestic until she married James Stewart, a well-to-do black shipper whose income afforded her several years of leisurely reading. But her comfortable life did not last. In 1829, Maria Stewart was widowed. Her husband left her an inheritance and a soon-to-be-born son. But the white executor of the estate swindled Stewart out of her bequest.

To support herself, Stewart turned from reading to writing and speaking. She had applauded the fiery *Appeal to the Coloured Citizens,* published in 1829 by her friend David Walker. Walker had hinted that God might instruct slaves to violently overthrow their masters, and upon Walker's death in 1830 Stewart took up his mixture of religion and revolution. In this she was encouraged by William Lloyd Garrison, who in 1831 helped her publish a pamphlet that caught the attention of Boston's literary circles. This pamphlet, "Religion and the Pure Principles of Morality, the Sure Foundation on Which We Must Build," promoted thrift and sobriety as a means for earning citizenship and stressed the importance of religious faith. "It is the religion of Jesus alone that will constitute your happiness here," she wrote.

Garrison supported Stewart's advocacy of rights for black women. She argued that discrimination against women and African Americans were entwined, preventing black women's full development and mocking Christian virtue. Claiming that black men contributed to the oppression of black women, she warned African American women not to be subservient to them. "How long," she asked, "shall a mean set of men flatter us with their smiles, and enrich themselves with our hard earnings?" Women, she concluded, must "promote and patronize each other," with a spirit that is "bold and enterprising, fearless and undaunted." Stewart urged black women to work together to end their oppression: "How long shall the fair daughters of Africa be compelled to bury their minds and talents beneath a load of iron pots and kettles? Until union, knowledge and love begin to flow among us." With barely 2,500 African Americans living in Boston in 1830, few black women heard Stewart speak. But

The Liberator's 3,500 subscribers helped spread her ideas. Inspired, black New Englanders formed the Female Anti-Slavery Society of Salem, Massachusetts, in 1832.

The first female public speaker in America whose speeches were published, Stewart set an example for black women of her day. However, the hostility she encountered wore her down. She left Boston in 1833. "I am about to leave you, for I find it of no use to me to try to make myself useful among my color in this city. God has tried me as if by fire. I can now bless those who have hated me, and pray for those who have used and persecuted me." Stewart moved to New York to teach in a colored school.

Self-Improvement and Education

"Instead of drinking grog or smoking tobacco, we should read the newspaper." Thus did Pittsburgh teacher Lewis Woodson implore his students to use their time and money for self-improvement. Maria Stewart shared this commitment to self-discipline and thrift. "I would implore our men," she admonished, "and especially our rising youth, to flee from the gambling board and the dance hall; for we are poor, and have no money to throw away." Free black Americans like Woodson and Stewart hoped self-improvement would convince white Americans that black people could be responsible and productive citizens. They believed African Americans should learn to read and write, to work outside of slavery, and to lead lives of Christian virtue.

The Pittsburgh African Education Society adopted this blueprint. "The intellectual capacity of the black man is equal to that of the white," said its constitution, "and he is equally susceptible of improvement, all ancient history makes manifest; and modern examples put this beyond a single doubt." Persuaded that "ignorance is the cause of the present degradation and bondage of the people of color in these United States," the Society erected a building to house a school, library, and lecture hall, open to all black people, enslaved and free.

The American Moral Reform Society (AMRS) also promoted black self-improvement. Established in Philadelphia in 1835, it aimed to reform all American society. At age sixty-nine, James Forten became the AMRS president. Less than half Forten's age, the eloquent William Whipper was its spokesman, exhorting "every *American*," regardless of race, to commit to "EDUCATION, TEMPERANCE, ECONOMY, and UNIVERSAL LIBERTY."

The reform spirit fostered many self-help societies. The Afric-Female Intelligence Society of Boston, the New York Female Literary Society, and others met regularly to read and debate history, science, and current events. In Philadelphia, dozens of black organizations modeled responsible citizenship by providing musical, educational, recreational, and burial services.

While self-help societies played a vital role, schools for black children proved even more crucial. During the 1830s, urban public schools excluded black students, so dedicated teachers founded separate schools for them. Most were, of course, in the North. These included Margaretta Forten's school in Philadelphia, Charles L. Reason's Free African School in New York, and the

New England Union Academy in Providence, Rhode Island. Even in the South, a few free black children—often the biracial offspring of white masters—studied with black teachers, such as Daniel Payne in Charleston.

Some philanthropic white people set up schools for black children. In Philadelphia, the Quaker-run Institute for Colored Youth opened in the 1830s, becoming the nucleus of a teachers' college that still survives. In 1832, white reformer Prudence Crandall opened a school for black girls in Canterbury, Connecticut. White townspeople, however, harassed Crandall and torched the school. Despite such incidents, teachers persevered.

From "African" to "Colored"

Working for better lives, free African Americans also focused on self-identity. Black communities traditionally honored their origins by using *African* in naming their organizations. By the 1830s, however, some black leaders suggested discontinuing this practice in order to remind their white neighbors that they and their children were Americans, not Africans.

During these years, many Americans—regardless of skin color or region—were reassessing the meaning of the word *American*. Across the nation, with new canals and railroads transporting citizens, immigrants, printed materials, and fugitive slaves to frontier communities, Americans increasingly encountered people different from themselves. As the new wave of European immigrants increased the number of Catholic congregations and Jewish synagogues, it also intensified native-born white Americans' resistance to newcomers' customs. Anti-immigrant tensions rose, so many black Americans sought to remind white Americans that they were not newcomers. Rather, they were "*colored Americans.*"

Names with Meaning

Free African Americans enjoyed a luxury unavailable to most slaves: choosing their children's names. Maria Stewart named her son after white abolitionist William Lloyd Garrison. The Montgomerys bestowed the Old Testament names Rebecca and Isaiah on two of their children; they named their youngest son for abolitionist William Thornton.

The Delanys also chose names reflecting black concerns as well as Christian values. In 1846, they named a son Toussaint L'Ouverture, honoring the Haitian revolutionary leader. Another son, Charles Lenox Remond, was named for the Massachusetts black abolitionist. Other sons' names were similarly chosen: Alexander Dumas for the black French author; St. Cyprian for the third-century black religious leader; Faustin Soulouque for a Haitian emperor; and Ramses Placido for ancient Egyptian monarchs and a Cuban revolutionary poet. Knowing the biblical promise that, in praise for liberating enslaved peoples, Ethiopia will "stretch forth her hands to God," the Delanys named their only daughter and last child Ethiopia.

Thus, as parents have done throughout time, the Stewarts, Montgomerys, and Delanys expressed their hopes and values through their children. Earlier generations of African Americans had selected names reflecting their new status (Freeman, Newman, or Trusty) and confirming their American-ness (John, James, or Mary). Reform-era black names bespoke knowledge of literature, history, and current events stretching far beyond the limits of a slave world.

The Abolitionist Movement

Recounting his life story in 1845, Frederick Douglass recalled the day he decided he would never be whipped again. "Whence came the daring spirit . . . I do not know. The fighting madness had come upon me, and I found my strong fingers firmly attached to the throat of the tyrant, as heedless of consequences as if we stood as equals before the law." Douglass's narrative of resistance, escape, and transformation from slave to abolitionist lecturer is among America's most celebrated stories. It chronicles a man's life as well as the subtleties of black–white abolitionist relationships. It also highlights African Americans' sharpened political consciousness and will to resist oppression.

Radical Abolitionism

By 1830, the abolitionist movement turned radical as reformers vowed to break laws, confront slaveholders, or commit violence, if necessary. Though the anti-slavery movement was not new, the mood of urgency was, as symbolized by the *Liberator*'s strident masthead: "I will not retreat a single inch, and I WILL be heard." Editor William Lloyd Garrison meant to provoke Americans into imagining a radically reformed society.

Frederick Douglass was twenty-nine when this daguerreotype was taken. Abolitionists displayed such images in their homes for inspiration.

Source: The Art Institute of Chicago. All Rights Reserved.

Radical abolitionism solidified with the 1833 founding of the American Anti-Slavery Society (AAS) in Philadelphia. Garrison led a white delegation to the first meeting that included Arthur and Lewis Tappan from upstate New York and a group of religious revivalists from Ohio. Meeting with James Forten and other influential black Philadelphians, these men shaped AAS's mission: to complete the abolition begun in some northern states during the American Revolution. The AAS took particular offense at the Constitution's implication that a black person was only three-fifths of a citizen. That clause, they said, was "a criminal and dangerous relation to slavery." The AAS promised to organize "in every city, town and village in our land," to send agents, enlist the press, and circulate literature to show "the guilt of the nation's oppression" against African Americans. Members also sponsored lectures where ex-slaves gave firsthand accounts of a plantation system most northern white people—and many free black people—had never seen.

Much leadership for the abolitionist movement grew out of the black churches, particularly the African Methodist Episcopal Church, the largest black denomination. AME membership soared from 7,000 in 1836 to 20,000 by the 1850s. AME congregations, already strong in Philadelphia and Baltimore, soon arose in dozens of southern cities. Black Baptist and Presbyterian congregations also flourished. Although manumissions decreased, the natural increase in black births resulted in a growing number of free black people in the South—from 180,000 in 1830 to 240,000 by 1850—to fill these churches. Small but tenacious Catholic, Episcopal, and Moravian congregations took root as well. The churches became the hub of black community life, offering friendship, education, entertainment, and, sometimes, information about gaining freedom.

Sending hundreds of organizers across northern and western states to link 2,000 affiliated groups, the AAS had 150,000 members by 1840. The traveling organizers preached to massive audiences, barraged Congress with antislavery petitions, and printed volumes about the immorality of slavery. Their most widely read literature included Garrison's *Liberator* and Lydia Maria Child's *Appeal in Favor of That Class of Americans Called Africans* (1833). Child, from a white New England family actively involved in reform, decried slavery and the difficulty free black people had in finding work: "We made slavery, and slavery makes prejudice." Echoing Garrison, her mentor, she insisted that free black people were "more temperate and more industrious" than the "foreign [white] emigrants who are crowding our shores."

In addition to white reformers like Child, Garrison helped recruit African Americans—including Frederick Douglass—to abolitionism. Born on a Maryland plantation in 1817, Douglass was the son of a slave woman and a white father he never knew. The planter's wife helped him learn to read as a child. Though a fight with his overseer crystallized Douglass's intent to escape, it took three years and two tries before he broke free. Finally, in 1838, disguised as a sailor, he made his way to New Bedford, Massachusetts. There he married Anna, a free woman he had met in Baltimore, where she was a domestic servant. In New England, Douglass worked closely with Garrison, describing his "education" at "Massachusetts University, Mr. Garrison, President." To avoid capture, the fugitive Douglass spent two years in England while American abolitionists raised funds to purchase his freedom. Free by 1845, Douglass regularly traveled on abolitionist lecture tours and spoke at Conventions of Free People of Color.

The urgent abolitionist mood generated a wave of antislavery activity. Almost every northern community formed a Vigilance Committee of black people

TABLE 8.1 ABOLITIONIST ORGANIZATIONS

ORGANIZATION/ YEAR FOUNDED	BLACK LEADERS	WHITE LEADERS	GOALS	STRATEGY
American Colonization Society/1816	Paul Cuffe (died before its founding), Edward Blyden, and Robert Campbell.	James Madison, James Monroe, and Henry Clay.	Gradual abolition; black education and resettlement outside the U.S.	Encourage southern manumission; establish schools for free black people.
American Anti Slavery Society (AAS)/1833	James Forten, John B. Vashon, and Charles Remond.	William Lloyd Garrison, Arthur and Lewis Tappan.	Immediate abolition.	Petition Congress to broaden the Constitution to outlaw slavery; circulate antislavery literature.
Salem Female Anti-Slavery Society/1832; Philadelphia Female Anti-Slavery Society/1833	Sarah Remond, Margaretta Forten, Sarah Mapps Douglass	Lydia Maria Child, Angelina Grimké, and Lucretia Mott.	Support AAS; encourage black education; pursue women's rights.	Raise money for AAS and for schools; confront AAS on its gender exclusion.
Philadelphia Free Produce Society/1838	Robert Purvis	James Mott and Isaac T. Hopper	Freeze slaveholders out of the American economy.	Produce and sell cotton cloth and sugar from free-labor growers.
American and Foreign Anti-Slavery Society/1840	Henry Highland Garnet and Samuel Cornish.	Arthur and Lewis Tappan, and James G. Birney.	Agitate Congress for abolition; mount an antislavery presidential campaign.	Protect American morality by denouncing slavery and refusing to have men and women work together.
Liberty Party/1840	Frederick Douglass and Martin Delany	James G. Birney	Establish an antislavery political party.	Challenge traditional presidential candidates.
American Missionary Association/1846	Henry R. and Tamar Wilson.	Lewis Tappan	Purge white churches of the sin of slavery.	Dispatch missionaries to start black schools and churches.

and a few white allies who harbored fugitives in their homes and circulated antislavery petitions. Their connections in ports and along inland trade routes helped runaway slaves stay in touch with those left behind. Finally, they supported free produce stores, which sold only products made with non-slave labor. In 1838, several dozen black and white Philadelphians founded the American Free Produce Society, which encouraged consumers to substitute local honey for slave-grown sugar and to shun slave-grown cotton. Following the *Liberator*'s call to be "as uncompromising as justice," they were determined to drive slave owners out of business.

Divisions among Abolitionists

Abolitionists agreed on their primary goal: ending slavery. But beyond this there was little unity of motivation or strategy. The primary concern of some white reformers, like the Tappans, was that slavery degraded white Americans' morality. The Tappans would not rent to black tenants or live near African Americans; like many reformers, they hoped free black people would go to Africa. Garrison, by contrast, confessed shame at being part of the white race, socialized with black friends, and published their writing. He also envisioned a society in which all races lived harmoniously. But he could be high-handed with abolitionists—especially black ones—who resisted doing things his way. In 1848, when he discouraged Frederick Douglass from starting a newspaper, Douglass concluded that Garrison resented black leaders and wanted to make decisions for them. Finally, there were white antislavery activists like Gerrit Smith, who embraced black Americans. In the 1840s, Smith donated a large tract of land in northern New York to start a black community, and chose to live there. In 1849, John Brown—who later tried to ignite a slave rebellion in Harpers Ferry, Virginia—moved his family to Smith's black settlement.

Even among free African Americans, there was little unity. Some black entrepreneurs in the North, perhaps wanting to protect thriving businesses or avoid reprisals from white people, remained silent. Others were too focused on mere survival to involve themselves in protests. Only gradually did these black Americans come to see their fate as intertwined with that of slaves.

Gender became another source of division among abolitionists. AAS leaders excluded women from decision making. Like most men of their time, they believed proper ladies should abstain from "promiscuous" gatherings—groups comprising both men and women. Thus, many AAS groups were founded specifically for women, such as the Philadelphia Female Anti-Slavery Society. Women's groups raised funds for black schools or established schools of their own. But they also joined public protests: Women constituted almost half the signers of an 1837 petition to abolish slavery in the District of Columbia.

Appreciating that abolitionist men like Garrison and Douglass believed women's voices should be heard, some women's groups also raised money for *The Liberator*. In 1848, when radical women gathered at Seneca Falls, New York, to write a declaration of women's rights, Douglass was a featured speaker. Though such male support was rare, many women found ways to make a difference. Lydia Maria Child went on the abolitionist lecture circuit,

The Pennsylvania Anti-Slavery Society Executive Committee, shown in this 1851 photograph, included both free African Americans and women. Quaker minister Lucretia Coffin Mott (front row, second from right) provided an important link between abolition and women's rights. Robert Purvis (at Mott's right) was one of Philadelphia's best-known black leaders.

as did Sarah Remond, a black middle-class woman. Frederick Douglass's wife Anna took a job in a shoe factory to support her husband's travels. Other women taught children, organized women's literacy programs, and attended political education meetings. In Boston, black women petitioned against segregated schools. In Salem, Massachusetts, they wrote a constitution "associating ourselves for our mutual improvement and to promote the welfare of our color."

Many black women now found a new platform to celebrate both race and gender. Elleanor Eldridge's *Memoirs* (1839), describing her grandfather's noble West African heritage and her brother's leadership among black New Englanders, set an inspiring example. Jarena Lee, whom Philadelphia AME bishop Richard Allen had refused a regular pulpit, became a traveling missionary for Allen's church (see Chapter 7). In 1839, Lee published her story, then joined the AAS, which now provided an outlet for black women's aspirations.

But the appointment of Abbey Kelley to the AAS executive committee in 1840 caused a rupture among abolitionists. Kelley was a tireless lecturer who advocated women's equality, exhorting abolitionists to "take a stand for all truths." Following Garrison's lead, she insisted that "moral suasion" to stir the public conscience was the only sure way to achieve equality. But her appointment alienated many male abolitionists who felt women should not be public leaders. The AAS splintered. Lewis Tappan led a walkout to establish the American and Foreign Antislavery Society, which rushed delegates off to

London to persuade the AAS international convention not to seat women. Sharing Tappan's conviction that women should play a subservient role, ex-slave Henry Highland Garnet became one of only six black men—all ministers—to join the American and Foreign Anti-Slavery Society. Over Garrison's objections that prejudice against women was no better than prejudice against slaves, male delegates banned women from policy-making sessions, consigning them to attend only social events.

This controversy in London crystallized abolitionist divisions. The movement fractured over questions of gender, leadership, the role of free African Americans, and expectations for black people's fate should abolition succeed. After 1840, the abolitionists' only common ground was the ending of slavery.

Violence against Abolitionists

The AAS's confrontational posture drew violent reactions from Southerners and Northerners who feared abolition might dislodge white people's superior social status. Yet many abolitionists welcomed public attacks, feeling they gained publicity and sympathy that ennobled their cause. When Lydia Maria Child's abolitionism drove subscribers away from her children's magazine, she started a sugar beet farm to promote alternatives to slave-grown sugar. As Garrison was preparing to speak before the Boston Female Anti-Slavery Society in 1835, a white mob that feared black labor competition looped a rope around his neck and dragged him through the streets. He survived only because he was arrested for inciting a riot. The martyrdom pleased Garrison, who viewed the antislavery cause as holy and deemed it better to "have brickbats [thrown at him] in the cause of God than to have wedges of gold in the cause of sin [slavery]."

Elijah Lovejoy was not so lucky. A New England teacher who embraced gradual emancipation, Lovejoy settled in Alton, Illinois, where he founded an abolitionist paper. But local white residents, worried that the newspaper would attract abolitionists to Alton, destroyed his printing press. Infuriated, Lovejoy vowed to defend his constitutional right to free speech. Several times the AAS replaced his equipment; several times angry mobs destroyed it. Finally, in 1837, Lovejoy's opponents destroyed his press and murdered him. Intending mostly to defend free speech, Lovejoy became what a New York black man called "the first martyr in the holy cause of abolition in the nation."

In Philadelphia, barred from meeting in most public buildings, a committee of black and white women who supported the abolitionist cause raised money and built Pennsylvania Hall. It opened in May 1838, with speeches by William Lloyd Garrison and Angelina Grimké, who two days earlier had married Presbyterian minister Theodore Weld. Outraged that black guests had attended the wedding, a white crowd mobbed the building. The following day, the crowd burned the empty building to the ground while the mayor and neighbors stood idly by.

Similar reprisals menaced free black people who agitated for citizenship. Between 1833 and 1838, more than three dozen race riots in northern cities targeted symbols of black independence: churches, businesses, meeting places, and prosperous black families. Often the instigators were white laborers who resented black workers' successes. But some were what abolitionist William Lloyd Garrsion called "gentlemen of property and standing"—owners of banks, transportation, and commerce that depended on southern cotton to keep northern textile mills profitable. White clergymen and intellectuals, armed with new pseudoscientific theories about black deficiency, added to the racist chorus. They contended that black Americans lacked the moral character or mental capacity to function as equal citizens.

In the wake of Nat Turner's Rebellion in 1831 (see Chapter 7), southern abolitionism dissolved. A handful of planters quietly continued manumission, but most vocal southern white abolitionists, afraid for their lives, abandoned the South. A few became northern abolitionist leaders. James G. Birney, a slaveholder who helped to develop a manumission policy, left Alabama and in 1837 became AAS's executive secretary. Sarah Grimké, sister of Angelina Grimké Weld and daughter of a prominent South Carolina slaveholding judge, moved to Philadelphia in the 1820s, breaking ties with the South and with her southern family.

By 1840, few remembered that U.S. presidents Jefferson, Madison, and Monroe—all three from the South—had suggested freeing slaves. The battle lines were drawn: Abolition was a northern movement; Southerners who sympathized had best keep quiet or leave the South.

Northern Black Press, Southern White Press

"The *Advocate* will be like a chain, binding you together as ONE," proclaimed New York City's *Weekly Advocate,* an antislavery newspaper, in its inaugural issue of January 1837. "We . . . are opposed to colonization [and] we hold ourselves ready to combat with opposite views," it continued, promising to "contain the news of the day and a variety of scientific and literary matter."

Other black entrepreneurs and communities launched black newssheets. These publications railed against slavery and debated emigration to Africa. Bolstered by the loyalty of their mostly black readers and the increasing reliability of mail delivery, more than a half-dozen black publications appeared by the 1840s. The earliest was John Russwurm's *Freedom's Journal,* begun in 1827. When Russwurm promoted relocating to Liberia, his partner, Samuel Cornish, established an alternative publication, *The Rights of All,* against relocation. Cornish's paper asserted that while a few African Americans might benefit from relocating to Africa, they would be abandoning defenseless slaves. The *Colored American,* begun in 1837, also discouraged black Americans from going to Africa.

Martin Delany's southern travels reinforced his commitment to the black press. In 1843, he launched *The Mystery,* dedicated to "the moral elevation of the Africo-American and African Race." Celebrating African heritage, its masthead proclaimed "all the wisdom of the Egyptians." The newsweekly brimmed with essays, reports from national correspondents, black merchants' advertisements, letters to the editor, and, of course, tirades against slavery. Delany even publicized his support for women's education. From the start, *The Mystery* was both a source of pride and a drain on Delany's resources. While it boasted more than 1,000 subscribers, Delany often could not collect the subscription fees.

While the mainstream white press lamented depressed cotton prices and an economic downturn that began in 1837, the white-owned *Anti-Slavery Standard* and the black-run papers covered debates important to black reformers. The *Standard* encouraged reformers to unite behind Garrison. But other black newssheets argued for racially separate organizations. Some black reformers echoed Douglass's concern over white abolitionists' efforts to control black people. So black publications, like the *Advocate* and *The Mystery,* tried to remain independent of white influence.

After several years of struggling with *The Mystery,* Delany joined Douglass and black Boston historian William C. Nell to launch *The North Star.* The new partnership proved just as frustrating as working alone. The newssheet's provocative writing attracted a following, but the paper struggled financially. Yet Delany believed in the power of the press. In 1848, he took to the road again, leaving his ailing wife and his children as he traveled through Maryland, Pennsylvania, Ohio, and Michigan seeking subscriptions.

Proslavery Americans also understood the power of the press. Southern post offices refused to deliver abolitionist tracts, sometimes burning them. Meanwhile, southern periodicals like the widely heralded *DeBow's Review* focused on agricultural management—but all discussions were shaped by proslavery arguments. These periodicals reminded readers that "slave labor is the source of all our wealth and prosperity . . . the basis of the most desirable social and political system the world has ever seen."

Through such publications, southern planters exchanged advice on maximizing the value of their human property. One planter likened his slaves to livestock. Noting that cattle "well cared for in winter were in better condition all the year," he was "cautious of exposing my Negroes in the winter" and recommended providing them with "good houses, good clothing, and good food." Other planters stressed careful attention to daily work schedules, discipline, diet, housing, and religious training. With good management, advised the press, a planter could avoid such pitfalls as *drapetomania*—a mental illness they believed caused slaves to run away—and *dyasthenia aethiopica,* which they said caused slaves to become careless and break tools. Still other planters offered advice on controlling slaves. Some slaves, they explained, "require stirring up, some coaxing, some flattering, and others nothing but good words."

The Gag Rule and Landmark Legal Cases

Tension over slavery underlay every congressional discussion. Though the Missouri Compromise of 1820 temporarily suppressed debate about whether slavery should spread to western territories, the controversy still percolated, bubbling up as senators Henry Clay of Kentucky, Daniel Webster of Massachusetts, and John Calhoun of South Carolina debated land policy in the West, banking issues in the East, and the division of authority between federal and state governments. Voters watched anxiously as these political stalwarts struggled over concerns.

Meanwhile, the burgeoning northern population foretold a decline in the political power of the South. As immigrants flooded northern cities, the balance in the House of Representatives tipped toward the North. Radical abolitionists, though never more than 5 percent of the North's population, were a strident minority. Many Southerners feared that if abolitionists were elected to Congress, they would limit or end slavery. Surveying their worn-out fields, southern planters yearned to take their slaves farther west, where they might establish new slave states and reclaim their congressional majority.

Fearing incendiary debate about antislavery petitions, Congress instituted the Gag Rule in 1836, consenting to receive antislavery petitions but agreeing to ignore them. Though free speech advocates like former president John Quincy Adams (now a representative) decried this ban on public discussion, the Gag Rule remained in effect for eight years.

In 1839, debate polarized around a dramatic court case after slave captives seized the *Amistad,* a Spanish slave ship. Though the mutiny occurred in international waters near Cuba, it became an American cause célèbre when a U.S. naval ship commandeered the vessel. Charged with piracy and murder, the slaves were imprisoned, awaiting settlement of the competing claims of the *Amistad* crew, the American navy, and the Spanish government.

Garrison, proclaiming that the case should awaken the "sympathy of all true-hearted, impartial lovers of liberty," insisted that the slaves had done what Americans had done in their own revolution: defended their rights and liberty. Abolitionist newspapers also decried Spain's disregard for 1818 international laws banning the slave trade.

Over several years, the *Amistad* case slogged through the American legal system. On appeal to the U.S. Supreme Court, John Quincy Adams came to the

To raise funds for the *Amistad* Africans' defense, abolitionists distributed lithographic copies of this painting of Joseph Cinque, leader of the mutiny, for one dollar apiece.

defense of the mutineers. Though not an avowed abolitionist, he opposed slavery and wanted international law upheld. In 1841, the Supreme Court agreed that the *Amistad* captives should be freed but not that the federal government should transport them to Africa. So abolitionists paid the captives' passage. In November 1841, from Sierra Leone their leader Sengbe Pieh (Joseph Cinque) "thanked all Merica people, for them send Mendi people home."

The *Amistad* episode was followed by a similar case two years later. This time, the outcome disheartened abolitionists. An American ship, the *Creole,* transporting slaves along the coast, was seized by the slaves and sailed to the Bahamas, where the slaves declared themselves free and under British protection. Daniel Webster, now U.S. Secretary of State, claiming the ship's deck was an extension of American soil, insisted that Britain compensate the owner for his loss. Northern abolitionists felt betrayed by their government. By extending American protection for slaveholders beyond U.S. borders, the federal government, they declared, implicated an unwilling North in the slave trade. Garrison urged northern states to secede from the Union—a "peaceable separation for conscience sake." To slaveholders, this call was further evidence that slavery was under siege.

Historians view the *Amistad* and *Creole* cases as landmarks, setting a precedent for extending abolitionism beyond individual conscience and into the courts, the constitution, and international law. The *Amistad* case also inaugurated the American Missionary Association (AMA), a Christian abolitionist organization that supported schools and missions for black people in Africa and the United States. The organization urged member churches to "purify" themselves by denying membership to slaveholding "sinners" and refusing to do business with them. The AMA did not aim to deprive southern planters of their property. Rather, it sought to cleanse Americans of the sin of slavery, sending missionaries to the American West to preach against it. But the AMA had an additional mission: ridding America of free black people.

Limitations and Opportunities

"The heart of the whites must be changed, thoroughly, entirely, permanently changed," wrote the New York black physician James McCune Smith to Gerrit Smith in 1846. Otherwise, the black man insisted, racial discrimination would never end. Growing restrictions on free African Americans in the South and new laws denying them the vote in the North made it clear that not enough white hearts were being changed by abolitionist agitation.

Meanwhile, as white Americans streamed across the Appalachian Mountains and the Mississippi River, the slavery issue and racial discrimination accompanied them. In Midwestern states like Ohio, Indiana, and Illinois, the 1787 Northwest Ordinance prohibited slavery. But individual state laws often barred black people from entering the state unless they could prove they had money. Some local laws prevented them from owning land. Yet the sparsely populated West seemed to offer greater freedom than the South or the North. The Republic of Texas offered free land to any American—black or white—who would homestead there and help outnumber Mexicans.

Disfranchisement in the North

When the Liberty Party nominated abolitionist James A. Birney for president in 1840, Martin Delany and Frederick Douglass campaigned for him. Developing from the AAS division, this was the first antislavery political party. One *Colored American* commentator wrote of the 1840 election: "We ought and must vote for the Liberty Ticket, with James G. Birney at the head, a gentleman, a philanthropist and a Christian." But only a small number of black men could vote, and the 7,000 votes cast for Birney merely underscored the irony of support from black leaders.

By the 1840s, black political power and participation had all but disappeared. It had not always been this way. Following the Revolution, as northern states phased out slavery, free black property owners became eligible to vote. But because few black men owned land, most could not exercise this right. Still, in New York, Pennsylvania, and the New England states, the presence of a few hundred black voters raised the possibility that eventually black voters could influence elections.

But even as many states began allowing men without property to vote, black men saw their access to the polls narrow. New York, for example, instituted in 1821 a property requirement for black voters only. In 1838, Pennsylvania revoked the black franchise, despite impassioned entreaties from black leaders who presented evidence of free black people's economic and social stability. Three years later, disfranchisement was narrowly defeated in Rhode Island. In Ohio, Michigan, and Wisconsin, black residents repeatedly—and unsuccessfully—petitioned state representatives for the franchise, reminding legislators that the Constitution prohibited taxation without representation.

The Texas Frontier

With increasing limits in the North and South, some African Americans looked west. Greenbury Logan, for example, headed for Texas. Injured in military service to the Republic of Texas, Logan asked for tax relief in 1841: "I came here in 1831 invited by Col. [Stephen] Austin," explained Logan. "Having no family with me I got one quarter league of land instead of a third, but I love the country and did stay because I felt myself more a freeman than in the [United] states. I am . . . permanently injured and can barely support myself now."

Logan was a free man in a territory severed from Mexico but not yet part of the United States. Indeed, Texas had a unique history. Many southern planters were among the 20,000 white Americans who accepted Mexico's invitation in the 1820s to settle Texas. These planters brought 2,000 slaves with them. When Mexico achieved independence from Spain in 1821 and began abolishing slavery, Texas became a pivotal part of U.S. politics. President Andrew Jackson's unsuccessful attempt to buy Texas from Mexico led the Mexican government to retract its invitation to American settlers in 1830. In turn, the Americans already living in Texas seceded from Mexico, inviting more Americans to help resist Mexican control. In 1836, Texans gained independence and set up the Lone Star Republic.

Fighting for Texas secession, Logan also unwittingly helped ensure the entrenchment of slavery. American planters petitioned Congress to annex Texas as a slave state, and the question of annexing Texas dominated the 1844 U.S. presidential election. Capitalizing on northern opposition to another slave state, the Liberty Party drew increased support from abolitionists and others who resented southern aggressiveness. Its 60,000 votes worried proslavery Americans, though Southerners continued to argue that most Americans favored annexing Texas. In 1845, Congress granted Texas statehood and allowed slavery there. In pursuit of regional compromise, it stipulated that as many as four more states might be carved from Texas, and in some of those states slavery would be prohibited.

As many feared, Mexico retaliated, sparking a two-year war, beginning in 1846. In 1848—only a few days after gold was discovered in California—Mexico capitulated. The Treaty of Guadaloupe Hidalgo gave the United States more than a million square miles that eventually became Texas, Arizona, New Mexico, Utah, and California. Overnight, Greenbury Logan was demoted from a citizen in an independent republic to a free black non-citizen in a slave society.

The annexation of Mexican territories had profound consequences. First, Texas's admission to the Union augmented slaveholders' representation in Congress. Second, with fertile soil for growing cotton, corn, sugarcane, and cattle, white Texans prospered, their exports contributing to a flourishing American economy. Third, slaves provided a stable workforce, distant from abolitionist agitation.

But many Americans—black and white, northern and southern—believed the slavery issue could tear the United States apart. As early as 1837, *The Colored American* warned "should Texas be admitted into the Union, farewell to the union of the States. Ten thousand discordant clashing elements and interests will be stirred up, that will only subside with a division of the Union. . . . From the Potomac to the extreme Southern boundaries, anarchy, [and] bloodshed [will] deluge the country."

Radicals like Garrison may have welcomed such discord as a way to dramatize the evils of slavery, but most Americans hoped to avert a clash. Pennsylvania Congressman David Wilmot tried to stop the spread of slavery, proposing in 1846 "neither slavery nor involuntary servitude shall ever exist" in any territories gained from Mexico. Known as the Wilmot Proviso, the measure passed in the northern-dominated House but was defeated in the Senate, where the South retained strength. The defeat of the Wilmot Proviso guaranteed the continuation of the controversy over extending slavery.

While war and rhetoric raged, hundreds of free black Texans worked as skilled artisans in sawmills and brickyards and as blacksmiths, tailors, tavernkeepers, and house servants. A few acquired substantial agricultural holdings. But slavery was the foundation of Texas agriculture. Ten years after Greenbury Logan's plea for tax relief, the slave population in Texas had swelled to nearly 60,000; by 1860, it had more than tripled again.

The Mountain West

Texas was just one western destination for African Americans. Lured by wagon trains or the promise of gold in California, some free black people chose the new frontier, while slaves had little choice but to accompany owners who

Trapper James Beckwourth's discovery of an obscure northern California pass through the Sierra Nevada Mountains resulted in the establishment of a town that still bears his name.

"JAMES P. BECKWOURTH IN HUNTER'S COSTUME."

migrated west. Hence, many free and enslaved black Americans ended up in the Rocky Mountain region—Utah, Oregon, and California—as slaves to Mormons or as free explorers, ranchers, or entrepreneurs. James Beckwourth is an example. Born in the South in 1798 to a slave mother and a white father, Beckwourth apprenticed with a blacksmith, then signed on with the Rocky Mountain Fur Company. A skilled scout and translator, he moved easily between local Indians and white settlers. He was adopted into the Crow Indian community, living with them for several years. Later he assisted U.S. troops against the Seminoles in Florida. In 1845, he joined rebel Mexicans in an abortive attempt to wrest California from Mexico. Moving to New Mexico, he joined the U.S. Army's campaigns against Mexico in 1847. He married four times—twice to Indian women, once to a Spanish woman, and finally, at age sixty-two, to an African American woman in Denver, Colorado. With this last wife, he returned to the Crow community, where he died four years later.

George Washington Bush went west hoping to gain political rights. A free man, he had served under Andrew Jackson in the War of 1812. In 1844, he was a cattle trader in Missouri when a wagon train bound for the Oregon Territory lumbered through town. With his wife, children, and four other families, Bush joined the expedition. Years later, a fellow traveler remembered Bush's concerns: "It was not in the nature of things that he should be permitted to forget his color. He told me he would watch, when we got to Oregon, what usage was awarded to people of color, and if he could not have a freeman's rights he would seek the protection of the Mexican Government in California or New Mexico."

In Oregon, Bush's companions had to help him get an exemption from local anti-black laws in order to receive his 640-acre homestead. Once over this hurdle, Bush put down roots. He introduced the region's first sawmill, gristmill, mower, and reaper, and fathered a dynasty of local leaders known for their generosity to less well-off neighbors.

The discovery of gold in California in 1848 occasioned an influx of black easterners seeking riches. Here, gold dust—not skin color—defined a man's worth. By 1850, nearly a thousand African Americans—mostly single men— were among the fortune-seekers. Even those who did not work directly in mining gained from the booming economy. As cooks, waiters, laundresses, tavernkeepers, and dockworkers in Sacramento, San Francisco, and many small towns, black newcomers enjoyed economic prosperity, even if they lacked citizenship privileges.

The Compromise of 1850

The gold rush brought 80,000 Americans to California, which qualified for statehood by 1850. But admitting California as a free state would upset the regional balance in the U.S. Senate. Thus, proposed statehood for California touched off a bitter congressional debate over whether slavery would extend to the newly gained territory. The controversy resulted in the Compromise of 1850, the last congressional attempt to ease regional tensions by giving something to both North and South.

The compromise contained four momentous provisions. First, California entered the Union as a free state, upsetting the balance of free and slave states. Second, the government authorized the creation of territorial governments in New Mexico and Utah, letting the settlers there decide whether to permit slavery. Third, legislators abolished the internal slave trade in the District of Columbia, but not slavery itself. The compromise's fourth provision, the Fugitive Slave Act, generated the most controversy. It denied accused fugitive slaves a jury trial, leaving their fate to federal commissioners, who were compensated for each fugitive slave case they adjudicated. When the commissioners ruled in favor of the fugitive, they received $5, but they received $10 for ruling in favor of the owner. The Fugitive Slave Act also compelled northern citizens to help apprehend runaways. Now it was not only illegal to assist a fugitive slave; anyone who refused to assist slavecatchers could be prosecuted.

Stephen Douglass, one of the main architects of the Compromise of 1850 in Congress, saw the ruling as the "final settlement" of the slavery question. As we will see in Chapter 9, he was gravely mistaken.

Conclusion

When Thomas Jefferson heard about the 1820 Missouri Compromise—Congress's first attempt to balance slave states and free states—he reacted by being "filled . . . with dread." Jefferson's anxiety was well founded. In the three decades between the Missouri Compromise and the Compromise of 1850, the controversy over slavery followed American settlers into every region of the continent and every aspect of public life. Many Americans sought reform, and for reformers, slavery was often a top priority. Shut out from public life, white and black women stepped forward not only to defend slaves but also to fight for their own rights.

During the reform era, African Americans sought ways to improve their own lives. Some negotiated a bit of latitude within the slave system; others escaped slavery altogether. Some free black people, like Martin Delany and James Forten, assumed leadership in the abolitionist struggle. Other free people sought to educate themselves, choose their own names, and shape their own communities on American soil or elsewhere. Still others, like John Horse and James Beckwourth, shifted their loyalties between enslaved people and a government that protected slavery.

Both white abolitionists and slaveholders defined black people as different from themselves, and William Lloyd Garrison was one of the few who could envision an interracial society as a positive thing. But for now, the possibility of a harmonious black and white society seemed remote. With the Compromise of 1850, the nation neared a crisis point.

Questions for Review and Reflection

1. How does the itinerary of Martin Delany's travels help us visualize the broad variation in the seeming sameness of "southern slavery"?

2. What were some of the dynamics of the early nineteenth century that underlay the alliance between abolition and women's rights movements? What stresses fomented discord among these allies?

3. To what extent did African Americans make a good decision when they focused attention on choosing a label for themselves as a group (colored *Americans*) and on names for individuals in their families? In other words, "what's in a name?" and how important is that question for today's Americans of color?

4. To what extent was mob violence against African Americans specific to black people, and to what extent was it one aspect of an era wherein *general* mob violence was the common version of societal discourse?

5. In the decades leading up to the civil war, the slavery debate was augmented by such variables as America's expansion into the West, the North's increasing population that gave it greater congressional power, the development of new technologies such as railroads and canals, and the discovery of precious metals. How might events have had a different outcome if even one of those variables unfolded differently?

A Prelude to War: The 1850s

Tragedy and Triumph at Christiana

Early on the morning of September 11, 1851, Joshua Kite and six other African American rebels crouched by the windows of a small stone farmhouse on a hill near Christiana, Pennsylvania. Kite was poised to resist his former owner, Edward Gorsuch. Accompanied by federal marshals, Gorsuch had journeyed more than 70 miles from Maryland to take his "boys" back "home."

Two years earlier, rather than awaiting the manumission promised by their master, twenty-one-year-old Kite and several other slaves had escaped from Gorsuch's farm. Crossing the Chesapeake Bay, they headed north. Arriving in Christiana, where they blended into a region populated by 3,000 free and fugitive African Americans, they found refuge among black neighbors, and sympathy from white antislavery Quakers.

Gorsuch had hired slave-hunters to help him locate the fugitives. But by the time he arrived in Christiana, the town had been alerted to his approach. Kite and dozens of his black neighbors stationed themselves at the home of local residents William and Eliza Parker. When a federal marshal challenged him, Parker dismissed the marshal's authority: "I told him I did not care for him nor the United States." Parker's wife threatened the escaped slaves with a corn cutter lest they attempt to surrender. Within minutes of Gorsuch's arrival, he had been shot to death, and his son was badly wounded. White onlookers offered water to the injured and then left them to their fate. Kite, Parker, and a few others escaped to Canada.

The Christiana Riot, as it came to be known, struck terror in the hearts of slaveholders while inspiring hope and pride in African Americans. For once, it was black men—not white—who had prevailed. Southerners demanded hangings, hoping that public executions of black fugitives and their white supporters

1849	Harriet Tubman escapes from slavery.
1850	Fugitive Slave Act requires private citizens to help capture runaways. The Underground Railroad steps up its efforts. Sojourner Truth publishes her life story and begins to lecture on abolition and women's suffrage.
1851	Joshua Kite and William Parker lead a standoff in Christiana, Pennsylvania. William and Ellen Craft's narrative of their escape is published.
1852	Harriet Beecher Stowe's *Uncle Tom's Cabin* is a bestseller.
1853	Mary Ann Shadd becomes the first female newspaper editor in North America.
1854	The Kansas-Nebraska Act establishes popular sovereignty. Fugitive Anthony Burns stands trial in Boston, a test case of the Fugitive Slave Act. Antislavery groups form the Republican Party.
1856	Popular sovereignty precipitates open warfare in "Bleeding Kansas."
1857	In *Dred Scott* v. *Sandford*, the Supreme Court rules that slaves are property protected in every state, that slaves are not entitled to use the courts, and that slaves and their descendants can never be citizens. Hinton Rowan Helper publishes *The Impending Crisis of the South*. George Fitzhugh publishes a defense of slavery.
1858	Lincoln–Douglas debates dramatize regional crisis.
1859	John Brown leads raid on a federal armory in Harpers Ferry, Virginia.

would deter further rebellion. Officials arrested nearly three dozen people, white and black. A recent law provided that aiding runaway slaves rather than turning them over to authorities was a federal crime, so the detainees were charged with conspiracy and treason—the latter punishable by death. Still, white jurors in Pennsylvania, where the trial was held, acquitted one man and dropped the charges against the rest. They viewed the slave hunt and the trial as a battle between states' rights and the federal government's attempts to erode those rights, and thus they had no interest in assisting slave hunters.

The episode dramatized the regional and racial tensions tearing at American society in the 1850s. The tensions were heightened by the Fugitive Slave Act of 1850, which required individuals to capture and return escaped slaves. Many white Northerners who had been undecided or indifferent about slavery now associated antislavery action with the right to make their own laws. Meanwhile, abolitionist sentiment in the North was growing. Newspapers regularly published harrowing accounts of slavery and daring escapes—many written by escaped slaves.

In contrast, white Southerners increasingly felt outnumbered in the federal government. With their slave-based economy and social system under attack by abolitionists, even white Southerners who did not own slaves often felt duty-bound to defend the institution. Only a few white Southerners viewed the slave system as a drag on the southern economy and a cancer on the nation.

The new militant mood of many African Americans reflected a mixture of defiance and fear. No black person, slave or free, could ignore slavery. The Underground Railroad, which provided a means of escape for slaves in the South, offered some hope to those who were enslaved, as did the growing abolitionist movement. Still, opportunities were limited even for those who were free. In Canada, former slaves could find freedom but few jobs. The American West offered dreams of gold and jobs, but efforts to extend slavery westward made it a risky place to settle. Even as reformers increased efforts to sway America's conscience, political and legal efforts tightened the grip of slavery. Convinced that Americans would never give up slavery peacefully, the boldest abolitionists encouraged a messianic figure, John Brown, who attempted to ignite a slave rebellion at Harpers Ferry, Virginia, in 1859.

Controversy over the Fugitive Slave Act of 1850

The Compromise of 1850, passed by Congress in that year, included a Fugitive Slave Act that strengthened federal regulations for apprehending runaway slaves. The new policy raised tensions for many Americans, northern and southern, white and black. The issues included federal authority versus state powers, constitutional protections of private property, individuals' protests against federal power, and black fugitives' security. Both Southerners and Northerners feared capture of federal power by the other. Southern planters increasingly worried that if the federal government acquired too much power, it might ban slavery. Northerners feared that if the federal government could legislate how they treated fugitive slaves, it might begin controlling other facets of their lives. And the prospect of abolishing slavery caused everyone to worry about property rights. If slaves were freed and slaves were property, wouldn't this amount to government seizure of property? If owners were compensated by the federal government, wouldn't this amount to Northerners being implicated in the purchase of slaves?

The rising regional tension was also felt in southern slave quarters, where masters' growing anxiety about rebellion often meant increased repression. And repression, combined with the increasing frequency of slave sales from the Upper South into the Lower South, spurred a dramatic rise in the number of escapes. As the slave grapevine reported growing defiance among northern white abolitionists, greater numbers of slaves became willing to risk all for freedom.

Controversy between the North and South also grew with the widening gulf between their economies. Many northern states had developed mills, factories, and extensive canal and railroad systems to move manufactured goods west and to transport raw materials to eastern cities. Southerners had extended their plantation system, which required many workers and vast stretches of land. People in both regions wanted to make sure their interests were adequately represented in Congress. But through the 1850s, as immigration swelled the North's population, its growing number of congressmen tipped the balance in Congress to the North.

Federal Power versus States' Rights

The U.S. Constitution protected the rights of slaveholders by providing that any person escaping bondage should be returned. Federal laws passed in the 1790s also required local officials to return fugitives to owners. But in 1826 Pennsylvania reformers had passed a "personal liberty" law banning the forcible return of slaves. In 1842, the U.S. Supreme Court upheld personal liberty laws in *Prigg* v. *Pennsylvania*, ruling that individual states were not obliged to help enforce these federal laws. Several northern states took this decision as permission to pass personal liberty laws *prohibiting* state officials from aiding slavecatchers.

These Northerners resented the Fugitive Slave Act provision whereby citizens who refused to help apprehend slaves could be charged with treason. This provision, they felt, overstepped federal authority. Now, as would-be fugitives could not find safety by crossing into a northern state, their desperation increased, as did the risks associated with escape. Fugitives would have to leave the country or find support in standing their ground in northern states, hoping local resistance to federal authorities would work in their favor. The standoff at Christiana was among the most dramatic of such clashes.

Westward expansion also raised the question of states' rights, specifically whether new territories would be slave or free. As we saw in Chapter 7, Congress approved the Missouri Compromise in 1820, dividing the 1803 Louisiana Purchase into a northern section without slaves and a southern section where slavery was allowed. In 1848, just as Mexico was ceding to the United States new territory that included California, Utah, and New Mexico, the discovery of gold in California sparked a rush westward. Congress responded by designing the complex Compromise of 1850, whereby California entered the union as a free state while the other territories acquired from Mexico might become slave states if their citizens so chose. Thus, the compromise established the principle of popular sovereignty: the right of local residents to decide whether their state would be slave or free.

Statehood for California gave the free states a 16–15 edge in the U.S. Senate, worrying Southerners, who got a more stringent Fugitive Slave Act in return. But ultimately the Compromise of 1850 only intensified conflict between

THE CHRISTIANA TRAGEDY.

First published in 1859 , this engraving of the Christiana incident remained popular for decades.

North and South. Even white Northerners without strong abolitionist sympathies became convinced that resisting slave-hunting federal marshals was an act of patriotism. Some northern state legislatures broadened personal liberty laws to include the right of state courts to override *any* federal legislation. Massachusetts boldly nullified the Fugitive Slave Act. This was the most flagrant attack a state could make on federal power: to instruct its citizens to ignore or defy a federal law.

Despite northern fears of a "slaveocracy," in which Southerners would spread guarantees for slavery throughout the country, many Southerners in Maryland and Virginia, like Edward Gorsuch, had been preparing to release slaves: As the region's economy shifted from tobacco to grain farming, hiring seasonal field hands was far cheaper than clothing and feeding slaves all year. Nonetheless, Gorsuch's slaves represented more than a financial investment (though a single slave might represent an investment of $2,000). To him slaves embodied the principles of property rights and personal honor. For Southerners like Gorsuch, slaves themselves were less important than the right of a man to maintain control of his property.

The Underground Railroad

In 1849, the same year Joshua Kite fled, another twenty-one-year-old slave escaped from Maryland. After a brief rest on the free soil of Pennsylvania,

Harriet Tubman retraced her steps to escort some of her family and friends over the same ground. Soon known as "Black Moses," Tubman made as many as three dozen trips into slave territory, leading hundreds of slaves to freedom, including her own parents. She seemed fearless. Armed with a pistol, she made it clear that she would use it on anyone, white or black, who threatened to sabotage her mission. Slaves revered her. Slaveholders feared what she represented: a new posture of black defiance. Some put a price of $40,000 on her head—equivalent to more than $1 million today. But she was never captured.

Tubman was among the best-known members of the abolitionist network known as the Underground Railroad, a community of African Americans and their white allies, called "conductors." Originally, the Underground Railroad used secret routes along rivers, seaports, and northern border communities to transport slaves from the South to freedom in Ohio, Pennsylvania, and New York. By 1830, conductors were taking a few runaway slaves as far as New England, Canada, Europe, and Mexico. Supported by Vigilance Committees—secret local networks—the Underground Railroad was at its most active during the 1850s as the national upheaval over slavery came to a boil. Of the estimated 100,000 slaves who escaped in this way, probably three-fourths did so after the 1850 Fugitive Slave Act intensified their desperation and their conductors' commitment.

Work in the Underground Railroad had personal meaning for many individuals. William Still, a black Philadelphian, discovered that a fugitive he "conducted" was his own long-lost brother. Still's coded records of runaways and those who helped them are invaluable to historians working to reconstruct this secret network. Levi Coffin, a white Quaker from North Carolina, moved to Indiana to better position himself to help. John Brown, a white New Englander, relocated to Kansas to further the abolitionist cause.

Fugitives themselves escaped by various methods and to various places. Oriented by the North Star of the Big Dipper constellation in the night sky and guided by moss on the north sides of trees, perhaps as many as 8,000 slaves per year fled the South on foot, horseback, or hidden in wagons. Some escaped by sea stowing away on ships headed as far as Canada and Britain, or as near as Cincinnati, Detroit, and the northern Mississippi River. Some journeyed on to California, the Pacific Northwest, and Texas. Others joined Native American communities in remote places like Nacimiento, across the Rio Grande in Mexico, where Seminole leader John Horse established a refugee outpost in 1849.

The Escape and Trial of Anthony Burns

The experience of Anthony Burns, a slave who escaped to Boston in 1854, exemplifies one way the Fugitive Slave Act played out in the North. Learning to read at a young age, Burns became a preacher in his local Baptist church in Virginia, where black and white congregants worshipped together. Hired out by Charles Suttles, his master, to work in Richmond, Burns escaped on a boat bound for Boston. Befriended by a white Quaker abolitionist, he quietly worked

With help from a northern Vigilance Committee, Henry "Box" Brown was shipped to William Johnson, a Philadelphia black abolitionist. This triumphant portrayal, using the biblical reference of "resurrection" to underscore the righteousness of Brown's escape, was published in 1854.

in a clothing shop. But he missed his family and could not resist sending a letter to his brother on the Suttles plantation. Suttles intercepted the letter and contacted Boston authorities. Burns was arrested and placed in leg irons in a federal courthouse.

Boston's abolitionists sprang to action. Lawyer Richard Henry Dana, condemning the Fugitive Slave Act as "the devil's license for kidnapping," called a protest meeting that drew several thousand angry people, including hundreds of black residents from the whaling town of New Bedford. In a frenzy, the crowd stormed the courthouse to free Burns, killing one federal official and wounding others. President Franklin Pierce sent troops and authorized "any expense" to uphold federal law. The next day, the abolitionists raised $1,200 to purchase Burns's freedom. But federal officials persuaded Suttles not to sell Burns; it was vital, they said, to use his case to test the Fugitive Slave Act in court.

Dana attempted to prove that Massachusetts's personal liberty law superseded the Fugitive Slave Act. But after the judge ruled that Burns must be returned, armed troops escorted him through an aisle of sobbing abolitionists who had draped buildings in black. By the time Burns was loaded onto a boat for Virginia, more than $100,000 had been spent to uphold Southerners' constitutional right to federal protection of their property.

Anthony Burns's story had a happy ending, as the Boston Vigilance Committee eventually succeeded in purchasing his freedom. But his trial deeply affected abolitionists. Charlotte Forten, a seventeen-year-old black Philadelphian, attended the public meetings and anguished over the ruling. "It is impossible to be happy now," she wrote, rededicating herself to abolitionist efforts. Abolitionism was a family tradition. The granddaughter of a prosperous black sailmaker and daughter of a respected abolitionist, she was well educated and well-to-do. Despite her privilege, she saw herself as an African American in a country that dehumanized all black people, and she empathized with slaves who suffered because of their race.

The Power of Stories

In her 1987 best-selling novel, *Beloved,* Toni Morrison describes a slave who so loves her child that she kills her rather than see her grow up in bondage. Morrison's fictional character was a composite of actual enslaved women who had been driven to this desperate act. In the 1850s, such tragic stories captured the attention of northern and southern audiences. A second wave of writing—often poetry, fiction, and historical accounts—came from northern African Americans who focused on the struggles of free black people. The writings of white abolitionists, such as William Lloyd Garrison, publisher of *The Liberator,* argued that unless white people destroyed slavery, they risked incurring God's wrath. White Southerners, in contrast, wrote to demonstrate that slavery was better than free labor systems.

Slave Narratives

In the dead of winter in 1848, William and Ellen Craft escaped from Georgia to freedom. William disguised himself as a servant to the light-skinned Ellen, who dressed like a man, posing as a slave owner's son. With the money saved from William's carpentry work, the Crafts traveled as paying customers on steamboats, staying in fine hotels along the way. Who, after all, would look in such places for runaways? The following year, the Crafts toured England, explaining to spellbound audiences that although their master had not treated them harshly, they escaped lest they bear a child who would be sold from them. In 1851, the Crafts published their experiences in a London newspaper, demonstrating the power of stories to move minds and hearts and to enlist British sympathies to the American antislavery cause. These African American–British networks—what one historian has called "an anti-slavery wall"—proved invaluable in coming years.

African American fugitives had dramatic stories to tell. The saga of former slave Henry "Box" Brown, published in 1854, provides an apt example of a slave narrative, a firsthand account that exposed the cruelties of slavery. Five years earlier, Brown had himself packed in a 2-foot-square crate and shipped by boat from Richmond to Philadelphia. As we saw in Chapter 7, Harriet Jacobs's *Incidents in the Life of a Slave Girl* (1861) constituted one of the most gripping stories of the cruelties inflicted on slave women. Sexual abuse and fear for their children often heightened slave women's desperation. Some took huge risks to free or protect themselves and their youngsters; others "freed" their children from bondage by killing them. Frederick Douglass, who had published his autobiography in 1845, released an updated version entitled *My Bondage and My Freedom* in 1855 that included his analysis of the effect of the Fugitive Slave Act. Long silenced, black Americans finally had a voice. They also had an audience hungry for their words.

Northern Black Voices

Northern African Americans told a different story of slavery and abolition. In 1826, Isabella Van Wageren, born a slave in upstate New York, walked away from an owner who reneged on his promise to free her. There was no daring escape, no long journey, no secrecy, for both slave and master knew that New York's gradual abolition law would free her the next year. Deeply religious, Van Wageren later reported that God had called her and told her to change her name to Sojourner Truth. A sojourner, she explained, is one who travels. She was to take to the road to tell the truth about the evils of slavery and the oppression of women.

In 1850, Truth published her life story, *Narrative of Sojourner Truth*. A spellbinding storyteller, Truth began to travel widely on the antislavery lecture circuit. She enjoyed public speaking, she said, because "I wanted to see what

Known best as a stalwart abolitionist and crusader for women's rights, Sojourner Truth was masterful at promoting her concerns. She distributed prints of herself like this one mounted on small cards to spread her reputation and raise money for her cause.

God would have me say." Truth emerged as a powerful voice for women's suffrage as well as African American rights. She secured a lasting reputation when she preached that if one woman—the biblical Eve—could turn the world upside down, then a united community of women could put it right again. Truth frequently claimed she could work as hard as any man, yet she challenged her audience, "Ain't I a woman?"

Most black Americans lacked the resources to publicize their plight, but others spoke for them. In 1855, Bostonian William C. Nell, America's first black historian, published two volumes documenting African Americans' participation in the American Revolution and the War of 1812 (downplaying the numbers who fought for the British, who promised them freedom). In 1847 William Wells Brown published the story of his life and escape from slavery. Six years later he published *Clotel,* a novel about Thomas Jefferson's mixed-race daughter that portrayed black Americans as complex human beings rather than as stereotyped slaves and fugitives. In 1857, Frank Webb published *The Garies and Their Friends,* about the social life of Philadelphia's black middle class. Webb's popular novel also helped white Americans put a human face on black men and women.

Francis Ellen Watkins also contributed to this black intellectual movement. Born free in 1825 and orphaned young in the slave city of Baltimore, she was raised by her uncle, an abolitionist shoemaker who was friends with Garrison. The uncle nurtured his precocious niece's writing talent and her strong social conscience. Before she was twenty, Watkins had published *Forest Leaves* (1845), a collection of poems. More volumes followed, including one introduced by Garrison. Lecturing on the antislavery circuit, she encouraged her listeners to boycott products resulting from slave labor.

White Abolitionist Appeals

White abolitionists also used stories of slavery's horror to advance the antislavery cause. One involved Margaret Garner, who fled with her family in 1856. When U.S. marshals located them in Ohio, the distraught Garner slit the throat of her infant daughter and struck two of her sons with a shovel to prevent them from being re-enslaved. Then she threw herself and one or perhaps more of her children—accounts vary—into the Ohio River. Still, she was captured before she could kill herself. She was sold into the Lower South, and her remaining children sold to different masters. Within days, abolitionists everywhere had begun recounting Margaret Garner's story.

In 1851, Harriet Beecher Stowe began publishing a serialized novel about slavery. Neither a historian nor an abolitionist, Stowe was a religious woman inflamed by the Fugitive Slave Act. Eventually titled *Uncle Tom's Cabin,* her story was sympathetic to southern slave owners as well as to slaves. Stowe characterized most white Southerners as decent, God-fearing people trapped in an economy supported by a tradition of bondage and cruelty. Only the overseer, Simon Legree, was presented as heartless. Stowe portrayed a tender friendship between Eva, an innocent white child, and Tom, a patient and loving elderly

Raised in a slave-owning Kentucky family, Thomas Satterthwaite Noble painted many slave scenes, including this one dramatizing the 1856 event of fugitive Margaret Garner attempting to destroy her children lest they be seized by federal authorities. The painting, done in 1867, several years after slavery's end, demonstrates the story's enduring hold on the public imagination.

slave who was devoted to his master's family and who took comfort in Christian faith. Stowe contrasted his acceptance of his lot with the rebellious young fugitive Eliza, fleeing to freedom across the icy Ohio River.

By allowing readers to empathize with most of her characters—black and white, northern and southern—Stowe reached many who had not previously advocated abolition. In 1852, when the serial was published as a novel, it immediately sold 300,000 copies. Quickly translated into several languages, *Uncle Tom's Cabin* became an international best seller, breathing new life into the antislavery movement.

Annoyed by Stowe's passive hero, Martin Delany claimed Stowe "knows nothing about us." In response, he published *Blake; or the Huts of Africa* (1852), a novel drawn on his reminiscences of his trip through the South. Henry Blake, the protagonist, was the antithesis of Uncle Tom. A rebel who escaped from slavery, Blake had no religious qualms against killing a white man. On his way to Canada, Blake urged other African Americans to contact "one good man or woman on [each] plantation" to incite rebellion.

Southern Views of Slavery

For different reasons, Southerners were also enraged by *Uncle Tom's Cabin*. Some Southerners claimed that because Stowe had never visited the South, she had no authority to condemn its ways. Others argued that brutal overseers like

Simon Legree were the exception. Southern novelist William Gilmore Simms said his novel, *Woodcraft* (1854), was "probably as good an answer to Mrs. Stowe as has ever been published." Using humor, Simms portrayed a plantation life in which the sense of loyalty and responsibility on the part of slave owners to both the land and slaves created a model society.

Other Southerners joined Simms's defense of slavery. Among the most persuasive was George Fitzhugh, an aristocratic Virginia lawyer. Fitzhugh held that southern slavery offered the most moral and humane system for both white and black Americans. Although Northerners were not slaveholders, he said, their system exploited weak individuals, while southern society protected them. In several works, including *Cannibals All! or, Slaves Without Masters* (1857), Fitzhugh argued that the North had abolished the name of slavery "but not the *thing*."

In Fitzhugh's view, the "thing" that dehumanized the North was the wage system, which made no provisions for workers' illnesses, pregnancy, childrearing, or old age. Industrialism forced owners to cast out all but the most efficient laborers. In contrast, said Fitzhugh, southern planters looked after slaves' welfare, for it was to their economic advantage to do so. Applauding Fitzhugh's publications, which articulated long-held views, many Southerners shifted from a defensive posture to defiance.

The Changing South

In 1857, North Carolinian Hinton Rowan Helper's *The Impending Crisis of the South, and How to Meet It* infuriated many Southerners with its assertion that the southern economy was fundamentally unsound. Helper looked at slavery from a purely economic point of view, arguing that it undermined both the livelihoods of non-slaveholding white people (such as himself) and the southern economy at large. By depressing the employment opportunities and wages of white workers, slavery kept southern industries and ports from expanding. *The Impending Crisis* was banned across the South; southern post offices refused to deliver it. Helper fled to New York, but suppression of his book did nothing to stop the forces transforming the South's society and economy.

Southern Society and Economy

During the 1850s, about 25 percent of the 8 million white people living in the South owned slaves, and only about 1 percent possessed as many as 300 slaves. A minority of the South's white men controlled almost all the region's slaves, yet they had disproportionate social and political influence. The nearly 55 million bales of cotton they produced annually accounted for more than half of the dollar value of all U.S. exports. Because northern textile mills relied on southern cotton, many northern congressmen sympathized with southern arguments that only slave labor could sustain the U.S. economy.

The South that Helper described was actually becoming several Souths, each with its own economy and social structure. In the Upper South (Virginia,

Maryland, and North Carolina), corn and wheat production was replacing tobacco, and the selling of surplus slaves to the Lower South was rapidly reducing the number of African Americans. In contrast, the Lower South (from South Carolina to eastern Texas), where cotton production dominated the economy, the black population swelled rapidly. The forested Appalachian Upcountry remained the preserve of struggling white farmers. In North Carolina, for example, most of the slave-owning planters were in the coastal region, while most white people (70 percent of the white population) living in the hilly western region held no slaves at all, and over two-thirds of those who owned slaves had fewer than ten.

Imbalances in southern demographics worried some white Southerners. The slave count climbed steadily, especially in the Lower South. Meanwhile, the free black population grew slowly—mostly in the Upper South—from 250,000 in 1850 to about 260,000 in 1860. More than one-third of free black people lived in cities, while less than one-quarter of the white population did. Though the birthrate for all black Americans, enslaved and free, decreased slightly, the free black population in the West more than quadrupled as free African Americans left the South. The more than two million European immigrants who arrived during these years settled almost exclusively in the North and West, giving these regions labor alternatives unavailable to the South. Most white Southerners feared losing control of the dependable labor that had once given them an economic advantage over the North.

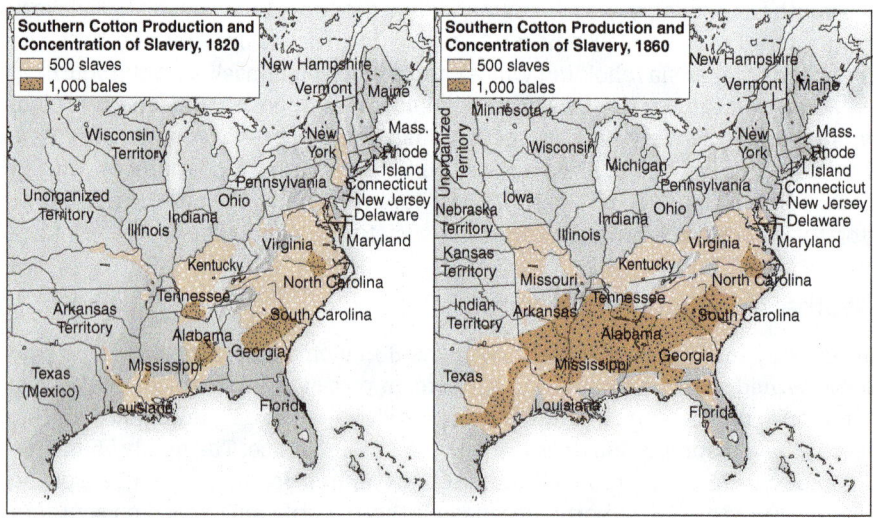

MAP 9.1   Southern Cotton Production and Concentration of Slavery, 1820 and 1860

Between 1820 and 1860, as cotton production eclipsed tobacco, the concentration of slaves shifted from the Upper South to the Lower South. Most slaves were now further isolated from the Atlantic coast and from the North.

In *The Impending Crisis,* Helper championed the cause of southern white farmers who struggled to make a living on small plots of land without sufficient labor. He decried their dependence on large planters to market their crops and the injustice of their taxes being used to compensate owners whose slaves were executed for crimes. Using statistics (some exaggerated), Helper argued that slavery deprived the South of funds for schools, roads, libraries, newspapers, and industries. Policies that maintained large planters' dominance kept poor white people isolated, ignorant, and dependent. Railroads built with slave labor, for example, connected cities but did not link to the hinterlands, as railroads in the North did. By retarding the South's industry, transportation, and commerce, Helper claimed, planters forced Southerners to import most finished goods from the North or abroad.

Historians are still debating how prosperous the South really was, but Helper identified real problems with its economy. Much land was mortgaged to banks in England or the North. Planters were often land rich but cash poor, unable to pay for labor. Sometimes the cost of acquiring and maintaining a slave worker exceeded the slave's productivity. Yet most planters were wedded to their way of life, even if it was in crisis.

"The World They Made Together"

With the large black-to-white ratio in many parts of the South, African Americans—including fugitives and even some black slaveholders—exerted surprisingly great influence. In theory, white Southerners controlled black lives, but the interdependence between slaves and owners was so intricate that one historian describes the black-and-white South as "a world they made together."

In the summer of 1855, Lucy Skipwith wrote to her absent master in Virginia: "We keeps up family Prayers every morning. I does the best I can teaching the children but I can never get more than two and sometimes three little ones on week days. My little girl Maria is beginning to write very well and is very anxious to write to you." Through the letters of Lucy Skipwith, who managed a plantation household during the 1850s, we can glimpse one example of the intricacies of plantation life. Lucy's master, John Hartwell Cocke, was a southern reformer who planned to Christianize his slaves, teach them thrift and temperance, and then free and dispatch them as missionaries to Liberia. To that end, in 1840 he established Hopewell, a cotton plantation in Greene County, Alabama. There he installed Lucy Skipwith's father, George, as head driver, and sometimes as overseer, of four dozen slaves.

George Skipwith, a man of independent spirit, often ignored overseers' authority. Yet Cocke tolerated him because slaves worked efficiently under his supervision. Lucy apparently inherited her father's strong sense of his own mind. Though Cocke set Hopewell's goals, the plantation's daily operation lay in the hands of the black Skipwiths. For over a decade, Cocke spent almost half of each year in Virginia. When he was at Hopewell, Lucy Skipwith was his personal servant. But when he was in Virginia, she set her own schedule and household priorities, managing sewing, weaving, cooking, and religious education. Taking advantage of Cocke's instructions to Christianize the slaves, she lobbied for black education and complained when work routines interfered. Thus Cocke's legal authority and power intertwined with the Skipwith's actual authority and power. The power was unequal, but the interdependence was inescapable.

The lives of most black slaves and their masters fell somewhere between what readers found in Harriet Beecher Stowe's meek Uncle Tom and Martin Delany's insurrectionist Henry Blake. White slaveholders believed they controlled their world, but in fact they depended heavily on slaves' ingenuity and loyalty. They had to tolerate countless acts of slave resistance—burned meals, deliberately broken tools, pilfered livestock, or sabotaged crops—even as they wavered between denying and fearing the system's instability. Every law, every policy, every move a master made was shaped by the desire to tighten control over potentially rebellious bondspeople.

Free Black People

By 1850, more than 200,000 free black people lived in the South. Most were clustered in the cities, where they worked as domestic workers or as carpenters, blacksmiths, or clothiers. Some of these African Americans were the children of masters. Others were slaves whose masters had allowed them to hire out their time; they had saved their money and purchased themselves or their families. It was not uncommon for a man to purchase his wife—while himself remaining enslaved—to protect her from sexual exploitation and assure that his children would be born free. But the free black person's life was precarious. If captured by an unscrupulous slave hunter, a free black man or woman might be sold to some distant location. Because black people were usually not allowed to testify in the courts, there was little recourse if a white person claimed a free black person as property.

Yet some southern free African Americans made a comfortable life. Often choosing not to leave the area where relatives were still enslaved, they opened schools or shops or made a living on the docks. A few even acquired substantial property—including slaves. By 1850, a few hundred black slaveholders owned 9,000 bondspeople. To be sure, most southern free African Americans, even those of substantial means, did not traffic in black people. But those who did were as free as their white neighbors to exploit their human property.

A few black planters grew wealthy. South Carolina's William Ellison owned more than five dozen slaves. William Johnson of Natchez left a diary of his career as landlord and farmer. A mixed-race man freed by his master, Johnson was twenty-three when he bought his first slave. When he died, he owned 400 acres. Like his white neighbors, he gambled, traveled, hunted, fished—and whipped his slaves. As he was in a position to lend money to some of his white neighbors, Johnson attained a status that was remarkable in the slave South.

In the weeks following the passage of the 1850 Fugitive Slave Act, Johnson's diary entries remained focused on produce, wool, livestock, and his white overseer and his slaves. However, a cryptic comment from late September suggests local tensions: "Young Jno [Jonathan] Gains shot a Black man that had ran away from Mr. Hutcheons this morning and killed him dead. This was done in the woods." Ironically, Johnson was shot to death in those woods the next year, apparently in a property dispute with another biracial planter. The only witnesses were black men—who were not allowed to testify in the courts. After two years in jail and many trials, Johnson's killer convinced a jury he was white. Because the murder of a black man by a white man was not considered a crime, the killer was acquitted.

Viewing black planters as potential allies in the cause of justifying bondage and suppressing slave insurrection, some white planters encouraged black slaveholding. But there were limits to what black slaveholders could do. They could not vote or escape racial insults, and they had no protection in the courts. Their status and freedom depended on not angering powerful white neighbors.

Black Exiles Abroad and at Home

The number of hospitable destinations for free black people in the United States shrank quickly during the 1850s. Ohio, for example, imposed a heavy tax on free black immigrants, while a new Illinois law halted black immigration completely. Maryland, long home to thousands of free African Americans, began to allow slave hunters to seize *free* black people entering from other states and sell them into bondage. Virginia laid a poll tax—a tax on voting—on free black residents, intended specifically to create funds to deport them to Africa. Minnesota revoked a long-held black right to vote. Other states followed suit until black men could vote only in Maine, New Hampshire, Rhode Island, Vermont, Wisconsin, and Massachusetts. In response, black leaders debated the best options for free black people, with some advocating that they leave the country that curtailed their freedoms. Some black people went to the American frontier; others left for Canada, Haiti, and Africa.

The Debate over Emigration

The divisions between the Holly brothers exemplified the debates over emigration taking place in free black communities in the 1850s. The son of a shoemaker, James T. Holly studied mathematics and classics in black schools in his native Washington, DC, and in Brooklyn, New York. In 1850, Holly and his older brother Joseph established themselves as bootmakers in Burlington, Vermont. But James Holly dreamed of a better life outside the United States. He was attracted by the argument that black Americans should save money to relocate to Africa or accept offers from groups like the American Colonization Society to help finance such a move. Joseph Holly, James's brother, insisted that expatriates were traitors, as they left enslaved black people without advocates. Expatriates, he said, were manipulated by white schemers intending to send the most talented (and therefore troublesome) black people to places where they could not incite slaves to rebel.

By 1852, James Holly had settled in Ontario, where he met the embittered Martin Delany. Two years earlier, Delany had gained admission to Harvard University's medical school. In 1850, only a few black doctors practiced in the United States, and most had been educated abroad. In 1849, Bowdoin College awarded medical degrees to two African American brothers, Thomas and John White, and Harvard's training would position Delany as the next black American doctor trained in his own country. However, white fellow students forced Delany to withdraw during his first year. Unable to enlist the support of Boston abolitionists, who felt they had more pressing battles to fight, Delany moved to Ontario with his wife and children. There, he became a leader of the black exile community.

Together, Delany and Holly formed the American Emigration Society. At its annual conventions, its leaders encouraged emigration to Canada, which offered citizenship and all-black communities. They also suggested the West Indies, Liberia, Haiti, and Central America as havens from discrimination.

But in the years before the Civil War, views changed. At first, Holly championed Canada, citing its proximity to the United States as ideal for aiding slaves. But influenced by white abolitionist James Redpath, who urged black people to leave "this bastard democracy in the United States," Holly soon recommended Haiti, where he and Redpath persuaded the government to give land to African American settlers. Meanwhile, Delany, fearing the United States would soon annex Canada, recommended Central and South America and the British Caribbean.

Safe Haven in Canada

In 1852, young Mary Ann Shadd touted Canada as a home for free black people. In a pamphlet, "Notes of Canada West," she compared opportunities in the British West Indies and Central America and concluded that the Great Lakes region of southern Canada, a short ferry ride from Detroit, "offers stronger inducements to colored people."

Indeed, Canada's government, hoping new black communities would be a buffer between white Canadians and rebellious Indians, offered citizenship and the vote to black immigrants after just three years' residency. Canada's invitation had wide appeal, and Ontario's black communities grew dramatically, attracting the principal players in the Christiana episode—William and Eliza Parker and some of the fugitive slaves—Martin Delany, and other disaffected African Americans. By 1860, several thousand black immigrants were living in Canada. While grateful for Canadian sanctuary, many resented their exile and their treatment as second-class citizens. Although several hundred black newcomers owned businesses and land, many had trouble finding work, and their wages were often lower than those of white workers.

Unlike Delany and many other Canadian immigrants, Mary Ann Shadd had never experienced slavery. Born in 1823 to free and relatively prosperous parents in Delaware, she had studied at Quaker schools. In the 1840s, the family relocated to Canada. Shadd's father, Abraham, was elected to the town council in Chatham—the first black person to win an elective office in Canada. In the late 1840s, Mary Ann Shadd returned to the United States to teach black children in Pennsylvania, Delaware, and New York. Then passage of the Fugitive Slave Act spurred her to return to Canada to teach fugitive slaves. In 1851 she accepted support from the American Missionary Association (AMA) to open a school. But she always felt uneasy about the AMA, suspecting it cheated black refugees by selling them Canadian land at inflated prices. In 1856, when the AMA withdrew its support from her school, she was relieved to regain her autonomy.

Shadd was mentored by Henry Bibb, a black newspaper publisher who had arrived in Canada with a more harrowing history. It had taken Bibb five attempts before he finally escaped from his master in Kentucky in 1842. Then he spent several years lecturing for the antislavery cause and campaigning for the antislavery Liberty Party. In 1849, settled in Detroit, Bibb published his *Narrative of the Life and Adventures of Henry Bibb, An American Slave, Written by Himself.* When the Fugitive Slave Act made him feel vulnerable in Detroit, Bibb moved to Ontario, where he felt safe enough to write to his former owner celebrating his own "work of self-emancipation." By 1852, Bibb was publishing his own newspaper, *The Voice of the Fugitive.*

Shadd and Bibb parted ways over education for black children, however, reflecting frustrations within black communities over how to carve out lives in a new country. The Canadian government provided schools for black immigrants, but they were inferior to those for white students. Shadd advocated independent schools. Black and white parents alike, she insisted, could pool their resources to educate children of both races. In contrast, Bibb, whose wife's independent school for black children had failed financially, felt African Americans could ill afford private schools and that government-supported all-black schools were better than no schools at all. Bibb had no faith that interracial schools would work.

In 1853, Shadd assumed editorship of the *Provincial Freeman,* an independent black newspaper. She was the first female newspaper editor, black or white, in North America. The paper gave voice to her views about emigration, community life, and education, and to her frustration with Bibb. Their feud over education played out in public, in their respective newspapers.

The Lure of the Frontier

While several thousand African Americans sought refuge in Canada in the 1850s, a small but steady stream went west. During the 1840s, a few fled to Texas—but by 1860, when some 300 free black Texans were outnumbered by a slave population grown to 183,000, white Texans acted to constrain free black peoples' rights. So black freedom-seekers moved on to the next frontier. By 1860, several thousand reached California. Another hundred made it to the Oregon Territory. In both regions, slavery was outlawed. Though these areas hardly extended a warm welcome, African Americans established themselves as tavernkeepers, laundresses, haulers, and shopkeepers. Others became scouts, cooks, livestock tenders, or gold prospectors.

Among the most colorful black westerners was free-born Mifflin W. Gibbs. As a twenty-two-year-old Philadelphian in 1850, Gibbs was recruited to the antislavery lecture circuit by Frederick Douglass and Charles Remond. But soon he was lured to California by the gold rush, where he learned of Biddy Mason, whose master had brought her from Utah to California in 1851. Encouraged by free black leaders, Mason petitioned the California courts for her family's freedom. In 1855, after three days of hearings, the courts declared the Masons free.

The abolitionist spirit in California energized Gibbs, who founded *Mirror of the Times,* the state's first black newspaper. He protested California's poll tax, which was imposed only on black voters. When he voted without paying the tax, officials seized goods from his clothing store, but Gibbs resisted. "With a fervor as cool as the circumstances would permit" he pledged "that the great State of California might annually confiscate our goods, but we would never pay the voters tax." When the courts restored his goods, Gibbs gloated, "No further attempts to enforce the law upon colored men were made."

Regional Crisis

"Are we incapable of self-government?" Martin Delany asked black Americans in an 1852 essay. Answering his own question, Delany insisted that only political power, not moral argument, could assure African Americans lives of dignity. Smarting after his humiliation at Harvard, Delany poured out his discouragement at the prospects for equality and justice in the country of his birth. "No people can have political power if they do not constitute a majority," he concluded.

Delany's concern about finding a place where black people could influence government policy mirrored regional concerns about representation. White Southerners despaired the loss of their majority in Congress. Western settlers worried that federal laws would favor easterners. As free black people sought influence, their leadership splintered. Meanwhile, white leaders' attempts to settle the slavery question with the Kansas-Nebraska Act of 1854 took the nation to the precipice of civil war. Regional compromise seemed all but impossible.

From Moral Suasion to Political Power

While some black Americans chose emigration, others, like Frederick Douglass, began exploring political methods to end slavery and gain citizenship. For more than a decade, Douglass promoted William Lloyd Garrison's concept of "moral suasion"—appealing to American consciences to end slavery. But increasingly convinced that this tactic was naive and unrealistic, Douglass moved toward political action after the 1839 founding of the Liberty Party. He came to believe that the U.S. Constitution—if it could be enforced—guaranteed African Americans citizenship. In 1848, he joined the Free Soil Party, a coalition led by New England abolitionists who wanted any territory gained from Mexico to be non-slave. The Free Soil Party ran an antislavery candidate for president in 1848. Though black men could vote in only a few states, Douglass helped design the party's platform.

Douglass also began to see a value in separate black organizations, and he encouraged black people to work with—but not within—white reform organizations. These ideas drew him away from other black leaders, who still believed biracial cooperation to change the hearts and minds of white Americans was the only way to achieve enduring racial peace. Through these differences in perspective, black leadership splintered in the 1850s.

The Kansas-Nebraska Act

In 1854, Illinois Senator Stephen A. Douglas reopened the question of slavery in the territories. Arguing that local people could best determine their region's needs, Douglas had a further suggestion for helping Americans remember their common interests. A railroad from Chicago to the Pacific, he argued, would benefit the whole nation's economy. For the railroad to succeed, however, white Americans would need to settle Kansas and Nebraska. Why not offer these new settlers popular sovereignty—that is, the right to decide whether to have slavery in their communities? Though some politicians feared the plan would lead to battles over community control, Congress passed the Kansas-Nebraska Act in May 1854.

Despite twenty years of political experience, Douglas had misjudged how Americans' anxieties about slavery could fuel their fears of conspiracies. When fugitive Anthony Burns was apprehended in Boston just two days after passage of the new act, northern reformers accused Douglas of plotting with others in the federal government to stir southern resentment against the North. Radical white abolitionists and even many moderate Northerners also worried that popular sovereignty would undermine the Missouri Compromise, as both Kansas and Nebraska were north of the line where slavery was to have been prohibited. Losing faith in Douglas's integrity, Northerners deserted his Democratic Party. Some switched to the antislavery Republican Party, a new coalition formed in 1854 when remnants of the Liberty Party joined with the Free Soil Party. Others opted for the two-year-old Know-Nothing Party, which condemned abolitionists and proslavery advocates alike to focus its fury on Catholics and recent immigrants who, they feared, would bring religion into America's carefully guarded separation between church and state.

In the wake of the Kansas-Nebraska Act, the opening of new territory, combined with the desire to stake a claim for a slave or non-slave community, sent many from both North and South rushing West. By 1856, the region was poised for confrontation.

"Bleeding Kansas"

The Kansas-Nebraska region soon erupted in violence. Southern settlers, frustrated that the federal government refused full support for slavery, rioted in the antislavery town of Lawrence, Kansas. In retaliation, the New England Emigrant Aid Society sent white radical abolitionists into the area, including John Brown and four of his sons. Brown, who had moved many times to fulfill his self-proclaimed mission for racial justice, killed several Southerners who had brought slaves to Kansas, and two of his sons died in the skirmishes. Newspapers called the area "Bleeding Kansas." Hearing reports from Kansas, Charlotte Forten, the black abolitionist in Boston, recorded both con-cern and exhilaration. "Mr. [Charles] Remond lectured for us this evening," she wrote. "I particularly liked what he said about Kansas. Everybody has so much sympathy for the [white] sufferers there, and so little for the poor slave, who for centuries has suffered tenfold worse miseries—still I am glad that something has roused the people of the North at last. . . . A very great political excitement prevails."

Anger over Kansas ignited chaos in Congress. During a debate over Kansas statehood in May 1856, Massachusetts abolitionist senator Charles Sumner passionately denounced the "crime against Kansas," holding Stephen A. Douglas responsible for the policy that precipitated violence. Two days later, South Carolina congressman Preston Brooks, nephew of a senator who had supported Douglas, stormed into the Senate and pounded Sumner with a cane. Disabled, Sumner could not return to Congress, but Massachusetts voters reelected him in 1857 so his empty chair would symbolize aboli-tionist sacrifice.

The *Dred Scott* Decision

As blood spilled in Kansas, the U.S. Supreme Court considered a crucial suit that had been in the courts for more than a decade. The suit centered on Dred Scott, a Missouri slave whose master had taken him from slave territory into Illinois and free Wisconsin Territory in the 1830s, and then back south. When the master died in 1846, his widow's brother, an abolitionist, helped Scott sue for his freedom on the grounds that he had lived on free soil.

Before the Fugitive Slave Act was passed, Missouri's local courts had judged Scott free. But in the post-Act hysteria, the state's supreme court over-turned this decision. After five more years of litigation, in March 1857 the U.S. Supreme Court reached its decision. Though there was considerable disagree-ment among the judges, the majority handed down three important rulings. First, the Court said Scott was not free, because to free him would deprive his owner of property without due process of law. Second, the Court said slaves were not entitled to use the courts, as only citizens had that right. Finally, the Court ruled that neither slaves nor their descendants could ever be citizens. The effect of the ruling was to overturn the Missouri Compromise, which pro-hibited owners from taking slaves north of the compromise line. No law, said the Court, could deprive a citizen of property anywhere in the United States.

The U.S. Supreme Court's ruling on the *Dred Scott* case evoked a wave of public sympathy for Scott, as this news story highlighting his family suggests.

While the ruling did not *enslave* free African Americans, it did encourage free states to strip away their few remaining rights as citizens. New York's radical black *Weekly Anglo-African* promised persistent opposition: "When you repeal the Fugitive Slave Law, reverse the *Dred Scott* decision, and give us the right of citizenship in the free states, and break up the internal slave trade between the slave states, then, and not until then, you may expect us to be silent."

The Lincoln–Douglas Debates

Running for reelection in 1858, Stephen Douglas was challenged by Abraham Lincoln, a Republican who accused Douglas of contradictions. The principle of popular sovereignty, said Lincoln, which Douglas had embedded in the Kansas-Nebraska Act, promised power to local residents. But the *Dred Scott* decision, which Douglas supported, gave power to the federal government. Though Douglas was reelected, Lincoln gained popularity for his more moderate approach. While not suggesting that Southerners do "what I would not know how to do,"—that is, abolish slavery—he warned that the nation could not exist "half-slave and half-free."

But Lincoln took contradictory stances as well. He argued both that the Constitution protected African Americans as citizens and that only white people should settle the West. While emphasizing that slavery was morally wrong, he stopped short of suggesting it be abolished. He condemned the *Dred Scott* decision, saying black people should be equal before the law, but he shied away from affirming intellectual or social equality. While contending that discrimination based on race could easily become discrimination based on eye color, height, or other physical characteristics, he offered no solutions. But he did predict a crisis.

John Brown at Harpers Ferry

The 1850s ended as they began—with bloody confrontation. On October 16, 1859, John Brown, by now a bent and aging warrior, ordered his twenty-one-man army, "Men, get on your arms; we will proceed to the ferry." The bearded, stooped, intensely religious leader was dedicated to purging society of the sin of slavery. He had spent months preparing for this day.

Brown represented abolitionists who believed violence was the only solution. They advocated direct action, calling slaves to rebellion. Brown began soliciting arms, information, recruits, and money to set up a sanctuary for runaways in the mountains reaching into the South. From this sanctuary, he envisioned a chain-reaction slave revolt penetrating the southern heartland. If they could "conquer Virginia," Brown told his followers, "the other southern states would nearly conquer themselves."

Arriving in Ontario, Canada, in the spring of 1858, Brown had already studied guerrilla warfare and was finalizing his plans. He consulted with Harriet Tubman, an expert on the southern terrain. He received donations from white New Englanders and black New Yorkers who were weary of ineffectual protests. He spoke with Frederick Douglass, who offered guarded encouragement but would not support violence. The Massachusetts State Kansas Committee—mostly Boston abolitionists—agreed to supply money and guns. Using passionate religious arguments to lure them from pacifism, Brown had recruited several young Iowa Quakers. He was ready to fashion an army. Martin Delany, Mary Ann Shadd, James T. Holly, and William Parker were among the Canadian refugees who listened to him with interest. Parker, Holly, and the Shadd family made tentative plans to join him. But Delany, feeling Brown was moving too slowly, turned his attention to emigration to Africa, sailing for Nigeria in the spring of 1859.

That summer, Brown's volunteers proceeded to Harpers Ferry, Virginia, an industrial village with a federal armory, which Brown planned to raid for its rifles. Located just east of the Appalachians, where the Shenandoah and Potomac rivers meet, Harpers Ferry seemed well situated as a base from which to launch an attack on the South. It had a substantial number of free African Americans who might lend their support, and it was only 50 miles from the nation's capital.

Brown assembled an army of sixteen white men and five black men, recruited from far afield, reflecting the broad reach of abolitionist networks. Only Shields

Green had once been a slave. John Anthony Copeland, a black North Carolinian studying at Oberlin College, brought along his uncle, Sheridan Leary, a mixed-race Oberlin resident who left behind his wife and baby daughter. Mixed-race Dangerfield Newby also joined the group, hoping to liberate his wife and children from slavery in Virginia.

When the insurrection began, Brown's men managed to seize a local farmer—George Washington's great-grandnephew—as a hostage. But the campaign to seize the arsenal failed. Brown's group had brought the wrong ammunition for the guns they carried. Holly, Parker, and the Shadd family were delayed in arriving from Canada. Reinforcements promised by Harriet Tubman never arrived. Not one local African American joined in. Most of Brown's freedom fighters, including two more of his sons, perished in the fray. Osborne Anderson, the only black rebel who escaped capture, returned to Canada. Unlike the Christiana confrontation, the raid at Harpers Ferry had no triumphant ending. This time Southerners got their hangings. On December 2, 1859, Brown went to the gallows for treason.

Yet Brown succeeded in stirring up America. Southerners worried the Harpers Ferry raid would spark full-blown war. Because of "a good deal of talk about Harper's Ferry," wrote one slave trader, "everybody nearly wants to volunteer to go to fight." The uncertainty caused slave prices to plummet. When Congress convened on December 5, lawmakers came armed. Hoping for southern support for a presidential bid, Stephen Douglas blamed the

John Brown asked that his execution be attended only by the "poor little, dirty, ragged bare headed and barefooted slave boys & girls led by some old grey headed slave mother." But fearing an attempt to rescue Brown, the authorities barred the public from the abolitionist martyr's scaffold. Still, many artists painted the scene Brown had envisioned anyway, some showing him as a Christlike avenging angel. More than two decades after the event, Thomas Hovenden, who had married an abolitionist, produced this fictional rendition of Brown kissing a black child.

Republicans for Brown's insurrection. Southern congressmen demanded an investigation to determine if the Republican Party had supported Brown. But when Abraham Lincoln and other white Republicans also condemned Brown, rumors of a plot subsided.

Though Brown's mission failed, William Lloyd Garrison, heretofore a pacifist, conceded the righteousness of the effort. Black and white abolitionists began describing Brown's raid as "noble." John Copeland, Brown's young black Oberlin recruit, wrote to his mother, "Could I die in a more noble cause?" Black poet Frances Ellen Watkins called Brown "the hero of the nineteenth century." Writing to Brown's wife, Watkins said: "Belonging to the race your dear husband reached forth his hand to assist, I thank you. Not in vain has [he] periled all. From the prison comes forth a shout of triumph. Enclosed I send you a few dollars as a token of my gratitude, reverence and love." Frederick Douglass eulogized Brown as "a human soul illuminated with divine qualities" who "saw slavery through no mist or cloud but in the light of infinite wisdom" and "loved liberty for all men." Memorials, songs, and poems helped Brown accomplish in death what he could not in life: stirring abolitionists to agree that the only way to end slavery was to "purge the land with blood."

Brown's army died with a dignity and conviction that drew wide admiration, but the day of his execution was a sad one. Hundreds of thousands of black Americans, weeping, lined the tracks as the train carried Brown's remains home from Virginia through Philadelphia to his farm in New York's Adirondack Mountains.

Conclusion

The congressional leaders who had fashioned the Missouri Compromise, the Compromise of 1850 (with its Fugitive Slave Act), and the policy of popular sovereignty struggled to provide political solutions to the slavery problem that was tearing apart the United States. Antislavery advocates sought to accomplish abolition by raising moral outrage. Proslavery forces called on constitutional and legal power to protect their property—and with the *Dred Scott* decision, the U.S. Supreme Court supported their claims. But both Southerners and Northerners knew the matter was far from settled.

The 1850s opened and closed with bloody confrontations over slavery. The slavery issue ignited conflict over the federal government's jurisdiction over states, federal protection of citizens' property, and the moral and religious implications of holding a person in bondage. As new settlement areas opened in the West and in Canada, Americans struggled to define how race related to citizenship and what individuals could do to defend their rights. Throughout the decade, cotton remained the nation's most profitable export crop, and the land and labor required to grow it became the subjects of hot debate and violence.

For black Americans, these developments had mixed implications. On the one hand, the Fugitive Slave Act increased the danger and desperation of slave life. But the same law helped create and publicize black heroes and chroniclers.

Inspired by accounts of courageous actions, more and more white Americans began to perceive slaves' fates as intertwined with their own. Nonetheless, an increasing number of Americans, black and white alike, began to share Abraham Lincoln's foreboding that the country would have to reach a crisis before the controversy could end.

Questions for Review and Reflection

1. In the decade that preceded the Civil War, African Americans increasingly developed a unique literary voice. What were some of the elements of that unique voice?

2. The antebellum world slaves and slaveholders made "together" consisted of many areas of connection and tensions. Why do you imagine that world did not shatter *sooner* than it did?

3. The political fortunes of Stephen Douglas and Abraham Lincoln rested on the institution of slavery. How well do historians understand the relationship of each of them to that institution?

4. Historians have long debated about whether John Brown was a visionary or a just a fanatic? What are some of the merits of each side of the debate and why do you suppose so few southern slaves joined in his rebellion at Harper's Ferry?

Civil War and the Promises of Freedom: The Turbulent 1860s

Martin Delany Becomes the First Black U.S. Army Major

The 1850s left some African Americans despairing of ever seeing an end to slavery in the United States. Abolitionist Martin Delany, who had settled in Canada in search of greater freedom, began to dream of a home in Africa. "Africa for the African race, and black men to rule them," he proclaimed.

In December 1860, Delany returned to America from an eighteen-month visit to England and Africa during which he made plans for a new black settlement. From Africa, following a meeting with Yoruban leaders, he wrote to New York American Methodist Episcopal (AME) minister Henry Highland Garnet, "I am happy to report that I have concluded a treaty . . . by which we secure the right of locating in common with the natives on any part of their territory not otherwise occupied." Pleased, Garnet contacted a "number of men who are willing to embark on this glorious enterprise, and who believe as I do— that there is a glorious future before Africa." But when Delany returned to the United States, he found the nation on the brink of a war that delayed his Africa plans for almost two decades.

Like that of thousands of others, Delany's life was redirected by the civil war that erupted in the spring of 1861. After the federal government eventually

1860	Frederick Douglass is attacked by an angry mob. South Carolina secedes from the Union.
1861	In February, seven states form the Confederate States of America. Confederate troops bombard Fort Sumter in Charleston Harbor in April. By May, Virginia, North Carolina, Tennessee, and Arkansas join the Confederacy. Union general Benjamin Butler labels fugitive slaves "contraband" and refuses to return them to masters.
1862	In May, Congress mandates that slaves seized as contraband not be returned to owners. President Lincoln issues a provisional Emancipation Proclamation. The Union army's first all-black unit is formed: the First South Carolina Volunteers.
1863	On January 1, the Emancipation Proclamation ends slavery in the Confederate states. The Fifty-fourth Massachusetts Regiment draws black soldiers from across the North. In June, Virginia's western counties abolish slavery and return to the Union as West Virginia. After Union victory at Gettysburg, France and Britain withdraw support of the Confederacy. In New York City, white rioters protest conscription and competition from black workers. The Fifty-fourth's performance at Fort Wagner gains the respect of skeptical white soldiers.
1864	Union general William Sherman begins a campaign from Chattanooga to Savannah. Congress mandates equity in black troops' pay. Abraham Lincoln is reelected by a narrow margin. The Equal Rights League is formed.
1865	Martin Delany becomes the first black major in the United States Army. Congress proposes the Thirteenth Amendment to the Constitution. Congress establishes the Freedmen's Bureau. Confederate general Robert E. Lee surrenders at Appomattox Court House. President Abraham Lincoln is assassinated. The Thirteenth Amendment abolishes slavery throughout the United States.
1866	Berea College, in Kentucky, opens as an interracial school. Congress proposes the Fourteenth Amendment. The Ku Klux Klan is founded in Tennessee.
1867	The Freedmen's Bureau opens Howard University in Washington, DC.
1868	The Fourteenth Amendment guarantees citizenship to any man born in the United States, regardless of race.

recruited black troops, Delany petitioned to serve as a surgeon. Receiving no answer, he journeyed to Washington, DC, to propose that northern black leaders help organize slaves into a fighting force. President Abraham Lincoln agreed and issued Delany a commission. Thus, in February 1865, the fifty-two-year-old Delany—who had been driven from Harvard's medical school, had been an expatriate in Canada, and dreamed of life in Africa—became the U.S. Army's first black major.

The Civil War set Northerners to debating whether it was more important to end slavery or to hold the nation together. Initially, they went to war not over slaves or black people, but to preserve the Union. Describing the conflict as "a white man's war," northern (Union) officials turned away free black men who volunteered for the army. President Lincoln envisioned resettling black people outside the United States, and slaves who escaped from the South (the Confederacy) to Union army camps were returned to their masters. But northern free black men and women insisted that the war *had* to be about black people. When the Union government could not raise enough white recruits, African Americans mustered 190,000 black volunteers whose battlefield achievements won their country's admiration.

Gradually, emancipation came to be seen as an effective military strategy by both the Union and the Confederacy, as both sides concluded that offering freedom could secure black people's loyalty. Meanwhile, free black people petitioned the Union for equal military pay, opportunities for education, and the right to vote.

The war signaled dramatic changes for black and white people alike. In the North, it stimulated the economy but also increased political and racial tensions. In the South, many white men needed little persuasion to enlist in the Confederate army, as the war ravaged their homelands. White slave owners even persuaded white men who did not own slaves that they should fight to uphold regional and family loyalty. At war's end, African Americans celebrated emancipation and embraced their new "citizenship." But they knew that without the right to vote, they were not yet full citizens. Only changes in the U.S. Constitution would grant them full citizenship.

While federal officials struggled to plan for 4 million freed black men, women, and children, southern states were forced to grant the franchise to black men. But black people's efforts to build a solid political structure in the South were complicated by economic woes and resistance to slaves' emancipation. These circumstances left the majority of black Southerners unable to attain better lives or protection from white violence. By June 1868, southern freedmen could cast a ballot—but most northern African Americans could not. So black people confronted the next hurdle: gaining the franchise for black men in the North.

"A White Man's War"

On December 10, 1860, while Delany was crossing the Atlantic Ocean, Frederick Douglass was speaking in Boston's Music Hall to commemorate John Brown's martyrdom. Douglass described a meeting the week before that had

By war's end, Martin Delany—having spent the first five decades of his life as an outsider in his native United States—achieved as much honor as his government had to offer: the highly dignified rank of major.

MAJOR MARTIN R. DELANEY.

been "invaded, insulted, captured by a mob of gentlemen." These were anti-abolitionists, and though most people assumed they were lower-class ruffians, Douglass knew better. "The leaders of the mob," he said, "were gentlemen . . . who pride themselves upon their respect for law and order." Many were northern textile manufacturers who profited from slave-produced cotton, and feared that abolition might mean the end of easy and inexpensive cotton supplies. But soon these "gentlemen" would be drawn into a war against their southern suppliers and customers. If slavery was the spark that ignited the war, the election of a new president fanned the flame.

The Election of Abraham Lincoln

For the 1860 presidential election, the Republicans hoped to appeal to both abolitionists and southern planters. Their platform called for prohibiting slavery in the territories but reaffirmed states' right to control local institutions. The Democratic Party split in two. Southerners called for protecting slavery in the West, while followers of Illinois senator Stephen A. Douglas favored a hands-off policy. With the splintering of the Democrats, Republican Abraham Lincoln won the presidency by a narrow margin—without the support of a single southern state.

Many Southerners thought the newly elected president was an abolitionist, but black Americans knew better. In a February 1860 speech, Lincoln condemned abolition as "extremism." Though he opposed the extension of slavery into the western territories, he also opposed interfering with it where it existed. Black Americans generally distrusted politicians. The usually optimistic

Frederick Douglass conceded, "[T]he very best that can be said of [the Republican] party . . . is that it is simply opposed to allowing slavery to go where it is not at all likely to go." In New York's *Weekly Anglo-African* newspaper, publisher Thomas Hamilton explained:

> *The two great political parties . . . entertain the same ideas. . . . [T]he Democratic party would make the white man the master and the black man the slave, and have them thus together occupy every foot of American soil. . . . The Republican party . . . with larger professions for humanity . . . oppose[s] the progress of slavery in the territories, . . . but . . . their opposition to slavery means opposition to the black man— nothing else. . . . We have no hope from either [Democrats or Republicans]. We must rely on ourselves, [and on] the righteousness of our cause.*

Nearly a year after Lincoln's election, New Jersey AME minister Jabez Campbell despaired that "the president is not now, and never was, either an abolitionist or an anti-slavery man. He has no quarrel whatever with the South upon the slavery question."

Southern States Secede

Convinced that Lincoln intended to eradicate slavery, South Carolina's legislators in December 1860 voted to withdraw from a union they felt threatened their right to hold slaves. Many South Carolinians who did not own slaves also voted to secede, as they felt excluded from a political system that could choose a president without a single southern electoral vote. They also worried about how thousands of free black people would fit into their society. Most Americans hoped a compromise would prevent war, but now that possibility vanished.

Cotton was also a catalyst for secession. By 1860, cotton production had expanded by 30 percent over two decades, and its value had more than doubled. Most Southerners could not envision a southern economy without cotton and could not imagine cotton without slaves. South Carolina and Mississippi, which depended heavily on cotton and slaves, were the first to secede.

By February 1861, Florida, Alabama, Georgia, Louisiana, and Texas had joined the Confederacy. Its constitution stressed each state's "sovereign and independent character." The new president was Jefferson Davis of Mississippi, brother of Hurricane Plantation owner Joseph Davis (see Chapter 8). Quickly raising an army, the Confederacy began seizing federal forts, post offices, and arsenals across the South. By April, Fort Sumter, in Charleston Harbor, was one of only three southern forts still under Union control.

In his March 1861 inaugural speech, Lincoln promised not to interfere with slavery, but he refused to accept secession. In early April, informed of supply shortages at Fort Sumter, he determined to send food but no arms or troops. But South Carolinians concluded that provisions would prolong Union control. On April 12, they fired on Fort Sumter and blockaded the harbor. The next day, Union forces, out of ammunition, surrendered.

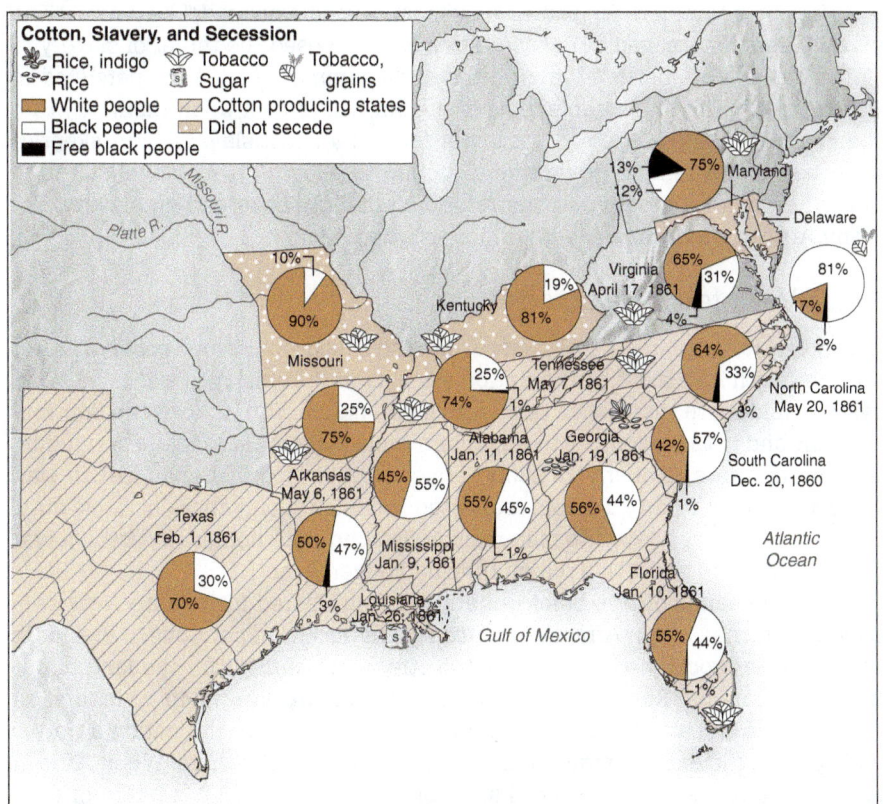

Cotton, Slavery, and Secession
- 🌾 Rice, indigo
- Rice
- 🌿 Tobacco
- 🍬 Sugar
- 🌱 Tobacco, grains
- ▨ White people
- ▨ Cotton producing states
- □ Black people
- ▨ Did not secede
- ■ Free black people

Maryland — 13%, 12%, 75%
Delaware — 81%, 17%, 2%
Missouri — 10%, 90%
Kentucky — 81%
Virginia, April 17, 1861 — 65%, 31%, 4%
Tennessee, May 7, 1861 — 25%, 74%, 1%
North Carolina, May 20, 1861 — 64%, 33%, 3%
Arkansas, May 6, 1861 — 25%, 75%
Alabama, Jan. 11, 1861 — 45%, 55%
Georgia, Jan. 19, 1861 — 55%, 45%, 1%
South Carolina, Dec. 20, 1860 — 42%, 57%, 1%
Texas, Feb. 1, 1861 — 30%, 70%
Mississippi, Jan. 9, 1861 — 50%, 47%, 3%
Louisiana, Jan. 26, 1861 — 56%, 44%, 1%
Florida, Jan. 10, 1861 — 55%, 44%, 1%

Atlantic Ocean

Gulf of Mexico

MAP 10.1   Cotton, Slavery, and Secession
The greater the investment in slaves and cotton, the more quickly and resoundingly came the vote for
secession. In the four states where cotton was unimportant and the free black population high, white soldiers
chose to fight on each side. At least 40 percent of Kentucky soldiers served in the Confederate army, as did
30 percent of Maryland volunteers, 25 percent of recruits from Missouri, and about 10 percent from Delaware.
More than 13,000 Delaware men fought for the Union.

  With the outbreak of war, Virginia seceded. Though its voters had
rejected secession early in 1861, Lincoln's call for troops changed their
minds. (The western counties, too mountainous for plantation slavery, later
broke away to form the new state of West Virginia). The secession of
Arkansas, Tennessee, and North Carolina brought the number of Confederate
states to eleven.

  Four slave states—Delaware, Maryland, Kentucky, and Missouri—did not
secede. These states grew tobacco and other crops, mostly on small farms.
With relatively few slaves and large free black populations, they accepted
Lincoln's claim that he was more interested in maintaining federal authority
than ending slavery, a system they were beginning to phase out anyway. They
sent thousands of troops to the Union army, but many young men from these
states also fought on the Confederate side.

Frederick Douglass welcomed secession. "God be praised," he wrote. "The slaveholders have saved our cause. They have exposed the throat of slavery to the keen knife of liberty." Through the early summer of 1861, he persisted in believing that the "inexorable logic of events will force it upon them . . . that the war now being waged . . . is a war for and against slavery." But skeptics observed that a federal government willing to allow "loyal" slaveholders to keep their chattel hardly demonstrated a commitment to ending slavery. Yet many African Americans shared Douglass's optimism.

Black Volunteers Rejected

Like most Northerners, Lincoln felt certain the South would soon collapse. After all, the North had most of the nation's banks and industry, a better railroad system, and more than twice the South's population. It outpaced the South in firearms and in the resources to repair and replace them. European immigrants, arriving at a rate of nearly 200,000 per year, could replenish men lost to war. Expecting quick victory, Lincoln requested recruits for only three months' duty. Even so, many eligible white men resisted leaving their homes to pursue a war they did not care about in a region they had never seen.

But thousands of free black Americans volunteered for military service— only to be turned away. African Americans sent dozens of petitions to President Lincoln. One proclaimed, "We cherish a strong attachment for the land of our birth and for our Republican Government. We are strong in numbers, in courage, and in patriotism, and . . . we offer to you and to the nation a power and a will sufficient to conquer rebellion." Lincoln ignored them. When African American attorney John Mercer Langston, a member of Ohio's board of education, offered to raise troops, Ohio's governor responded, "Do you not know, Mr. Langston, that this is a white man's government; that white men are able to defend and protect it? When we want you colored men we will notify you." In Cincinnati, police forced a black recruiting station to remove the American flag. "We want you . . . niggers out of this," police officers declared. "This is a white man's war."

War and Freedom

Union leaders hoped that blockading southern ports and seizing southern cities would quickly end the conflict. In July 1861, Union troops marched toward Richmond, the Confederate capital. But on July 21, Confederate soldiers stopped them cold near Manassas Junction, less than 30 miles out of Washington. The Confederacy's success there—known as the Battle of Bull Run—caught Union leaders off guard.

On the heels of this defeat, some black Americans again hoped Lincoln would accept black soldiers, but again they were disappointed. Most white Northerners shared Lincoln's conviction that black soldiers were a bad idea— they were possibly cowardly and undisciplined, probably a threat to white civilians. Not until 1863 would official black Union regiments form, even then under some white officers who doubted black soldiers' courage and ability.

Slaves as Contraband

Within weeks of the firing on Fort Sumter, slaves fleeing to Union-held Fort Monroe, near Hampton Roads, Virginia, were put to work. Commanding general Benjamin Butler declared them "contraband"—enemy property seized in war—arguing that returning them to owners was counterproductive. Butler reasoned that planters who joined the Confederate army had abandoned their human property. "Have [slaves] not assumed the condition [i.e., freedom] which we hold to be the normal one of those made in God's image?" he asked.

Butler was not alone in thinking that war changed the status of slaves. General John C. Frémont, an abolitionist, harbored similar notions. Declaring military law in Missouri in August 1861, Frémont proclaimed that "real and personal property of those who shall take up arms against the United States . . . is declared confiscated, and their slaves are hereby declared free men." Lincoln reversed this policy and promptly removed Frémont from command of the Army of the West. But Congress soon passed the Confiscation Act, authorizing confiscation of "property used for Insurrectionary Purposes." Through the summer of 1861, field commanders followed Frémont's example, liberating thousands of slaves and using them as cooks, laborers, spies, and sometimes as armed soldiers.

Meanwhile, local communities made their own military plans. By the end of 1861, the First Kansas Colored Infantry had organized. Its slaveholding Cherokee commander, at first supporting the Confederacy, soon transferred his loyalties to the Union (which he thought was likely to win) and declared his unit open to "all persons, without reference to color . . . willing to fight for the American flag." In 1862, Union general David Hunter, in charge of captured coastal South Carolina, organized the First South Carolina Volunteers, the Union's first all-black fighting unit comprising primarily ex-slaves. In Kentucky, a "general stampede" of slaves (as one white officer described it) arrived at Hart County's Camp Nevin. Union officers put many to work building fortifications. When the army moved on, these workers accompanied them and began to move onto the battlefield.

New Roles for Southern Slaves

In spring 1862, when Joseph Davis heard that Union forces had seized New Orleans, he abandoned Hurricane Plantation near Vicksburg, Mississippi, leaving it in the hands of his trusted slave, Ben Montgomery. Montgomery wrote regularly to Davis, reporting that some slaves had gone to Vicksburg to help build Union fortifications, others had disappeared, but many remained on the plantation. In June, Union forces swept through Hurricane, destroying what remained of the previous year's cotton crop. Montgomery survived by starting a small business, tanning leather and making shoes to sell to neighbors. When Union admiral David D. Porter arrived at Hurricane in the spring of 1863, he set Montgomery and his talented son, Isaiah, to repairing machines on Union boats. But deeming them too talented to be jeopardized in the South, he soon sent them north to Ohio.

Some slaves cast their lot with the Confederacy. Hearing stories of Yankee cruelty, or worried about reprisals if the South won the war, many chose to remain in familiar surroundings, or went to war as servants to masters they knew and trusted. Others were pressed to remain with their masters. By 1865, fearing defeat, some Confederate leaders grew desperate enough to recruit black regiments with the promise of freedom.

Like Ben Montgomery, other black people, free and enslaved, remained in the South but took on new roles. In Kentucky in 1862, a free black man known only as Mr. Bradwell organized his slave neighbors to grow and sell livestock and produce. The group raised $700 to erect their own Methodist church building.

But many bondspeople fled their masters. A Georgia slave who escaped recalled how she "had been reading so much about the 'Yankees' and was . . . anxious to see them. The [southern] whites would tell their colored people not to go to the Yankees, for they would harness them to carts . . . in place of horses." But, she understood, they said "those things to frighten them. . . . I heard that the Yankee was going to set all the slaves free." One Louisiana house servant and his mother stole a mule from their master and "traveled eighteen miles to a plantation . . . where the Yankees had a camp." In May 1862, South Carolina's Robert Smalls, an experienced steamboat pilot, stowed his family aboard the *Planter* and delivered the ship to the Union navy near Charleston. The Union converted the *Planter* to a warship and appointed Smalls captain.

The Port Royal Experiment

Early in 1862, the Union army seized the Sea Islands off the coast of South Carolina. The few white islanders fled, abandoning meals in their kitchens,

Organizations sponsored by northern philanthropists sent young women into the South to teach black people. Though one black volunteer wrote proudly, "We think it noble work, and will do it nobly," some observers have commented that the black teachers in this photograph seem to be marginalized as the white people take center stage.

crops in the fields, and thousands of bewildered slaves. As Union leaders debated whether the slaves were contraband or recruits, northern abolitionists arrived, bringing food, clothing, and volunteer teachers. One was twenty-four-year-old Charlotte Forten, from a free black family in Philadelphia. Arriving at Port Royal in October 1862, she recorded her excitement as she "commenced teaching the children [the song] 'John Brown' . . . [and] felt the full significance of that song being sung here . . . by little negro children . . . whom the glorious old man died to save."

Federal officials encouraged teaching in Port Royal, but they also set black residents to cultivating cotton, which the government could sell abroad and to factories in the North. Ex-slaves were angry to discover that "freedom" meant only more of the familiar backbreaking labor. One black woman, hoeing cotton at Port Royal under the new wage system, complained to a Union agent that the New England manager of her plantation gave her less clothing, shoes, and food than had her former master.

The system introduced at Port Royal was replicated in numerous places throughout the South as Union forces liberated one area after another. Northerners, both black and white, showed up to help slaves with the transition to freedom. Held to a strict regimen of schooling and manual labor, many former slaves were disappointed in the so-called freedom. After the war, the rebuilding of the South became known as "Reconstruction." One historian has described the Port Royal experiment as a "rehearsal for Reconstruction."

Near Hurricane plantation, in the winter of 1863, Admiral Porter set up contraband camps like those at Port Royal. He invited Quaker missionaries to set up schools, and he pressed black refugees into tilling confiscated land—for scanty wages or none. In this Mississippi outpost, more than one-third of the black population died as malnutrition and poor sanitation lowered resistance to pneumonia, smallpox, measles, and malaria.

Emancipation as Military and Political Strategy

In the summer of 1862, Frederick Douglass wrote to Charles Sumner, a white abolitionist and Massachusetts senator, "The events taking place seem like a dream." He was describing a series of federal policies gradually overriding Lincoln's official position that the war was not about ending slavery. As the war dragged on, undermining slavery became both a goal of the war and a strategy for weakening the South. Congressional leaders agreed with General Butler: Returning slaves to their masters only aided the enemy. In the spring of 1862, Congress forbade commanders to return captured or fugitive slaves.

Emancipation Possibilities

As the war unfolded, Union leaders confronted thorny issues. How would they mount a long-distance campaign to retake the rebellious South? How would they maintain Northerners' confidence in federal authority? How would they keep foreign nations—some dependent on southern cotton—from aiding the Confederacy? By 1862, Union officials concluded that African Americans could have immense strategic value in dealing with these challenges.

Throughout 1862, Lincoln tried to strike a balance between keeping northern abolitionists' support and persuading the South to cease hostilities—all while trying to avoid alienating slave states loyal to the Union. Many northern white Americans who opposed slavery made it clear they did not want black people as social or political equals. Walking a tightrope, Lincoln proposed that the federal government free slaves and compensate their masters. Congress voted him down.

With Southerners absent and reformist Republicans dominant, Congress set out to define black Americans as people rather than property. In a symbolic move, it abolished slavery in the District of Columbia—the only area of the United States where it had the power to do so. With similar symbolism, Congress established diplomatic relations with Haiti and Liberia, two black nations ruled by former slaves. Then the secretary of state made a public event of issuing a passport to Henry Highland Garnet as a "*citizen* of the United States." A well-known black Bostonian, William C. Nell, was made a postal clerk, becoming the first African American to hold a federal civilian appointment. Lincoln even signed a second Confiscation Act, freeing any slave entering Union-held territory and allowing Union soldiers to seize "all property"— including slaves—in areas they captured. Though each step was a token, each also eroded slavery and elevated free African Americans. Black hopes were raised. When slavery was banned in the nation's capital, the editor of New York's *Anglo-African* exulted, "Henceforth, whatever betide the nation, its physical heart is freed from the presence of slavery."

Lincoln made clumsy overtures toward African Americans, reiterating his abhorrence of slavery but insisting that his goal was holding the nation together, not ending slavery. Frederick Douglass described the Lincoln administration as "fighting the war with only one hand" in refusing to allow black troops. In August, inviting Douglass and other black leaders to the White House, Lincoln suggested relocating slaves—and any interested free black people—to Central America. Feeling betrayed, Douglass reflected, "Abraham Lincoln is . . . the miserable tool of traitors and rebels. . . . [He] seems to possess an ever increasing passion for making himself appear silly and ridiculous." But Douglass's son Lewis became one of several hundred African Americans who volunteered to relocate to Chiriqui, in today's Panama.

Some black Americans grew increasingly skeptical of all federal policy. They suspected that Garnet had been recognized as a citizen because he endorsed Lincoln's plan to remove black people from the United States, and that Nell got a postal clerkship only because Massachusetts had an abolitionist governor. Disillusioned and frustrated, a few prominent African Americans insisted black people should not fight in a war that would not free slaves. Others imagined opportunities abroad. Uncharacteristically, Frederick Douglass considered moving to Haiti. But Delany, declaring Haiti "a small island, with no prospect of additional territory," favored "Africa . . . a vast continent peopled by one of the great, enduring . . . absorbing races of the earth." Hoping to gather recruits for African resettlement, Delany crisscrossed the North and West, and found support for emigration. "If this war should result in the abolition of slavery, as we hope it may," wrote a black New Yorker in the *Weekly Anglo African*, "it will not ameliorate the condition of the free black man one iota. . . . The scanty pittance of social toleration which is here and there grudgingly doled out to us . . . illustrat[es] the more strikingly the rule which everywhere excludes us."

But most black people yearned to fight for justice in the America of their birth. In a black newspaper, Isaiah Wears of Philadelphia explained: "To be asked, after so many years of oppression . . . by a [white] people who have been so largely enriched by the black man's toil, to pull up stakes . . . and go . . . is unreasonable and anti-Christian." Douglass agreed, publicly stating he would stay in the United States. Sarah Remond, fiery sister of abolitionist Charles Remond, campaigned to keep Britain from aiding the South. "Let no diplomacy of statesmen," she implored, "no intimidation of slaveholders, no scarcity of cotton, no fear of slave insurrections, prevent the people of Great Britain from maintaining their position as the friend of the oppressed negro."

The Emancipation Proclamation

The Battle of Antietam finally prompted Lincoln to stop waffling on the fate of slaves. By mid-1862, the Union navy had blockaded southern seaports and captured Memphis and New Orleans. With Union commanders poised to control the Mississippi River, Confederate general Robert E. Lee tried to push the war into the North to disrupt railroad lines that supplied Washington, DC. On September 17, Lee's troops met General George McClellan, at Sharpsburg, on Antietam Creek. The bloodiest one-day battle of the war ensued; more than 22,000 soldiers perished or suffered injuries.

Lee retreated to Virginia. Had McClellan pursued Lee, he might have won a decisive victory. But the Union general, characteristically timid and slow to act, missed his chance. Nonetheless, as Antietam was a southern defeat, England and France began to doubt the South could win. More significantly, the battle moved the cautious Lincoln to action. First, he removed McClellan from duty. Second, on September 22, the president surprised the nation by offering a provisional promise of freedom to slaves in the Confederate states.

In this preliminary emancipation proclamation, Lincoln chose his words carefully. Emphasizing that he was not planning to free slaves in states loyal to the Union, he promised that any Confederate state that rejoined the Union by January 1, 1863 would also be allowed to retain slavery. The effect was to free slaves only in areas where the Union had no control. Moreover, the order would be void if the war ended before that date. Though aware of its limitations, Frederick Douglass made the best of the promise: "We shout for joy that we live to record this righteous decree." Everywhere, Lincoln's emancipation promise lifted black spirits. In New Orleans, where the newspaper

TABLE 10.1 THE FEDERAL POWER STRUGGLE, 1861–1865

During the Civil War, a federal power struggle ensued among the military, Congress, president, state governments, and Supreme Court on the status of slaves and Confederate lands.

DATE	MILITARY	CONGRESS	PRESIDENCY	SUPREME COURT
1861	General Benjamin Butler accepts freed slaves at Union army post in Hampton Roads, Virginia, declaring them "contraband."	Congressional Confiscation Act seizes Confederate farms, and frees all slaves employed by Confederate military; abolishes slavery in District of Columbia.		Supreme Court rules that wartime exigency allows the president to institute a blockade of southern ports, and that the president and military can suspend the right of *habeas corpus*.
	General Benjamin Butler declares fugitive slaves in Georgia, Florida, and South Carolina to be free.		Lincoln reverses Butler's emancipation order.	
1862	Over Lincoln's disapproval, General David Hunter organizes freemen into First South Carolina volunteers.		Lincoln objects to congressional plan to confiscate land, on grounds that it would deprive heirs of their rightful inheritance.	
		In response to Lincoln's Constitutional concerns, Congress amends Confiscation Act, allowing confiscated land to revert to heirs of Confederates.		
1863	General John Frémont frees slaves of Missouri residents who are in rebellion.		Lincoln reverses General Frémont's order freeing Missouri slaves.	
			Lincoln issues Emancipation Proclamation, abolishing slavery	

			in states still in rebellion, but promises amnesty to southern states where 10% of citizens take loyalty oaths, and state agrees to free slaves. Lincoln offers amnesty to states that comply with loyalty-oath requirements; Arkansas and Louisiana comply.	
		Congress refuses to seat Arkansas and Louisiana representatives pardoned by Lincoln.		
1864	Sherman's "Field Order #15" designates 80,000 acres of confiscated land in South Carolina for rent or purchase by freedmen. Military field officers claim right to try civilians.	Congress passes Wade-Davis Bill, requiring that, for readmission, a majority of a Confederate states' citizens must swear allegiance to Union.	Lincoln pocket-vetoes Wade-Davis Bill.	In *Ex Parte Vallandighan*, Supreme Court refuses to rule on whether military has wartime jurisdiction in civilian offenses.
1865		Congress establishes Freedmen's Bureau. Congress refuses to seat ex-Confederates who have not sworn allegiance to the Union. Congress passes Thirteenth Amendment, abolishing slavery in *all* states and territories. It is ratified by 27 states.	Andrew Johnson grants "amnesty and pardon" to most Confederate citizens, restoring their confiscated land, and exiling thousands of black farmers from their land.	

L'Union served a vibrant mixed-race community, an editorial urged readers to drop "the craven behavior of bondage" and to "stand up under the noble flag of the union." One black observer recalled that in Washington, DC, "men squealed, women fainted, dogs barked, songs were sung, and cannons began to fire at the navy yard." Philadelphia's *Christian Recorder* thanked "God and President Lincoln" even while the editor expressed his hope that "Congress will do something for those poor souls [slaves] who will still remain in degradation."

In December 1862, when Union troops tried again to capture Richmond, they were stopped at Fredericksburg, Virginia. As the year ended, southern leaders declared that the Confederate states would not return to the Union.

So on January 1, 1863, as promised, Lincoln declared that any slave living in Confederate territory was "then, thenceforward, and forever free." One Virginia slave remembered the day: "It was wintertime and mighty cold, but we danced and sang right out in the cold . . . then we [left] the plantation, carrying blankets and pots and pans and chickens piled on our backs." In Port Royal, where black Americans jubilantly read aloud the new order, Charlotte Forten called this "the most glorious day this nation has yet seen." She wrote, "I was in such a state of excitement. It all seemed . . . like a brilliant dream." The news traveled throughout the slave South: Lincoln might finally liberate slaves—if the North could win the war.

"Men of Color, to Arms!"

Martin Delany responded to the Emancipation Proclamation by proposing the "Corps D'Afrique," a private black army to aid Union forces. But before he could organize it, Lincoln authorized Massachusetts governor John Andrew to raise the first northern black regiment—the Massachusetts Fifty-fourth. Andrew sent a team of black leaders to recruit in other Union states. With renewed hope, Delany joined the team.

But many white Northerners doubted black men would be good soldiers. One northern reformer at Port Royal, appalled at General Hunter's plans for a southern black regiment, wrote, "Plantation negroes will never make soldiers. . . . Five white men could put a [black] regiment to flight." But Colonel Thomas Wentworth Higginson disagreed. A white Massachusetts abolitionist and Unitarian minister, he ignored his West Point comrades' warning that commanding black troops would ruin his career. "It needs but a few days," he insisted, "to show the absurdity of doubting the equal military availability of these people, as compared with whites. There is quite as much . . . courage . . . as much previous knowledge of the gun, & there is readiness of the ear."

After the Emancipation Proclamation, black leaders buried their philosophical differences. Instead they united to recruit black soldiers. Posters proclaimed: "Men of Color, To Arms!" Sarah Woodson, sister of reformer Lewis Woodson, urged listeners "to accept the means which God has placed in your power." New York minister J. W. C. Pennington exhorted: "The only wise and safe course is to [join the army and] press rapidly into the heart of the slave country, and [secure] the Proclamation of freedom." While a few thought black Americans should withhold support until they got citizenship, the rhetoric of the New York *Anglo-African* is representative: "Should we not with two centuries of cruel wrong stirring our heart's blood, be but too willing to embrace any chance to settle accounts with the slaveholders? . . . Can you ask any more than a chance to drive bayonet or bullet into the slaveholders' hearts?"

Black communities sent more than 190,000 black enlisted men and over 7,000 officers to Union service—constituting 10 percent of the North's total fighting force. Most volunteers came from unremarkable circumstances, but sons of renowned black leaders also enlisted. Alongside Delany's seventeen-year-old son, Toussaint L'Ouverture Delany, marched Frederick Douglass's sons Lewis and Charles. Sojourner Truth sent off her grandson James Caldwell, observing wryly that this was yet another example of how "the niggers always have to clean up after the white folks." Even as they worried that if captured they would be immediately killed, black men volunteered in record numbers.

Colored Troops

At Camp Meigs near Boston, the Massachusetts Fifty-fourth received just two months' training before heading south in July 1863 to launch a night attack on Fort Wagner, in the Charleston harbor. Led by their young white colonel, Robert Gould Shaw, the regiment withstood relentless shelling that left Shaw dead and many others wounded. Toussaint L'Ouverture Delany received injuries

These pictures show the transformation of a slave into a freedman. After Contraband Jackson fled to the Union army, he was mustered into the 79th U.S. Colored Troops as Drummer Jackson. Abolitionists produced such visual renditions to show how changes in clothing and occupation transformed African Americans' posture, facial expression, and confidence.

from which he never recovered. Though its objective was not won, the Massachusetts Fifty-fourth earned wide recognition for its battlefield performance. For bravery at Fort Wagner, Sergeant William Carney was the first black serviceman to be awarded the Congressional Medal of Honor, the military's new medal. The poet Frances Ellen Watkins Harper captured the moment in a poem: "Bearers of a high commission/To break each brother's chain/With hearts aglow for freedom, They bore the toil and pain." The *New York Tribune* wrote that the regiment "made Fort Wagner such a name to the colored race as Bunker Hill has been for ninety years to the white Yankees."

Other black regiments showed similar bravery and discipline. Louisiana's First and Third Native Guards helped establish Union control at Port Hudson, near Vicksburg, in May 1863, and at nearby Milliken's Bend, three black regiments held off a division of Texans. One black observer wrote, "The bravery displayed before Port Hudson by the colored troops was applaudingly received here by persons who have not been looked upon as friendly to the movement [of raising black troops]."

By summer 1863, support for black units came from surprising places. Sidestepping her pacifism, white Quaker abolitionist Lucretia Mott offered her farm near Philadelphia as a training camp for black recruits. In Ohio, the

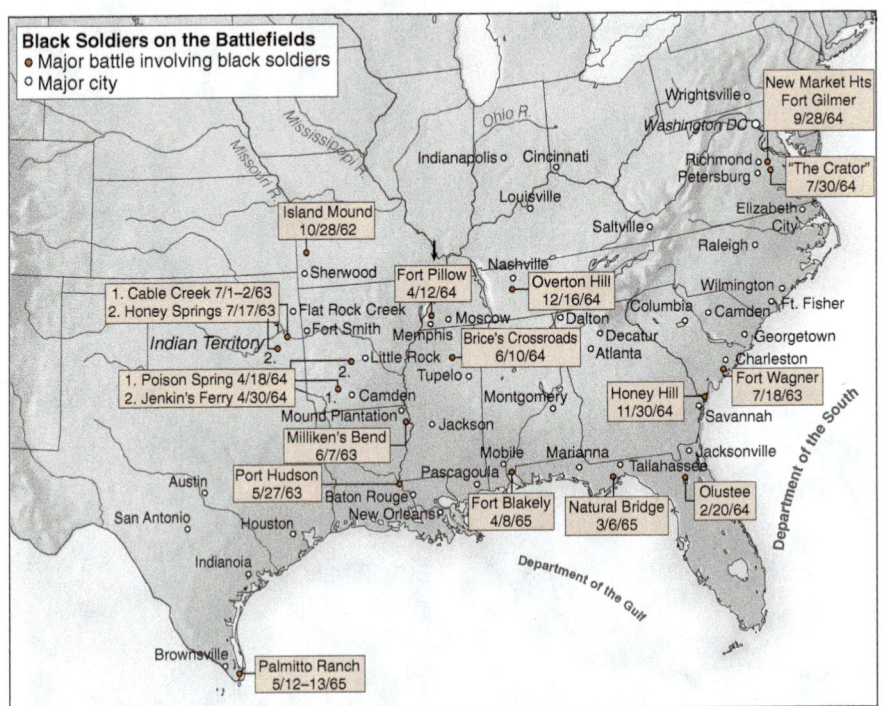

MAP 10.2 Black Soldiers on the Battlefields

This map shows some of the more than two hundred Civil War engagements in which black soldiers participated. In all, black soldiers served in battles as far north as Maryland, as far south as Florida, and as far west as the Indian Territory. A number of black men rose to the rank of sergeant during the Civil War, and more than a dozen received the Congressional Medal of Honor.

governor who had rebuffed John Mercer Langston's offer of aid now requested his help in recruiting.

Northern black soldiers took great pride in their regiments. Before setting off into battle, the Sixth Colored Infantry dedicated its regimental flag. "Soldiers," the speaker urged, "under this flag let your rallying cry be 'for God, for freedom, and our country.' If for this you must fall, you fall the country's patriots, heroes, and martyrs." The Sixth carried its flag at Petersburg, Dutch Gap, and New Market Heights in Virginia; at Fort Fisher in Wilmington, North Carolina; and at the Battle of Olustee in the Florida swamps. Not just a battle-field marker, the flag had a symbolic meaning that extended beyond the battle-field and even beyond the war. When the Sixth disbanded at war's end, its banner was in tatters. Still, Sergeant Major Thomas Hawkins, a Congressional Medal of Honor winner, was honored to receive it from his comrades. For many years, the flag dropped from public view, but it now resides in a museum, where it helps Americans remember the part played by African American patriots and heroes in the preservation of the Union.

Yet military service did not necessarily bring glory. Black soldiers often got the toughest assignments and longest guard duty. Some were relegated to building fortifications, growing food, or tending livestock. For them, war continued the drudgery of slavery. For those captured in battle, death might follow, as the Confederate army labeled black soldiers "insurrectionists." The worst incident occurred at Fort Pillow, Tennessee, on the Mississippi River, where, on April 12, 1864, more than 300 black prisoners were massacred.

This lithograph, produced thirty years after the Battle of Olustee, attests to the conflict's enduring symbolic importance.

The Fight for Equal Pay

Black recruits often earned less than half the pay of white soldiers. In August 1863, Frederick Douglass beseeched President Lincoln to end this blatant inequity. As Douglass later recalled, Lincoln explained that black soldiers were "a serious offense to popular prejudice" so unequal pay "seemed a necessary concession to smooth the way to their employment at all as soldiers."

Meanwhile, black soldiers at the front petitioned Secretary of War Edwin Stanton. In the fall of 1863, the Massachusetts Fifty-fourth refused to accept any pay until their salaries matched that of white soldiers. One regiment member remembered, "Four months we have been working night and day under fire . . . patiently, waiting for justice." After more than a year of pressure from northern abolitionists, and the horror of black sacrifice at Fort Pillow, Congress passed legislation equalizing pay in June 1864.

Black Women and War

Black women also advanced the cause of black freedom. Dozens of black women labored alongside Clara Barton, nursing wounded soldiers in Baltimore. Fugitive slave leader Harriet Tubman returned to the South as both nurse and spy, her information helping to secure a Union victory at the Combahee River. Tubman reported that one slave woman rejoiced, "Oh! Praise de Lord! I'd prayed seventy-three years, and now he's come and we's all free." Mary Elizabeth Bowser, a literate servant in the Confederate presidential mansion, feigned mental illness to gain access to Jefferson Davis's military secrets, which she passed to Union officers. In Washington, DC, Elizabeth Keckley, a free black seamstress employed by Mrs. Lincoln, helped raise relief money for southern black people. "If the white people can give festivals to raise funds for the relief of suffering soldiers, why should not the well-to-do colored people . . . do something for . . . suffering blacks? The next Sunday I made a suggestion in the colored church," Keckley said, "and in two weeks the 'Contraband Relief Association' was organized, with forty working members." This was one of dozens of black groups that raised money for southern contraband camps.

But in the South, as the Civil War disrupted households, many black women and children were set adrift. Unlike black men, they were not thought useful to the Union army in the war effort. Yet as large numbers of black women, some with children, arrived at Union camps, white troops sometimes put them to work in the fields alongside black men and assigned them to heavy labor. Other women worked as cooks, nurses, or livestock tenders, seldom receiving the pay they were promised. Learning they might be separated from husbands or assigned to housekeeping for white people, some black women collected their families and traveled to nearby towns, where Confederates paid for such services.

Single or widowed women often accepted help from northern relief agencies, or tried to fend for themselves. Nearly 6,000 Natchez, Mississippi, black women were dependent on American Missionary Association philanthropy or on funds raised by northern black women for relief and education. Other women huddled in camps outside towns, vulnerable to Confederate raids and to Union officers who might coerce them into field labor. One woman, probably typical of many, reported trading sex for pay because "we women had to make a living." Still, some newly freed women were able to find paid work, save money, and buy a home, even during the war.

1863: The Tide Turns

After losses to the Confederates in 1862, in May 1863 Union general Ulysses Grant won five battles in three weeks at Vicksburg. Union victory seemed within reach, but a draft met surprisingly strong resistance in the North.

Victory at Gettysburg

At first, as Confederates marched north into Pennsylvania, Lincoln's call for volunteers got a quick response. In a three-day clash at Gettysburg in July 1863, northern troops led by General George Meade shot down more than half of the Confederate troops sent into the battle. By the time Confederate forces retreated from this bloodiest battle of the war, more than 23,000 Union soldiers and 28,000 Confederates had perished or been injured.

The Union victory at Gettysburg proved a turning point. Now European nations definitively withdrew their support from the South. Britain canceled contracts to build warships for the Confederacy, as British dependence on northern wheat outweighed its need for cotton, which it now imported from India and Egypt. British popular opinion, massaged into abolitionist sympathies by dozens of black abolitionists, helped solidify this decision. France, too, distanced itself from the Confederacy.

President Lincoln bestowed symbolic importance on this battle by traveling to Gettysburg in November 1863 to deliver his memorable address dedicating the battlefield as a cemetery. Before a somber audience, he declared that the Gettysburg victory foretold "a new birth of freedom" in a nation that had been "conceived in liberty and dedicated to the proposition that all men are created equal."

Anti-Draft Riots

Along with Union gains came setbacks, especially the difficulty in finding new recruits. In the spring of 1863, Congress enacted a draft law requiring three years military service for every man between ages twenty and forty-five. (Those who could pay a fee or find a substitute were exempted.) Shortly after the Gettysburg victory, when New York newspapers printed a list of draftees, hundreds of young white men rioted in New York City. Convinced that black men would take their jobs while they were off fighting, the white draftees stormed a building where a draft lottery was taking place. For more than a week mobs vandalized factories and shipyards where war supplies were manufactured or transported. Black workers were randomly attacked on the streets, and black neighborhoods were ravaged.

Why such resistance to the draft? Many of the rioters were poor immigrants who resented the provision allowing wealthier men to avoid service. Falling wages also provoked the outbursts. Military purchasing had inflated prices, but earnings had not kept pace. Thus, poorly paid white factory workers, seeing their standard of living decline, were frustrated and viewed black workers as the source of the troubles. The protesters claimed that black workers lowered wages by settling for less money than white workers. Moreover, the rioters resented black men and women who carved out successful lives. As black New Yorkers struggled to defend themselves, more than one hundred black and white people died. Troops were called from the battlefield to crush the uprising. In the end, Union draft officers looked the other way while 10 percent of young white men ignored their call or deserted after entering the army. In Detroit, Philadelphia, and other cities, as the Democratic press fanned fears of job competition, white workers replayed the New York riots, resisting the draft by attacking black Americans.

Grant and Sherman Lead Union Victories

By early 1864, victories at Vicksburg and Gettysburg had solidified the North's advantage. Now black troops were under Union general Ulysses S. Grant's command in Virginia when he confronted Confederate general Robert E. Lee. "By arming the negro we have added a powerful ally," Grant told Lincoln. "They make good soldiers, and taking them from the enemy weakens [the South] as it strengthens us." In June 1864, when Lee's forces stopped Grant's at the outskirts of Petersburg, Virginia, both sides suffered high casualties in a siege that lasted nine months.

African American soldiers also accompanied Union general William T. Sherman in May 1864 as he began his march from Tennessee through Georgia to the sea and north into South Carolina. One black Rhode Island recruit described the southern white people he encountered: "We could see signs of smothered hate [for] both our color and [our] present character as Union soldiers. But, for once [I] walked fearlessly and boldly through the streets of a southern city, without being required to take off my hat at every step, or to give all the side-walks to the planters' sons." During this eight-month campaign, Union troops systematically destroyed everything in their path: bridges, railroads, factories, warehouses, barns, crops, and homes all went up in flames. By the time Sherman reached Savannah in December 1864, he had severed the South's transportation and supply routes.

While Sherman swept through the South, the 1864 presidential election revealed a precarious political situation as politicians and federal officials in Washington clashed over the management of the war, of slaves, and of procedures for reunification. The Democrats called for an immediate end to the war. Weary of war, Republicans could not unite behind Lincoln. The Radical faction nominated Frémont and the Republican (National Union) faction nominated Lincoln, with Andrew Johnson, a Democrat from Tennessee, for vice president. Only Sherman's victories in Georgia assured Lincoln's reelection. He won by a mere 40,000 votes out of 4 million cast, revealing that Northerners (Southerners did not vote) had mixed feelings about the war.

"Forty Acres and a Mule"

Sherman's success marked another turning point for former slaves. In January 1865, after he took Savannah, black ministers petitioned Sherman for land on which they and their people could raise food for their families. The general responded with Special Field Order No. 15, granting thousands of acres of confiscated land along the Florida, Georgia, and South Carolina coast to black families in 40-acre plots. Sherman also gave them mules to work the acreage.

News of Field Order No. 15 spread quickly. Many ex-slaves and northern reformers concluded the government should provide *all* freed people with "40 acres and a mule." But some white leaders doubted the legality of confiscating and redistributing property, and black leaders who had worked their way up the economic ladder worried that free land might foster laziness and undermine the capitalist economy they now embraced. Both black and white leaders also feared that, at war's end, white resentment of land grants might spark riots. South Carolina's Alonzo Ransier, an African American soon to win election to the U.S. House of Representatives, advised people to "buy lands by saving their money, and not to expect confiscation or the possession of lands that were not theirs."

But most ex-slaves disagreed. Some suggested the states buy land at tax auction, then resell it to freedmen at reduced costs if they would improve it with a dwelling and farm it. Modeled after the 1862 Homestead Act, this plan never saw the light of day. One landless South Carolinian concluded: "At the close of the war [we] were set free without a dollar, and without a foot of land [or] the wherewithal to get the next meal even. The labor of these people had for two hundred years cleared away the forests and produced crops that brought millions of dollars annually. . . . Did they get any portion of it? Not a cent. . . . Four million people turned loose without a dollar . . . [by those] whose duty it was to feed them. My opinion is that the government should have done it."

An Incomplete Victory

By the time Major Martin Delany arrived in Charleston on April 3, 1865 to organize a black fighting force, the war was nearly over. On April 9, Confederate general Lee surrendered at Virginia's Appomattox Court House.

Across the nation, black rejoicing took many forms. Young black soldiers hurried home with the news to West Chester, Pennsylvania, where they rang the courthouse bell. Black residents in New York celebrated with a parade. Thomas Morris Chester, the black war correspondent for African American newspapers, sent word to Philadelphia: "The colored population was wild with enthusiasm. Old men thanked God in a very boisterous manner, and old women shouted upon the pavement as high as they ever had done at a religious revival."

On April 14, ex-slave Robert Smalls sailed into Charleston Harbor on the steamship *Planter,* which he had stolen for the Union early in the war. Now a gunboat captain, Smalls joined the Union flag-raising celebration at Fort Sumter—four years, almost to the day, after its fall. There sixty-year-old white abolitionist William Lloyd Garrison stood beside the son of slave rebel Denmark Vesey and numbers of other veteran abolitionists when Delany recorded the buoyant mood: "The Union flag," he said, "now symbolizes freedom for all, without distinction of race or color."

In Texas, the Union army arrived on June 19 to announce victory ("Juneteenth" celebrations still mark the day). One black woman who had fled slavery and survived in the wild for several years now had, it was told, "freedom not of the swamp, but of the world." At a New Orleans Fourth of July parade in 1865, a black military officer "declared that slavery was dead and will be buried so deep that the judgment will not find it!"

But the idea of freedom proved more exhilarating than the reality. Freed slaves had few resources with which to provide for or protect themselves—and no power to acquire them. Across the South, state governments were in disarray, local economies broken, and cities and farms in shambles. Black and white families alike desperately needed food, shelter, medical care, and reassurance. One black Floridian wrote, "Nobody had his bearings. The freed people had no homes and no names except such as they inherited from their owners. They [did not know] whether to rejoice because they were free or to be cast down at their new condition of . . . responsibility and homelessness." In New Orleans, Frank Bell recalled his experience: "When war am over [the master] won't free me, says I'm valuable to him in his trade. He say, 'Nigger, you's supposed to be free but I'll pay you a dollar a week and iffen you runs off I'll kill you.'" In South Carolina, Nancy Johnson repeatedly sent her four hungry children back to her former master for food. Still, there was progress, too. Eventually, Nancy Johnson opened a successful boarding house, and her grandchildren all finished college.

The Assassination of President Lincoln

Within days of the South's surrender, Confederate sympathizer John Wilkes Booth killed Abraham Lincoln in a theater. Setting aside earlier disappointments with Lincoln, Delany eulogized him as "the humane, the benevolent, the philanthropic, the generous, the beloved, the able, the wise, great and good President of the United States." Delany suggested a fitting memorial would be a statue depicting a kneeling African woman with tear-filled eyes cast to heaven, to be funded by a penny from every African American man, woman, and child. Delany's vision was never realized.

Other black Americans also memorialized Lincoln as their savior, creating a legend that remained untarnished for more than a century. The black New

Orleans *Tribune,* having criticized the living Lincoln, now linked him with the most radical abolitionist: "Lincoln and John Brown are two martyrs. . . . Both have willingly jeopardized their lives for the sacred cause of freedom." Black people in the Sea Islands, where the Port Royal system still tied black people to the land, passed a resolution praising "the wisdom and Christian patriotism [Lincoln] displayed" in the "most memorable act proclaiming Liberty to our race."

The Thirteenth Amendment

In February 1865 the Thirteenth Amendment to the U.S. Constitution, ending slavery everywhere in the United States and its territories, was passed by Congress. By December 18, 1865, twenty-seven states (including eight in the South) had ratified the premise that "neither slavery nor involuntary servitude, except as a punishment for crime, shall exist within the United States." Once again, celebrations followed. In Boston, black and white abolitionists crowded into Music Hall, where William Lloyd Garrison reported being moved by the "deeply religious and moral significance" of outlawing slavery.

But the Thirteenth Amendment did not include the franchise. Even as black people celebrated, Delany urged them to organize for the right to vote. Augusta, Georgia's *Colored American* reported that a black convention in South Carolina called for "equal suffrage [to] be conferred in common with white men as a protection from hostility, and because all free governments derive their power from the consent of the governed." In the North and South, Equal Rights Leagues, many led by black veterans of antebellum abolitionism, took up the franchise battle. Only the vote could safeguard the freedom promised by the Thirteenth Amendment.

Reuniting Black Families

With slavery vanquished, thousands of liberated black Americans sought lost family members. Northern and southern black newspapers published notices like this one: "I have a mother somewhere in the world. I know not where. She used to belong to Philip Mathias in Elbert County, Georgia, and she left four of her children there about twenty-three years ago. . . . I ask all who read this to inquire for her. Her name was Martha and I heard that she was carried off to Mississippi by speculators."

Similar heart-wrenching appeals testified to African Americans' longing to be reunited with loved ones. Some had been separated by slave sales or war. Others hoped to locate relatives who had escaped to the North or were returning from exile. Fugitive slave James Davis, heading home from Canada, yearned to hear from his family. "Write me word how Johnny is getting on," implored his notice. "I am in East Boston but I feel very lonesome. I don't see any colored ladies & gentlemens." From Cincinnati, Ben Montgomery and his family returned home to Hurricane Plantation in 1865. They reopened their old store but now served the free black farmers who leased confiscated land from the government.

The Freedmen's Bureau

In 1865, Congress established a Freedmen's Bureau to allocate work, supplies, and abandoned and confiscated southern lands among freed black people. Bureau agents also delivered medical, educational, and legal services and helped set up hospitals, schools, and stores. The bureau assigned Delany a post in South Carolina.

The federal government sent troops to impose political order in the South, but the Freedmen's Bureau was charged with repairing the region's social and economic order. It encouraged white planters to revive their farms, urged black workers to accept jobs, monitored contracts between landowners and workers, and pressed both to treat each other as employers and employees, not owners and property. Bureau agents followed the Port Royal model in blending education, philanthropy, and paid labor.

As the extent of the South's devastation became clear, Congress renewed the Freedmen's Bureau charter in 1866. Bureau agents now expanded their reach, working to reunite families and helping black refugees write or read letters and newspaper notices for lost kin. Reuniting families sometimes involved legal battles with local and national courts, as local governments tried to replace slavery with other forms of servitude. Maryland's oppressive apprentice system was a typical example, finally overturned by the Supreme Court in 1868. In the process, the bureau established African Americans' right to seek justice in the Maryland courts.

Black Codes and Sharecropping

Maryland's system of separate laws for black people was part of a larger southern legal pattern known as Black Codes. After the Civil War, the federal government restored citizenship privileges and statehood to former Confederate states whose white leaders swore allegiance to the United States. By 1869, many southern states had elected new officials and reorganized law enforcement to restrict black people's movement, economic and social prospects, and access to legal recourse. Alabama gave former slave owners the right of first refusal for black apprentices. Georgia banned interracial marriage. North Carolina required the death penalty if a black man raped a white woman (in all other instances, rapists were fined).

Many contracts promoted by the Freedmen's Bureau bound black workers to repetitive tasks, long hours, low wages, or compensation in produce rather than cash. When the dream of "40 acres and a mule" evaporated, the Bureau pressured black freedmen to accept an owner–tenant relationship known as *sharecropping*. In such arrangements, a landowner provided about forty acres and some of the seeds and supplies to plant cotton, corn, wheat, oats, or rice. In return, the tenant gave the landlord a percentage, or share, of the resulting crop.

Advocated by the Freedmen's Bureau to suppress vagrancy, sharecropping encouraged blatant exploitation. Many landowners manipulated the cost of supplies so it exceeded the tenant's share of crop production. This ploy kept the tenant perpetually indebted to the owner and, therefore, tied to the land. Other landowners found excuses to dismiss tenants just before their compensation was due. Such incidents made black people wary of entering into contracts. "I am opposed to working under a contract," wrote one black South Carolinian. "I expect to stay in the South . . . but not to hire myself to a planter. . . . I have seen some men hired who were turned off [of the land] without being paid."

"Times are very hard, and hard to get money," wrote South Carolina ex-slave Celia Johnson in 1868, resigning herself to a farming contract. As often as men, women suffered their employers' violent resentment of the postwar changes. One Georgia county agent reported that a landowner had "cursed and abused" a freedwoman working for him "when she told him she was as free as he. On this he kicked her in the head and knocked her down seriously hurting her."

By 1869, sharecropping was supported by Black Codes. Black adults who failed to enter into contracts, or who broke them, could be arrested for vagrancy and imprisoned. Prisoners, in turn, were leased to farmers or commercial concerns, and the wages from their labor went to state coffers. A ball and chain attached to the ankle kept prisoners from escaping as they toiled on county roads and private railroads. Freedmen's Bureau agents declined to interfere with such practices, believing they brought order by preventing black vagrancy. But few black Southerners described their new conditions as free.

Black Education

The Freedmen's Bureau was overwhelmed by land and labor issues, but it did a better job of providing other services. Between 1866 and 1872, it distributed more than 21 million food rations and widespread medical care to distressed Southerners, both black and white. But its most enduring influence was on black education. In its sixteen years, it established more than 4,000 schools for former slaves, many of which survive today.

Private organizations often helped develop black schools. In 1868, Samuel Chapman Armstrong organized a black boarding school near Hampton Roads, Virginia. The curriculum at Hampton focused on self-discipline, hygiene, and manual skills, and aimed to produce skilled, responsible workers. Other schools aimed to develop black leaders. Established by the Freedmen's Bureau in 1867 and named after Bureau director and Union general Oliver O. Howard, Howard University in Washington, DC, offered a rigorous and varied curriculum, including degrees in law and medicine. Lincoln University in Pennsylvania and Wilberforce in Ohio, supported by the American Missionary Association, shared Howard University's focus on liberal education.

So, too, did the innovative Berea College in Kentucky. Opened in 1858, Berea was suspended during wartime but reopened in 1866 with a program similar to Hampton's. Students put their manual training to use in maintaining the school's buildings and grounds. Berea's abolitionist founder, Reverend John Fee, welcomed black and white students and hired an integrated faculty. To this day, Berea remains racially integrated, tuition-free, and graduates are expected to commit their lives to social reform ideals.

The Rise of the Ku Klux Klan

Even while black Southerners pursued self-improvement, they remained aware of white Southerners' bitterness over the war, the demise of slavery, and the federal military presence in the South. In Tennessee in 1866, angry white Southerners formalized their hatred in an organization known as the Ku Klux Klan. Billing itself as the protector of the Old South's noble traditions, the Klan united resentful Confederates from many walks of life. Led by a former Confederate general, the Klan used hoods and fiery crosses, secret codes, and night raids to scare black Americans away from taking advantage of new opportunities. Thousands of so-called night riders systematically threatened, maimed, or killed to keep black people out of politics. Nevertheless, between 1867 and 1870, southern black men gained the right to vote, while most of their

northern counterparts could not legally cast a ballot. They were determined to leverage this power.

The Fourteenth Amendment

Race-based hatred showed black Southerners what black Northerners had long understood: True equality comes from political power only. As early as February 1862, Frederick Douglass laid out his vision of the war's outcome: "No war but an Abolition war; no peace but an Abolition peace; liberty for all, chains for none; the black man a soldier in war, a laborer in peace; a voter at the South as well as at the North; America his permanent home, and all Americans his fellow countrymen. [Then] our glory as a nation will be complete."

Following Douglass's lead, black Northerners began organizing for the right to vote during the war. In 1864, more than a hundred African Americans from eighteen states (including states still in the Confederacy) gathered in Syracuse, New York, to create the National Equal Rights League. They insisted the war was about citizenship as well as slavery.

To secure citizenship rights for black people, the Republican Congress in 1866 proposed the Fourteenth Amendment, aimed at overriding the Supreme Court's 1857 *Dred Scott* ruling that African Americans were not citizens. The amendment, stating that "no state shall make or enforce any law which shall abridge the privileges or immunities of citizens in the United States," protected citizens' rights from violation by state governments. It also promised that "when the right to vote at any election is denied to any of the male inhabitants of such state . . . the representation [in Congress] shall be reduced in proportion." To regain representation in Congress, Confederate states had to ratify the

Fourteenth Amendment. As they did, federal troops began to leave, and the Freedmen's Bureau began to close down.

But black Americans did not consider the job done until black men had the right to vote everywhere. The National Equal Rights League expanded rapidly, linking New York, Michigan, Pennsylvania, and Ohio with Tennessee, Louisiana, and North Carolina. Proclaiming that "it is the duty of every colored citizen to obtain a repeal of [any state] law which disfranchises him on the soil on which he was born," members repeatedly petitioned state legislatures for the franchise implied under the Fourteenth Amendment.

Thus, securing the right to vote became paramount in the postwar years. The black editor of the Atlanta paper *Loyal Georgian* spoke for many when he wrote, "The colored man owes it to the martyrs who have fallen to procure his right to—upon their graves reared to liberty—*vote* and vote *right*. Let the Republicans of the North know the strength and character of the colored voter in the South." The *Arkansas Freeman* agreed: "The colored voters hold the power to strike out for themselves" and "demand their rights." In Mississippi, black planter P. B. S. Pinchback told African Americans that voting was essential "if they wanted to be men." For decades to come, black people equated manhood with the right to vote.

Conclusion

What began as a "white man's war" in 1861 evolved over four years into a conflict where black men fought to end slavery. Former slaves assumed leadership positions in the military, and a president who wanted to deport black people issued the Emancipation Proclamation freeing them. Congress followed with the Thirteenth Amendment to the Constitution, finally eradicating slavery. Federal soldiers, the Freedmen's Bureau, and private agencies moved into the South to build a new society that included African Americans as free people, not slaves.

Postwar freedom brought black Southerners real advances—reunited families, increased land ownership (in some regions), and rising literacy rates. The Fourteenth Amendment guaranteed citizenship to anyone born in the United States. But these advances came only in the South, and only under pressure from Congress. Moreover, black freedom sparked white hate groups in the South, bent on restricting black progress.

In Washington, meanwhile, the struggle over ending slavery and defining new roles for black Americans highlighted rivalries among the legislative, judicial, and executive branches of the federal government, as well as between these units and the military. For African Americans, the struggle did not end with the war's conclusion. As we will see in the next chapter, the federal government gradually concluded that black citizens in the North should also have the right to vote. In February 1869, when Congress proposed the Fifteenth Amendment, giving the franchise to all black men, African Americans' hopes stirred again. Nonetheless, it required intense pressure from the federal government to ratify the amendment that made the African American man a voter, finally fulfilling Frederick Douglass's dream.

Questions for Review and Reflection

1. How did the original definition of the Civil War as "a white man's war" affect the strategies adopted by—and the relationships between—both white and black Americans?

2. What are the broader lessons to be learned—both from the 1860s and in later times—from the Port Royal experiment?

3. Imagine yourself as a field reporter for the *Christian Recorder* during the Civil War. (The *Christian Recorder* was the only black newspaper to publish throughout the war.) What should be the focus and the priorities that shape your reports from the battlefront?

4. Why wasn't the Thirteenth Amendment enough?

CHAPTER 11

Post-Civil War Reconstruction: A New National Era

Emanuel Fortune Testifies before Congress

"They always spoke very bitterly against it," said Florida Republican Emanuel Fortune, describing his white neighbors' reaction to the idea of black people voting. Those neighbors told Fortune, "The damned Republican party has put niggers to rule us, and we will not suffer it." Fortune was testifying before a congressional committee investigating Ku Klux Klan threats and violence against black Southerners. After the Civil War, when anger in many southern white communities erupted in violence, some white Southerners targeted black men like Fortune who organized voters or ran for office. "I got information that I would be missing some day and no one would know where I was, on account of my being a leading man in politics," Fortune recalled.

Emanuel Fortune's story typified the experience of black political leaders who emerged in the postwar period. Relatively young—Fortune was thirty-nine in 1871—these leaders were new to politics. Just a few years earlier, they had been outsiders—many of them slaves. Now they had a political voice. Fortune, for example, had participated in the 1868 constitutional convention that qualified Florida—part of the Confederacy during the war—to reenter the Union by guaranteeing black suffrage and ratifying the Fourteenth Amendment, which defined citizens as anyone born in the United States, guaranteed them the equal protection of the laws, and provided for a reduction in congressional representation for any state that denied the vote to some of its citizens. The fact that a black man could run for office and get elected by a black constituency demonstrated those new rights. But the threats Fortune received also

1865	In March, Congress charters the Freedmen's Bureau and the Freedmen's Savings and Trust Bank.
	In December, the Thirteenth Amendment, ratified by twenty-seven states, abolishes slavery throughout the United States.
1866	Over President Andrew Johnson's veto, Congress passes the Civil Rights Act granting citizenship and civil rights to African Americans.
	In Pulaski, Tennessee, the secretive Ku Klux Klan is formed.
1868	Congress carries out impeachment proceedings against President Andrew Johnson.
	Johnson is acquitted in May, when the Senate fails, by one vote, to reach the two-thirds vote necessary for conviction.
	The Fourteenth Amendment is ratified, guaranteeing citizenship to African Americans and requiring southern states to approve it before gaining readmission to the Union.
1869	Congress proposes the Fifteenth Amendment to protect "the right of citizens of the United States to vote."
	Mary Ann Shadd Cary tries to register to vote in Washington, DC, and petitions Congress when officials deny her.
	Over the issue of black civil and voting rights, the women's rights movement splits into two rival organizations.
1870	The Fifteenth Amendment is ratified.
	Seven southern legislators become the first black men elected to the United States Congress.
	Congress passes the Ku Klux Klan Act to protect voting rights, also known as the Enforcement Act, making it a federal offense to interfere with franchise rights guaranteed by the Fifteenth Amendment.
1871	The District of Columbia is granted self-rule.
	After holding a series of hearings on Ku Klux Klan violence, Congress enacts a second Ku Klux Klan Act.
1872	At the National Colored Men's Labor Convention in Washington, DC, Frederick Douglass and Mary Ann Shadd Cary champion manual laborers' rights.
	The Freedmen's Bureau is dismantled.
	Black leaders endorse the reelection of Republican presidential candidate Ulysses S. Grant for president, pleased that he advocates annexing the Dominican Republic, with its majority black population.
1873	Beginning in September, the Panic of 1873 plunges the United States into economic depression.
	In the *Slaughterhouse Cases,* Supreme Court narrows the scope of the Fourteenth Amendment.
1874	The Freedmen's Savings and Trust Bank fails.
	The Virginia legislature reorganizes election districts to dilute the black vote.
1875	Congress passes the Civil Rights Act, guaranteeing black Americans access to public accommodations.
1876	Harriet Purvis is elected the first black president of the American Woman Suffrage Association.

(Continued)	1877	A compromise between Congress and the Republican Party over the disputed presidential election results in complete withdrawal of federal troops from the South. The Republican Party establishes a separate Black and Tan Party, segregating black Americans from the mainstream Republican Party. A nationwide railroad workers' strike in July elevates Peter Clark, the first known African American socialist, to leadership.
	1878	The Liberia Exodus Joint Stock Company sends the ship *Azor* to Africa.
	1879	The Kansas Exodus Joint Stock Company sends emigrants west to Kansas.

highlighted the risks run by southern black men who dared to claim seats at the political table. He described Jackson County, Florida, in 1869 as being in "such a state of lawlessness that my life was in danger at all times."

Fortune was prepared to fight back. He was remembered by friends as a "dead shot, and he *would* shoot." Despite threats, he never relinquished his political commitment. Over the next ten years, he served as city marshal, Republican national convention delegate, county commissioner, clerk of the city market, and state congressman.

Fortune's testimony before Congress reveals the realities of the postwar South. White Southerners complained bitterly about what they called "black rule" as African Americans took positions as sheriffs, justices of the peace, county clerks, and school superintendents. Even so, only a few dozen black Americans occupied positions of real authority. Few actually ran for office, and many black voters, intimidated by threats or actual violence in the open southern polls, where a vote was public knowledge, supported white politicians.

With the South's return to the Union after the Civil War, race relations in that embattled region took center stage. For the first dozen years after the war—a period that became known as Reconstruction—the federal government sent troops and agents to restore order and aid slaves' transition to freedom. Federal and private agencies opened schools, distributed food and medicine, and intervened in legal disputes between freed people and their white neighbors. In what many Northerners considered a new national era, the federal government aimed to heal the war-torn South and make it more like the North, physically, economically, socially, and politically. While repairing fields, roads, and homes was foremost, many Northerners hoped the South would soon have new railroads, factories, banks, and wage laborers as well.

Reconstruction extended to the national level, as black men were elected to Congress and Republican presidents appointed African Americans to positions of authority. During this era, black leaders made access to the polls their highest priority, believing African Americans could vote into office leaders who supported their goals, such as farm ownership and jobs that would allow them to be independent of white landowners. They also wanted education for their children, as literacy would, in turn, provide opportunities for entrepreneurship and political power that would lift people out of poverty.

But most northern and southern white Americans hoped to "reconstruct" a system that tied black Americans to menial roles. A few white Americans envisioned former bondspeople becoming successful landowners or entrepreneurs, although certainly not equal members of society. Though slavery had been outlawed, persuasion, local statutes, intimidation, and widespread prejudice kept black people tied to agricultural and service jobs in both the South and the North.

As we saw in Chapter 10, resentful southern planters also began instituting Black Codes to keep black people subservient. These laws were backed by violence, threats, or economic reprisals, such as dismissing black farm workers who tried to vote or who encouraged others to do so. The presence of the federal Freedmen's Bureau in the South, which aimed to help former slaves become full citizens, infuriated many white Southerners. These planters hoped to reconstruct the old agricultural system in which wealthy white men made the laws, leaving both white and black poor people powerless.

But black Americans had sweeping ambitions: strengthening their communities economically, reassembling their families, and protecting themselves from violence and intimidation. All these goals hinged on acquiring and protecting political rights, navigating the shifting and sometimes treacherous tides of southern and federal politics. Washington, DC—seat of the national government—symbolized the complexities of the new era. From across the nation, black Americans seeking employment and federal protection streamed into the capital city.

But federal sympathy toward freedmen and freedwomen waned after a decade of Reconstruction efforts, and federal promises went unfulfilled. Discouraged by slow progress, some black Americans again directed their hopes elsewhere—to African or to western frontiers.

Postwar Reconstruction

On February 25, 1870, an ambitious, urbane Southerner arrived in Washington, DC, with a mission: to ensure that the federal government treated black people as full citizens. That man was Hiram Revels—African Methodist Episcopal Church (AME) minister, former Union recruitment officer, and advocate of education for black people. The first black American to be elected to Congress, Revels soon discovered how fervently white congressmen resented his presence. His public service career—beginning before the Civil War and continuing until his death in 1901—reveals much about how emancipation transformed black people and about the complexities of Reconstruction.

Radical Reconstruction

Revels found Congress dominated by a coalition of northern representatives known as Radical Republicans. These politicians aimed to protect and promote the interests of black Southerners and to punish white Southerners for the Civil War. Simultaneously, Congress clashed with the president over how to define and protect black rights. Though the war had ended, sectional tensions remained. Because black Southerners could not yet vote, southern white aristocrats returned to the congressional seats they had vacated with secession. In response,

Radical Republicans, still in the majority, asserted Congress's right to refuse to seat southern congressmen who had not yet sworn Union allegiance. Led by Pennsylvania representative Thaddeus Stevens and Massachusetts senator Charles Sumner (who returned to the Senate in 1860), they strategized on how to get southern black candidates seated in Congress in order to drive southern white men from the legislature.

Radical Republicans pounded the South with new policies. In early 1867, Congress passed three new Reconstruction acts. The first divided the South into five military districts, sending federal troops to maintain order and protect freed people. The second required former Confederate states to draft constitutions guaranteeing black male suffrage. The third stipulated that former Confederate states could send congressmen to Washington only after state legislatures had ratified the Fourteenth Amendment. This amendment, ratified in 1868, was the most important product of the Reconstruction era. It affirmed black people's citizenship, removing any ambiguity left from the *Dred Scott* case of 1857. It also denied former slave owners' claims that they should be compensated for their lost "property." Fortune, a delegate to Florida's constitutional convention, helped pass these provisions. To build support for punishing Southerners, Congress also established a committee to investigate southern antiblack violence.

Presidential Reconstruction

Black people across the nation hoped the Fourteenth Amendment would secure them a place in their nation's economic, political, and social life. However, a milder form of Reconstruction proposed by President Abraham Lincoln and favored by his successor, Andrew Johnson, enabled the white South to resist. Hoping to heal sectional bitterness, Lincoln and some Northerners favored a nonpunitive approach. The South, they contended, did not possess the authority to leave the United States. Hence, southern states had always remained in the Union, and thus technically did not need to rejoin.

When Lincoln was assassinated in April 1865, the presidency fell to Vice President Andrew Johnson. A former Democratic senator from Tennessee, Johnson also favored a lenient Reconstruction policy. Reversing Congress's Confiscation Act of 1862, which had allowed the federal government to seize Confederates' property without compensation, Johnson offered to pardon and to restore the property of former Confederates who took an oath of allegiance to the Constitution. He also promised to restore their confiscated land. He acknowledged North Carolina's new constitution, which, following Republican guidelines, gave black men the vote, and encouraged other Confederate states to reestablish state governments.

Thus, black rights became the focus of Johnson's power struggle with Congress in the postwar era. He vetoed Congress's Civil Rights Act of 1866, which gave limited legal rights to African Americans, as well as a bill to renew the Freedmen's Bureau. But Radical Republicans overrode both vetoes and passed both bills. Johnson still opposed the Fourteenth Amendment because he felt it violated southern states' rights to control their citizenship. During the 1866 midterm campaign, he urged southern states not to ratify it.

Tension between Johnson and Congress reached a climax when the president tried to remove Secretary of War Edwin Stanton, who was encouraging military officers stationed in the South to ignore communications from the president. Seeking to undermine Johnson's authority, Congress passed the Tenure of Office Act, which blocked Johnson from firing Stanton and guaranteed tenure of office to anyone appointed with the Senate's approval. When Johnson dismissed Stanton anyway, Republicans promptly called for the president's impeachment on the grounds that he had violated the Tenure of Office Act and other charges. A three-month impeachment trial failed to remove Johnson, however, because the two-thirds majority required in the Senate fell one vote short. Once more, the contest for power between the South and branches of the federal government—ostensibly about black issues—only diverted federal attention from black people's needs.

The Fifteenth Amendment

The Fourteenth Amendment should have secured black freedom everywhere, but even as congressional policies gave southern black men the franchise, northern black men with political ambitions had to head south to fulfill them. In a bitter irony, southern black men, so recently liberated from slavery, had more opportunities for political leadership than did black Northerners. Many northern states still banned black men from voting. The *New York Tribune* put the matter bluntly: "They who desire the Right of Suffrage for Blacks of the South oppose the extension of the same right to Blacks of the North." Across the North, Equal Rights Leagues advocated for full political equality.

By the 1868 elections, northern voters had enough of the tug-of-war in Washington. They elected moderate Republicans who distanced themselves from the Radicals' platform and supported the new president: military hero Ulysses S. Grant. With conservative governments victorious in Virginia by 1869 and in North Carolina and Georgia by 1871, aggressively pro-black Reconstruction all but vanished.

Now that Congress had a conservative southern contingent, even moderate Republicans—most of whom had rejected a black suffrage amendment—began to see that northern black voters could be useful. So in February 1869, moderate Republicans proposed the Fifteenth Amendment, prohibiting federal and state governments from limiting the franchise because of "race, color, or previous condition of servitude." To return to the Union, former Confederate states had to ratify this amendment. Mississippi was among the first to comply. Upon its readmission, black voters sent state senator Hiram Revels to Washington to finish out the Senate term vacated by Jefferson Davis in 1861. As a black Pittsburgh teacher commented, "The Republican party had done the Negro good [in passing the Fifteenth Amendment], but they were doing themselves good at the same time." When Revels took his seat in Congress, he was as much a symbol as a politician. To black Americans and Radical Republicans, he embodied black enfranchisement and the South's defeat. To moderate Republicans, he represented a concession to Radical Republican schemes that would preserve the Republican majority in Congress.

Hiram Revels helped recruit the first black Civil War regiments in Maryland and Missouri. After his U.S. Senate service, he returned to Mississippi and became president of Alcorn, a Reconstruction-era black college. This photo of Revels with his wife and five daughters was taken in about 1870.

Black Suffrage and Woman Suffrage

The passage of the Fourteenth and Fifteenth Amendments exposed the fragility of the northern white and black reformer alliance. With Emancipation, war's end, and the Thirteenth Amendment, many white abolitionists, satisfied that black rights would come in due course, diverted some of their energies to promoting full citizenship for women. This connection between black rights and women's rights had been marked since Frederick Douglass attended the 1848 Women's Rights Convention at Seneca Falls, New York. Douglass and Elizabeth Cady Stanton had long been friends, as Douglass backed Stanton's claim that "the power to choose rulers and make laws was the right by which all others could be secured."

During the war, Stanton had circulated petitions supporting the Thirteenth Amendment outlawing slavery. When it was ratified, she expected antislavery leaders like Wendell Phillips to support her women's agenda in return. At issue for her was the word *male* in the Fourteenth Amendment. Previously, women had assumed they were citizens. The new amendment, which specified voters as "male inhabitants," underscored women's exclusion from the political process. Furious, Stanton refused to support the Fourteenth and Fifteenth Amendments. "My question is," she challenged Phillips, "do you believe the African race is composed entirely of males?" Stanton's friendship with Douglass also soured, as Douglass argued that the right to vote was more crucial for black men than for women. "The government of this country loves women," he contended, "but the Negro is loathed." Douglass feared a bill giving women the vote could not pass, even in a Radical Republican Congress.

TABLE 11.1 THE FEDERAL POWER STRUGGLE 1865–1877

Black newspapers recognized that often white Americans' interest in Reconstruction involved a power struggle among the three branches of government rather than the best interests of black people or the South. African American concerns frequently faded into the background. Below are some of the battles that took place during the Reconstruction years.

DATE	CONGRESS	PRESIDENCY	SUPREME COURT
1865	Establishes Freedmen's Bureau.	Andrew Johnson grants "amnesty and pardon" to most Confederates, restoring confiscated land, and exiling thousands of black farmers from their land.	
1866	Passes Thirteenth Amendment, abolishing slavery in all states and territories; ratified by 27 states. Expands Freedmen's Bureau authority and over Johnson's veto empowers it to try civil cases for freedmen. Over Johnson's veto, passes three Civil Rights Acts, including one that vacates the 1857 *Dred Scott* decision and grants citizenship to black Americans. Passes Fourteenth Amendment, guaranteeing citizenship and requiring Confederate states' approval; ratified in 1868.	Johnson vetoes a two-year extension for Freedmen's Bureau. Johnson vetoes Civil Rights Acts.	In *Ex Parte Milligan*, rules that neither the president nor Congress has legal power to allow other agencies to try civilian cases, except in theater of war.
1867		Enforces provisions of Civil Rights Acts.	In *Cummings* v. *Missouri*, rules that government may not require voters to take oaths of past loyalty.
1868	Passes Tenure of Office Act, forbidding the president to remove Secretary of War Edwin Stanton. Impeaches Johnson; conviction fails by one vote.	Removes military officers from duty, including Secretary of War Edwin Stanton.	Agrees to hear a southern state's case regarding the constitutionality of Reconstruction Acts. Outlaws Maryland's race-based apprentice system.
1869	Passes Fifteenth Amendment guaranteeing suffrage, requiring Confederate states to ratify; ratified in 1870.		Upholds congressional authority to shape Reconstruction.

		In *Texas* v. *White*, rules that Confederate officials had never left Union, since secession was illegal.
1870–71	Passes Ku Klux Klan Acts. Moderate Republicans refuse to seat black Louisiana Senator P. B. S. Pinchback.	
1872	Passes Amnesty Act Dismantles Freedmen's Bureau.	
1873		In the *Slaughterhouse Cases*, rules that only the rights of federal citizenship are protected under the Fourteenth Amendment; other rights at state discretion.
1875	Passes Civil Rights Act guaranteeing freedmen access to public accommodations.	
1877	Compromise installs Rutherford B. Hayes as president; federal troops withdrawn from South.	

The question of whether women had as much right to vote as freedmen found few sympathizers, even among Radical Republicans. Most reformers adopted a "black men first" strategy. By opposing the Fourteenth and later the Fifteenth Amendments, Stanton found herself linked to antiblack forces. The issue split the women's movement. Remaining true to her abolitionist principles that black male suffrage was more important than women's suffrage, Lucy Stone founded the interracial American Woman Suffrage Association (AWSA). She was soon joined by Harriet Purvis, who became its first black president in 1876. Other reformers sought to promote the cause of women *and* African Americans equally. "If colored men get their rights, and not colored women theirs, colored men will be masters over the women. . . . I am glad to see that men are getting their rights, but I want women to get theirs," said Sojourner Truth in an 1867 speech. Frances Ellen Watkins Harper and Mary Ann Shadd Cary agreed. They joined Stanton and Susan B. Anthony in the National Woman Suffrage Association in 1869. Cary, who shared Anthony's interest in divorce reform and support for women entrepreneurs, drafted a woman-suffrage statement to the House of Representatives and led a group of women who attempted to register to vote in the District of Columbia elections in 1869.

But soon Cary and other black women were put off by Stanton's and Anthony's impulsive rhetoric about "black [male] beasts" gaining the ballot before white women. In 1871, Cary broke away, establishing the Colored

A woman who made her living by words, Frances Ellen Watkins Harper (1835–1911) often canonized black heroes in poetry. A staunch advocate of temperance and the franchise for women, she agonized over the tensions tearing at reformers' alliances as rival groups argued about the Fourteenth and Fifteenth Amendments.

Woman's Progressive Franchise Association, which aimed to "take an aggressive stand against the assumption that men only [should vote]." Thus, in one of the nation's greatest ironies, enfranchisement for African Americans severed alliances between black leaders and white female reformers. When the Fifteenth Amendment was ratified in 1870, Douglass resumed his advocacy of women's suffrage and slowly rebuilt his friendship with Stanton. But the contest between race progress and gender reform continued into the twenty-first century.

Elected Black Leaders

Revels's election as the first black man to serve in the U.S. Senate was a mixed victory, as northern and southern congressmen questioned his eligibility: Had he been a citizen of the United States for the required nine years? After all, the Fourteenth Amendment granting citizenship had been ratified only two years before. By arguing that he had some white ancestors and therefore had been at least *partly* a citizen before 1868, Senator Revels succeeded in taking his seat.

Within months, six other African Americans joined Revels in Congress, thanks to the rising number of southern black voters. To represent South Carolina, Georgia, Alabama, and Mississippi came former slaves and freemen born in the North and the South. All seven knew their fellow congressmen would feel—at best—ambivalent about their presence. Yet they set out to help maintain a Republican majority in Congress and to sustain its commitment to African Americans. Black Americans celebrated what promised to be a new national era. Douglass, who had long argued that the black man must be "a voter at the South as well as at the North," envisioned a day when black Northerners would have the voting strength to elect black representatives.

THE FIRST COLORED SENATOR AND REPRESENTATIVES.
In the 41st and 42nd Congress of the United States.

This popular portrait of the seven black congressmen, from spring of 1873, includes several who were ending their term and several just arriving. Missing is Pinckney Benton Stewart Pinchback, elected to the Senate from Louisiana in 1872.

Black congressmen were pragmatic about the limits of their new power. Familiar with the ways of white Southerners, they recognized the need for compromise to accomplish their goals. Revels reassured those white Americans who feared politically powerful black men: "The white race has no better friend than I. I am true to my own race. I wish to see all done that can be done . . . to assist [black men] in acquiring property, in becoming intelligent, enlightened . . . citizens . . . but at the same time, I would not have anything done which would harm the white race." Yet Revels lobbied for integrated schools. Segregation, he said, "is wicked. . . . I hold it to be the duty of this nation to discourage it, because it is wicked, because it is wrong." Recognizing the atmosphere of violence in which black politicians operated, he recommended self-defense. "We all have to go armed in the South," he reported, "ready at a moment's warning to sell our lives if it is necessary." Delicately balancing humility, resolution, and self-protection, Revels worked for political progress.

Blanche K. Bruce, also from Mississippi, hoped compromise with white Southerners could spur black progress. A well-educated man who had held local offices, Bruce was elected to the Senate in 1874. Even as he joined southern white senators lobbying for federal funds to improve Mississippi's ports, he advocated full citizenship for Chinese and Native Americans—groups that, he figured, would then support the Republican Party.

Many black congressmen looked for ways to gain white allies. Revels and Alabama's Benjamin Turner were among those African Americans voting for the Amnesty Act of 1872, which would end restrictions on former Confederates' political participation. Revels explained to his constituency that accommodating white Southerners "got colored mechanics in the United States Navy Yard for the first time." With compromise and accommodation, Bruce negotiated alliances that brought black people jobs in post offices, customs offices, and Freedmen's Bureau offices across the South. Black representatives in Washington also cut deals that brought black cadets to West Point and the Naval Academy. Maneuvering through Washington's corridors of power, black politicians understood that their constituents were vulnerable and their own positions fragile. They sought issues on which they could negotiate with white allies without trading away too many black political gains. The balancing act demanded constant attention and vigilance.

Some black congressmen refused to compromise or negotiate. "In my state, since emancipation there have been over five hundred loyal men shot down by the disloyal men there, and not one of those men who took part in committing those outrages has ever been brought to justice," said Congressman Jefferson Long of Georgia. "Those disloyal people still hate this Government, [and] when loyal men dare to carry the 'stars and stripes' through our streets, they are turned out of employment." But outspoken black congressmen like Long found it hard to push their agenda. Too few in number and too new to politics, they struggled to represent their constituents' concerns. Sometimes simply being heard was all they could hope for. For example, Long voted against the Amnesty Act, knowing this would further isolate him in a Congress bent on reconciliation. Richard Cain, a representative from South Carolina, also voted no. "I want to see a change in this country," said Cain, a northern-born minister whose calling had taken him South to fight for black justice. "Instead of colored people being always penniless, I want to see them coming in with their mule teams and ox teams, with their corn and potatoes to exchange for silks and satins. I want to see children coming to enjoy life as it ought to be enjoyed." Cain doubted that reinstating political rights to Confederates would help realize this vision. Several other black congressmen also voted no on amnesty. Even red-inked letters from the Ku Klux Klan warning of "doom sealed in blood" could not deter these men from speaking out—knowing their arguments fell on deaf ears.

Young black congressmen sought counsel from seasoned political activists like Douglass. The esteemed black leader befriended them, often hosting them at his home. Yet even Douglass misread the political realities of Reconstruction. In the 1872 presidential race, he supported Republican President Ulysses S. Grant's bid for reelection. When Grant suggested annexing the Dominican Republic as a haven for African Americans, Douglass believed in Grant's goodwill. But others did not. Douglass's abolitionist friend Senator Charles Sumner, who chaired the Senate Foreign Relations Committee, suspected that annexation was a scheme to enrich white land speculators. Even when Grant refused to include black representatives at a White House dinner discussion on annexation, Douglass continued to support him. With support from the black voters Douglass helped deliver, Grant won reelection—but neither annexation of the Dominican Republic nor a federal appointment for Douglass materialized. Black people now had another reminder that their vote wielded little influence unless they could enlist support from powerful white allies.

TABLE 11.2 THE BLACK MEN WHO WENT TO CONGRESS IN 1870

Most African American congressmen were young, ambitious, and outspoken. All represented the South, though some were born in the North. Some brought prestigious educational credentials; others brought a wisdom born of life experience. Here is a look at the first seven black men who were elected to Congress. Most went on to fruitful careers following their terms in Congress.

NAME/ STATE/AGE IN 1870	BACK-GROUND	PRIOR EXPERIENCE	SERVICE IN CONGRESS	POST-CONGRESS EXPERIENCE
Blanche K. Bruce (1841–1898) Mississippi 29 years old	Born slave in Virginia to master and slave woman.	Studied at Oberlin College; Mississippi tax assessor, superintendent of education, alderman, sheriff.	Senate, 1875–1881. Supported seating of P. B. S. Pinchback, Mississippi River flood control and port development, citizenship for Chinese and Native Americans, dissolving all-black regiments.	1881–1893: Register of the Treasury and DC Recorder of Deeds; trustee of Howard University.
Richard H. Cain (1825–1887) South Carolina 45 years old	Born free in western Virginia, to black mother, Cherokee father.	Studied at Wilberforce College; delegate to SC state constitutional convention; served in SC state senate.	House of Representatives 1873–1874; 1877–1879. Opposed Amnesty Act; supported woman suffrage, education, and land.	1878: Encouraged South Carolinians to support Liberia exodus.
Robert DeLarge (1842–1874) South Carolina 28 years old	Born free in Virginia.	SC constitutional convention (1868) and state legislature.	House of Representatives, 1871–1873. Removed from office 2 months before his term expired because a white opponent won the contested election. Supported Amnesty Act, black land ownership.	Magistrate in Charleston.
Robert Brown Elliott (1842–1884) South Carolina 28 years old	Born in South Carolina to free black parents.	Passed SC bar in 1867; editor of black Republican newspaper, the *South Carolina Leader*;	House of Representatives, 1871–1875. Supported suppression of Ku Klux Klan,	Lawyer in New Orleans, Louisiana.

(continued)

TABLE 11.2 (*Continued*)

NAME/ STATE/AGE IN 1870	BACK- GROUND	PRIOR EXPERIENCE	SERVICE IN CONGRESS	POST- CONGRESS EXPERIENCE
		SC constitu- tional conven- tion; assistant adjutant-general of SC.	protection of black vote.	
Jefferson Long (1836–1900) Georgia 34 years old	Born a slave in Georgia to slave mother and white father.	Tailor.	House of Representatives, 1871–1873. Supported Ku Klux Klan Acts, opposed amnesty for ex- Confederates.	Tailoring busi- ness suffered because of his continued organizing for the Republican Party.
John Roy Lynch (1847–1939) Mississippi 23 years old	Louisiana slave freed when Union army seized Natchez, 1863.	Elected justice of the peace; Mississippi legislature speaker of the house.	House of Representatives, 1872–1876. Supported civil rights legislation.	Delegate to four national Republican conventions; appointed by President Benjamin Harrison to be auditor of the U.S. Treasury for the Navy Department.
Pinckney Benton Stewart Pinchback (1837–1921) Louisiana 33 years old	Born free to Georgia planter and an emancipated slave.	Louisiana state senator; lieutenant governor; acting governor.	Senate: elected in 1872, but never allowed to assume office. Advocated education, women's suffrage.	U.S. Customs inspector; cotton planter; owner of a Mississippi riverboat company; admitted to Louisiana bar in 1886; helped found Southern Normal School.

Local Politics in the South

"When we opened the school a party of armed men came to my house, seized me, carried me out and threw me in Thompson's Creek after they had belabored me with the muzzles of their revolvers . . . [saying] they 'did not want . . . any damned nigger school in that town and were not going to have it,'" Texas state senator George Ruby recalled in testimony about obstacles facing southern black politicians at the state and local levels. These politicians often had to craft political strategies and alliances simply to ensure constituents' safety, and in the South black politicians had few white allies. Nor did Radical Republicans intercede on their behalf. Even the presence of federal troops could not deter threats such as those Ruby endured merely for opening a school.

Ruby quickly learned the Texas political terrain. Born in New York and educated in New England, he had lived for a while in Haiti but returned to the United States to work for the Freedmen's Bureau. Assigned to build schools in Texas, he also represented Galveston County at the 1868 Texas constitutional convention, where he gained enough visibility to be elected to the State Senate. One of only two black state senators in Texas, Ruby had a constituency mainly of black voters and the minority of white politicians who sought federal assistance for rebuilding the state's infrastructure, refurbishing the Galveston port, and establishing an educational system benefiting poor Texans of all races.

Like Revels and other black leaders at the national level, Ruby used compromise and negotiation. He supported white Texans as well as black for patronage positions, and he tolerated the new state laws segregating public travel, parks, and even Republican political events. In return, he hoped to gain white support for laws that would restrain the Klan, give citizenship and the franchise to Native Americans, and promote schools and other services for freed people. He also hoped to limit Black Codes, those state or local laws restricting African Americans' employment choices, land ownership, mobility, and other opportunities.

Ruby's strategy reflected his understanding of southern political realities. In the postwar era, southern politics took one of three forms: the political middle (the vast majority of white Southerners), the political right, and the radical left. The political middle, or "moderates," included entrepreneurs, professionals, and farmers who had concluded even before the war that the South needed to modernize—to diversify its economy, develop technology and industry, and gain federal subsidies for geological surveys, railroads, factories, and ports. Moderate white Southerners were not much interested in economic advancement for African Americans, but they envisioned black laborers as part of the new South, working in factories as well as in fields. They welcomed alliances with black leaders who could help persuade black communities to meet moderate white people's goals. As long as leaders like Ruby stayed "in their place" and were deferential to white people, white moderates supported black education and voting rights.

South Carolina planter Wade Hampton exemplified white moderates. Hampton believed black and white southern leaders should unite in rebuilding the South. "Does not that glorious southern sun above us shine alike for both of us?" he asked. But Hampton and other moderates made no overtures toward social integration, viewing class and racial divisions as natural for society.

Black leaders like Ruby knew white moderates could help black people obtain access to education and jobs in agriculture or factories. Martin Delany was another who advocated black–white alliances. Filling in as editor for South Carolina's *Missionary Record,* he developed a blueprint for black–white cooperation. He felt certain that "the black man and the white man must work together . . . [to] bring about the redemption of the state and prosperity and happiness for the whole people." "The black men of this state are dependent on the whites, just as the whites are dependent on them," he wrote in 1873. Thus, he advised black Southerners to relinquish "hatred and resentment" and to be "polite, pleasant, agreeable, ever ready and obliging." Persuaded by Hampton's argument that "when all our troubles and trials are over, [black and white

Southerners] will sleep in that same soil in which we first drew breath," Delany supported Hampton's successful bid for governor of South Carolina in 1876.

At the political right stood what some might call radical reactionaries, a small but significant group of white Southerners. These included dislocated plantation owners who had lost their economic system and a few struggling white farmers emotionally invested in the South's old way of life, which had given even poor white people a higher status than black people. Their anger at the ravages of war prevented them from embracing any part of a new order that enabled African Americans to progress beyond a servile role. Intent on reviving the prewar agricultural economy, radical reactionaries needed laborers to work the land, and they wanted freed slaves to do the job. They had little interest in modernizing the South. They were most often the instigators of violence against black people, and black politicians did their best to avoid them.

The South's radical left—the third political group—argued that poor black people had more in common with poor white people than with wealthy black ones. That is, class was more important than race in working to achieve goals. Seeking unity among poor people regardless of race, they were concerned with universal education, more equitable land policies, better contracts for renters, and the rights of the poor. Some of their ideas were rooted in socialism, a political belief that government should distribute wealth equally among all its citizens. This philosophy, which defined economic circumstance as more important than race or ethnicity, gained favor with many of the world's poor in the late nineteenth century.

As steel and mining industries began to modernize southern cities like Birmingham and Atlanta, a black laborers' movement, allied with white radicals, gathered momentum. A small but vocal minority of southern white labor organizers embraced black radicals like Lucy Parsons, an organizer of Texas's Socialist Workingmen's Party, which advocated interracial labor unions, and Peter Clark of Cincinnati, who urged industrial workers to put class unity above racial division. Parsons, married to a white Texas socialist, exemplified what conservative white Southerners feared: miscegenation, or sexual liaison between black and white people. Though such "race-mixing" was common under slavery, white planters feared that in post-slavery times, mixed-race people would feel entitled to the privileges of white Americans.

Only the most optimistic of black Americans joined the socialist ranks. Most soon recognized that white socialists had little power to effect real change. However, the idea of political parties that subordinated racial differences to class loyalty remained alive for decades, even helping to shape the rhetoric of the 1984 presidential debates. In the 1890s, when the Populist Party emerged to put many of these concerns on the national agenda, poor black Southerners were among its strongest supporters.

White Backlash

Even outside the South, white Americans found many ways to keep black people "in their place." Immediately after Congress introduced the Thirteenth Amendment abolishing slavery, white-on-black violence intensified in the North. The same night President Abraham Lincoln was assassinated, an Ohio mob torched the main building of the black Wilberforce University. The blaze destroyed all of Delany's correspondence, manuscripts, and African art collections. "The hand that placed the torch," wrote Delany, was "leagued in sentiment with the same dastardly villains who struck down the greatest Chief Magistrate [Lincoln] of the present age."

Indeed, that hand had a broad span. In Philadelphia and San Francisco, in the late 1860s, white trolley riders shoved black people off when they tried to board. In Rochester, New York, in the winter of 1867, Douglass's son-in-law was so badly menaced by white drivers that he quit the taxi trade. That same winter, in the Freedmen's Bureau offices in Washington, DC, General Oliver O. Howard had to threaten to fire his white clerks to get them to accept black coworkers.

In the South, members of the Ku Klux Klan, cloaked in white hoods, galloped on horseback to the homes of black political leaders and their supporters who tried to vote, or those who had become economically comfortable, or supposedly did not show due deference to whites. The attackers often dragged black people out of their homes and whipped or tortured them. Sometimes they killed them, mutilated them, set them on fire, or hanged them from trees—a practice that became known as *lynching*.

Between 1868 and 1876, while an estimated 20,000 black people were murdered by the Klan, southern officials looked the other way. Many victims had been active in local politics. One Alabama woman said the Klan had murdered her husband because "he just would hold up his head and say he was a strong Radical." Klan members beat people who, like Ruby, did nothing more radical than build a school or exude confidence. Another woman reported that the "Ku Klux came to my house and took us out and whipped us, and then said 'don't lets hear any big talk from you, and don't sass any white ladies.'"

Klan tactics helped end Republican Party control in Georgia in 1870, as terrified black voters stayed away from the polls. The following year, Mississippi Klansmen burned dozens of black churches and schools, torturing and killing the ministers and teachers. Klansmen also harassed and murdered the few poor or idealistic southern white citizens who supported socialist groups and advocated racial equality. Still, many black Southerners refused to be intimidated. Exclaimed one black Alabaman: "The Republican party freed me, and I will die on top of it. I vote every time."

The Enforcement Acts

The Fifteenth Amendment gave all black American men the right to vote—but securing that right in practical terms presented an entirely separate challenge. Affirming the federal commitment to the Fourteenth and Fifteenth Amendments, Congress passed two Enforcement Acts in 1870 and 1871—also known as the Klan Acts because they attempted to protect black voters from Klan violence. Both acts defined interference with a person's right to vote as a federal offense punishable by fine or imprisonment. In the summer of 1871, responding to Freedmen's Bureau reports of continued attacks against black Southerners, Congress collected testimony from Fortune and hundreds of others to learn whether southern voters indeed were still unable to express their political views safely. The hearings produced thirteen volumes of testimony.

After Emanuel Fortune's death in 1903, his son, journalist Timothy Thomas Fortune, reported, "It was natural [for him] to take the leadership in any independent movement of Negroes."

But the Enforcement Acts did not stop the violence. In Louisville, Kentucky, white people pummeled black residents who exercised their court-won right to ride the trolley cars. In Colfax, Louisiana, long-simmering racial hatred led local black men to arm themselves and patrol the town. In a confrontation on Easter Sunday, 1873, when the black militia and a white posse exchanged fire, more than a dozen white men were killed or wounded and two dozen black men injured. About three dozen black men were arrested and executed without a trial. Douglass's *New National Era* reported that in the wake of the incident, the local White League, with guns and cannons from neighboring states, randomly shot, stabbed, and beat black citizens. They intended, they said, to set an example for "every parish in the State [so] we shall begin to have some quiet and niggers will know their place."

Racial violence also broke out in the North. A white mob murdered Octavius Catto, a Union major and beloved school principal, at his Philadelphia polling place. Catto's leadership in the Pennsylvania Equal Rights League had made him a target. A friend lamented, "The Ku Klux of the South are not by any means the lower classes of society. The same may be said of the Ku Klux of the North. Both are industriously engaged in trying to break us down." Black Americans experienced yet another instance of their government's inability to protect them.

The Freedmen's Bank

If reconstructing the nation politically posed daunting challenges, establishing a firm economic foundation for African Americans proved even more difficult. In 1865, Congress chartered the Freedmen's Savings and Trust Company to offer black people the chance to save money and purchase land and farm equipment. In

1870, the *New National Era* gave glowing reports of the bank's progress. Though Congress did not monitor the bank's operations, thousands of black depositors in Washington, Baltimore, New York, and other cities trusted it. Year by year, coin by coin, they accumulated nest eggs they hoped would give them financial autonomy.

But the bank soon fell on hard times. In its first years, well-known white bankers—along with Freedmen's Bureau director Oliver Howard and a national board of four dozen trustees—oversaw operations. They upheld the congressional mandate of investing depositors' money in government securities. But in 1870, during a postwar building boom and railroad expansion, Congress amended the bank's charter, enabling the managers to invest deposits in real estate and railroads. In the next few years, several white members of the bank's board made speculative loans in these enterprises. By the time the enterprises failed, these white board members had resigned, leaving mostly black trustees to repair the damage.

Desperate to maintain black people's confidence in the bank, the trustees called on Douglass to replace the white bank president. Douglass did so, even investing $10,000 of his own money. Yet he could not salvage the bank and had to preside over its closing in July 1874. As the savings of thousands of African Americans evaporated, some blamed the bank's failure on Douglass, and his reputation was seriously tarnished. Discouraged that Congress had offered no assistance, many African Americans also lost their faith in the federal government, convinced it had abandoned them yet again.

Washington, DC, in the New National Era

The seat of both hope and disappointment, Washington, DC, became a magnet for black Americans. By 1870, they constituted more than 30 percent of the city's population of 132,000, up from 10 percent just ten years before. Due in part to its proximity to the South, the city's black population soon eclipsed even that of Philadelphia and Baltimore, in both absolute numbers and proportion. The nation's capital offered black people greater economic and social opportunities than any other city. Along with federal protection and political power came black organizations and businesses and plentiful jobs in the federal bureaucracy.

The Black Elite

Drawn by the federal government and Howard University, many accomplished African Americans settled in the capital city. Douglass moved to Washington during the 1870s, working with his sons to publish the *New National Era*, which chronicled the political progress of the Republican Party and its new black constituency. Douglass himself launched what would be a quarter-century-long career in government service as the District of Columbia Recorder of Deeds and as director of U.S. diplomatic relations with Haiti. John Mercer Langston, the Oberlin-educated lawyer and Equal Rights League activist, came to Washington from Ohio to direct the law curriculum at Howard University. Langston also served as counsel to the city Board of Health, collecting vital statistics and monitoring the city's health measures.

Douglass and Langston were central figures in a growing cadre of Washington intellectuals. Anticipating ties with well-read companions and sophisticated conversation with like-minded colleagues and friends, they encouraged those with similar tastes to join them. Black poets, essayists, novelists, and public speakers responded to the call. Literate women such as Frances Ellen Watkins Harper, Maria Stewart, and Charlotte Forten were among them. Harper became a frequent lecturer, while Stewart taught in the public schools and served as a matron at the Freedmen's Hospital, established by the Freedmen's Bureau to provide medical care for Washington's black population. Though long retired from public speaking, she kept her feminist drive, publishing her speeches on women's rights in 1878. Charlotte Forten arrived in Washington from the South Carolina Sea Islands in 1864, exhausted and ill after eighteen months of teaching. In the capital city, she became one of fifteen black female clerks employed in the Treasury Department.

The black elite of Washington—around 2 percent of the city's black population—included lawyers, doctors, teachers, publishers, and business owners. Many were of mixed-race background, and their families, free a generation or more, had been able to educate themselves and establish businesses or professions that gave them influence far beyond their small numbers. They provided employment for many black newcomers. For example, James Wormley's hotel near the White House drew praise from guests even as it provided a handsome living to its black proprietor and steady employment for black workers. These individuals led black social clubs, churches, schools, and social service agencies. Some even lived in integrated neighborhoods. They sent their children to the growing number of African American colleges and universities. A few young people attended the small number of white colleges—including Bowdoin, Amherst, Oberlin, and the University of Pennsylvania—that accepted black students. Thus the black people in these wealthy, educated circles prepared their children and grandchildren to become Washington's future leaders.

Shopkeepers and service workers formed the core of Washington's black middle class. They enjoyed the chance to associate with Washington's black politicians and intellectuals and with renowned social activists such as Sojourner Truth. In 1874, Truth became the first African American to take communion at the white Metropolitan Methodist Church. She also spoke before the white congregation of First Congregational Church, where General Oliver Howard called for desegregation. She focused her attention, however, on the desperate situation of black people outside in the streets. Seeing black "men and women taking dry bread from the government to keep from starving," she set out to get "land for these people, where they can work and earn their own living." She had the ear of General Howard, who offered money and moral support for her plan to help freedmen obtain farmland in the West under the 1862 Homestead Act. Truth also assisted Freedmen's Bureau agents in relocating refugees from Washington to Ohio and Michigan.

The Black Working Class and Poor

Like Truth, Cary was concerned with the plight of ordinary black people. Widowed in 1860 with two children to raise, Cary moved to Washington

A woman of strong opinions, Mary Ann Shadd Cary caught the attention of outspoken white women, including fellow Washington lawyer Belva Lockwood. Throwing her energies into Lockwood's 1872 presidential campaign, Cary hoped to show her support not only for black rights but also for women's leadership.

permanently in 1869. Believing black people needed their own legal counseling, she became Howard University's first female law student. Encouraged by her family, Cary also assumed leadership in other areas where she felt black communities needed to make progress. She left Howard University in 1871 to go on the lecture circuit, speaking out about the need to ensure that young African Americans gained access to education and employment opportunities—a notion that became a theme for black leaders in the century ahead. In 1873 she and Douglass spoke before the National Colored Men's Labor Convention, stressing the need for programs that would teach black youth job skills such as blacksmithing, dressmaking, and carpentry.

That year, a panic brought economic depression. Overinflated railroad speculation, reduced European demand for American farm products, and the failure of powerful American banks cut job opportunities for all Americans, especially unskilled black workers. In 1874, Cary wrote two articles to provoke black parents' thinking about employment for their sons: "We have members of State Legislatures . . . [and] aspirants in the field of letters, all of which is enjoyably rose-tinted and gilded as compared to the past; but we, no more than others, can afford to build at the top of the house only. . . . [T]he craftsman, the architect, the civil engineer must all come through the door opened to us by the mechanic." Cary believed most young black workers would be more able to benefit from training in—and finding work in—manual trades than in intellectual or political leadership roles. In succeeding years, many black leaders—including Booker T. Washington—echoed her concern for the fate of the average worker.

Cary's views on the lack of economic opportunities for African Americans deepened when she saw the widespread poverty in the nation's capital. More than three-quarters of Washington's black families lived in alleys near to large houses where they served as laundresses, porters, handymen, and domestic servants. In the crowded alleys around the Capitol and along the Potomac River lived those who worked in government service. In many of these black households, teeming with family members and boarders, conditions were as bleak as those under slavery. Malnutrition, poor health, violence, and alcoholism abounded. Fish from local rivers and lakes and vegetables from urban gardens helped ward off starvation, but some black people resorted to prostitution and petty theft in order to survive. Others returned home to the familiar rural South. As the black historian John Hope Franklin observed, "It was one thing to provide temporary relief for freedmen, and another to guide them along the road to economic stability and independence."

Despite these difficulties, many freed people built vibrant communities in the capital city. The streets of Washington's poor black neighborhoods rang with the shouts of children playing games, adults performing music, and residents regaling each other with stories. But there was typically a large gap between these people and black political leaders, who were often economically well off, at least comparatively. Some black leaders—both social advocates and politicians—lost touch with the needs of ordinary black people. While they took seriously their role as advocates for racial and economic justice, their own lives came to include second homes at summer resorts, international travel, and interracial marriages. While such leaders sometimes seemed to forget the impact of slavery on the present generation, Cary was one leader who never forgot. She dedicated her life to working for economic stability and independence for the poor.

Political Patronage and Politics

In 1871, Congress established a local government for the District of Columbia consisting of a governor, eleven commissioners appointed by the president, and twenty-two delegates, elected by popular vote, with the power to make local laws. Though the District had no voice in Congress or in national politics, as the states did, respected black leaders—including Douglass and AME bishop James A. Handy—were elected as delegates and hence had a say in local politics. The new structure was seen by many northern leaders as an improvement over the city charter that had expired in 1870.

Though African Americans were in a minority in this interracial governing group, the restructured District government signaled a friendly attitude toward black residents, and dozens of loyal black Republican supporters were rewarded with political patronage jobs in such agencies as the Board of Health and the Recorder of Deeds Office, Patent Office, Treasury Department, Post Office, public schools, and municipal utilities. Hundreds more found employment as government clerks and service workers. Local ordinances outlawed racial segregation in public services, and operators of hotels, restaurants, concert halls, and theaters paid fines and had licenses suspended if they did not comply. The Civil Rights Act of 1875, though soon to be overturned by the Supreme Court, reinforced open access to public accommodations.

Steady cash wages—a first for most black people—allowed for middle-class lifestyles for some, and elevated others to elite status. Black service workers were sometimes able to save money and buy property of their own. A government salary allowed Douglass to move to Cedar Hill, an estate in nearby Anacostia. Even as she railed against segregated schools, Cary's position of principal at the American Missionary Association's Lincoln School placed her in Washington's professional class. These developments mirrored a phenomenon unfolding across the nation. In staggering numbers, African Americans left the countryside, relocating to urban areas where some made economic progress and began participating in local politics. They headed for Detroit and Cincinnati, for New York, Philadelphia, and Pittsburgh. Black communities flourished in Baltimore, Charleston, Galveston, Richmond, and Jacksonville. Many cities had enough black residents to support a black press, and black newspapers proliferated.

The End of Reconstruction

Radical Reconstruction brought important gains to black Southerners: schools, varied economic possibilities, and the franchise. Efforts to diversify the economy, increase access to the polls and leadership positions, and reunite families separated by slavery also improved black lives. In 1867, in New Orleans, African Americans won the right to ride the public trolley cars. Through protests and negotiations, they persuaded the car companies to admit "our citizens into all the cars, without any distinction as to color." In many southern states, Radical Republican governments passed laws granting black people access to soda fountains, opera houses, railroads, and steamboats. In 1875, Congress certified these gains in a Civil Rights Act banning discrimination in public places across the country. But the act constituted the last piece of civil rights legislation until the 1950s.

Waning Federal Sympathy

Even as the Civil Rights Act was passed, many reformers pulled back from the enormous effort required to remake a former slave society. The same 1870 elections that brought black congressmen to power also swept away the Republican majority in the House of Representatives. With the crumbling of Republican power, African American progress began to disintegrate as well. In the South, as federal troops were gradually withdrawn, black political organizations withered away. In 1869, Mississippi had 87,000 registered black voters; eleven years later, it had just half that number. Radical Republican governments in southern states gave way to conservative white Democratic ones. White Southerners called these developments "redemption." A black Louisianan saw it differently in 1877: "The whole South—every state in the South—had got into the hands of the very men that held us slaves."

The Supreme Court encouraged the retreat from black causes by limiting the scope of the Fourteenth Amendment. In the *Slaughterhouse Cases* (1873), it distinguished between citizenship of the United States and citizenship of a state, saying that the amendment applied only to the former and that states had the right to define citizenship and its accompanying rights for their residents. In 1883, the Court heard several cases in the course of which it overturned the 1875 Civil Rights Act. In their rulings, the justices distinguished between political rights (guaranteed by the Constitution) and social rights (pertaining to public accommodations), which involved citizens' private lives. The Court declared the federal government had no authority over social rights. The stage was now set for the so-called Jim Crow laws, which limited the rights of African Americans for the next seventy-five years.

The Compromise of 1877

The 1876 presidential contest was so close that it fell to the House of Representatives to adjudicate disputed electoral votes. The agreement Republicans and Democrats worked out became known as the Compromise of 1877: Southern congressmen agreed to concede the presidency to Republican candidate Rutherford B. Hayes, while Republicans agreed to allow white Southerners to control local elections and local ordinances on black employment contracts and racial separation. The few remaining federal troops were withdrawn from the South, federal intervention in southern state affairs ceased, and the U.S. government agreed to appoint at least one Southerner to the president's cabinet. Across the South, state governments now lay firmly in the hands of the white "redeemers," who regained local power to deny true citizenship privileges—such as the vote—to thousands of African Americans. The national Republican Party distanced itself from black interests, entrenching segregated "Black and Tan" parties in an increasingly segregated South. For white Americans, the era of Reconstruction had ended.

African Americans on the Move

"I made the outside box [for Julia Haven] and her coffin, in Smith County, Tennessee. And another young colored lady . . . they committed an outrage on her and then shot her, and I helped to make her coffin." In the spring of 1880, seventy-year-old Benjamin "Pap" Singleton used these examples of women who had been raped and killed to help a Senate committee understand why black people were fleeing the South. The investigation was launched after both Democrats and Republicans claimed the other was conspiring to provoke black people to migrate. Republicans accused Democrats of wanting to gain control of the South by expelling black voters; Democrats said Republicans wanted to spread their influence outside the South. Singleton knew better: Black people were fleeing the South to avoid rape, murder, and mutilation.

The Exodusters

Benjamin Singleton, a former Tennessee slave who had escaped via the Underground Railroad through Detroit into Canada, returned to his home state after the war. Like many black Americans, Singleton soon took advantage of the 1862 Homestead Act, which offered 160 acres of government land free to anyone who would live on it, improve it, and pay a small registration fee. With other black Tennesseans, he started the Edgfield Real Estate and Homestead Association to establish a new black settlement in Kansas. Several families who had visited Kansas, he said, "brought back favorable reports. . . . Three or four hundred . . . went into Southern Kansas . . . and formed a colony there, and bought about a thousand acres of ground." Comparing their projects to the exodus of the biblical Hebrews from Egyptian bondage, the thousands of black Americans who went west with groups such as the Kansas Exodus Joint Stock Company in the late 1870s called themselves *Exodusters*.

Recruiters for the new black settlements took posters such as this one to local meetings across both North and South.

Ho for Kansas!

Brethren, Friends, & Fellow Citizens:
I feel thankful to inform you that the
REAL ESTATE
AND
Homestead Association,
Will Leave Here the

15th of April, 1878,

In pursuit of Homes in the Southwestern
Lands of America, at Transportation
Rates, cheaper than ever
was known before.
For full information inquire of
Benj. Singleton, better known as old Pap,
NO. 5 NORTH FRONT STREET.
Beware of Speculators and Adventurers, as it is a dangerous thing
to fall in their hands.
Nashville, Tenn., March 18, 1878.

One of the many posters calling on southern blacks to leave for Kansas.

The town of Nicodemus in Graham County, Kansas, on the Solomon River typifies these new African American frontier communities. By 1880, 700 black settlers had moved to Nicodemus, but many encountered stiff resistance even as they left home. To retain the South's cheap labor force, white Southerners tried to sabotage the planned black exodus. Singleton told Congress how armed white men blocked Mississippi River crossings to black travelers, seizing them and even hacking off their hands. "Now see if you can go to Kansas and work," they said. White sheriffs arrested black travelers for breach of contract (if they were contracted to a planter) or for vagrancy (if they were not). Despite these tactics, black people continued to head west. Between 1870 and 1880, the African American population in Kansas doubled to more than 40,000.

At first white Kansans welcomed the Exodusters. Eager to increase the population of farmers and defend themselves from belligerent Native Americans, some Kansas communities raised money to help black newcomers pay land fees. But black homesteaders, with few tools or work animals, found independent farming hard. Discouraged, many Exodusters ended up in Topeka, where they hunted for work. But this city was also home to displaced white Southerners seeking jobs. Racial intimidation and lynchings became so common that the Republican mayor of Topeka, once sympathetic to African Americans, suggested the money raised for black relief might better go to returning black refugees to the South—especially agitators "who were always talking politics."

Some black leaders like Douglass urged black families to stay aggregated in the South. Only with large numbers, they contended, could black voters exert power and influence. But Douglass wrote from the relative safety and comfort of Washington. It was people like Singleton who experienced the southern predicament firsthand: "We don't want to leave the South," he wrote in 1881, "and just as soon as we have confidence in the South I am going to . . . persuade every man to go back, because that is the best country; . . . we love that country . . . but [by leaving] we are going to learn the South a lesson."

The Western Frontier

Beyond Kansas, numerous African Americans found adventure and fortune in Nebraska, Colorado, North Dakota, and along the Pacific coast. Closed out of northern and southern economy and politics, black families headed for these new frontiers. Nancy Lewis told how she and her husband, a Civil War veteran, established their Nebraska farm in the 1870s. By 1880, they counted among 2,000 black Nebraskans. Virginia-born Barney Ford, a one-time barber and ship's steward, journeyed to Denver and by 1874 had opened a prosperous hotel. Two of Douglass's sons were also among Denver's thousand African Americans. Cowboy Nat Love's prowess in an 1876 rodeo in Deadwood City, North Dakota, gained him the nickname "Deadwood Dick." His autobiography, *The Life & Adventures of Nat Love, Better Known in the Cattle Country As Deadwood Dick* (1876), promoted the escapades of some of the thousands of black cowboys. But when the book was later published as one of many mass-market stories of the West, Love's African heritage was omitted.

Some black Americans got all the way to California. By 1880, as many as 6,000 were there, and several hundred had settled in each of the other western states and territories. These pioneers included cowboys, farmers, shopkeepers, prospectors, and service workers such as barbers, laundresses, and domestic

Finishing a term as a forager (raider) for the Confederate army, Isom Dart was among the cowboys who drifted west. Joining a group of cattle thieves, he was arrested in Texas, Colorado, and Wyoming. Legend has it that he was never imprisoned.

servants. Biddy Mason, who remained in California after the courts declared her free, purchased property, ran a grocery store and boardinghouse, supported black schools, and helped establish the West's first AME church.

To Africa

Driven by the same hope and frustration that motivated western migration, other black Americans looked east to Africa. In the postwar years, Delany revived his dream of claiming a black nationality there. "We have no chance to rise from beggars," he argued. "Men own the capital that we work who believe that my race have no more right to any of the profits of their labor than one of their mules." Cain, a disillusioned ex-congressman, echoed Delany's despair: "The colored people of the South are tired of the constant struggle for life and liberty and prefer going where [there are] no obstacles . . . to . . . their liberty." Partnering with AME minister Henry McNeal Turner, Delany recruited settlers for Liberia. Turner had been born free in South Carolina in 1834, studied in the North, and served as pastor for a Washington, DC, church before the Civil War. After a stint as an army chaplain, he stayed in Georgia, working for the Republican Party and the AME church. By 1877, he shared Delany's dismay at the federal government's abandonment of black Southerners.

In the spring of 1878, thousands of black Americans watched the launching of the *Azor* from Charleston's wharf. Led by Delany and Turner, and with support from Cain, the Liberian Exodus Joint Stock Company had raised more than $6,000 to purchase the ship, which now carried some 200 settlers to Africa. Other black families invested thousands more. But expenses exceeded the company's capital, and the Exodus Company soon lay in financial shambles. After delivering its first settlers, it collapsed without establishing a permanent community. Though the effort represented yet another failed dream, the image of an African homecoming remained in the black imagination. Future generations would try again.

Conclusion

Emanuel Fortune's testimony in 1871 before the congressional committee investigating the Ku Klux Klan revealed the violence underlying post-Civil War southern politics. The politics of this war-torn region was no longer merely a regional concern of Southerners and a few abolitionist Northerners. The challenges facing African Americans now dominated the national agenda.

The federal government had outlawed slavery, extended equal rights to all citizens, and mandated that all black men could vote, but the law had little to do with reality. Though Revels and other black men represented southern states in Congress, white supremacist groups such as the Ku Klux Klan used threats, torture, and murder to scare southern black voters away from the polls. Still, many black politicians sought common ground to negotiate compromises with southern white politicians. Sometimes they urged their black followers to accommodate some aspect of racial oppression in return for economic gains or political representation. At the far margin of the political spectrum, radicals tried to bridge the gap between the wealthy and the disaffected by envisioning a society that transcended divisions of race and class. All these strategies aimed to enable black people to move toward economic and social equality.

By 1877, African Americans seemed destined to be shunted aside again. With the Compromise of 1877, the federal government withdrew from helping freed slaves gain political rights and economic security. In the postwar era, black politicians had seats in Congress and in state legislatures. But with the end of Reconstruction, black politicians began returning to the South to manage their personal lives and to try to forge working relationships with white neighbors. Most white people in the North and the South expected black Americans to stay in the South, resigning themselves to menial jobs, limited political power, and continued deference to white people. Indeed, in the coming decades, southern black laborers seemed doomed to jobs that ensured only subordination and debt, and black leaders understood these as the limitations within which they must operate.

Though Washington, DC, the federal capital, continued to attract black people seeking jobs and a strong black community, the American frontier and Africa lured others who dreamed of better opportunities and fresh ideas. By 1879, with the passing of many antebellum black leaders, the black cause desperately needed new energy and direction. The ratification of the Thirteenth, Fourteenth, and Fifteenth Amendments had promised African Americans access to political participation. Now, with Black Codes, poverty, and violence circumscribing those promises, black Americans needed new leadership.

Questions for Review and Reflection

1. The American political practice of democracy is a complex phenomenon. What can we learn about it from Reconstruction-era debates and the final passage of the Fourteenth and Fifteenth Amendments?

2. The late-nineteenth-century black congressmen walked a treacherous political, social, and racial tightrope as they sought to juggle multiple constituencies, contradictory goals, and their own personal safety. In retrospect, which of their strategies seem to have been most farsighted?

3. In the wake of the Civil War, Congress acceded to pressure to have the federal government intercede to secure African Americans' rights. What were some of the long-range effects of that government posture?

4. The western "frontier" offered new possibilities for African Americans. How did the black frontier experiences compare with those of white compatriots?

CHAPTER 12

The Post-Reconstruction Era

Booker T. Washington Teaches Black Self-Sufficiency

"My life had its beginning in the midst of the most miserable, desolate, and discouraging surroundings," recalled Booker T. Washington in 1901, after he had earned worldwide renown as an expert on educating the poor. By that time his work had opened doors and shaped destinies for hundreds of black and white Americans.

Like millions of post-Civil War southern black people, Washington began his life in poverty. As a child, he worked in a coal mine, but as a teenager he began to rise above his "discouraging surroundings." Hearing about Hampton Normal and Agricultural Institute in Virginia, a new school for freed slaves, Washington made his way there in 1872. Passing a practical entrance exam—which required him to sweep the floor of a shed—he convinced the white school head, Samuel Chapman Armstrong, that he deserved a scholarship.

Working as a janitor to help pay his way, Washington soon learned Armstrong's recipe for ex-slaves' success in modern America: manual labor education along with training in hygiene, thrift, and deference to white Americans. After Washington graduated from Hampton in 1875, Armstrong asked him to return to teach Native American students. Washington was part of what he described as an "experiment being tried for the first time by General Armstrong, of educating Indians at Hampton." Could he help Armstrong prove that education could "civilize" Indians as well as African Americans?

Washington discovered that his Indian students learned well. "I found that in the matter of learning trades and in mastering academic studies there was little difference between the coloured and Indian students." Watching the willingness of black students to assist the Indians taught Washington how

1880	In *Stauder* v. *West Virginia,* the U.S. Supreme Court rules that excluding black people from jury duty is unconstitutional.
1881	T. Washington becomes head of Tuskegee (Alabama) Normal and Industrial Institute.
	A new Tennessee law requiring separate railroad cars for black people and white people becomes a model for other states' Jim Crow laws.
1882	Congress passes the Chinese Exclusion Act, which prohibited new immigration from China.
1883	George Washington Williams publishes *The History of the Negro Race in America from 1619–1880,* one of the first histories of black Americans.
	Declaring that Congress lacks authority over public accommodations, the Supreme Court reverses the Civil Rights Act of 1875.
	Congress passes the Pendleton Act, which replaced some political patronage positions in the civil service with a merit system.
1884–1885	At an international conference in Berlin, Belgium, England, France, Germany, and Italy agree to partition Africa.
1886	The Colored Farmers' Alliance is established, allying with the white National Farmers' Alliance.
	In Chicago's Haymarket Square, black Americans join a workers' rally.
	Knights of Labor leader Terence Powderly shares a Richmond, Virginia, speakers' platform with black New York labor leader Frank Ferrell.
1887	Edward Blyden publishes *Christianity, Islam, and the Negro Race,* a call to African Americans to revere their African heritage.
	John Alexander graduates from West Point Military Academy and joins the Ninth Cavalry in Nebraska.
	Congress passes the Dawes Act, which redefines some communal Indian tribal lands as individual family homesteads.
1889	Black women's rights advocate Ida B. Wells becomes part-owner of the *Memphis Free Speech and Headlight.*
	William Bush is elected to Washington's first state legislature.
	When Congress opens Oklahoma to settlement, 10,000 black Southerners stake homestead claims.
1892	Anna Julia Cooper publishes *A Voice from the South by a Black Woman of the South.*
	The lynching of Thomas Moss in Memphis, Tennessee, sparks antilynching campaigns among black Americans.
	Colored Farmers' Alliance representatives help found the Populist Party.
1893	George Washington Carver's paintings are displayed at the Chicago Columbian Exposition.

1894	Zeke Miller is appointed deputy marshal in Oklahoma Indian Territory.
1895	Frederick Douglass's death marks a transition to new black leaders.
	At the Cotton States and International Exposition in Atlanta, Georgia, Booker T. Washington delivers his Atlanta Compromise speech, outlining his social and economic program.

(Continued)

educational programs might foster not only intellectual growth but also social responsibility. Years later, he wrote, "I have often wondered if there was a white institution . . . whose students would have welcomed . . . companions of another race in the cordial way that these black students at Hampton welcomed the red ones. How often I have wanted to say to white students that they lift themselves up in proportion as they help to lift others." Throughout his career, Washington frequently evoked images of lifting and climbing, of improving one's own life while helping others to succeed.

Washington expanded Armstrong's educational formula into a broad philosophy of black self-sufficiency that inspired many African Americans in their own rise from slavery. By 1881, with Armstrong's help, Washington became head of Tuskegee Agricultural and Mechanical Institute, an Alabama school modeled after Hampton.

Washington used his own life story as an example of how the powerless could rise. His combination of perseverance, skill, and luck made his climb from poverty to power as remarkable as that of contemporary white industrialists like Andrew Carnegie and John D. Rockefeller. Such stories taught a simple but profound lesson: Acquiring a valued skill and working hard could bring economic success. This lesson made practical sense to many black Americans.

In the harsh decades after the Civil War, Booker T. Washington was an exception. Most black Southerners did not advance in just one generation after slavery. Only about one in three African Americans had access to schooling, and only one in a thousand attended college. During the years Washington attended Hampton and established Tuskegee, millions of black Southerners had no homes and suffered from hunger, illness, and humiliation. In 1877, the federal government officially ended military control of the South and thus the era of Reconstruction. The South came back under the control of former slave owners who continued to envision black people only as their servants. Most black Southerners eked out an existence by farming someone else's land. During these years, most white Southerners sought to reinstate an economic system much like slavery—with laws and violence to back it up. In trying to build a "New South" of industry and factories, white and black Americans found it difficult to break away from the old farming economy.

Meanwhile, as white intellectuals developed pseudoscientific theories that white people were superior to dark-skinned peoples, African Americans sought educational opportunities to convince the world they were morally and intellectually able to contribute to American society. Education, therefore, became the centerpiece of African American strategies for progress. Many black leaders set out to train teachers, or became educators themselves. Some African Americans sought social and economic opportunities in the nation's cities. A few fortunate ones received federal appointments in Washington, DC. Others settled in all-black towns to escape white domination. In an age of industrialization, some black people found allies in white workers who believed class unity was more important than racial disunity. Unions helped black workers garner a fair wage; farming alliances helped protect farmers from exploitation. Other black people again looked to the western frontier and Africa to make a new life and escape the growing violence of the late-nineteenth-century South.

Rebuilding the South

"Many are sick and in bad condition generally," Mississippi planter Isaiah Montgomery wrote in 1879. He was describing his farm workers who had fled because they could not pay their debts. Montgomery sympathized with these tenants, as he was trapped in the same labor system and in constant danger of losing his farm. Montgomery was one of the few black Southerners who owned a large plantation, but his African American tenants fared no better than those who worked for white landowners. Although he dreamed of an independent black economy, Montgomery's plight and that of his workers typified the South's economic situation in the decades following the Civil War, especially as worldwide demand for southern cotton declined. Three-quarters of the nation's four million black citizens lived in southern states, and most farmed or share-cropped someone else's land. By 1880, droughts and epidemics further under-mined an economy ravaged by war.

Montgomery's situation highlighted the dilemma of many African Americans in their hard rise from slavery. Even black Southerners who managed to obtain land found themselves in desperate straits. People with fewer resources sank into abject poverty. In ever-growing numbers, the families who worked Montgomery's land left him. Some headed for black settlements in Kansas; others drifted aimlessly. With each departure, Montgomery lost more of his livelihood, including his investment in the provisions he had purchased for his workers, expecting to be repaid when crops were harvested.

Farm Labor and Poverty

In the post-Reconstruction era, many white and black farmers were locked in a cycle of poverty. Following the war's devastation of the plantation economy, three new forms of agriculture emerged. The most common arrangement for landless rural workers was *sharecropping*, whereby a landlord provided seed, housing, and tools in return for a share of the resulting crop. The constraints of sharecropping—the landowner retained control over when and how crops would be planted, tended, harvested, and sold—evoked bitter memories of slavery. It was viewed as a last resort by impoverished black farm workers.

Share tenancy was an option for farmers who had a little money to invest. Landlords provided the housing but tenants chose the crop, provided the seed, and set their own schedule for harvesting and selling. This system offered farm workers more autonomy than did sharecropping. *Tenant farming* offered the greatest autonomy of the three systems. Tenants paid cash to landlords to rent farmland. Renters lived where they wished, often choosing to put some distance between themselves and their landlord. They also made their own decisions about what to plant and how and when to tend and market their crops.

Farming imposed financial hardships on farm owners and workers who had to borrow to cover expenses until crops were sold. The merchants who provided food, clothing, and other necessities charged high interest, forcing borrowers deeper into debt. Saddled with this *crop lien*, as it was called, few could make a profit.

Farming someone else's land left workers vulnerable to fraud. The prevalence of oral agreements and low literacy among farmers meant landowners and merchants could easily misrepresent contracts and balances due. Ex-slave Henry Baker of Alabama recalled, "In all my dealings as sharecropper, renter or tenant, I never made no contract; everything was done by word of mouth." Once mired in debt, farmers found it hard to get out. They passed debt down to their children, who found themselves shackled to the land just as tightly as their forbears had been under slavery.

Reliance on a long-standing barter economy exacerbated the situation. Because purchases and payments were made mostly with crop shares rather than cash, owners and tenants were bound together, mutually dependent. In the North, cash transactions shaped the economy, but until Southerners produced something that Northerners or Europeans wanted to buy, little cash could flow into the South. The cashless economy allowed those who possessed wealth, goods, land, or literacy to hold back those who did not. Southern agriculture also lagged behind other regions. Because southern farmers lacked cash, they could not mechanize, as farmers on the Great Plains were doing. Instead, they carved their land into ever smaller and less efficient rental plots.

Hard times intensified conflict between landowners and tenants. Most landlords had the power to win disputes, but black farmers sometimes prevailed. For example, Alabama share tenant Sarah Fitzpatrick won a legal battle against her white landlord. With no written contract, Fitzpatrick's family watched their debt grow, even as the landowner dispensed only "what they wanted me to have: so much corn, potatoes, and shoes, and a house to live in, [and] a little money at Christmas." When cotton prices slumped, Fitzpatrick's son wanted to postpone selling their crop until prices rebounded. The landowner insisted on selling, but the Freedmen's Bureau arranged for legal

TABLE 12.1 DIVISION OF CROP PRODUCTION

Tenant farming, *which gave both landowner and laborer the most freedom, was rare, as cash was scarce in the postwar South. A* share wage *arrangement was the least attractive, as landowners' profits were dependent upon laborers' skill, diligence, and luck; laborers seldom could avoid sinking into hopeless debt.*

CONTRACT-ING PARTY	TENANT FARMING	SHARE TENANCY	SHARE CROPPING	SHARE WAGES
Landlord	Receives cash rent.	Receives one-fourth of cotton crop; one-third of grain crop. Provides housing.	Receives one-half of cotton and grain crops. Provides housing. seeds, and tools.	Receives two-thirds to three-fourths of cotton and grain crops. Provides housing, seeds, and tools.
Laborer	Pays cash rent.	Receives three-fourths of cotton crop; two-thirds of grain crop. Receives housing.	Receives one-half of cotton and grain crops. Receives housing, seeds, tools.	Receives one-third to one-fourth of cotton and grain crops. Receives housing, seeds, and tools.

Based on F. W. Loring and C. F. Atkinson, *Cotton Culture and the South Considered with Reference to Emigration* (Boston: A. Williams, 1869), pp. 25–26; J. R. Dodge, *Report of the Commissioner of Agriculture . . . for the Year 1876* (Washington: GPO, 1877), pp. 131–135; Eugene W. Hilgard, ed., *Report on Cotton Production in the United States,* 2 vols. (Washington: GPO, 1884).

help. The Fitzpatricks won that round, but they could never save enough to purchase land.

In most southern states, fewer than 25 percent of black residents owned land (in Florida, the figure was 50 percent). With the end of the Freedmen's Bureau in 1872 and the federal government's withdrawal from the South in 1877, black farm workers were on their own. They lost access to legal assistance, and many who had purchased land were cheated out of it.

Even Isaiah Montgomery, who owned several parcels of mortgaged land, had to give up. Squeezed between workers who could not pay their debts and creditors who nevertheless demanded payment, Montgomery saw his land sold at auction. Without land to hold them together, the family scattered. One brother moved west to the Dakota Territory, where, freed from the constraints of the southern farming economy, he acquired more than 1,000 acres.

Jim Crow

Frustrated by southern intransigence during Reconstruction, federal officials gradually stopped investing time, effort, and money in southern freedmen. The

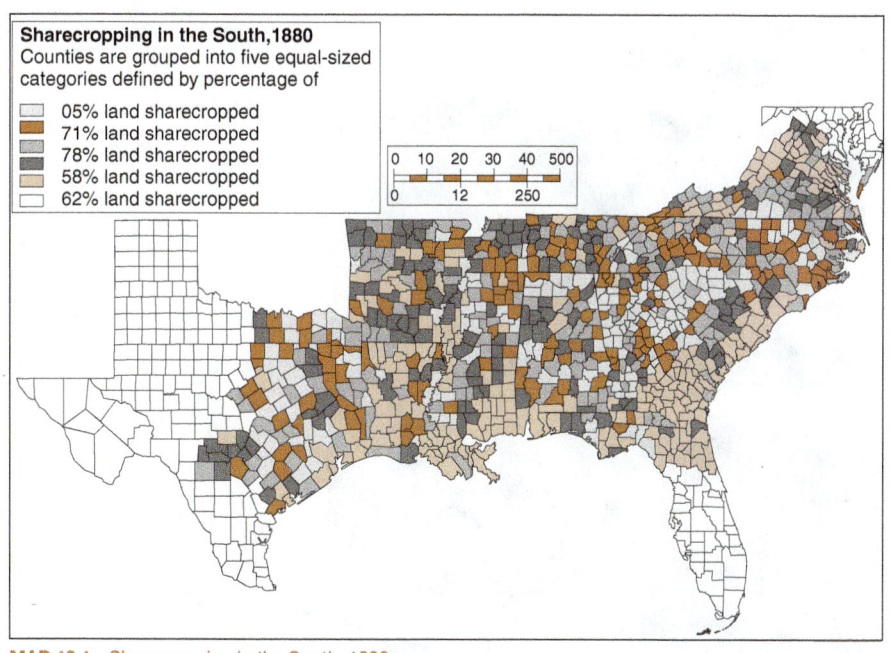

MAP 12.1 Sharecropping in the South, 1880

In the post-Reconstruction era, landless black and white Southerners were pressed into farming others' land.

From Roger L. Ransom and Richard Sutch, *One Kind of Freedom: The Economic Consequences of Emancipation,* 2nd ed. (Cambridge: Cambridge University Press, 2001), p. 93. Reprinted with the permission of Cambridge University Press. Data from U.S. Census Office, Tenth Census (1880); *Report of the Production of Agriculture* (Washington: Map 12.1)

Supreme Court vacillated between expanding the rights of black Americans and whittling them away. In *Stauder* v. *West Virginia* (1880), the Court said that black Americans could not be excluded from juries. But in 1883 the Court struck down Congress' 1875 Civil Rights Act, declaring it unconstitutional and concluding that while Congress might bar *states* from discriminating, it had no authority to prevent *individuals* or private entities from doing so. Congress could not declare "by law that all persons shall have equal accommodations in all inns, public conveyances, and places of public amusement." In *Hall* v. *Cuir* (1887), the Court specifically decreed that states could legislate segregation on public transportation. As the protection afforded by federal laws slipped away, the new category of state and local statutes known as *Jim Crow laws* took root, restricting African Americans' rights. Probably named for a minstrel character who mocked black people, Jim Crow laws helped institute racial segregation across the land.

In the early 1880s, Jim Crow policies became more formalized. In 1881, after Tennessee passed a law requiring black and white people to ride in separate railroad cars, other southern states quickly followed. Many rewrote constitutions to mandate separate schools and to ban black patrons from white-run

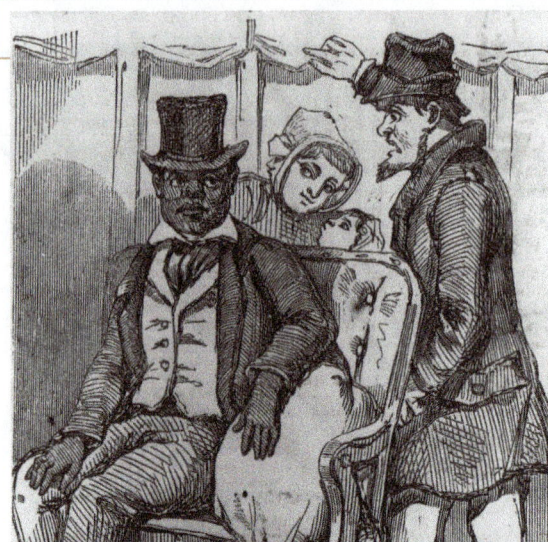

Negro Expulsion from a Railway Car.

NEGRO EXPULSION FROM RAILWAY CAR, PHILADELPHIA.

hotels, barbershops, restaurants, and theaters. These laws laid the legal foundation for racial separation and exclusion.

Racial segregation had been rare in the old slave South. Black and white people had long lived in close proximity. House slaves often slept in owners' bedrooms, and slaves frequently attended public celebrations with their masters. But now that all Southerners were free citizens, Jim Crow laws required black Americans to defer to white people in public places. And Jim Crow was not limited to the South. At first a few northern states passed half-hearted civil rights protections, but by 1890, most northern states also had laws and customs segregating black people from white people.

The Rise of Booker T. Washington

While federal protection for black Americans waned in the 1880s, the old national black leadership was fading as well. In the antebellum years, black leaders had focused on one thing: ending slavery. Now the venerable Frederick Douglass, age seventy-three in 1890, was slowing down. When Sojourner Truth died in 1883, black communities lost their best-known women's suffrage lecturer. The deaths of Henry Highland Garnet (1882) and Martin Delany (1885) silenced the most persuasive voices advocating African colonization. Now black communities searched for new leaders who understood the plight of southern freed people.

Wishing to project an air of dignity and learnedness, Booker T. Washington always dressed formally and preferred to be photographed holding a book.

By the mid-1880s, Booker T. Washington emerged as one such leader. After a year of teaching at Hampton, Washington joined Olivia Davidson in Tuskegee, Alabama, where she was helping organize a teachers' training school. Davidson reported that the state "agreed to aid in the purchase of a farm with a view to having an industrial school, where students can work to pay their expenses and at the same time pursue their studies." Applying the habits of hard work and perseverance, Washington and Davidson persuaded local white residents to support the school financially. The Tuskegee founders assured supporters that education would turn ex-slaves into well-trained, cooperative workers who would not challenge the southern system of social segregation.

Under Washington's leadership, Tuskegee flourished. Opening with thirty students in July 1881, the school outgrew its first building in three months. The students renovated the building, beginning an enduring tradition of student maintenance of school facilities. Washington married Davidson in 1885, and when she died four years later, the school had more than 400 students. Over the next two decades, Tuskegee grew to over 2,000 acres, dozens of buildings, and a faculty of nearly 200. In the next century, it sent forth thousands of graduates who possessed agricultural, craft, or industrial skills as well as a strong work ethic and the commitment to inspire others to lift themselves out of poverty.

Washington shaped his understanding of southern poverty into a broad social philosophy. Even with black representatives in Congress, no African American leader had devised a remedy for the economic and social deprivation Washington witnessed daily. In his travels, he saw large families sharing one-room houses with dirt floors. As under slavery, the demands of cotton dominated their lives. Meals scraped together were eaten in the fields. Fresh fruits and vegetables were scarce and malnutrition common. Even the typical diet of pork fat and cornbread was often procured on credit. Medical care was unavailable. Washington worried that black politicians had not grasped the urgency of the situation. He believed that black people first had to gain skills and literacy. Only then, when they were indispensable to the southern economy, would they rise out of poverty, achieve racial integration, and gain political power. But for now, he often told audiences, it would be best not to challenge racial segregation and to accept the Jim Crow system in return for land, work, and protection from violence.

The New South

Black Southerners were not alone in seeking economic equilibrium. The prewar South, based on agriculture and unpaid labor, had died just as industrial capitalism was reshaping the Western world. In northern Europe and the American North, more and more people made their living not by physical labor but by investing in banks, factories, and transportation systems. In capitalist economies, workers were paid in cash and it was up to them to find housing, food, and other essentials.

After the war, many Northerners and some white Southerners envisioned industrial capitalism in a "New South" based on factories, banks, and railroads. Indeed, iron deposits transformed Birmingham, Alabama, into a steel-based industrial center. New railroads helped Memphis, Tennessee, build lumber, paper, cottonseed oil, beer, and drug industries. Railroads also gave Richmond, Virginia, a way to transport the products of its flour mills and steel foundries. In Richmond's more than four dozen tobacco factories, workers used new machinery to make ready-rolled cigarettes. New textile mills in Montgomery, Alabama, and Greensboro, North Carolina, turned local cotton into cloth instead of sending it north for processing.

Thirty years after emancipation, seventy-two-year-old ex-slave Levi Coppin recalled that he had fared well in capitalism. "There were several days that I shed tears on account of our homeless conditions," he recalled, "but I fixed my course and set my stakes to deal in real estate, and . . . the Lord has blessed my efforts. I have built since freedom eighty-seven houses in Americus [Georgia], and have sold one hundred and sixteen vacant lots to both white and colored people. I have experimented in fish raising for twenty years, and have had four ponds."

Coppin's story was rare. Those black Southerners who took wage jobs discovered that with economic independence came new vulnerabilities. No longer sheltered by masters, they were pummeled by boom and bust cycles. They lost jobs in economic downturns and had no resources for getting out of poverty and despair. But many white Americans believed that black status was due not to circumstance but to innate racial traits.

Social Darwinism

Europeans had long assigned racial traits to Africans, using race to predict personality, behavior, and intellectual capacity. With the publication of the British scientist Charles Darwin's *Origin of Species* in 1859, Western scientists grew more confident about their predictions. Darwin argued that species "evolved" as they adapted to changes in their environment through a process he called *natural selection*. In each succeeding generation, the vigorous individuals who survived the changing challenges of nature competed with each other to mate with similarly hearty individuals. This, suggested Darwin, was nature's way of constantly perfecting a species by weeding out those who could not adapt to change.

In a sociological expansion of Darwin's biological theory, many white Americans described natural selection as operating in human societies to weed out the unfit. This pseudoscientific theory, known as Social Darwinism, was introduced to America by sociologist William Graham Sumner. It fueled discussions about public policy, especially when Sumner argued that private charity and public intervention on behalf of the poor were useless—even dangerous. But the theory was also used to support so-called scientific analyses and predictions. Social Darwinists concluded that black Americans had difficult lives because they were unable to adapt to modern society. Thus, Darwin's theory of evolution lent scientific justification to social inequity; in a competitive marketplace, only the most vigorous would survive, and successful competitors deserved the rewards they gained. It followed that those who were unsuccessful were also undeserving. While a few reformers pointed to Booker T. Washington's success as invalidating the theory, most white Americans believed that race was the reason that those who had been slaves remained poor.

The same views fueled rising prejudices against immigrants. In 1882, Congress banned Chinese immigration for ten years; the ban was later extended. A second act prevented paupers and criminals from entering the country. At the same time, ideas about racial superiority led white Americans and Europeans to claim they had a "white men's burden" to bring civilization and Christianity to Africa and other supposedly backward regions of the world. Throughout Africa, European conquerors taught religion while coercing Africans into harvesting gold, diamonds, and exotic woods for export to the white world. Social Darwinist views made it acceptable to exploit black labor for capitalist gain.

Education: Making a Living and a Life

"Thursday was city election day," wrote Ida B. Wells in 1884. "I was not interested in anything but the School Board & both colored men were [defeated]; we now have an entirely white board." Like Booker T. Washington, Wells emerged as a black leader in the post-slavery era. She too had high hopes that education would uplift her race—but she did not trust white school boards to represent black students' interests. Though born to a slave family, Wells had never been meek or accommodating toward white people. Only sixteen when her parents died, she supported herself by teaching. Her diary recorded her outrage at racial discrimination and her conviction that students must resist it. Unlike Washington, Wells believed black education should go beyond workplace skills, to give students liberal arts training that prepared them to think independently. She also felt teachers should motivate students to challenge racial injustice.

Black Schools: Practical Training and Liberal Arts

Many black schools had sprung up in the South by the 1880s. Some were legacies of the American Missionary Association (AMA) or the Freedmen's Bureau. Others were offshoots of black church schools that taught basic literacy to children and adults. Still others were makeshift classrooms developed by local black communities. Like Hampton and Tuskegee, these schools taught manual labor. Practical skills, teachers argued, would enable freed people to find jobs, protect themselves from exploitation, and build schools for the next generation. Booker T. Washington believed learning to make a living should take precedence over agitation for social equality.

But more and more black people insisted their schools teach literature, art, and music, disciplines that would develop academic skills and demonstrate black aptitude for good citizenship. Moreover, appreciation of liberal arts enabled black people to make a life, not just a living. Among the best known academic schools was the AMA's Colored High School. Founded in the 1860s, it grew into Fisk College in Nashville. By the 1880s, it was turning out graduates who became lawyers, ministers, civil service workers, teachers, and college professors. But like many other schools (most of which did not survive), Fisk struggled financially during its first years. The AMA planned to close it in 1871, but its music teacher organized students who "began to help our school by going Fridays and Saturdays to neighboring towns to give concerts."

One of those students, sent "to sing the money out of the hearts and pockets of the people," was Ella Sheppard. She recalled that at first slave songs "were never used in public, [because they] were associated with slavery and the dark past, and they were sacred to our parents, who used them in their religious worship." But after "two or three slave songs were sung at the close of a concert," the singers found that "the demand of the public changed this. Soon the land rang with our slave songs." Traveling to England and Russia in 1871,

Henry Ossawa Tanner, the son of a middle-class black Philadelphia minister, studied art with the white painter Thomas Eakins. In a career spanning four decades, Tanner painted classical religious works as well as scenes that celebrated—and romanticized—African Americans. In this 4-foot-tall painting, *The Banjo Lesson* (1893),Tanner used the meagerness of black possessions to dignify African Americans' music, domestic tidiness, family tenderness, and the transmission of cultural wealth from older generations to the young.

Source: Henry Ossawa Tanner, "The Banjo Lesson" 1893. Oil on canvas. 49" × 35 1/2". Hampton University Museum, Hampton, Virginia.

the Fisk Jubilee Singers raised enough to pull their school out of debt and to hire new liberal arts faculty. They built pride in black Americans and earned admiration from white people.

The accomplishments and loyalty of Fisk's students and faculty inspired hundreds of schools elsewhere. Some offered an ambitious array of courses; others, little more than reading lessons. Virginia State College, near Petersburg, taught liberal arts and agriculture starting in 1882—the first black college founded under an 1862 law granting tracts of public land on which states could build agricultural schools. When the college opened with one hundred students and seven black faculty, Ohio lawyer John Mercer Langston was its first president. In Topeka black teacher E. H. White founded a night school in 1881 so that "mothers, fathers, young men and ladies whose opportunities . . . have not been such that they could acquire an education" could have a "regular program" of instruction. In Greensboro, black and white congressmen sponsored another land-grant school, North Carolina Agricultural and Technical Institute, which accepted its first students in 1897, and soon became fondly known as "A & T." Six decades later, students at A & T would be leaders in the modern civil rights movement.

Believing education prepared individuals for success, some white liberals supported schools for poor people, including Hampton and Tuskegee. In their view, these experiments could demonstrate that education raised the prospects of the disadvantaged. Cynics accused congressmen and northern white philanthropists of supporting southern black schools only to ensure that black people were tracked into menial jobs in the South. Indeed, many upper-class northern white people wanted to keep their distance from black people. Regardless of motivation, money from Northerners was often matched by southern white donors eager for workers trained for the factories of the "New South."

Some northern philanthropists, such as Andrew Carnegie and Julius Rosenwald, helped establish southern schools with an academic curriculum. Spelman College, a liberal arts school for black women, opened in Atlanta in 1881. Hartshorne College, a liberal arts school for women in Richmond, soon followed. New northern schools included Philadelphia's Berean Institute, which began taking students in 1884.

Both manual-skills and academic schools fostered personal and racial pride. Faculty encouraged students to excel, reminding them their successes brought honor to the entire race. As the school song of the M Street High School in Washington, DC, expressed it, black schools aimed to "strengthen and hearten and quicken with life/minds fettered by darkness, hearts deadened by strife." Nevertheless Booker T. Washington insisted that practical training should form the core of freedmen's education. He worried that liberal arts students at schools like Howard University and the M Street High School "knew more about Latin and Greek when they left school, but they seemed to know less about life and its conditions as they would meet it in their homes." The education of liberal arts graduates, he declared, would make them too self-centered to perform community service. In Washington's view, education was less about academic subjects than about the development of self-esteem, the improvement of home life and health, and dedication to community progress. With lessons in hygiene, nutrition, and home economics along with integrity, self-discipline, and long-range planning, Tuskegee turned out healthy, industrious, thrifty, and well-mannered graduates. Equally important, Washington claimed, these young men and women were dedicated to improving economic and social conditions for *all* African Americans—not just for themselves.

Segregated or Integrated Schools?

"The subject of race pride is to my mind one of the most important and worthy to be considered at this time," black Boston lawyer Edward Everett Brown told an audience in 1888. "Why should any man of African descent be ashamed of his race?" he asked. "In every department of industry in its higher scientific branches, the Negro is proving . . . beyond any question that he is the equal and in many cases the superior of his Anglo-Saxon brother." Other African Americans also used racial pride as a defense against Social Darwinism. But black educators pondered how to develop their students' minds and confidence. Would students fare best competing in integrated schools or in all-black institutions?

Advocates of integrated schools insisted the only way for black citizens to gain access to the resources of mainstream America was to learn the ways of white society. They believed prejudice would evaporate if people from different races got to know each other, as Washington had experienced with his Indian students at Hampton. They also felt that by competing with white students while young, African Americans could avoid being intimidated by white people as adults. Well-off black families sent their children to integrated, white-operated schools and colleges, such as New England boarding schools, Oberlin College in Ohio, Harvard and Amherst in Massachusetts, Wesleyan College in Connecticut, and the University of Pennsylvania.

Other educators advocated all-black schools. Philadelphian Jacob C. White, principal of Roberts Vaux Consolidated School, believed that by "educating ourselves, by and through ourselves," African Americans would acquire the confidence to resist racial injustice. Dedicated black teachers would serve as role models. Black students would learn about their own heritage and gain self-confidence and the commitment to uplift the race. Educated in the Quaker-sponsored Institute for Colored Youth, White had mastered Latin and mathematics, literature and pedagogy, and chess and baseball. Like Booker T. Washington, he promoted industrial education and attention to cleanliness and integrity. Yet White also advocated liberal arts training.

The debate over the merits of separate and integrated schools soon became moot. By century's end, schools and neighborhoods were segregated in both North and South. A few public schools in Boston, New York, Chicago, and New Orleans remained integrated, but this, too, would change in the early twentieth century.

Education and Gender Identity

Believing education should shape pride in one's gender as well as one's race, numerous black women set out to prove themselves to black men as well as to white America. Many drew inspiration from Howard University Law School graduate Charlotte Ray, who passed the Washington, DC, bar in the 1870s to become the nation's first black woman lawyer. Mary Ann Shadd Cary completed Howard's law program in 1883 at the age of sixty. That same year, Lucy Moten became the first woman to head Washington's Miner Normal School, where she encouraged young teachers to expand minds rather than simply train workers.

Studying at Fisk and then at Harvard in the 1880s and 1890s, young scholar William Edward Burghardt (W. E. B.) Du Bois also connected education to gender identity. He concluded that only a liberal arts curriculum could shape young African American boys into men. The importance of manhood surfaced often in the rhetoric of black Americans. Whether it involved voting, owning land, earning a good wage, or protecting black women from exploitation, manhood seemed to symbolize the achievement of racial justice and equal education.

The Lure of Cities

In the post-Reconstruction era, many black Americans connected cities with new opportunities. Edward Booker, for example, established a gambling operation in Detroit. He enjoyed the dynamism of urban life and profited from the temptations it offered. Starting as a saloonkeeper, he bought a building in which he hosted gambling and prostitution. Then he expanded further by purchasing a racehorse, a gaming rooster, and a fighting tomcat. By 1887, he earned $30,000 a year, in a time when the average black man earned less than $100. But Booker died penniless, a victim of debt and his own passion for gambling. His story illustrates both the economic possibilities and the pitfalls of urban life.

Urban Community Life

African Americans constituted less than 10 percent of northern urbanites in the 1880s, yet those who ventured to northern cities found considerable economic and social opportunities. When enough black people settled near each other, black businesses could develop. Earning cash wages, black people began using banks. In 1888, Maggie Lena Walker responded to this new development by opening the nation's first black bank in Richmond, Virginia.

Black communities continued to thrive in cities along the waterways that once had served the Underground Railroad. Now towns along the railroads offered employment as well. Black people found jobs loading freight cars and ships, repairing wharves and railbeds, and serving as cooks, stewards, and porters. After railroad baron George Pullman was embarrassed by newspaper coverage of discrimination against the Fisk Jubilee Singers on his trains, he pledged to integrate his sleeping cars and give work to black porters. At eastern railroad hubs like New York, Philadelphia, and Baltimore, many black people found work.

Urban work also allowed for leisure time. Domestic workers got days off to use as they chose. And when white people left the cities in the summer, black laundresses, theater doormen, and caterers visited friends or relatives or took summer jobs at resorts in Saratoga, New York, and Newport, Rhode Island. Thus, they combined a change of scene with seasonal service work in hotels.

In the cities, black churches flourished. Church members gathered to worship and to celebrate weddings, holidays, and other special events. Black churches also served as venues in which to discuss politics and raise money for charities. Church groups hosted picnics, dances, and the offices of burial insurance and savings and loan societies. Through these institutions, black urbanites learned about upcoming concerts, debates, lectures, and professional black baseball games, as well as job opportunities. In these ways, places of worship nurtured both religious and secular life. Leadership in church activities also prepared men and women to be leaders in business, politics, and the arts.

The influx of black newcomers made many urban communities highly stratified. Philadelphia's black society, for example, had distinct layers. The several hundred black families who had been in the city before the Civil War enjoyed social privileges that separated them from recent arrivals. Black politician Gilbert Ball owned a comfortable house in an integrated neighborhood. But the majority of black newcomers had few financial resources. They crowded into mostly black neighborhoods characterized by high crime, dirty streets, polluted water, and high rates of illness and mortality—foreshadowing the all-black ghettoes soon to come. In 1880, the majority of Philadelphia's 32,700 black residents (up from 22,100 a decade before) could not read. They lived from hand to mouth, relying on churches or other social agencies to help them find housing, employment, and access to reading and food programs.

Newer cities such as Topeka were also divided by class. Between 1865 and 1880, Topeka's black population more than tripled. When the Exodusters poured into Kansas during the early 1880s (see Chapter 11), Topeka's population became almost one-quarter black. Black Topekans established their own stores, churches, schools, recreation clubs, and newspapers, even though more than two-thirds of black men and one-third of black women worked in unskilled occupations. The city's First African Baptist Church welcomed the poor, while the Second Baptist Church was home to most middle-class black people. Many Southerners who had come to Kansas hoping for a plot of land to farm had found racial hostility and no work. When Sojourner Truth visited Kansas in 1879 and saw widespread poverty, she was so distressed that she traveled through other urban black communities to raise money for relief.

Nevertheless, those fortunate enough to find steady employment sometimes gained middle-class status. Henry Clay Wilson is an example. Starting out as a housepainter in Topeka, he saved his money and soon owned a fifteen-chair barbershop. His business served white customers primarily, and the profits enabled him to purchase a controlling interest in a nearby recreation park where black churches held their outings. Wilson's small social circle included a real-estate agent, doctor, lawyer, newspaper publisher, and restaurant owner. More than two-thirds of these black leaders could read, a proportion twice that of the general black population. Their experience helped confirm African Americans' conviction that education was the way out of poverty.

Despite a legacy of Reconstruction race riots, black Memphis was thriving by the 1890s, thanks to the leadership of black saloon-owner Robert Reed Church. The son of a black woman and a white riverboat captain, Church learned the liquor business while working on his father's steamship. When a yellow fever epidemic in 1878 caused a mass exodus from Memphis, he remained in the city, buying up vacated property. Over the next twelve years, Memphis grew from a town of 20,000, of whom two-thirds were black, to a city of 100,000, of whom half were black. With financial help from Church, Memphis installed sewers to reduce the incidence of disease.

Federal Appointments

On February 27, 1885, Laura Hamilton Murray "went down to Washington" to see Grover Cleveland "going to the Capitol to take [his] oath." Cleveland was the first Democratic president since the Civil War. Like many other black Americans, Murray felt apprehensive about the Republican Party's loss of power. "Well we are now living under a new administration," Murray wrote in her diary. "How it will terminate who can tell."

Since Reconstruction, Washington, DC, had attracted black men and women with its abundance of federal jobs. The city became even more of a magnet in 1883, when Congress passed the Pendleton Act. Prompted by a public outcry against favoritism in federal appointments, the act established a merit-based civil service open to black and white applicants alike. Murray's husband, from Ohio, was one of hundreds of black people who passed the civil service exam. Landing a clerkship in the War Department, he moved with his family to Washington. There, Laura Murray kept her eye on Washington politics. She believed that only federal authority could prevent local leaders in the North and South from rescinding black Americans' right to vote or from blocking their access to the courts.

Under President James Garfield, black men had obtained numerous federal appointments: Henry Highland Garnet became minister to Liberia; Frederick Douglass, District of Columbia Recorder of Deeds; Blanche K. Bruce, Registrar of the Treasury; and John Mercer Langston, minister to Haiti. Former congressman Robert Brown Elliott worked in the Treasury Department. Even though the number of African Americans in Congress steadily declined after 1876, these federal positions continued to be open to African Americans under the administrations of Cleveland and subsequent presidents.

Black Towns

As discussed in Chapter 8, black and white Americans alike had established utopian settlements designed to cure society's ills. One such town was New Philadelphia, an isolated agricultural village peopled by black fugitives. Frank McWhorter, a former slave who bought his own and his family's freedom, organized this town in the 1830s at a site in Illinois, across the Mississippi River from St. Louis.

Stimulated by the emergence of enough free black people to settle and sustain them, other black towns sprang up after the Civil War, especially where residents had access to a rail connection and a nearby industry where there was work. The most successful black towns, then, became black suburbs of larger industrial cities—safe havens from white intrusion. For example, Brooklyn, Illinois, a few miles from New Philadelphia, was home to black railroad employees and workers in nearby coal mines and the sprawling St. Louis National Stock Yards.

Some black towns benefited from the cooperation of white capitalists and black leaders. Mound Bayou, Mississippi, is an example. Established in 1888, it was led by Isaiah Montgomery, the black farmer who had lost his plantation, but not his vision of an independent black economy. When the owners of the Louisville, New Orleans, and Texas Railroad sought to create a rail hub, Montgomery served as liaison between black settlers and white investors. He named the hub Mound Bayou. A modest down payment and a five-year mortgage was all a family needed to move in. Within a decade, Montgomery had sold 15,000 acres in the town and its surrounding area to almost 2,000 black settlers. As the new residents cleared land to build their homes, Montgomery helped them sell felled trees for railroad ties. Booker T. Washington praised Mound Bayou as a model of black enterprise and leadership, and he raised money for its development. The town thrived for several years beyond

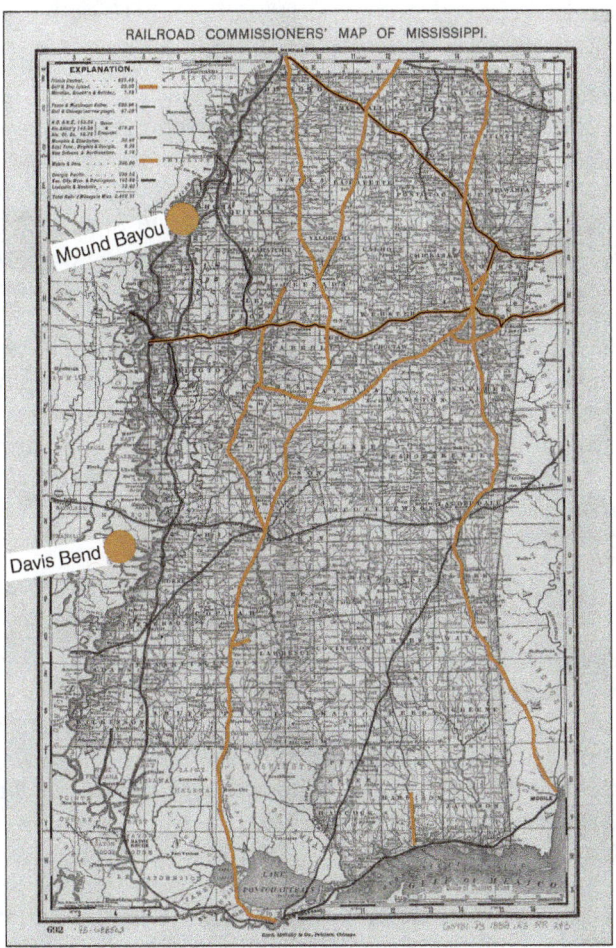

MAP 12.2 Isaiah Montgomery's Mississippi

This 1895 map of Mississippi shows Mound Bayou's location along railroad routes that bisect the northwest corner of the state. Hurricane Plantation, at Davis Bend, lies more than one hundred miles to the south, just below Vicksburg. By the end of the twentieth century, Mississippi's major transportation routes had changed little. Vast sections of the state still had only secondary roads.

Montgomery's death in 1934, despite a foundering cotton market and the subsequent demise of the railroad.

Though most of the nation's three dozen black towns lay within 500 miles of Mound Bayou, a few were scattered through states from New Jersey to Texas. However, based in rural life and values, most could not keep pace with industrializing America. Local stores could not compete with the mail-order houses like Sears & Roebuck and Montgomery Ward. By the 1930s, when automobiles began to make the rail junction irrelevant, many black towns were abandoned or absorbed into other municipalities.

The Economics and Politics of Unity

"One of the objects of [the Knights of Labor] is the abolition of distinctions that are maintained by class, creed, color, or nationality," proclaimed New York African American labor leader Frank Ferrell to a Richmond audience in 1886. In the last decades of the century, the New South's industries attracted unions like the Knights of Labor, which welcomed black and white workers. Northern white workers had organized strikes since at least the 1830s, but black people helped lead labor organizing in the post-Reconstruction South. In 1881, for example, a group of black laundry women in Atlanta initiated a successful strike for higher wages.

As modern capitalism seemed to force workers into longer workdays and shrinking wages, tensions between laborers and captains of industry sometimes cut across racial lines even where Jim Crow laws worked to keep the races separate. Around the country, labor unions sprang up to unify industrial wage earners. Sometimes, as in the Chicago and Omaha stockyards that housed farm animals awaiting shipment, the interests of farmers and laborers merged into political coalitions.

Unions

Like Frank Ferrell, white workers, even in the South, began to realize that class unity mattered more than racial disunity. The union Ferrell represented, the Knights of Labor, promoted the idea that all laborers, shopkeepers, and farmers had a common interest in replacing capitalism with a system in which workers owned the means of production. The Knights sought sweeping reforms of banking and tax systems and an end to child labor.

By 1886, the Knights of Labor had 700,000 members nationwide, 60,000 of whom were black. Many state chapters, such as Virginia's, met in segregated units. Segregation caused problems at the Knights' national convention in Richmond that year. New York units protested segregated hotels by housing themselves in their own tents to pressure the Knights' president, Terence Powderly, who then agreed to share the podium with Ferrell. Powderly, a white railroad machinist, was ambivalent, stating that he did not advocate equality between the races. On southern speaking tours, he usually addressed black members in segregated meetings. Nonetheless, most black workers stuck with the union, hoping to gain bargaining power. After the Richmond convention, African American membership in the Knights of Labor increased.

Across the nation, union locals followed the New York example, treating their black peers as allies in the economic struggle and promoting new black leaders. Among those leaders was Lucy Parsons, a light-skinned African American with Mexican American and Native American ancestors. Parsons was an anarchist—a person who aimed to overthrow a government unresponsive to workers' needs. There were enough disgruntled laborers in 1880s America that her speeches found ready ears. In Texas, after the Civil War, Lucy married Albert Parsons, a white former Confederate who became the outspoken pro-black Republican editor of the Waco *Spectator*. After Albert was shot in the leg and threatened with lynching for promoting black equality and mixed-race marriages, the couple fled Texas.

In the 1870s, the Parsons settled in Chicago, where they edited the radical labor newspaper *The Alarm*, published by the Knights of Labor. They also helped organize Chicago's participation in a nationwide workers' strike on May 1, 1886, in support of the eight-hour workday. During the strike, confrontations among strikers, strikebreakers, and police left several people dead and others wounded. Tensions rose when workers staged a mass protest against police brutality three days later in Haymarket Square.

The so-called Haymarket Riot unleashed bloody mayhem. A dynamite explosion and the death of seven policemen led to murder convictions for

Lucy Parsons, whose revolutionary rhetoric included racial, class, and gender issues, refused to be hemmed in by black leaders who felt she should focus on race only.

protest organizers, among them Albert Parsons. He went to prison, and his wife continued to organize workers while raising funds to appeal his case. Though Albert Parsons was executed in November 1887, Lucy Parsons remained committed to their cause. For the next fifty years she edited labor newspapers, demonstrated for the unemployed and homeless, and raised money for what she deemed "a common humanity, the same red blood whether that of African or Caucasian." Many black organizers criticized Parsons' approach, urging her to put racial issues above class concerns. But she persisted in agitating on behalf of the dispossessed regardless of race or background. At the 1905 founding convention of the Industrial Workers of the World (IWW), an international and color-blind union, she was the only female speaker.

T. Thomas Fortune, black editor of the *New York Age* (and son of the bold Florida Reconstruction politician Emanuel Fortune), spoke for many African Americans when he praised labor unions for uniting the races in pursuit of economic justice. However, in the wake of the Chicago violence, union loyalties fell apart. Many Knights members who disliked direct confrontation and strikes dissociated themselves from the union. The American Federation of Labor (AFL) soon eclipsed the Knights of Labor. This new union also courted black members. Led by New York cigar maker Samuel Gompers, the AFL united those workers who still believed strikes and boycotts could force employers to provide better hours, wages, and workplace conditions.

Interracial Alliances and Populism

Urban labor union action was mirrored by farmers who established alliances or cooperatives. To protect themselves against economic exploitation, farmers created cooperative ventures that could bypass—or stand up to—overcharging suppliers and high-priced shipping. Founded in Texas in 1886, the Colored Farmers' National Alliance and Cooperative Union represented thousands of black farmers in a dozen states. Since the Alliance could sometimes negotiate lower rates from suppliers and shippers, soon members of the white National Farmers' Alliance made overtures to their black peers. As with the Knights of Labor, white farmer unions did not favor full racial equality. But allying with black farmers enabled both groups to negotiate favorable transportation, marketing agreements, and bulk purchase prices. These deals proved especially valuable when the cost of supplies to bale cotton suddenly shot up. White farmers' alliances understood that by including black cotton growers in their sales agreements, they could also prevent black farmers from undercutting wholesale prices.

These new class loyalties had profound political implications. United in their resentment of landowners, black and white sharecroppers in North Carolina teamed up with local Knights of Labor units to elect black and white state legislators pledged to protect small farmers. This same coalition sent a black congressman to Washington to champion workers' rights. These efforts gave rise to the populist movement, in which black and white activists worked for federal restrictions on railroads to protect farmers and workers.

Populism spread throughout the rural South. In 1890, populists helped elect white lawyer Tom Watson to Congress, who shook the halls of Congress with his radical oratory: "Every laborer [should] understand that the cause of labor is the same everywhere; . . . every farmer, white and black [should] understand that the cause of the farmer is the same; . . . every producer, white and black, [should] understand that the cause of the producer is the same; and thus [they should] march shoulder to shoulder to the redress of grievances, demanding laws [to] . . . insure justice to all." In February 1892, Watson's prophecy was realized when representatives from the integrated Knights of Labor, the Colored Farmers' Alliance, and the Dakota Alliance joined to form the Populist Party. The new organization included not only farmers but also woman suffrage advocates and urban reformers with radical ideas for redistributing wealth and restricting the power of corporations and railroads. The Populists chose James Beard Weaver from Iowa as their 1892 presidential candidate. Rural Midwestern support for populism ran strong, and Weaver won more than one million popular votes, for twenty-two electoral votes. But on Election Day, many white Southerners supported the Democratic Party, fearing that splitting the white vote might endanger white dominance in the South.

Thus, the populist tide turned almost as soon as it crested. That same November, Watson was voted out of Congress. By the following spring, the economy deteriorated as rail companies went bankrupt, banks failed, 15,000 businesses closed, and agricultural prices plummeted. During the severe depression that followed, many white workers began seeing black people as competitors, not allies. Watson retracted his pro-black rhetoric, and other populists accepted the southern argument that even a poor white person was racially superior to any black person. In northern cities, populists refused to join unions that had African American members. AFL leaders gradually withdrew their commitment to black laborers—first by forming separate local organizations and then by sponsoring completely segregated black unions.

After endorsing Democratic candidate William Jennings Bryan in 1896, the Populist Party faded away. Local pockets of populists lingered for decades, yet most white union organizers had all but forgotten that they had briefly envisioned racial cooperation.

Finding a Place to Uplift the Race

"The situation on the island that caused me to leave more than anything else was the 1893 storm," said a South Carolina woman, describing her departure from the South. "We had been growing corn and cotton. Then here come 'long the storm. It blow down the little out-buildings, killed our turkeys and destroyed the crops. Water spread out all over our place. We had worked hard many years takin' care of the soil. Water just washed it all away." The woman "didn' think I was leavin' for good when I left." Yet she spent the rest of her life in New York City. Her life story underscored the reality that the abolition of slavery did not end black Americans' struggle to put down roots. With only a tenuous grasp on their lives and fortunes, few black Southerners could plan for the future. A storm, an illness or accident, an economic downturn—any of these calamities could dislodge them.

Subjected to racial discrimination, poverty, and isolation from mainstream America, a new generation of black Southerners set off in search of more welcoming places. The destinations they chose in these last decades of the nineteenth century were not new, but black Southerners themselves had changed. The war and the hopes and disappointments of Reconstruction had increased their willingness to risk all for the promise of a better life.

Migration within the South

Frederick Douglass worried that a black exodus from the South would leave African Americans "in the deepest trouble without a home." But most black Southerners relocated from one part of the South to another. Of the almost 200,000 African Americans who moved to Texas between 1870 and 1890, most came from other southern states. Many gained a foothold in Texas as independent farmers and ranchers. By 1900, another 40,000 black newcomers had joined them. But even as African Americans streamed into Texas, thousands of black Alabamans headed for Mississippi to work on cotton farms, joined by almost 30,000 black Americans arriving from the North and West. Thus Mississippi, which lost many native black people to Arkansas and Louisiana, experienced a net gain in its African American population. By 1890, 750,000 black Americans called Mississippi home—the highest number and greatest proportion of black people of any state in the country. For many African Americans, the South *was* home. They intended to make a life there, despite Jim Crow laws and racial violence.

Western Soldiers, Pioneers, and New Opportunities

In the late nineteenth century, many black people followed the western trail African American pioneers had blazed years before the Civil War. A few families had pushed West in wagon trains, but most went West as part of the army or railroad gangs. After the war, some black Americans stayed in the West as soldiers and homesteaders.

Beginning in the late 1860s, the federal government formed new military units to fight Indian wars and serve as local police. The Ninth and Tenth Cavalries, created in 1867, merged with the Twenty-fourth and Twenty-fifth Infantries in 1869. Over the next half-century, 20,000 black soldiers staffed military bases in the West, with troops that included both northern and southern recruits as well as seasoned Civil War soldiers who had never been discharged.

Following military service, some veterans helped lay track or build roadbeds. Thus, military installations and railroad stops sometimes became the settings for new black communities.

Military life brought adventure and steady pay, but in some respects it resembled slavery. Black soldiers often found themselves in service roles: cooking, building camps, or hauling supplies and water for white soldiers. Sometimes the Native Americans against whom they fought jeered at them, calling for the black soldiers to join forces against white men.

Despite hardships and discrimination, soldiers like Thomas Boyne and John Alexander made a career of the army. A member of the Ninth Cavalry's Troop C, Boyne received a Congressional Medal of Honor in 1882 for bravery in New Mexico's Indian wars. The Ninth Cavalry was also home to Alexander, West Point's second black graduate. Arriving in Nebraska in 1887, he was promoted to first lieutenant in 1893—one of only a handful of black officers who nevertheless inspired other black men to pursue a military life.

The cattle business drew other black people West. White ranchers, desperate for help driving cattle to the Kansas stockyards, recruited an estimated 8,000 black, Indian, Mexican, and mixed-race cowboys. These newcomers—about one-quarter of all cowboys—sometimes became ranchers in their own right. In isolated western towns, black men also found work in laundries,

Black congressmen who fought for entrée into West Point and the Naval Academy figured that that military service would give black men a leg up in America: public respect, a pension, and positioning for rewarding careers. Often this was the case. Charles Young of Kentucky, who followed his father into military life, graduating from West Point (1889), was the first black man to attain the rank of colonel in the regular U.S. army. A commander of the 10th United States Cavalry, he served in Mexico, in the Philippines, and, briefly, as director of California's Sequoia National Park—the first African American to hold such a post in the nation's new national park system. Upon his death in 1922, services were held for him in the amphitheatre of Arlington National Cemetery.

post offices, freight concessions, and blacksmith shops, while women (often single, widowed, or abandoned) worked as midwives, laundresses, shopkeepers, or prostitutes.

Western towns also offered work in mining. Helena, Montana, had a small band of black gold miners. African Americans were particularly welcomed in the mining town of Buxton, Iowa. A group of Quakers had founded Buxton as a multiethnic model community with substantial homes instead of the makeshift shacks often found in mining towns. Buxton also had churches of several denominations for both black and white residents. Mining gold, coal, copper, lead, and silver was backbreaking, dirty, and dangerous, but for many the pay made it worthwhile.

The Oklahoma Territory presented opportunities to acquire land and set up businesses and homesteads. With the Dawes Act of 1887, Congress reassigned Indian communal lands to individual families. In 1889, Oklahoma lands became fair game for homesteaders. Ten thousand African American settlers joined the land rush. Civil War veteran David Franklin and his family, for example, established a prosperous ranch near the Washita River. The Franklin family sent their seven children to college. One son, Buck Colbert Franklin, became a lawyer who fought Jim Crow laws and lived to see his own son, John Hope Franklin, become a world-renowned historian.

During these same years, young George Washington Carver traveled the Midwest. Hearing of the new all-black towns, Carver left his Missouri birthplace and hitched a ride to Kansas. After witnessing the lynching of a black man accused of raping a white girl, he decided to move on. He settled in Minneapolis, where he opened a laundry, bought land, and taught himself to read, hoping to go to college. But in 1885, he was turned away from a Presbyterian college in Kansas because of his race.

Carver eventually gained admission to a white agricultural college in Iowa, where he studied chemistry and botany. When Booker T. Washington persuaded him to join Tuskegee in 1895, Carver became the school's only faculty member with an advanced degree from a white institution. The accomplished scientist enhanced the school's reputation. Tuskegee also gained an able artist: Carver's paintings had been displayed at the Chicago Columbian Exposition in 1893. For more than four decades, Carver trained black scientists and carried on agricultural research, proposing solutions to the South's problems of boll weevil infestation, tobacco diseases, and overworked soil. His work with peanuts, which gained him wide recognition from white agriculturalists, inspired many black men to study science.

Antidiscrimination laws also drew black people West. Admitted to the Union in 1889, the state of Washington protected interracial marriage and integrated schools. Of the few hundred African Americans who lived there in 1890, most clustered in Seattle. There they worked in hotels, restaurants, and shipyards while building a close-knit community with their own AME church. The state's franchise laws gave black women the vote and permitted them to serve on juries. Thanks to the vigorous advocacy of the local group of the Knights of Labor, black Washingtonians faced less discrimination on the job than did workers in other states.

Seattle's black leaders also helped to build community institutions. William Bush made substantial financial contributions to build roads and bridges. In 1889, he won election to Washington's first legislature. Horace Cayton, a former Mississippi slave, established the *Seattle Republican,* which promoted black rights and Republican loyalty.

Rethinking Africa

During the 1880s, a few black Americans looked once more toward Africa. Black scholar George Washington Williams poured years of research into *The History of the Negro Race from 1619–1880 . . . As Slaves, As Soldiers, and As Citizens* (1883). His book focused on the three subjects that defined his life: Christianity, Africa, and Christianity *in* Africa. Williams was part of a small circle of late-nineteenth-century black Americans who sought liberation through African colonization.

Volunteering to help Belgium's king Leopold Christianize Africa's Congo region, Williams traveled to Africa in 1885. When he returned to the United States in 1889 he tried to enlist the help of the federal government in Leopold's central African railroad. Rebuffed by President Benjamin Harrison, Williams went back to Africa, where he soon saw that Leopold's railroad scheme was nothing but "fraud and trickery." The Belgian king had cheated tribal leaders out of their land, while white foremen brutalized Congolese workers.

In a long "Open Letter to Leopold II," Williams criticized the Belgian monarch for failing to keep his promise of "fostering care, benevolent enterprise, [and] honest and practical effort" to "secure the welfare" of the Africans. Meanwhile, he tried to convince black Americans that establishing Christian missions in Africa would enable them to reclaim their lost racial heritage. Williams continued writing about Africa until his death in 1891, but his ideas appealed to only a minority. Most black Americans had little interest in Africa during the late nineteenth century.

Yet other intellectuals also tried to focus black Americans' attention on Africa. Writer Edward Blyden, long associated with the biracial American Colonization Society, published *Christianity, Islam, and the Negro Race* in 1887. In it he acknowledged African American ties to the Muslim faith, but he believed that by adopting Christianity—the religion of Europe—Africans would have a better means for resisting a European takeover. Blyden's program, known as *Ethiopianism,* called attention to the biblical story in which Ethiopia commanded a divinely protected empire.

Henry McNeal Turner also dreamed of Africa. After an unsuccessful repatriation attempt in 1879, he made his first trip to the vast continent in 1891. But Turner lamented that he had waited too long to make the voyage: "I have just strolled as far out in the direction of Boporo—the Eden of West Africa—as my strength would permit. I have seen the African in his native town and hut, rather dwellings, and I have just had a long weep or cry at the grand field for missionary operation here, and that I am too old now to engage in it." The fifty-seven-year-old Turner returned to the United States to launch *The Voice of the Mission,* a newspaper promoting missionary work. Over many years, his entreaties inspired a few thousand black Americans to cross the Atlantic to Liberia.

Terror and Accommodation

"If you will kill us, turn our faces to the West." These were the last words of Thomas Moss before a mob of white men lynched him and two other black men near Memphis in the spring of 1892. Historians do not know whether Moss was making a spiritual allusion or suggesting that black people go West in search of justice. But, his death riveted international attention on lynching.

Lynching has a long history in Western society. In the United States in the years after the Civil War, however, white mobs used lynching specifically to enforce racial inequality. Lynching escalated in frequency as state laws curtailed black people's citizenship rights. Particularly in the South, African Americans who had successful businesses, stood up to white people's insults, ran for office, or voted risked incurring white people's wrath. Mere friendliness or eye contact with white women could get a young black man killed.

A year after Moss's death, his friend Wells told his story to a Boston audience. She recounted how a local white storeowner, displaced by Moss's successful Peoples Grocery, incited a confrontation in which police officers were wounded. Afterward, an angry white mob dragged Moss and two other black men from their jail cells, as Wells put it, to "do what the law could not be made to do . . . [teach] a lesson to the Afro-American that he must not shoot a white man—no matter what the provocation." The three black men fought back, but the mob mutilated their bodies and gouged their eyes out.

Campaign against Lynching

Wells knew how to get heard. Her 1893 Boston speech was not the first time she called attention to racial injustice. In 1884, she refused to leave the Ladies Coach reserved for white women on a Jim Crow train in Tennessee, sinking her teeth into the arm of the conductor who tried to remove her. Moss's death unleashed the full extent of her fury. For the newspaper she had co-owned since 1889, *Free Speech and Headlight,* she wrote a long account of his murder—the first of many articles in her campaign against lynching. The piece was printed while Wells was in New York visiting fellow black journalist T. Thomas Fortune. In her absence, white supremacists vandalized her office. Fortune told her, "I'm afraid you will have to stay in New York."

So Wells went to work for Fortune's *New York Age,* launching a war of words and rallying 250 women to raise funds to publish a report on lynching. Money came from as far away as Seattle, where women in the tiny AME church had recently formed a Woman's Christian Temperance Union chapter. Investigating the circumstances of more than 700 southern lynchings in the previous decade, Wells published a detailed study in 1893. The report concluded that lynch mobs frequently targeted successful black men and black men accused of raping white women who had in fact initiated the relationship. In 1889, 150 black lynchings were reported across the country. In 1892, the year Thomas Moss lost his life, there were 250 such murders.

Wells's campaign, which Douglass helped her plan, galvanized black communities. Wells admired Douglass, often quoting his vision of America as a "composite" nation of many peoples and cultures. Douglass, in turn, valued Wells's focus on women's rights and social justice. He wrote an introduction to *A Red Record*, her next study of lynching, published in 1895. Though black politicians failed to secure passage of federal antilynching laws, the number of lynch mob attacks in Memphis and around the country declined after 1893. Wells had exerted a measurable impact.

The Atlanta Compromise

Organizers of the 1895 Cotton States and International Exposition in Atlanta invited Booker T. Washington—a speaker they hoped would please both black and white audiences—to address the crowd. In his address, he did not publicly decry lynching or challenge white racism. Instead, he presented a blueprint for southern progress. Hoping to inspire black dreams and allay white fears, he urged black people to stay in the South, accommodate themselves to racial discrimination, build their economic strength, and bide their time.

"One third of the population of the South is of the Negro race," Washington began the speech for which he is best remembered. "No enterprise seeking the material, civil or moral welfare of [the South] can disregard this element of our population." Using a metaphorical story of passengers dying of thirst on a ship lost at sea, he reminded his audience that when told to "cast down your bucket where you are," the passengers discovered fresh water in the salt ocean. Urging patience, he encouraged black Americans to "cast down your bucket in making friends of the people by whom we are surrounded." "Cast it down in agriculture, mechanics, in commerce, in domestic service, and in the professions," he implored. At the same time he urged white Southerners not to hire new immigrants but to "'Cast down your bucket where you are.' Cast it down among the eight millions of Negroes whose habits you know." He reminded them of loyal black workers who "without strikes and labour wars, tilled your fields, built your railroads, and helped make possible the progress of the South." He promised that black workers would be "the most faithful, law-abiding and unresentful that the world has seen."

Though he saw the destinies of black and white Southerners as intertwined, Washington advocated racially separate social circles, where black and white workers would be "separate as the fingers, yet one as the hand in all things relating to mutual progress." In other contexts, however, he hinted of a future in which black people were full citizens and in which black enterprise would eventually bring equality. "No race," he said, "that has anything to contribute to the markets of the world is long in any degree ostracized."

Widely publicized, the speech catapulted Washington to a position of visibility, influence, and power never before held by even so revered a black

American as Douglass, who had black and white admirers in the North and in the South. Some black leaders applauded Washington's speech. New York journalist T. Thomas Fortune, who had in 1883 hailed those "from Denmark Vesey to Nat Turner, from . . . Frederick Douglass and Henry Highland Garnet," who had protested "against injustice," now echoed Washington's request for patience. Isaiah Montgomery of Mound Bayou, one of Mississippi's delegates to the exposition, was also inspired by Washington's speech.

But many African Americans distanced themselves from Washington and his ideas. "It is supreme folly to speak of Mr. Washington as the Moses of the race," wrote one black Atlanta newspaper. "If we are where Mr. Washington's Atlanta speech placed us, what need have we of a Moses?" African American leaders who favored more immediate and direct demands for equal political rights labeled this speech "Washington's compromise."

Conclusion

The first generations of African Americans born into emancipation struggled to find a place to establish families, make a living, and educate themselves in a hostile white society. The Civil War had left the South with social, economic, and political problems that Reconstruction alone could not solve. After 1877, black and white Southerners tried to rebuild their economy and forge a new relationship with each other. Poverty mired black and white workers in a cycle of debt and a mood of despair. Jim Crow laws bound African Americans to menial jobs and subjected them to racial discrimination. Pseudoscientific theories of Social Darwinism prompted white people to shun African Americans. Against a backdrop of racial violence, migration, and relocation, black Americans struggled to forge alliances with white farmers and industrial workers, but it was often difficult for black people to shed the slave past.

Out of this climate of hopelessness, Booker T. Washington rose up to lead African Americans into the twentieth century. He urged his followers to gain education and work skills and to remain in the South as they lifted themselves above their "discouraging surroundings." Hoping to reduce the violence against southern black people, Washington assured white Southerners that black workers would accommodate old racial hierarchies. He opposed aggressive leaders like Wells and Du Bois, who pressed for education that would include the liberal arts, lay the foundation for what Du Bois called the development of men, and encourage students to stand up to racial injustice. For these leaders, "manhood"—which included personal dignity, and economic and political power—seemed to be missing from Washington's goals. Though Washington and the Tuskegee Institute dominated black strategies in the early decades of the twentieth century, black people left the rural South in droves. They headed for southern and northern cities, all-black towns, the western frontier, and Africa. As soldiers, rail workers, radical political activists, missionaries, and journalists, they plowed fresh ground in new places.

In 1896, the election year following Washington's Atlanta Compromise speech, a political movement known as Progressivism emerged. One aspect of Progressivism included black and white intellectuals who came together to design solutions to what one observer described as "the problem of the twentieth century . . . the problem of the color line."

Questions for Review and Reflection

1. The American Civil War ended just as the Atlantic world was fully embracing cash-wage capitalism. How might the southern rebuilding/reconstruction have been different if the Atlantic world had remained firmly bound by an agrarian economy based upon barter?

2. How might Reconstruction have been different had Social Darwinist theories not emerged at this time?

3. What were some of the advantages/disadvantages of Booker T. Washington's social and economic strategies for late-nineteenth-century America? How valuable would his ideas be in today's world?

4. What factors promoted interracial populism in the 1890s? What doomed it?

"Colored" Becomes "Negro" in the Progressive Era

Mary Church Terrell and the NACW

The applause was deafening. As Harriet Tubman, now in her seventies, entered the Washington, DC, meeting hall in the spring of 1896, a crowd of several hundred rose to its feet. Tubman had arrived to help launch the National Association of Colored Women (NACW), a federation of forty urban black women's clubs from around the nation. Inspired by Ida Wells Barnett's anti-lynching campaign, which demonstrated women's power to unite and finance a common cause, the NACW planned to focus on children and home life. Members envisioned black families creating the cornerstone of a strong national community, teaching children to seek personal success while helping others. The NACW adopted the motto "lifting as we climb," echoing Booker T. Washington's credo.

As NACW members honored Tubman for her leadership in the slave past, they chose Mary Church Terrell as their president to lead them into the future. Wealthy and well educated, Terrell had developed her worldview amid the hope and violence of the Reconstruction South. Her father, Memphis businessman Robert Reed Church, born the enslaved son of a white master, eventually became one of America's wealthiest black men. After white ruffians shot him while ransacking his saloon, Church testified in the courts against his attackers. His actions defined him as a "race man"—determined to defend the possessions and honor of all African Americans. In her childhood, Mary Church absorbed her family's commitment to struggle for racial justice. With a master's degree from Oberlin College, she married a lawyer and settled in Washington, DC.

1896	Republican William McKinley defeats Democrat William Jennings Bryan for president.
	The National Association of Colored Women is founded.
	Lyrics of Lowly Life establishes Paul Laurence Dunbar as a major poet.
	In *Plessy* v. *Ferguson*, the U.S. Supreme Court upholds segregation.
1897	W. E. B. Du Bois and other black intellectuals form the American Negro Academy.
1898	Spanish-American War establishes the United States as an imperialist power.
1899	Scott Joplin's "Maple Leaf Rag" establishes ragtime as an American musical form.
1900	First Pan-African Congress meets in London.
	Black Americans seek to establish the Afro-American Party.
	Booker T. Washington launches the Negro Business League.
1901	In *The Guardian*, William Monroe Trotter criticizes Booker T. Washington.
	The assassination of President William McKinley elevates Theodore Roosevelt to the presidency.
1903	In *Souls of Black Folk,* W. E. B. Du Bois introduces his notion of a black "Talented Tenth."
1905	Du Bois, Trotter, and other opponents of Booker T. Washington found the Niagara Movement.
1906	President Roosevelt dishonorably discharges an entire company of black soldiers in Brownsville, Texas.
1908	Race riot in Springfield, Illinois, stirs white reformers to join the fight for racial justice.
1909	The Niagara Movement merges with white reformers to form the National Association for the Advancement of Colored People (NAACP).
	The National Afro-American Press Association links black journalists across the United States.
1910	Boxer Jack Johnson defeats Jim Jeffries, the "Great White Hope."
1911	Alfred Charles Sam helps establish an international black trade network.
	The National Urban League unites community centers.
	Arthur Schomburg helps found the Negro Historical Society of Research.
1913	President Woodrow Wilson segregates federal civil service.
1914	Marcus Garvey establishes the Universal Negro Improvement Association.

1915	The NAACP protests the film *Birth of a Nation*.
	The NAACP achieves its first legal victory in *Guinn* v. *United States*, outlawing Oklahoma's grandfather clause.
	Carter G. Woodson founds the Association for the Study of Negro Life and History.
	Booker T. Washington dies.
	African American leaders meet at Amenia, New York, to seek ideological compromise.

Terrell's commitment to resisting racial injustice strengthened the NACW. In her first speech as president, she proclaimed, "In Union there is strength . . . the colored women of the United States [have] banded together to fulfill a mission." African American women needed their own organization, she said, "because our peculiar status in this country . . . demand[s] that we stand by ourselves in the special work for which we have organized." She maintained

Mary Church Terrell, the first president of the National Association of Colored Women, saw a strong home life, education, self-discipline, and good hygiene as essential to improving the lives of African Americans. This image shows Terrell in her typically impeccable attire.

that "only through good homes . . . [can] people . . . become really good and truly great."

NACW members resolved to go beyond charity work and cultivate "fine, cultured, women" with "better homes, purer homes." The organization shared Booker T. Washington's concern for teaching hygiene, home economics, and self-discipline. Members urged personal grooming, good manners, and practices such as reading to children and disciplining them with reason rather than physical punishment. Eventually representing more than 50,000 black women in 1,000 clubs across the United States, the NACW also promoted kindergartens and childcare facilities at which black children could learn while their mothers earned a living.

Improving colored Americans' lives was also part of the Progressive movement that swept America at the end of the nineteenth century. Progressives, who came from all races and political parties, sought to perfect society. Progressive ideas influenced everything from political and scientific theories to architecture and religion, sparking schools of social work, city planning organizations, and urban community centers for the disadvantaged. The NACW's mission and strategy embraced Progressive ideas such as women's rights. Like white female reformers, black female reformers disputed women's supposed inferiority. They declared that colored women's dual oppression of race and gender made them "the most interesting women in the country." One NACW founder described broad goals: "The old notion . . . that woman was intended by the Almighty to do only those things that men thought they ought to do is fast passing away. In our day and in this country, a woman's sphere is just as large as she can make it."

NACW leaders represented the new intellectual black leadership. Born after Emancipation, well educated, and sometimes economically independent, such women faced the future with optimism and confidence. But as we will see in this chapter, they encountered staggering challenges. With its *Plessy* v. *Ferguson* decision upholding racial segregation, the Supreme Court led a backlash against federal protections for black citizens. Convinced by pseudo-scientific racism that defined African Americans as inferior, state and local governments initiated new laws and customs—often enforced by violence—increasingly restricting black freedom and opportunity.

New leaders launched a variety of legal and cultural counterattacks. Seeking to accommodate or combat racial segregation, they promoted unity and racial pride. Some hoped to earn their country's respect through military service in the Spanish-American War. Others looked to the National Association for the Advancement of Colored People (NAACP) and the Urban League to help improve their lot.

In cities such as New York a proud black identity emerged, encouraged by the churches and enhanced by the arts, literature, and sports. Yet powerful ideological and social pressure from the white majority prevented many black Americans from achieving social or economic progress. As World War I erupted, the NAACP led the campaign to replace "accommodation" to racial segregation with confrontation to this injustice.

Racial Segregation

"Another Jim Crow Car Case, Arrest of a Negro Traveler Who Persisted in Riding with the White People," announced the New Orleans *Daily Picayune*, reporting Homer Plessy's challenge to segregation laws. Plessy boasted he would "sooner go to jail than leave the spirit of the Thirteenth and Fourteenth Amendments." On June 7, 1892, this black shoemaker violated the 1890 Louisiana Separate Car Act, which used race to assign people to "white" or "colored" passenger train cars. He boarded a train in New Orleans and sat down in the car reserved for white people. Plessy might have gone unnoticed, since the heritage that defined him as colored—one black great-grandfather—hardly showed on his pale skin. But Louisiana law declared that any person who had "one drop of Negro blood" was "colored." The "race clerk"—a railroad employee responsible for keeping track of local family relationships—identified Plessy and had him arrested. Plessy welcomed the arrest, for he wanted to challenge the unjust law. A $500 bond, posted by supporters, kept him out of jail while his case proceeded through the courts.

"Separate but Equal"

Supported by the New Orleans Citizens Committee, formed specifically to test the legality of separate train cars, Plessy and his allies aimed to use public opinion and the courts to force the federal government to protect the right to equal access to public services. Like Plessy, many black people in New Orleans had a mixed heritage. Called Creoles, they had French or Native American as well as black ancestors. One such person was newspaper editor and lawyer Louis Martinet, whose *Crusader* advocated voting rights. Like many black men, poor white men were subject to local "grandfather clause" laws that excluded them from voting because their landless grandfathers had not been allowed to vote. The franchise, the *Crusader* argued, was an issue "in which all the common people, whether colored or white, are vitally interested."

In July 1892, Plessy's lawyers argued before the New Orleans District Court that the Fourteenth Amendment prohibited states from making or enforcing "any law which shall abridge the privileges or immunities of citizens." But the court ruled against Plessy, saying the state's right to regulate intrastate trade allowed it to require separate cars. Plessy's appeal to the Louisiana Supreme Court also failed. This court ruled that the Separate Car Act treated black and white people equally, prohibiting both from sitting in integrated cars. Plessy then appealed to the nation's highest court.

The appeal failed. In 1896, eight Supreme Court justices concluded that though the Fourteenth Amendment guaranteed "absolute equality of the two races before the law, . . . in the nature of things it could not have been intended to abolish distinctions based upon color, or to enforce . . . a commingling of the two races upon terms unsatisfactory to either." Upholding Louisiana's Separate Car Act, the Court stated that as long as "equal" services were

Robert James Harlan, the mixed-race half-brother of Justice John Marshall Harlan, accumulated a fortune during the California gold rush, which he invested in Cincinnati real estate. In 1875, after raising a black regiment that became the Ninety-fourth Ohio Battalion, he was commissioned as a colonel by President Rutherford B. Hayes. Serving in the Ohio Legislature in the 1890s, Harlan worked to repeal Jim Crow laws.

provided for black citizens, states could legislate that those services be "separate." It did not rule on how *equal* would be defined, and indeed train cars for colored patrons were seldom of equal quality. The justices noted that "the enforced separation of the races [does not mark] the colored race with a badge of inferiority."

The sole dissenter in the *Plessy* case was Justice John Marshall Harlan, a former slaveholder. Harlan warned that this decision was as harmful as the *Dred Scott* decision had been and would erode the Fourteenth Amendment's guarantees that had overturned *Scott*. Harlan cautioned that court rulings that reduced black Americans to inferior status would "stimulate [white] aggressions, more or less brutal, upon the admitted rights of colored citizens." But few white Americans heeded these warnings.

The *Plessy* decision shaped American racial policies and limited black people's civil rights for more than a half-century. Now that states and local governments had legal approval for racial segregation, the New Orleans Citizen's Committee dissolved. "It was better," committee members said, for African Americans "to suffer in silence than to attract attention to their misfortune and weakness." Changing his plea to guilty, Plessy paid the $25 fine for riding in the "wrong" car. The militant *Crusader* ceased publication. Many African Americans came to believe in this era that continuing political agitation "would not only be fruitless but decidedly dangerous."

Across the nation, new state and local laws segregated more and more facilities. In the South, public transportation and public services were segregated, as were schools. The New Orleans Catholic Diocese divided its parishes into black and white. In at least one Mississippi cemetery, the body of a black person was dug up and reburied in a segregated burial ground. Even in the North, communities segregated schools, libraries, prisons, hospitals, and cemeteries. Hotels, theaters, and restaurants followed. Northern urban neighborhoods rapidly became all black or all white, with African Americans typically concentrated in older areas. White workers moved to new suburbs and used the new electric streetcars and rail lines to commute to their jobs.

Jim Crow laws also affected the political process. In 1898, when the Supreme Court upheld Mississippi's poll tax, many southern states adopted some combination of grandfather clauses, poll taxes, literacy tests, and "understanding clauses" that required a potential voter to interpret parts of the Constitution. These tests were applied unequally; white applicants might be given nursery rhymes to interpret, while black applicants might be asked to read the Bible in Latin. These practices quickly erased the black franchise. In Louisiana, the number of black voters dropped from 130,000 in 1890 to just 1,300 in 1900. Some southern states passed "white primary" laws, which banned African Americans from running or voting in primary elections. By limiting the franchise to upper-class white men, southern politicians reestablished the hierarchy of pre-Civil War America.

For many black people, the *Plessy* ruling reinforced Booker T. Washington's view that African Americans had best concentrate on economic progress, not legal and political equality. Frugality, integrity, and job skills, Washington argued, would bring success in the only areas in which black Americans could control their destiny.

Progressivism and White Supremacy

The decline of Populism (see Chapter 12) coincided with the rise of Progressivism. Fueled by the social dislocation of rapid industrialization, urbanization, and the arrival of new immigrants, the Progressive movement united a disparate group of reformers who shared the belief that society could be improved. Progressives included opponents of corruption in local government, woman suffrage activists, critics of big business, social workers, agricultural reformers, and temperance advocates.

Ideas of civilization, politics, and social management merged with Progressive ideas about race. The popular view of many white people at this time was that the genes (which they called bloodlines) of white people were superior and should thus be passed along to future generations to ensure a strong civilization. White people should avoid mating with nonwhites, lest "inferior" traits dilute their bloodlines. Most white Progressives shared this view and sought to wall off white Americans from so-called inferior races.

Through the 1890s, a pseudoscience called *eugenics* took hold. Eugenics equated physical characteristics with a person's quality. In *Eugenics: The Science of Human Improvement by Better Breeding* (1910), Charles Davenport proposed that racial traits were inherited and that choosing the right mate could ensure human progress. Eugenicists believed that the presence of inferior individuals could threaten a whole society's progress. These ideas blended with Progressive notions of bettering society through scientific understanding and buttressed ideas about the superiority of white people. In settlement houses, Progressives sought to "Americanize" immigrants, teaching them English and American dress and cuisine. White female reformers tried to improve black communities through public health, education, and social work. Programs to train African Americans in skilled trades and to reform criminals and derelicts grew out of such experiments. Yet for all their talk about improving society, most white Progressives only wanted African Americans and immigrants to behave like middle-class white Americans. They were not interested in absorbing whatever strengths these newcomers or their cultures might bring to white society.

Pointing to Booker T. Washington and others who had elevated themselves, some Progressives also supported black self-help organizations such as the NACW. But this limited sympathy toward and curiosity about black Americans did not stop segregation and racial violence. By 1900, some white Americans who had previously supported black rights now advocated racial separation and the curtailment of black freedom. Democratic senator William Jennings Bryan, a leader of the interracial Populist Party in the early 1890s, eventually concluded that "white supremacy promotes the highest welfare of both races." William Dean Howells, editor of the widely read *Harper's Magazine,* allowed the publication to poke fun at African Americans by depicting them as buffoons or children. As one Yale professor put it, "The Negro's day is over. He is out of fashion."

"Colored" Becomes "Negro"

As racial separation accelerated following the *Plessy* decision, black leaders resurrected the decades-old issue of identity, believing that the right term for themselves would help unite black Americans and garner white people's respect. Plessy used the term *colored* in his legal case, yet he identified himself as Creole to honor both his African background and his French blood. White Americans increasingly used the term *negro,* the term by which scientists now designated people with dark skin. Could this designation serve black self-identity? One Philadelphia minister quickly objected to *negro* as "a miserable misnomer," too close to the word *nigger* and "full cousin to the term 'darkey'"—both words used during slavery. When the *AME Church Review* suggested that spelling *negro* with a capital *N* would dignify it, many black Americans agreed. The NACW joined the appeal to have colored Americans referred to as *Negroes.*

Some black people thought *Afro-American* more clearly conveyed the merging of American and African cultures. Others saw the term as too narrow: "Some of us have . . . some of the blood of all races," they protested; "we are descendants of all continents." Yet black Americans well understood that U.S. law did not regard them as "descendants of all continents." The presence of any known African ancestry defined a person as "Negro," consigning him or her to second-rate status. But by 1915, most black and white Americans had adopted the term *Negro.*

The Problem of the "Color Line"

"The problem of the twentieth century is the problem of the color line," announced thirty-two-year-old W. E. B. Du Bois in July 1900. Speaking to the Pan-African Conference in London, he proclaimed that "the question [was] how far differences of race . . . will hereafter be made the basis of denying to over half the world the right of sharing . . . the opportunities and privileges of modern civilization." Expressing unity with the "millions of black men in Africa, America and the Islands of the Sea, [and] the brown and yellow myriads elsewhere," he predicted that "if by reason of carelessness, prejudice, greed and injustice the black world is to be exploited and ravaged and degraded, the results must be deplorable, if not fatal—not simply to them, but to the high ideals of justice, freedom and culture which a thousand years of Christian civilization have held before Europe." Seeking to arrest the imperialism evident at the Berlin Conference of 1884–1885, in which European nations had sanctioned the division of Africa among themselves, Du Bois called on these nations to "respect the integrity and independence" of the "darker peoples."

The mixed-race Du Bois had spent more than a decade developing his vision of an international alliance of colored peoples. He concluded that the color line—the line that divided black people and white—was a global problem that held people back in every way. In the United States that line was ever more deeply pronounced.

Pan-Africanism

The term *Pan-Africanism* had been coined by a Trinidadian organizer of the conference to embrace all those who took an international stand against racism. Du Bois interpreted it to mean that the world's colored peoples should unite against white imperialism at home and abroad. "In this the closing year of the nineteenth century, there has been assembled a congress of men and women of African blood, to deliberate solemnly upon the present situation and outlook of the darker races of mankind," he said. Conference funding and speakers came from many black organizations, including the NACW. Their goals ranged from full inclusion in American democracy to temporary or permanent racial separation. Even Booker T. Washington initially backed the Pan-African Conference, though he and Du Bois would soon be bitter rivals.

Du Bois's experiences at Fisk, Tennessee's renowned black college, had opened his eyes in many ways. Growing up in western Massachusetts with few black peers, he had moved comfortably among white classmates. But in his teens, a white girl's refusal to exchange visiting cards with him took him by surprise. The incident reminded him that he was "shut off from their world by a vast veil." At Fisk, he was deeply moved by Jubilee Hall, built with money raised by the Jubilee Singers. It "seemed ever made of the songs themselves, and its bricks were red with the blood and dust of toil. . . . [It] was full of the voices of my brothers and sisters, full of the voices of the past." He felt "thrilled to be for the first time among so many people of my own colour or rather of such extraordinary colours, who it seemed were bound to me by new and exciting external ties." Du Bois later recalled: "Into this world I leapt with enthusiasm: henceforth I was a Negro."

For Du Bois, being Negro was as much a mission as an identity. He held some ideas in common with the intellectuals of his day—for example, that membership in a given race implied common characteristics. But he rejected the notion that white people were more intelligent or morally superior. Determined to bring honor to his race, he earned in 1895 the first history doctorate ever awarded a black man by Harvard University. Soon after, Washington invited the young scholar to teach at Tuskegee. Du Bois declined, accepting a position at Wilberforce College in Ohio. He was then hired by the University of Pennsylvania to produce a study evaluating black potential. *The Philadelphia Negro: A Social Study* (1899) profiled 40,000 black Americans in the city. It showed how black people defied huge odds to build vibrant communities through their churches and educational institutions. But "color prejudice" impeded economic progress. *The Philadelphia Negro* reflected the Progressive idea that poor people could fashion better lives if social planners improved their environment.

After publishing *The Philadelphia Negro,* Du Bois joined the faculty at Atlanta Baptist College (soon to become Morehouse College), the South's premier black liberal arts school. There he continued to study black business, education, labor unions, churches—even prison life. He also joined with other black intellectuals to establish the American Negro Academy to promote lectures, meetings, and publications of black scholars. He believed an academic education and the franchise would give African Americans the stature and self-confidence to master economic challenges. Liberal arts education, he contended, would enable them to be good citizens and to make wise choices for themselves and their society. By the time he spoke before the Pan-African Conference, Du Bois's reputation as a scholar and teacher gave him an authoritative voice on the subject of worldwide racism.

Black Americans and the Spanish-American War

In his London speeches, Du Bois connected "the problem of the color line" in the United States with America's recent war with Spain. That venture had secured U.S. control over Cuba, Puerto Rico, Guam, and the Philippine Islands in the same year that Hawaii was annexed. American officials saw the dark-skinned native peoples of these islands as incapable of governing themselves. Insisting they wanted to improve the lives of the native peoples—to "establish system where chaos reigns"—the American occupiers made sweeping changes in these places, establishing missionary schools and hospitals and introducing new forms of agriculture and commerce. But Du Bois knew that U.S. improvements meant the seizure of mines, farmlands, and resources and the consigning of local colored residents to menial jobs.

The Spanish-American War erupted in 1898. The American battleship *Maine,* which had been dispatched to Cuba, a Spanish colony, to protect American citizens there, exploded and sank, killing dozens of American soldiers. The incident gave American imperialists a chance to declare war against Spain, ostensibly to help liberate Cuba and the Philippines from Spanish rule.

Thousands of black soldiers fought in the Spanish-American War. However, for many, the call to service exposed a conflict between loyalty to their race and loyalty to their country. As Kansas City's black newspaper *American Citizen* put it, "Uncle Sam [should] keep his hands off other countries till he has learned to govern his own." Black Republicans such as Calvin Chase, editor of the Washington *Bee,* announced, "The Negro has no reason to fight for Cuba's independence. . . . He is as much in need of independence as Cuba is." Still, other black journalists urged loyalty to the U.S. government. "America is the land of our birth," said the Cleveland *Gazette.* "As citizens and patriots, let us be ready and willing to do our part . . . our full duty, and to do even more than others in the hour of the nation's peril." Other African Americans echoed Du Bois's conviction that racial issues in United States reflected an international pattern. "The dark-skinned inhabitants of these islands will be the victims of race prejudice," predicted Richmond's black newspaper, *The Planet.* Events in the Philippines justified the comparison. After the war, when the Filipinos realized that the United States intended to replace Spanish control with its own, they mounted a resistance that lasted five years. More than 14,000 Filipinos died, and some white soldiers relished the opportunity to slaughter them. It was "like killing the niggers back home," wrote one soldier from the South, "more fun than a turkey shoot."

Racism reverberated at home. Barely a week after twenty-two black American soldiers died on the *Maine,* a white mob in Lake City, South Carolina, torched the home of black postmaster Fraser Baker, killing Baker and his child and wounding several others. When the murders went unpunished, Barnett took Baker's case to the White House. Pointing out that the

In addition to serving in the Spanish-American War, many black soldiers were stationed on the western frontier to fight Indians and protect white settlers. Life as a soldier was another means for leaving the South.

U.S. government had compensated Italy and China when Americans lynched those nations' citizens, Barnett argued that the country should "do as much for its own." North Carolina's George Henry White, the only black representative in Congress, made a similar case, but both Congress and President William McKinley dismissed the appeal. McKinley remained silent the following year when a race riot in Wilmington, North Carolina, left dozens of black Americans dead or wounded. A black refugee from the city condemned the irony of race murders "while the nation was on its knees thanking God for having enabled it to break the Spanish yoke from the neck of Cuba."

The Brownsville Incident

Du Bois returned from the Pan-African Conference to an America where the political influence of black people was declining. Despite the development of the Afro-American Party (an embryonic race-based political party), Representative George White, completing his term in 1901, would be the last African American in Congress for more than three decades. With the Democrats outspokenly racist, many black voters halfheartedly cast their ballot for Republican incumbent McKinley. In 1901, McKinley's assassination put Vice President Theodore Roosevelt in the Oval Office. A Progressive New Yorker, Roosevelt sought Booker T. Washington's advice about African Americans. When the president crossed the color line, inviting Washington to dine at the White House, many black Americans dared to hope the federal government might again support black rights. In 1904, they helped reelect Roosevelt.

But two years later, the president dishonorably discharged the entire Twenty-fifth Infantry regiment, many of them recently returned from the Philippines. These black soldiers were stationed near Brownsville, Texas, where local white residents resented their presence. On August 14, some unidentified men fired dozens of shots, wounding several white residents. The presence of military rifle cartridges led federal investigators to blame black soldiers. Roosevelt dismissed the regiment with no trial and no possibility of appeal.

In Boston, black journalist William Monroe Trotter called the mass discharge "meanness, injustice, and unwarranted cruelty." Privately, Booker T. Washington also condemned it. "There is no law, human or divine," he told friends, "which justifies the punishment of an innocent man." But he refrained from public comment and discouraged followers from "going too far" in protesting.

Accommodation or Agitation?

The Brownsville incident provided a sharp reminder of African Americans' political powerlessness and of divisions within the black community. More and more black people refused to accept Washington's admonitions about "going too far." His passivity on Brownsville marked the beginning of the end of his singular influence among black people. Some of Washington's former admirers such as Terrell and Barnett now sought leaders who would openly condemn racism.

Until the Pan-African Conference, Du Bois and Washington had been allies, though they had disagreed about how to achieve racial progress. Washington's lack of response to Brownsville deepened their division. As the twentieth century dawned, black people faced a dilemma: Should they follow Washington's strategy, accommodating racial injustice and waiting patiently for white people to see them as worthy, or should they confront injustice head-on, agitating for immediate equality?

Opposition to Washington

"We have come to protest forever against being shut off from equal rights with other citizens, and shall remain forever on the firing line in defense of such rights," wrote Trotter in 1901. A proponent of direct resistance to racial injustice, the twenty-nine-year-old Trotter was in Boston producing the first issues of *The Guardian,* a news weekly focused on black political concerns. Occupying the building in which William Lloyd Garrison had launched the *Liberator* in 1831, Trotter, like Garrison, passionately advocated full and immediate equality for African Americans. The son of a Boston realtor, Trotter graduated from Harvard in 1895, where he met Du Bois. He shared the older man's disdain for Booker T. Washington's political patience and emphasis on vocational education. In *The Guardian,* Trotter criticized Washington's programs while promoting the immediate dismantling of segregation.

Though he admired Washington's accomplishments, Du Bois felt slave origins had narrowed the southern leader's vision. African Americans, Du Bois argued, should insist on immediate full inclusion in the society their labor had built. The small but vocal group of intellectuals who followed Du Bois and Trotter viewed Washington's accommodation strategy as shortsighted. Despite these criticisms, Washington continued to promote caution and patience. He and his followers worried that Du Bois and Trotter encouraged poor black Americans to pursue unrealistic goals. When Washington spoke in Boston in 1903, Trotter and others publicly challenged his conciliatory style. Washington had the hecklers arrested and encouraged his allies to withhold advertising from any newspaper that refused to endorse the more moderate Tuskegee approach. His loyal friend T. Thomas Fortune, editor of the *New York Age,* supported him.

Living daily among southerners scarred by slavery, Washington continued to focus on helping them acquire survival skills. By ingratiating himself to wealthy white philanthropists and villifying African Americans who stood in his way, he reaped results. Hundreds of southern black people from disadvantaged backgrounds benefited from education at the Tuskegee Institute. Demonstrating the value of Washington's strategy, they made a respected place for themselves in black communities. But to the minority of black Americans who followed Du Bois—most from privileged backgrounds—respect in the black communities was not enough. Far removed from black southerners, Trotter and Du Bois agitated for a world where black men and women did not have to compromise their dignity to make a living.

The rivalry between Washington and Du Bois dominated black discourse between 1900 and 1915. The year that Trotter heckled Washington, Du Bois published a collection of essays, *The Souls of Black Folk*, describing Washington as leading a "cult" with an ignorant, "unquestioning following." Du Bois conceded that Washington, "beginning with so little, has done so much." But his limited vision, argued Du Bois, which discouraged African Americans from seeking political power and publicly protesting injustice, perpetuated cowardice and passivity. Vocational education, Du Bois added, could make workers but it could not make men.

In *The Souls of Black Folk*, Du Bois argued that the color line stunted black Americans' "spiritual strivings." Capturing the dilemma of black people's divided loyalties, he described how the American Negro "ever feels his Twoness—an American, a Negro . . . two warring souls in one dark body whose dogged strength alone keeps it from being torn asunder." Du Bois dedicated himself to understanding and dignifying the "spiritual strivings" of African Americans—who he felt shared a special racial consciousness with the other "darker peoples of the world."

For Du Bois, black consciousness had a lyrical and almost religious quality. Born out of suffering and an African mysticism stretching back through centuries, black consciousness gave dark-skinned peoples a unique depth of soul. People of "Negro blood," he proclaimed, had a "message" of spirituality and high morality "for the world." Influenced by Darwinist ideas, he also suggested that a small minority of African Americans were socially and intellectually superior to the rest. The race should unite, he said, to develop "the Talented Tenth," who would "guide the Mass away from the contamination . . . of the Worst, in their own and other races." Du Bois later recanted this arrogant notion.

Chicago Democrat Julius Taylor, the black editor of the *Broad Axe*, felt Republican politics—with which Washington was allied—did not help African Americans gain the franchise or access to other than menial jobs. In 1899, he predicted that "the time is not far distant when Booker T. Washington will be repudiated as the leader of our race, for he believes that only mealy-mouthed Negroes like himself should be involved in politics."

Despite growing opposition, in 1905 Washington was among the most powerful men in America. A central operator among Republicans—often helping black workers secure service jobs in Republican homes and businesses—and a savvy strategist for black enterprise, he had secured the loyalty of rising urban black entrepreneurs (many of them Tuskegee graduates) by establishing the Negro Business League in 1900. Consulted by presidents and white capitalists, and supported by their charity, he affected the lives of thousands of black Americans, most of whom idolized him. Former slave Daniel Dowdy of Oklahoma City recalled, "He is the father of industrial education and you know that sho' is a great thing."

The Niagara Movement and the NAACP

Washington's stranglehold on black leadership prompted a backlash. In 1905, William Monroe Trotter, W. E. B. Du Bois, and Morehouse College president John Hope invited two dozen black leaders—mostly northerners—to meet at Niagara Falls in Ontario, Canada. There they formalized opposition to Washington's idea of gradual progress. Soon 400 strong, the Niagara Movement, as the group became known, agitated for federal legislation guaranteeing equal rights for black citizens.

Sensing the threat to his power, Washington tried to undermine the Niagara Movement by sending spies to meetings and warning that federal workers who supported Du Bois would lose their jobs. He also discouraged both black and white financiers from backing the movement. But a 1908 race riot in Springfield, Illinois—Abraham Lincoln's hometown—catalyzed support for the movement among influential white Progressives. White Kentucky-born socialist William E. Walling called for a national organization of "fair-minded whites and intelligent blacks" to speak out boldly against racial violence and injustice.

Heirs to the nineteenth-century abolitionist movement responded. In the spring of 1909, journalist Oswald Garrison Villard (grandson of William Lloyd Garrison) joined Walling and white Progressives, such as settlement house founder Jane Addams, to establish the National Negro Committee Conference. Washington refused their invitation, but Du Bois and John Hope attended as representatives of the Niagara Movement. Poet Alice Ruth Moore, Barnett, and Terrell were there too. The conferees called for government protection of Fourteenth Amendment rights and southern black voters, guarantees for African Americans' physical safety, and fair access to education. They also formally opposed Tuskegee's focus on industrial and manual training.

The committee met again in 1909 to establish the National Association for the Advancement of Colored People (NAACP). The organization flourished as more white Progressives joined, including *Harper's* editor William Dean Howells. Du Bois inaugurated the NAACP's magazine, *Crisis,* and remained its editor until 1934. The organization had a compelling mission: to ensure that African Americans be "physically free from peonage, mentally free from ignorance, politically free from disfranchisement, and socially free from insult." To accomplish this, it aimed to design test cases forcing the courts to dissolve racial segregation. Led by an interracial board of directors, the NAACP soon had fifty branches and more than 6,000 members. Washington declined to join. So did Ida Wells Barnett. Preferring to be out in the streets with working people, she found the NAACP's legalism too slow-moving.

A few black Americans sought a middle ground between Washington and Du Bois. One was John Hope, a cofounder of the Niagara Movement. Though he had witnessed racial violence and deprivation firsthand as a child, Hope's horizons were broadened by his education at Rhode Island's elite Brown University. In 1906, when he became the first black president of Morehouse College, he urged both vocational and liberal education. He inspired others who sought black unity. Buck Colbert Franklin, who studied at Morehouse, named his son John Hope Franklin in honor of the great educator. The grandson of a slave, Buck Franklin had grown up in Oklahoma and had Choctaw Indians in his extended family. After graduating from Morehouse, Franklin returned to Oklahoma and became a lawyer, seeking to repeal Oklahoma's grandfather clause. Though he lived in Rentiesville, an all-black town, he agitated against segregated schools.

Buck Franklin embodied the ideals of both Du Bois and Washington. Like Du Bois, he supported the NAACP. Like Washington, he was dedicated to hard work. Near the end of his life, he wrote in his autobiography: "At best, the road ahead for the American Negro is going to be rough, and there will be no way for the weak or timid to make it. Those with strength, with creative genius, potential, courage, faith and hope, will make it if they are willing to work hard. They must be clean and presentable, for outer cleanliness advertises inner cleanliness. If you live across the tracks and have something the other fellow needs, he will come to you for it."

Black Culture

"He was kind to all of us musicians that would just, as I say, 'flock' around him, 'cause he was an inspiration to us all. We always treated him as 'daddy' to the bunch of piano players." So Arthur Marshall remembered composer Scott Joplin. Marshall had studied with Joplin in the early 1890s, when Joplin was playing in Sedalia, Missouri, at the black Maple Leaf Club. Joplin also composed music, and in 1896 registered the copyright for his first musical score, "Crush Collision March." He called his music "rag" because of its "ragged rhythm." Joplin soon would be "daddy" to ragtime, a musical form that captured the imagination of both white and black Americans.

Black culture crossed the color line. International audiences had thrilled to performances of the Fisk Jubilee Singers in the 1870s. Penetrating the African interior, Europeans had been captivated by African sculpture. After Du Bois attributed a mystical spirituality to black Americans, many white intellectuals developed the romantic notion that the world's colored peoples were naturally artistic. White audiences also admired black athletic talent.

Black artistic and athletic ability were not new. What was new was white America's growing appreciation of black expression, especially when it blended with the familiar. Joplin's mixture of classical European music, complex African rhythms, and his own north Texas heritage proved an enticing combination.

Music, Poetry, Composition

The son of a free mother and an enslaved father, Scott Joplin determined to bring honor to his race. Encouraged by his mother to study piano with a

Black artists were supported by philanthropists like Sarah Breedlove "Madam C. J." Walker, America's first black female millionaire. One of twenty children in a Mississippi family, Walker established an international network of beauty parlors. Walker had a worldwide payroll of 5,000 black women by 1910, when she turned forty-three years old. When she died nine years later, she bequeathed most of her wealth to charity. She also left instructions that her company always be run by a woman.

German musician, he had a grounding in European music traditions as well as his mother's memories of southern black expression. He also studied music at a local college run by the Freedmen's Bureau and the Methodist Church. Shortly after publishing "Crush Collision March," Joplin published "Maple Leaf Rag," the composition that would make him "the king of ragtime composers," he told his friend Marshall. Joplin's prediction came true. By 1900, the thirty-two-year-old Joplin was the first black American to earn a living writing music.

Just as Joplin's music caught the nation's attention, so did the lyrical poetry of Paul Laurence Dunbar. Like Joplin, Dunbar had grown up hearing southern black rhythms in his mother's voice. Dunbar's mother encouraged her son to master the speech styles of white Americans as well as the sounds of black America. Also like Joplin, Dunbar never lost sight of a racial mission.

During high school, Dunbar submitted poems and essays to newspapers across the country. Several black papers printed his advice that black Americans should settle in the West. Frederick Douglass saw great promise in the young poet when he heard him read "Ode to Ethiopia," with its "pledge of faith unwavering" to "the Mother Race" of African Americans who "have the right to noble pride." Dunbar felt deeply honored when Douglass accepted the gift of a book and invited the poet to stay with him. "It would do me good to have you up there in my old study just working away on your poetry."

In his work, Dunbar embraced both patriotism and race pride. "A Columbian Ode," memorialized Christopher Columbus's voyage to America and proclaimed allegiance to the American flag. Dunbar's approach was simple: "Let the work have a message . . . a story to tell, a living man or woman to present, a lesson to deliver—clear, strong, and unmistakable." His popular *Lyrics of a Lowly Life* (1896), exemplified this poetic style that appealed both to unschooled audiences and sophisticated intellectuals.

Dunbar often expressed "self-doubts" about his work. He hoped "that there is something worthy in my writings and not merely the novelty of a black face associated with the power to rhyme." When *Harper's Weekly* editor William Dean Howells reviewed Dunbar's third book of poetry, *Majors and Minors,* in 1896, the young artist's success was assured. Howells did "not remember any English-speaking Negro" who was Dunbar's equal, comparing him to the venerated Scottish poet Robert Burns. "I have sometimes fancied that the Negro *thought* black and *felt* black, that they were racially so utterly alien and distinct from ourselves that there could never be common intellectual and emotional ground." But in Dunbar's writing, Howells found "white thinking and white feeling in a black man." He speculated that through art, others might discover that "God hath made of one blood all nations of men." From then on, Dunbar's readings and royalties made him the first black American to support himself with a literary career.

Dunbar never lost sight of his modest beginnings, and his writing celebrated both slave dialect and formal European writing styles. In an 1895 letter to the black poet Moore (whom he married three years later), he asked "whether or not you believe in preserving by Afro-American—I don't like the word—writers those quaint old tales and songs of our fathers . . . or whether you, like so many others think we should ignore the past and all its . . . literary materials." Dunbar walked a fine line between preserving his ancestors' expressiveness and making them a laughingstock. His writing celebrated a variety of black and white leaders, including the Haitian revolutionary Toussaint L'Ouverture and the black New England poet Phillis Wheatley, and white heroes like President Theodore Roosevelt and Robert Gould Shaw, the Civil War commander of the Fifty-fourth Massachusetts.

When Dunbar died in 1906, the black bicycle racer Major Taylor voiced the impact of the poet's success: "I am thinking seriously of taking up this work where poor Paul Laurence Dunbar had to leave off." Taylor himself had achieved international fame as an athlete. Yet inspired by Dunbar, he dreamed of becoming a poet.

Thanks to Dunbar's literary trailblazing, other black artists began finding appreciative audiences. In 1900, James Weldon Johnson and his brother J. Rosamond Johnson became the first black songwriters on Broadway. Many of their so-called coon songs mocked black and foreign characters. Unlike Dunbar, they seemed to care little whether art expressed dignity or had a "message." The popular black press believed that any successful black performer was an inspiration to the race, but also grew critical of black dialect and the degrading "coon songs." In the late 1890s, several journals defined a new mission for black music. Best-known was the *Negro Music Journal,* started by pianist J. Hillary Taylor. Published in Washington, DC, the *Journal* extolled music's power to teach young musicians "how to be industrious, studious, patient, benevolent, loving, unselfish, and refined."

Sports

By the time Tuskegee organized the first black intercollegiate track meet in 1893, competitive sports had become a vital part of black life. Some African Americans were introduced to sports as seasonal workers in fashionable white vacation spots like Atlantic City, New Jersey; Saratoga, New York; and Newport, Rhode Island. In spare time spent in the shadow of America's most luxurious playgrounds, they used the facilities during off-hours to practice baseball, tennis, golf, or horsemanship.

Baseball afforded the biggest sports opportunity. Until 1887, white baseball teams sometimes had black players. But that year, when the Chicago White Stockings refused to play a New Jersey team with a black team member, black athletes were prohibited from the major leagues. By 1900, the Colored Baseball Leagues emerged, with professional teams in Chicago, New York, Philadelphia, and Norfolk, Virginia. On these teams, baseball greats like Spottswood Poles—known as "the black Ty Cobb"—made their careers. Poles batted .440 for New York's Lincoln Giants in 1911.

Some athletes broke the color line in sports. By 1896, Major Taylor had bested some of the world's finest white cyclists. A founding member of the Colored Wheelman's Association, he was a favorite with black and white spectators. In 1902, given a hero's sendoff by Booker T. Washington and a crowd of Tuskegee students, Taylor went to compete in Sydney, Australia, where he emerged victorious. Returning home, he eventually retired to a black community in New England, opened a bike repair shop, and devoted his time to his church.

Other sports figures overestimated the level of acceptance black athletes could expect from white fans. One example was professional boxer Jack Johnson, who won more than five dozen fights between 1897 and 1910. Johnson beat white champion Tommy Burns in 1908, and in 1910 he defeated the "Great White Hope" Jim Jeffries, whom many white Americans had hoped would secure the championship on behalf of the white race. Thumbing his nose at white America, Johnson married a white woman in 1911, and when she died, another white woman. This time he was convicted of a federal violation: transporting a woman across state lines for "immoral" purposes. He escaped imprisonment only by leaving the United States. After losing his title in Cuba in 1915, he returned to America in 1920 and served his one-year sentence. Feeling betrayed by what they called Johnson's "shenanigans" with white women, many black Americans no longer found him glamorous.

Closed out of mainstream America, black artists and athletes developed their talent anyway. Sometimes, when their dreams complemented white

Americans' values, black heroes like Joplin, Dunbar, and Taylor enjoyed a moment of fame that transcended the color line. At other times, as with Jack Johnson, they paid dearly.

Black Progress

"How can the multiplication of Negro mechanics help to solve the so-called race problem, when those who are already skilled cannot obtain employment?" Speaking in Nashville in 1899, AME minister Charles S. Smith bluntly assessed the dire economic prospects of black Americans. He challenged the Tuskegee philosophy of encouraging industrial and agricultural skills. "When . . . was it written that the universal position of the Negro should be that of a tiller of the soil?" Observing that "the acquisition of scientific agriculture cannot possibly profit the masses of the Negroes to any great extent, seeing that they are not the owners of the soil," Smith also criticized Booker T. Washington's insistence that black people stay in the South. Smith deplored Washington's provincialism, and felt that if the Tuskegee leader would travel to "Europe, West and southwest Africa, South America, and the Caribbean, . . . he may find some of his view modified." Smith contended that as long as more than three-quarters of all black people worked someone else's land, their economic prospects remained grim.

Many black Americans were illiterate; they could neither read Dunbar's poems nor comprehend the views of black intellectuals. Instead, "plain negro

As the Fugitive Slave Act had done in 1850, the Plessy decision reinforced some black Americans' inclination to move to Canada. In 1899, 52-year-old Mattie Mayers, inspired by a promotional advertisement, gathered up her ten children and her husband, Joseph, and left Oklahoma. Having moved multiple times since the Emancipation Proclamation, she lived at several places in Canada before acquiring a farm near Edmonton, Alberta. She lived there until 1953, when she died at age 104.

men and women, not any better or whiter than other American negroes," as planter Isaiah Montgomery described them, made their way as best they could. Texas's 500,000 black residents typified the lot of "plain American negroes." More than half were farmers, but only one-third of those farmers owned their land. Fewer than 200 of the state's black residents engaged in professional careers such as medicine or businesses like barbering or blacksmithing. In 1910, Dallas had two black female dentists, Austin had a black female physician, and Galveston had a woman-run private black hospital. Yet few black women held skilled jobs. More than half of the black women in Texas worked in agriculture. Another third labored in domestic or laundry services. Black men in Texas made their way as lumberers, dockworkers, or cowboys, or, after oil was discovered in 1900, they went to work in the oil fields. A few signed on with the railroad as Pullman porters or cooks. But none of these occupations was secure. Across America, black Americans believed that by improving their social and economic environment, they could brighten their political and financial prospects. In this they were aligned with Progressive ideas. But Progressives and American society generally also saw African Americans as a problem—the "Negro Problem."

Harlem and the Urban League

In New York, Philip A. Payton sought to raise the quality of housing for black families. His Afro-American Realty Company, formed in 1904, acquired five-year leases on luxurious new brownstones in Harlem, on Manhattan Island in New York City, for which the builders had not found white buyers. Payton rented the brownstones to black tenants, then purchased other rental properties nearby. By sharing housing, extended families and groups of friends were able to afford the desirable location. By 1915, about 50,000 black people lived in more than a thousand buildings in Harlem's twenty-three square blocks. By 1930, the population had risen to 200,000.

Black institutions followed. The NAACP moved its national office to Harlem by 1915. T. Thomas Fortune relocated his *New York Age* to the neighborhood. Black churches bought property, and social service agencies set up their offices there. Indeed, Harlem became known as the place where African Americans could expect a warm welcome, where they were not a problem. It was a magnet for black Americans of every class.

One of the most enduring improvement organizations spawned by Harlem's dramatic growth was the National Urban League. In contrast to the NAACP, which focused on court battles, the Urban League tackled issues of working-class city life, from negotiations with police and public officials to mediation with employers or landlords to neighborhood organizing.

Like the NACW and the Negro Business League, the Urban League started out as a national organization linking local community centers. One center affiliated with the Urban League was the White Rose Mission, a settlement house that offered services to newcomers similar to those white Progressive women provided for European immigrants, including temporary housing, child care, and job counseling. White Rose founder Victoria Earle Matthews, inspired by the idea of "lifting" her race, believed that "the Afro-American woman . . . deserves . . . active sympathy and cooperation." Poet Alice Ruth Moore taught evening classes at White Rose, adding a cultural component to the mission's programs.

Other cities offered similar services. In Philadelphia, an interracial coalition organized the Armstrong Association. Lugenia Burns Hope, wife of educator John Hope, helped establish the Atlanta Neighborhood Union, with nurseries, playgrounds, and a tuberculosis care center. Chicago's Negro Fellowship League, started by Barnett, helped southern newcomers adjust to city life. All these enterprises came under the National Urban League umbrella.

The National Urban League was the most overtly political of early twentieth-century organizations. It encouraged black urbanites to vote, join unions, and petition local governments for equal services. Like the NAACP, the Urban League received some support from liberal white Progressives. But there was an important distinction between the NAACP and the Urban League. Strongest in northern cities, the NAACP was dominated by educated and sophisticated men and women, often of mixed race and usually from families that had long been free. While its political agenda included black people of all classes, its membership and social gatherings often did not. By contrast, the Urban League reached out to a broad spectrum of black city-dwellers, welcoming uneducated newcomers. By 1915, the League was also gathering annual statistics on housing and employment among black urbanites—a tradition it continues today.

Churches and Clubs

In all the urban places where black people clustered, black churches connected them. A network of more than 6,000 AME churches stretched from Atlanta to Seattle, San Francisco to Boston. Baptist and Methodist churches also flourished, their membership exceeding the AME's by the early twentieth century. Congregations in northern and western cities enabled black migrants to preserve connections to the South, linked through families and friends in "sister churches."

Black churches had a bold social mission as well. They were places where people could learn to read and write or to feed families. They served as recreation centers, voting information centers, employment agencies, and savings and loans institutions. Incubators of black talent, they sponsored Sunday schools and sports teams and encouraged orators, writers, singers, and athletes. Churches helped send black youth to college and supported entrepreneurship. When Texan Richard Henry Boyd in 1897 established the National Baptist Publishing Board to publish religious literature for black people, local churches supported him. In 1907, black churches inaugurated the Associated Correspondents of Race Newspapers (ACRN) to provide accurate information to black newspapers across the country. Soon to become the National

Afro-American Press Association, members included Fortune of the *New York Age* and Robert Sengstacke Abbott, whose weekly Chicago *Defender* soon reached a circulation of 250,000. Black churches also fortified racial pride by placing ads in *Crisis* for "the Negro doll," designed by Nashville's National Negro Doll Company. Dominated by "plain American Negroes," black churches spent little time debating the merits of various black strategies. Members were loyal to the Republican Party and to Booker T. Washington, and they raised spirits with Bible study and song.

The Progressive spirit also gave rise to college fraternities and sororities. Alpha Phi Alpha, the nation's first black fraternity, began at Cornell University in 1906 when Robert Ogle and seven other black students, refused entry to the library, formed a study group. In 1911, Kappa Alpha Psi followed at Indiana University. Within the next few years, fraternities Omega Psi Phi and Phi Beta Sigma and sororities Alpha Kappa Alpha and Delta Sigma Theta were founded at Howard University. As they fanned out across the country, black alumni used these connections to cement business partnerships and social networks.

TABLE 13.1 BLACK ORGANIZATIONS FOR PROGRESS, 1895–1915

During the Progressive era, many black organizations defined new directions for the future of African Americans. Overcoming the isolation of slavery that had made for slow social and economic progress, black Americans created united communities. Ten of the more influential organizations are listed below.

ORGANI-ZATION	FOUNDING	PUBLICA-TION	AUDIENCES	TARGETED STRATEGY
National Association of Colored Women (NACW)	1895: Ida Wells Barnett; Mary Church Terrell; Fannie Barrier Williams; Rosetta Douglass Sprague.	*The Woman's Era*	Local black women's clubs	Establish kindergartens, childcare centers, and women's educational facilities, to "lift as we climb."
American Negro Academy	1897: Alexander Crummel; W. E. B. Du Bois; Paul Laurence Dunbar.		African American intellectuals	Promote study, conferences, and publications of African Americans' scholarly work.
Negro Business League	1900: Booker T. Washington.	*Negro Business League Herald*	African American entrepreneurs	Personal contact from Washington or his agents to encourage networking.
National Association for the	1909: Niagara Movement members	*Crisis*	Northern and Midwestern urban black	Challenge segregation in franchise and

Advancement of Colored People (NAACP)	W. E. B. Du Bois, William Monroe Trotter, John Hope; white Progressives Jane Addams, Joel Spingarn, Mary White Ovington.		middle class; white liberals	public services through court cases and appeals to public conscience.
Negro National Press Association	1909: T. Thomas Fortune; William S. Pittman; Robert S. Abbott; Robert L. Vann.		Black journalists around the world	Circulate accurate information among black newspapers.
National Urban League	1910: Victoria Earle Matthews; Lugenia Burns Hope.	*Opportunity*	Working-class people in northern and southern cities	Support black public and private efforts for economic justice.
Negro Historical Society of Research	1911: Arthur Schomburg; W. E. B. Du Bois; Alain Locke; Carter G. Woodson.		Black intellectuals around the world	Collect and disseminate information to raise black solidarity and self-esteem.
Akim Trading Company	1911: Chief Alfred Sam.	*African Pioneer*	"The best Negro farmers and mechanics"	Procure land in West Africa and establish reciprocal trade with black Americans.
Universal Negro Improvement Association (UNIA)	1914: Jamaican Marcus Garvey.	*The Negro World*	Urban and rural poor in the United States, South America, the Caribbean, and Africa	Create a separate international black economy, creating "a universal confraternity."
Association for the Study of Negro Life and History (ASNLH)	1915: Carter G. Woodson.	*Journal of Negro History*	Black and white academics	Encourage and publish historical research.

Churches and schools aimed to instill pride in black youngsters. In segregated schools, for example, black teachers celebrated revolutionaries like Crispus Attucks and Toussaint L'Ouverture. By the 1920s, students would sing "Lift Every Voice and Sing," an inspiring anthem, composed by James Weldon and J. Rosamond Johnson, that honored black Americans' struggles and triumphs. Thousands of black youths developed black consciousness at segregated Young Men's and Young Women's Christian Associations (YMCA and YWCA), which served as much-needed recreation centers.

New Charismatic Leaders

Of all the urban places where organizations sought to better the lives of black Americans, none was more vibrant than Harlem. The neighborhood brimmed with creative black people. Among them was newcomer A. Philip Randolph, the Florida-born graduate of the Cookman Institute in Daytona Beach. Arriving in New York in 1911 at age twenty-two, Randolph intended to become an actor. But then he became aware of the plight of black workers, now increasingly excluded from labor unions except for the revolutionary Industrial Workers of the World (IWW), which welcomed wage workers "no matter what your color." So Randolph diverted his attention from acting to labor organizing. Studying and teaching economics at City College and at the Rand School of Economics, he became convinced that the U.S. economy needed overhauling—but not overthrowing. His marriage to wealthy widow Lucille Green, a partner in Madam C. J. Walker's beauty business, gave him the means to pursue his interests. Developing an interest in socialism, Randolph studied politics and labor organizing, and built a small but dedicated following by 1915.

Another charismatic Harlem newcomer was "Chief" Alfred Charles Sam, "the self-styled Moses of the colored race." A Ghanaian who had studied at African missionary schools, Sam founded the Akim Trading Company on the premise that "the civilised Negro is responsible to develop Africa." He hoped to promote trade between Africans and African Americans while expanding Christianity in Africa. Sam bought land in Britain's Gold Coast colony to trade in mahogany and rubber and purchased the steamship *Liberia* to settle African Americans there.

By 1914, the Akim Trading Company had recruited black farmers, businesspeople, and professionals through nearly 200 emigration clubs in Oklahoma and Texas. Despite arrest and a federal investigation for mail fraud, Sam launched an excursion to the Gold Coast. Ultimately epidemics decimated the settlers there, and Sam's mysterious disappearance ended the venture. But a few settlers remained in Africa, helping plant Western ideas in established African towns. Like similar back-to-Africa movements, Sam's dream foundered on lack of funds and over-reliance on a charismatic leader.

Other black visionaries congregated in Harlem. In the spring of 1911, a small informal group known as the Men's Sunday Club created the Negro Historical Society of Research. Members included established intellectuals like W.E.B. Du Bois, Harvard-educated Carter G. Woodson, and young men like Alain Locke, the first black Rhodes scholar. To raise black Americans' appreciation for their heritage, Woodson established the Association for the Study of Negro Life and History (ASNLH) four years later, and soon began publishing the *Journal of Negro History,* which celebrated the achievements of black Americans. In these efforts, Woodson received encouragement from his friend Jesse Edward Moorland, who had a large library of books, manuscripts, graphics, and newspaper clippings on black heritage. "The achievements of the Negro properly set forth," Woodson said, "will crown him as a factor in early human progress and a maker of modern civilization." Similar groups were launched in other cities. Philadelphia's American Negro Historical Society claimed that "no country can tell its history truthfully until all its scrolls are unrolled."

An important founding member of the Men's Sunday Club was book collector Arthur Schomburg. The child of Puerto Rican immigrants who had settled in Harlem, Schomburg developed an interest in black history when a fifth-grade teacher told him that black people had no past, no heroes, no great moments. Determined to prove otherwise, he began gathering literary and artistic works by people of African descent, developing contacts with collectors in other cities. Schomburg enjoyed the company of his intellectual colleagues, but he distrusted white people and preferred the company of the black working class.

Schomburg and other lay historians were enthusiastic about the work of Jamaican black nationalist Marcus Garvey. Though many intellectuals considered Garvey brash and overbearing, Schomburg eagerly read Garvey's writing in the London-based *Africa Times and Orient Review*. He admired Garvey's focus on Toussaint L'Ouverture and on the writings of Edward Blyden, a former teacher and missionary in Liberia.

Schomburg became an ardent supporter when Garvey established his Universal Negro Improvement Association of Jamaica in 1914. This organization promoted socially and economically separate American black communities with an orientation toward Africa. Schomburg admired Garvey's focus on working class issues. For Schomburg, "Negro improvement" applied to both middle-class and poor black people.

The "New Abolition"

In response to race riots in 1915, the Chicago *Defender* counseled its black readership, "If you must die, take at least one with you." This cry of rage, which got the paper banned in many cities, rose from the frustration that underlay black struggles for progress. Black leaders saw their choices limited to emigration, separate communities within the United States, agitation for full civil and political rights, or accommodation of white supremacy. W. E. B. Du Bois chose agitation, using the *Crisis* to protest disfranchisement and racial violence. In 1912, he and the NAACP began to receive assistance from white New York intellectual Joel E. Spingarn. A man of enormous energies, Spingarn inaugurated what he called "the New Abolition"—a movement calling for an end to racial segregation and for full and immediate equality for African Americans. Two years earlier, the impulsive Spingarn had purchased the Heart of Hope Club, a suburban New York service organization for destitute black people. Seeking advice about how to manage it, he had written to Du Bois, initiating a lifelong partnership. Now, crisscrossing the country on "New Abolition" tours, Spingarn spoke before 70,000 people in two dozen cities, where his efforts helped establish an NAACP presence. Spingarn also got NAACP literature distributed to white campuses and civic organizations. "There is no such thing as a 'Negro problem,'" Spingarn insisted. "It is an American problem, for while injustice exists, the whole country is in danger."

On "New Abolition" tours, Spingarn and Du Bois reminded Americans of the deterioration of black rights. In 1911, Baltimore had been the first city to mandate segregated neighborhoods, pushing the *Plessy* decision and Progressive ideas about social management to new levels. Fears of race-mixing led northern states such as New York, Massachusetts, and Michigan to consider laws against interracial marriage and the forced sterilization of white people who "tainted" white "blood" by mating with inferior races. Spingarn cited the continuing horror of lynchings—such as the burning alive of a black man in Coatesville, Pennsylvania, in 1911. "All we ask is absolutely fair treatment among men regardless of color."

The NAACP Legal Assault

Spingarn contended that if legal obstacles were removed, black Americans could be part of mainstream America, and he cited NAACP successes. NAACP cases had enabled black student Carrie Lee to petition for a room in Smith College's dormitories, helped a black boy gain admittance to New York's Central Preparatory School, successfully challenged housing discrimination in Louisville, Kentucky, and desegregated a New York theater. In *Guinn* v. *United States* (1915), the Supreme Court outlawed Oklahoma's grandfather clause.

But Spingarn and the NAACP also met defeats. The NAACP could not overturn President Woodrow Wilson's 1913 order mandating segregation in federal employment facilities. It had failed to persuade the National Board of Censorship to ban *Birth of a Nation* (1914), a movie that depicted the Ku Klux Klan as heroes and black Americans as brutes. Showing the film in the White House, Wilson praised it as "history written with lightning."

Although most black leaders reluctantly supported Republican candidates, Du Bois had backed Wilson in 1912, believing he would protect black rights. Trotter also supported Wilson, though he was cynical about national politics. Before Wilson's inauguration, he wrote, "The clouds are lowering and a feeling of foreboding is creeping over the Colored people." In 1914, Trotter met with Wilson to protest racial segregation in federal offices. "Two years ago you were thought to be a second Lincoln," Trotter admonished the president. "Have you a New Freedom for white Americans and a new slavery for 'your Afro-American fellow citizens'? God forbid."

The End of Booker T. Washington and Accommodation

Though more and more black men and women disagreed with him, Booker T. Washington continued to promote accommodation and to believe that fulfilling white America's expectations offered African Americans their best hope for physical safety and economic success. Then, in November 1915, he collapsed during a speaking tour in New York. A man of provincial tastes—he seldom left the South and was uninterested in African heritage—Washington asked to be taken home. "I was born in the South," he said, "I have lived and laboured in the South, and I expect to be buried in the South." He died at Tuskegee a few days later.

After Washington's death, it was revealed that the man who had promoted accommodation also had harbored a white-hot rage at racial injustice. He had secretly contributed to efforts challenging grandfather clauses. He had quietly met with industrialists to improve conditions for black train travelers and had donated money for court battles against segregation and disfranchisement. He had even written an essay stating that segregation was "unjust" and "embitters the Negro and harms the moral fiber of the white man." In a telling comment, Washington said, "That the Negro does not express this constant sense of wrong is no proof that he does not feel it."

With Washington's death, the day of the docile, accommodating colored person drew to a close. Increasing numbers of Negroes—who now insisted on a capitalized *N*—would soon confront injustice head-on.

The Amenia Conference

At this juncture Du Bois set out to ease the tension between those who sought an immediate end to segregation and racial injustice and those who counseled patience and accommodation. With white reformer Joel Spingarn he hosted a meeting at Spingarn's summer estate near Amenia, New York. Tuskegee sent Emmett J. Scott, and when the meeting opened in August 1916, there were many NAACP supporters and old allies of Washington.

An upbeat mood infused the conference. Delegates drafted a statement affirming both liberal and industrial education for young black people. The statement recognized the "peculiar difficulties" of black southerners who supported Washington's philosophy of pursuing economic progress but postponing the goal of integration to avoid incurring the wrath of white southerners. The delegates ended by pledging to support African Americans in any plan that sought racial progress.

Trotter chose not to attend the conference but felt cheered by its outcome. "In this celebration the big chiefs buried the hatchet and smoked together the pipe of Peace," he wrote in *The Guardian*. Predicting that black leaders, "with a united front and unbroken ranks," would "turn to renew the warfare against race discrimination, segregation, and lynching," he concluded, "This is the spring-time of the race's hopes in America."

Conclusion

During the Progressive era, the first generation of African Americans born after emancipation reached adulthood. They hoped to erase the color line and to choose how and where they would live and how they would be identified— colored, Afro-American, negro, Negro. Through government and military service, economic endeavors and artistic pursuits, community building and protest, the men and women of this new generation sought to educate their children and gain white Americans' respect. Though they faced daunting challenges, new black leaders and everyday African Americans built churches, organizations, and publications dedicated to progress and improvement. While Booker T. Washington urged restraint as he sent forth thousands of Tuskegee graduates trained in manual skills, Du Bois called for immediate full political and legal equality. But a few successes in the courts and a new dignity in the name *Negro* were not enough to offset the blow dealt by Plessy's legal defeat. Jim Crow restrictions increased everywhere.

In the coming decades, as thousands of black Americans left the South, the organizations and ideas born in the Progressive era gained momentum. The NAACP would chip away at legal restrictions. Organizations like the NACW, Urban League, YWCA, and YMCA would help a growing minority of black Americans climb painstakingly into the American middle class—even while the great majority still barely eked out an existence. But the big gains for African Americans in the years after 1915 would come with the development of black culture and arts romanticizing ancient Africa in a rebirth—a renaissance—of black poetry, fiction, and music.

Questions for Review and Reflection

1. The Progressives of the early twentieth century manifested ambivalent and contradictory attitudes toward America's "race question." Explore some of the elements of that ambivalence.

2. To what extent did "Pan-Africanism" capture the issues facing black Americans in the Progressive Era?

3. Booker T. Washington and other black leaders disagreed about what would constitute racial progress. What was there about black constituencies that made it difficult to unite on one strategy?

4. What qualities did Progressive-Era black leaders have in common?

CHAPTER 14

The Making of a "New Negro": World War I to the Great Depression

Thomas Edward Jones to the European Front

In June 1918, First Lieutenant Thomas Edward Jones crossed the Atlantic Ocean to serve as an American soldier in France. The previous year, the United States had entered Europe's Great War to support Britain and France against Germany and Austria. Struck by the magnitude of what lay ahead, Jones began keeping a diary. "Day clear and cool. Saw my first whale after many days of watching," he wrote on June 21. Fearing German submarine attacks, soldiers slept in life preservers, and Jones quoted the black poet Paul Laurence Dunbar to describe the anxiety: It felt as if they were sleeping with "one eye shet [shut] and one eye open." Assigned to medical duty in the infirmary, Jones reported a night with "about 30 cases of acute gastritis, cause undetermined, Both white and colored."

A child of slaves, Jones had left the South and earned a medical degree at Howard University in 1912, becoming one of 3,000 licensed black physicians in the United States. But his rural southern experience, education, and his ocean crossing could not prepare him for what he experienced during World War I: a warm welcome by the French people, the horror of trench warfare, and the vicious racism of white American comrades-in-arms. Arriving in France in June 1918, Jones found the "French people extremely courteous," and he enjoyed

Chronology

1915	In this single year, more than 1.5 million African Americans leave the rural South for war industry jobs.
1917	United States enters World War I. Marcus Garvey incorporates his Universal Negro Improvement Association (UNIA). *Buchanan* v. *Warley* outlaws residential segregation. Emmett Scott becomes advisor to the U.S. War Department.
1918	Leonidas Dyer introduces bill to make lynching a federal crime. Armistice ends fighting on the Western Front.
1919	President Woodrow Wilson proposes a League of Nations to promote international cooperation. Urban race riots across the nation underscore the depth of America's racial divisions. Garvey establishes the Black Star shipping line to promote world-wide commerce among black people. In *State* v. *Young,* the West Virginia Supreme Court rules that courts cannot exclude black jurors. With "If We Must Die," the Jamaican-born poet Claude McKay promotes art-as-protest.
1920	Republican Warren G. Harding is elected president. Nineteenth Amendment grants suffrage to black and white women. One-third of the U.S. black population lives in cities.
1921	A race riot in Tulsa, Oklahoma, levels the black neighborhood.
1922	Garvey is indicted for mail fraud.
1923	Harding dies; Calvin Coolidge becomes president.
1925	A. Philip Randolph organizes the Brotherhood of Sleeping Car Porters. With NAACP help, Chicago doctor Ossian Sweet convinces courts of his right to defend his home against white attackers.
1926	Carter Woodson inaugurates Negro History Week.
1927	President Coolidge pardons and deports Garvey. In *Nixon* v. *Herndon,* the U.S. Supreme Court overturns laws excluding African Americans from primary elections.
1928	Herbert Hoover is elected president.
1929	The stock market crashes.
1930	Half of America's black population lives in cities.

dinners at a "swell hotel." With a degree of freedom he had never experienced before, he visited a French mineral-water spa and used his medical skills to treat a white baby.

Jones's diary entries took on a more ominous tone beginning on August 21, 1918. That day, he wrote, he was "busy preparing to leave for the trenches" in the critical battle zone of the Argonne Forest. Until October 4, when his all-black 368th Infantry "left Argonne forest . . . cold, hungry and weary," Jones's notes were brief and grim. "Took our positions in line at Argonne . . . quite a few casualties due to . . . shells"—including Jones's own shell wound. The mission was reported as failed, and his unit was labeled as cowards. Later investigations, however, uncovered the 368th's bravery in the Argonne Forest mission, and the cowardice of their white officers. The unit was commended, and Jones was rewarded with a promotion, the French *Croix de Guerre* (France's highest military honor), and the American Distinguished Service Cross. He also returned home with a lifelong friendship with an Italian-American soldier whose life he saved.

Often American racism followed black troops abroad. Though they shared the battlefield with white soldiers, black soldiers were relegated to segregated regiments and their white comrades-in-arms constantly reminded them of the meaning of race in America. Jones recalled one white "captain who called our boys God Damned Niggers."

Though Jones's background was similar in some ways to that of his fellow soldiers, he had unique experiences as well. At age nineteen, having graduated from Lynchburg High School in Virginia, he moved to Washington, DC, where he supported himself with odd jobs. He joined the volunteer National Guard and worked his way up to first lieutenant. Twenty years older than the typical soldier, Jones was almost thirty-seven in 1917 when the United States declared war on Germany. After the Argonne Forest Campaign, he earned a promotion to captain, becoming one of a few dozen black soldiers in World War I decorated for bravery.

Returning to America, Jones joined the staff of Freedmen's Hospital, the federal black hospital in Washington, DC. There his war record, professional accomplishments, and participation in the local National Association for the Advancement of Colored People (NAACP) eventually brought him to the attention of the White House. Secretary of State Harold Ickes appointed Jones to head the hospital in 1939. But despite this recognition, Jones remained acutely aware of the persistent mistrust white Americans felt toward black people.

This chapter examines how World War I and its aftermath reshaped black Americans' lives. On the front lines, black soldiers encountered the horrors of war while facing racism from white soldiers. On the home front, the war accelerated African Americans' exodus from the rural South to northern and southern cities, where they found plentiful jobs because of the booming war industry.

The postwar era saw the growth of a large and influential black movement. Charismatic Jamaican immigrant Marcus Garvey encouraged black people to build an economy separate from that of white Americans. His message appealed to poor and working-class black people, many of whom used his ideas to build their own confidence, pride, and economic self-sufficiency.

The Harlem Renaissance, a flowering of black artistic expression nourished by black entrepreneurs, artists, writers, and intellectuals, reverberated in black neighborhoods across the nation. Harlem also nurtured black musical innovations such as ragtime and jazz—new styles all Americans embraced.

"Over there" . . . and Back Here

"On account of our meeting, the Negro race was more united and more ready to meet the problems of the world than it could possibly have been without these beautiful days of understanding." Thus W. E. B. Du Bois recalled the 1916 Amenia Conference that brought together his supporters and those of Booker T. Washington. But with the United States' entry into the world war a year later, black unity fractured.

Black Americans and World War I

While European nations had been embroiled in war since 1914, U.S. president Woodrow Wilson had struggled to keep America neutral. But in April 1917, spurred by German attacks on U.S. shipping, the United States declared war on Germany. As in the Spanish-American War, African Americans were divided over how to respond to their country's military call. While a new popular song celebrated American participation in the war "over there," many black people were wary. They questioned whether black men should join segregated units and fight overseas to make the world "safe for democracy" when they did not have full political and social rights at home.

Du Bois supported the NAACP's position that patriotism should come first. "Let us, while this war lasts," he wrote in the *Crisis,* "forget our special

In this painting, artist Alan Werner uses photographic images and impressionistic symbols to capture defining aspects of Thomas Jones's life: his graduation from Howard University, his military uniform with its Distinguished Service Cross and Buffalo Soldier insignia, his installation by Eleanor Roosevelt as medical director of Freedmen's Hospital in 1939. The backdrop of this painting depicts the farm Jones purchased in Maryland. As a resident of Washington, DC, he was disenfranchised; in Maryland, he could—and did—vote.

grievances and close our ranks shoulder to shoulder with our own white fellow citizens and the allied nations fighting for democracy." He hoped African Americans' military service abroad would win them respect and legal equality at home. Others opposed sending black soldiers overseas. In the *Guardian*, William Monroe Trotter urged black Americans to boycott the military until it agreed to integrated units and black officers. "As this nation goes forth to fight the 'natural foe of liberty,' let Americans highly resolve that all shall have liberty within her borders," he insisted. Eventually, Du Bois came to share Trotter's view.

More than 400,000 black volunteers and draftees joined the army, constituting 20 percent of America's military force. But their hopes for respect soon dissolved. Even as the first black servicemen landed in France in the summer of 1917, dozens of Twenty-fourth Infantry soldiers in Texas were court-martialed and sentenced to death for disobeying Houston's Jim Crow laws. Stung by the irony that the Twenty-fourth Infantry had served with distinction during the Spanish-American War, Howard University professor Kelly Miller lashed out at Wilson: "The Negro, Mr. President, in this emergency, will stand by you and the Nation. Will you and the Nation stand by the Negro?"

Secretary of War Baker took steps to raise black troops' morale, establishing training for black officers and recruiting Tuskegee's Emmett J. Scott as a "confidential advisor" to the War Department on issues regarding black troops. However, racial tensions mounted among troops in Europe. The problem had several sources. First, some black regiments drew criticism because poor training hurt their performance. Second, white officers in charge of black units often ridiculed their own troops. Third, military leaders could not always impose strict segregation in troop transport and housing, and name-calling and practical jokes were the result. Indeed, First Lieutenant Thomas Jones reported open hostility between black and white soldiers aboard the ship that conveyed his unit to and from Europe. Finally, unreliable supply lines meant delays that further damaged troop morale.

The experience of three all-black units in France—the 368th, 369th, and 371st—illustrates some of the frustrations black soldiers faced. The 368th and 371st arrived first, and set a high standard. Secretary of War Baker praised the 369th Infantry as the best all-round regiment sent to France. This unit later won the French *Croix de Guerre*, for helping capture a railroad junction in the fall of 1918. Throughout the Great War, the 369th never lost a foot of ground and never had a man captured. The unit included baseball hero Spottswood Poles, who is credited with planning exhibition games that introduced baseball to France. The 371st Infantry also served with distinction, capturing German prisoners and shooting down several German airplanes near Verdun. Its white commander, Southerner William Hayward, reported that his men "never flinched or showed the least sign of fear. They will go down in history as brave soldiers." Admiring the men's discipline and dedication, U.S. general John J. Pershing declared, "I cannot and will not discriminate against these soldiers."

By the time Jones and the 368th Infantry reached France in June 1918, however, discrimination toward black soldiers was the norm. Field officers as well as officials back in Washington did not want black soldiers to grow accustomed to the level of respect and authority they received abroad. Despite the praise for the 369th and 371st, orders came down that no black man would be promoted above the rank of captain. Scott's protests were in vain. As officer vacancies opened in black units, they were filled with white men. By August 18, when Jones's unit—the 368th—hunkered down in the trenches, the black officer staff had dwindled by more than 30 percent.

Reports pouring into the United States rarely emphasized black soldiers' successes. After two weeks in battle, fifty deaths, and several hundred more casualties, the 368th was labeled cowardly and summarily recalled from the Argonne campaign. Commanders far from the front had deemed its mission a failure. But Scott pressed for an investigation; the 368th's bravery came to light. It had captured a crucial German stronghold and pushed the battle line six miles into enemy territory, even as two white officers fled and a nearby white unit broke ranks. Convinced by the evidence, the investigators recommended the unit for commendation, not punishment. In January 1919, the 368th Infantry was awarded the Distinguished Service Cross, America's second-highest military honor, as well as the prestigious French Croix de Guerre. As part of what Jones described as "a gala day" of celebration, the troops were "decorated with flowers by ladies."

After the war in Europe ended with an armistice signed on November 11, 1918, black soldiers returning home often got a hero's welcome. Crowds of black and white spectators turned out to cheer them in New York, Cincinnati, and St. Louis. When Jones, now promoted to captain, entered Washington's Asbury Methodist Church, the congregation rose and sang "Praise God from Whom All Blessings Flow." In New York, the jazz band of the black Fifteenth Regiment, playing for the victory parade, received so enthusiastic a response that it cut twenty-four records the next spring. Both war and jazz helped gain respect for black Americans at home.

Despite honoring black war heroes, white America was not yet ready to embrace racial equality. Victory celebrations ended, and American race relations resumed their prewar tension. Across the nation, white mobs rioted against black veterans and civilians. In Crisis, Du Bois summarized black soldiers' frustration: "We return. We return from fighting. We return fighting. Make way for Democracy." Jamaican Claude McKay, soon one of the nation's best-known black poets, advised black people to resist: "If we must die, let it not be like hogs/Hunted and penned in an inglorious spot," he began one poem. "Like men we'll face the murderous, cowardly pack/Pressed to the wall, dying, but fighting back!"

The Great Migration

Arriving in Philadelphia by 1916, Hughsey Childs was part of a group that decided to "name a church after Morris Chapel in Greenwood [South Carolina]." Typical of the black migrants streaming out of the South to northern cities after

1915, he intended to stay connected to southern family and friends. He was joined by George Bailey, described as "a very ambitious man [who] opened his first community market [in 1916], and by 1922, he was the second Negro member of the Frankford Grocers' Association." Bailey married a Greenwood woman, and together they made his store the news center linking black Philadelphians and South Carolina relatives. In 1916, an article in the AME *Christian Recorder* described such newcomers as "vigorous, active, ambitious men and women . . . [who] will equal the best we've got here; for all of us are immigrants."

Southern migrants came for economic opportunity, but many also felt they were running for their lives. One New Orleans resident said he came north to escape "the lynchman's noose and the torchman's fire." A black newspaper predicted African American immigrants would "suffer in the North. Some of them will die . . . [but] any place would be paradise compared with [the danger in] some sections of the South."

Even before the United States entered World War I, African Americans had begun migrating. But the black exodus accelerated during the 1920s, in what historians call the Great Migration. By 1930, half of black Americans had left the southern countryside. During the first phase of the Great Migration, between 1900 and 1915, most migrants simply moved from the South's rural areas to its cities. Depleted soil, and the boll weevil that destroyed cotton crops, displaced farmers, who sought new livelihoods in the railroad, furniture, and metal industries of such places as Atlanta, Birmingham, and San Antonio.

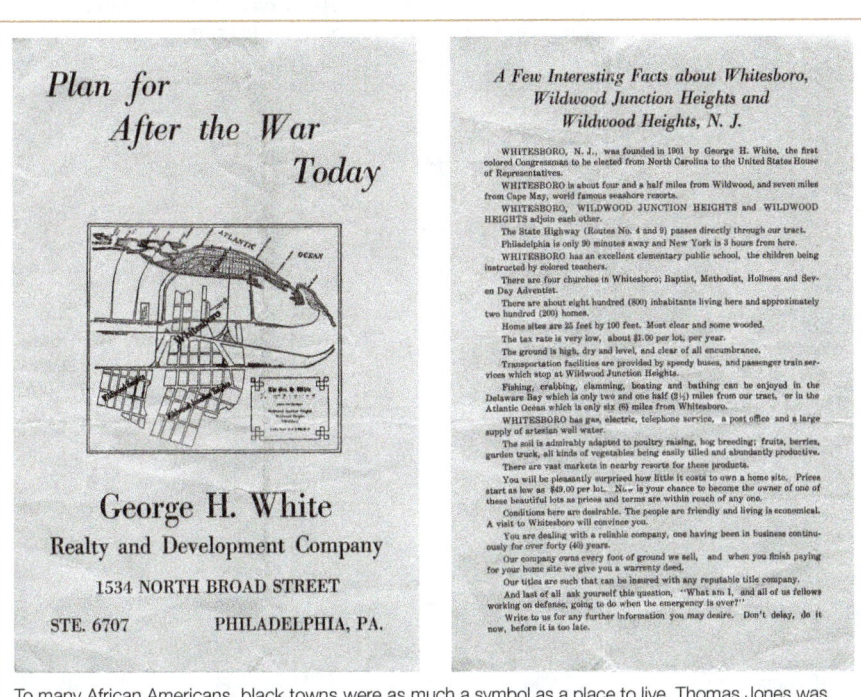

To many African Americans, black towns were as much a symbol as a place to live. Thomas Jones was one of dozens of black people who bought property in towns like Whitesboro. Yet he never lived in this tiny outpost, which remained a black town into the 1950s.

When the war began in Europe, northern U.S. factories stepped up production of ammunition, food, and textiles to aid Britain and France. To meet increased demand for labor, these factories recruited black workers from the South who, because of their limited employment opportunities, would accept lower wages than would white people. Typically, a small group (or just one person) moved to a town easily accessible by rail or river. When they found jobs, friends and family joined them. This second phase of the Great Migration created whole urban neighborhoods, complete with family, church, or friends, from a particular community in the South.

Between World War I and 1930, an estimated two million black people left the South. Some headed for border states such as Missouri and Illinois. Others traveled farther north or west. Still others formed separate black communities in far-flung sections of the United States or even abroad. Large cities, such as Chicago, Detroit, New York, Washington, and Los Angeles, together absorbed more than 800,000 black newcomers in this period.

TABLE 14.1 BLACK AMERICANS MOVE TO THE CITIES, 1910 AND 1930

By 1930, Chicago, New York, and Philadelphia were America's "black" cities, with the highest number of black residents. In some northern cities, the African American population grew by more than 300 percent, increasing both the number and the proportion of black residents. The southern urban black population also increased somewhat.

	1910		1930	
	BLACK POPULATION	PERCENT OF TOTAL POPULATION	BLACK POPULATION	PERCENT OF TOTAL POPULATION
Chicago	44,000	2	234,000	6
New York (Manhattan)	61,000	2	225,000	11
Philadelphia	84,000	5	220,000	11
Baltimore	85,000	15	142,000	17.6
Washington, DC	94,000	28	132,000	27
New Orleans	89,000	26	130,000	28
Detroit	6,000	1	120,000	7
Atlanta	52,000	33	90,000	32
Los Angeles	15,500	2.6	38,900	3
Denver	6,000	2	7,200	2.5
San Francisco	2,400	4.7	3,800	6
Seattle	2,894	9	3,300	9

Race Riots and Revival of the Klan

Wherever African Americans moved, racial hatred followed. In cities outside the South, black workers found jobs at factories, railroads, and docks—but they also bore the brunt of resentment and competition from poor white people also desperate for work. Often the tensions between the two groups turned violent. For example, in the summer of 1916, white workers on strike at the Aluminum Ore Company in St. Louis, Missouri, attacked black workers who had come to fill vacant jobs. Similar antagonisms sparked a four-day riot across the Mississippi River in East St. Louis. A Missouri senator reported that "over 100 Negroes were mangled or beaten to various degrees of help-lessness." But President Wilson, who viewed racial separation as the best way to manage American society, refused to meet with a delegation of riot refugees. With the Great Migration, black Americans found the old white atti-tudes of discrimination and intimidation traveled with them to their new urban homes.

Throughout the nation, people died in street confrontations. A 1921 upris-ing in Tulsa, Oklahoma, where oil drilling had attracted a large black commu-nity, was one of the worst. A policeman accused a black man of assaulting a white woman and threw him in jail. Young Buck Franklin witnessed the sub-sequent rioting. A group of black veterans, he recalled, "fired up the crowd by telling . . . how they spent nights in foxholes and how winning a battle [depended on good] strategy." Incited by these men who had fought for democ-racy abroad, several people barricaded the courthouse to protect the prisoner from a gathering lynch mob. Franklin and hundreds of others were arrested. Released from jail several days later, Franklin found his neighborhood a smok-ing ruin. The accused attacker was ultimately found innocent, but more than fifty black people had perished in the riots. Upwards of a thousand residents of Greenwood, Tulsa's black neighborhood, suffered property losses their insur-ance companies refused to reimburse. Appeals to President Warren Harding went unanswered.

Threats of lynching accompanied riots. On the decline since Ida Wells Barnett's 1890s campaign, lynching picked up again during the first years of the Great Migration. Fifty-eight black people lost their lives to lynch mobs in 1916—most in the South, but a few in the North. In 1919, more than seventy people perished, some in military uniform. Wives warned husbands and parents cau-tioned sons about traveling alone. Every family knew of men who had myste-riously disappeared, only to be found drowned, hanged, or beaten. Black women or girls considered "uppity" (disrespectful to white people) risked rape by white men as well as lynching.

Horrified by the violence, Missouri congressman Leonidas Dyer introduced a bill in 1918 to make lynching a federal crime. The NAACP lobbied in support of the Dyer Bill, but few in Congress were interested. Though President Wilson eventually denounced lynchers as "betrayers" of democracy, the Dyer Bill was never passed. Only rising outrage and increasingly strict neighborhood segre-gation produced a decrease in lynching in subsequent decades.

In 1915, the dormant Ku Klux Klan came alive again. The organization continued to target African Americans, but now it also attacked Jews, Catholics, and dark-skinned immigrants from eastern and southern Europe. Its terrorist tactics spread quickly across the nation. With three million members nationwide by the mid-1920s, the Klan had units in northern and western cities such as Pittsburgh, Los Angeles, and Seattle. Klan members held political office in Denver, Colorado, and Portland, Oregon. The organization flourished particularly in the Midwest, where white and black southern refugees concentrated in towns along the Mississippi River. From Indianapolis, home to at least 12,000 members, the Klan published its newsweekly, *The Fiery Cross*. The publication touted the group's conviction that darkness (and dark-skinned people) signified sin, and that nonwhite residents should leave the United States.

Eugenics—the old Progressive notion that racial characteristics indicated intellectual and social worth—added fuel to the Klan's revival. In 1920, the Government Printing Office published *Defects Found in Drafted Men,* describing physical dimensions and markings gathered when the Surgeon General's staff examined military recruits. The study legitimized the Klan by attributing negative meanings to the physical characteristics of black and immigrant men. "Swarthy skin" and "slanty eyes" were among the descriptions used to label those whom eugenicists considered prone to drunkenness and crime. These ideas circulated widely through the white population.

Black Americans and the Red Scare

Though interracial violence peaked in the summer of 1919, most white Americans remembered the violence as aimed at "Reds" rather than at black people. In 1917, a revolution in Russia overthrew the government and established a communist or "Red" regime (named for the color of the revolutionaries' flag). Promising equality to the dispossessed and an intention to unite the workers of the world in a new political and economic order, the revolutionaries abolished private property and established collective ownership of fields and factories. They aimed to end capitalism, unequal profits, and labor exploitation. Worried that low-paid U.S. workers would be ripe targets for revolutionary organizers, Attorney General A. Mitchell Palmer stirred up a "Red Scare" against political radicals in the United States, urging citizens to ostracize those suspected of harboring revolutionary ideas. In the summer of 1919, in violation of constitutional rights, federal agents kicked down doors and barged into homes and offices, intimidating and arresting thousands of citizens and deporting hundreds of noncitizens. Prejudice against outsiders hardened into public policies. Believing the United States should maintain the dominance of white Protestant people, Congress limited the numbers of immigrants from places other than northern Europe.

Black Americans were similarly suspect and oppressed. The Justice Department launched an investigation of *Crisis* and other black periodicals, seeking evidence of disloyalty to the United States. A few African Americans did read radical publications and support communist programs. Indeed, A. Philip

Randolph, who established a New York Socialist club in 1917, held "capitalism the cause of lynching." Randolph was convinced racism would persist until black and white workers achieved economic equality. He and his wife, Lucille, repeatedly—and unsuccessfully— ran for political office on a Socialist Party ticket.

Frustrated with exclusive white unions, in 1925 Randolph organized the Brotherhood of Sleeping Car Porters (BSCP) with a membership of black men who carried baggage, made beds, and served meals on sleeping-car trains. A few white unions, including the International Ladies Garment Workers' Union (ILGWU) and the longshoremen's unions, began to open up to black workers. Though racial discrimination—such as refusal to protest unequal pay—sometimes crept into union policies, membership in these organizations did bring benefits. In particular, union members gained increased wage protection and a sense of dignity for themselves and their families. In many unions, the members embraced the communist belief that socioeconomic differences posed a far greater problem than racial differences did. However, these radical views attracted only a minority of black Americans.

The Challenge of Garveyism

"We never heard one syllable from the lips of Woodrow Wilson, touching anything relative to the destinies of the Negroes of America or England or of the world," Marcus Garvey told a Baltimore audience in 1918. He was reminding listeners that the president's concern for the self-determination of oppressed minorities in Europe did not extend to American Negroes. The dynamic young Jamaican had already published political tracts and organized laborers in Central America, the Caribbean, and England. Now he spoke out to white America and challenged African Americans with a bold new program of racial unity: the Universal Negro Improvement Association (UNIA).

Admiring Booker T. Washington's book *Up From Slavery*, Garvey had written to the Tuskegee leader about establishing an industrial school in his native Jamaica. After Washington's death, he contacted Washington's successor, Robert Russa Moton, and visited Tuskegee in the spring of 1916 to learn more about its manual skills curriculum and to outline his own schemes "for the advancement of my people." Garvey next traveled north to Harlem. Du Bois announced in *Crisis:* "Mr. Marcus Garvey, founder and president of the Universal Negro Improvement Association of Jamaica, is now on a visit to America." Finding a welcoming audience in the United States, Garvey extended his tour.

At first, Du Bois promoted Garvey's fund-raising, but soon a bitter rivalry divided the two men. Garvey envisioned separate black nations in many locales across the world. If geographic separation were not possible, black people should at least maintain racially separate and independent economic and social institutions. Du Bois, in contrast, wanted to gain equal access for black Americans within America's existing economic, political, and social framework. Though both men advocated Pan-Africanism—the idea that people of African heritage from around the world should unite—they had different ideas about achieving it. Garvey's bold programs—so popular that even Garvey was astonished—challenged traditional black leaders and their black intellectual followers by appealing to poor black people, desperate for a ray of hope.

The Universal Negro Improvement Association

Bustling with black-owned businesses serving nearly 200,000 black residents, Harlem was the ideal place for Garvey to recruit. But Harlem was only the beginning. By 1917, Garvey had publicized his separate-economy plan in thirty-eight states. African American newcomers to northern cities responded enthusiastically to his call for racial separation. One observer described Garvey as a powerful speaker who could "throw his voice around three corners." Crowds as large as 100,000, by some estimates, heard him describe the East St. Louis riots as evidence of a "conspiracy" to exterminate black people. (The idea of genocide conspiracies resurfaced in black protests for decades to come.)

At the end of 1917, Garvey set aside his plan to establish an industrial training school in Jamaica and moved his headquarters to Harlem. He incorporated the UNIA as an umbrella encompassing economic, philosophical, social, and even religious enterprises. His weekly newspaper, *The Negro World,* had an international circulation that eventually topped 200,000. With English, Spanish, and French editions, it became the world's most widely circulated paper devoted to black issues.

"The Universal Negro Improvement Association advocates the unity and blending of all Negroes into one strong, healthy race," the organization proclaimed. Its program combined the Urban League's goals of decent jobs and housing with the entrepreneurial spirit of Booker T. Washington's Negro Business League. Garvey's message also contained a religious element. Redefining Christianity to make God black and the Devil white, he used religion to reinforce race pride. Promoting self-help and self-reliance, he chastised those who would "depend upon the other races for a kindly and sympathetic consideration of their needs, without making the effort to do for themselves."

The UNIA gained power both from its goals (autonomy for black peoples) and its methods (appeals to ordinary people who felt excluded by black intellectual organizations). Garvey aimed to attract the masses and to inspire them to self-discipline and united action. He solicited donations from black people, promising jobs and returns on investments. Through investments and contributions from some of the poorest African Americans, the UNIA soon controlled assets worth hundreds of thousands of dollars in dozens of cities. By 1925, the organization claimed 6 million members in 900 branches across the United States, Central and South America, Britain, and West and South Africa. Black people around the world recognized the UNIA—and Garvey.

Marcus Garvey hired James Van Der Zee, Harlem's premier black photographer, to create an extensive portfolio promoting the UNIA's activities. Van Der Zee took many photographs like this one, which captures the Garveyites' power to dominate a neighborhood. Week after week, thousands of listeners poured into the streets to hear Garvey speak. Garvey organized parades of men and women who wound through the streets on foot, on horseback, or in motorcades, dressed in military-style uniforms or the white garb of the Black Cross nurses. For Garvey, the martial dress and parading conveyed the message that "we Negroes have fought and died enough for white people; the time has come to fight and die for ourselves."

"Negro Nation"

Styling himself as heir to the Tuskegee tradition, Garvey frequently quoted Washington and adapted Washington's challenge for the UNIA letterhead: "Up, you mighty race!" Using the same rhetoric of racial superiority voiced by eugenicists, he told black veterans of World War I: "It was you, the superman, that brought back victory." Like the eugenicists, Garvey advocated racial separatism to promote the "purity of the Negro race and the purity of the white race." Committed to racial pride, he refused to take advertisements in *The Negro World* for the hair straighteners and skin bleachers that sustained most black publications. The UNIA, Garvey bragged, did not need such help to shape "men and women who are able to create, to originate and improve, and thus make an independent racial contribution to the world." Consistent with the mood of his day, he opposed "rich blacks marrying poor whites" and "rich or poor whites taking advantage of Negro women."

Setting a goal of "Negro producers, Negro distributors, Negro consumers," Garvey conceived this "Negro nation" as a global political and economic network. In 1919, he incorporated the Black Star Line, a commercial shipping operation headquartered in Harlem, to develop trade with African nations. By 1924, the company had grown into the Black Cross Navigation and Trading Company, which transported emigrants to Africa and promoted international commerce. Under the Negro Factories Corporation, Garvey turned out uniforms for the UNIA's recruiters and its Black Cross Nurses. A thriving laundry kept two delivery trucks busy. Next came black doll factories, Caribbean grocery stores, restaurants and a hotel, tailoring shops, and a printer that served most of Harlem. The UNIA also acquired property in Philadelphia, Chicago, Pittsburgh, Detroit, and other locations around the world. By 1920, it had more than 300 employees, and plans to set up a bank. In short, Garvey exhorted "Negroes [to] get busy building a nation of your own" and to place "race *first* in all parts of the world."

Pan-Africanism

Garvey had an ambitious plan to "plant the banner of freedom on the battle plains of Africa." Claiming he was called to "redeem Africa," he designated himself "Provisional President of the African Republic" and imagined a bold transformation of the entire African continent: "Steamships must be bought and built. . . . In Liberia railroads must be built. Industrial plants must go up."

While sharing Garvey's commitment to making Africa a central component in black American identity, Du Bois denounced Garvey's arrogant self-promotion as "Provisional President." "Africa belongs to the Africans," Du Bois said. "They have not the slightest intention of giving it up to foreigners, white or black. Liberia is not going to allow American Negroes to assume control and direct her government. Liberia . . . is for Liberians."

Nevertheless, inspired by plans for a League of Nations that had emerged from the Versailles Peace Conference after World War I, Du Bois organized the Second Pan-African Congress in 1919. Delegates from fifteen countries, meeting in Paris, proposed that an international committee assume control of Germany's African colonies and an international code of laws protect all peoples from imperialism. Subsequent Pan-African congresses, contesting treaty arrangements that gave Germany's African colonies to European war victors, called for "the development of Africa for the Africans and not merely for the profit of Europeans." Though Garvey did petition the League of Nations for African independence, he and his followers did not support Du Bois's wider call for the independence of colonized peoples across the world. Garvey's Africa-centered plan had more followers than Du Bois's Pan-African agenda.

Garvey's Decline

Garvey was not above collaborating with his adversaries if he believed black people might gain by it. Even while threatening to "whip" the Ku Klux Klan, for example, he conspired with white segregationists to plan for separate black colonies. In his most outrageous move, Garvey met with Klan leader Edward Young Clarke to seek Clarke's aid in establishing African colonies. Describing this 1922 meeting in Atlanta, Garvey reported, "I was speaking to a man who was brutally a white man, and I was speaking to him as a man who was brutally a Negro." As both men advocated racial purity and a ban on interracial marriage, Clarke promised Garvey economic support. But such tactics helped precipitate Garvey's downfall, as some UNIA members resisted taking racist money.

At the same time, white authorities were becoming alarmed by Garvey's defiant posture and economic power. As early as 1917, federal immigration officials began watching Garvey, seeking an excuse to deport him. By 1919, they worried that "a doctrine of [independence] of the Negro, for the Negro" might incite revolution among "those elements of our population that have a just cause of complaint." They studied Garvey's speeches, tracked his travels, and solicited complaints from disgruntled investors in the Black Star Line.

Following Garvey's meeting with Clarke, outraged black leaders and the black press joined white America's campaign against the charismatic Jamaican. Du Bois mocked Garvey as "a little fat black man, ugly but with intelligent eyes and a big head." The Urban League's newspaper, *Opportunity,* called Garvey's financial programs "a gigantic swindle." One-time Garvey admirer A. Philip Randolph now sought "to drive Garvey and Garveyism in all its sinister viciousness from the American soil."

At first, Garvey dismissed critics with a victor's bravado, denouncing them as "big Negroes . . . doctors and lawyers and other professionals . . . [who] feel they are not part of the other negroes . . . and who call themselves 'aristocrats' and 'gentlemen.'" Taunting the NAACP, Garvey reported he had "visited some of the so-called negro leaders, only to discover that they had no program, but were mere opportunists living off their so-called leadership while the poor people were groping in the dark." He bragged about his influence over people he termed "the small negroes."

But even as Garvey's belligerence was uniting his white and black enemies, his influence among the black masses also began declining. Few believed the permanent segregation of the races that he called for would bring them economic progress. Then, in 1922, the U.S. government convicted Garvey of mail fraud. He spent five years in jail before President Calvin Coolidge pardoned him, on the condition that he leave the country. Small pockets of UNIA members remained for many decades, holding property and promoting segregationist programs. But they were only vestiges of the largest and most powerful mass movement of black Americans the nation would see until the mid-century civil rights movement.

The NAACP and the Urban League in the 1920s

Garvey's meteoric rise temporarily stalled the momentum of other black organizations. The NAACP's experience offers an apt example. Its membership peaked in

1920, with 300 branches and 50,000 members in the United States and abroad. But by the time writer James Weldon Johnson was named the NAACP's executive secretary in 1921—the first black man to hold this position—the UNIA boasted a far larger membership. Some NAACP supporters were turning away from political involvement. Retired bicycle racing star Major Taylor, for example—who regularly read *Crisis* and was a friend of Du Bois—was focusing, instead, on day-to-day affairs, including his local Baptist church, his bike and auto repair shop, and his daughter. By 1930, NAACP membership had shrunk to about 30,000. Meetings were sparsely attended, and the organization struggled financially.

Nevertheless, the NAACP had imaginative and committed workers, like the biracial, blond, blue-eyed Walter White, who infiltrated white supremacist groups and whose reports Du Bois summarized in the *Crisis*. More significantly, the organization continued its legal assault on segregation and discrimination. Chipping away at segregated courts, schools, and neighborhoods, it sought to make racial exclusion so morally reprehensible and expensive that white Americans would abandon the policy. In its first decade, NAACP lawyers had won rulings against residential segregation in Kentucky and Chicago (*Buchanan* v. *Warley*, 1917) and against all-white juries (*State* v. *Young*, 1919). In 1923, in *Moore* v. *Dempsey*, it won protection of the right to a fair hearing in a courtroom. In 1927, in *Nixon* v. *Herndon*, the courts upheld the right of African Americans to participate in election primaries.

Drawing on the talents of white counsel and dedicated black lawyers like Tulsa's Buck Franklin and Howard University Law School dean Charles Houston (a World War I veteran of the 368th Infantry) the NAACP sought equal pay for black schoolteachers and janitors and equal access to state colleges and graduate schools. It also inaugurated what became a decades-long campaign for integrated neighborhoods. Houston insisted that only concerted and consistent legal pressure would dismantle restrictive covenants—private agreements among homeowners not to sell to so-called unacceptable buyers. In one California case, the NAACP successfully kept Booker T. Washington, Jr., from having his home sold out from under him.

The NAACP also stepped in to help when, across the nation, white people used violence to keep black Americans out of their neighborhoods. When black physician Ossian Sweet moved into a white Detroit neighborhood, a mob attacked his home. A shot from Sweet's house killed one of the attackers, and Sweet was indicted for murder. In 1925, his NAACP legal team, including white lawyer Clarence Darrow, convinced a local judge that the Sweet family had acted in self-defense. But the NAACP also suffered numerous legal defeats. Over and over, the courts declared themselves powerless to prevent private citizens from blocking home sales to black people.

Serving poor city-dwellers, the Urban League also saw a decline in membership during the 1920s. By the time the U.S. economy slumped in 1930, the number of cities with Urban League offices dropped from twenty-seven to sixteen. With limited means, the organization could not attract strong leadership. Nevertheless, it kept providing social services, including day nurseries, employment and housing assistance, dental clinics, and home economics courses. It also gave financial support to black social work students.

New Beginnings in the City

"The number of the day was often some combination of the last three digits in the Dow Jones," said Otis Mack. The elderly black man recalled numbers running in America's era of illegal gambling. With so many doors closed to legitimate economic advancement, Mack chose crime over low-paid factory work. Born Theodore Roosevelt McCluskey, he changed his name to Otis Mack when he escaped the Klan in Georgia and made a new life in southern Ohio, where he found employment in the steel mills. But dreaming of making more money, Mack teamed up with the white gambling network in Cincinnati and Dayton. He collected cash from black men and women who placed bets in the illicit lottery system, took his cut, and delivered the rest to white gangsters (known as "bankers") in Youngstown, Ohio. He then returned any winnings to his clients. With money in his pocket and a reputation for integrity, Mack gained the respect of his family and community.

Most urban migrants did not choose a life of crime, but Mack's story illustrates the types of opportunities black Americans grasped in their impatience to make a better life. It also exemplifies black people's transition to a cash economy. With the relative abundance of urban jobs in the 1920s, black workers were no longer trapped in the perpetual debt and barter typical in rural areas. In the cities, black workers who earned cash wages could set their own spending priorities.

Increasingly, black people lived in cities. In the South, the proportion of African Americans living in cities rose from less than 25 percent in 1920 to almost 33 percent by 1930. Yet even as the black South became urbanized, the North outpaced it. More than 80 percent of black residents of the North, Midwest, and West became urban—with men and women migrating in equal numbers. White Americans moved to the cities as well, but black migrants came faster, and in larger numbers. Whereas in 1920 only one-third of the nation's black population lived in cities (compared to more than half of the white population), by 1930 almost half was urban, while the white urban population increased only slightly.

In the postwar years, the black migration to Chicago outpaced the flow to East Coast cities. New York had recently replaced Washington, DC, as the northern black urban center. Now Chicago eclipsed Harlem. Still, large numbers of black people also headed for New York, Washington, Cleveland, Detroit, Pittsburgh, or Philadelphia, where employers in industries ranging from oil refining to auto manufacturing sought their labor. In smaller numbers, black migrants also set out for western cities—Denver, San Francisco, Los Angeles, Seattle, and Portland—where mining or livestock-handling jobs beckoned.

A Rising Standard of Living

Working for wages in cities, African American women and men enjoyed the freedom afforded by a cash income. Service workers in hotels, excursion boats, and laundries who now joined the cash economy could choose whether to spend more on housing and less on food, or vice versa. Or they could decide to share housing and thereby reduce costs enough to have their children attend school instead of working. Black drivers, gardeners, maids, and nannies who increasingly replaced white immigrant domestic workers also had this freedom of choice. Women outnumbered men in such service work, but some also made significant progress in fields such as nursing, social work, and teaching. Black women also outnumbered white women in the workforce, constituting more than half the 120,000 women working in industry in 1920. The federal government continued to provide jobs as mail carriers and civil service workers. Railroads also offered steady employment for thousands of black porters, janitors, and cooks. By 1920, the census reported that almost one-third of the country's 110,000 dockworkers were black.

The rising standard of living inspired feelings of optimism and black unity. In 1921, James Weldon Johnson of the NAACP republished a poem calling on black Americans to "lift every voice and sing" and to proclaim "the harmony of liberty." Set to music by his brother, songwriter J. Rosamond Johnson, the work was quickly adopted as the "Negro National Anthem." Children in black schools across the country sang it every morning, and still do so today.

Segregated Neighborhoods

As black Americans migrated to the cities, upper-class white Americans fled to the suburbs, where they walled themselves off from black people. Increasingly clustered into black neighborhoods, many African Americans had little contact with white people. The occasional white visitor in a black neighborhood—such as Thomas Jones's Italian-American war buddy—encountered curiosity and apprehension among black passersby.

Thus segregation became more entrenched, making it difficult for most black and white Americans to imagine the humanity of the other race. Though black people were everywhere—driving limousines, preparing food, or tending children—they became "invisible," as African American author Ralph Ellison later phrased it. Most white Americans saw African Americans not as mothers, sons, or daughters with social networks and personal ambitions; they saw black people only as service providers and as beings somewhat less than human. The black theologian Howard Thurman reported how a white child had clobbered him with a board while assuring him "this doesn't hurt you." Even the black athletes, jazz enthusiasts, and intellectuals who were visible to Americans were generally seen as one-dimensional performers rather than as full human beings.

Black homeownership rose steadily in every region, reaching an average of 25 to 30 percent of the urban black population. However, in contrast to white neighborhoods, which were becoming segregated by class, religion, or ethnicity, black neighborhoods saw middle-class and lower-class families living side by side. The spacious and well-kept brownstone or brick houses of black lawyers, doctors, teachers, journalists, and ministers intermingled with the more modest and crowded homes of laborers and domestic workers.

Some well-off black families enjoyed a comfortable lifestyle. Children read widely, studied piano or ballet, and prepared for college. Bridge clubs, tennis tournaments, and museums and lectures occupied adults' leisure time. These families might be members of the NAACP or serve on the governing board of the local YMCA, YWCA, or Urban League. Summer vacations in resort areas or Europe expanded their horizons. From a young age, children in well-heeled black families were groomed for leadership. Adults sought their opinions during dinner conversations about current events. They also encouraged youngsters to treat adults as equals, often by addressing family friends by first names (sometimes preceded by "Aunt" or "Uncle") or by professional titles. The use of "sir" and "ma'am" was discouraged, as it evoked memories of slavery. Children were told to "look people in the eye and speak up" in conversation with anyone, black or white. Well-off black parents also reminded their children that privilege obliged them to advocate for their race.

Though they shared neighborhoods with middle-class African Americans, working-class black urbanites lived very different lives. Residences often housed several generations of family or boarders. Children played in the street and seldom advanced past high school. Most women worked as factory laborers, seamstresses, or domestics—sometimes in the homes of their better-off black neighbors. More often than in wealthy families, women raised children alone and children worked to supplement family income. Working-class people more often spent leisure time picnicking or playing sports rather than reading. They were more likely to be members of the UNIA or the Urban League than of the NAACP. Many also relied on the social services provided by the local Ys or the Urban League.

As in the rural South, urban working-class children grew up under watchful eyes of aunts and grandparents, family and friends, learning to respect and accept discipline from a wide network of adults who looked out for them. Drawing on southern traditions, working-class parents taught children to cherish and respect their elders and teachers, to address them as "Mr. Jay" or "Miss Lisa," and to call them "sir" or "ma'am." Children learned to show deference to those in authority by casting their eyes down and refraining from talking back.

When working-class black children succeeded in school or completed high school or college, the whole neighborhood rejoiced. Girls often received special encouragement. For example, a brother might forego his own education to put his sister through teachers' college so she could avoid the risk of sexual exploitation that came with many domestic-service jobs. After graduation, many of these newly minted teachers married the uneducated manual laborers who had made the same sacrifice for *their* sisters. Such successes in the North enabled a great many people to send money to family members remaining in the South.

Most black urbanites had a "church home." Working-class families, often at home in Baptist or AME congregations, found Bible teaching, church suppers, and excursions a welcome respite from the week's labors. Well-off black Americans attended primarily Episcopal, Presbyterian, or Catholic churches. For most wealthy black churchgoers, the churches were not the major center of social life or leadership for their members, although their ministers often devoted time to black progress organizations such as the NAACP.

The Harlem Renaissance and the "New Negro"

"Until recently," wrote black Rhodes scholar Alain Locke, "except for occasional discoveries of isolated talent, the main stream of [black literary] development has run in the special channels of 'race literature.'" But now, he continued, "we are presenting the New Negro in a national and even international scope, establishing new contacts, founding new centers, finding a new soul." A Philadelphia-born Harvard PhD, Locke observed that until the 1920s, "the Negro has been more of a formula than a human being." The "formula" created by white Americans stereotyped black people as childlike, incapable of subtle or creative thought, and dependent on white people. In a cultural movement that became known as the Harlem Renaissance, black artists and writers sought a new black identity—self-defined by African Americans.

Locke's book, *The New Negro* (1925), aimed to show that the suffering African Americans endured during slavery had fostered nobility in the black race. He wanted black Americans to use this nobility to shape a rich new creative expression—that of the New Negro—that would speak to and for *all* Americans.

Locke concluded that black arts had been energized by "a new vision of opportunity, of social and economic freedom. Harlem, he said, was "the first concentration in history of so many diverse elements of Negro life. It has attracted the African, the West Indian, the Negro American; the Negro of the North, and of the South; from the city and from the town and village; the peasant, the student, the business man, the professional man, artist, poet, musician, adventurer and worker, preacher and criminal, exploiter and social outcast. . . . [T]heir greatest experience has been the finding of one another. The pulse of the Negro world has begun to beat in Harlem."

The Negro Genius

Benjamin Brawley's book *The Negro Genius* (1925) outlined his conviction that the New Negro genius, while drawing on African inspiration, was also uniquely American. "We emphasize no connection between primitive African art and that of the Negro in America to-day. An individual sculptor may receive some inspiration from a piece of African carving, but that would not say that his own culture was basically African." At the same time, however, Brawley echoed the prevailing view that race conferred certain personal characteristics. He declared that "the temperament of the American Negro is primarily lyrical, imaginative, subjective; and his genius has most frequently sought expression in some of the arts." Brawley was sure that "the blacks are the singers and the seers."

Many creative African Americans sought to boost black people's confidence in their ability to wrest nobility from adversity. In poems such as "If We Must Die," Claude McKay advised black Americans to fight racism. As much political theorist as artist, McKay wrote both poetry and fiction inspired by Harlem and by his travels abroad. His novel, *Home to Harlem* (1928), celebrated urban black communities, and his experiences in Russia and France informed his poems. Charles Waddell Chesnutt, who for three

Photographer and jazz musician James Van Der Zee retouched negatives to achieve special effects, and he posed subjects with painted landscapes, furnishings, animals, flowers, or poetry. Sometimes he achieved drama by hand-coloring prints or speckling negatives. Starting out as a darkroom assistant in a New York City department store in 1914, Van Der Zee opened his own Harlem studio the following year and earned a handsome living from it as well as from his music. This photograph of a gathering place for well-to-do women in a beauty salon reflects the continuing reverence for the cosmetic company millionaire Madam C. J. Walker.

decades had published fiction exploring interracial friendship and love, received the NAACP's 1928 Spingarn Medal for his "pioneer work as a literary artist depicting the life and struggle of Americans of Negro descent." Novelist Jean Toomer embarked on a spiritual quest that took him through Protestantism, Quakerism, and non-Western expressions of spirituality before he settled on Catholicism. In 1928 he published the novel *Cane,* which explored a man's search for racial identity. Like other black intellectuals of his day, Toomer—the grandson of Reconstruction Mississippi senator P. B. S. Pinchback—helped define the New Negro as a person in the process of proud self-definition.

Langston Hughes

In 1921, nineteen-year-old James Mercer Langston Hughes, a student at New York City's Columbia University, was transfixed by black New York, recalling, "I didn't want to do anything but live in Harlem." Like many African Americans, Hughes was fascinated by what he called the "great dark city." In Harlem, Hughes experienced connections within his own heritage that stretched from Africa through America, from North to South, from city to town and village. In Hughes's veins flowed many streams of American history.

Born in Missouri, Hughes's heritage extended to the Powhatan Indians, and he was related to Henry Clay, an influential white Kentucky senator from the pre-Civil War era. But Hughes was also the grandson of a man who had died in John Brown's attempt to incite bondspeople to overturn slavery. His grandmother "looked like an Indian. My mother was a newspaper woman and a stenographer. My father lived in Mexico City. My granduncle [African American John Mercer Langston] had been a congressman and there were heroic memories of John Brown's raid and the underground railroad in the family storehouse." Hughes soon became known as a leading figure in American culture, a role he maintained for more than four decades. His poem "The Negro Speaks of Rivers" (1921) brought him international fame. In it Hughes linked the civilizations of ancient African valleys of the Euphrates, Congo, and Nile rivers to the Mississippi River valley of his own youth. Defining the New Negro as a blending of cultures, he described the depth of the black soul: "I've known rivers/Ancient, dusky rivers. My soul has grown deep like the rivers."

Distinguished by sharp wit and insightful social commentary, Hughes's poetry and political essays earned awards from black publications and found audiences in many languages. Hughes eventually created a satirical character named Jesse B. Semple ("just be simple") to dramatize black people's ability to survive the absurdities of American life by maintaining a sense of humor. In one essay, Semple tells a census-taker, "I've been laid-off, fired and not rehired, Jim Crowed, segregated, insulted, underfed, under-paid, undernourished, and everything but undertaken—but I'm still here." Thus Hughes defined the "New Negro" as the embodiment of a new, resolute attitude.

Zora Neale Hurston

Floridian Zora Neale Hurston arrived in Harlem in 1925 to attend Barnard College. Studying with Franz Boas, an anthropologist who spoke out against eugenicists, Hurston sought to prove that experiences, not inherent racial traits, defined a person's potential. As the daughter of the mayor of an all-black town, Hurston had a childhood insulated from the daily indignities of racism. When she witnessed racial stereotyping in New York, she often countered it with offhand humor. Her coined word "Negrotarians," for example, described white patrons who fawned over black artists. Through humor she made peace with the fact that for many years she was supported by a white patron whom she referred to as "Godmother."

In her writings, Hurston interwove the dialect of black Southerners with the language of white scholarship. At first, many black male writers ridiculed her writing as trivial, yet it appealed to both black and white audiences because it reflected humor and her own experience. Hurston's first publication, *John Redding Goes to Sea* (1921), is a fictionalized biography of her own restless and ambitious father. She also wrote a series of commentaries about northern intellectuals. In essays such as "The Hue and Cry About Howard University" (1925) and "How It Feels to Be Colored Me" (1928), she cautioned the black literati—whom she called "niggerati"—against taking themselves too seriously.

In 1927, the black writer Wallace Thurman satirized Hurston as Sweetie May in his play *Infants of Spring*. Wryly applauding Hurston's success, Thurman gave Sweetie May these lines: "Being a Negro writer is a racket and I am going to make the most of it while it lasts. Sure I cut the fool. But I enjoy it too. My ultimate ambition is to become an anthropologist. I get my tuition paid at Columbia. . . . I find queer places for whites to go in Harlem: out of the way primitive churches, sidestreet speakeasies. . . . About twice a year I manage to sell a story. It is acclaimed. I am a genius in the making. Thank God for this literary renaissance. Long may it flourish."

Best remembered for her novel *Their Eyes Were Watching God* (1937), Hurston also described the rural Southerners she knew best in *Mules and Men* (1935), an oral history study of the rural South. This and her autobiographical *Dust Tracks on the Road* (1942) became classic portraits of southern black culture.

The New Negro Woman

Hurston was one of the most flamboyant of a new breed of black women who pursued goals outside the limits of domestic work, field labor, or child care. *The Messenger* had a name for such women: "New Negro Woman with a Revolutionary Orientation." Wartime had offered them new economic and social roles. Organizing the Circle for Negro War Relief, black women helped recruit and encourage black soldiers, while black nurses volunteered for the Red Cross. In 1917, the National Association of Colored Women (NACW) launched a fund-raising campaign to purchase Frederick Douglass's Washington,

DC, home as a memorial. Its success was a testimony to black women's financial power and ability to unite in a common cause. Shrugging off servile and dependent roles, they demonstrated that they could overcome the double disadvantage of gender and race.

While many African American women worked within organizations, others pursued individual goals. During the war, Bessie Coleman became fascinated with airplanes. Obtaining her pilot's license in France, she returned to the United States to perform flight stunts before spellbound crowds—and she insisted that they be integrated. Lucy Diggs Slowe, the first women's national champion of the American Tennis Association, the oldest African American sports organization in the United States, later became Howard University's first black dean of women. Singer Marian Anderson earned international acclaim after she won a competition that gained her a performance with the New York Philharmonic Orchestra in 1925.

It was as if a glacier had begun to melt, sending rivers of fresh opportunity into black women's lives. African American women had always worked, but in a cash economy they could now set personal goals beyond husband and family. Now mothers could counsel their daughters to "always keep some sort of little job of your own, and make sure you put aside a little money and time for yourself." Heeding this advice, the New Negro woman surveyed her options from all vantage points. Amy Ashwood is an example. In 1914, just seventeen years old, she helped organize Jamaica's UNIA women's auxiliary, which, she said, should ensure women's economic independence. Ashwood soon moved to New York to help develop *The Negro World*. In 1919, she and Marcus Garvey were married in a lavish ceremony. Though they worked together to expand the UNIA's reach in the United States, Ashwood gained attention for her independence and willingness to disagree with her husband. She divorced Garvey in 1922; then she moved to England, where she continued lecturing and organizing for black women's rights and greater autonomy for married women.

The Harlem Renaissance and White America

Some influential white intellectuals found inspiration in black culture. Playwright Eugene O'Neill and photographer Carl Van Vechten romanticized black life as they listened to black poetry or viewed black art in brothels, gambling houses, and nightclubs. Some black writers also reached white Americans. Rudolph Fisher's novel *Walls of Jericho* (1928), which explored class tensions among Harlem's black residents, found a wide audience. So did the works of Nella Larsen, daughter of a Danish white woman and a Caribbean black father. Larson's *Quicksand* (1928) and *Passing* (1929) were autobiographical novels about being of mixed race. Readers of all skin colors hungered for "real" stories of black life. Bicyclist Major Taylor's autobiography appeared in 1928. Even boxing champion Jack Johnson got his autobiography, *Jack Johnson: In the Ring and Out* (1928), published—written while he was inside federal prison. Langston Hughes assessed the mood: "We younger Negro artists . . . now intend to express our individual dark-skinned selves without fear or shame. If the white people are pleased, we are glad. If they are not, it doesn't matter. We know we are beautiful. And ugly too. . . . If colored people are pleased, we are glad. If they are not, their displeasure doesn't matter either."

Harlem and black culture were indeed in fashion. A'Lelia Walker, heiress to the fortune of the hairstyling millionaire Madam C. J. Walker, hosted parties attended by black and white artists and intellectuals who helped publicize black culture. *Harlem Shadows,* Arthur Schomburg's collection of poems celebrating black art and artists, was published in 1922. In 1925, when the New York Public Library hosted its first exhibition of black art and literature, Schomburg lent his collection of "the Negro in old New York." The following year, the New York Public Library bought Schomburg's holdings. Soon his friend Jesse Moorland donated his library of African American works to Howard University, where he was teaching.

It took decades for the nation as a whole to seek to understand black people's contributions, but during the Harlem Renaissance, the New Negro planted the seeds of a cultural tradition that bloomed again in the 1950s and 1960s—when another generation of disaffected black and white Americans rediscovered its value.

The Jazz Age

"The music from the trumpet at the Negro's lips is honey mixed with liquid fire." With these words, Langston Hughes described the new music called jazz. But among black intellectuals, Hughes's opinion was in the minority. Many black Americans distanced themselves from the sensuous music that brought white attention to black culture. Jazz music's improvisational style, they argued, only reinforced the stereotype that black people were impetuous and lacked intellectual discipline. Other black people criticized this "folk art" because it was born in brothels and performed in speakeasies—illegal bars that opened during the decade of Prohibition, when the government outlawed alcohol. But jazz was not just a musical innovation. At a time when all other social institutions in the United States were segregated, a few jazz clubs brought together music lovers of all races.

Some historians consider jazz the only truly American art form. Rather than deriving from another culture, it was born in the United States from a blend of European and African percussion, horn, and piano melodies. Many jazz artists were trained in the disciplined formality of classical piano. But jazz was feel-good music, embracing a bewildering array of forms—from spirituals and the mournful tones of the blues to the aggressive percussion of marching band rhythms, from the asymmetry of ragtime to the staid patterns of European tradition. Jazz offered deep, throaty voices, and provocative brass, woodwind, and percussion sounds. Building on written scores, band members improvised during performances. Thus jazz was always in motion, always transforming something familiar into something new. Hughes felt that jazz embodied a cultural richness that opened new doors for black Americans. Through jazz, Hughes commented, "Josephine Baker goes to Paris, Robeson to London, Jean Toomer to a Quaker Meeting House, Garvey to Atlanta Federal Penitentiary . . . and Duke Ellington to fame and fortune."

The Chicago Style of Jazz

"I ain't supposed to be in this band; they're too *good*," worried Louis Armstrong when he arrived at the Lincoln Gardens jazz club on Chicago's South Side in 1922. Invited there by his mentor, Joe "King" Oliver, Armstrong wondered whether he had made a mistake in leaving his hometown of New Orleans, where Oliver had befriended the teenage Armstrong, teaching him to play the trumpet. By 1918, when Oliver moved to Chicago, jazz music was sweeping through black communities everywhere. But Armstrong quickly mastered the Chicago music scene, which savored personal charisma and chemistry. Established performers like Fletcher Henderson, Clarence Williams, and Ma Rainey each had a unique style that up-and-coming jazz performers tried to copy or improve upon.

Improvising duets with Oliver, Armstrong became the envy of musicians. "I just made duets to whatever Oliver played," Armstrong said, "and we never did have to write it down." He later reported, "I was *home*." Jazz also soon found a worldwide home. When black horn player James Reese Europe arrived in wartime France with New York's Fifteenth Regiment, his band not only played "Memphis Blues" but also performed a lively innovation of the French National Anthem. French audiences thronged to hear what they called "sunburned Americans" with their "trick instruments" that seemed to speak words amid the complicated rhythms. James Reese Europe sealed the future of jazz with the French people.

Black Women Sing the Blues

With the introduction of radio and the emerging technology of sound recording, jazz helped create new celebrities, including female vocalists. Radio broadcasts featured Bessie Smith, whose first hit recording in 1923, "Down Hearted Blues," sold 800,000 copies. This recording helped popularize the blues, a slow, haunting music characterized by falsetto singing and personal storytelling woven out of southern black hardship. Over the next few years, Columbia Records reproduced dozens of Smith's performances. So did the Black Swan recording studio, one of several black "race record" companies that employed only black workers. Peddled by newsboys on street corners, these recordings did so well that in 1928 Smith was earning $2,500 a week—perhaps ten times what the average jazz musician earned in a month.

Jazz opened a new world to many other black women. Ethel Waters from Chester, Pennsylvania, began her singing career at age thirteen, billing herself as "Sweet Mama Stringbean" and singing in Baltimore nightclubs. She reportedly was the first to sing W. C. Handy's "St. Louis Blues." In 1920 her recording of it proved an instant hit, and white singer Sophie Tucker came to study with her. Across the country, singers like Ma Rainey and Ida Cox from Georgia and Victoria Spivey from Texas were among some 200 black women recruited by record companies to produce more than 5,000 recordings. In 1929, fourteen-year-old Eleanora Gough spent hours listening to Louis Armstrong on the radio. Soon she changed her name to Billie Holiday and began making recordings herself, developing her own unique style.

Political Goals and Setbacks in the 1920s

"Even in New York it costs an elevator man 365 hours of extra labor and $400 a year to be colored," noted Harlem minister Adam Clayton Powell, Sr. Citing the pay disparity between black and white workers, Powell was reacting to an employment agency advertisement that blatantly offered $90 per month for a white elevator boy for an eleven-hour workday, and $65 per month for a twelve-hour workday if the elevator boy were colored. Though the employment situation was better in cities than in rural areas, a gap still existed between white and black pay. As the robust economy of the early 1920s faded, the gap widened.

In the immediate postwar years, black people sometimes got a hearing from national politicians who sought support from the growing urban black voting bloc. During the 1920 presidential campaign, Republican Warren G. Harding held a "Colored Voters Day." Denouncing lynching, he also declared that "if the United States cannot prevent segregation in its own [military] service, we are in no way a democracy." Many African American leaders took heart at Harding's comments, but after his landslide victory, achieved with the help of urban black votes, Harding backed away from the Dyer antilynching bill.

Harding died in 1923. When Vice President Calvin Coolidge assumed the presidency, he initially showed support for black voters' concerns. He pardoned the soldiers of the Twenty-fourth Infantry who were serving life sentences for the Houston riot. He also pardoned Marcus Garvey on the condition that he leave the country. But because Coolidge did not support the antilynching bill or attempt to desegregate federal facilities, he failed to win the wholehearted allegiance of black Americans. Black voters were no longer a predictable Republican bloc.

In the 1928 presidential campaign, neither the Republicans nor Democrats made much effort to woo African Americans. Black men and women hoped Republican Herbert Hoover's Quaker background would lead him to champion racial justice. But Hoover expressed little interest in black issues. His Democratic opponent, Al Smith, made overtures to the black community, offering to issue a statement supporting black rights. He persuaded a few NAACP members to vote Democratic, but when election day came, Hoover won the presidency.

Increasingly, black voters felt torn between the Democratic Party (whose policies of protecting wage earners were popular among northern workers) and the Republican Party (which had abolished slavery). With African American leaders and voters divided, the Communist Party gained some ground among black working people in the 1920s. In Harlem rallies, party members proclaimed support for "social equality" and for a class solidarity that should supersede race. Through the next decade, communists attracted an increasing number of black workers and intellectuals in northern cities—and gained a small foothold in the rural South.

In some local elections, unified urban voting put black men into office. In Chicago's South Side in 1925, African Americans were the decisive factor in electing Republican Adelbert Roberts to the Illinois legislature—the state's first black congressman. Illinois voters also sent Republican Oscar de Priest to the U.S. House of Representatives in 1928—the first-ever northern black congressman and the first black man in Congress since 1901, when North Carolina's George L. White left office. But as on the national level, local political issues influenced black party loyalties. Concerns about housing, school boards, and local protections for jobs and patronage shaped how black men and women voted.

At the decade's end, black leaders faced the crisis that challenged all of America, and indeed the world. The collapse of the American stock market in October 1929 sent shock waves through the international economy, throwing hundreds of thousands out of work. Black commentators described black workers as the "last hired, and the first to be fired." Civil rights gains stalled in an atmosphere of economic desperation.

Conclusion

World War I accelerated change in every aspect of life. Thousands of Southerners left rural homes for urban opportunities, and many African Americans felt optimistic about their prospects. This optimism was reinforced by dynamic postwar leadership that helped open new horizons in employment, housing, cultural expressions, and expanded racial pride. By 1930, transformed by war, migration, prosperity, and some legal and political victories, America's young black people had expectations and attitudes unimaginable just two decades earlier. The majority of black Americans still bore the scars of slavery, but many were better educated, healthier, wealthier, and more confident than their parents. The NACW offered women examples of independence, the NAACP posited integration as an achievable goal, and the Urban League paved the way to the middle class for many. Under Garvey's leadership, the UNIA propelled thousands of working-class black people toward self-improvement.

The Harlem Renaissance and the Jazz Age lit a spark of hope in the spiritual life of black Americans. In poetry and prose, the visual arts, drama, music, scholarly pursuits, and business, a generation shaped a distinctive black identity. But the first three decades of the twentieth century confirmed Du Bois's prediction: The problem of the twentieth century was the problem of race. The combined efforts of artists, writers, lawyers, teachers, union organizers, churches, and common laborers were needed for the agonizingly slow progress toward racial equality.

Questions for Review and Reflection

1. World War I helped to stimulate new self-definitions and new expectations among African Americans. What were some aspects of the social and political demands that arose out of black communities? How were these demands manifested?

2. How do the goals and strategies outlined by Garvey and Du Bois help us understand some African American visions for a new role in an international community?

3. In the years after World War I, how did life in urban communities change African Americans? How did African Americans change America's cities?

4. In the 1920s, some black men and women used their talents and skills to pierce the armor of American racism. What aspects of their legacy have been enduring?

The New Politics of the Great Depression

The Scottsboro Boys

"The next time you want by, just tell me you want by and I let you by," Haywood Patterson remembered telling the young white hobo who stepped on his hand as both clung to the side of a freight train on March 25, 1931. Nineteen years old at the time, Patterson was himself a hobo. He had joined thousands of other people riding the rails in search of work as the Great Depression tightened its grip on Americans. This day, he was traveling across northern Alabama on his way to Memphis. Patterson had encountered hardship even before the stock market crash of 1929 that sent the economy reeling. His parents, Janie and Claude Patterson, had worked as sharecroppers on a Georgia farm. Like many other black farmers, the couple struggled to pay off the debts that tied them to their white landlord. When his father found work in Chattanooga and moved the family there, young Patterson felt compelled to leave school after the third grade to help support his younger siblings. Venturing throughout the South and as far north as Ohio looking for employment, he found only temporary, low-paying jobs. Through hard experience, Patterson learned that he had to stand up for himself. But he could hardly have anticipated how much his life would change as a result of his brief confrontation with a white teenager.

> *"Nigger, I don't ask you when I want by," the teen shouted. "What you doing on this train anyway?"*
>
> *"Look, I just tell you, the next time you want by, you just tell me you want by and I let you by."*
>
> *"Nigger bastard, this is a white man's train. You better get off. All you black bastards better get off!"*
>
> *"You white sonsofbitches, we got as much right here as you,"* Patterson yelled back.

1929	The stock market crashes, signaling the beginning of the Great Depression.
1931	After eight of nine black youths accused of rape in Alabama are sentenced to death, Communists launch "Free the Scottsboro Boys" campaign.
1932	In *Powell* v. *Alabama,* the Supreme Court rules that the Scottsboro defendants must be retried because Alabama officials violated the Fourteenth Amendment by denying them adequate legal counsel.
1933	Democrat Franklin Delano Roosevelt becomes president and immediately launches the New Deal. Robert Weaver, named race relations advisor in the Interior Department's Housing Division, is the Roosevelt administration's first African American appointee. W. E. B. Du Bois and other black leaders gather in Amenia, NY, to discuss the NAACP's future direction.
1934	Du Bois is forced from editorship of the NAACP's *The Crisis.*
1935	Mary McLeod Bethune founds the National Council of Negro Women and receives the Spingarn Medal from the NAACP. Du Bois publishes *Black Reconstruction in America.* In *Norris* v. *Alabama,* the Supreme Court again overturns the conviction of a Scottsboro defendant.
1936	The National Negro Congress is formed, with A. Philip Randolph as president. Bethune becomes director of the Division of Negro Affairs of the National Youth Administration (NYA) and organizes the Federal Council on Negro Affairs, better known as the Black Cabinet. With black support, Roosevelt wins presidential election by a landslide.
1937	Alabama officials agree to drop charges against four of the Scottsboro defendants, but others remained imprisoned. Randolph's Brotherhood of Sleeping Car Porters gains union recognition. Joe Louis becomes world heavyweight champion.
1938	In *Missouri ex rel. Gaines* v. *Canada,* the U.S. Supreme Court rules that states must provide equal, even if separate, educational facilities for African Americans.
1939	Marian Anderson sings to a large audience at the Lincoln Memorial after being denied the opportunity to perform at Daughters of the American Revolution's Constitution Hall. Jazz singer Billie Holiday popularizes the antilynching song "Strange Fruit."
1940	The NAACP Legal Defense and Educational Fund is established under the leadership of Thurgood Marshall. Richard Wright publishes *Native Son.* President Franklin Roosevelt announces that African Americans will have equal opportunities in the military but rejects calls for desegregation of Armed Forces.

As the two shot retorts back and forth, other hobos on the train watched with growing interest. Soon the argument escalated into a fistfight between the black and white youths. Most of the white hobos retreated by jumping off the slow-moving train and complaining to local authorities that a gang of blacks wielding knives and guns had assaulted them.

When the train arrived in Paint Rock, the next stop in Alabama, the sheriff was waiting with an armed posse. By this time, some of the black riders had already gotten off the train. But deputies roped Patterson and eight others together and took them to the county jail in Scottsboro. The arrestees would soon be known as "the Scottsboro boys," though the oldest was nineteen years old. Two were thirteen. All nine were poor, illiterate or barely literate, and bewildered by the allegations against them. A deputy initially told Patterson, who knew two of the other arrestees, that the group would be charged with assault and attempted murder. Yet only after the inmates had languished in jail for hours did they learn the true seriousness of their situation.

Patterson recalled that two young white women were brought to the jail. He had paid little attention when he had seen them in Paint Rock standing with the white hobos and wearing men's clothing.

"Do you know these girls?" a deputy asked the prisoners. Patterson and the others said no.

"No? You damn-liar niggers! You raped these girls."

Charged with rape, a capital offense in Alabama, the Scottsboro defendants now faced the possibility of death in the electric chair—that is, if they managed to avoid being lynched by the mob of whites who gathered as lurid accounts of the alleged crime spread. There had been twenty-one reported lynchings in the United States the previous year, nearly all involving southern black men who were murdered before they could stand trial. Fearing bad publicity for the state, Alabama's governor and the local sheriff agreed to call in the National Guard to ensure that the defendants received a trial.

The trials began in Scottsboro on April 6, just twelve days after the arrests. They unfolded in a climate of mob vengeance that made it clear the defendants had no chance. Angry white people gathered inside and outside the courtroom. Some insisted that the trials were a waste of taxpayers' money, given that the defendants must certainly be guilty. The headline of a *Huntsville Times* editorial read, "DEATH PENALTY PROPERLY DEMANDED IN FIENDISH CRIME OF NINE BURLY NEGROES." The sixty-nine-year-old white defense attorney who reluctantly agreed to accept the cases had little time to prepare and was hesitant to challenge the stories of the white accusers.

Yet the testimony of Victoria Price and Ruby Bates contained numerous inconsistencies and improbabilities. Like the defendants, the two women were unemployed vagrants. They claimed that armed black men had brutally raped them, but medical examinations revealed no evidence of sexual assault. No weapons were found on the defendants. But such considerations did not deter the prosecutors. Within four days, all-white juries had convicted eight of the nine defendants, who were then sentenced to death. Jurors deadlocked in the case of the youngest defendant, Roy Wright. A mistrial resulted in his case when eleven of the twelve jurors insisted on the death penalty after the prosecutors asked only for life imprisonment.

In previous years, the Scottsboro case might have attracted little attention outside the South, and the defendants would have been promptly executed. But in 1931 economic catastrophe was reshaping American politics. People of all races had begun questioning their country's political and economic institutions and considering radical solutions to their problems. Insisting that the Depression demonstrated the failure of capitalism, members of the United States Communist Party saw the Alabama case as a chance to unite workers of all races against what they called the Scottsboro Frame-Up. Though few African Americans embraced revolutionary socialism, the Communist-led Scottsboro campaign spurred various forms of black militancy, especially in urban areas. During subsequent years, black non-Communists worked with Communists to stage numerous mass protests—rallies, marches, rent strikes, economic boycotts—to try to vanquish discrimination. The Scottsboro campaign also prompted heated debates about the future of the National Association for the Advancement of Colored People (NAACP), the nation's oldest and largest civil rights organization.

Presidential politics also influenced the fate of the Scottsboro defendants and the lives of most African Americans. Franklin D. Roosevelt's New Deal offered an alternative to radicalism. Although Roosevelt's first priority after winning the presidency in 1932 was to restore confidence in the economic system, his administration provided relief assistance to ease the anguish of joblessness and hunger. New Deal employment and job training programs brought hope to those without work. Despite racial bias in the administration of some of these programs and Roosevelt's failure to support civil rights legislation, most African Americans appreciated the New Deal and some benefited from it. In the 1936 election, many black voters switched allegiances from the Republican Party of Abraham Lincoln to the Democratic Party of Roosevelt. Moreover, Roosevelt's black appointees—often called the Black Cabinet—testified to the gradual incorporation of African Americans into the New Deal coalition, which came to include numerous black workers who joined the expanding industrial union movement.

The cultural explosion of the Harlem Renaissance could not survive the economic downturn of the Great Depression. Yet black writers, artists, and entertainers of the 1930s still managed to reach large multiracial audiences and influence the nation's popular culture as never before. By the early 1940s, mobilization for a new war in Europe further transformed American race relations, as wartime labor needs opened new opportunities for black workers. Meanwhile, the bestseller status of Richard Wright's provocative novel *Native Son* (1940) revealed the growing impact of black intellectuals on the nation's cultural mainstream—even as Wright's doomed young protagonist, Bigger Thomas, symbolized persistent racial divisions.

African Americans in Desperate Times

"I did not know in that spring of 1931 that I was about to join an estimated 200,000 to 300,000 homeless boys—and a smattering of girls—between twelve and twenty, products of the Depression, who rode freights or hitchhiked from town to town in search of work," twenty-year-old Pauli Murray recalled. Unlike the Scottsboro defendants, Murray's time as a hobo was limited to one cross-country trip that ended without misfortune. She was a college student at New York's Hunter College at the time of the 1929 stock market crash, but had been forced to quit school when laid off from her waitress job. "I became one of those marginal workers who felt the first shocks of the Depression."

Although Americans of all races and backgrounds were profoundly affected by the worsening economic crisis of the 1930s, black Americans such as Pauli Murray experienced special hardships due to the added burden of racial discrimination. African Americans who had fewer employment opportunities than whites even during the best of times were especially hard hit by the crisis. As the nation's overall unemployment rate reached 25 percent, the black unemployment rate was twice that in many cities. In once-thriving Detroit, as automobile plants laid off workers in the early 1930s, the unemployment figure for black workers exceeded 60 percent. One of thousands of African American migrants who had flooded into New York during the Harlem Renaissance, Murray and other black people encountered intensified competition for urban jobs as the economy deteriorated.

In the South, floods and boll weevil infestations made conditions even more dire. At the beginning of the 1930s, one of every two African Americans lived on farms, most as sharecroppers dependent on white landlords. The fall in cotton prices—from twenty cents per pound in the early 1920s to five cents by 1933—led to farm foreclosures and still more hardship for tenants working land owned by others. Everywhere, African Americans sought answers to the problems confronting them.

Du Bois Ponders Political Alternatives

"The Scottsboro, Alabama, cases have brought squarely before the American Negro the question of his attitude toward Communism," W. E. B. Du Bois editorialized in the September 1931 issue of the NAACP's journal *The Crisis*. As the Scottsboro cases and the Communist-led campaign to free the defendants captured widespread attention during the early 1930s, Du Bois insisted that the Communist Party was cynically using the Scottsboro campaign to persuade African Americans "to join the Communist movement as the only solution to their problem." At the same time, he was convinced that the NAACP, which he had helped found to fight racial discrimination, needed to combat economic deprivation as well.

Du Bois had stirred controversy when he urged black voters to support the Socialist Party in the 1928 election. But three years later, he found himself on the defensive as Communist organizers spearheaded efforts to organize industrial workers and increasingly competed with the NAACP for the support of African Americans. In an editorial, Du Bois conceded that Communists had "made a courageous fight against the color line among the workers." But he doubted whether white workers would ever turn toward socialism or ally themselves with black workers. Throughout the history of the Negro in America, "white labor has been the black man's enemy, his oppressor, his . . . murderer," Du Bois insisted.

Du Bois concluded that the NAACP's strategy of achieving *gradual* reform held greater promise for African Americans than the Communists' radical effort to overthrow capitalism. "Negroes know perfectly well that whenever they try to lead revolution in America, the nation will unite as one fist to crush them and them alone," he wrote. Though most African Americans shared Du Bois's skepticism about the Communist Party, a small minority found the party a source of hope in a time of desperation. Exerting influence far beyond their numbers, these black Reds ignited an unprecedented upsurge of African American political militancy.

Black Reds

"WOULD YOU RATHER FIGHT OR STARVE?" Seventeen-year-old Angelo Herndon spotted this provocative headline on a leaflet he found on a Birmingham street as he walked home from work in June 1930. At first he guessed the leaflet was a call to military service. But reading more closely, he saw it was an invitation to attend a meeting of Birmingham's Unemployment Council. Herndon had a job. Nevertheless, he had struggled to survive since leaving home at age thirteen to work as a coal miner, as his father had done for most of his life. Lying about his age, Herndon had labored in the mines of Kentucky and northern Alabama before landing a job in Birmingham loading coal onto railway cars. He found the working conditions harsh, as white bosses assigned black workers to the most dangerous and lowest-paying jobs. And even those jobs were insecure. "Mines and factories were closing down; businesses failed, banks crashed," Herndon recalled. "Workers who had never been out of jobs before suddenly found themselves tramping vainly in search of new employment."

Herndon went to the Unemployment Council meeting, where he heard Communist organizers, both black and white, urge workers to unite against "the bosses." Ignoring warnings from relatives about associating with "Reds," Herndon soon became a Communist organizer. He had once admired "big Negro leaders" such as Du Bois, but now he thought such "self-appointed leaders" were "lined up on the side of the capitalist class." Though Herndon had dropped out of school, he struggled to read Karl Marx's *Communist Manifesto* and concluded that the Communist Party offered him "a purpose in living, in doing, in aspiring."

The Communist Party's success in recruiting black workers such as Herndon resulted from its decision during the 1920s to combat racial discrimination as well as economic oppression. After its founding in 1919, the party had initially attracted only a handful of black members. Notable among them were the Harlem Renaissance writer Claude McKay (who soon abandoned radical politics) and a few black nationalists affiliated with the secretive African Blood Brotherhood. The party scored greater successes, however, in the late 1920s, when it took the position that African Americans were an oppressed national group with the right of self-determination in the South's "Black Belt," where they formed a majority. The party stepped up recruitment of African Americans and established the League of Struggle for Negro Rights to fight lynching and other forms of racism. Herndon was impressed that the party "fought selflessly and tirelessly to undo the wrongs perpetrated upon my race. Here was no dilly-dallying, no pussyfooting on the question of full equality for the Negro people."

The Scottsboro Campaign

The Scottsboro trials in 1931 gave the Communist Party an opportunity to demonstrate its commitment to black rights. Within days of the verdicts, William Patterson, the African American head of the Communist-sponsored

Haywood Patterson (seated) and seven other "Scottsboro Boys" facing death sentences confer with defense lawyer Samuel Liebowitz in March 1933, shortly before the beginning of Patterson's second trial on rape charges.

International Labor Defense (ILD) (and no relation to defendant Haywood Patterson) sent the ILD's lead attorney to meet with the defendants and their parents. A graduate of the University of California's law school, Patterson had risked his successful legal practice in Harlem to join the Communists. After studying Marxist theory during a stay in the Soviet Union, he quickly became one of the party's most influential black members.

The NAACP also sent lawyers to Alabama, but the ILD team argued convincingly that its strategy of combining legal appeals and mass protests offered the best chance for saving the defendants. Du Bois and NAACP executive secretary Walter White complained that the Communists were manipulating the poorly educated defendants, but the defendants saw things differently. Explaining his decision to place his fate in the hands of Communists, Haywood Patterson noted that the ILD representatives "were the first people to call on us, to show any feelings for our lives, and we were glad."

The Communist Party launched a nationwide "Free the Scottsboro Boys" campaign. As the defendants awaited execution, scheduled for July 1931, Communists in Harlem held boisterous rallies and led marchers along Lenox Avenue demanding "Death to Lynch Law" and "Smash the Scottsboro Frame-Up." Several demonstrations featured appearances by Janie Patterson, Haywood Patterson's mother. Angelo Herndon joined the Scottsboro effort, organizing a mass meeting of workers and a defense committee. Speakers at such gatherings called on workers of all races to prevent the "legal lynching" of the Scottsboro defendants. ILD lawyers appealed the convictions, thereby staving off the executions and buying time to mobilize support. In *Powell* v. *Alabama* (1932), the Supreme Court ruled that the Scottsboro defendants be retried because they had been denied adequate legal counsel.

To the dismay of NAACP leaders, the Communist Party's enthusiastic support of the Scottsboro defendants proved to be an effective recruiting tool in black communities. Although some black ministers barred Communist organizers from their churches, the Scottsboro campaign attracted support from many sources. Early in 1932, Langston Hughes visited Alabama's Kilby Prison, where the defendants waited. The experience inspired Hughes to spread the news about "eight black boys and one white lie." His one-act play, *Scottsboro, Limited*, portrayed black workers uniting to smash an electric chair. Though Hughes did not join the Communist Party, the Scottsboro campaign brought him into close contact with party activists, and he agreed to serve as president of the party's League of Struggle for Negro Rights.

Clamping Down on Black Radicalism

Langston Hughes risked his career as a writer by associating himself with the Communist-led Scottsboro campaign, but black Communists working in the South, such as Angelo Herndon, took more serious risks. Even without the Red label, black political activists in the region often came under violent attack from the Ku Klux Klan. Herndon recalled finding a Klan handbill at his front door warning "Alabama is a good place for good negroes to live in, but it is a bad place for negroes who believe in SOCIAL EQUALITY." Members of Alabama's

Croppers and Farm Workers Union learned this lesson when they were violently attacked at a meeting near Camp Hill.

Herndon moved to Atlanta in 1932 to continue his organizing activities and soon became the central figure in another major protest campaign. After he led a thousand black and white workers to Atlanta's courthouse to demand increased economic relief, he was arrested for "attempting to incite insurrection." Facing a possible death sentence, Herndon defiantly turned his 1933 trial into a forum on injustice. He proclaimed to the jury, "If the State of Georgia and the City of Atlanta think that by locking up Angelo Herndon, the question of unemployment will be solved, I say you are deadly wrong. If you really want to do anything about the case, you must go out and indict the social system."

Like the Scottsboro trials, Herndon's plight provided a rallying point for Communists, who began organizing demonstrations on his behalf. Black attorney Benjamin J. Davis, Jr., a graduate of Harvard Law School, volunteered to defend Herndon at no charge. Though lacking trial experience, Davis devoted all his energies to the case. When Herndon was nonetheless convicted and sentenced to twenty years on a Georgia chain gang, the undaunted Davis appealed the conviction (the Supreme Court overturned Herndon's conviction in 1937) and resolved to continue working on behalf of workers. As Davis explained, "I entered the trial as [Herndon's] lawyer and ended it as his Communist comrade." Davis later became editor of the *Harlem Liberator* and began a rise to political prominence that culminated in 1943, when he won election to the New York City Council—the first Communist to hold such a position in the United States.

Election of 1932

Herndon's imprisonment revealed the considerable obstacles facing Communist organizers in the South. Yet even in northern cities, the party found it difficult to garner mass support in black communities. As the 1932 presidential election approached, the Communist Party attempted to strengthen its black support by running a black vice presidential candidate—James W. Ford, a Fisk graduate radicalized by his military experiences in World War I. Still, few African Americans felt comfortable casting their vote for a controversial party that had no chance of winning a national election.

Though Republican candidate Herbert Hoover had presided over the economic tailspin, many black voters retained their traditional Republican ties, viewing Democratic candidate Franklin D. Roosevelt with skepticism. Roosevelt's record as governor of New York had shown him to be liberal on many issues, but he had never supported civil rights reforms. Roosevelt's 57 percent majority in the election was achieved without substantial black support, though Democrats made gains in northern black communities. The Communist ticket received slightly more than 100,000 votes, less than 1 percent of the total turnout and considerably less than the Socialist Party candidate Norman Thomas, who was favored by Du Bois as a nonrevolutionary alternative to the major candidates.

On taking office in March 1933, Roosevelt's first priority was to restore confidence in the economic system. He said nothing about addressing racial problems.

In addition to regulating the banking system and securities trading, the new president quickly won passage of the first of a series of measures that became known as the New Deal. The National Recovery Administration (NRA) established codes to stabilize prices in certain industries, but its minimum wage guidelines did not apply to the menial job categories in which most black people worked. However, the Federal Emergency Relief Administration's funds for local agencies did provide food and shelter for unemployed African Americans. As the New Deal gradually shifted its focus from reviving capitalism to providing jobs and training for those in need, increasing numbers of black workers benefited from federal programs.

Black Militancy

For the NAACP, the upsurge of Communist agitation and the launching of Roosevelt's New Deal posed a dilemma. Under the leadership of Walter White, the nation's largest civil rights organization struggled to build a mass following in black communities while also attracting the support of powerful white leaders. White's initial reluctance to involve the NAACP in the controversial Scottsboro case drew criticism from African Americans who saw the group as overly cautious. Although Du Bois initially agreed with White that the Communists were exploiting the Scottsboro case, he came to agree with the Communists' view that mere legal assistance to the Scottsboro defendants "will never solve the larger Negro problem but that further and more radical steps are needed."

A New Course for the NAACP

As the economy spiraled downward in the early 1930s, Du Bois and other NAACP members grew increasingly dissatisfied with White's dedicated but uninspiring leadership. At the organization's annual convention in 1932, Du Bois argued that the NAACP should abandon the notion of working "*for* the black masses but not *with* them." While rejecting calls for revolution, Du Bois urged delegates to seek economic as well as political change and to view America's racial problems through an international lens. In 1933, he provoked debate within the NAACP with an essay in *The Crisis* titled "Marxism and the Negro Problem."

Du Bois also called on the best-educated black leaders—his "talented tenth"—to define economic as well as civil rights goals for the NAACP. He handpicked the thirty-three people who met in Amenia, New York, at the estate of NAACP board chairman Joel Spingarn in August 1933. Du Bois made certain that invitations went to up-and-coming young professionals and academics, many from Howard University, including the political scientist Ralph Bunche, the economist Abram Harris, and Law School dean Charles Houston. The Fisk sociologist E. Franklin Frazier, another brilliant young scholar who would soon join Howard's faculty, also participated. Like Du Bois, these scholars had studied at leading research universities (Bunche and Houston at Harvard, Harris at

Columbia, and Frazier at the University of Chicago). They shared the leftist views of many white intellectuals of the period and hungered to devote themselves to the cause of social justice. Most agreed with Du Bois's dismissal of Communist calls for violent revolution. Yet they saw enormous promise in interracial efforts to unionize industrial workers. They exerted considerable influence over the discussions, sometimes even pushing Du Bois toward a greater emphasis on economic rather than racial concerns.

But the young intellectuals at the Amenia Conference proved unable to shift the NAACP's direction—a failure that disappointed Du Bois, who then took on the task himself. In a January 1934 *Crisis* editorial titled "Segregation," Du Bois questioned the NAACP's single-minded devotion to integrationist policies. He feared that these policies implied a "distaste or unwillingness of colored people to work with each other, to cooperate with each other, to live with each other." Instead, he wrote, "it is the race-conscious black man cooperating together in his own institutions and movements who will eventually emancipate the colored race."

White and other NAACP leaders worried that some readers might mistake the *Crisis* editor's views for the organization's official position. When the organization's board ordered Du Bois to stop using the journal to criticize NAACP policies, Du Bois resigned. "If I criticize within, my words fall on deaf ears," he wrote. "If I criticize openly, I seem to be washing dirty linen in public." Du Bois then left New York for Atlanta University, where he had already accepted President John Hope's invitation to teach. Sixty-six years old, Du Bois now began a new, remarkably productive period of study, scholarship, and activism that would last almost three decades. In 1935 he published *Black Reconstruction in America,* a controversial reinterpretation that suggested a "general strike" by slaves had contributed to Union victory and stressed the role of the black masses in Reconstruction's democratic initiatives.

Within the NAACP, White had prevailed over Du Bois. Nonetheless, Du Bois's criticisms, together with the nation's economic collapse and new developments in the Scottsboro cases, finally forced a shift in the NAACP's direction. When Scottsboro defense lawyer Samuel Leibowitz asked for help in preparing for a third set of trials, White agreed to support a Scottsboro Defense Committee led by moderates rather than Communists. For Haywood Patterson and the other defendants, this development made little difference. They were convicted once more but this time were spared the death penalty. In 1937, however, the committee gained the release of four of the defendants, though Patterson and the others remained imprisoned.

Walter White continued the NAACP's efforts to pass federal antilynching legislation, and Charles Houston, named head of its new legal department, launched a new campaign against school segregation. Houston had been the first African American editor of the *Harvard Law Review,* and as dean of Howard Law School he had been a strict taskmaster, unwilling to accept anything less than excellence. Thurgood Marshall, one of his students, remembered, "He used to tell us, in our first year, to look at the man on your right and look at the man on your left, and bear in mind that two of you won't be here next year. Well, that sort of kept your feet to the fire." Howard students sometimes

Instrumental in training a new generation of civil rights lawyers, Charles Houston was legal counsel to the NAACP. He worked with Thurgood Marshall in a legal assault against segregation in the United States.

derided Houston as "Iron Shoes" or "Cement Pants," yet he, along with his colleague William Hastie (also a distinguished Harvard graduate), transformed Howard's law school into a training ground for attorneys who would spearhead the civil rights movement. Marshall stuck it out and graduated first in his class in 1933; he would later replace his mentor as director of the NAACP's legal campaign.

At the NAACP, Houston and the lawyers he recruited sought to identify cases that would expose obvious racial inequities, especially in the field of public education, then force states to undertake the expensive and often impractical task of living up to the separate-but-equal standard of *Plessy* v. *Ferguson*. When the University of Missouri Law School rejected the application of a black resident, Lloyd Gaines, Houston filed suit arguing that Gaines was denied "equal protection" rights guaranteed by the Fourteenth Amendment. In 1938, the Supreme Court accepted the argument. In *Missouri ex rel.* v. *Canada*, the court declared that Missouri must make legal training available to qualified residents regardless of race. Previously focused on its unsuccessful antilynching campaign, the NAACP now broadened the battlefield to secure civil rights for African Americans.

Black Nationalists

NAACP leaders understood that enforcing the separate-but-equal principle was simply a means toward the eventual goal of integration, but for some African Americans, integration was not the goal. The Depression also spurred the emergence of black nationalists, often street-corner orators who attracted followings in New York and other cities. In Chicago, where the Ethiopian Peace Movement and the National Movement for a Forty-Ninth State sprang up, a firebrand named Sufi Abdul Hamid initiated a "Don't Buy Where You Can't Work" campaign that soon spread to other cities. Hamid later gained the nickname "Harlem Hitler" when he moved to New York and launched boycotts targeting Jewish businesses, a tactic that attracted considerable support in black communities. In Detroit, former Garveyite Elijah Poole joined the Nation of Islam, a small sect established by itinerate peddler Master Fard Muhammad. The Nation's founder claimed that Allah (God) was a black man who would someday return "the so-called Negro" to a position of superiority over "white devils." Poole, who changed his name to Elijah Muhammad, became the group's new leader when his predecessor mysteriously disappeared in 1934. While most unconventional black religious figures experienced only fleeting success during the Depression, Muhammad managed to retain a small yet loyal following through the 1940s and 1950s.

During this volatile decade, the educator and historian Carter G. Woodson continued to be one of the most articulate proponents of the black nationalist tradition. Though not affiliated with any black nationalist group, Woodson stressed the need for African Americans to rely on their own resources. Woodson also drew attention to African American historical achievements. In 1915 he founded the Association for the Study of Negro Life and History, and in 1926 he initiated Negro History Week. In his influential book, *The Mis-Education of the Negro* (1933), Woodson denounced educational institutions that estranged black students from the black masses while failing to provide them with the practical knowledge needed to uplift the race. Higher education, he argued, should serve "as preparation to think and work out a program to serve the lowly rather than to live as an aristocrat." Woodson further insisted that black advancement should be "based on the scientific study of the Negro from within to develop in him the power to do for himself what his oppressors will never do to elevate him to the level of others."

Social Gospel Ministers

Neither Du Bois nor Woodson saw most African American religious leaders as positive forces for social change. An agnostic who rarely attended church, Du Bois once complained that "pure-minded, efficient, unselfish" black ministers were far outnumbered by "pretentious, ill-trained men" who were often "dishonest and otherwise immoral." Not surprisingly, Du Bois had omitted ministers from his Amenia invitation list. Woodson similarly saw black clergymen as among those who had been "mis-educated." Most African American ministers, he charged, borrowed their ideas from "the oppressors of the race" and were either illiterate or "trained to drift away from the masses." He believed they were unprepared to confront the real, everyday problems burdening black Americans. He also despaired that the scant resources of African Americans were divided across their numerous denominations and self-governing churches. Yet Woodson applauded the minority of clergymen "who today are endeavoring to carry out the principles of Jesus long since repudiated by most Christians." He was referring to black clergymen who advocated a "social gospel" version of Christianity to address the economic problems of the Great Depression.

Among these social gospel advocates was Martin Luther King Sr., pastor of Atlanta's Ebenezer Baptist Church. In 1935 King led a voting rights march through downtown Atlanta, and he later orchestrated an effort to raise the salaries of black public school teachers to the levels of their white counterparts. Adam Clayton Powell, Jr., was another minister who combined religious and political leadership. After succeeding his father in 1937 as pastor of Abyssinian Baptist Church in Harlem, he became a crusader for social justice. Powell helped form the Greater New York Coordinating Committee for Employment, which used picketing and boycotts to pressure businesses to hire more black workers.

As the large urban black churches turned increasingly to college-educated ministers such as King and Powell for leadership, others without educational credentials also played important roles in African American religious life. One of the most unconventional was the largely self-educated, charismatic preacher George Baker, better known as Father Divine. Arriving in New York shortly before World War I, Divine convinced a growing number of white as well as black followers that he was "the true and living God." Followers in his integrated Peace Missions were prosecuted for disturbing the peace, but when the judge who sentenced him to a year in jail suddenly dropped dead, Divine added to his legend by asserting, "I hated to do it."

Many self-serving cult leaders simply enriched themselves at the expense of gullible followers. But Divine's movement, which reached as far as California, proved a complex blend of idealism and hucksterism. While stressing spiritual enrichment rather than political activism, Divine nonetheless encouraged his followers, mostly female, to support the Scottsboro and Herndon defense campaigns and similar causes. Despite frequent financial and sexual scandals, he developed self-help programs, such as Peace Kitchens, that responded to the material as well as spiritual needs of his "angels." Even Du Bois grudgingly acknowledged that Divine's movement "helped many people who need help."

Activist Black Intellectuals

Charles Houston's transformation of Howard's law school helped make the university an exciting intellectual center. Many college campuses buzzed with political activism during the Depression. But black students at black colleges in the South were discouraged from political expression by college presidents, who had to answer to white trustees. Even at Howard, Mordecai Johnson, the university's first black president, suppressed student protests. Nonetheless, Johnson worked to attract talented black faculty members. Many had scholarly credentials that would have gained them teaching positions at leading, predominantly white universities—if racial barriers had not existed in academia. These included Rayford Logan in history, Sterling Brown in literature, and Charles Drew in medicine, as well as Amenia Conference participants Abram Harris, Ralph Bunche, and E. Franklin Frazier. Several of these professors tested Johnson's constraints on political activism. For example, Bunche joined the Scottsboro Defense Committee. Howard law professor William Hastie joined with recent Williams College graduate John Aubrey Davis to found the New Negro Alliance, which launched boycotts against businesses that discriminated against black workers.

International events, especially the rise of fascism in Europe and the stirrings of anticolonialism in Africa, further intensified political militancy among black intellectuals. During these years, Bunche—who wrote his doctoral dissertation on French colonialism in Africa—met with many African leaders, including Kenya's Jomo Kenyatta, who would later lead an independence movement in his country. In 1936, Bunche's influential *World View of Race* predicted that racial conflict would soon give way to "the gigantic class war which will be waged in the big tent we call the world."

The success of Roosevelt's New Deal eventually convinced Bunche and other activist intellectuals that the United States could solve its economic problems without revolution. By the mid-1930s, some of the outspoken intellectuals who had attended the Amenia Conference had considered or accepted positions in New Deal agencies. Even some Communists gladly took federal jobs as the Roosevelt administration began providing employment and other direct aid to the unemployed. Federal employment programs—most notably those under the Works Progress Administration (WPA)—restored hope to millions of Americans and contributed to Roosevelt's growing support in black communities.

Although New Deal programs addressed economic rather than racial problems, they forced African Americans to rethink their political views. Instead of revolutionary activism or mass protest, it was the Roosevelt administration that emerged as the most significant new political force of the 1930s, and it was a Roosevelt appointee who emerged as the most influential African American of the period.

A New Deal for African Americans?

"Don't you realize this is the first such post created for a Negro woman in the U.S.?" pleaded Aubrey Williams, head of the National Youth Administration (NYA). Williams wanted Mary McLeod Bethune to join his New Deal agency, which provided training and part-time jobs for students so they could stay in school. Two weeks earlier, Bethune had caught President Roosevelt's attention when he heard her report that NYA wages of $15 to $20 per month "meant real salvation for thousands of Negro young people" and brought "life and spirit" to people "who for so long have been in darkness." After concluding her moving testimony, Bethune recalled "a stillness in the room" and tears in the president's eyes. Impressed by Bethune's accomplishments as an educator and her forthright manner, Roosevelt decided she should join his administration as director of the NYA's Division of Negro Affairs.

Mary McLeod Bethune

Initially, Bethune hesitated to leave her position as founding president of Florida's Bethune-Cookman College, but she recognized the historic significance of Roosevelt's invitation and accepted. "I visualized dozens of Negro women coming after me, filling positions of high trust and strategic importance." When Aubrey Williams took Bethune to the White House to discuss her new role with Roosevelt, she assured the president, "I shall give it the best that I have." Roosevelt observed to Williams, "Mrs. Bethune is a great woman. I believe in her because she has her feet on the ground; not only on the ground, but deep down in the ploughed soil."

In 1935, Mary McLeod Bethune founded the National Council of Negro Women. Franklin D. Roosevelt appointed her director of the Division of Negro Affairs of the National Youth Administration, a position she occupied from 1936 to 1943. She was particularly well suited to this role because it allowed her to reach the nation's black youth with her zeal for education. Roosevelt also considered her one of his foremost advisors in the unofficial "Black Cabinet" of black appointees in his administration.

Even before she accepted the position that would make her Roosevelt's most influential black appointee, Bethune had demonstrated remarkable perseverance and leadership. Born in 1875 in Mayesville, South Carolina, the fifteenth child of former slaves, she had left cotton farming to gain a formal education, eventually training to become a missionary in Africa. But she then realized, "Africans in America needed Christ and school just as much as Negroes in Africa." After teaching in various places including Chicago's slums, she used her savings of $1.50 to found a small girls' school in Daytona Beach, Florida. Yet it was her shrewd appeals to white businessmen vacationing in Florida and to black entrepreneurs—such as hair-care distributor Madame C. J. Walker—that enabled Daytona Normal and Industrial Institute to flourish. In 1923, the school merged with the nearby Cookman Institute to become Bethune-Cookman College.

The following year, Bethune was elected president of the National Association of Colored Women (NACW). Walking the middle ground between racial militancy and accommodation, she emerged as the most revered black educator of the period after Booker T. Washington's death. She also became a major figure in the NAACP and the National Urban League. Republican presidents Calvin Coolidge and Herbert Hoover sought her advice on racial issues.

As Bethune's national influence grew, organizations around the country invited her to speak. Known for her distinctive flair for fashion—long capes, colorful jewelry, and a cane carried for "swank"—and her strong sense of racial pride, she often said of herself, "Look at me, I am black, I am beautiful." Her down-to-earth, direct manner enabled her to get along with a wide range of people. These included Langston Hughes, who traveled with her through the South in 1931. Hughes recalled that Bethune "was a wonderful sport, riding all day without complaint in our cramped, hot little car, jolly and talkative, never grumbling." During the trip, Bethune's many friends and admirers provided housing and food. Their generosity prompted Hughes to remark that chickens fled upon Bethune's arrival: "They knew some necks would surely be wrung in her honor."

Bethune's ability to collaborate with people who held differing views served her well as a New Dealer. For example, she jauntily deflected racial slights as she carried out her duties. When a White House guard called her "Auntie," she quipped, "Which one of my brother's children are you?" She realized that Roosevelt himself was no racial liberal, at least at the start of his presidency, but a patrician accustomed to seeing blacks in subordinate roles. He was also reluctant to support civil rights reforms that would offend the southern segregationist politicians, nearly all of them Democrats, who provided crucial support for his New Deal programs.

But Roosevelt did select a few white proponents of racial equality—such as Bethune's boss, Aubrey Williams—for important posts in his administration. Secretary of the Interior Harold Ickes, a progressive who once headed the Chicago NAACP, appointed the New Deal's first black official, the Harvard-trained economist Robert Weaver. Bethune and Weaver, both "advisors for Negro affairs," became visible symbols of racial progress. Rather than setting New Deal policies, even on racial issues, they persuaded powerful whites to follow their recommendations. The talented black professionals joining the Roosevelt administration also included William Hastie, who left the Howard law faculty to become assistant solicitor of the Interior Department.

Among the dozen or so black appointees of the Roosevelt administration, Bethune was the most visible and effective. Although previously a Republican, she soon developed an intense loyalty to President Roosevelt. She not only gained the president's confidence but also forged strong ties with his politically active wife, Eleanor Roosevelt. Bethune encouraged the First Lady's growing commitment to racial equality and often influenced the president through her. Even before her appointment, the NAACP had honored Bethune with its annual Spingarn Medal, and she had become the nation's best-connected black leader. Drawing on her rich array of contacts, she brought together all the major black women's organizations to form a new umbrella group, the National Council of Negro Women.

Black Critics of the New Deal

Despite her awareness of racial bias in some New Deal programs, Bethune served as a restraining influence on more critical black appointees, such as Robert Weaver and William Hastie. Weaver, an expert on labor policies, understood the limitations as well as the benefits of the New Deal with respect to African Americans. In a 1935 article published in the Urban League's journal *Opportunity,* he noted that there had been racial "abuses" in the distribution of relief payments. "We can admit that we have gained from the relief program and still fight to receive greater and more equitable benefits from it," he wrote. Weaver's concerns were shared by other black intellectuals, both inside and outside the Roosevelt administration. In 1935, John P. Davis, a black economist who had collaborated with Weaver to monitor the impact of federal programs on African Americans, persuaded Bunche to call a conference at Howard University billed "The Status of the Negro under the New Deal." Although most participants supported the New Deal, some voiced strong criticisms of Roosevelt's policies.

Early the following year, as Roosevelt began preparing his reelection campaign, Benjamin Davis, Ralph Bunche, and other black critics of the New Deal convened a major gathering that drew more than 800 representatives of 585 black organizations to Chicago. This conference led to the formation of the National Negro Congress, with black labor leader A. Philip Randolph as president and John P. Davis as executive director. Although internal disputes between Communists and non-Communists soon weakened the new organization, it initially strengthened bonds between established African American organizations, such as the NAACP and the Urban League, and black activists (including Bunche, Randolph, and Davis) who saw the New Deal as merely the first step toward more far-reaching social change. As Randolph's keynote speech insisted, "The New Deal is no remedy. It does not seek to change the profit system. It does not place human rights above property rights, but gives business interests the support of the State."

Bethune did not participate in the Chicago conference. But later in 1936, she provided a forum for constructive criticism of the New Deal when she invited Weaver and other black officials of the Roosevelt administration to a meeting at her home. This gathering resulted in the formation of the Federal Council on Negro Affairs, an informal group that journalists soon described as the Black Cabinet. Though no member of the group actually held a cabinet position (thirty years later, Weaver would become the first African American to hold such a position), the so-called Black Cabinet enabled the growing number of black New Dealers to exchange views on the racial impact of New Deal programs. Bethune's leading role in the group also enhanced her visibility as a symbol of black participation in the Roosevelt administration.

By the 1936 election, Roosevelt's savvy appointments of African Americans had convinced many blacks that the New Deal, despite its limitations, was their best available political option. Even members of the Communist Party shifted their stance regarding the New Deal from open hostility to more measured criticism. Facing the rising threat of German fascism but encouraged by the success of industrial union movements in the United States, American Communists adopted a Popular Front strategy—joining with liberals and non-Communist socialists to resist fascism and to seek reforms short of revolution. The party's decision to cede control of the Scottsboro cases to the Scottsboro Defense Committee was part of this strategy.

The 1936 election marked a historic shift in black political allegiance, as a majority of black voters abandoned the Republican Party to support the Democrat Roosevelt—who won by a landslide. A historian later estimated that Roosevelt captured an overwhelming 81 percent of Harlem's black vote and exceeded his nationwide 61 percent in many other black communities. For the first time, African Americans became part of the northern liberal-labor coalition that competed with southern conservatives for control of the Democratic Party.

After the election, Bethune asserted herself as forcefully as she thought prudent against racial bias in New Deal programs. In her view, gradual progress through New Deal reforms offered far more potential than "the quicksands of revolution or the false promises of communism or fascism." Indeed, the early years of Roosevelt's second term marked the high point of New Deal social programs. In addition to providing food and shelter to unemployed men and women, Bethune's NYA, the WPA, and the Civilian Conservation Corps (CCC) offered jobs and training to needy individuals of every race. For many black workers, these programs provided the best wages they had ever received.

Still, some black people continued to voice discontent with racial bias in New Deal programs. Rather than seeking to muzzle these criticisms, in 1937, Bethune called on black leaders to address them at a conference at Howard University. "Until now," she said, "opportunities have not been offered for Negroes themselves to suggest a comprehensive program for the full integration of benefits and responsibilities of American democracy." The report that resulted from the National Conference on the Problems of the Negro and Negro Youth provided a balanced assessment of Roosevelt's programs, conceding that black Americans had received unprecedented benefits from the New Deal. But it bluntly acknowledged the New Deal's limitations: "It is a matter of common knowledge that the Negro has not shared equitably in all of the services the Government offers its citizens." The delegates proposed that the federal government take over administration of New Deal programs from state and local officials to prevent further racial discrimination.

Gains and Setbacks

The criticisms of the New Deal expressed at various conferences foreshadowed the assessments of historians who have studied the New Deal. These scholars have concluded that Roosevelt did little to confront racism and racial discrimination. He sought to appeal to black voters without supporting civil rights reforms that would alienate southern segregationists or northern workers who competed with black people for jobs and housing.

Some of the New Deal's deficiencies had long-term consequences that widened the economic gulf between white and black Americans even further.For example, when the Agricultural Adjustment Administration gave subsidies to farm owners who reduced production and purchased machinery (such as the mechanical cotton picker), black sharecroppers and farm laborers suffered. Moreover, labor unions were not prohibited from maintaining racially exclusive practices, and federal housing programs often reinforced existing patterns of racial segregation. Most significant, the exclusion of farm workers and domestic servants from the Social Security program had a damaging effect on the very categories in which black workers predominated.

Yet, despite their limitations, government social programs delivered much needed benefits to many African Americans. In addition to providing direct relief, such as food, New Deal programs gave training and jobs to black workers who had previously been unemployed or restricted to menial jobs and domestic service. African Americans also benefited from the rapid expansion of the union movement following passage of the National Labor Relations Act (called the Wagner Act, after its Senate sponsor), which protected workers' right to join unions and bargain collectively. In 1937, the Brotherhood of Sleeping Car Porters won a major victory when the fiercely antiunion Pullman Company recognized its right to bargain on behalf of porters and maids who worked on the trains. The Brotherhood's president, A. Philip Randolph, then affiliated his union with the American Federation of Labor (AFL), even though many AFL craft unions excluded black workers. As the AFL's most prominent black labor leader, Randolph became a persistent critic of racial discrimination in the labor movement.

Although the Wagner Act did not prevent unions from excluding black people or prevent employers from firing nonunionized black workers, it did strengthen the new Congress of Industrial Organizations (CIO), which organized workers by industry rather than by craft, as the AFL did. Recognizing that black replacements (often labeled "scabs") could undermine strikes, CIO organizers energetically recruited black workers, targeting especially those working in Detroit's automobile factories. This strategy contributed to the success of United Auto Workers' strikes at General Motors, Chrysler, and Ford. Such successes strengthened Bethune's conviction that, on balance, the New Deal improved African Americans' lives. She would later recall of her decade of service in the Roosevelt administration, "More than once I proposed pretty drastic steps to end the hideous discriminations and second-class citizenship that make the South a blot upon our democracy." When she asked Roosevelt "why this couldn't be done at once or that done immediately," the president pointed to political realities. But Bethune wrote that Roosevelt expected Americans to achieve racial equality in time. "That day will come," she quoted the president as saying.

Black Artists and the Cultural Mainstream

In New Orleans, sixteen-year-old Margaret Walker heard her parents discussing an upcoming visit by Langston Hughes. The white president of the college where they taught had told them that Hughes charged a fee of $100 and that he didn't think one hundred people would pay a dollar apiece to come to hear a Negro poet. But one *thousand* people came. That night, Walker later recalled, "was one of the most memorable in my life." At the reception after the reading, she nervously handed Hughes a manuscript of her poems. "He said I had talent," she recalled, "and urged my parents to send me to school in the North, where I would have more freedom to grow."

Margaret Walker and the Works Progress Administration

After Walker graduated from Northwestern University in 1936, she found work with the WPA's Writers' Project, one of many New Deal programs that provided jobs for people who would otherwise have been unemployed. For many black artists, actors, musicians, and writers, these federal jobs were an opportunity to earn a living while developing their craft. Walker's project was to write a guide to Illinois—part of a nationwide research effort to produce touring and historical guides for every state. She was able to support both herself and her sister on her salary of $85 a month.

For Walker, the job meant far more than just a wage. Working for the WPA, she believed, helped end "the long isolation of the Negro artist" and fostered "a great deal of exchange between black and white writers, artists, actors, dancers, and other theater people." A supervisor in her office was author Richard Wright, already a leading force in Chicago's black community. When she had first heard him speak at a meeting of Chicago's South Side Writers' Group, she was fascinated by his observations on "the sad state of Negro writing" and by his writings. "Even after I went home," she recalled, "I kept thinking, 'My God, how that man can write!'" Over the next year, Walker and Wright had long conversations about their literary ambitions. The Writers' Project, Walker later recalled "turned out to be one of the best writers' schools I ever attended." "The greatest significance of the WPA," she concluded, was that it accomplished what nobody believed possible: "a renaissance of the arts and American culture, with the appearance of spectacular artists or artistic figures, phenomenal programs, and immortal creative work."

The WPA gave early, crucial support to many talented African Americans. Ralph Ellison, who would later write the prize-winning novel *Invisible Man*

(1952), worked for the Writers' Project in New York. Zora Neale Hurston, soon to achieve prominence for her novel *Their Eyes Were Watching God* (1937), conducted fieldwork for the Writers' Project in Florida, interviewing former slaves as part of an effort to preserve the fading memories of those once held in bondage. Aaron Douglas created murals for the New York Public Library, while Jacob Lawrence gained early training as a painter in the federally sponsored Harlem Arts Center. Oberlin graduate Shirley Graham worked for the Federal Theater Project directing plays, including *Swing Mikado* (1939), a jazzy adaptation of the Gilbert and Sullivan play with black actors.

Paul Robeson and the Black Role in Hollywood

As federal programs fueled advances in African American culture, the expanding entertainment industry also accelerated the entry of black artists and entertainers into American mass culture. Despite the Depression—or perhaps owing to it—large numbers of Americans bought mass-produced novels and records, attended movies, and went to nightclubs and dance halls in the 1930s. Nearly everyone listened to the radio. More than ever before, black entertainers attracted white fans. Still isolated in mostly separate social worlds, black and white Americans nevertheless now danced to the same commercially popular variant of jazz and blues called swing. Although white executives dominated the entertainment industry and catered mainly to white consumers, African American musicians, singers, and dancers had reason to hope. Like Langston Hughes, they found that their talents could make them a decent living. As entertainer Paul Robeson sardonically observed in 1935, "In a popular form, Negro music, launched by white men—not Negroes—has swept the world."

Robeson's star shown so brightly that he was willing to accept the risks that came with his leftist political ties. During the 1920s, he had earned admiration in Harlem, first as a professional football player. (He had been an All-American football star and a Phi Beta Kappa student at Rutgers.) Then he attracted notice as an actor and singer during the heyday of the Harlem Renaissance. His fame spread quickly following critically acclaimed performances in the Broadway production of Eugene O'Neill's *Emperor Jones* (1925). He also played a starring role in black filmmaker Oscar Micheaux's *Body and Soul* (1925) and had a brief but memorable part singing "Ol' Man River" in the 1929 Hollywood musical *Show Boat*. Despite the onset of the Great Depression, Robeson's continuing success as an entertainer brought him personal wealth, a home in London, and freedom to expand his political and cultural contacts. He became acquainted with leftist radicals, such as the Jamaican Marxist writer C. L. R. James, and with African nationalists, such as Nnamdi Azikiwe (later president of Nigeria) and Jomo Kenyatta (later president of Kenya). By 1934, Robeson had resolved that "in my music, my plays, my films, I want to carry always this central idea: to be African."

But Robeson made this decision at a time when Hollywood studios cast black actors in comic bit roles—mainly as servants, porters, or menial laborers—in films whose plots focused on white characters. Stepin Fetchit, who depicted slow-witted, slow-moving racial stereotypes, was the highest-paid black actor

As an actor, the charismatic Paul Robeson was one of the first black men to play serious roles in the primarily white American theater. He also performed in a number of films, including a remake of *The Emperor Jones* (1933).

in Hollywood. He established a model for subsequent black comics who demeaned themselves to get laughs. In 1935, jazz pioneer Louis "Satchmo" Armstrong clowned and played his trumpet in *Pennies from Heaven* (1936), starring white actor Bing Crosby, and thereafter took similar cameo movie parts. Child actor Shirley Temple's hit films included roles for talented blacks; in *The Little Colonel* (1935), Hattie McDaniel played Mammy and Bill "Bojangles" Robinson danced. Despite the limitations of such roles, the presence of African Americans in Hollywood films attracted black ticket buyers. It also enabled the major studios to quash competition from independent black film producers such as Oscar Micheaux. Some black performers (and their fans) saw even these stereotypical Hollywood roles as personal and racial breakthroughs. McDaniel, who won an Academy Award for her performance—again as "Mammy"—in the 1939 epic *Gone With the Wind,* defended her roles emphatically: "I'd rather play a maid than be one."

The Swing Era

While Robeson harbored reservations about trends in the entertainment industry, many African American musicians welcomed them. By the mid-1930s, the swing phenomenon took jazz from the small clubs in the black sections of New Orleans, Chicago, and New York to bigger nightclubs and urban radio stations throughout the nation. Swing musicians, black and white alike, revolutionized popular music in the United States and around the world. As a struggling student, Pauli Murray savored Harlem's Apollo Theater as one of the "bright spots." There, she said, "we could sit in the balcony for twenty-five cents and see the great Negro entertainers in the heyday of their youth—Ethel Waters, Jackie (Moms) Mabley, the one-legged dancer Peg Leg Bates, tap dancers Peter, Peaches, and Duke, comedian Galley de Gaston, and the great bands led by such extraordinary musicians as Duke Ellington and Cab "Hi Di Ho" Calloway."

The appeal of these performers transcended racial lines. Both Ellington and the flamboyant Calloway were headliners at New York's Cotton Club, which, significantly, relocated from black Harlem to midtown Manhattan. By the mid-1930s, the bands of Ellington, Calloway, Count Basie, Fletcher Henderson, and Chick Webb were facing competition from highly popular white bandleaders such as Tommy Dorsey, Glenn Miller, and Benny Goodman, often called the "King of Swing." After blues singer Billie "Lady Day" Holiday began performing with white bands, she redirected her career by singing regularly at New York's Café Society, a hangout for bohemians and leftists of all races. It was there in 1939 that she introduced "Strange Fruit," a haunting antilynching song with lyrics written by a white Communist schoolteacher.

The popularity of swing music enabled some black performers to reach white audiences, but the tradition of southern blues music was kept alive in small clubs and juke joints. Blues musicians Leadbelly and Josh White appealed to northern leftists who appreciated authentic expressions of southern black working-class consciousness. Robeson himself continued to sing traditional African American music, although his film acting increasingly overshadowed his singing career. The tradition of black sacred music also remained vibrant as gospel singing evolved in new directions in big-city church choirs

Billie Holiday transformed familiar songs with her intensely personal interpretations.

featuring stirring compositions, including "Precious Lord, Take My Hand," by Thomas A. Dorsey, often called the Father of Gospel Music.

African Americans would continue to debate whether the growing popularity of black musical styles was a positive or negative trend. Many African Americans resented entertainers who perpetuated racial stereotypes while performing before white audiences. Nevertheless, most black entertainers were widely admired in black communities. More than ever before, successful black entertainers also became unofficial racial representatives. When the NAACP awarded its annual Spingarn Medal to opera singer Marian Anderson in 1939, the honor was a testimony to a performer who had broken racial barriers. That year, after she was denied permission to perform at Washington's Constitutional Hall (owned by the Daughters of the American Revolution), Eleanor Roosevelt and Secretary of the Interior Harold Ickes invited Anderson to give an open-air concert at the Lincoln Memorial. On a chilly Easter Sunday, 75,000 fans came to hear her.

Native Son and the Decline of Leftist Radicalism

"Generally speaking, Negro writing in the past has been confined to humble novels, poems, and plays, prim and decorous ambassadors who went a-beggin to white America," Richard Wright complained in his 1937 "Blueprint for Negro Writing." Wright's essay concerned literature, but his criticisms applied as well to black entertainers and artists who compromised their integrity to gain white acceptance. During his career, Wright struggled to break free of constraints that prevented him from honestly depicting "Negro life in all of its manifold and intricate relationships." During his formative years in the South, his ambition had been stifled by the Jim Crow system and his own family. He had found a way out through his exposure to literature that "evoked in me vague glimpses of life's possibilities." After migrating to Chicago during the late 1920s, he still struggled to make a living, but he eventually recognized that his writings could make readers aware of what black people endured. Then, when he attended meetings of the John Reed Club, a Communist-affiliated group of artists and writers, his feelings of alienation gave way to hopes for a united working class. "Out of the magazines I read came a passionate call for the experiences of the disinherited," he remembered. "It did not say: 'Be like us and we will like you, maybe.' It said: 'If you possess enough courage to speak out what you are, you will find that you are not alone.'"

Wright joined the Communist Party, but his political views continued evolving as he gained confidence as a writer. He saw himself as a revolutionary, but his writings rarely discussed Marxism. Instead, in his journalistic pieces about Chicago's black community, he avoided the tendency of some Communist writers to see African Americans only as potential working-class allies. He sought to convey the complexities of American race relations—in particular, the ways in which shared experiences shaped African American political attitudes. His vivid description of the massive street celebration that followed Joe Louis's knockout victory in 1935 over former heavyweight champion Max Baer reflected his understanding of the broad appeal of black sports heroes such as Louis.

By the time he wrote "Blueprint for Negro Writing," Wright was willing to criticize Communists for insisting that black writers be political propagandists. He urged them instead to match the dedication displayed "in the Negro workers' struggle to free Herndon and the Scottsboro Boys" while still paying attention to the distinctive racial or "nationalist" aspects of African American culture. That culture, he believed, derived largely from the religious life and folklore of black people rather than just from their work experiences. Black writers, he added, must understand this culture to reach black readers. "Marxism is but the starting point," he continued. "No theory of life can take the place of life."

In 1938, Wright, now in New York, sent Margaret Walker a special-delivery letter asking for news clippings about a sensational story then breaking in Chicago. A young African American accused of rape and murder had been captured by the police and forced to confess to five major crimes. Wright saw the accusations against this black youngster not as another Scottsboro-type episode of class and racial oppression but as a basis for a more complex story. Rather than assuming that the young man was innocent, Wright made his character guilty. Then he sought to imagine the circumstances that might have led his black protagonist—Bigger Thomas—to kill a white woman who sympathized with Communist efforts to help African Americans. *Native Son*, published in 1940, became the first best-selling novel by a black author.

Many readers of *Native Son* were shocked by Wright's raw language—especially his vivid depiction of the killing of Mary Dalton. Although Wright did not justify Thomas's crime, he allowed readers to see it as resulting from a series of tragic misunderstandings rooted in racial and class differences. *Native Son* revealed not only the wide gulf that separated Thomas and his employer, Dalton's wealthy father, but also the gulf between Thomas's perspective and that of Communists who saw him solely as a victim of oppression. When Mary Dalton asks Thomas to drive her and her Communist boyfriend, Jan Erlone, to a black restaurant, Thomas becomes increasingly uncomfortable and resentful as Jan's probing questions prod him to reveal that his father was killed in a southern antiblack riot.

> *"Listen, Bigger," Jan replied, "that's what we want to stop. That's what we Communists are fighting. We want to stop people from treating others that way. I'm a member of the Party. Mary sympathizes. Don't you think if we got together we could stop things like that?"*
>
> *"I don't know," Bigger said; he was feeling the rum rising to his head. "There's a lot of white people in the world."*
>
> *"You've read about the Scottsboro boys?"*
>
> *"I heard about 'em."*
>
> *"Don't you think we did a good job in helping to keep 'em from killing those boys?"*
>
> *"It was all right."*
>
> *"You know, Bigger," said Mary, "we'd like to be friends of yours."*
>
> *He said nothing.*

Wright's narrative illuminates the enormous racial barriers that prevented Bigger, Mary, and Jan from seeing one another as individuals rather than as black or white. After returning to the Dalton home, Bigger carries the intoxicated Mary to her bedroom. Sexually aroused by her helpless condition, he also fears being discovered in a white woman's room and quiets Mary by pressing a pillow over her face, inadvertently suffocating her. Eventually caught after a massive search, he is tried for murder. As in the Scottsboro case, the Communist Party provides Thomas with legal assistance. Yet even his well-intentioned lawyer can never fully understand what led Thomas to kill Dalton and then his own girlfriend to avoid getting caught. Condemned to die, Thomas eventually perceives that his crime came not only from racial and class oppression but also from his own choices.

Richard Wright's growing disenchantment with the Communist Party was shared by other black intellectuals who had once been drawn to Communist-led campaigns. Langston Hughes wrote to a friend, "I am laying off of political poetry for a while, since the world situation, methinks, is too complicated." Ralph Ellison, who became Wright's protégé after arriving in New York from Tuskegee Institute, distanced himself from his mentor's Communist friends. A friend of Margaret Walker's advised her to "get to know" leftist writers but to avoid "getting to be a part of them and all they represent."

Much had changed since the early 1930s, when Communists staged massive protests on behalf of the Scottsboro defendants. A decade later, the case had faded from public view. In 1938 Alabama officials quietly released one of the four defendants still in prison, but two of the other defendants would wait until 1944 before they were paroled. Haywood Patterson, labeled a troublemaker by prison officials, would languish in prison cells until 1948, when he escaped to Michigan, where he avoided extradition attempts. He enjoyed a few years of freedom in Michigan before being imprisoned once again. Patterson resembled Bigger Thomas in age and impoverished background, but he was largely forgotten by the time Wright's doomed fictional character captured the nation's attention. Looking back on all that he had endured, Patterson concluded shortly before his death that the Scottsboro campaign had advanced the cause of civil rights. "I guess my people gained more off the Scottsboro case than any of us boys did. It led to putting Negroes on juries in the South. It made the whole country, in fact the whole world, talk about how the Negro people have to live in the South."

Conclusion

By the time *Native Son* achieved bestseller status, Communist radicalism had been largely supplanted by New Deal liberalism. Still, the party's attention to civil rights issues and its innovative use of mass militancy made a lasting impact on American race relations. In a broad sense, leftist agitation and publications expanded popular awareness of racial discrimination and encouraged appreciation for African American art, music, and literature. Yet, as New Deal programs moderated some of the hardships of the Great Depression and as Communist leaders turned their attention from civil rights issues to the threat of German Nazism, black militancy continued to evolve in new directions. The outbreak of war in Europe prompted black protests against segregation in the military and discriminatory hiring practices in war-related industries. The NAACP's legal campaign, now under the direction of Thurgood Marshall, moved ahead with increasing confidence. Many African Americans had suffered during the Great Depression, but they had also shared experiences with Americans who were not black. Black Americans still faced widespread discrimination and segregation, but in important ways the political, economic, and cultural changes of the 1930s had brought them closer to the nation's political, economic, and cultural mainstream.

Questions for Review and Reflection

1. How did national political and economic factors influence the outcome of the "Scottsboro boys" legal case, and how did this incident in turn influence the politics and race relations of the 1930s?

2. How did the Great Depression affect the status of African Americans in the nation's social, economic, political, and cultural life?

3. Discuss the differences distinguishing the tactics and strategies used by the NAACP and by the Communist Party to bring about racial and economic change.

4. In what ways were African Americans especially affected by the New Deal? What were the strengths and limitations of Roosevelt's policies as they applied to African Americans?

5. Discuss the racial implications of changes during the 1930s in American popular culture—including music, movies, literature, etc.

Fighting Fascism Abroad and Racism at Home

A. Philip Randolph Challenges President Franklin D. Roosevelt

"Which class were you in at Harvard?" President Franklin D. Roosevelt asked A. Philip Randolph, head of the Brotherhood of Sleeping Car Porters, as they began their White House meeting on June 18, 1941. Randolph knew the question was small talk, and the attempt at flattery fell flat. Randolph had attended Cookman Institute in Florida and took night classes at New York City College. "I never went to Harvard, Mr. President," he responded. He became increasingly impatient as Roosevelt chatted amiably with Walter White of the NAACP and T. Arnold Hill of the Urban League. "Mr. President, time is running on," Randolph finally interjected. "You are quite busy, I know, but what we want to talk with you about is the problem of jobs for Negroes in defense industries."

This was Randolph's second visit to the White House. The previous September the three black leaders had urged Roosevelt to end racial discrimination in the military and in the defense industries already supplying weapons to Great Britain in the European war ignited by Germany's invasion of Poland in September 1939. Although war industries, not New Deal programs, were finally ending the Great Depression, black Americans were still shut out of jobs. As head of the nation's largest black union, Randolph was determined to end job discrimination, brashly proposing in early 1941 that African Americans stage a massive march on Washington. "Black people will not get justice until the administration leaders in Washington see masses of Negroes—ten, twenty, fifty

1940	William H. Hastie is appointed War Department advisor on racial issues. Franklin D. Roosevelt is elected for third term as president.
1941	To avert A. Philip Randolph's threatened march on Washington, Roosevelt establishes the Fair Employment Practices Committee (FEPC). The Japanese attack on Pearl Harbor, on December 7, draws the United States into World War II.
1943	Hastie resigns in protest over continuing segregation and discrimination in the armed forces. James Farmer and other civil rights activists form the nonviolent protest group that later becomes the Congress of Racial Equality (CORE). Twenty-five African Americans and nine white Americans die in a Detroit race riot, spurred by conflicts over housing and jobs. A race riot in Harlem also reveals racial tension.
1944	In *Smith* v. *Allwright,* the Supreme Court declares that "white primary" laws violate the Fifteenth Amendment. At Port Chicago, California, a naval supply ship explodes, killing 320 men, including 202 African American munitions loaders. Gunnar Myrdal's *An American Dilemma,* a landmark study of race relations in the United States, is published.
1945	Roosevelt dies, and Harry S. Truman becomes president. World War II ends.
1946	Hastie is appointed governor of the U.S. Virgin Islands. In *Morgan* v. *Commonwealth of Virginia,* segregation on interstate buses is ruled unconstitutional.
1947	CORE and the Fellowship of Reconciliation (FOR) launch a two-week Journey of Reconciliation through the South to test compliance with the *Morgan* decision. Brooklyn Dodgers second baseman Jackie Robinson breaks color bar in major league baseball. *To Secure These Rights: The Report of the President's Committee on Civil Rights* calls for federal leadership in civil rights reform.
1948	In *Sipuel* v. *Oklahoma State Board of Regents,* the Supreme Court rules that states must admit qualified African Americans to previously all-white graduate schools when no comparable black institution is available. In *Shelley* v. *Kraemer,* the Supreme Court rules that racially restrictive housing covenants are not legally enforceable. Truman issues Executive Order 9981, calling for "equality of treatment and opportunity" in the military.
1949	Paul Robeson's controversial speech in Paris against the Cold War prompts condemnations from the NAACP and baseball star Robinson.

thousand—on the White House lawn," he insisted. Randolph's idea quickly became a movement, as his associates mobilized support in numerous cities.

Now, with the march just two weeks away, the meeting at the White House was the last chance for negotiation. Despite pressure from the administration, Randolph refused to call off the protest unless African Americans had "jobs, not promises." He pressed the president to issue an executive order banning discrimination in defense plants, but Roosevelt objected: "If I issue an executive order for you, then there'll be no end to other groups coming in here and asking me to issue executive orders for them, too. In any event, I cannot do anything unless you call off this march of yours."

"I'm sorry, Mr. President," Randolph firmly replied. "The march cannot be called off."

After intense discussion, Roosevelt backed down. On June 24, he issued Executive Order 8802 authorizing a Fair Employment Practices Committee (FEPC) to ensure "full and equitable participation of all workers in the defense industries, without discrimination because of race, creed, color, or national origin." Although some black activists regretted that Randolph had not won an end to segregation in the military, the threatened march produced the most significant presidential order on behalf of African Americans since Reconstruction. Randolph had demonstrated the potential of mass activism to achieve federal civil rights reforms. "A tall, courtly black man with Shakespearean diction and the stare of an eagle," NAACP leader Roy Wilkins later recalled, "had looked the patrician Roosevelt in the eye—and made him back down."

Randolph's confrontation with Roosevelt reflected growing African American militancy and the increasing importance of black voters in the Democratic Party's New Deal coalition. During the previous decade, as the Roosevelt administration sought to end economic depression and then to prepare for American involvement in the spreading war, black Americans increasingly expected that federal power would be used to address both racial and economic issues. In August 1941, Roosevelt raised these expectations when he met with British leader Winston Churchill to sign an Atlantic Charter affirming that the war against "Nazi tyranny" in Germany was also intended to secure democratic principles, such as "the right of all peoples to choose the form of government under which they live." Although Churchill quickly clarified that the charter would not apply to Great Britain's colonial possessions, it fed the hopes of African Americans that the war would bring democracy to not only European colonies but also southern states where black Americans were prevented from voting.

As during previous wars, African Americans contributed to World War II mobilization, but they also challenged segregation and seized employment opportunities created by wartime needs for military personnel and industrial labor. Although wartime civil rights militancy was often locally rather than nationally organized, significant black support was evident in the NAACP, Randolph's March on Washington Movement, and, to a lesser extent, the Communist-backed National Negro Congress.

When the wartime alliance of the United States and the Soviet Union gave way to Cold War hostilities, growing anticommunism fostered bitter ideological divisions among black leaders. While most NAACP leaders identified with the

American government's efforts to combat communism at home and abroad, black leftists such as W. E. B. Du Bois and Paul Robeson strongly criticized Cold War policies and tried in vain to push the new United Nations to act against not only colonialism but also racial discrimination within the United States. The 1948, presidential election proved a turning point in the decline of black leftists, who backed the Progressive Party candidate Henry Wallace. In contrast, NAACP leaders and their liberal allies supported the victorious Democratic incumbent, Harry S. Truman, and they emerged from the election confident that their strategy of litigation and lobbying would soon bring major civil rights reforms.

African Americans in the Armed Forces

On the morning of December 7, 1941, Dorie Miller, Mess Attendant, second class, was collecting laundry on the battleship USS *West Virginia*, stationed at Pearl Harbor in Hawaii, when he heard the call to battle stations. Japanese planes were attacking American naval forces. Finding his station already destroyed by a torpedo, he raced to the deck and began carrying wounded sailors to safety. After moving the ship's mortally wounded captain to a first aid

Mess Attendant Dorie Miller was awarded the Navy Cross for his courage in battle aboard the USS *West Virginia* during the Pearl Harbor attack.

"above and beyond the call of duty"

DORIE MILLER
Received the Navy Cross
at Pearl Harbor, May 27, 1942

station, Miller returned to the bridge, behind a 50-caliber antiaircraft machine gun. Although not trained to use the weapon, he fired at attacking Japanese planes, shooting down at least two and perhaps as many as five. When the ammunition ran out, he was ordered to abandon the heavily damaged ship.

For his extraordinary courage in battle, Miller was awarded the Navy Cross and promoted to mess attendant, first class. Though his heroism brought him fleeting fame, it did little to open opportunities for black sailors. His experience proved emblematic of the experience of African Americans in the U.S. Armed Forces during World War II. Even as they contributed to the war against fascism—and especially the superior race doctrines of German leader Adolf Hitler—they faced racism within their own ranks. Yet for African Americans whose political perspectives were shaped by the Great Depression, the war was a new chance to fight racial discrimination by linking this cause to the democratic ideals for which the United States claimed to be fighting.

William H. Hastie and Jim Crow in the Military

Though A. Philip Randolph's threat to march on Washington prompted concessions from Roosevelt, military leaders maintained a segregated military in which black recruits were assigned menial roles. Army chief of staff George C. Marshall expressed the prevailing view: "The settlement of vexing social problems cannot be permitted to complicate the tremendous task of the War Department and thereby jeopardize discipline and morale." In the U.S. Navy, African Americans such as Miller served as stewards and cooks. In the Army, they were assigned to all-black support or service units, such as the Quartermaster Corps, under white officers—most of them southern, in part because some military leaders believed that southern whites had a special understanding of black soldiers. At the beginning of 1940, the United States had only two African American military officers—Colonel Benjamin O. Davis and his son, Lieutenant Benjamin O. Davis, Jr., whose desire to train as a pilot had been frustrated by the Army Air Corps' refusal to give flight instruction to black candidates.

Black women who wanted to join the military faced similar obstacles. At the start of the war, they could volunteer only for segregated units of the Women's Auxiliary Army Corps (WAAC). The Navy's auxiliary, the WAVES (Women Accepted for Volunteer Emergency Service), did not admit black women volunteers in any capacity until the final year of the war. Despite a campaign led by Harlem's Mabel K. Staupers, the Army and Navy Nurse Corps refused to recruit black nurses until President Roosevelt intervened in 1944— just in time to build black support for his reelection.

The Roosevelt administration was forced to make overtures to black voters following a racial incident during the 1940 presidential election. On a campaign stop in New York City, Roosevelt's press secretary inadvertently kicked a black policeman who blocked his way as he rushed to catch up with the presidential party boarding a train. To counter the negative publicity, the president ordered Colonel Davis promoted to brigadier general and asked William H. Hastie, dean of Howard University's law school, to join the War Department as civilian advisor on racial issues. Hastie was at first "skeptical" about what "a person with no authority of his own" could accomplish, but he accepted the position hoping "to work effectively toward the integration of the Negro into the Army and to facilitate his placement, training, and promotion."

Hastie soon found he could do little to alter military recruitment and promotion policies. Although the 1940 Selective Service Act forbade racial discrimination, military officers assumed that segregation was necessary to maintain white soldiers' morale. Secretary of War Henry L. Stimson was adamant about keeping black soldiers under white officers. "Leadership is not embedded in the Negro race," he reflected in his diary. Yet Hastie was also well placed to collect information about black discontent in the military. One of his former assistants recalled, "Black GIs who thought they were being wronged would say, 'Goddamn it, I'm gonna write to Hastie.'" Write they did. Aeron Bells, a black college graduate from Houston, fumed, "I fail to see why I WILL BE FORCED TO SHED MY BLOOD on Democracy's battlefields as a Private and [not allowed] to volunteer as an officer candidate." Three black soldiers who had qualified as aviation cadets complained of "going from one basic training to another and getting no nearer to the Air Corp[s]." "The operative theory in the War Department was that blacks were not adequate soldiers, because they lacked courage and were too stupid to master the intricacies of modern warfare," recalled Coleman Young, future Detroit mayor, who served more than three years but never was assigned overseas.

When Hastie learned of plans to establish a segregated flight training school at Tuskegee, he decried the foolishness of duplicate facilities: "Why in the name of common sense should all this elaborate special machinery be set up to train Negro flyers?" Although convinced the segregation policy was wrong, he finally acquiesced, relieved that African Americans would finally receive flight training. Benjamin O. Davis, Jr., joined the initial group of pilot trainees at Tuskegee.

But complaints about discrimination in promotion and training opportunities were not the worst Hastie heard. A group of black soldiers at Jackson Air Base in Mississippi reported that they were "treated like wild animals here, like we are unhuman. The word Negro is never used here, all they call us are nigger do this, nigger do that." In April 1941, a black soldier at Fort Benning, Georgia, was found hanging from a tree with his hands tied behind his back. At Fort Dix, New Jersey, military police killed two black privates and wounded five others.

Hastie warned Stimson that such incidents would jeopardize military preparedness. "So long as we condone and appease un-American attitudes and practices within our own military and civilian life, we can never arouse ourselves to the exertion which the present emergency requires," he wrote in September 1941. Discontent, he explained, seethed beneath the surface: "Most white persons are unable to appreciate the rancor and bitterness which the Negro, as a matter of self-preservation, has learned to hide beneath a smile, a joke, or merely an impassive face." Hastie argued it was impossible to train a black soldier to fight "a foreign enemy" while he was treated "as less than a man at home."

After the Pearl Harbor attack in December 1941, the United States allied with Britain and the Soviet Union against the Axis alliance of Japan, Germany, and Italy. Hastie again pleaded with Stimson to end racial discrimination, and black leaders, including Mary McLeod Bethune, petitioned Roosevelt to end "the persistent, contemptuous rejection of the earnestly proffered services of the colored American" by placing black representatives on defense policy boards. But black advisors like Hastie had little impact. In early 1943, he resigned, complaining that the War Department lacked "will and understanding." The resignation of the War Department's highest-ranking black official drew attention to racial problems in the military, as did articles Hastie later published. Many black Americans admired Hastie's willingness to express his dissent publicly, and the NAACP awarded him its highest honor, the Spingarn Medal—not only for his War Department work but also for his earlier contributions to the group's legal effort.

The Double-V Campaign

Early in 1942, the *Pittsburgh Courier*, the most widely circulated black newspaper in the United States, launched the "Double-V Campaign"—for victory over the Axis on the battlefront and victory over racial prejudice on the home front. The campaign sought to push the nation to live up to the democratic principles expressed in the Atlantic Charter. The NAACP agreed that the war effort should be two-pronged: "We will fight, but we demand the right to fight as equals in every branch of the military, naval, and aviation services." Randolph also kept the spirit of his March on Washington Movement alive, urging supporters "to win the peace, for democracy, for freedom and the Brotherhood of Man without regard to his pigmentation, land of his birth or the God of his fathers." He warned that black Americans were unlikely to respond to the "close ranks" argument W. E. B. Du Bois had used in World War I. "Negroes made the blunder of closing ranks and forgetting their grievances in the last war," Randolph asserted. "We are resolved that we will not make that blunder again."

Du Bois himself conceded that World War I "did not bring us democracy" and after Pearl Harbor warned: "We close ranks again but only, now as then, to fight for democracy . . . not only for white folk but for yellow, brown and black." Few were as willing as Du Bois to link their cause to that of other oppressed groups, but World War II soon broadened the perspectives of African Americans. Langston Hughes predicted the war would "eventually shake the British Empire to the dust. That will shake Dixie's teeth too, and crack the joints of Jim Crow South Africa."

Yet racial gains did not come without struggle. Even as black resentment increased, military leaders stubbornly retained segregation policies. In defense industries, only acute labor shortages caused black employment to rise, from 3 percent of all employees in 1942 to 8 percent in 1944—still less than the proportion of black workers in the nation's workforce. But even this gain came in the face of stiff resistance from some white employers and workers. The Fair Employment Practices Committee established by Roosevelt could investigate discrimination but lacked enforcement powers.

Polls conducted by the *Pittsburgh Courier* during the early years of the war revealed considerable black discontent. One found that 82 percent of *Courier* readers were unconvinced by statements from U.S. leaders "about freedom and equality for all peoples, including the American Negro." Readers overwhelmingly supported Mahatma Gandhi and other Indian leaders who were demanding an end to British colonial rule of their nation as a price for backing the war. In response to the question "Do you feel that the Negro should soft pedal his demands for complete freedom and citizenship and await the development of the educational process," almost nine out of ten said no. In June 1942, a secret federal survey confirmed these attitudes. Nearly one-fifth of black respondents believed they would be treated better under Japanese rule than by the American government; another third thought they would be treated "about the same."

While most African Americans remained loyal to the United States, black antiwar activism was sufficiently widespread to prompt a crackdown by the Federal Bureau of Investigation (FBI) in 1942. More than eighty black critics of the military draft were arrested. Nation of Islam leader Elijah Muhammad was sentenced to a five-year prison term, and, in 1943, black pacifist Bayard Rustin, who had worked with Randolph on planning the March on Washington Movement, was sentenced to three years in prison for refusing to submit to military induction.

As the Army increasingly filled its ranks with conscripts rather than volunteers, protests by black soldiers became more frequent. Although Roosevelt issued an executive order in December 1942 banning racial discrimination within the military, black newspapers and leftist periodicals published numerous reports of discrimination and black resistance. Jackie Robinson, an Army second lieutenant and a former sports star at the University of California, Los Angeles (UCLA), was court-martialed but acquitted during the summer of 1944 for refusing to take a seat in the back of a bus near Camp Hood, Texas. When black film star Lena Horne noticed that German prisoners of war were seated in front of black soldiers for her performance at Fort Riley, Kansas, she left the stage to sing for her black fans in the rear. At Fort Huachuca, a military camp in the southern Arizona desert with the largest single concentration of black troops, a 1942 riot left three soldiers dead and others facing mutiny charges. Even a quickly arranged visit from General Benjamin Davis failed to calm racial tensions.

The worst racial incident of the war occurred at the naval ammunition base at Port Chicago, northeast of San Francisco. On July 17, 1944, a fully loaded ship exploded, killing 320 men, including 202 ammunition loaders, all of whom were black. It was the single deadliest accident of the war, accounting for 15 percent of all black naval casualties. Four days later, the Naval Court of Inquiry concluded the black seamen were at fault, absolving their white supervising officers, who often ignored safety commands and made bets to see whose crew could load the most cargo. The surviving seamen cleaned up the debris and human remains, but 258 refused to resume loading bombs without new safety procedures. "I wasn't trying to shirk work," one recalled. "But to go back to work under the same conditions, with no improvements, no changes, the same group of officers that we had, was just—we thought there was a better alternative, that's all."

Told they could be charged with mutiny and possibly face death by a firing squad, 208 seamen agreed to return to work. They were given bad-conduct discharges and docked three months' pay. The remaining fifty were charged with mutiny, leading to the largest mass court-martial in naval history. Thurgood Marshall, sent by the NAACP to observe the proceedings and support the defendants, remarked, "This is not fifty men on trial for mutiny; this is the Navy on trial for its whole vicious policy toward Negroes." The seamen "just want to know why they are the only ones doing the loading," he explained. "They wanted to know why they are segregated, why they don't get promoted." Despite Marshall's efforts, forty-four were convicted of organized mutiny, dishonorably discharged, and sentenced to between eight and fifteen years in prison. Only after the war were these sentences reduced.

The Port Chicago explosion dramatically demonstrated the constraints on black sailors, but by the time of the deadly accident attitudes were changing. Benjamin Davis, Jr., commander of the 99th Pursuit Squadron that trained at Tuskegee, recalled that questions about the unit's readiness were allayed by its combat performance in Italy. "All those who wished to denigrate the quality of the 99th's operations were silenced once and for all by its aerial victories over Anzio on two successive days in January 1944," Davis remembered. The 99th and Tuskegee Airmen Squadrons compiled a remarkable record in combat, escorting American bombers on 1,578 missions against German targets without a single loss. Grateful bomber crews called them the "Red-Tailed Angels," for the distinctive bright red paint on the tails of their planes.

Colonel Benjamin O. Davis, the leader of the 332nd Fighter Pilot Squadron (the 99th was added to the 332nd), the only all-African American unit in the U.S. Air Force, at an airbase in Rametti, Italy, in 1945.

The combat successes of the Tuskegee Airmen and the performance of black troops in combat elsewhere persuaded a military advisory committee to recommend abandoning the general policy of not assigning black soldiers to combat roles. Nonetheless, most black soldiers who participated in the Allied D-Day invasion of Europe in June 1944 served in logistical roles only. A black quartermaster regiment known as the Red Ball Express gained renown for transporting supplies to the front despite heavy enemy fire. As in the Civil War, however, the military's reluctance to use black soldiers in combat receded as casualties mounted and as African Americans constituted an increasing proportion of available troops. Late in 1944, black soldiers helped repel the last major German counteroffensive—known as the Battle of the Bulge.

During the final months of the European war, Allied Supreme Commander Dwight D. Eisenhower authorized an "experimental" departure from the military's segregation policy when he assigned about forty black soldiers as replacements in white units that had suffered heavy losses. In addition, 2,500 black volunteers were placed in predominantly white infantry units. In a subsequent study of this experiment, white officers reported that the black troops performed "very well" in combat, but top military officials belittled the study's conclusions and suppressed it. In the Pacific, the first black enlistees in the Navy's Marine Corps were sent to guard munitions dumps, although they were pressed into battle at the island of Iwo Jima when their posts came under fire.

Thus, for many African American soldiers, World War II offered more opportunities to fight racism within the military than to engage in combat against fascism abroad. A protest during the closing months of the war against a segregated officers' club at Freeman Field in Indiana revealed the extent of black militancy and foreshadowed postwar civil rights protests. Sixty-nine black officers were arrested for trying to enter a base club that violated the military's own ban on racial restrictions. Coleman Young, one of those arrested, recalled that "there was nearly a full-scale mutiny on the base. The black troops refused to gas airplanes or to carry out the basic daily operations of the post." Eventually most charges were dropped, the club was integrated, and fifty years later the Air Force made an official vindication.

Racial Issues on the Home Front

"We did not plan our arrest intentionally," Pauli Murray wrote to a friend. "The situation developed, and we applied what we knew of *Satyagraha* on the spot." In her autobiography Murray described this technique, which Gandhi had used in India's independence struggle, as "nonviolent resistance coupled with good will." In March 1940, when Murray and a friend were jailed in Petersburg, Virginia, for refusing to obey segregation laws on an interstate bus, they put the idea into practice. They drafted a Statement of Facts, carefully recording the details of their arrest and imprisonment, and a polite memo to the prison deputy saying they would cooperate with prison regulations. Murray remembered that the deputy was unsettled; he knew how to deal with hostility, but not with "courteous behavior which nevertheless revealed a clear demand for justice." The NAACP attorneys who came the next day praised the Statement of Facts: "Trained attorneys could hardly have done a better job." Nevertheless, the women were quickly convicted, and the subsequent NAACP appeal was unsuccessful. But Murray had learned an important lesson: "that creative nonviolent resistance could be a powerful weapon in the struggle for human dignity."

Pauli Murray and "Jane" Crow

Teaching in New York for the Works Progress Administration (WPA), Murray had become immersed in Depression-era radicalism and aligned with a small socialist—but anticommunist—group. "The study of economic oppression led me to realize that Negroes were not alone but were part of an unending struggle for human dignity the world over," she later wrote. Fighting for social justice also increased her sense of pride: "Seeing the relationship between my personal cause and the universal cause of freedom released me from a sense of isolation, helped me to rid myself of vestiges of shame over my racial history, and gave me an unequivocal understanding that equality of treatment was my birthright and not something to be earned."

In 1941, Murray entered Howard University's Law School, where her mentors included Dean William Hastie and others involved in the NAACP's legal campaign. She was excited to be in a place where students helped research key discrimination cases. "When a case was to be presented to the Supreme Court," she recalled, "the entire school assembled to hear dress rehearsal arguments." But her experience at Howard, where she was held up for ridicule as the only woman in her class, made her aware of "the twin evils of discriminatory sex bias, which I quickly labeled Jane Crow."

Murray joined the Fellowship of Reconciliation (FOR), an international pacifist organization founded in 1914, and soon learned of black activists using

Denied admission to law school at the University of North Carolina in 1938 because of her race, and to Harvard University because of her gender, Pauli Murray worked to dismantle both types of barriers.

Gandhian tactics to resist segregation. James Farmer, a graduate of Howard's school of religion and FOR's first "race relations secretary," had helped found a civil rights organization in Chicago that later became the national Congress of Racial Equality (CORE). Murray was even more drawn to Bayard Rustin, another black pacifist on FOR's staff, whose background in the Depression-era left somewhat paralleled her own. In addition, as Murray experienced gender discrimination, Rustin was marginalized as a homosexual in a period before this sexual orientation could be acknowledged even within radical political circles.

Murray's growing commitment to Gandhian ideas was realized when the Howard campus mobilized to protest the arrest of three female undergraduates for challenging segregation at a nearby lunch counter. Murray became an informal legal advisor for student groups planning nonviolent action, and in the spring of 1943, she joined a protest at the Little Palace Cafeteria, where students who had been refused service at the buffet line took their empty trays to open seats, sat down, and opened books to read. After a few days of these "sitdowns," the restaurant owner agreed to serve African Americans. "We were jubilant," Murray recalled. "We had proved that intelligent, imaginative action could bring positive results." Noting that twelve of the nineteen Howard protestors were female, she observed, "We women reasoned that it was our job to help make the country for which our black brothers were fighting a freer place in which to live when they returned from wartime service."

Wartime Race Riots

Murray's jubilation over successful protests against segregated facilities in Washington faded quickly in the summer of 1943, when racial violence exploded in several American cities. Detroit endured the most deadly riot of all. But "few Negroes were surprised," she claimed, as "the racial tensions that produced it had been building steadily throughout the war." Racial antagonism was evident wherever black workers competed for jobs previously monopolized by white people and for the limited supply of decent, affordable housing. But Detroit was a special case, as its booming auto plants, converted to the production of tanks and airplanes, attracted 50,000 African Americans between 1942 and 1945. Under pressure, the black–white alliances created by the Congress of Industrial Organizations (CIO) broke down. Thousands of white United Auto Workers (UAW) members walked out at one plant to prevent the promotion of eight black UAW members, and Packard employees staged a "hate strike" when three black women were hired as drill operators. In February 1942, three black families moving into the federally funded Sojourner Truth Housing Project were menaced by a white mob armed with knives, clubs, and guns. National Guardsmen restored order, but as more violence threatened, city officials promised that subsequent public housing projects would not disrupt the racial composition of surrounding neighborhoods, a policy soon adopted elsewhere.

These isolated racial clashes set the stage for the widespread violence that broke out in June 1943, following a fistfight between a black man and a white man at a Detroit amusement park. Within hours, rioting had spread to many areas of the city and continued the following day. White mobs attacked black workers, and black rioters looted white-owned stores. More than 6,000 federal troops restored order, but the city was devastated. Twenty-five African Americans (seventeen shot by police) and nine white people died; at least 700 other people were injured. Property loss was extensive. Murray wrote to government officials proposing that a national commission conduct a full investigation. She also noted that President Roosevelt was "strangely silent about the worst racial outbreak to occur in the nation since 1919."

In an article entitled "Negroes Are Fed Up," Murray predicted further riots. No sooner than it was published, the prophecy proved true. In Harlem, on August 1, 1943, word that a white policeman had killed a black soldier drew 3,000 residents into the streets. The next day Murray walked through the area and was astounded "that human beings could have accomplished such utter destruction so swiftly and ruthlessly." Harlem, she wrote, "was like a bombed-out war zone." She caught its mood in the aftermath: "The undercurrent everywhere and from every lip was 'These riots had to come.'"

The NAACP's New Legal Thrust

The upsurge of black discontent during World War II put pressure on the normally cautious NAACP head, Walter White, to establish new branches and expand membership. Though the organization welcomed the rapid growth of dues-paying members, many activists like Murray were discouraged by its reluctance to support mass militancy at the local level. Yet Murray was also encouraged by the legal efforts spearheaded by the NAACP lawyers at Howard. Hastie assisted Thurgood Marshall, head of the NAACP's Legal Defense and Education Fund, on the case of Lonnie Smith, a black physician in Houston who had tried to vote in the Texas Democratic primary. In 1944 an appeal brought the NAACP its most significant victory of the war years, when the U.S. Supreme Court ruled in *Smith* v. *Allwright* that racially exclusive "white primaries" violated the Fifteenth Amendment. The decision had special importance in southern states, where the Democratic Party's long-standing dominance meant that victors in its primaries faced only token Republican opposition in the general elections. Although black Southerners attempting to vote still faced other obstacles, such as literacy tests, poll taxes, and outright violence, the decision marked a major step in the long struggle to eliminate barriers to black voting.

While the Court deliberated the *Smith* case, Murray provocatively suggested during a civil rights seminar that the NAACP's litigation strategy was flawed because it did not directly challenge the *Plessy* v. *Ferguson* doctrine of separate but equal. "One day during class discussion, in a flash of poetic insight," she recalled, "I advanced a radical approach that few legal scholars considered viable in 1944—namely, that the time had come to make a frontal assault on the constitutionality of segregation per se instead of continuing to acquiesce in the *Plessy* doctrine." Murray's comment foreshadowed the approach the NAACP would adopt within a decade and brought her to Hastie's attention. Impressed by her activism and sharp legal mind, Hastie suggested she pursue advanced legal training and return to serve on Howard's faculty. With his support, she applied to a master's program at Harvard Law School, only to learn that women were not admitted. She appealed her rejection and even contacted Eleanor Roosevelt to secure a presidential letter of support, but Harvard refused to change its position. Losing her first battle "against 'Jane Crow,'" as she put it, only strengthened her resolve to be not only a civil rights attorney but also "an unabashed feminist as well."

Accepting an offer to continue her legal studies at the University of California's Boalt Hall School of Law, Murray spent the summer of 1944 in Los Angeles. Her research interests were spurred by the difficulties she and a friend encountered finding an apartment in south-central Los Angeles, where black workers in the booming shipbuilding and aircraft industries competed for housing with whites. Though Murray and her friend succeeded in renting a place on the racial border, they were threatened with legal action. Murray refused to move and began researching the housing issue, drawing on sociological and psychological studies of the harmful effects of racial segregation. Years later, Howard professor Spottswood Robinson told her that her research paper had helped the NAACP legal team prepare arguments for two landmark cases: *Shelley* v. *Kraemer* (1948), which ruled that racially restrictive housing covenants were not legally enforceable, and *Brown* v. *Board of Education* (1954), striking down school segregation.

At Boalt Hall, Murray developed ideas about overturning *Plessy* as she wrote her master's thesis on equal opportunity in employment. Her views were also shaped by her roommates at Berkeley's International House, where more than thirty nationalities were represented. "Over coffee and cigarettes, I listened to heated conversations on the rights of small countries and the responsibilities of large ones and to frequent expressions of resentment over the 'superman complex' of the United States," she later wrote. "There were laments over 'forgotten Africa' and proddings from Zionists on the right of Palestinian Jews to a homeland." Murray appreciated that she was "learning to see the civil rights struggle within the wider context of all human rights."

Finishing her degree in 1945, Murray passed the California bar exam and took a job as a deputy state attorney general. At age thirty-five, with three degrees to her credit, her accomplishments were considerable. She was recognized by the National Council of Negro Women as one of twelve outstanding women in American life for 1945, for her devotion "to the humanities and to the creation of a better life for all people." Her experiences had included hobo life during the Depression, militant civil rights activism, reporting urban riots, and graduate legal studies at a leading university. Yet her prospects in postwar America were uncertain. The promised position in the Attorney General's office disappeared once white male lawyers returned from wartime service to claim former jobs. Marshall told her no positions were available on his NAACP legal team. Murray knew major law firms would not hire a black woman. The elation she felt over the Allied victory in World War II was tempered by doubts about her future.

TABLE 16.1 POLITICAL AND CIVIL RIGHTS ORGANIZATIONS

Congress of Racial Equality (CORE)   An interracial group formed in the early 1940s by pacifists to combat segregation and racial discrimination using nonviolent tactics. With the Fellowship of Reconciliation (FOR), CORE launched a two-week Journey of Reconciliation in 1947 to test compliance with the Supreme Court's *Morgan* decision banning segregation on interstate buses.

Civil Rights Congress (CRC)   A protest organization led by William L. Patterson, the CRC had close ties to the Communist Party and was labeled a subversive group by the Truman administration.

Council on African Affairs (CAA)   Founded in 1937 by Paul Robeson and Max Yergan, the CAA mobilized African American support for African struggles against European colonialism and white domination.

Leadership Council on Civil Rights (LCCR)   A national coalition of civil rights proponents initiated in 1950 by A. Philip Randolph, the NAACP's Roy Wilkins, and Jewish leader Arnold Aronson.

Legal Defense and Education Fund (LDEF)   In 1940 the NAACP created a separate legal wing under Thurgood Marshall's leadership to bring suits to combat segregation and racial discrimination.

March on Washington Movement (MOWM)   Although Randolph called off his threatened march in 1941 in return for Roosevelt's executive order establishing a Fair Employment Practices Committee (FEPC), the March on Washington Movement continued to stage rallies and other protests against racial discrimination in employment and military service.

National Association for the Advancement of Colored People (NAACP)   Headed by Walter White, the nation's oldest and largest civil rights organization greatly expanded its membership during World War II.

Postwar Dilemmas

Murray's uncertainty was shared by many African Americans as World War II came to an end. The civil rights gains of the war years were limited. Despite concessions, segregation in the military was still the norm. The FEPC had the power to investigate discrimination but not to compel minority hiring. Roosevelt made no commitment to continuing it after the war. His death on April 12, 1945, raised new questions: Where would President Harry S. Truman stand on civil rights issues? The signals were ominous when Mary McLeod Bethune's request to meet with the new First Lady was diverted to a White House aide with a query: "Mrs. Truman wants to know whether or not she should see these people."

Racial Understanding and Racist Violence

Despite uncertainties about the future, race relations were better understood at the end of the war than in previous eras, thanks to the work of social scientists who rejected racist assumptions. Gaining the most attention was Gunnar Myrdal's monumental study, *An American Dilemma: The Negro Problem and*

Modern Democracy (1944). Myrdal, a Swedish scholar, drew on the research of leading black scholars such as Ralph Bunche, E. Franklin Frazier, and Charles S. Johnson. Myrdal's overall theme was that the race problem was solvable if white Americans would acknowledge the contradictions between the treatment of black Americans and the nation's democratic ideals. Although some leftist intellectuals questioned whether white Americans would uphold ideals that contradicted their interests, Myrdal's work set the optimistic tone for many subsequent studies by black scholars of African American life and black–white relations. His associate St. Clair Drake collaborated with Horace R. Cayton on *Black Metropolis* (1944), a classic study of the Chicago black community. Former New Dealer Robert C. Weaver published *Negro Labor: A National Problem* (1946), and the Harvard-trained historian John Hope Franklin published a pioneering African American history textbook called *From Slavery to Freedom* (1947).

While these studies increased popular understanding of the status of African Americans in the United States, the eradication of racial discrimination required more than enlightened scholarship. Demobilization proved disruptive, as war veterans returned and factories shifted out of wartime production, cutting wages and laying off workers, both black and white. Racial conflicts and labor unrest increased, as nearly 5 million workers participated in nearly 5,000 strikes in 1946. The job prospects for African Americans—historically the last hired and first fired—were also clouded by new technology that reduced the need for unskilled labor. Nonetheless, black workers were determined to retain jobs gained during wartime labor shortages, and the more than 900,000 returning black veterans were equally determined to continue the fight against racial discrimination.

In the South, racial violence demonstrated that African Americans, even veterans in uniform, could expect no changes in Jim Crow. The most serious incident occurred in February 1946, when a black veteran in Columbia, Tennessee, defended his mother after a white repairman slapped her in a dispute over charges. After the veteran threw the repairman through a plate glass window, a white mob led by Ku Klux Klansmen and local police assaulted black residents (two deaths were reported) and destroyed homes and businesses in the black section of town. A few days later, Columbia police killed two black suspects being held for questioning. When twenty-five black residents were charged with attempted murder, Marshall and other NAACP lawyers convinced an all-white jury to acquit all but two defendants.

Altogether, in the wave of racial violence between June 1945 and September 1946, fifty-six African Americans died. In Georgia, white men killed Macio Snipes, a veteran who had been the first African American in Taylor County to vote in the Democratic Party primary. On a secluded road near Monroe, several dozen white men killed two black married couples. This widely publicized incident prompted sixteen-year-old Morehouse College student Martin Luther King, Jr., to write in protest to the *Atlanta Constitution*: "We want and are entitled to the basic rights and opportunities of American citizens: The right to earn a living at work for which we are fitted by training and ability; equal opportunities in education, health, recreation, and similar public services; the right to vote; equality before the law; some of the same courtesy and good manners that we ourselves bring to all human relations."

Colonialism and the United Nations

As southern segregationists sought to sustain white supremacy in the postwar period, European colonialists attempted to preserve their domination in Africa and Asia. Soldiers from India, Kenya, Senegal, and other colonies who fought for the Allies returned to civilian life determined to realize the democratic ideals of the Atlantic Charter. Political scientist Bunche was uniquely positioned to understand the relationship between the African American struggle for civil rights and the emerging African and Asian movements for national independence. During the 1930s he had become not only an outspoken critic of segregation but also an expert on African colonization. Through his academic studies, Bunche recognized the increasing militancy of African nationalists, whom he met in his travels. His *World View of Race* (1936) described European imperialism as "a product of modern capitalism." Influential in the NAACP, Bunche questioned its emphasis on civil rights to the neglect of economic reform.

Yet Bunche also saw cause for optimism in the anticolonial implications of the Atlantic Charter. During the war, he left academic life to take a position as an Africa expert with the Office of Strategic Services (OSS) and later as a State Department advisor on colonial policies. In spring 1945, as a member of the U.S. delegation in San Francisco drafting the charter for the new United Nations, he was in a position to influence the deliberations. But he was torn between his belief that dcolonization was "the best guarantee of world security" and his awareness that he represented the Truman administration, which was reluctant to put too much pressure on Britain and France and was itself under pressure from southern Senators who opposed giving the world body the authority to intervene in the "domestic jurisdiction" of member states. Although disappointed that the charter did not call for an end to colonization and racial discrimination, Bunche and the NAACP representatives at the conference (Walter White, W. E. B. Du Bois, and Mary McLeod Bethune) did gain concessions when delegates established a Commission on Human Rights, to be chaired by Eleanor Roosevelt.

Truman's policies at the U.N. conference were shaped by concerns thrust on him by Roosevelt's death. Though the war with Japan was still not over, relations between the United States and its communist ally, the Soviet Union, were already deteriorating. A year later, the changed international climate was sharply etched in a speech by Britain's wartime leader Winston Churchill, who warned that an "Iron Curtain" had descended on Europe, dividing the "free world" from the communist nations aligned with the Soviet Union.

Cold War Split in African American Politics

In 1946, Pauli Murray found herself in the unexpected position of testifying before the U.S. Senate about the character of one of her Howard professors. President Truman had nominated Hastie as governor of the U.S. Virgin Islands, but southern segregationist senators, led by Mississippi's James O. Eastland, objected. To discredit Hastie, they implied he had once associated with communists and might be disloyal, pointing to his past ties with leftist groups such as the National Negro Congress. Murray recalled the satisfaction she felt "looking Senator Eastland straight in the eye" and describing Hastie as "a man of principle and not of 'party line.'" Hastie denied any communist affiliation, although he readily acknowledged working with civil rights reformers representing a wide range of views. Hastie was confirmed as the first African American governor of a U.S. territory, but his interrogation was an inkling of things to come. As the United States and the Soviet Union faced off in the Cold War, any criticism of America was liable to charges of being "communist inspired," and the intensification of anticommunism brought about major divisions in African American politics.

Loyalty Issues and Internationalist Appeals

In the chilling atmosphere of the emerging Cold War, some African Americans saw a continued opportunity to expose the contradiction between America's ideals and its racial practices. But many who had associated with the Communist Party in the 1930s found themselves on the defensive. Langston Hughes responded to criticism of his outspoken Depression-era poems by insisting he had never been a communist. Richard Wright published an apologetic article, "I Tried to Be a Communist," in the *Atlantic Monthly*. Others with no communist connections grew cautious, worried about appearing disloyal. NAACP leaders Marshall and White carefully aligned themselves with the anticommunist but increasingly pro-civil rights Truman administration.

Du Bois and Robeson, however, doubted that Truman would take strong action on behalf of civil rights. They believed the United Nations should become

In 1947 W. E. B. Du Bois presented to the United Nations his "Appeal to the World" document detailing the consequences of racial discrimination against African Americans.

a forum for bringing international pressure to bear on U.S. racial policies, even if this proved embarrassing to the Truman administration, which saw civil rights reform in the context of the international struggle against communism. In 1947, Du Bois brought the issue of racial discrimination in the United States to the attention of the U.N. Human Rights Commission by submitting an "Appeal to the World" detailing the consequences of racial discrimination against African Americans. The document benefited from contributions by many experts on racial matters, including Bunche, Hastie, and Rayford Logan of Howard University, and had initially been supported by the NAACP, which in 1944 had rehired Du Bois to direct its research office. American officials, however, were determined to suppress Du Bois's petition, especially after the Soviet Union agreed to sponsor it, and the commission rejected it. Du Bois denied that the petition played into the hands of the Soviet Union, but the controversy over the "Appeal" produced serious infighting within the NAACP. Eleanor Roosevelt, chair of the U.N. commission, threatened to resign from the NAACP's board in protest. White removed Du Bois instead. Eighty years old, Du Bois soon moved on to become vice chairman of the leftist Council on African Affairs, which Robeson had cofounded in the late 1930s to aid national liberation struggles in Africa.

The considerably younger Robeson emerged as the most energetic and popular proponent of an African American leftist perspective during the early postwar years. Since the 1930s, his career as a singer and actor was laced with political activism, though during the war his public stands in favor of CIO unions, civil rights, and the Soviet Union—then America's ally—attracted little opposition. But after the war, he sparked controversy when he largely abandoned his career to sing and speak at civil rights rallies, often on behalf of the Council on African Affairs and the Crusade Against Lynching, a protest group he had helped organize.

At a massive rally against lynching held at Madison Square Garden, Robeson shared the podium with Henry A. Wallace, Roosevelt's vice president until displaced by Truman at the 1944 Democratic Convention and later secretary of commerce until Truman fired him. While Wallace denounced America's "get tough with Russia policy," Robeson denounced lynching, pointing to the irony of trying Nazis for crimes against humanity while America ignored its own crimes. When the Crusade Against Lynching held a rally in Washington, Robeson expressed shame "that here in the capital of the world's first genuine democratic government, it is necessary to seek redress of a wrong that defies the most fundamental concept of that precious thing we call democracy." Then he led a delegation to the White House, where he bluntly contradicted Truman's contention that the United States and Great Britain represented "the last refuge of freedom in the world." When Robeson warned that African Americans might have to defend themselves if the government would not, Truman abruptly announced that the meeting was over.

By this time, Truman was stepping up efforts to combat communism abroad and at home. Increasingly concerned about communist takeovers in Europe, in March 1947, he announced that the U.S. government would provide military and economic aid to Greece, Turkey, and other imperiled nations. This new Truman Doctrine was accompanied by policies designed to combat communist subversion within the United States. The Justice Department, ordered to prepare a list of "subversive organizations," cited not only the Communist Party but also the National Negro Congress, the Civil Rights Congress, the Council on African Affairs, and many other groups devoted to civil rights reform. At the same time that Truman put leftist civil rights advocates on the defensive by labeling them as subversive, he strengthened his appeal among African Americans by backing the far-reaching recommendations of his Civil Rights Commission, released early in 1947 as a report titled *To Secure These Rights.*

Even as Truman announced his pro-civil rights policies, Robeson was under investigation by the FBI and the House Committee on Un-American Activities (HUAC), which was scrutinizing the movie industry in search of communist influences. Robeson was already resigned to being shut out of Hollywood, but the HUAC investigation led to blacklisting, which adversely affected the careers of many in the industry, including some black actors. During the communist "witch hunts," as these investigations came to be called, entertainers were not the only ones under suspicion. As pressures for political conformity increased, investigative agencies turned their attention to any outspoken black leader with a leftist background.

The 1948 Election and the Decline of the Black Left

When, at the end of 1947, Wallace announced he would run for president on the Progressive Party ticket, Robeson immediately announced his support, as did Du Bois. But White and other NAACP leaders remained loyal to Truman and the Democrats, so the campaign further split black political leadership. Truman responded to the Progressive Party challenge by portraying himself as a staunch opponent of communism, both at home and abroad. Recognizing the need for black votes to beat his Republican opponent, New York governor Thomas Dewey, Truman recruited Hastie to campaign on his behalf in black communities and, early in 1948, announced wide-ranging civil rights proposals that included antilynching legislation and a permanent Fair Employment Practices Committee.

But even as Truman planned his reelection strategy, A. Philip Randolph launched a campaign to desegregate the armed forces. When Truman proposed a Cold War military draft, Randolph saw an opportunity to prod the president. In March 1948, leading a delegation of black leaders that included Charles Houston, he warned Truman, "Mr. President, Negroes are in the mood not to bear arms for the country unless Jim Crow in the Armed Forces is abolished." As with Roosevelt seven years before, Randolph urged Truman to issue an executive order. When Truman failed to act, Randolph told the Senate Armed Services Committee that he would urge African Americans to refuse to serve in a segregated military. When the draft was reinstituted without a segregation ban, Randolph joined Bayard Rustin, his former colleague in the March on Washington Movement, to found the League for Nonviolent Civil Disobedience to encourage black draft resistance.

Faced with Randolph's threat of civil disobedience, Truman offered more civil rights concessions, but his support of a pro-civil rights platform at the Democratic National Convention in the summer of 1948 split his own party. Southern Democrats led by South Carolina's Strom Thurmond walked out to form the States' Rights Party, or "Dixiecrats." Ironically, this split gave Truman a freer hand on civil rights issues, as he now had no need to appease the Dixiecrats. Ten days later, he strengthened his black support by issuing Executive Orders 9980 and 9981 banning racial discrimination in federal employment and in the armed forces. As Randolph had in 1941 called off the March on Washington after gaining concessions from Roosevelt, he also agreed to call off threatened civil disobedience after gaining them from Truman. The first presidential candidate to campaign in Harlem, Truman kept up his attacks on Wallace supporters by charging that the Progressive Party was dominated by communists and communist sympathizers.

The 1948 presidential campaign was thus a decisive confrontation between the moderate approach to civil rights reform favored by Truman and his black supporters, and the far-reaching changes sought by Robeson, Du Bois, and Wallace. Most black voters opted for Truman, as he was more likely to win the election and so to deliver on his promises. Black votes in key northern states gave the president a razor-thin victory over Dewey. Wallace attracted just 2 percent of the vote, slightly less than Thurmond received.

In the aftermath of Wallace's overwhelming defeat, the ideological boundaries of African American politics—and American politics in general—narrowed. The exceptional conditions of the Depression and World War II had encouraged an upsurge in black militancy and political experimentation that could not survive the Cold War. The internationalism and Pan-Africanism of Robeson and Du Bois were increasingly obscured by their communist associations, which made them targets of anticommunist zealots and government prosecutors. By the end of the 1940s, eleven prominent Communists, including New York City's only black councilman, Benjamin J. Davis, had been convicted of violating the Smith Act, which outlawed Communist Party membership. The Civil Rights Congress, led by veteran Communist William Patterson, also came under attack. Du Bois himself was prosecuted in 1950 but was ultimately acquitted of the charges brought against him.

While noncommunist activists such as Randolph and Rustin were not persecuted in comparable ways, they did not thrive in the Cold War political climate. Disbanding the League for Nonviolent Civil Disobedience, Randolph concentrated on ending discrimination in the labor movement, while Rustin became increasingly active in pacifist protests against nuclear arms.

Era of NAACP Dominance

As urban black voters began to affect state and local elections as well as presidential contests, significant civil rights reforms were achieved in some areas. In addition to electing liberal white politicians who favored civil rights, black voters elected two African Americans to Congress—New York's Adam Clayton Powell, Jr., and Chicago's William L. Dawson. By the end of the decade, both had sufficient seniority to influence national legislation affecting African Americans. The NAACP increased its effectiveness by forging ties with liberal politicians, labor unions, and Jewish organizations in an alliance formalized in 1950 with the creation of the Leadership Conference on Civil Rights.

Though the NAACP failed to achieve antilynching legislation, its litigation produced some highly visible victories. In 1946, the Supreme Court accepted Marshall's arguments that Irene Morgan's arrest for refusing to accept segregated seating on an interstate bus was unconstitutional (the same issue for which Pauli Murray had been arrested earlier in the decade). The *Morgan* v. *Commonwealth of Virginia* (1946) ruling did not prevent Rustin and others, however, from being arrested the next year during bus rides testing enforcement of the decision in the South. Next, Marshall supported leftist activist Heman Sweatt's challenge to racial barriers at the University of Texas Law School and Ada Lois Sipuel's similar challenge at the University of Oklahoma Law School. *Sweatt* v. *Painter* (1947) and *Sipuel* v. *Oklahoma State Board of Regents* (1948) forced states to make equal educational facilities available to black professional students. Marshall also supported a lawsuit against racial covenants that excluded black home buyers and owners from many neighborhoods. *Shelley* v. *Kraemer* (1948), outlawing court enforcement of these covenants, was a major victory in this area.

Marshall's Legal Defense and Education Fund (LDEF) not only undermined the legal foundations of the separate-but-equal doctrine but also provided a substitute for mass protest. With growing support from white liberals and foundations, Marshall matched the legal resources of his segregationist opponents. He tapped the expertise of Howard scholars such as Charles Houston, Hastie, and Spottswood Robinson and worked closely with legal experts from liberal and Jewish groups. By 1948, his talented staff included graduates of Howard Law School: Robert Lee Carter, a veteran who was his chief aide; Oliver Hill, Marshall's classmate; and Constance Baker Motley, the first woman attorney on the NAACP staff. Although Murray was not on the staff, the Marshall team moved closer to the position she framed at Howard: a direct attack against the separate-but-equal doctrine of *Plessy* v. *Ferguson*.

TABLE 16.2 SUPREME COURT CASES, 1944–1950

Smith v. Allwright (1944)   In a Texas case, the Supreme Court declares that "white primary" laws violate the Fifteenth Amendment.

Morgan v. Commonwealth of Virginia (1946)   The Supreme Court bans segregation on interstate buses, but the ruling has little immediate effect on southern practices.

Sipuel v. Oklahoma State Board of Regents (1948)   The Supreme Court decides in an Oklahoma case that states must admit qualified African Americans to previously all-white graduate schools when no comparable black institution is available.

Shelley v. Kraemer (1948)   The Supreme Court rules that racially restrictive housing covenants are unenforceable.

Sweatt v. Painter (1950)   The Supreme Court rules that states must make equal educational facilities available to black professional students.

Racial Dimensions of Postwar Popular Culture

In a 1949 article published in Russian in the Soviet Union, Paul Robeson described the enormous influence of "Negro folk music" on American culture. He drew particular attention to his own repertoire of spirituals, work songs, and "songs of protest . . . directly calling the Negroes to the struggle for their rights, and against lynch-law, against their exploiters, against capitalists." His dismay was evident as he contrasted modern African American musical trends with the folk music and protest songs he performed before audiences of leftists and labor activists. He worried that these traditional music forms had been displaced in popularity by jazz and blues, which to him expressed "the emotional state of the individual" rather than the collective concerns of black people. Robeson saw ominous political implications in the rise of "commercial jazz," which, he said, had "prostituted and ruthlessly perverted many splendid models of Negro folk music and has corrupted and debased many talented musicians in order to satisfy the desires of capitalist society."

Although some black artists and performers of the period shared Robeson's perspective, most sought success within the constraints of the capitalist system and Cold War liberalism he denounced. Even within the African American cultural world, others who were more willing to adjust to postwar trends in American mass culture had already displaced Robeson. Langston Hughes now offered far gentler social criticisms in his humorous Chicago *Defender* columns, which he reprinted in 1950 as *Simple Speaks His Mind*. By the late 1940s Richard Wright moved from Marxism toward existentialism (a philosophical movement focusing on individual existence), increasingly interpreting his sense of alienation in personal rather than class terms.

Decline of Swing and the Rise of Rhythm and Blues

The commercialized jazz that Robeson derided was itself being displaced in popularity during the late 1940s. The big bands of the swing era found it difficult to survive in the postwar period, although popular singers such as Ella Fitzgerald, Nat "King" Cole, Sarah Vaughn, and Billie Holiday sustained their careers as individual recording stars. The increasing blandness of heavily orchestrated swing music provoked a revolt by talented young jazz musicians—notably saxophonist Charlie Parker, trumpeter Dizzy Gillespie, and pianist Thelonious Monk—who left the big bands to form small ensembles playing a faster tempo, more intense, and experimental jazz style known as bebop.

But neither swing nor bebop generated as much enthusiasm as gospel and "race music," the name applied to the rhythm and blues that began to be played on city radio stations. While Robeson condemned the commercialization of African American culture, others saw opportunities in this trend. In 1948, WDIA Memphis became the first radio station to switch to all-black programming, and the following year, Atlanta's WERD became the nation's first black-owned radio station. Many other stations responded to the growth of black purchasing power by hiring black disc jockeys. In Chicago, Arthur Bernard Leaner achieved wealth and fame when he changed his on-air name to Al Benson and developed a down-to-earth patter. A few politically engaged artists and intellectuals sought to develop uplifting radio programs on African American history, but in the aftermath of depression and war, black city workers often preferred rhythm-and-blues entertainers such as Memphis Slim, the Staple Singers, and B. B. King.

Black Americans in Hollywood

If Robeson's political views had little impact on the recording industry, they had even less impact on the Hollywood film studios, where opportunities expanded for black actors willing to accept the limited roles offered them. Former Cotton Club singer Lena Horne's scenes in films such as *Panama Hattie* (1942) and *Swing Fever* (1943) made her a favored pinup girl for black soldiers during the war, but they were often cut by southern censors so as not to offend white audiences. Performers such as Horne, Ethel Waters, Eddie Robinson, Butterfly McQueen, and Bill Robinson often chafed at having to play racially stereotyped roles, but they were also seen as racial pioneers and sources of racial pride. Most avoided taking public stands on political issues, but some were blacklisted for being identified with left-wing groups. Canada Lee, a former boxer and product of the Federal Theater Project, was among the most successful of the black actors of the 1940s—starring not only in films such as *Lifeboat* (1944) but also in the Broadway adaptation of Richard Wright's novel *Native Son*— until he was charged with having communist ties. Blacklisted in Hollywood after he refused to denounce his friend Paul Robeson as a Communist, Lee found work only in films made outside the United States, such as *Cry the Beloved Country* (1950), an antiapartheid film made in South Africa.

Jackie Robinson and the Major Leagues

It was hardly surprising that outspoken entertainers such as Lee and Robeson would find it hard to thrive in a political environment encouraging conformity. More surprising was the sudden emergence of another black personality— Jackson "Jackie" Robinson—who achieved enormous popularity just as the careers of Lee and Robeson began to decline. Indeed, the contrasting career paths of Robeson and Robinson, who broke the color barrier in Major League Baseball in 1947, crossed during the late 1940s as the two men became symbolic figures in the contentious political conflicts of the Cold War.

Although Robeson and Robinson were different in important ways, both began adulthood as exceptional athletes. Robeson was an All-American football player at Rutgers and a varsity athlete in three other sports, while Robinson earned an All-American honorable mention as a UCLA football player, was a top scorer in basketball, and excelled as a broad jumper in track. Both pursued sports careers after leaving college. Robeson played two seasons of professional football at a time when black players were still accepted, but racial bars in the National Football League restricted Robinson to occasional semiprofessional football games before he was drafted into the military in 1942.

Robeson, however, was not only an exceptional athlete but also an outstanding student and a gifted orator, while Robinson struggled in the classroom

As a player for the Brooklyn Dodgers, Jackie Robinson was named Rookie of the Year in 1947 and won the National League batting title and Most Valuable Player award in 1949.

and left UCLA before graduation. Robeson's multifaceted intellectual interests as well as extensive travels abroad contributed to his cosmopolitan outlook, his connection to left-wing politics, and his deep interest in African culture. In contrast, Robinson was more singularly focused on athletics, and his experiences in the Army and then as a baseball player for the Kansas City Monarchs of the Negro National League shaped his adult outlook.

Although both chafed at racial restrictions—as evidenced by Robinson's challenge to bus segregation while in the military—by the late 1940s, they had arrived at differing conclusions about how to respond. Robeson increasingly sacrificed his performing career to immerse himself in radical politics, while Robinson agreed to suppress his aggressiveness in order to participate in the desegregation experiment of Brooklyn Dodgers executive Branch Rickey. "I'm looking for a ball player with guts enough not to fight back," Rickey explained when he signed Robinson to a contract. In 1943, Robeson had pleaded in vain with Major League club owners to sign black baseball players, but Rickey carefully orchestrated Robinson's entry into the major leagues while insisting he was not giving in to black protesters and political leaders. He saw desegregation as making moral and economic sense, given the untapped talent of black athletes and the need to attract black fans.

Robinson spent a year playing for the Dodgers farm team in Montreal before playing his first game with the Dodgers on April 11, 1947. His skill gained him acceptance from white players. Following Rickey's instructions to ignore racist taunts and provocations, Robinson led the team in runs scored, led the league in bases stolen, and was named Rookie of the Year.

The significance of Robinson's achievement extended beyond baseball. He attracted enormous attention from the press and appeared on the cover of *Time* magazine. To many African Americans, he was a hero, while white Americans admired his talent and his refusal to retaliate against provocations. He demonstrated to black Americans that opportunities were expanding and confirmed to white baseball fans that the nation was living up to its ideals of fair play. Like heavyweight boxing champ Joe Louis and Olympic gold medalist track star Jesse Owens, Robinson became a reassuring racial symbol, talented in his field yet, unlike Robeson, untainted by radicalism and political militancy.

Robinson's career symbolized broad social trends that enabled a few African Americans to experience success while collective racial gains remained modest and gradual. Those who went to the ballparks to cheer for Robinson returned after the game to mostly segregated neighborhoods. While some observers saw white Americans' acceptance of Robinson as signaling broader racial tolerance, he also served as a model for gradual or token racial reform that did not touch the lives of most African Americans. Qualified black players continued to be excluded from many major league teams; twelve years would pass before the Boston Red Sox became the last team to sign a black player.

Robinson's ascendancy during the late 1940s contrasted dramatically with Robeson's decline. The National League's Most Valuable Player of the 1949 season, Robinson led the Dodgers to the World Series (they lost to the New York Yankees) and led the league in batting percentage and stolen bases. Robeson, for his part, endured a torrent of criticism after he attended the Congress of World Partisans of Peace in April 1949 and suggested that African Americans would "not make war on the Soviet Union." When reports of his comments appeared in the press, black leaders such as A. Philip Randolph, Bayard Rustin, Roy Wilkins, and Mary McLeod Bethune denounced his views as unrepresentative.

In the midst of this controversy, the House Committee on Un-American Activities invited Robinson to testify regarding the Robeson controversy. In remarks prepared with the help of Rickey and Urban League head Lester B. Granger, Robinson disassociated himself from Robeson's comments but also insisted that racism was a real problem, not "a creation of Communist imagination." He affirmed his loyalty to the United States and expressed confidence that black Americans could win their struggle against racial discrimination "without the Communists and we don't want their help." White patriotic organizations applauded Robinson for repudiating Robeson. Film footage of this testimony was included as the climax to a Hollywood film biography, *The Jackie Robinson Story* (1950), in which Robinson depicted his own struggle.

By the end of the decade, Robinson had emerged as a major black spokesman. Robeson, in contrast, faded from public view after a mob disrupted his Peekskill, New York, concert in September 1949, and news of the riot led to cancellations of his scheduled appearances. Denied the right to perform in the United States, the State Department also stripped him of his passport to travel.

If Robeson's descent to obscurity represented the fate of the black left during the early years of the Cold War, Robinson's sudden fame represented a type of racial progress that soon emerged in its stead. With the exception of his congressional testimony, Robinson steered clear of political controversy during his initial years in the major leagues, but he opposed racial discrimination in his own way. By the late 1950s, a revival of mass black activism pushed him toward support of the civil rights movement, especially once his playing career ended. He became a Republican rather than a leftist radical, but he spoke out on racial issues and was willing to use his extraordinary success in baseball as a platform for influencing the desegregation of American life.

The decades following Robinson's breakthrough became an era of First Negroes—pioneers in fields from which the race had previously been excluded. Other African Americans who rose to prominence during the 1950s followed Robinson's model of overcoming prejudice through excellence and cautious activism that stayed within the confines of Cold War anticommunism. Thus, even as Robeson's star faded, Robinson and other African Americans came to prominence in new civil rights struggles that were different, yet ultimately more powerful than previous ones.

Conclusion

The social stresses of World War II transformed African Americans, feeding discontent and political militancy as well as rising expectations. During the war, A. Philip Randolph, William Hastie, Pauli Murray, and other civil rights activists pressed for racial reform. They discovered, however, that winning a world war was more readily accomplished than overcoming long-standing racial barriers. After the war, the United States seemed at a crossroads. African American scholars, political leaders, and cultural stars struggled to bring home the democratic ideals for which the nation had fought abroad. The Cold War fueled both the leftist agitation of W. E. B. Du Bois and Paul Robeson and the more conventional litigation strategy of Thurgood Marshall and his staff of NAACP lawyers. Moreover, the increasing political power of African Americans and the growing effectiveness of the NAACP brought significant gains such as President Truman's executive order ending segregation in the military.

By divorcing itself from the left and adhering to President Truman's loyalty program, the NAACP secured its position as the dominant African American organization on the national political scene. Its legal victories encouraged optimism that African Americans could achieve gains by identifying the cause of civil rights with the fight against communism. The success of a few talented individuals offered promise of progress for all African Americans. By the early 1950s, Jackie Robinson and a few other black athletes were playing in baseball's major leagues, Bunche had won a Nobel Peace Prize for his diplomatic work at the United Nations, Hastie had become the first African American federal appeals court judge, Gwendolyn Brooks had become the first African American poet to win the Pulitzer Prize, and Ralph Ellison had published *Invisible Man*, the first novel by an African American to win the National Book Award. Yet major civil rights legislation and collective racial advancement remained elusive. During the 1950s, the NAACP's continuing legal victories had the ironic effect of encouraging grassroots activism that would ultimately pose growing challenges to the group's dominance in the civil rights field.

Questions for Review and Reflection

1. In what ways did World War II intensify the African American freedom struggle? In what ways did it hinder the freedom struggle?

2. How did black soldiers and black Americans on the home front respond to segregation and racial discrimination in the war effort?

3. How did political divisions among African Americans affect their struggles for civil rights gains during the 1940s?

4. How did Gunnar Myrdal's *An American Dilemma: The Negro Problem and Modern Democracy* (1944) reflect and affect trends in American racial relations?

5. How did the Cold War affect the African American freedom struggle?

CHAPTER

Emergence of a Mass Movement against Jim Crow

Barbara Johns Leads a Student Strike

Just before 11:00 A.M. on April 23, 1951, the phone rang in the principal's office at Robert R. Moton High School in Farmville, Virginia. In a muffled voice, the caller said that two Moton students were in trouble at the bus terminal and then hung up. The call—a ploy to lure Principal Boyd Jones away from the building—succeeded. As soon as he headed to the bus station, a student delivered forged notes to the school's teachers, signed with a facsimile of the principal's characteristic *J*, saying that all teachers and students were to report immediately for an assembly. After Moton's 450 students filed into the central hall, which doubled as the auditorium, the stage curtain swung open, revealing a group of student leaders. At the rostrum stood sixteen-year-old Barbara Rose Johns, who announced that the assembly was for students only; emphasizing her point, she rapped her shoe on a bench while shouting to the teachers, "I want you out of here!"

Then Johns began what one of the student leaders called "her soliloquy." Moton's school buildings were totally inadequate, Johns told the students. The white high school in Farmville had a gymnasium, cafeteria, locker rooms, infirmary, and an auditorium with fixed seats; Moton had none of these. When Moton's student body outgrew the building's 180-student capacity, the Prince Edward County school board put up three temporary structures covered with tar paper. Some people said the "tarpaper shacks" looked like a poultry farm. Teachers had to stop teaching to stoke the sometimes dangerous woodstoves that made close by students too hot but left those farther away too cold. "We

BARBARA JOHNS LEADS A STUDENT STRIKE

will not accept these conditions," Johns told the students. "We will do something. We will strike."

Johns assured the students that they would not be punished if they stuck together because the local jail was not big enough to hold them all. Exiting the school, they paraded with already made placards: "We Are Tired of Tar Paper Shacks—We Want a New School." The students overwhelmingly decided not to consult their parents first but to act on their own. The next day they rode buses to school but stayed outside, protesting on the school grounds.

According to her family, Johns had been quiet and studious before she took charge of the student protest. She had read widely—notably Booker T. Washington's *Up from Slavery,* Richard Wright's *Native Son,* and other books she found in the library of her uncle, Vernon Johns, an outspoken pastor who had once been president of Virginia Seminary. The Reverend Johns had inspired his young niece's rebelliousness before he left Farmville to become pastor of Dexter

Avenue Baptist Church in Montgomery, Alabama. "I used to admire the way he didn't care who you were if he thought that something was right," Barbara Johns said of her uncle. As she became increasingly angered by Moton's makeshift facilities, a teacher challenged her to do something, and she did.

In the hectic first day of the strike, the students called the NAACP office in Richmond. Johns and Carrie Stokes, president of the Moton student council, followed up with a letter to veteran NAACP lawyer Spottswood Robinson: "We hate to impose as we are doing, but under the circumstances that we are facing, we have to ask for your help." Two days later, Robinson and his longtime NAACP associate Oliver T. Hill stopped by Farmville to meet with the students, who were told to bring their parents. "I had a horror of talking to a group of these kids with no adults around," Robinson recalled. After the meeting, the two attorneys were sufficiently impressed by the students' determination to agree to help them, if they agreed to seek desegregation rather than merely better facilities. "What made us go ahead," Robinson explained later, "was the feeling that someone would have to show them something before they would go back to school."

The strike at Moton was planned and led by students. When other students suggested they should defer to the adults who had been working for years to get the county school board to approve a new black school, Johns rejected the advice, citing scripture: "A little child shall lead them." In a later interview, she said, "We knew we had to do it ourselves, and if we had asked for adult help before taking the first step, we would have been turned down." One student leader recalled Johns predicting, "We could make a move that would broadcast Prince Edward County all over the world." Events proved her right, as the strike at Moton became a lawsuit that was combined with other desegregation cases to become *Brown* v. *Board of Education of Topeka,* the most important and successful legal effort in the NAACP's long compaign to end segregation in schools.

But Johns was not a party to the suit she helped initiate. After threats to her and a cross burning on the school grounds, her parents feared for her safety and sent her to live with her Uncle Vernon in Montgomery, where she finished high school. Her leadership, however, left a legacy of student activism that continued to grow in the following years.

Johns and the Moton students bypassed their parents to appeal directly to the NAACP, which during the early 1950s dominated African American politics at the national level. Under Thurgood Marshall's leadership, the NAACP Legal Defense and Education Fund had achieved major victories, most notably the Supreme Court rulings against segregated graduate and professional schools. During a time when black leftist leaders such as W. E. B. Du Bois and Paul Robeson faced Cold War repression, the NAACP, with more than a thousand local branches, was the leading force in African American activism. The NAACP's reliance on litigation and lobbying was shown to produce major legal and legislative victories.

Within the NAACP, however, some members remained dissatisfied with the slow pace of civil rights reform. Local black activism eventually posed a challenge to the NAACP at the national level, as impatient members were eager to experiment with new protest tactics.

The year-long Montgomery bus boycott movement that began late in 1955 was an important turning point because it demonstrated that many African Americans were ready for more militant forms of civil rights activism. The boycott also revealed that a black community could remain united in struggle for more than a year. Although Martin Luther King, Jr., was but twenty-six years old at the start of the boycott, he emerged as a nationally known civil rights leader and the head of his own organization, the Southern Christian Leadership Conference (SCLC). But still younger activists soon pushed his group as well as the NAACP toward greater militancy. The students who braved mobs to desegregate Little Rock Central High School in 1957 and the black college students who launched a wave of sit-in demonstrations in 1960 inspired an upsurge in grassroots protests through the South. By the spring of 1960, when student protest leaders formed the Student Nonviolent Coordinating Committee (SNCC), it was apparent that the southern freedom struggle was beyond the control of any single leader or organization.

The Road to *Brown* v. *Board of Education of Topeka*

"The complete destruction of all enforced segregation is now in sight," Thurgood Marshall confidently announced in June 1950, about ten months before the student walkout in Farmville. He was encouraged by the success of two NAACP suits challenging segregation in graduate and professional schools. The first involved George W. McLaurin, a black man in his sixties who had been admitted to the formerly all-white University of Oklahoma graduate school of education but forced to sit apart from other students, even in the library and cafeteria. The second case involved Heman M. Sweatt, a Houston mail carrier who had applied to the University of Texas Law School but was instead referred to a hastily established black law school in a basement at Texas State University for Negroes (later Texas Southern University).

Using expert testimony from social scientists to support their position, Marshall and other NAACP lawyers argued that under such conditions neither McLaurin nor Sweatt could receive educational opportunities equal to those of white students. Ruling in *McLaurin* v. *Oklahoma State Board of Regents* and *Sweatt* v. *Painter*, the Supreme Court agreed. Marshall was exuberant. The *McLaurin* case seemed particularly important because the Court held that separation from other students violated the Fourteenth Amendment's equal protection provision: "such restrictions impair and inhibit his ability to study, engage in discussions and exchange views with other students, and, in general, to learn his profession." Marshall saw broad implications in the Court's finding that racial isolation hindered the education of black students, as the same reasoning could be applied to the elementary and high school levels.

The Attack on "Separate But Equal"

Soon after the *McLaurin* decision, Marshall convened a meeting of NAACP lawyers to determine whether the time had come for a frontal attack on the separate-but-equal doctrine. Thus far, the NAACP had challenged the *Plessy* v. *Ferguson* precedent piecemeal, forcing states on a case-by-case basis to improve educational facilities—that is, to live up to the *equal* side of the equation. Now Spottswood Robinson and others argued for a challenge to racial separation itself. Robert Lee Carter, Marshall's top assistant, noted that in a California case involving Spanish-speaking children, *Mendez* v. *Westminster School District* (1946), a federal appeals court had accepted the idea that segregating students implied that they were inferior and thus violated their right to equal treatment. Carter also cited research showing that racism caused psychological damage. By the end of the meeting, Marshall was convinced. Acknowledging that schools provided children with their "most important contact with organized society," he announced to reporters, "We are going to insist on nonsegregation in American public education from top to bottom—from law school to kindergarten."

For Marshall, the decision to attack the separate-but-equal doctrine was a crucial turning point in his career as head of the NAACP Legal Defense and Education Fund. Previously, he had steered a moderate course. He had cooperated with FBI director J. Edgar Hoover to purge anyone suspected of communist ties from the NAACP's ranks, but he took a political risk when he investigated desegregation in the military. Within a month, his extensive evidence of continued discrimination against black soldiers spurred full implementation of Truman's executive order calling for military desegregation. Yet even with these achieve-

George W. McLaurin, the first African American student at the University of Oklahoma's Graduate School of Education, is forced to sit apart from white students. Although permitted to eat in the school's cafeteria, he was also assigned to a separate table there. In 1950 the Supreme Court ruled that such discriminatory treatment violated the Fourteenth Amendment's "equal protection" guarantee.

ments behind him, Marshall knew the frontal attack on *Plessy* might fail. Oliver Hill, Marshall's friend since their student days at Howard Law School, recalled that Marshall was "cautious" about risking the gains that had been achieved. "His prevailing sense, I think, was that we just couldn't afford to lose a big one," Hill remembered. What if black teachers and administrators lost their jobs when public schools were desegregated? But most African Americans saw equalization efforts as ineffective and enforced segregation as wrong. "They were just fed up with what we called 'doghouse education,'" Judge William Hastie observed, "and it was clear that the segregation fight was going to be pushed at the secondary- and elementary-school level."

The NAACP's School Desegregation Suits

The conditions endured by Moton High students were not unusual; about two of every five African American children attended classes in schools that were segregated by law and that were rarely equal in quality to the schools provided for white children in the same area. In 1950, twenty-one states, many of them outside the South, maintained segregated public schools (see Map 17.1). Marshall and his colleagues had to select the right cases, however, to launch a frontal attack on *Plessy*. As in Farmville, they had to find black plaintiffs—students as well as their parents—willing to take the risks associated with challenging racial segregation.

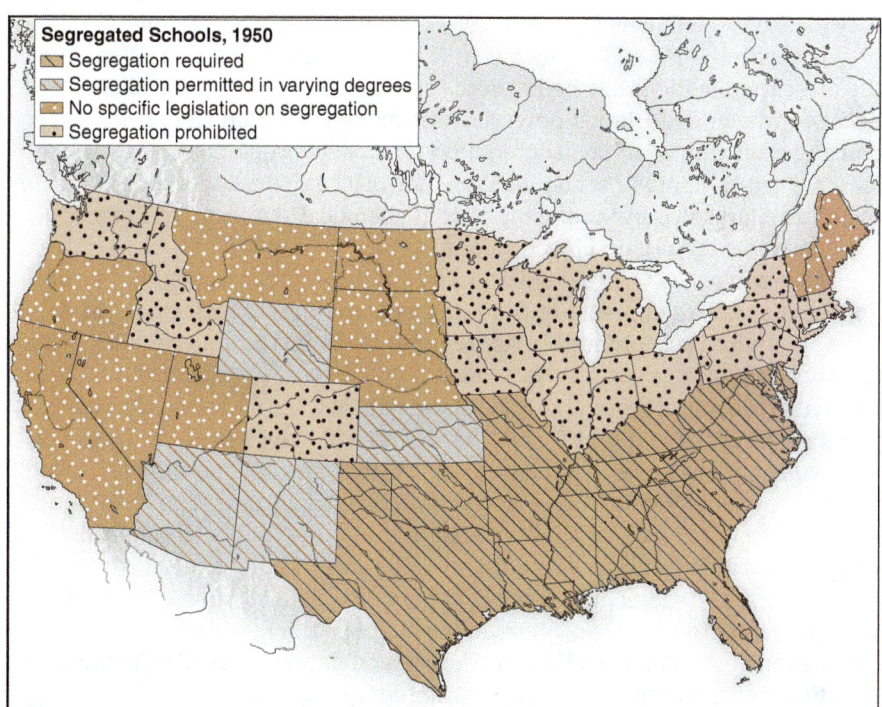

MAP 17.1 Segregated Schools, 1950

In 1950, twenty-one states, including several outside the South, maintained segregated public schools.

At first the NAACP lawyers focused their energies on *Briggs* v. *Elliott,* a case initiated in the late 1940s in predominantly black Clarendon County, South Carolina. As in Virginia's Prince Edward County, the black plaintiffs from Clarendon initially sought to improve facilities for black students, some of whom had to walk seven miles to dilapidated black schools while white students used buses. Racial disparities in South Carolina's spending for the 1949–1950 school year were stark: $179 per white student; $43 per black student. When the case first reached court in 1949, a sympathetic white South Carolina judge, J. Waties Waring, privately indicated to Marshall that a suit seeking desegregation rather than equal facilities might succeed. Thus, when the NAACP's revised suit was heard by a three-judge panel in May 1951, Marshall used the opportunity to argue that, even if funding were equalized, racial inequalities would persist. At the request of the NAACP, social psychologist Kenneth Clark traveled to Clarendon County to study the psychological effects of segregation by administering a test he and his wife, Mamie, had developed. The Clarks found that black children who were shown two dolls—one black and one white—generally considered the white doll prettier and smarter than the black doll, indicating that feelings of racial inferiority had been instilled at an early age. Eleven of the sixteen black children who took this test in Clarendon County said the black doll looked "bad." When asked to select the doll most like themselves, Clark reported, "Many of the children became emotionally upset when they had to identify the doll they had rejected." He testified that segregation caused black children "to reject themselves and their color and accept whites as desirable" and concluded they had been "definitely harmed in the development of their personalities."

Although the NAACP lawyers lost the case in a 2–1 decision (Waring was the dissenting judge), they believed the trial record would be useful on appeal because it included Clark's powerful testimony regarding the psychological damage caused by enforced segregation. Even as worried South Carolina officials rushed to improve school facilities for black children to head off further litigation, Marshall grew confident he could demonstrate that Jim Crow education inevitably stigmatized black students.

Meanwhile, another case had made its way through federal courts. In Topeka, Kansas, the parents of third-grader Linda Brown had sought to enroll her in the white school four blocks from her home instead of the black school twenty-one blocks away. The facts in *Brown* v. *Board of Education of Topeka* differed greatly from those in the South Carolina and Virginia cases because the facilities for black and white children in Topeka, even the plaintiffs agreed, were substantially equal. All children went to the same schools from junior high on; only Topeka's elementary schools were divided by race. The case put the constitutionality of segregation front and center. Carter wrote to Marshall, "The more I think about this case, the more importance I think it will have." In the summer of 1951, federal judges ruled against Brown, but evidence presented in the case supported Clark's contention that segregation retarded "the education and mental development of Negro children" and deprived them of "some of the benefits they would receive in a racially integrated school system."

In June 1952, the Supreme Court announced it would hear appeals in the *Briggs* and *Brown* cases in October, but then accepted an appeal of the *Davis* case involving Moton High students and postponed oral arguments until December. In November, the court added a case from the District of Columbia—*Bolling* v. *Sharpe,* which had been initiated by veteran NAACP lawyer Charles Hamilton Houston before his death in 1950. Three days later it added still another case—*Belton* v. *Gebhart,* from Delaware. The five cases from different parts of the country would be considered together.

The *Brown* Decision

Marshall worked fast to keep up with the Court's additions. At the NAACP headquarters in Manhattan, he and his staff prepared a 256 page legal brief that brought together years of legal, historical, and social science research. "When we were preparing for the *Brown* decision, sometimes we slept there," one staffer recalled. The responsibility weighed heavily on Marshall. He knew he would have only one chance to persuade the nine justices on the merits of school desegregation and that the NAACP's reputation as well as racial progress depended on the outcome. Once the brief was submitted, he shifted his headquarters to Washington, DC, where he practiced mock arguments with Howard students and professors. In the *Brown* case, Marshall faced a formidable legal team, headed by South Carolinian John W. Davis, a former solicitor general of the United States who had argued more cases before the Supreme Court than any lawyer of his time. Although some of his assistants were better at preparing legal briefs than he was, Marshall did have formidable assets, including his ability to inspire his staff and win courtroom victories through extensive preparation. Characteristically, Marshall paid respect to Davis's legal reputation by inviting him to lunch shortly before the two met in court.

When arguments began on December 9, 1952, the Supreme Court's chambers were filled. Arguing on behalf of the South Carolina students, Marshall responded effectively to the probing questions of justices about how desegregation could be implemented. Davis scored points by quoting Du Bois's argument, made in the 1930s, that black children were better off in educational settings where they were accepted, but Marshall kept the focus on the destructive consequences of enforced racial isolation. Discounting other justifications for segregation, Marshall concluded its purpose was to stigmatize black Americans: "The only thing it can be is an inherent determination that the people who were formerly in slavery, regardless of anything else, shall be kept as near that stage as possible, and now is the time, we submit, that this court should make it clear that is not what our Constitution stands for."

Marshall hoped the Supreme Court would rule by the spring of 1953, but instead, the justices asked for further arguments regarding the intentions of the framers of the Fourteenth Amendment and indicated their uncertainty about the Court's ability to enforce school desegregation. As it turned out, this delay was crucial to the outcome. The Court was badly divided when the case began, but after the death of the chief justice, President Dwight D. Eisenhower appointed Earl Warren, Republican governor of California, as the new chief justice. Still haunted by his role as California's attorney general in the internment of Japanese Americans during World War II, Warren was quietly determined to remedy the racial injustices that affected African American children. Behind the scenes, he sought to reach a consensus with other justices, knowing that a ruling favoring desegregation needed the broadest possible support. A new climate of opinion was also evident in the Justice Department's friend-of-the-court brief, which generally backed the NAACP's position that public school segregation was unconstitutional.

On May 17, 1954, Marshall was at the Supreme Court when Warren announced the decision in the *Brown* case. The decision was unanimous. "We conclude that in the field of public education the doctrine of 'separate but equal' has no place," Warren read to the crowded chamber. "Separate educational facilities are inherently unequal. Therefore, we hold that the plaintiffs and others similarly situated for whom the actions have been brought are, by reason of the segregation complained of, deprived of the equal protection of the laws guaranteed by the Fourteenth Amendment."

Marshall told reporters the decision was "the greatest victory we ever had." NAACP leader Roy Wilkins remembered the ruling as "one of life's sweetest days. We had won a second Emancipation Proclamation." Major issues remained unresolved: How would the ruling be enforced, given widespread southern opposition? How broadly would the ruling be applied against segregation in other areas, such as public buildings, restaurants, hotels, and motels? Even as he celebrated with other NAACP staff members, Marshall cautioned, "I don't want any of you to fool yourselves, it's just begun; the fight has just begun."

Attorneys George E. C. Hayes, Thurgood Marshall, and James Nabrit celebrate the 1954 *Brown* decision.

Building on the *Brown* Breakthrough

In January 1954, shortly before the *Brown* decision, Vernon Johns returned to Dexter Avenue Baptist Church in Montgomery, Alabama, where he had served as pastor until his combative personality led to his ouster (his niece Barbara Johns had moved to Philadelphia following her marriage in 1953). After trying unsuccessfully to regain his pastorate, Johns had gone back to his farm in Virginia, occasionally accepting invitations to preach. A guest sermon he delivered in Atlanta at Martin Luther King, Sr.'s Ebenezer Baptist Church gave him an opportunity to meet King's oldest son, a Boston University doctoral student in theology who was already gaining a reputation as an outspoken young preacher. Johns knew King, Jr., had been invited by Dexter Church to be a candidate for Johns's former position as pastor. After the younger King delivered a well-received trial sermon at Dexter, he and Johns had a wide-ranging dinner discussion at the home of Ralph Abernathy, the young pastor of Montgomery's First Baptist Church. Although Johns was much older than King and Abernathy, who were in their twenties, the three ministers shared a strong commitment to the Social Gospel, which stressed the need for justice as well as salvation. King listened intently to Johns's assessment of the Dexter congregation, which had dismissed him for his controversial stance on racial and class inequities. King admired Johns as "a real iconoclast" who "never allowed conditions of injustice to come to his attention without lashing out." He took to heart Johns's credo: "Any individual who submitted willingly to injustice did not really deserve more justice."

The dinner conversation reflected the simmering discontent felt by many African Americans in the mid-1950s, as legal victories culminating in the *Brown* decision had stirred hopes and fueled impatience, especially for younger black Americans, such as Abernathy and King, who saw the South through the prism of a rapidly changing world. Both looked to anticolonial movements in Africa and Asia as models for what should be happening in the United States, and both were skeptical of Cold War anticommunism. They sympathized with the views expressed at the 1955 Bandung (Indonesia) Conference of African and Asian nations seeking to remain neutral in the Cold War. They regretted that the United States and its allies failed to offer alternatives to communism to those struggling against European colonialism. Both were NAACP members but were impatient with national NAACP leaders such as Marshall and Roy Wilkins, Walter White's replacement, who sought reforms through litigation and lobbying rather than mass protest.

Although Marshall realized that implementing the *Brown* decision would not be easy, he could hardly have predicted the intensity of both grassroots black activism and the white resistance it provoked. Recognizing the "considerable complexity" posed by "the wide applicability of this decision" and "the great variety of local conditions," the Supreme Court itself delayed implementation of its decision, announcing in May 1955 that school districts would be required to desegregate only "with all deliberate speed." This announcement signaled segregationists that they could devise strategies to avoid compliance. Southern state legislatures passed hundreds of laws and resolutions limiting enforcement of *Brown*. Virginia cut off state aid to all desegregated schools, and when the courts struck down this measure, some school systems—including public schools in Prince Edward County, where the Moton High School walkout had taken place—closed rather than desegregate. Private schools, often subsidized with public money, made education available to white students, but many black students like those at Moton High had no schools to attend.

While southern politicians urged resistance to the *Brown* decision, white support grew for groups such as the Ku Klux Klan, which used violence and threats of violence to intimidate southern black people, and the white Citizens Councils, which used economic pressure—such as threatening the jobs of black civil rights proponents—to achieve the same ends. In May 1955, the Reverend George Lee, a voting rights proponent, was killed in Belzoni, Mississippi. In a case that stunned the nation, white men in Leflore County, Mississippi, brutally murdered Emmett Till in 1955. The black youngster from Chicago was visiting relatives when he allegedly insulted a white woman in a country store. Three days later, the teenager's mangled body was found at the bottom of the Tallahatchie River. An all-white jury quickly acquitted the two men charged with the crime, despite the testimony of Till's great uncle, who witnessed the abduction and identified its perpetrators. When Till's mother requested an open-casket funeral, news photographs conveyed the horror of southern racism.

The brutal racial violence of Till's murder outraged African Americans, but it was a lesser indignity associated with white supremacy that sparked a mass protest movement in Montgomery a few months later. Montgomery's black community had built a strong foundation for sustained struggle against segregation. On May 21, 1954, just days after the *Brown* decision and a few days before King, who accepted Dexter's call, delivered his first sermon, Dexter member Jo Ann Robinson wrote to the city's mayor warning that segregation practices on local buses might prompt a boycott by black riders. Robinson, a professor at Alabama State, was head of Montgomery's Women's Political Council (WPC), founded by another Dexter member, Mary Fair Burks, in the late 1940s. And Dexter member Rufus Lewis had founded the Citizens Club about

---

TABLE 17.1 POLITICAL AND CIVIL RIGHTS ORGANIZATIONS

Legal Defense and Education Fund (LDEF)   The NAACP's separate legal wing, led by Thurgood Marshall.

Montgomery Improvement Association (MIA)   Group organized in 1955 under King's leadership to continue the Montgomery bus boycott.

National Association for the Advancement of Colored People (NAACP)   Headed at the national level by Roy Wilkins, the NAACP's branches throughout the South often became centers of protest activity.

Southern Christian Leadership Conference (SCLC)   King was the founding president of this regional organization formed in 1957 to sustain the momentum of the Montgomery movement.

Student Nonviolence Coordinating Committee (SNCC)   Organization established in 1960 by student sit-in leaders with the assistance of Ella Baker.

the same time to promote voting, especially among black war veterans. When King established a Social and Political Action Committee at Dexter to encourage its members to support the NAACP and to become registered voters, Robinson, Burks, and Lewis all quickly joined.

Thus, King discovered that some members of Montgomery's NAACP branch were primed for action. E. D. Nixon, an organizer for the Brotherhood of Sleeping Car Porters, had long struggled to invigorate the group, serving as branch president and eventually statewide head of the NAACP. Rosa Parks had been its secretary since the mid-1940s. Nixon, Parks, and others were inspired by King's forceful denunciations of African Americans who tolerated segregation as "mental slaves" and his exhortation at an NAACP gathering,: "we've come a long way, but we have a long way to go." In the spring of 1955, they became keenly aware of the potential impact of the *Brown* decision when fifteen-year-old Claudette Colvin, arrested for refusing to give up her seat on a bus to a white man, told policemen, "It's my constitutional right to sit here."

The Montgomery Bus Boycott and the Southern Christian Leadership Conference

Around noon on December 1, 1955, forty-two-year-old Rosa Parks left her job as a seamstress at a department store to spend her lunch break with Fred Gray, the young black attorney who defended Colvin after her arrest. As secretary of Montgomery's NAACP branch and advisor to its youth group, Parks knew Colvin and admired Gray's willingness to take civil rights cases with little hope of monetary reward. In his modest office above an auto shop, Gray shared with

Rosa Parks is arrested for her role in the Montgomery bus boycott.

Parks his regret that the Colvin case had not been used to challenge bus segregation; Colvin's subsequent pregnancy had made some black leaders hesitant to support her. In October, eighteen-year-old Mary Louise Smith was arrested under similar circumstances, but this case had also failed to mobilize Montgomery's black residents. That afternoon, as she took a bus home from work, Parks herself was arrested and charged with refusing to obey the local rule that black bus riders sit in the rear seats and give up middle seats to standing white passengers.

News accounts later depicted Parks as a tired seamstress to emphasize that an ordinary black woman had protested bus segregation, but Gray and local civil rights advocates were aware of her history of activism. In the 1930s, Parks's husband, Raymond, had joined the controversial campaign to free the Scottsboro defendants. Spurred by the World War II Double-V campaign, Rosa Parks had managed to register and vote for the first time in 1946. By then she was working closely with Nixon. In summer 1955, she attended a workshop on "Racial Desegregation: Implementing the Supreme Court Decision" at Tennessee's Highlander Folk School, where she was inspired by Septima Clark, head of its innovative education program. "If only I could catch some of her spirit," Parks remembered thinking as she left Highlander, unaware that her own dignified yet spirited resistance to segregation would soon ignite a sustained struggle.

A Community Revolts

Parks's arrest was unexpected, but long threads of black resistance to segregation had converged in Montgomery in December 1955, enabling a solitary act of defiance to grow into a mass movement. As news of the arrest spread, key leaders of Montgomery's black community quickly agreed that a collective response was needed. Nixon posted bail for Parks—using his own home as security—and urged her to allow her arrest to become a rallying point against segregation. Despite her husband's warning—"Rosa, white folks will kill you"—she agreed. Nixon then began calling other civil rights proponents, including Robinson, who had already started mobilizing her WPC colleagues for a one-day boycott of the Montgomery city bus system. With two of her students, Robinson stayed up most of the night duplicating leaflets urging Montgomery's black residents to support the boycott. "Another Negro woman has been arrested and thrown in jail because she refused to get up out of her seat on the bus for a white person to sit down," the leaflet read. "This has to be stopped. Negroes have rights, too."

After Fred Gray agreed to be Parks's attorney, Nixon informed Thurgood Marshall at the NAACP's New York office about the boycott plans. But the Montgomery protest remained locally led. Nixon made certain the city's black ministers were contacted, and they agreed to support the boycott, calling for a rally the evening of the boycott at Holt Street Baptist Church. "It was then that the ministers decided it was time for them, the leaders, to catch up with the masses," Robinson recalled.

On Monday, December 5, the day of the boycott, black residents overwhelmingly supported the protest. Many buses on routes through black neighborhoods were empty. That afternoon, the city's black leaders determined to continue the boycott, organizing as the Montgomery Improvement Association (MIA), at Ralph Abernathy's suggestion. Although Parks, Nixon, and Robinson initiated the movement, there was general agreement that a minister was needed to sustain the effort. In fact, Nixon was pleased when King, nominated by Dexter member Rufus Lewis, was elected president of the group. "I always knowed," Nixon reflected, "that one day this fight would reach a point where better educated and better talkin' folks would have to take over."

Martin Luther King, Jr., and Boycott Leadership

King had been pastor of Dexter only a year before the boycott began, but he had already demonstrated a commitment to social justice and exceptional abilities as an orator. The son of an Atlanta minister who led civil rights marches in the 1930s, King responded to his "inescapable urge to serve society" by studying for the ministry at Crozer Theological Seminary in Pennsylvania. While a graduate theological student at Boston University, he met music student Coretta Scott, an Alabama native who had campaigned for the Progressive Party in the 1948 election while she was an Antioch College undergraduate. Discovering their shared commitment to social justice, King told Scott he rejected communism but still believed that "a society based on making all the money you can and ignoring people's needs is wrong." After the two were married, King finished his theology courses and accepted an invitation to succeed Johns as Dexter's pastor. Despite worries about returning to the South to raise a family in the "bonds of segregation," he and his wife decided they had "a moral obligation to return—if only for a few years."

Hours after becoming head of the MIA, King delivered his first major speech as a protest leader. Although he had little time to prepare, his words stirred the overflow crowd at Holt Street Baptist Church by linking their bus boycott to the broader cause of social justice. "And you know, my friends, there comes a time when people get tired of being trampled over by the iron feet of oppression," he proclaimed. Calling on his listeners to remain nonviolent and true to Christian principles, he identified their cause with the traditional values of the nation: "If we are wrong, the Supreme Court of this nation is wrong! If we are wrong, God Almighty is wrong!" He concluded by predicting—correctly—that the events in Montgomery would be long remembered: "When the history books are written in the future, somebody will have to say, 'There lived a race of people, a black people . . . who had the moral courage to stand up for their rights. And thereby they injected a new meaning in the veins of history and of civilization.'"

King's moving speeches strengthened the resolve of the city's black residents. His effectiveness as a leader also derived from his ability to work closely with local leaders such as Parks, Gray, Nixon, Robinson, and his close friend Abernathy. But privately, King continually fought feelings of inadequacy in the face of the leadership role suddenly thrust upon him. Late in the evening of January 27, a particularly threatening phone call prompted self-doubts. "The people are looking to me for leadership," he thought, "and if I stand before them without strength and courage, they too will falter." Then he remembered feeling a divine presence that quieted his fears. "It seemed as though I could hear the quiet assurance of an inner voice saying: 'Stand up for righteousness, stand up for truth; and God will be at your side forever.'"

Despite one black newspaper's depiction of him as "Alabama's Gandhi," King was initially skeptical about the nonviolent strategy Mahatma Gandhi had used to free India from British colonial rule. He even applied for a gun permit during the early weeks of the boycott. Yet, when his home was bombed at the end of January 1956, he calmed the angry crowd outside by repeating the biblical injunction, "He who lives by the sword will perish by the sword." His understanding of Gandhian ideas deepened with the arrival a few weeks later of veteran black pacifist Bayard Rustin, who had worked with A. Philip Randolph during the 1940s in the March on Washington Movement and later in the military desegregation campaign. Rustin quickly gained King's confidence, advising on strategy and dissuading him from using armed guards. The presence of an "outside agitator" from New York soon attracted controversy and critical news coverage, however, for Rustin had been a communist as a young man and had been arrested as a homosexual in 1953. Rustin decided he should leave Montgomery, but he continued to advise King and mobilized northern support for the boycott.

With diversified leadership and almost total support from Montgomery's black residents, the bus boycott withstood violent attacks and intimidation from white employers. Dexter members continued to play major roles in the MIA. Jo Ann Robinson edited its newsletter, while Rufus Lewis headed the transportation committee, which created an elaborate carpool system for former bus riders. King's close friend Abernathy also provided crucial leadership for the boycott movement. Yet boycott leaders were also responding to the determination of MIA members. There was much truth in Claudette Colvin's assertion, "Our leaders is just we ourself."

In February 1956, white officials tried to suppress the Montgomery movement by indicting eighty-nine MIA stalwarts on charges of conspiring to boycott. Rather than being intimidated, the MIA activists proudly surrendered themselves at the courthouse. King's defense attorneys insisted that residents had stayed off the buses as a protest rather than as an organized boycott. This argument did not dissuade the judge from convicting King (whose fine and jail sentence were quickly appealed), but it did reflect King's oft-stated view that

---

TABLE 17.2 SUPREME COURT CASES, 1950–1956

Sweatt v. Painter and McLaurin v. Oklahoma State Regents (1950)   The Supreme Court declares racially segregated facilities for graduate schools unconstitutional.

Brown v. Board of Education of Topeka (1954)   The Supreme Court unanimously overturns 1896 *Plessy* decision by ruling that public school segregation is unconstitutional.

Browder v. Gayle (1956)   The Supreme Court upholds lower court ruling banning segregation on Montgomery, Alabama, buses.

the goal was "not to put the bus company out of business, but to put justice in business." When King emerged from the courthouse, he was cheered by hundreds of supporters.

King's trial attracted nationwide press coverage. While he often downplayed his role in the boycott—"I neither started the protest nor suggested it"—he became its best-known participant, appearing on the cover of *Time* magazine and receiving numerous speaking invitations. King's articulate statements on the broader significance of the Montgomery movement attracted widespread attention, as did his advocacy of nonviolence and racial reconciliation even in the face of violent provocations. King's rapidly growing national influence led to tensions with NAACP leaders, who supported the MIA's legal effort to desegregate the city's buses but also saw King as a potential competitor. Although some reporters erroneously concluded that the NAACP's national leaders had orchestrated the boycott, Marshall conceded that "our people in the South are actually way ahead of us on this thing." Despite their reservations about the Montgomery movement, however, Marshall and Wilkins publicly supported it and even invited King to address the NAACP's annual national gathering in June 1956. While avoiding criticism of NAACP leaders, King used the occasion to appeal for greater militancy.

The Montgomery boycott demonstrated that African Americans, though often poor, could be a powerful force when united. Not only did the boycott hurt the bus company, but a related MIA boycott of Montgomery's stores put pressure on merchants. Yet city officials still refused to make concessions. Finally, an NAACP-sponsored suit against segregation on city buses prevailed. In November, as MIA leaders were in a Montgomery courtroom seeking to prevent local officials from shutting down carpool operations, the Supreme Court, in *Browder v. Gayle,* affirmed a lower court ruling that segregated seating on city buses was unconstitutional. On the morning of December 21, 1956, after a protest lasting 381 days, King, Nixon, and Abernathy became the first black bus riders to sit legally in the front section of a Montgomery bus.

The Founding of SCLC and King's Widening Influence

"Old Man Segregation is on his death bed," King announced as the boycott came to its end. "But history has proven that social systems have a great last-minute breathing power, and the guardians of a status-quo are always on hand with their oxygen tents to keep the old order alive." King added that segregation still existed, not only "in the South in its glaring and conspicuous forms" but also "in the North in its hidden and subtle forms. But if democracy is to live, segregation must die." Thus, even as he celebrated the success of the boycott, King turned the energies of MIA members toward new objectives, such as voter registration and desegregation of educational and recreational facilities.

Grassroots protests against segregation were springing up all over the South, outside the control of any national organization or leader, including King himself. In May 1956, students at Florida A&M University launched their own bus boycott, which soon spread to the city of Tallahassee under the leadership of the Reverend C. K. Steele and the Tallahassee Inter-Civic Council. The following month, black activists in Alabama reacted to that state's banning of the NAACP by forming the Alabama Christian Movement for Human Rights, with fiery Birmingham minister Fred Shuttlesworth as leader. Three days after the Montgomery boycott ended, Steele and others were arrested for attempting to ride Tallahassee buses on a desegregated basis. Then Shuttlesworth's home was bombed. The next day King telegraphed Shuttlesworth's supporters, urging them to carry on and, "if necessary, fill up the jails of Birmingham."

King and other leaders recognized the need for a regional organization to sustain the momentum of the Montgomery movement. With Rustin's behind-the-scenes help, King, joined by Shuttlesworth and Steele, organized a conference of southern black leaders that was held in January 1957 in Atlanta. Although the gathering was disrupted when King and Abernathy rushed back to Montgomery following the bombing of four churches, including Abernathy's, the sixty participants formed the Southern Negro Leaders Conference, which later became the Southern Christian Leadership Conference (SCLC). King was selected to head the new group and help draft a "Statement to the South and Nation" that linked the southern black struggle to global politics:

> Asia's successive revolts against European imperialism, Africa's present ferment for independence, Hungary's death struggle against communism, and the determined drive of Negro Americans to become first class citizens are inextricably bound together. They are all vital factors in determining whether in the Twentieth Century mankind will crown its vast material gains with the achievement of liberty and justice for all, or whether it will commit suicide through lack of moral fibre.

King's growing international prominence became evident when African independence leader Kwame Nkrumah invited him to attend Ghana's independence ceremonies in March 1957. The leader of the first sub-Saharan African nation to free itself from colonialism, Nkrumah had personal ties to African Americans, having attended college in the United States during the 1930s and 1940s. King traveled to the ceremonies as part of an American delegation that included older and more established black leaders such as A. Philip Randolph, New York Congressman Adam Clayton Powell ,Jr., and United Nations official Ralph Bunche.

Upon his return, King found himself much in demand. He agreed to support a campaign against South Africa's white government and its harsh apartheid policies. He also participated in the Prayer Pilgrimage at the Lincoln Memorial in May 1957 to mark the third anniversary of the *Brown* decision. Although Randolph, Wilkins, and other established leaders had organized the event, the 25,000 demonstrators gave their most sustained applause to King's rousing closing. "Give us the ballot, and we will no longer plead to the federal government for passage of an anti-lynching law," he proclaimed. "We will by the power of our vote write the law on the statute books of the South and bring an end to the dastardly acts of the hooded perpetrators of violence." The *New York Amsterdam News* concluded King had become "the number one leader of sixteen million Negroes in the United States."

Yet King's rapid rise to prominence did not clarify the roles he and the SCLC should play in the civil rights movement. SCLC's Crusade for Citizenship had the ambitious goal of registering three million black voters but made only modest progress in overcoming racial barriers to voting, such as literacy tests and poll taxes. Even the Civil Rights Act of 1957, which passed despite a filibuster by Strom Thurmond and other segregationist senators, did little to stimulate SCLC's voting rights campaign. By the end of 1957, King faced complaints from within his own organization. Birmingham's Shuttlesworth, who had been beaten by chain-wielding segregationists when he tried to enroll his daughters in an all-white school, urged the SCLC to take the initiative against civil rights opponents "rather than waiting to defend ourselves." Impetus for continued militancy in the southern civil rights struggle would not come from King or the SCLC. Instead, just as in Farmville and Montgomery, the first stirrings of revolt were localized acts of rebellions, and black teenagers once again took the lead in challenging segregation. Films focused on rebellious youth such as *Rebel Without a Cause* (1955), with James Dean and Sal Mineo, and *Blackboard Jungle* (1955), with Sidney Poitier, signaled the arrival of a new consciousness among young people of all races. By 1957, the nation had become aware of teenage rebelliousness in the form of juvenile delinquency and the craze for rock-and-roll music. The enormous popularity of white singer Elvis Presley and black performers such as Fats Domino and Little Richard demonstrated that the nation's youth had left behind the musical tastes of their parents. During the fall of 1957, as Little Richard reached the top of the music charts with "Lucille" and "Long Tall Sally" and many television viewers turned to American Bandstand, a group of black high school students in Little Rock began a new stage in the civil rights struggle.

The Little Rock Nine

"I think that the first day was probably the most afraid I ever was," fifteen-year-old Minniejean Brown observed as she recalled her arrival at Little Rock's previously all-white Central High School for the fall term of 1957. Brown was one of nine black students to take part in the desegregation effort initiated by Daisy Bates, head of the NAACP's local branch. Selected on the basis of their academic excellence and willingness to become racial pioneers, the nine students worked closely with Bates to prepare themselves for the hostilities they expected to face. The evening before the first day of school, Arkansas Governor Orval Faubus announced he was sending National Guardsmen to deal with the anticipated violence. When the nine black students arrived on the morning of September 4, they quickly realized that the Guardsmen were positioned to block them from entering the school, not to protect them from a jeering mob of white segregationists. "I don't think we dared turn back to the mob," Brown recalled. She found it confusing that those in the mob hated her, even though they knew nothing about her. "I mean if they knew me a little bit, then they could say they hated me, but to not know me at all just seemed so strange."

Constitutional Rights versus Mob Violence

The students who became known as the Little Rock Nine were unable to enter Central High School on September 4, but they were determined to prevail over Governor Faubus and mob violence. The following day, Bates arranged for them to meet to walk to the school together. Elizabeth Eckford, one of the nine, did not get word of the plan, however, because there was no phone in her home. An angry crowd quickly surrounded her when she approached the school alone. Confused and frightened, she sat tensed on a bench until a white woman intervened and walked her to safety. The other eight students walked together to the school entrance, only to be turned back once again by Guardsmen with bayonets.

Faubus achieved a temporary victory by assigning National Guardsmen to prevent integration, but Marshall and other NAACP lawyers obtained an injunction against the governor's use of Guardsmen. When the nine students again encountered an angry mob on returning to Central High on September 23, Little Rock police escorted them into school through a delivery entrance. "The policemen seemed really scared, which kind of scared me," Brown remembered. Facing the threat of mob vengeance, the black students were finally taken away hastily in police cars.

The drama of black teenagers braving mob violence attracted international press coverage and transformed the Little Rock Nine into heroes of the civil rights movement. "It was the first time white Americans had seen black children in the newspaper," Brown recalled with pride. President Eisenhower,

White students jeered (left) as Elizabeth Eckford tried to make her way to the Little Rock Central High School entrance.

though reluctant to intervene, realized Faubus could not be allowed to block implementation of a federal court decision. After another day of mob violence, Eisenhower nationalized the Arkansas National Guard, shifting their command from the state to the federal government. He also ordered the 101st Airborne Division to Little Rock, the first time since Reconstruction that a president had sent federal troops into the South to enforce the Fourteenth Amendment.

With military escorts, the students were finally able to attend school. Although the paratroopers were withdrawn in November, federalized Guardsmen remained through the rest of the school year. "I was actually embarrassed that I had to go into the school with soldiers, which is the reverse of how it should be," Brown remembered. "*They* should have been embarrassed that I had to go into the school with soldiers." At first, Brown thought being front-page news was "kind of cool." Despite facing violence, she and the other black students realized the importance of their racial breakthrough. "You could see we were representing the race," she recalled.

But once mob violence dissipated and daily press coverage declined, Brown found that getting through the school year was a challenge of its own. "I had no experience, really, with white people," she remembered. "It was all so new." Like the other black students, she was the target of taunts and hostile acts—"kicking, spitting and throwing lighted pieces of paper at us." For Brown, the harassment culminated in "the chili incident." In December, as she carried her tray to a cafeteria table, several boys pushed chairs in front of her. "I stood there and said to myself, 'I'm gonna wait.'" Then she started forward, and they blocked her again. "I opened my hands, and the whole thing, tray, milk, butter, roll, and chili spattered all over these four guys." Brown recalled that she "walked out of the cafeteria as if I was queen of everything," then nearly collapsed. Ernest Green, one of the other black students in the cafeteria, remembered a dead silence, broken by applause from black workers in the cafeteria.

As result of the incident, Brown was suspended. A few months later, after a second suspension for "verbal retaliation after provocation," she was expelled. With Bates's help, Brown was able to continue her schooling at New York's New Lincoln High School, living with Mamie and Kenneth Clark, whose research had contributed to the *Brown* decision. The remaining eight students completed the school year in Little Rock, and in June 1958 Ernest Green became the first black student to graduate from Central High. Although Green recalled that there was no applause when he received his diploma, he was satisfied to have finally "cracked the wall."

Stirrings of Grassroots Revolt

As the Little Rock Nine approached the end of their first term at Central High, Ella Baker arrived in Atlanta to take on the task of running the SCLC's headquarters and revitalizing an organization that had accomplished little in the year since its founding. Baker was aware that King and other SCLC leaders had made some gains at the local level, but they were ministers who had less history of involvement in the civil rights movement than she did. The fifty-four-year-old

Baker had organized consumer cooperatives in New York City during the Depression years before joining the NAACP staff in 1940. As the NAACP's director of branches, she traveled extensively, and her contacts with grassroots leaders convinced her that Walter White's bureaucratic leadership often stifled local initiative. Discouraged, she resigned in 1946. During the early 1950s, she headed the NAACP's New York branch and led an effort to end the de facto—as opposed to de jure, or legally imposed—segregation of New York's school system. After Rosa Parks launched the Montgomery bus boycott, Baker joined with Rustin and leftist white lawyer Stanley Levison to form In Friendship, to raise funds for southern civil rights activities. It was Rustin and Levison who convinced King that Baker was the right person to organize the SCLC's headquarters. Although she was disturbed that the decision was made without consulting her—"I don't like anyone to commit me"—she left New York for Atlanta.

As Baker did her best to invigorate the SCLC, a few local movements, often involving young people, were developing without much guidance from regional or national groups. In 1958, members of NAACP Youth Councils in Wichita, Kansas, and Oklahoma City began using the "sit-down" tactic to desegregate lunch counters. Teenagers in St. Petersburg, Florida, tried to integrate a public swimming pool. In October 1958, over 10,000 students joined baseball star Jackie Robinson and actor Harry Belafonte in a Youth March for Integrated Schools in Washington, DC.

During 1959, there were other indications of African American impatience with the pace of civil rights reform. Lorraine Hansberry's highly acclaimed play *Raisin in the Sun,* opening on Broadway, touched on concerns that fueled black militancy in the 1960s: racial discrimination in housing and employment, generational differences among African Americans, and increasing identification with Africa. A television documentary, *The Hate That Hate Produced,* drew attention to the racial separatist doctrines of the Nation of Islam and Malcolm X.

National civil rights leaders could ignore the Nation of Islam, given its small following, but they took more seriously a challenge from Robert F. Williams, head of the NAACP's branch in Monroe, North Carolina, who suggested in 1957 that members arm themselves against Klan attacks. Two years later, he called for retaliation against an all-white jury that had acquitted a white man of raping a black woman. Though the NAACP suspended Williams, King, as the nation's best-known advocate of nonviolence, felt compelled to respond. In an extended rebuttal, King blamed black impatience on "half-hearted and inadequate" federal enforcement of the *Brown* decision. Insisting that calls for "retaliatory violence" would "mislead Negroes into the belief that this is the only path," he argued that forceful nonviolent tactics were more effective than "a few acts of organized violence." But nonviolence, he said, required "dedicated people, because it is a backbreaking task to arouse, to organize, and to educate tens of thousands for disciplined, sustained action."

In 1956, King had called for greater militancy in his address to the NAACP convention, but three years later the controversy concerning Williams served as a reminder that King's own organization, the SCLC, had done little to stimulate nonviolent protest movements in the South. By the end of 1959, Ella Baker was concerned that the organization was devoting its resources to "routine procedures for promoting registration and voting" rather than developing "potential leaders" for "a vital movement of nonviolent direct mass action" throughout the South. What was needed, she believed, was "the development of people who are interested not in being leaders as much as in developing leadership among other people." King recognized the validity of some criticisms of his leadership and planned to leave Dexter church and to devote all his time to the SCLC. But, Baker wondered, would he risk directly involving himself and the SCLC in local protest campaigns? Was he the kind of "creative leader" who could stir up "dynamic mass action"?

The Student Sit-In Movement

Having grown up in Chicago and attended Howard University, Diane Nash remembered feeling "stifled and boxed in" after transferring to Nashville's Fisk University in 1959. She found it difficult to adjust to the segregation she experienced living in the South for the first time. Moreover, she saw segregation as responsible for the South's "slow progress in industrial, political and other areas" and "the weakening of American influence abroad as a result of race hatred." Nash's outlook brightened, however, when she heard about James Lawson's nonviolence workshop, which had already attracted students from several of Nashville's other black colleges.

Nash was immediately impressed by Lawson, a black theology student deeply committed to using nonviolent tactics to bring about social change. In the early 1950s, he had chosen to go to prison rather than serve in the military. Paroled to the Methodist Board of Missions, he spent three years as a missionary in India, where he studied Gandhian ideas. Returning to the United States, he became a field secretary of the Fellowship of Reconciliation, the pacifist group that in the 1940s had hired Bayard Rustin and James Farmer to work on race relations.

Discussing his plans with King in 1958, Lawson moved to Nashville to enroll at Vanderbilt University's divinity school. With support from the SCLC's Nashville affiliate, Lawson began training students in the Gandhian philosophy of nonviolent resistance. Some of his initial recruits were black students studying to become ministers, notably John Lewis, Bernard Lafayette, and James Bevel of American Baptist Theological Seminary. Nash, though raised a Catholic, found she had much in common with the other participants. She began to see nonviolent tactics as "applied religion" designed "to bring about a climate in which there is appreciation of the dignity of man and in which each individual is free to grow and produce to his fullest capacity." By November 1959, Nash and others in Lawson's workshop had begun "test sit-ins" at Nashville department stores. Before they could put their ideas into practice, however, four teenagers in Greensboro, North Carolina, began a new stage of the southern civil rights struggle.

Spread of the Sit-ins

"We always got together and talked about the events that were occurring across the nation and the world," David Richmond recalled of his "bull sessions" with Izell Blair, Franklin McCain, and Joseph McNeil. The four first-year students at North Carolina A&T College had belonged to NAACP youth groups in high school, but they decided on their own to take action as they talked about the racial discrimination confronting them off-campus. "We challenged each other," Richmond remembered. Late in the afternoon of February 1, 1960, they walked into a Woolworth's "five-and-dime" store where black students often bought school supplies but were not allowed to eat. They sat down at the lunch counter. The black woman who worked behind the counter chastised them, "You know you are supposed to eat at the other end." The four students were not sure what would happen, but they remained seated until the store closed, when they promised to be back in the morning when it opened.

The word *sit-in* had not yet been coined, but the four Greensboro students discovered that other students were eager to use this simple tactic to put segregationists on the defensive. The next morning, about thirty students occupied most of Woolworth's lunch-counter seats. By the third day, students had formed the Students Executive Committee for Justice to coordinate protests that culminated at the end of the week in a march of several thousand students from the A&T campus to Greensboro's downtown. Meanwhile, black students at nearby black colleges launched similar protests. By the end of the first week, the sit-in movement had spread through North Carolina to all-black Hampton

Students stage a sit-in at a Woolworth's store in Greensboro, North Carolina.

Institute and elsewhere in Virginia. The first major arrests of the sit-in campaign came as police in Raleigh, North Carolina, took away forty-one students on February 12.

Spurred by news of these protests, Nash and other workshop participants organized a campaign in Nashville that began on February 13 with a sit-in by 124 carefully trained and disciplined black students. On February 27, police arrested student protesters who had occupied all the seats at a downtown lunch counter, but more students quickly took their places. In all, eighty-two demonstrators, including Nash, were arrested that day, and sixty more the following week. Black residents supported the students with a boycott of downtown businesses. On April 19, a bomb exploded at the home of Alexander Looby, a black city councilman who had served as legal counsel to the arrested students. Rather than deterring the protests, this violence prompted 2,500 demonstrators to march silently to City Hall, where Nash forced the mayor to concede that segregation was wrong. Soon afterward, the campaign achieved its first major concessions when several businesses ended their segregation policies.

During the spring, student-led sit-ins achieved similar success in other communities. Although black colleges had experienced protests before, these had usually been about student rules or poor food in dining halls. Suddenly, students on dozens of campuses were willing to risk jail to expand the meaning of the *Brown* decision and speed the pace of racial change. By the end of the school year, more than 3,000 students had been arrested.

A New Racial Pride

By forcing concessions from white leaders, student activists transformed their self-image. They became, as Nash put it, "suddenly proud to be called 'black.'" Acting independently rather than on behalf of a civil rights group, the students grew evermore confident of their ability to direct campaigns without adult leadership. Although many of the students were affiliated with NAACP youth groups or supported by NAACP branches, the new movement offered an implicit challenge to the cautious strategy of the nation's oldest civil rights group. While NAACP leaders gave public support to the sit-ins, they privately questioned their usefulness. Marshall only reluctantly agreed to provide legal assistance to students "who violated the sacred property rights of white folks." King, in contrast, applauded the students for taking their "honored places in the world-wide struggle for freedom." He was particularly impressed by their willingness to remain nonviolent despite provocation and to go to jail to achieve change. Yet, although he sympathized with the student protesters, he remained reluctant to involve his group in a direct action campaign.

For Ella Baker, the sit-in movement was what she had hoped for: mass militancy at the local level. Impatient with King's cautious leadership and disenchanted with the SCLC's failure to build on the momentum of the Montgomery bus boycott movement, she saw the student activists as "refreshing indeed" to those like herself "who bear the scars of battle, the frustrations and the disillusionment that come when the prophetic leader turns out to have heavy feet of clay." She admired the strong desire of student activists to remain independent of adult leadership. The local student protest groups seemed to confirm her view that the civil rights movement did not need a "strong, savior-type leader" like King. By this time, Baker also knew the male clergymen who ran the SCLC wanted to replace her with a male minister who would be less contentious.

Aware that her time in the SCLC was limited, Baker proposed that the group sponsor a meeting of student sit-in leaders from across the South. She invited more than one hundred young people to discuss nonviolent philosophy and tactics at an Easter weekend leadership training session at North Carolina's Shaw College in Raleigh, where she had been an undergraduate in the 1920s. Nearly 300 students showed up, including a dozen southern white students. Both King and James Lawson were invited to speak. Lawson's address came close to capturing the tone of student militancy, especially when he criticized the NAACP for stressing "fund-raising and court action rather than developing our greatest resources, a people no longer the victims of racial evil who can act in a disciplined manner to implement the constitution."

Baker resisted pressure to have the students at the meeting affiliate with the SCLC or other existing civil rights groups. "I thought they had the right to direct their own affairs and even make their own mistakes," she later explained. The students decided to form the Student Nonviolent Coordinating Committee (SNCC—pronounced "snick"), selecting Fisk student Marion Barry as chairman. The statement of purpose Lawson drafted for the new group affirmed "the philosophical or religious ideal of nonviolence as the foundation of our purpose, the presupposition of our faith, and the manner of our action." Unable to afford its own quarters, SNCC had its first office in SCLC's Atlanta headquarters, where Baker still worked. As SNCC leaders met over the next few months, many found that Baker's ideas about organizing coincided with their own desire to keep their local sit-in groups free from the control of older and more cautious civil rights organizations and leaders. "She was much older in terms of age," Nashville activist John Lewis recalled, "but I think in terms of ideas and philosophy and commitment she was one of the youngest persons in the movement." Most of the students affiliated with SNCC also admired King, but they increasingly saw themselves as spearheads of the southern civil rights struggle. Although King was barely in his thirties, there was already a generational gulf dividing student advocates of civil disobedience and the somewhat more cautious SCLC leaders.

Even when King, after moving to Atlanta, joined students in an October 1960 sit-in at a department store, he did so only at their prodding, later admitting he took part "only as a follower, not a leader." His arrest, however, attracted national attention and unexpectedly played a crucial role in the 1960 presidential election. When Georgia authorities released the protesters after several days in jail, they promptly rearrested King on charges of violating conditions of his earlier parole for driving in Atlanta with his Alabama driver's license. King was then sentenced to six months at hard labor—"all over a traffic violation," he complained. King feared for his life at Georgia's Reidsville State Prison; as a prominent black leader, he was sure to be the target of prison violence. Civil rights advocates mobilized to have King released on bond, and Democratic candidate John Kennedy telephoned Coretta Scott King to express concern while his brother and campaign manager Robert Kennedy worked behind the scenes. After a Georgia judge agreed to release King, news of John Kennedy's intervention strengthened his support among black voters and helped achieve his narrow win over Republican Richard Nixon.

Conclusion

The 1950s are often viewed as a period of complacency and conformity in the United States, but the spread of civil rights activism shows that discontent simmered in many black communities. To be sure, Cold War anticommunism had quieted the once powerful voices of W. E. B. Du Bois and Paul Robeson, but youthful political activism emerged as a major challenge to NAACP dominance at the national level. Less than two years after the organization achieved its great victory in the *Brown* case, the Montgomery bus boycott demonstrated that many black southerners were eager to challenge the Jim Crow system and speed the pace of racial reform. As a result of the boycott's success, Martin Luther King, Jr., emerged as a major civil rights leader whose stature, in time, surpassed that of NAACP leaders Roy Wilkins and Thurgood Marshall.

But King himself was a product of the Montgomery boycott movement rather than its initiator. Like many subsequent local protests of the late 1950s and afterward, the boycott was a grassroots movement that relied on the initiatives of local activists more than existing civil rights groups. In the decade following the student strike at Moton High, young leaders initiated many local protest movements and forced older, more established leaders to follow. Moreover, the Little Rock Nine managed to force the hand of the federal government by refusing to back down in the face of mob violence. When President Eisenhower reluctantly sent troops to Little Rock, young black people elsewhere learned a lesson that shaped subsequent African American politics: local protests could break down racial barriers and capture the attention of the nation and even the world. By the early 1960s, King's prominence in the civil rights movement was well established, but the wave of sit-ins made clear that the increasingly militant African American freedom struggle was not under the control of any one leader or organization.

Questions for Review and Reflection

1. What made *Brown* v. *Board of Education of Topeka* unique in comparison to similar cases the NAACP had been working on to fight segregation in

education? How was the argument used to fight segregation in this case a departure from the NAACP's previous legal approach?

2. Discuss the strengths and weaknesses of W. E. B. Du Bois's argument, made during the 1930s, that African American children were better off in educational settings where they were accepted.

3. To what extent was the *Brown* v. *Board of Education Topeka* critical to the subsequent progression of the civil rights movement?

4. Was Martin Luther King, Jr., essential to the success of the Montgomery Bus Boycott or would the boycott and the broader civil rights struggle have expanded even without his influence and involvement?

5. What effect did the desegregation of Central High School and the student "sit-in" movement have on the role of black students in the modern African American freedom struggle? What accounts for the growing impact of youthful black activism?

CHAPTER 18

Marching toward Freedom, 1961–1966

Freedom Riders Challenge Segregation

"We can't let them stop us with violence," Diane Nash told James Farmer during the 1961 freedom ride campaign. "If we do, the movement is dead." Nash, a leader in the Nashville Student Movement and the new Student Nonviolent Coordinating Committee (SNCC), had just turned twenty-three. Farmer, age forty-one, had a lifetime of experience with civil rights activism. He had been Nash's age when he helped found the Congress of Racial Equality (CORE). This was his second freedom ride, having participated in CORE's 1947 Journey of Reconciliation, which involved sending black and white volunteers on a bus ride through the South to test local compliance with a Supreme Court ruling banning segregation in interstate transportation. In the freedom ride campaign that began in May 1961, Farmer joined twelve other riders, seven of them white, on two buses that left Washington, DC, on a trip that was intended to culminate in New Orleans. The riders purposely disregarded signs designating waiting rooms and restrooms as "Colored Only" and "Whites Only." The activists soon found that while bus companies might be willing to comply with antisegregation laws, white segregationists in the Deep South were not.

Farmer and the other participants encountered increasing violence as they ventured farther into the South. In Rock Hill, South Carolina, several riders were assaulted. Outside Anniston, Alabama, someone in an angry mob threw a firebomb into the bus. The freedom riders escaped, but a photograph of the burning bus became front-page news across the nation. When the second bus arrived at Birmingham, the riders were savagely beaten with pipes and baseball

1961	Black students continue the freedom ride campaign. The voting rights advocate Herbert Lee is killed by a white state legislator who is later absolved. The Interstate Commerce Commission (ICC) implements desegregation in transportation facilities. Hundreds are arrested in the Albany Movement's desegregation campaign in Georgia.
1962	The Albany Movement's protest campaign subsides. James Meredith desegregates the University of Mississippi.
1963	King writes "Letter from Birmingham Jail" during decisive civil rights campaign. President John F. Kennedy proposes civil rights legislation to desegregate public accommodations. NAACP leader Medgar Evers is murdered outside his home in Jackson, Mississippi. At the March on Washington for Jobs and Freedom, King delivers "I Have a Dream" speech. Dynamite blast set by segregationists kills four black girls at 16th Street Baptist Church in Birmingham.
1964	The Mississippi Freedom Summer Project seeks to register black voters. Three civil rights workers murdered at start of Mississippi "Freedom Summer" Project seeking to register black voters. President Lyndon B. Johnson signs Civil Rights Act of 1964. The Mississippi Freedom Democratic Party fails to displace the all-white regular delegation at the Democratic National Convention in Atlantic City. Martin Luther King, Jr., receives the Nobel Peace Prize.
1965	Malcolm X is killed while speaking in Harlem. Police attack voting rights protesters attempting to march from Selma to Montgomery. President Lyndon B. Johnson signs the 1965 Voting Rights Act. Police arrest in Watts section of Los Angeles ignites four days of rioting.
1966	Civil rights leaders continue James Meredith's March Against Fear. SNCC chair Stokely Carmichael ignites controversy with his call for "Black Power."

bats. Ignoring warnings of violence, Birmingham police were conveniently absent. In light of the attacks, Farmer decided to call off the ride. Then he got a phone call from Nash.

> "Would you have any objections to members of the Nashville Student Movement, which is SNCC, going in and taking up the Ride where CORE left off?" she asked.
> "You realize it may be suicide," Farmer warned.

"We fully realize that," replied Nash, unfazed. "Let me send in fresh nonviolent troops to carry the Ride on. Let me bring in Nashville students to pick up the baton and run with it."

Though she had only recently been a student at Fisk, Nash was a movement veteran. A participant in James Lawson's workshops on nonviolence, she had been instrumental in the sit-ins that desegregated Nashville lunch counters. Earlier in 1961, she had joined an antisegregation "jail-in" in Rock Hill, serving a thirty-day jail sentence to make the point that nonviolent demonstrators should not accept bail money and thereby become dependent on the financial and legal assistance of others. Returning to Nashville, she dropped out of Fisk to devote herself full-time to the movement, working for both SNCC and the Southern Christian Leadership Conference (SCLC). "I'll be doing this for the rest of my life," she told a *Jet* magazine reporter.

After gaining Farmer's reluctant assent, Nash informed Birmingham minister and civil rights leader Fred Shuttlesworth that students would be arriving to continue CORE's campaign. She quickly mobilized support in Nashville, securing financial backing from black ministers in the local SCLC affiliate and recruiting student volunteers. Ten young people stepped forward. "Several made out wills," she recalled. "A few more gave me sealed letters to be mailed if they were killed. Some told me frankly that they were afraid, but they knew this was something that they must do, because freedom was worth it."

The Nashville contingent left for Birmingham on May 17, the seventh anniversary of the *Brown* decision, but as they arrived, Birmingham's notoriously racist police chief, Theophilus Eugene "Bull" Connor, ordered the new freedom riders taken to the Birmingham jail. The following night, he released them at the Alabama state border. They walked in the dark to a black farmer's home, where they telephoned Nash. She immediately sent a car to return them to Birmingham, even as news reports claimed they were back at their campuses. "The police chief wasn't going to get off that easily," Nash explained.

Within days, more freedom riders gathered at Shuttlesworth's home in Birmingham. Injecting new energy into the southern struggle, they boarded buses, undeterred by the mob assault in Birmingham. They encountered more violence when they arrived in Montgomery. Martin Luther King, Jr., who had declined Nash's request to join the freedom ride campaign, responded to the Montgomery violence by addressing an evening rally at a local black church. White rioters laid siege to the packed church, keeping occupants inside until U.S. marshals and the Alabama National Guard were called in to restore order.

Thus, within a week of Nash's decision to continue the freedom ride, student activists had prodded Farmer and King toward greater militancy and forced state and federal officials to intervene on their behalf. Segregationist violence had only made student protesters more determined. The youthful freedom riders were, in Nash's words, "dead serious. We're ready to give our lives."

Nash's determination to resume the freedom rides soon had major consequences for the southern civil rights movement. During May and June of 1961, the Freedom Ride Coordinating Committee she headed attracted a growing number of activists, including veterans of the sit-ins of the previous year, and this cadre spearheaded a determined assault against the bastions of Jim Crow in the rural Deep South. The freedom rides and the subsequent voting rights efforts in the Deep South posed a challenge to newly elected president John F. Kennedy. In January 1961, the forty-three-year-old Kennedy announced in his inaugural address that the torch had been passed to a new generation born in the twentieth century, but the young president could not have anticipated that during his administration still younger African Americans, many of them college students, would pick up the torch of advancing the cause of human rights. By 1961, thirty-two-year-old King had already become better known and more influential than older black leaders such as CORE's Farmer and the NAACP's Roy Wilkins and Thurgood Marshall. But Nash and other impatient SNCC workers were taking the initiative away from King.

Black students spearheaded the desegregation protests of the early 1960s, but African Americans of all ages and backgrounds would soon become more militant. Although student activists saw their direct action tactics as preferable to King's more cautious approach and the NAACP's reliance on litigation and lobbying, these alternative strategies did not necessarily conflict with one another. The increasing diversity of organizations and leaders made the civil rights struggle more difficult for anyone to control or suppress. Like Roosevelt, Truman, and Eisenhower, President Kennedy tried to avoid taking a stand on divisive and controversial civil rights issues, but he and his successor, Lyndon B. Johnson, were forced to respond to escalating demands for major civil rights reforms. Overcoming decades of southern intransigence, African Americans prodded national leaders to enact the Civil Rights Act of 1964 and the Voting Rights Act of 1965. But even these reforms did not allay the festering racial discontents that became evident as southern mass protests gave way to mass insurrections in the urban North.

By the mid-1960s, the civil rights struggle had become a liberation struggle aiming not only to eliminate racial barriers but also to deal with poverty and the legacy of past injustices. Having overcome the Jim Crow system, African Americans engaged in intense debates about the future direction of the struggle. Influenced by black nationalist leaders such as Malcolm X, some activists who had once used nonviolence to bring about desegregation began to call for black power and racial separation. As the focus of the black struggle shifted from the rural South to the urban North, established black leaders such as King were challenged by younger activists more willing to act militantly to achieve ever more ambitious goals.

Grassroots Struggles in the Deep South

The Mississippi prison called Parchman Farm seemed a throwback to slavery. "I'd heard about Parchman in the same way I'd heard about Mississippi—in tones of horror and terms of brutality," freedom rider John Lewis recalled. A recent graduate of Nashville's American Baptist Theological Seminary, Lewis was the youngest of the original group of CORE freedom riders. He had been beaten in Rock Hill and knocked unconscious in Montgomery. He still wore head bandages from the latter assault when he rode another bus from Montgomery to Jackson, Mississippi.

After Lewis and dozens of freedom riders were arrested in Jackson, they were sent to Parchman, where most served sixty-day sentences. They were forced to stand naked for two and a half hours after being strip-searched. "I could see that this was an attempt to break us down, to humiliate and dehumanize us, to rob us of our identity and self-worth," Lewis later wrote.

Although Mississippi officials expected that Parchman would deter further freedom rides, imprisonment produced a new sense of community and commitment among the riders. Lewis recalled exchanging ideas with Stokely Carmichael, the fast-talking, self-confident Howard University philosophy major who sharply questioned the Christian-Gandhian principles of the Nashville student activists. "He was as different from me as night from day, both in personality and in philosophy," Lewis recalled, "but for some reason I liked him." After his release, Lewis returned to Nashville, but the experience had changed him. "If there was anything I learned from that long, bloody trip of 1961, it was this—that we were in for a long, bloody fight here in the American South."

The freedom riders' determination set them on a collision course with the Kennedy administration. Their slogan—"Freedom Now"—and their demand for attention to civil rights were at odds with the determination of the new president to focus on Cold War concerns such as removing Fidel Castro's new revolutionary government in Cuba. Black voters had played a crucial role in Kennedy's election, but the administration feared alienating southern white Democrats if it supported civil rights reforms. In June, when Nash joined a delegation that met with Attorney General Robert Kennedy, she rejected Kennedy's plea that the freedom riders concentrate on voter registration rather than direct action protests like the freedom rides. The administration went ahead with plans to arrange financial backing for efforts to register black voters. Although student activists recognized the importance of voting rights and welcomed the prospect of funds for full-time staff members, Nash felt the Kennedy administration merely wanted to redirect the student's militancy toward less controversial goals.

During the summer of 1961, an increasingly bitter conflict arose within SNCC between those such as Nash who wanted to continue desegregation protests and those who favored a shift toward voting rights efforts. Lewis joined Nash in rejecting the administration's financial incentives for voter registration. "Direct action was what had gotten us this far," he explained. "SNCC had been created and built on the foundation of confrontation—disciplined, focused, aggressive, nonviolent confrontation." As the conflict threatened to split SNCC apart, the group's advisor, Ella Baker, fashioned a compromise that divided the organization into a voter registration wing and a direct action wing under Nash. This organizational division became unimportant, however, as

SNCC field secretaries sent to Mississippi and southwest Georgia soon found that segregationist opposition to any kind of civil rights activity was far more intense in rural areas of the Deep South than in the cities, where most of the sit-ins had occurred. In addition to rigorously enforcing segregation laws, southern white officials restricted black political participation through literacy tests, poll taxes, intimidation, and outright violence. Although black residents constituted almost half of Mississippi's population, less than 5 percent were registered to vote. "We would learn almost immediately that voter registration was as threatening to the white establishment in the South as sit-ins and Freedom Rides, and that it would prompt the same violent response," Lewis recalled.

Voter Registration in Mississippi

SNCC's first voter registration project was in the southwest Mississippi town of McComb in Amite County. Bob Moses, the twenty-six-year-old black high school teacher from New York who directed the McComb project, had been inspired to join the southern movement after seeing newspaper photographs of "sullen, angry, determined" sit-in demonstrators. In the summer of 1960, Moses accepted Bayard Rustin's invitation to work in SCLC's headquarters in Atlanta, but his skepticism about King's top–down leadership style drew him to Ella Baker and the student activists affiliated with SNCC. The next summer, Moses returned to the South and contacted local McComb leaders willing to provide housing for a small staff of SNCC field secretaries. As he and the staff tried to convince local residents to risk registering to vote, voting right proponents quickly became targets for violence.

Late in September 1961, a white member of Mississippi's legislature shot and killed Herbert Lee, a black Amite County resident who had helped Moses. Although the shooting of the unarmed Lee occurred in front of several witnesses, a coroner's jury accepted the legislator's claim of self-defense.

Meanwhile, SNCC workers faced another crisis when McComb teenagers became involved in sit-in protests. Although Moses focused on voter registration activities, other SNCC workers conducted nonviolence workshops in McComb that soon led to sit-ins and the jailing of five high school students. When the students were released after a month in jail, they were prevented from returning to school. Early in November, over one hundred students protested this decision and Lee's killing by marching to McComb's City Hall, where Moses and other SNCC workers joined them. As the demonstrators attempted to pray, police began to make arrests, and white onlookers suddenly attacked Bob Zellner, then SNCC's only white field secretary, gouging his eye. The melee ended with the arrest of Moses and ten SNCC workers, who were sentenced to four months in jail for contributing to the delinquency of minors.

The SNCC workers were released in December while their convictions were appealed, but the expulsion of student activists and the jailing of most of SNCC's staff marked the end of the first phase of the organization's venture into Mississippi. Moses abandoned voter registration activities in the McComb area and moved to Jackson, the state capital, where Nash, now married to fellow Nashville activist James Bevel, was already working on behalf of both SCLC and SNCC. Moses recognized the McComb effort as merely "a tremor," a small step toward weakening southern racism in its Mississippi stronghold. "We knew some of the obstacles we would have to face," Moses commented. "We had some general idea of what had to be done to get such a campaign started. And we began to set about doing this."

During 1962, Moses brought together a capable staff under the auspices of the Council of Federated Organizations (COFO), a joint effort of the NAACP, SNCC, and other civil rights groups active in the state. COFO field secretaries—most of them affiliated with SNCC—focused on the Mississippi Delta, where the state's black residents were concentrated. Most of Moses's recruits were young black people, but he also worked closely with older grassroots leaders in the Delta, including longtime NAACP activists. Facing violence and economic retaliation, only a few black Delta residents were willing to venture to county courthouses, where often hostile voter registrars administered literary tests. When plantation worker Fannie Lou Hamer tried to register, she lost her job and her home and was severely beaten in jail. Rather than being deterred, however, Hamer later joined SNCC's staff—becoming, at age forty-five, its oldest member.

As in McComb, segregationist resistance in the Delta was fierce. In February 1963, when Moses survived a highway ambush that left an SNCC worker seriously wounded, he began to doubt whether the campaign in Mississippi could succeed without outside assistance. Although he continued to rely mainly on Mississippi-born organizers, he announced that civil rights workers from outside the state would help organize mass demonstrations in Greenwood to build public support for voter registration. Moses realized there would be no major changes in Mississippi unless the federal government and the rest of the nation became aware of conditions there. He became increasingly convinced that helping poor and often ill-educated black Mississippians to register required a fundamental change in voting requirements. He questioned Mississippi's literacy test for voting when the state had failed to provide adequate educational opportunities for black children. Adopting the "one man, one vote" slogan of African nationalists, Moses insisted, "The country owed blacks either the right to vote as a literate or the right to learn how to read and write *now*."

The Albany Movement

While voting rights workers gained a foothold in Mississippi, other civil rights activists, many of them veterans of the sit-ins and freedom rides, launched voting rights campaigns elsewhere. Focusing on areas where segregationist resistance was strong, SNCC transformed itself from a committee of student sit-in leaders into a group of full-time community organizers. SNCC field secretaries not only went to Mississippi but also accepted invitations from grassroots activists in Selma, Alabama; Danville, Virginia; and Cambridge, Maryland. As SNCC's youthful staff, many of them only recently students, gained confidence in their organizing abilities, they also became more willing to criticize older civil rights leaders, including King. Some were disappointed that King had not joined the freedom ride campaign, but there were also tensions over broader issues. While the NAACP continued to emphasize litigation and lobbying Congress for broad civil rights reforms, King's SCLC reacted cautiously to the upsurge of southern protest campaigns. Both groups supported SNCC's organizing efforts, but conflicts between them increased as SNCC workers forged ties with militant local leaders. These conflicts were especially evident in southwest Georgia, where both SNCC and SCLC attempted to provide help and guidance for the Albany Movement.

SNCC organizers arrived first. Late in the summer of 1961, Virginia Union Seminary graduate Charles Sherrod teamed with Nashville sit-in veteran Cordell Reagon to establish SNCC's Southwest Georgia Project. By November, students initiated protests and forged strong ties with older leaders who formed the Albany Movement, with osteopath Dr. William G. Anderson as president. As protests and mass marches escalated in December, the rapid growth in black support seemed to confirm the effectiveness of SNCC's strategy of working closely with grassroots leaders. Then Anderson's decision to invite King to speak at a mass rally on December 15 soon escalated tensions between SNCC and SCLC. SNCC workers applauded King's willingness to be arrested during a march to City Hall, but, after King promised to remain in jail through Christmas, they were disappointed that he allowed himself to be released on bail.

King explained that his release was part of a compromise settlement that included integration of Albany's train station and the release of the other jailed demonstrators. But SNCC activists believed that continued protests might have achieved even greater concessions and were disturbed that King and his SCLC colleagues had reached the settlement without consulting them. Reporters covering the Albany protests began to note conflict between SNCC's bottom–up organizing strategy, which relied on long-term involvement in a community and close ties with grassroots leaders, and King's top–down leadership style.

The following July, when King and SCLC treasurer Ralph Abernathy returned to Albany to face charges for the December protest, they announced they would go to jail rather than pay fines. But the effort to put pressure on white officials by staying in jail fizzled when Albany's police chief Laurie Pritchett arranged for bail. "This was one time that I was out of jail and I was not happy to be out," King recalled. Upon his release, protests resumed, but King halted demonstrations after some black residents threw bottles and stones at police. When he tried to hold a prayer vigil at City Hall, he was once again arrested but his sentence was suspended. By this time, SNCC's own organizing efforts had stalled as Albany police arrested demonstrators without using the brutal tactics that attracted press attention and federal intervention.

By the end of 1962, despite hundreds of arrests in Albany, neither SNCC nor SCLC had achieved tangible gains. As in SNCC's Mississippi campaign, the

Southwest Georgia Project could not overcome segregationist resistance without substantial outside support.

The Nationalization of Civil Rights

"The largest industrial city in the South, Birmingham had become, in the thirties, a symbol for bloodshed when trade unions sought to organize," King wrote to explain the SCLC decision to launch its first major civil rights campaign there early in 1963. "It was a community in which human rights had been trampled for so long that fear and oppression were as thick in its atmosphere as the smog from its factories." King's failure to achieve major concessions in Albany left him increasingly vulnerable to criticism and eager for another chance to prove that nonviolence could work. Local SCLC leader Fred Shuttlesworth's home and church had been bombed during the 1950s, and numerous other acts of racist violence had given Birmingham the nickname Bombingham. Police chief Bull Connor's efforts to expel student freedom riders in the spring of 1961 also symbolized the intransigence of the city's segregationists. Alabama's newly elected governor, George C. Wallace, expressed the racism of many white officials when he declared in his inaugural address, "I say, segregation now! Segregation tomorrow! Segregation forever!"

King and the Children's Crusade

On Good Friday morning, April 12, 1963, King met with his SCLC colleagues in Birmingham's Gaston Motel to discuss a decision that would shape the outcome of their campaign. Sit-ins at libraries, lunch counters, and stores in the downtown area, as well as marches, had resulted in hundreds of arrests. Prodded by Shuttlesworth and younger activists, King realized that he had to join those in jail to sustain the campaign, but he also realized that imprisonment would prevent him, the primary SCLC fundraiser, from obtaining additional bail money. King went to an adjacent room where he stood alone to ponder his dilemma. "What would be the verdict of the country about a man who had encouraged hundreds of people to make a stunning sacrifice and then excused himself?" King whispered, "I must go." As anticipated, the police arrested him and other marchers for "parading without a permit," but King's jailing increased the campaign's national support. Singer and actor Harry Belafonte helped to raise sufficient bail bonds to sustain the movement, and President Kennedy phoned Coretta Scott King to express concern about her husband's arrest.

While jailed, King learned that eight white clergymen had publicly denounced the Birmingham campaign as "unwise and untimely." Seizing the opportunity to defend his protest strategy, he began drafting a response. King's eloquent "Letter from Birmingham City Jail" argued that white resistance to black equality had forced blacks to move outside legal channels and create a crisis rather than wait forever for change: "When you are harried by day and haunted by night by the fact that you are a Negro, living constantly at tiptoe

Arrested numerous times during his lifetime, it was in Birmingham that Martin Luther King, Jr., defended his protest strategy in his eloquent "Letter from Birmingham City Jail."

stance, never quite knowing what to expect next, and are plagued by inner fears and outer resentments; when you are forever fighting a degenerating sense of 'nobodiness'—then you will understand why we find it difficult to wait." Seeing himself as caught between the "force of complacency" in black communities and the "force of bitterness and hatred" represented by black racial separatists, King insisted that he offered "the more excellent way of love and nonviolent protest."

After King's jailing, the Birmingham demonstrations increased in intensity, and so did the arrests. By early May, more than 3,000 had been jailed. Faced with the possibility that Birmingham officials, like those in Albany, would crush the movement through mass arrests, SCLC leaders followed the urging of James Bevel to allow children to participate in marches. It was a risky decision, but it greatly expanded the demonstrations. "For the first time in the civil rights movement, we were able to put into effect the Gandhian principle: 'Fill up the jails,'" King observed. On May 7, after thousands of schoolchildren marched into Birmingham's business district, police used fire hoses and police dogs to disperse them. Worldwide news coverage of the police attacks and the chaos in Birmingham's downtown proved decisive in Kennedy's decision to send a

Justice Department official to negotiate between civil rights advocates and the city's white leaders.

Concerned that continuing protests would severely damage the city's economy, some local businessmen privately indicated they would negotiate a settlement. King was caught between Kennedy administration officials seeking to suspend the protests and Shuttlesworth and other local leaders who wanted to continue them until concessions were actually implemented. Although relations between King and Shuttlesworth frayed as they debated whether to call off the demonstrations, the two were finally able to agree on a settlement calling for gradual desegregation of public facilities and a modest expansion of jobs for black workers. City officials also agreed to release jailed demonstrators. In his first major victory since the Montgomery bus boycott, King jubilantly proclaimed that "the walls of segregation" would crumble in Birmingham.

Just as the protests subsided, however, a bomb exploded at the home of King's brother, a Birmingham minister involved in the movement, and an unexploded bomb was discovered near the room King often used at the Gaston Motel. In response, angry demonstrators clashed with police. King feared the truce would unravel in violence, but President Kennedy mobilized federal troops to restore order. Rather than give in to segregationist intimidation, Birmingham's white leaders reaffirmed the agreement negotiated with protesters.

By this time, the Birmingham protests had sparked others elsewhere in the nation. An estimated 930 protests took place in more than one hundred cities during the spring and summer of 1963. In contrast to the student-led sit-ins of 1960, some of these mass demonstrations involved large numbers of working-class blacks, and large-scale protests occurred in northern as well as southern cities. Chicago experienced major protests against public school segregation, and San Francisco police arrested hundreds of demonstrators demanding job opportunities in downtown hotels. King and other leaders of national civil rights organizations tried with only modest success to guide the escalating mass marches and demonstrations of 1963. The protests indicated that the civil rights movement had become national in scope.

James Baldwin and the New Black Militancy

The difficulties black leaders faced in controlling the protests were largely hidden from public view, but they did not escape notice by the gifted black writer James Baldwin. Born in Harlem, Baldwin was deeply affected by the changing climate of American race relations during the 1950s and 1960s, even though he had left the United States in 1948 to live in Paris. "I left America because I doubted my ability to survive the fury of the color problem here," he once explained. When he took an assignment from a magazine in the late 1950s to travel through the South to report on the freedom struggle, the resulting perceptive articles soon made him an influential spokesperson for the new black militancy.

Baldwin was particularly interested in King, seeing him as increasingly "beleaguered"—caught between "his enemies in the white South" and black Americans who had become "bitter, disappointed, skeptical." When Baldwin first interviewed King in 1957, he was impressed by the Montgomery minister's singular abilities as a preacher. By 1961, however, Baldwin realized King faced a difficult challenge as he attempted to steer a path between militancy and moderation.

In a 1961 essay entitled "The Dangerous Road Before Martin Luther King," Baldwin predicted the problems King would face as he moved beyond the traditional accommodationist role played by black leaders such as Booker T. Washington, who had aimed "not to make the Negro a first-class citizen but to keep him content as a second-class one." King, according to Baldwin, would have to "break, at last, with the habits and attitudes, stratagems, and fears of the past" in order to remain an effective leader. Baldwin concluded that the southern civil rights struggle would transform African American identity: "The Negro who will emerge out of this present struggle . . . will not be dependent, in any way at all, on any of the props and crutches which help form our identity now."

Baldwin's journalistic investigation of the black struggle brought him into contact with not only King and black student protesters but also followers of the Nation of Islam's Elijah Muhammad and the group's outspoken minister, Malcolm X. As a Harlem native, Baldwin understood why many disillusioned urban blacks had turned from Christianity toward the racial separatism of the Black Muslims. After interviewing Malcolm in 1961, Baldwin came to share the Muslim minister's skepticism about the use of nonviolent tactics to achieve civil rights reforms. "In the United States, violence and heroism have been made synonymous except when it comes to blacks, and the only way to defeat Malcolm's point is to concede it and to ask oneself why this is so," Baldwin remarked. He added, "There *is* no reason that black men should be expected to be more patient, more forbearing, more farseeing than whites; indeed, quite the contrary."

Early the following year, Baldwin described the increasingly militant mood of black Americans in a best-selling book of essays, *The Fire Next Time*. He shocked many white readers with his question, "Do I really want to be integrated into a burning house?" Asking whether "the four-hundred-year travail of the American Negro should result merely in his attainment of the present level of the American civilization," he concluded that the "only thing white people have that black people need, or should want, is power—and no one holds power forever."

In May 1963, Baldwin invited civil rights leaders and politically active entertainers such as Belafonte and Lena Horne to a meeting at Attorney General Robert Kennedy's New York apartment. Baldwin hoped the group would convey the dissatisfaction black Americans felt in the aftermath of the Birmingham campaign. A former freedom rider angrily berated Kennedy, the president's brother, and several black participants sharply questioned the Kennedy administration's failure to respond to black civil rights demands.

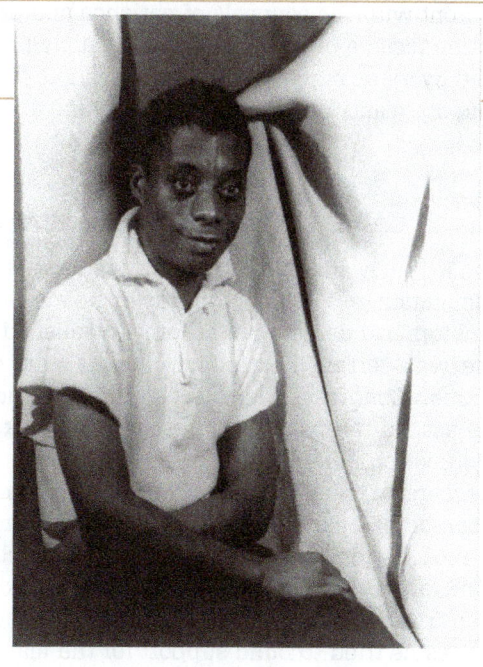

In *The Fire Next Time* (1962), James Baldwin expressed the increasingly militant mood of black Americans.

This angry exchange reflected the changing mood of many African Americans in the North who admired the sacrifices of southern civil rights protestors yet saw few changes in their everyday lives. Black Americans recognized the need for new civil rights legislation, but they also knew that legislation to eliminate de jure, or legally mandated, segregation in the South would have no effect on the widespread de facto, or actual, segregation in the North.

After Robert Kennedy told the president about the intensity of feelings expressed at the New York meeting, the two concluded that black discontent would not be assuaged without major new civil rights legislation. King had previously seen President Kennedy as lacking emotional involvement with racial issues: "He had never really had the personal experience of knowing the deep groans and passionate yearnings of the Negro for freedom, because he just didn't know Negroes generally and he hadn't had any experience in the civil rights struggle." But Kennedy's view began to change after Alabama's Governor Wallace barred black students trying to enter the University of Alabama, despite a Supreme Court order calling for desegregation.

This challenge to federal authority and the mass protests in Birmingham were clearly on President Kennedy's mind on June 11, 1963, when he delivered a nationally televised address explaining the need for civil rights legislation to desegregate public accommodations. He asked white Americans to contemplate the plight of black citizens: "Who among us would be content to have the color of his skin changed and stand in his place? Who among us would be content with the counsels of patience and delay?" Kennedy declared that the nation faced a "moral crisis" and that civil rights demands could not be "quieted by token moves or talk." He pleaded, "It is time to act in the Congress, in your state and local legislative body, and above all, in all our daily lives."

March on Washington for Jobs and Freedom

The Kennedy administration proposed an act to end racial segregation and discrimination, but its passage was by no means assured. Filibusters by southern senators had defeated or severely weakened previous civil rights bills, and no one was certain Kennedy would risk his other priorities to push the act through Congress. The president realized, however, that he also faced risks if the act did *not* pass, given escalating black discontent. During the spring of 1963, veteran civil rights and labor leader A. Philip Randolph added to the pressure on Kennedy by calling for a march on Washington. It was the same tactic he had used to wrest concessions from President Franklin D. Roosevelt in 1941. Randolph hoped the proposed march would similarly push Kennedy's hand as well as give discontented black people a nonviolent outlet for their frustrations.

As he tried to build support for the march, Randolph found black leaders far from united, with some fearing the march might turn into a massive act of civil disobedience. Therefore, Randolph, King, and other national civil rights leaders met with President Kennedy on June 22 at the White House. While assuring the president of their support for new civil rights legislation, the delegation also made clear that it would have to pass quickly to prevent black discontent from exploding into violence. When Kennedy initially objected to the march, Randolph responded, "Negroes were already in the streets. It is very likely impossible to get them off." Further, he advised Kennedy, "If they are bound to be in the streets in any case, is it not better that they be led by organizations dedicated to civil rights and disciplined by struggle rather than to leave them to other leaders who care neither about civil rights nor about nonviolence?" Kennedy decided to support the efforts of established leaders such as Randolph to remain in control of planning the event, and his administration behind the scenes to secure funding for the major civil rights groups.

The March on Washington for Jobs and Freedom, on August 28, 1963, was the largest civil rights demonstration ever held. Randolph, Bayard Rustin, and other march organizers drew more than 200,000 supporters to the Lincoln Memorial. Many arrived by chartered buses sponsored by black churches and local organizations all over the country. The march brought together many black leaders associated with earlier racial advances. Former baseball star Jackie Robinson was there, as was CORE leader James Farmer, Urban League head Whitney Young, and U.N. diplomat Ralph Bunche. Roy Wilkins spoke on behalf of the NAACP, graciously announcing the death of the organization's founder, W. E. B. Du Bois, the night before in Ghana, where he had been living in self-imposed exile.

Despite the display of unity, there were signs of impending splits. The Nation of Islam forbade members from attending the event, although Malcolm X observed from the sidelines. Baldwin was invited to attend but not to speak. Female activists were conspicuously missing from the initial list of speakers, prompting Pauli Murray, then working on behalf of President Kennedy's Commission on the Status of Women, to express dismay. Randolph headed off this budding controversy by adding Dorothy Height, head of the National Council of Negro Women, to a delegation that met with Kennedy. March organizers also revised the program to recognize Rosa Parks, Daisy Bates, and Nash Bevel.

Elected as SNCC's chair earlier that summer, John Lewis found himself caught between the mostly moderate leaders of the march and an increasingly militant SNCC when planning his speech. Despite giving in to Randolph's pleas that he soften criticisms of the proposed civil rights act, Lewis expressed disappointment that it did not protect voting rights workers. He derided "politicians who build their careers on immoral compromises and ally themselves with open forms of political, economic, and social exploitation."

King's famous "I Have a Dream" speech, which concluded the program, was a memorable summation of themes that had guided previous efforts by African Americans to "demand the riches of freedom and the security of justice." Calling on America to live up to the ideals expressed in the Constitution and the Declaration of Independence, King proclaimed, "Now is the time to lift our nation from the quicksands of racial justice to the solid rock of brotherhood. Now is the time to make justice a reality for all of God's children." Despite "the difficulties of today and tomorrow," King insisted, "I still have a dream. I have a dream that one day this nation will rise up and live out the true meaning of its creed—we hold these truths to be self-evident, that all men are created equal."

The march's optimism faltered a few weeks later when a bomb placed in a Birmingham church killed four black schoolgirls. Civil rights activists reacted with anger and resolve. Diane and James Bevel drafted plans for an even more determined voting rights campaign in Alabama. King joined a delegation of black leaders who warned President Kennedy that "the Negro community is about to reach a breaking point." Although black leaders had consistently advocated nonviolence, King added, "More and more we are faced with the problem of our people saying, 'What's the use?' . . . I am convinced that if something isn't done to give the Negro a new sense of hope and a sense of protection, there is a danger we will face the worse race riot we have ever seen in this country."

The assassination of President Kennedy in November 1963 made Americans of all races uncertain about the nation's future. Kennedy's successor, Lyndon B. Johnson, was a Texan who had identified himself with the Democratic Party's southern wing while serving as the Senate's majority leader in the 1950s. But he had also refused to sign the Southern Manifesto attacking the *Brown* decision. One of Johnson's first actions on becoming president was to call King to assure him that he would work for passage of Kennedy's proposals for civil rights reform.

Freedom Summer and the Mississippi Freedom Democratic Party

Mississippi civil rights workers came to the March on Washington hoping to draw attention to the violence and intimidation that had stalled the Council of Federal Organizations (COFO) voter registration campaign. Responding to an upsurge of racial violence in 1963 that the U.S. Commission on Civil Rights described as "a complete breakdown of law and order" in Mississippi, Bob Moses proposed the recruitment of hundreds of white students for a 1964 summer project. "These students bring the rest of the country with them," he explained. "The interest of the country is awakened, and when that happens, the Government responds to that interest." But some of COFO's staff agreed with Stokely Carmichael, who warned that a large number of white students would undermine the development of self-reliant local black leadership. The ensuing debate exposed growing racial tensions in the southern movement, which SNCC chair John Lewis understood as influenced by anti-colonial movements. Black activists were, he said, "conscious of things that happen in Cuba, in Latin America, and in Africa." Pointing to changes in dress (the sports coats of sit-in protesters had given way to jeans and work shirts) and the growing preference of black students for natural hairdos, he added, "I think people are searching for a sense of identity, and they're finding it."

The Freedom Democratic Party and the 1964 Summer Project

Despite internal debates, the COFO staff mobilized for a decisive struggle in 1964 to win political rights for black residents. Recognizing that Mississippi's all-white Democratic Party was unlikely to accept black participantion, COFO joined with black and a few white Mississippi residents to form the Mississippi Freedom Democratic Party (MFDP) as an alternative. "We decided to form our own party because the whites wouldn't even let us register," MFDP leader Hamer later explained. During the summer of 1964, COFO staff members worked with white volunteers to register thousands of prospective voters in the new party. Then delegates chosen by the new party intended to go to the national Democratic convention to convince President Johnson and other national Democratic leaders that they, rather than the all-white "regular" Democrats, should be seated as the legitimate Democratic Party in Mississippi.

The 1964 Summer Project attracted more than a thousand volunteers. Most were affluent college students, but some were doctors, lawyers, and teachers. The contrast between their backgrounds and those of COFO staff became evident in June when the volunteers arrived for training. Some staff members did not suppress their resentment, especially when volunteers seemed to lack understanding of the dangers that awaited them.

These dangers became evident when the trainees learned that a volunteer in Mississippi was missing. Andrew Goodman and two veteran civil rights workers, James Chaney and Mickey Schwerner, had left Meridian to investigate the burning of a black church near the town of Philadelphia. When they did not return, Moses immediately suspected they had been killed.

While the earlier killings of black Mississippians had attracted little press attention, the disappearance of two white activists, Goodman and Schwerner, became front-page news. The FBI, previously reluctant to protect civil rights workers, launched a massive investigation, and military personnel assisted in the search. "It is a shame that national concern is aroused only after two white boys are missing," Lewis observed. In August, the bodies of all three were found in an earthen dam. Mississippi officials refused to press murder charges against the killers, who included law enforcement officers, although several were later convicted on lesser federal charges of interfering with the civil rights of the victims.

While the search for the missing workers was going on in Mississippi, President Johnson gained passage of the civil rights legislation Kennedy had proposed. Yet, although the Civil Rights Act of 1964 resulted in the removal of "whites only" signs in many parts of the South, the Summer Project served as a reminder that the new legislation was not enough. Residents of rural areas like the Mississippi Delta were more concerned about political and economic gains than about desegregation of restaurants and hotels. Although the Civil Rights Act in time brought profound changes not only for black southerners but also for other victims of discrimination, including women, segregationist resistance remained strong in the Deep South. Only a few thousand black Mississippi residents were able to register officially to vote in the fall election, even though more than 80,000 had filled out MFDP registration forms.

The Summer Project made breakthroughs in other areas, such as literacy classes and "freedom schools" for black children. For the first time, many students learned about their rights as citizens and about African American history. Ideas drawn from the freedom school experiment later influenced the rise of alternative schools in black communities throughout the nation.

The 1964 Democratic Convention

The Summer Project ended with the MFDP's challenge to the seating of the all-white regular delegation at the Democratic National Convention. The MFDP delegates supported President Johnson, while many white delegates hinted they would support conservative Republican candidate Barry Goldwater to protest Johnson's civil rights policies. The MFDP also presented evidence to the credentials committee that black voters had been prevented from participating in Mississippi electoral politics. Hamer told committee members of being beaten after attempting to register in 1962. "If the Freedom Democratic Party is not seated now," she concluded, "I question America." Johnson faced a dilemma. If he supported the MFDP challengers, he risked losing the white southern Democrats. A compromise proposal gave the MFDP two at-large seats along with a promise to ban discrimination within the party at the next

"If the Freedom Democratic Party is not seated now, I question America." Challenging the all-white delegate seating at the Democratic National Convention, Fannie Lou Hamer testified about the mistreatment of black people attempting to register to vote in Mississippi.

convention. But the MFDP delegates rejected this compromise, believing they had risked their lives and that Johnson should also be willing to take political risks. Hamer scoffed at Johnson's offer: "We didn't come all this way for no two seats."

After the convention and even after Johnson's landslide win over Goldwater in the November election, the gulf widened between veterans of the southern struggle, who felt betrayed, and the liberal Democrats who supported Johnson. Having brought white volunteers to the state, Moses was disappointed that the Summer Project had not brought victory. For Lewis, the lesson of the Democratic convention was "when you play the game and go by the rules, you still can lose, if you don't have the resources, if you're going to disrupt the natural order of things." Other SNCC workers expressed their bitterness in even blunter terms, reflecting the racial tensions that later divided SNCC. Carmichael was convinced African Americans "could not rely on their so-called allies" because many of them had "closer ties to the national Democratic Party."

After several former Summer Project volunteers from the University of California, Berkeley, spearheaded the Free Speech Movement in the fall of 1964, northern white students elsewhere began to display some of the militancy associated with the southern struggle. SNCC staff members who remained after the Summer Project were exhausted but also exhilarated. Much had been accomplished in the three years since the McComb Project confronted white supremacy in the Deep South. Yet some now questioned SNCC's commitment to nonviolence and interracialism. An anonymous paper for a staff retreat also exposed tensions over gender issues, as women activists complained they were often assigned mundane tasks rather than decision–making roles. Acknowledging growing doubts about SNCC's future, Moses likened it to "a boat in the middle of the ocean. It has to be rebuilt in order to stay afloat. It also has to stay afloat in order to be rebuilt."

Malcolm X and the Freedom Struggle

When John Lewis and ten SNCC colleagues accepted Harry Belafonte's invitation to tour West Africa soon after the Democratic convention, they found that little news about SNCC had crossed the Atlantic, but African students often expressed admiration for Nation of Islam leader Malcolm X. "Back in America, we were considered radical by the mainstream elements of both the movement and society in general," Lewis observed. In Africa, however, "we were dismissed as mainstream, and it was Malcolm who was embraced." When Lewis and another SNCC worker had a chance encounter with Malcolm X in Nairobi, they were surprised that the black nationalist leader was eager to talk. "The man who sat with us in that hotel room was enthusiastic and excited—not angry, not brooding." Having just attended a meeting in Cairo of Third World nations—those that refused to be aligned with either the United States or the Soviet Union in the Cold War—Malcolm was convinced African nations should push the United Nations to address American racial issues. "He got most enthusiastic about his idea of bringing the case of African Americans before the General Assembly of the United Nations and holding the United States in violation of the United Nations' Human Rights Charter," Lewis recalled.

Break with the Nation of Islam

After becoming the best-known spokesman of the Nation of Islam, Malcolm grew increasingly dissatisfied with the apolitical stance of Elijah Muhammad, who had led the group since the 1930s. In 1962, Malcolm was dismayed when Muhammad advised restraint after Los Angeles police killed a Nation of Islam member during a raid. The following year, after the murder of Mississippi NAACP leader Medgar Evers and the Birmingham church bombing that killed four children, Malcolm felt constrained by his role as Muhammad's spokesman. "I made comments—but not what should have been said about the climate of hate that the American white man was generating and nourishing." Rather than standing on the front lines of struggle, Malcolm felt the Nation of Islam

By the early 1960s, Malcolm X was becoming increasingly dissatisfied with the Nation of Islam. He left the group in 1964 to form the Organization of African American Unity. He was assassinated in 1965.

was being bypassed by the new militancy. "It could be heard increasingly in the Negro communities: 'Those Muslims *talk* tough, but they never *do* anything, unless somebody bothers Muslims.'"

Malcolm's loyalty to Elijah Muhammad was tested when he was ordered to refrain from public statements after he called Kennedy's assassination a case of "chickens come home to roost." Even while serving his ninety-day suspension, Malcolm refused to stay out of public view. In February 1964, he accepted boxer Cassius Clay's invitation to attend his fight against heavily favored heavyweight champion Sonny Liston in Miami. Malcolm knew the brash young challenger and Olympic gold medalist had secretly joined the Nation of Islam. Clay's self-promotion—"I am the greatest," he proclaimed—set him apart from the Nation of Islam's ranks, but Malcolm appreciated Clay's charisma and potential influence in black communities. Malcolm was at ringside when Clay stunned the sports world by defeating Liston. The following morning, Clay again shocked boxing fans by acknowledging his affiliation with the Nation of Islam. Soon afterward, he announced he was abandoning his "slave name" for a new name, Muhammad Ali.

In the spring of 1964, Malcolm's hajj to Mecca—the pilgrimage required of Muslims—led him to realize that some of Elijah Muhammad's religious teachings were in conflict with orthodox Islam. Upon his return, Malcolm announced he was leaving the Nation of Islam to form the Organization of African-American Unity (OAAU) in order to bring together black militant groups. "I'm not out to fight other Negro leaders or organizations," he told reporters. "As of this minute, I've forgotten everything bad that the other leaders have said about me, and I pray they can also forget the many bad things I've said about them." Most members of the Nation of Islam refused to join Malcolm's new group. Even Ali decided his loyalty to Elijah Muhammad transcended his friendship with Malcolm. Nonetheless, freed from the constraints of his Nation of Islam role, Malcolm was more able to express the festering racial discontent that was becoming evident in black urban communities. In July 1964, the shooting of a fifteen-year-old Harlem youth by an off-duty white policeman sparked three days of rioting that left one Harlem resident dead. Soon afterward, five black residents died in a riot in Rochester, New York.

The Final Months

By the time he met SNCC activists in Nairobi, Malcolm was seeking to build ties with militant civil rights activists. His sense of the international implications of the African American freedom struggle paralleled the views of earlier black leaders such as Du Bois, and SNCC members were coming to see him as a potential ally, especially since they planned to expand their organizing efforts into northern inner-city black communities. Soon after Malcolm and the SNCC workers returned to the United States, this convergence of perspectives became evident in a proposal that SNCC establish "an African Bureau or Secretariat" to expand the group's contacts in Africa and "with any other countries or groups of people in other countries who can be help to us and the Cause." For his part, Malcolm invited Hamer and SNCC's Freedom Singers to participate in a Harlem rally, where he pledged support for the voting rights campaign.

Malcolm toned down his earlier harsh criticisms of national civil rights leaders. At a gathering arranged by Juanita Poitier, wife of actor Sidney Poitier, he attempted to find common ground with Randolph, Young, and Height. Malcolm had tried to start a dialogue with King, writing to him on several occasions. King rebuffed these entreaties, however, and their brief encounter in 1964 outside a Senate hearing room was limited to cordial greetings. When New Yorkers welcomed King after he accepted the 1964 Nobel Peace Prize, Malcolm attended the event and spoke with members of King's staff. But he made clear that a gulf still lay between their perspectives. "I don't want the white man giving me medals," he commented afterward.

In early February 1965, Malcolm accepted SNCC's invitation to come to Alabama, where SNCC and the SCLC were involved in a major voting rights campaign. "I believe they have an absolute right to use whatever means are necessary to gain the vote," he affirmed at a rally in Selma. Shortly after his rousing speech, Malcolm assured Coretta Scott King, who was in Selma on behalf of her jailed husband, that he had not come to make things more difficult for voting rights workers. "I really did come thinking that I could make it easier," Malcolm explained. "If the white people realize what the alternative is, perhaps they will be more willing to hear Dr. King."

Malcolm's speech in Selma was the most visible indication of his desire to ally himself with black veterans of the civil rights movement, but less than three weeks later he was dead. Members of the Nation of Islam assassinated him on February 21 as he began a speech at New York's Audubon Ballroom. Even while he attempted to forge strong bonds between the OAAU and other black groups, Malcolm's relations with his former associates in the Nation of Islam had deteriorated into hostility. In *Muhammad Speaks,* his former protégé Louis X (later Farrakhan) denounced him as a traitor "worthy of death" for his sharp criticisms of Elijah Muhammad."

Facing fierce opposition from Nation of Islam loyalists and unable to attract many of his former associates to his new group, Malcolm died before he could transform the African American freedom struggle from within. Despite the gulf between Malcolm's view and his own commitment to nonviolence, John Lewis believed Malcolm "had come to articulate better than anyone else on the scene—including King—the bitterness and frustration of black Americans." King wrote a note of condolence to Malcolm's widow: "While we did not always see eye to eye on methods to solve the race problems, I always had a deep affection for Malcolm and felt that he had the great ability to put his finger on the existence and root of the problem."

The assassination of Malcolm X did not destroy his influence in the African American freedom struggle. Many of his ideas—especially his advocacy of a positive racial identity and his pan-Africanism—coincided with the conclusions many black activists had drawn from their own political experiences. With the 1965 publication of Alex Haley's *Autobiography of Malcolm X,* Malcolm's life and thoughts reached an audience that far exceeded those who had heard him speak during his lifetime.

Voting Rights and Violence

The day before Malcolm X's Harlem funeral, twenty-six-year-old Jimmy Lee Jackson died of a gunshot wound incurred during a voting rights demonstration in Marion, Alabama. In the weeks after Malcolm's visit to Alabama, the campaign was marked by repeated Freedom Day marches to voter registration offices and escalating clashes between demonstrators and police. On several occasions Jackson had tried to register to vote, but Alabama officials had blocked him and others, using intimidation and violence. Fewer than one in five black Alabama residents of voting age were registered, most of them in the state's urban areas. On February 18, 1965, as Jackson and his family marched from a black church toward the Marion courthouse, state troopers ordered them to disperse. Jackson and his mother and grandfather took refuge in a café, but troopers followed and beat them, knocking Jackson against a cigarette machine before shooting him in the stomach. When Jackson died on February 26, civil rights workers from SNCC and SCLC pledged to step up their protests. Soon a voting rights campaign that had been largely ignored outside

Alabama captured the nation's attention and led to the passage of major civil rights legislation.

The Selma-to-Montgomery March

Reacting to Jackson's death, Diane and James Bevel proposed a march from Selma to Montgomery—about 50 miles—to confront Governor Wallace. The idea quickly gained support. King and other SCLC officials saw the Selma protests of 1965 as comparable to the Birmingham campaign of 1963. Through carefully orchestrated events, they would draw the nation's attention to brutal forces of repression—with sheriff Jim Clark in the Bull Connor role—and thereby prod President Johnson to introduce new voting rights legislation, just as the Birmingham protests had prompted passage of the 1964 Civil Rights Act. Late in 1964, Johnson had told King that southern congressmen, whose votes he needed for his Great Society social legislation, would prevent passage of new voting rights legislation, but King was not convinced. "The President said nothing could be done," King recalled. "But we started a movement."

As in Albany, Georgia, SNCC workers had already set up a project in Selma before King's arrival, and they saw themselves as more connected than SCLC staffers to the local black leaders. Resentment of King became evident at meetings planning the march to Montgomery, and SNCC chair John Lewis was one of the few SNCC members who favored participating in the march.

Lewis was surprised that King had left Selma to deliver a sermon at his Atlanta church, as he lead about 2,000 demonstrators from Brown's Chapel on Sunday, March 7, to march to Montgomery. Along with SCLC's Hosea Williams, Lewis led marchers across Pettus Bridge on the outskirts of Selma, where they confronted a large contingent of state troopers and Sheriff Clark's deputies. The marchers were ordered to disperse, and the combined police force chased them back across the bridge with tear gas and billy clubs. Lewis, who suffered a fractured skull, was one of several marchers injured. News photographs and television coverage of the violence at Pettus Bridge—activists called it "Bloody Sunday"—shocked civil rights supporters throughout the nation and drew hundreds more sympathizers to Selma.

When the marchers regrouped, many directed their anger not only at Alabama officials but also at King, because of his absence during the march, and at the federal government for failing to intervene. Even SNCC workers who had opposed the march now argued for its resumption to demonstrate that police violence would not prevail. King was with those in the lead when the second march crossed Pettus Bridge and again ran into a police barricade, but he drew more criticism by telling marchers to turn around rather than risk further violence. That evening a group of white Selma residents killed James Reeb, a northern white minister who had joined the march.

During the next few days, SCLC officials secured a federal court order allowing a march, but by this time relations between SCLC and SNCC had seriously deteriorated. Rather than favoring further nonviolent protests to gain sympathy from northern liberals, many SNCC organizers in Alabama concluded they should build independent black-controlled movements in the rural areas around Selma. Nevertheless, SCLC's strategy produced its intended result. In a March 15 televised address, President Johnson announced he would propose voting rights legislation to Congress. Referring to the freedom song that had become the anthem of the movement, Johnson assured the nation "We Shall Overcome."

The march began again on March 21. It was the culmination of a stage of the African American freedom struggle that led to passage of the landmark Voting Rights Act of 1965, but it was also the last major racial protest campaign to have substantial white support. When the marchers reached Montgomery, King delivered one of his most memorable speeches. Standing on the capitol steps, within sight of Dexter Avenue Church where he had first emerged as a boycott leader, he asked how much more sacrifice would be required to overcome segregation. The movement must not abandon its nonviolent principles, he told the crowd. "Our aim must never be to defeat or humiliate the white man but to win his friendship and understanding. . . . We seek . . . a society at peace with itself, a society that can live with its conscience."

TABLE 18.1 POLITICAL AND CIVIL RIGHTS ORGANIZATIONS

Congress of Racial Equality (CORE) A civil rights protest group led by James Farmer that initiated the Freedom Ride campaign of 1961.

Council of Federal Organizations (COFO) A Mississippi coalition of the NAACP, SNCC, CORE, and other civil rights groups involved in voter registration.

Lowndes County Freedom Organization (LCFO) An independent Alabama political party formed in 1966 with the assistance of SNCC organizers; the party became identified with its symbol, a black panther.

Mississippi Freedom Democratic Party (MFDP) An interracial alternative to Mississippi's all-white "regular" Democratic Party; the MFDP challenged the seating of the regular delegation to the 1964 Democratic Party convention.

National Association for the Advancement of Colored People (NAACP) Headed by Roy Wilkins, the NAACP sought to achieve civil rights legislation through governmental lobbying and legal efforts to end discrimination.

Nation of Islam A religious organization headed by Elijah Muhammad that advocated racial separatism.

Southern Christian Leadership Conference (SCLC) Martin Luther King, Jr., was president of this regional organization composed of black ministers.

Student Nonviolent Coordinating Committee (SNCC) Civil rights protest group formed in 1960 by student sit-in leaders with the assistance of Ella Baker.

The Voting Rights Act of 1965

In August, the legislation President Johnson introduced became the Voting Rights Act of 1965. It eliminated many of the obstacles that had prevented black southerners from voting. Use of literacy tests was suspended, and federal registrars were authorized in areas with a history of discrimination. The act was part of a series of governmental efforts in 1964 and 1965 intended to transform newly gained civil rights into tangible gains. "You do not take a person who, for years, had been hobbled by chains and liberate him, bring him up to the starting line of a race and then say, 'You are free to compete with all the others,'" Johnson explained in a Howard University speech in June 1965. Johnson's "War on Poverty" included an Equal Opportunity Act with the goal of ending poverty and unemployment through job training programs, adult education, and loans to small businesses. The Johnson administration also secured legislation to help poor people by providing food stamps and educational programs such as Head Start for preschool children. Community action programs were instituted to encourage poor people to organize in their own communities. A new Department of Housing and Urban Development (HUD) had responsibility for low-rent housing and urban renewal programs. Its first secretary was Robert Weaver, a member of the unofficial Black Cabinet under President Roosevelt.

Johnson's Great Society proposals had a major impact on American society, but as with Roosevelt's New Deal, the results were uneven and did not improve the lives of all African Americans. While programs such as Medicare and student loans intended for middle-class Americans received ample funding, Johnson's War on Poverty got only a small portion of government spending. In addition, by the summer of 1965, Johnson was shifting his attention from the Great Society programs to the escalating conflict in Vietnam, where thousands of American troops had been sent to counter communist forces. Moreover, following passage of the Voting Rights Act, it became clear that civil rights reforms had produced rising expectations among black Americans. The death of the Jim Crow system in the South did not obscure the reality that segregation, racial discrimination, and poverty still existed throughout the nation.

The Voting Rights Act was the last major victory of the African-American freedom struggle, but few black activists found time to celebrate. Within days of President Johnson's signing of the act, the arrest of a black man in Los Angeles led to several days of deadly violence that began in the Watts section of the city and then spread through south-central Los Angeles. More than thirty black residents were killed by police, and National Guardsmen were sent to the city. Newspapers called the violence a riot, but some residents saw it as a rebellion—an expression of widespread resentment of police brutality and harassment and of white-owned businesses in black residential areas. Violence in Los Angeles demonstrated that civil rights laws had done little to relieve the problems of black residents in America's large cities.

Visiting Los Angeles as the violence subsided, King talked with residents to try to understand what had happened. "At a time when the Negro's aspirations were at a peak, his actual conditions of employment, education, and housing were worsening," he acknowledged. He predicted the Watts insurrection was "the beginning of a stirring of a deprived people . . . who had been bypassed by the progress of the previous decade." The stirring that King predicted was actually the beginning of a major new stage of black militancy and political development.

Black Power

Stokely Carmichael, skeptical about the usefulness of the Montgomery march, focused on contacting local leaders in the rural areas surrounding Selma. Soon afterward, he became director of a new project in Lowndes County, which had no registered black voters even though most residents were black. The Lowndes County staff believed a new approach was needed to deal with the entrenched segregationist resistance in rural Black Belt areas such as Lowndes County. They expected to demonstrate that black organizers working with local black leaders could build a new kind of militant movement. Like the Mississippi Freedom Democratic Party, the Lowndes County Freedom Organization (LCFO) was independent of Alabama's white-controlled Democratic Party. It was registered as a legitimate political group able to field candidates in elections.

During the march through Mississippi, Stokely Carmichael, chairman of the Student Nonviolent Coordinating Committee, delivers a "black power" speech to a crowd in front of Mississippi State Capitol in March 1966.

The significance of the new group's emblem—a snarling black panther—was unmistakable. "The black panther is an animal that when it is pressured it moves back until it is cornered," explained LCFO leader John Hulett, "then it comes out fighting for life or death. We felt we had been pushed back long enough and that it was time for Negroes to come out and take over." Soon known as the Black Panther Party, the new political group captured the imagination of SNCC staff members who believed African Americans, in the North as well as the South, should abandon interracial alliances and non-violent principles and instead create independent, black-controlled political institutions.

For years, John Lewis had thought of Carmichael as a colleague, even a friend. Although the two argued often since they met in Mississippi's Parchman Prison during the 1961 freedom rides, they respected each other's commitment. Lewis had been arrested more than twenty times since the early 1960s, and Carmichael had acquired his own reputation for fearlessness as a SNCC project director in Mississippi and Alabama. During the Summer Project of 1964 they became reacquainted. They both backed SNCC's decision to oppose the escalation of American military involvement in Vietnam, but Lewis was a conscientious objector to all wars, while Carmichael accepted Malcolm X's view that "any means necessary" should be used in the black freedom struggle. Lewis was disturbed as SNCC moved away from its earlier nonviolent ideals, while Carmichael's staff sometimes carried weapons, and many voting rights meetings in Lowndes County were protected by armed guards.

When SNCC gathered in May 1966 for its annual meeting, Lewis did not expect serious opposition to his continuing as chair, though he knew that some staff members saw him as out of touch and that his critics were prepared to back Carmichael as his replacement. Indeed, when the vote was taken, Lewis was overwhelmingly reelected, and Ruby Doris Robinson, a veteran of the 1961 Rock Hill jail-in, was selected to replace James Forman as executive secretary. Under normal circumstances, this would have ended the matter, but others challenged the vote. Some staff members saw the anti-Lewis campaign as an opportunity to infuse the group with racial separatist ideas. "What it was about, in the end, was who was 'blackest,' and it was hard to tell where the lines were drawn," Lewis recalled.

After arguing until dawn, exhausted staff members narrowly voted to elect Carmichael as SNCC's new chair. News reports of the leadership change framed it as a sign that the interracial civil rights coalition, responsible for previous reforms and new federal legislation, was weakening. Carmichael was quoted as advising white civil rights workers to begin focusing their energies on white communities. For Lewis, who resigned from SNCC a few months later, the vote marked the end of an era that extended back to the group's founding in 1960. "Wounds were opened that would never heal," he recalled. "I didn't consider it so much a repudiation of me as a repudiation of ourselves, of what we *were,* of what we stood for."

Soon after his election, Carmichael gained national attention during a protest march that began with the shooting of James Meredith, who had desegregated the University of Mississippi in 1962. When a sniper shot Meredith during his solitary "march against fear" across Mississippi, civil rights leaders gathered at his Memphis hospital bedside and pledged to continue the march. Carmichael, King, and newly elected CORE chair Floyd McKissick then met at the church where James Lawson, once the mentor of the Nashville student group, served as pastor. They quickly called for supporters to join them at the spot where Meredith had been shot.

The Mississippi march was an unexpected event that brought together many veterans of earlier civil rights campaigns. But, as marchers assembled, King quickly noticed changes. Younger activists made it clear they did not accept nonviolent principles or welcome white participation. When some marchers began to sing the civil rights anthem "We Shall Overcome," a few young black marchers countered that the title should be changed to "We Shall Overrun." At the end of the first day, when march leaders gathered, King insisted they remain committed to nonviolent principles, but he faced strong opposition from members of SNCC, CORE, and the Deacons for Defense, a group of Louisiana activists who offered to provide armed protection for the march. When Carmichael suggested that white participation in the march should be deemphasized, King realized the movement was abandoning its earlier ideals. "As I listened to Stokely, I thought about the years that we had worked together in communities all across the South, and how joyously we had then welcomed and accepted our white allies in the movement."

The next day, walking at the front of the column and heading south to the Mississippi Delta, King and Carmichael continued their dialogue. Carmichael had heard that black people responded enthusiastically to the slogan "Black Power," a shortened version of the phrase "black power for black people" used by SNCC workers in Lowndes County. His first opportunity to use the slogan publicly came after police in Greenwood arrested him for erecting tents at a local black school so marchers could rest for the night. After his release, Carmichael announced at a rally, "This is the twenty-seventh time I have been arrested. I ain't going to jail no more." He argued that African Americans had been demanding freedom for six years and had gotten nothing. "What we gonna start saying now is Black Power." He shouted the slogan repeatedly; each time the audience shouted back, "Black Power!" Again and again, members of the audience shouted in unison the slogan that suddenly galvanized their emotions.

The two words had been combined long before. Richard Wright used them as the title for his book on African politics, written in the early 1950s, and Paul Robeson had spoken of black power during the same years. Although the two words were initially just a new slogan in a movement that had produced so many, they soon came to symbolize a major shift in the self-concept of many African Americans. The civil rights legislation of the mid-1960s had opened doors of opportunity, but the struggle to achieve change had produced aspirations for even greater changes. As James Baldwin had observed in 1963, the removal of racial barriers had forced African Americans to consider whether racial integration should be the central goal of the black struggle.

King recognized that the "black power" slogan expressed the widespread discontent of African Americans who remained poor and powerless despite civil rights reforms. Nevertheless, he told Carmichael that he believed the slogan "carried the wrong connotations"; press accounts had already implied it called for violence. And it alienated potential white allies. But Carmichael disagreed: "Power is the only thing respected in this world, and we must get it at any cost. Martin, you know as well as I do that practically every other ethnic group in America has done just this. The Jews, the Irish, and the Italians did it, why can't we?"

> *"That is just the point," King countered. "No one has ever heard the Jews publicly chant a slogan of Jewish power, but they have power. We must use every constructive means to amass economic and political power."*
> *"What we need is a new slogan with 'black' in it," Carmichael insisted. When King countered that the slogan would confuse white allies and isolate African Americans, Carmichael admitted, "Martin, I deliberately decided to raise this issue on the march in order to give it a national forum, and force you to take a stand for Black Power."*

King laughed with resignation: "I have been used before. One more time won't hurt."

Conclusion

Carmichael's call for black power reflected the undeniable fact that previous civil rights reforms had not brought racial equality. The southern civil rights protests of the early 1960s and the voting rights campaign in the Deep South had torn down the Jim Crow system of legally enforced segregation. The gains had been important, but deadly racist violence had produced many martyrs, and the slow pace of change had produced festering resentment. Ten years after the *Brown* decision, almost 98 percent of southern black students still attended predominantly black schools. More generally, most black Americans still lived in predominantly black communities and still experienced living conditions inferior to those of most white people. The "black power" slogan expressed the determination of black Americans to achieve "freedom now," but the vagueness of the phrase also indicated the uncertainty many felt about their identity as American citizens.

During the late 1960s and early 1970s, African Americans continued to seek the power to change their lives for the better. Many civil rights veterans turned their attention to the complex problems of the volatile urban black ghettos. King's nonviolent principles were tested in Chicago, launched in 1966, and in a Poor People's Campaign during 1968. SNCC also established organizing efforts in northern cities. But for many civil rights veterans, their experiences in the South were scant preparation for the difficult challenges they faced in urban black communities. They would discover that black power and black unity were elusive goals.

Questions for Review and Reflection

1. What factors explain the growing tensions between SNCC and SCLC and the increasing criticisms of King by SNCC workers?

2. Discuss the relative importance of the Freedom Rides, the Birmingham Campaign, and the Selma-to-Montgomery march as crucial turning points in the civil rights struggles of the 1960s?

3. How successful were Malcolm X and Martin Luther King, Jr., in providing ideological and tactical guidance for the mass protests of the 1960s?

4. What was the purpose of the March on Washington? Did it achieve its goals?

5. Explain the emergence of and sudden popularity of the "Black Power" slogan.

CHAPTER 19

Resistance, Repression, and Retrenchment, 1967–1978

Hubert "Rap" Brown Proclaims Black Power

"Violence is as American as apple pie," Hubert G. "Rap" Brown proclaimed on July 24, 1967, as he stood on a car trunk before a cheering crowd of hundreds of supporters in Cambridge, Maryland. The previous month, Brown had been elected as the new chair of the Student Nonviolent Coordinating Committee (SNCC). Though just twenty-three, he was a veteran of the 1964 Mississippi Summer Project, a leader in Howard University's SNCC-affiliated Nonviolent Action Group, and overall director of SNCC's Alabama projects. Now he had returned to Cambridge, where in 1963 he had worked with local leader Gloria Richardson in a protest campaign that drew broad support from black workers as well as students. Known within SNCC as an advocate of armed self-defense, Brown sounded the themes of racial pride and militancy that had characterized the speeches of his predecessor, Stokely Carmichael. But Brown went further, bluntly warning, "If America don't come around, we're going to burn it down." Rejecting Martin Luther King's ideal of a "beloved community," Brown advised against loving the "honky" (a derisive term for white people). "Shoot him to death, brother," he announced, "because that's what he is out to do to you."

No violence occurred during Brown's speech, but later in the evening he was slightly wounded when caught in an exchange of gunfire between police

1966	Huey Newton and Bobby Seale found the Black Panther Party.
1967	Martin Luther King, Jr., publicly condemns the Vietnam War. In *Loving* v. *Virginia,* Supreme Court outlaws state laws banning interracial marriage. Extensive racial violence erupts in Newark, Detroit, and dozens of other American cities. The FBI secretly initiates a counterintelligence program (COINTELPRO) against black militants. Thurgood Marshall becomes the first African American Supreme Court Justice.
1968	Tet Offensive in Vietnam strengthens antiwar sentiment. The National Advisory Commission on Civil Disorders reports that the nation is "moving toward two societies—one black, one white—separate but unequal." King is assassinated in Memphis.
1969	Republican Richard Nixon becomes president and Spiro Agnew vice president after calling for "law and order" during campaign.
1970	Police kill two black student protesters at Mississippi's Jackson State College.
1971	The Supreme Court overturns boxer Muhammad Ali's 1967 conviction for draft evasion. An inmate uprising at New York's Attica prison ends after police storm facility.
1972	New York Representative Shirley Chisholm opens her campaign for president. The National Black Political Convention is held in Gary, Indiana.
1973	African Americans are elected mayors of Los Angeles, Detroit, and Atlanta.
1974	President Richard Nixon resigns following the Watergate scandal. White residents of South Boston resist desegregation with violence.
1976	With black support, former Georgia governor Jimmy Carter is elected president.
1977	Televised miniseries "Roots" achieves record ratings. Andrew J. Young becomes United Nations ambassador.
1978	In *University of California Regents* v. *Bakke,* the Supreme Court rules against quotas for minority medical school applicants.

and black residents. He left Cambridge before early morning fires engulfed a black elementary school and several businesses. The next day Spiro T. Agnew, Maryland's recently elected Republican governor, arrived to inspect the damage. Announcing that state officials would "immediately arrest any person inciting to riot," Agnew said of Brown, "I hope they pick him up soon, put him away, and throw away the key." The governor refused to meet with local black leaders unless they first agreed to shun "lawlessness" and denounce Brown and other black power advocates.

Despite lack of evidence that Brown was responsible for the Cambridge violence, Maryland officials charged him with arson and arrested him. But Brown remained defiant. "We are on the eve of a Black revolution," he predicted from jail. Brown was released on bond, but in September he was rearrested for carrying a weapon across state lines while under indictment. Although again released on bond, he was prohibited from traveling. "Whatever they do to me is not going to stop the revolution," Brown insisted.

The Cambridge violence was neither the most deadly nor the most destructive racial outbreak of the "long, hot summer" of 1967, but it signaled a new era in American politics by focusing national attention on Brown and Agnew and the opposing forces they represented. Expressing the nation's volatile racial emotions in their inflammatory rhetoric, the two men suddenly rose from obscurity to national prominence and came to symbolize the growing divide between "black power" militants and white "law and order" politicians.

Some supporters of Agnew and Brown considered them moderates rather than extremists. Agnew had been elected governor with considerable black and liberal support. Brown had been expected to draw less public attention than had the more flamboyant Carmichael during his tumultuous year as SNCC chair. In more peaceful times, Brown and Agnew might have avoided controversy, but both were soon caught up in the turbulent racial climate of the late 1960s. By threatening armed rebellion against the nation's established political order, Brown expressed the anger felt by many African Americans. But his fiery speeches inadvertently strengthened white support for police suppression of black militancy. While Congress considered antiriot legislation (labeled the "H. Rap Brown law" by some reporters), FBI director J. Edgar Hoover condemned not only Brown and Carmichael but also King as "vociferous firebrands." Agnew's acerbic criticisms of black militants soon made him a popular figure in national Republican circles, and the following year he unexpectedly became the party's vice presidential candidate.

During the years following the summer of 1967, American society remained divided over racial issues. The interracial coalition that had made possible the passage of major civil rights legislation in the mid-1960s splintered, with bitter disputes over the Vietnam War and over policies developed to implement civil rights reforms—especially busing to achieve school desegregation and affirmative action efforts intended to reverse historical patterns of racial exclusion. The assassination of King and the white backlash against black militancy were major setbacks to those seeking civil rights reforms through nonviolence and interracial cooperation. But the black power movement faltered as well, due to external repression and internal divisions. Although black power militancy encouraged racial pride and expressed resentment of long-standing racial injustices, racial unity and power proved elusive. As black militant groups struggled to survive during the 1970s, black scholars, writers, and artists gave substance to black power rhetoric through their perceptive depictions of African American life and history. The revolutionary objectives sought by Brown and other black power advocates were not achieved, but a new generation of black elected officials protected previous civil rights gains and worked with increasing effectiveness within the American political system.

A New Racial Consciousness

During 1967, the year of H. Rap Brown's rise to notoriety, twenty-three-year-old Angela Davis returned to the United States after two years of graduate study in Germany. Although she had been abroad as black power militancy captured the nation's attention, Davis was, like many black students of the period, receptive to the new trend in African American politics. She remembered the dynamite attacks against the homes of black families, including hers, who attempted to move into formerly all-white Birmingham neighborhoods. She was also aware that her mother, a teacher, had a long involvement in civil rights causes extending back to the Scottsboro campaign of the 1930s. As a teenager, her parents sent her to a private high school in New York that was known for its leftist-oriented curriculum. Davis was drawn to Marxist ideas, which offered her a way of making sense of the racism she had experienced in the South. "What had seemed a personal hatred of me, an inexplicable refusal of Southern whites to confront their own emotions, and a stubborn willingness of blacks to acquiesce became the inevitable consequences of a ruthless system which kept itself alive and well by encouraging spite, competition, and oppression of one group by another," she remembered. She enrolled at Brandeis University, majoring in French literature. Davis was spending her junior year in Paris when she learned that acquaintances of hers were among the four children killed in the 1963 bombing of Birmingham's Sixteenth Street Baptist Church. After graduating with honors, she spent two years studying philosophy in Frankfurt before returning to the United States for graduate studies with noted philosopher Herbert Marcuse at the University of California, San Diego. There, as she prepared herself for an academic career, Davis was quickly swept up in the swift currents of black political militancy.

The political climate Davis encountered when she returned to the United States was notable not only for Brown's call for revolution but also for a much broader transformation of African American attitudes and American race relations. Years of civil rights activism, Malcolm X's militant ideas, and racial insurgences in major cities had affected the views of large numbers of young people, especially black college students. Campus visits by speakers such as Carmichael and Brown often stimulated the formation of black student organizations. Escalating protests against the war in Vietnam and the military draft added to the climate of racial militancy and confrontations with authority. Heavyweight champion Muhammad Ali's decision to refuse military induction—"No Vietcong ever called me Nigger," the boxer remarked—was but the most publicized of many convergences of black militancy and antiwar dissent.

Davis's initial contacts with SNCC activists in southern California strengthened her leftist orientation, but the new black consciousness was at least as much a cultural phenomenon as it was a form of political radicalism. While

Heavyweight boxing champion Muhammad Ali refused military induction during the Vietnam War, citing his status as a minister of the Nation of Islam.

Brown's provocative speeches expressed the anger felt by many African Americans, black power militancy often assumed less combative forms. Many black students began to set themselves apart by abandoning hair-straightening products and adopting "natural" or "Afro" hair styles or, less commonly, wearing African-style clothing. Although poet-singer Gil Scott-Heron would later warn black radicals, "The Revolution will not be Televised," African American popular culture conveyed a new sense of racial identity and political urgency. Even popular Motown singers such as Marvin Gaye sometimes injected political messages in their songs. Some proponents of black cultural nationalism pointedly rejected the tradition of black leftist politics, arguing that black politics should be rooted in distinctively African or African American values. Harold Cruse's *The Crisis of the Negro Intellectual* (1967) claimed that black leftists of the 1930s and 1940s had been misled by the white—often Jewish—leaders of the Communist Party. Cruse, who had once been a Communist himself, lamented the failure of African Americans to develop a political strategy that emphasized the role of black cultural institutions.

Davis rejected Cruse's argument and joined the Communist Party's Che Lumumba Club during 1968, but the black cultural transformation of the late 1960s would exert a more enduring influence on African Americans than would the political militancy of the late 1960s. Neither Davis's leftist views nor Cruse's advocacy of cultural nationalism encompassed the complex mixture of trends affecting African Americans in the years following the passage of historic civil rights legislation. Black radicalism and separatism coexisted uneasily with racial trends that brought African Americans closer to the mainstream. Thus, the year of Brown's rise to notoriety was also the year that Thurgood Marshall was named the first black Supreme Court justice, that Edward Brooke of

Massachusetts became the first black U.S. senator since Reconstruction, that the Supreme Court in *Loving* v. *Virginia* outlawed state laws banning interracial marriage, and that Carl Stokes of Cleveland, Ohio, and Richard Hatcher of Gary, Indiana, became the first black mayors of major cities.

It was also the year that black actor Sidney Poitier became Hollywood's most successful male actor. Although sympathizing with leftist causes during the 1940s, in the 1950s Poitier avoided political controversy by playing roles suggesting that racial divisions could be bridged. He had won acclaim for his portrayal of an embittered black man in the stage and film versions of Lorraine Hansberry's *A Raisin in the Sun,* but he usually played characters able to suppress anger. In 1964, for *Lilies of the Field,* he became the first African American to win a best actor Academy Award. In 1967, in *Guess Who's Coming to Dinner,* he played a successful doctor who charms the parents of his white fiancée, and in the police drama *In the Heat of the Night* he played a police detective who gains the grudging respect of a southern white sheriff. Such roles brought Poitier to the pinnacle of Hollywood success, but he was also constrained by the stereotypical aspects. Stung by black criticisms of his integrationist screen image, Poitier began rejecting the kind of roles that had made him a star, turning to film directing and more challenging roles in independent films.

King and the Wars against Communism and Poverty

Martin Luther King was also reassessing his future in light of black power controversies and the upsurge in racial violence. Troubled by the increasing discontent in black communities, he did his best to steer a middle course between agitators like Brown and Carmichael and more moderate civil rights leaders, such as NAACP leader Roy Wilkins or Whitney Young of the Urban League. He regretted that his differences with SNCC's new leaders had become embittered and public. He also would have preferred to stay out of the increasingly intense national debate about the war in Vietnam. He did speak out when Georgia legislators objected to SNCC's antiwar stance by refusing to seat former SNCC staff member and newly elected state representative Julian Bond. But otherwise King limited himself to calling for a negotiated settlement of the conflict while encouraging his wife, Coretta, to continue her long-standing peace activism.

Nonetheless, King felt guilty that his cautious calls for negotiations had done nothing to slow the escalation of the war. "At best, I was a loud speaker but a quiet actor, while a charade was being performed," he admitted later. Like other civil rights advocates, King saw the African American freedom struggle as stalled—unable to transform legal rights into better living conditions for many poor black people. The political coalition that had achieved major civil rights reforms seemed to be disintegrating due to white resentment of black militancy and disputes over the war. King worried that his public criticism of President Lyndon Johnson's war policies would end his access to the White

Leading the march against the Vietnam War are Dr. Benjamin Spock, the famed pediatrician who wrote an enormously popular advice book for parents, and Dr. Martin Luther King, Jr., on Chicago's State Street, March 25, 1967.

House and alienate many SCLC donors. But as American bombing and troop levels increased and antiwar demonstrations intensified, images of burned and wounded children pushed him closer to a decisive stand on the war issue. In particular, he was disturbed by a photograph, in the January 1967 issue of the leftist magazine *Ramparts,* that showed a Vietnamese mother holding her dead baby, killed in an American air attack. He decided he must take a stand. "Never again," he vowed to himself, "will I be silent on an issue that is destroying the soul of our nation and destroying thousands and thousands of little children in Vietnam."

Three months later, on April 4, King made public his views on the war in an address to an overflow audience at New York City's Riverside Church. Challenging those who said he should stick to racial issues, he charged that the war consumed funds that might otherwise be used to fight poverty in black communities. He also noted that black casualties in the war were disproportionately high. "We were taking the black young men who had been crippled by our society," he charged, "and sending them eight thousand miles away to guarantee liberties in Southeast Asia which they had not found in southwest Georgia and East Harlem." It was difficult, King said, to persuade African Americans to remain nonviolent while the nation used "massive doses of violence" in Vietnam: "I knew that I could never again raise my voice against the violence of the oppressed in the ghettos without having first spoken clearly to the greatest purveyor of violence in the world today: my own government." He warned, "A nation that continues year after year to spend more money on military defense than on programs of social uplift is approaching spiritual death."

Former SNCC chair John Lewis, in the audience at Riverside Church, recalled the speech as King's "greatest," and Stokely Carmichael was pleased when he heard King deliver his antiwar message at Atlanta's Ebenezer Baptist Church. Many white antiwar activists also applauded King's stand, but the NAACP's Wilkins was sharply critical, concerned that the war issue would split the civil rights movement. Thurgood Marshall, then U.S. solicitor general, advised King not to divert his energy from civil rights reform. FBI Director Hoover sent Johnson an ominous private note depicting King as "an instrument in the hands of subversive forces seeking to undermine our nation."

Despite intense criticism, King refused to back down. "The ultimate measure of a man is not where he stands in moments of convenience, but where he stands in moments of challenge, moments of great crisis and controversy," King told SCLC staff. King also believed it was necessary to move beyond civil rights legislation to eliminate economic inequities in the North as well as the South. He found that the problems facing the Chicago Freedom Movement, SCLC's first northern venture, were in some respects more difficult than southern legalized segregation. When he had confronted southern racists in Birmingham and Selma, northern white liberals and Democratic politicians at least offered verbal support, but white mobs in the Chicago suburb of Cicero responded to his "open housing" marches with bricks and bottles as well as with racist epithets. "I can say that I had never seen, even in Mississippi, mobs as hostile and hate-filled as in Chicago," King remarked.

Moreover, the Democratic machine of Mayor Richard Daley outmaneuvered King by publicly supporting his goals while refusing to make concessions. Although SCLC's Operation Breadbasket, directed by former North Carolina A&T student activist Jesse Jackson, did increase employment and franchise ownership opportunities for African Americans, the Chicago campaign produced few tangible gains. By the spring of 1967, King had become disgusted with the failure of Chicago officials to implement an open housing agreement. "The city's inaction," he warned, was "another hot coal on the smoldering fires of discontent and despair that are rampant in our black communities."

Racial Violence and White Repression

"If every Negro in the United States turns to violence," King remarked in 1967, "I will choose to be that one lone voice preaching that this is the wrong way." During that summer, King's determination was tested as racial violence spread through dozens of the nation's urban black communities. An especially deadly insurgency erupted on July 13 in Newark, New Jersey, after a crowd objecting to the arrest of a black taxi driver began throwing rocks at police. The following six days of civil disorder resulted in twenty-three deaths, more than 1,000 injuries, and widespread property damage. Soon afterward, still more deadly violence occurred in Detroit following a police raid on an illegal bar in a black neighborhood. Police were unable to regain control until National Guardsmen and army paratroopers arrived. The death count in Detroit reached forty-three, and arrests exceeded 7,000.

King feared that such racial violence would strengthen the influence of black power leaders who challenged his nonviolent strategy. He lamented the growing popularity of Frantz Fanon's *The Wretched of the Earth* (1961), which promoted violence as a "psychologically healthy and tactically sound method for the oppressed," and of *Black Power: The Politics of Liberation in America* (1967), by Stokely Carmichael and political scientist Charles Hamilton, which depicted African Americans as a colonized group. But King also recognized that violence was inevitable, given the nation's neglect of the deeply rooted social inequities affecting African Americans. "The nation waited until the black man was explosive with fury before stirring itself even to partial concern," he lamented.

King also found it increasingly difficult to counter the rising influence of black power proponents. In July 1967 he declined to attend the National Conference on Black Power held in Newark, which attracted 1,000 delegates and revealed the growing popularity of black power ideas. Several SNCC workers, including Brown, spoke, and all the major civil rights organizations, including SCLC, were represented, although NAACP and Urban League leaders continued to denounce the black power slogan. The most influential figures at the conference, however, were not veterans of the southern struggle but black nationalists from northern cities who spoke for discontented ghetto residents.

Newark poet and dramatist Amiri Baraka set the tone for the meeting when he appeared wearing bandages from a police beating and spoke approvingly of his city's recent "rebellion of black people for self-determination." Once in the circle of Beat poets that included Allen Ginsberg, Baraka (then known as Leroi Jones) had become politically active after touring Cuba in 1960 with a delegation of writers. Following Malcolm X's assassination in 1965, Baraka became an outspoken black nationalist, leaving his white wife and moving to Harlem. His 1965 poem "Black Art" set the agenda for militant black writers—"we want poems that kill"—and his writings inspired the Black Arts Movement of the late 1960s. Shortly before the Newark conference, he adopted the cultural nationalist perspective of Maulana Karenga, a former UCLA graduate student and "master teacher" of the black nationalist US group, whose slogan was: "Wherever we are, US is."

While black power proponents saw themselves as expressing black urban discontent, their speeches were less a cause than an outgrowth of the continuing urban violence, which was usually ignited by resentment of police. Nonetheless, white critics of black militancy, such as Maryland governor Agnew and FBI director Hoover, insisted that black power speeches caused violence. After the extensive racial violence of the summer of 1967, Hoover convinced Johnson to unleash a secret counterintelligence program (COINTELPRO) "to expose, disrupt, misdirect, discredit, or otherwise neutralize the activities of black nationalist, hate-type organizations and groupings, their leadership, spokesmen, membership, and supporters and to counter their propensity for violence and civil disorder." Among the groups selected for "intensified attention" were SNCC, CORE, the Louisiana-based Deacons for Defense, and the Nation of Islam. Even SCLC was on Hoover's list, despite King's well-known opposition to black nationalist ideas.

At about the same time Johnson approved COINTELPRO, he also established a National Advisory Commission on Civil Disorders to determine the root causes of the urban violence. Its report, issued in 1968, predicted that the nation was "moving toward two societies, one white, one black—separate and unequal." Still, Johnson did little to respond to its call for "a greatly enlarged" national commitment to action.

Although King's antiwar stance angered Johnson, both men were dismayed by the destructive impact of racial violence and antiwar dissent on the interracial coalition that had made possible Johnson's landslide victory in 1964. The Democratic Party's support among northern white workers declined as calls for black power contributed to a "white backlash." The deterioration in relations between African Americans and Jews also weakened the party, since both groups had traditionally supported Democratic liberalism. King viewed black anti-Semitism as "immoral and self-destructive," but he could do little to stem black resentment of Jewish store owners in black communities. Black-Jewish conflicts were exacerbated by the June 1967 war in the Middle East. Jews who had previously supported the civil rights struggle were angered when black activists in SNCC and other groups voiced support for the Palestinian struggle against Israel.

The Poor People's Campaign and Memphis

By the fall of 1967, King concluded that dramatic steps had to be taken to reverse the cycle of escalating racial violence and declining white support for racial reform. Addressing SCLC's annual meeting, he called for "restructuring the whole of American society" insisting that "the problem of racism, the problem of economic exploitation, and the problem of war are all tied together." Later in the year he announced that SCLC would "dramatize the whole economic problem of the poor" through a Poor People's Campaign that would bring the poor of all races to Washington to "place the problems of the poor at the seat of government of the wealthiest nation in the history of mankind."

TABLE 19.1 POLITICAL AND CIVIL RIGHTS ORGANIZATIONS

Black Panther Party Formed in 1966 by Huey Newton and Bobby Seale, the party initially emphasized armed self-defense but also developed "survival programs" for black communities.

Congressional Black Caucus Founded in 1971 by black representatives to develop legislative strategies to deal with the concerns of African Americans.

National Black Feminist Organization (NBFO) A loosely organized group formed in 1973 to promote the interests of black women.

National Black Political Assembly Formed to carry on the effort begun at the 1972 National Black Political Convention in Gary, Indiana, to build an independent national black political force.

People United to Serve Humanity (PUSH) Led by Jesse Jackson, PUSH used the threat of boycotts to prod major corporations to make economic concessions.

As King traveled to build support for the campaign, Johnson remained preoccupied with the war in Vietnam, which was diverting funding from his antipoverty efforts and other Great Society programs. Disturbed that "not a single basic cause of riots has been corrected," King began to complain in speeches that the "dream" he had described at the March on Washington in 1963 had turned into a "nightmare."

In March 1968, King accepted an invitation to join a march in Memphis, where black sanitation workers had gone on strike. He hoped that a resolution of this dispute would give momentum to his broader effort on behalf of black people. Disheartened when a few demonstrators disrupted the march by breaking windows in downtown stores and facing press criticism of his failure to control them, King felt compelled to return to the city to show that nonviolent tactics could still be effective. On April 3, he stayed at the black-owned Loraine Motel, while his staff tried to obtain a march permit and convince young gang members not to disrupt this protest.

When King spoke at a mass rally that evening, he assured the sanitation workers that justice would prevail. "I just want to do God's will, and He's allowed me to go up to the mountain," he told the cheering audience. "And I've looked over, and I've seen the Promised Land. I may not get there with you, but I want you to know tonight that we, as a people, will get to the Promised Land!"

The following day, April 4, as King stood on the balcony outside his motel room, an assassin killed him with a single rifle shot. A white escaped convict, James Earl Ray, later confessed to the killing, although he then claimed he was a "patsy" acting for others—a claim made more credible by later revelations of the FBI's extensive COINTELPRO activities against King.

News of King's death prompted deadly outbursts of racial violence in more than one hundred communities. As buildings burned within a mile of the White House, President Johnson proclaimed April 7 a day of national mourning. He also sent 20,000 troops, many of them trained for service in Vietnam, to quell the uprisings, which took forty-six lives. Carmichael warned that further violence would follow the death of "the one man of our race that this country's older generations, the militants and the revolutionaries and the masses of black people would still listen to." But John Lewis expressed dismay at the suggestion that violence was the only adequate black response: "What way was this to respond to the death of one of the most peaceful leaders of our time?"

King's funeral in Atlanta's Ebenezer Church was officiated by longtime friend Ralph Abernathy, who succeeded him as SCLC president. Among the tens of thousands of mourners were black leaders, including Roy Wilkins, Thurgood Marshall, and Jackie Robinson, who had criticized King's antiwar stand. Both Carmichael and Lewis represented SNCC. Presidential candidate Robert Kennedy, Vice President Hubert Humphrey, and former vice president Richard Nixon were also there in a brief moment of national unity. But the shared grief did not bridge the deep political divisions that had hampered King's work during his final years. The Poor People's Campaign was disbanded by early summer. Without King's leadership, SCLC's effectiveness declined.

Black Soldiers in Vietnam

For Army Major Colin Powell, King's death came as an "abrupt reminder" that "racism still bedeviled America." During his training at Fort Benning's Ranger school in Georgia, Powell, the son of Jamaican immigrants, had said he felt "plunged back into the Old South every time I left the post." But he and other black officers rejected the subsequent trend toward black power militancy. "We heard the radical black voices—Stokely Carmichael, Eldridge Cleaver, and H. Rap Brown with his 'Burn, baby, burn!'—with uneasiness," Powell recalled. "We were not eager to see the country burned down. We were doing well in it." Yet he understood the sources of the growing racial anger. "Each of us had experienced enough racial indignities to understand the riots unleashed in black ghettoes in the wake of the King assassination."

Like previous wars, Vietnam profoundly affected the lives of many African Americans. For black soldiers, the war offered an opportunity to demonstrate once again that they were prepared to fight for freedom on many fronts. But controversies in the United States over civil rights and black power reverberated in Vietnam, even as disagreements about American intervention affected the civil rights and black power movements. On both the home front and the battlefields, the backdrop of violence shaped the way racial issues were viewed and discussed. Daily newscasts brought the war to the television sets of civilians; some called it the "living room war."

Back in 1962, when Powell first arrived in Vietnam as a military advisor, few Americans paid attention to the ongoing civil war of the Vietnamese. The conflict had its roots in the American reluctance during the 1940s to support anticolonial movements, especially those seen as Communist-inspired. In 1954, after Vietnamese nationalists had defeated France, the United States opposed the reunification of previously French-controlled South Vietnam with North Vietnam, led by Communist nationalist Ho Chi Minh. Powell was among the more than 16,000 American advisors sent by President John F. Kennedy to prop up a pro-American South Vietnamese regime that had little popular support. Though Powell was convinced that it was "right to draw the line against communism anywhere in the world," he began to doubt that the war could be won without a major escalation of American involvement.

By the time Powell returned for his second tour in Vietnam in 1968, more than a half-million American troops were there. In August 1964 President Johnson had used the pretext of a North Vietnamese attack on U.S. naval forces in the Gulf of Tonkin to secure a congressional resolution authorizing military force to resist Communist aggression. Despite sending more and more troops to Vietnam, Johnson found that victory was elusive against a determined guerrilla army backed by North Vietnamese regular troops. Unlike the military advisors of the earlier period, the American combat soldiers Powell saw in 1968 were often draftees rather than volunteers. African Americans were about 11 percent of the nation's population; yet more than 16 percent of military inductees during 1967 were black, and the proportion of black soldiers was often even higher in combat units. Young black men were less likely than white men to escape the military draft by going to college or volunteering for National Guard service.

Like the rest of the nation, the American troops in Vietnam were racially divided. "Young blacks, particularly draftees, saw the war, not surprisingly, as even less their fight than the whites did," Powell observed. "They had less to go home to. This generation was more likely to be reached by the fireworks of H. Rap Brown than the reasonableness of the late Martin Luther King."

By the time he finished his tour in 1969, Powell was disillusioned with the conduct of the war. He rejected "the one-size-fits-all rationale of anticommunism" that had led to American involvement in a war rooted "in nationalism, anticolonialism, and civil strife beyond the East-West conflict." He was also disturbed that "poorer, less educated, less privileged" young men had been victims of "raw class discrimination," while "sons of the powerful and well placed" avoided combat service. Although this war saw the full desegregation of the armed forces, it also served as a reminder that the military was not isolated from the racial problems affecting American society as a whole. "We understood the bitterness of black GIs who, if they were lucky enough to get home from Vietnam in one piece, still faced poor job prospects and fresh indignities," Powell remembered.

The Rise and Fall of the Black Power Militancy

While Colin Powell served as an officer in Vietnam, the Black Panther Party for Self-Defense was urging black men not to "fight and kill other people of color in the world" who were "being victimized by the white racist government

Black Panthers march in New York to protest the murder trial of cofounder Huey P. Newton in Oakland, California, on July 22, 1968.

of America." Bobby Seale and Huey Newton, who had become friends while attending a junior college in Oakland, California, formed the party in October 1966. Dissatisfied with existing black political groups, they believed that more militancy was needed. Seale, the party's chairman, and Newton, its minister of defense, drafted a ten-point platform that included far-reaching demands, but the party's initial popularity was due largely to its call for an immediate end to police brutality against black people. Insisting that the Second Amendment of the U.S. Constitution gave them the right to carry weapons, armed Black Panthers began "patrolling the pigs" (their derogatory term for police) to observe and report police misconduct. The new group gained national press coverage in the spring of 1967 when a contingent of Black Panthers, most of them wearing the group's distinctive black leather jackets and black berets, carried their weapons to California's capitol to protest proposed gun control legislation. That October, police charged Newton with killing an Oakland policeman who had stopped a car containing Newton and another party member. The party's subsequent "Free Huey" campaign soon made the group the best-known and most controversial black militant group of the late 1960s.

The Emergence of Eldridge Cleaver

The effort to mobilize support for Newton soon brought together black militants from many different backgrounds and with varied political perspectives. Eldridge Cleaver, who became the party's minister of information shortly before Newton's arrest, quickly emerged as the key figure in this effort to build support. A gang member in Los Angeles during his youth, Cleaver's political evolution had begun as he was serving a prison term for rape. Raping white women, he initially thought, was "insurrectionary," a way of "trampling upon the white man's laws" by "defiling his women." But then he decided that he had "gone astray—astray not so much from the white man's law as from being human, civilized." Like Malcolm X, Cleaver educated himself in prison. He wrote insightful essays, later collected in the bestseller *Soul on Ice* (1967), which brought him to the attention of white sympathizers who gained his release from prison. In his writings, Cleaver derided James Baldwin, whose *The Fire Next Time* (1963) had expressed the black militancy of the early 1960s, as a victim of self-hatred and homosexuality. He called instead for a bold black heterosexual masculinity: "We shall have our manhood. We shall have it or the earth will be leveled by our attempts to gain it."

Cleaver's prominence as a writer and his forceful presence as a speaker contributed to the rapid growth of the campaign to free Newton. In the fall of 1967 Cleaver gained the backing of California's newly organized Peace and Freedom Party, which appealed mainly to antiwar activists. Other leftist groups also offered support, appreciating that Black Panthers rejected racial separatism. In his effort to build black support, Cleaver looked to Stokely Carmichael, whose travels were attracting international attention. In Cuba, Carmichael had met Fidel Castro and gained notoriety for calling the summer's black urban rebellions the beginning of a revolution. In North Vietnam, he met

Vietnamese leader Ho Chi Minh, who recalled once hearing Marcus Garvey speak in Harlem. By the time Carmichael made additional stops in several African nations, his status as the nation's foremost black militant had been confirmed. Cleaver and Seale met with Carmichael, persuaded him to speak at "Free Huey" rallies planned for February 1968, and invited him to become the Black Panther Party's prime minister.

Seale and Cleaver hoped Carmichael's support would lead to an alliance with SNCC and invited other SNCC leaders, including H. Rap Brown, to help build the party. Well-attended rallies in Los Angeles and Oakland attracted a wide array of black leaders, ranging from Los Angeles black nationalist Maulana Karenga to Berkeley city councilman Ronald V. Dellums. These rallies marked a period of rapid expansion for the Black Panthers, with dozens of chapters forming in cities throughout the nation. The party's recruits included college students, but many of the rank-and-file members were "street brothers" like Cleaver. Black women also filled the party's ranks, although armed black males shaped its public image.

High Tide of Black Rebellion

The growth of support for the Black Panthers was only one aspect of the upsurge in racial militancy during 1968. The explosion of racial anger that followed King's assassination in April signaled that the nation was indeed close to chaos, if not revolution. Discontent continued to grow on college campuses as well as in urban ghettoes. Although black colleges had been relatively quiet in the years since the 1960 sit-ins, student activism became widespread during the late 1960s. Clashes between police and students at Mississippi's Jackson State and at Houston's Texas Southern left three students dead. Early in 1968, an assault by police and National Guardsmen on unarmed student demonstrators at South Carolina State College resulted in the deaths of three students and the wounding of several dozen more. Black students at predominantly black Bowie State College in Maryland, Tuskegee Institute in Alabama, and Howard University in Washington, DC, seized buildings and called strikes to protest white governance and the lack of black studies programs. Students at predominantly white colleges and universities also protested. An extended strike at San Francisco State University that began in 1967 led to the creation of the nation's first Black Studies department. Black students armed with guns took over the student union at Cornell University, wresting concessions that included the formation of an Africana Studies and Research Center.

Some black athletes also expressed their discontent by supporting the Olympic Project for Human Rights, an effort spearheaded by San Jose State University professor and former athlete Harry Edwards. Recognizing the growing involvement of black athletes in professional and college sports, Edwards believed that collective protests by athletes could bring about change. The Olympic Project sought to convince black athletes to boycott the 1968 Olympics in order to draw attention to racial issues in sports, such as the decision of boxing authorities to strip Muhammad Ali of his heavyweight title due to his refusal to be drafted. Boycott supporters also demanded the exclusion of South

Extending gloved hands skyward in racial protest, Tommie Smith and John Carlos stare downward during the playing of the U.S. national anthem at the Olympic Games in 1968.

Africa and Rhodesia from Olympic participation until these nations stopped practicing racial apartheid. A poster for the movement read, "RATHER THAN RUN AND JUMP FOR MEDALS, WE ARE STANDING UP FOR HUMANITY."

A few major sports stars, including UCLA basketball player Lew Alcindor (later Kareem Abdul-Jabbar) decided against participating in the Olympics, but most black athletes were unwilling to pass up this chance to compete. Track legend Jesse Owens, a star of the 1936 Olympics, denounced the boycott. The 1968 Olympics began in Mexico City soon after police killed hundreds of students demonstrating against the Mexican government, and worried Olympic officials threatened to retaliate against any protest by an athlete. Nonetheless, when San Jose State track stars Tommie Smith and John Carlos stood on the platform to receive their medals for winning the 200-meter sprint, they held up their fists in a "black power salute" as the U.S. national anthem was played. Kicked off the U.S. team, they were expelled from Mexico.

Targeting the Black "Messiah"

The sports careers of Ali, Smith, and Carlos suffered because of their stands, but many black militants paid an even higher price. Soon after the Black Panther Party rallies in February 1968, the FBI stepped up COINTELPRO by developing plans to prevent "a coalition of militant black nationalist groups." The bureau targeted men such as Carmichael and King as leaders who might become the "messiah" able to unify the militant black nationalist movement. In addition, local police, sometimes with FBI assistance, began to crack down on the Black Panthers and other black militant groups.

Faced with these external threats, black militants were also more vulnerable due to internal divisions stemming from leadership competition and ideological differences. The tendency of Cleaver and other black militant leaders to threaten violence and revolution made white Americans more willing to see police repression as justifiable. The Black Panther Party endured the brunt of repression by the FBI and local police agencies. On April 6, just two days after King's assassination, Oakland police wounded Cleaver and killed Bobby Hutton, the sixteen-year-old Black Panther treasurer, after stopping a car containing a group of Black Panthers. During the following months numerous confrontations with police occurred in Oakland and other places where the party had established chapters. "The violent phase of the black liberation struggle is here, and it will spread," Cleaver insisted.

Despite such bravado and the rapid growth in party membership, the black unity the Black Panthers displayed at the rallies quickly devolved into competition and conflicts. Carmichael increasingly disagreed with Cleaver over the party's ties with white leftists. Plans for an alliance between the Panthers and SNCC floundered due to misunderstandings and FBI plots, such as sending anonymous messages to SNCC leaders suggesting Panthers might kill them. Other FBI "dirty tricks" worsened relations between the Black Panthers and Karenga's US organization. Cleaver did not help matters by ridiculing Karenga as a "pork-chop nationalist" allied with "pigs" (police). Tensions reached a breaking point in January 1969, when members of US killed two Panthers after verbal clashes on the UCLA campus.

Even as they depicted themselves as the spearhead of a black revolution, the Black Panther Party's leadership was beset with mounting legal problems. In September 1968, Newton was found guilty of manslaughter in the death of an Oakland policeman and sentenced to a prison term of two to fifteen years. Although his lawyers eventually won a new trial, he would not clear himself of these charges until the end of 1971. Seale also faced serious charges stemming from speeches he delivered to demonstrators outside the Democratic National Convention in Chicago in 1968. Along with seven white leftist leaders, he faced trial in 1969 on charges of violating the antiriot law Congress had passed in response to H. Rap Brown's speeches. Seale was also implicated in the murder of a Black Panther in Connecticut. Although Seale's conviction on the Chicago charges was later overturned on appeal and he was acquitted of the murder charges, his legal problems left him little time for party activities.

With Newton still in jail and Seale awaiting trial, a threat of reimprisonment for violating parole prompted Cleaver to choose exile. Carmichael, who criticized Cleaver's ties with white leftists, began to distance himself from the Black Panthers. He eventually resigned his position and moved to Guinea to become political secretary for exiled Ghanaian leader Kwame Nkrumah. Seeking to reverse its decline, the Black Panthers tightened rules for members and instituted purges. But these moves only weakened the group further, sometimes removing loyal members while overlooking actual police agents.

From his prison cell, Newton sought to deemphasize confrontations with police and instead stress survival programs, such as free breakfasts for children. Despite this policy change, police repression continued. In December 1969, a nighttime raid by Chicago police resulted in the deaths of Fred Hampton and Mark Clark, two leaders of the Panthers' Chicago chapter. Although Chicago authorities claimed the Panthers had initiated the gunfire, subsequent investigations revealed they had been sleeping and that only one of many bullet holes in the apartment had been caused by a shot from inside.

Attica and the Eclipse of the Black Panthers

In July 1970 the FBI named the Black Panthers as the nation's "most dangerous and violence-prone of all extremist groups," but by then the party was severely weakened by repression and internal conflict. As the party's survival programs replaced its earlier emphasis on "picking up the gun," groups such as the Black Liberation Army and the Republic of New Africa attempted to assume the role as revolutionary spearhead. But these groups also endured police attacks and infiltration by FBI informers. The Black Panthers also influenced the growing activism of prison inmates, such as George Jackson, whose published prison letters rallied support for black prisoners. Angela Davis, dismissed from the UCLA faculty due to her Communist Party membership, was one of those drawn to the Jackson campaign. A gun used in a California courthouse shooting resulting in four deaths, including that of Jackson's younger brother, was traced to Davis, and she was placed on the FBI's most-wanted list. Captured in October 1970, she was later tried and acquitted. In 1971 George Jackson and two other prisoners were killed during an escape attempt.

Jackson's death soon sparked a four-day revolt at Attica Correctional Facility in New York. Prisoners demanding better living conditions took over the prison and invited several well-known black power figures to come and investigate their complaints. The Attica revolt revealed both the militancy of politically aware black prisoners and the willingness of white authorities to crush black militancy with superior power. When police and state troopers retook the prison, they shot to death forty-three people, including ten of the guards being held hostage.

Although the deadly tactics to crush the Attica revolt were widely criticized, there was considerable popular support for law-and-order policies. By this time, the influence of the Black Panthers and other black radicals had declined dramatically. Although Cleaver continued to advocate revolution from abroad, Newton expelled him and his supporters from the party. The inflammatory speeches of Cleaver and other Black Panthers not only led to repression but also damaged the party's black support. Rather than attributing the decline of the Black Panthers entirely to the police and FBI repression, Newton acknowledged that his group had contributed to its own decline.

By the early 1970s, black power militancy was no longer a significant political force. Instead of Black Panthers with guns, popular films turned black militancy into entertainment. In 1969, Sidney Poitier starred in *The Lost Man,* a low-budget film made in Paris, in which he left behind his previous screen persona to play a black militant who finances revolutionary struggle through robbery. Independent black filmmaker Melvin van Peebles reached far more viewers with *Sweet Sweetback's Baadasssss Song,* released two years later. Starring in his own film, van Peebles played a pimp who retaliates for the beating of a black boy by assaulting two police officers. Although the flimsy plot consisted mainly of an extended chase, the film earned many times its cost of production. Its leading character was violent and sexually aggressive in ways that Poitier had not been allowed to be. Audiences in black communities cheered as the film ended with the message "A BAADASSSSS NIGGER IS COMING BACK TO COLLECT SOME DUES."

The surprise success of van Peebles convinced Hollywood that there was a large black audience for films featuring violence-prone black male heroes. During the next few years, more than a dozen black action films were released. *Super Fly* (1972) starred Ron O'Neal as a Harlem cocaine dealer, while several *Shaft* films starred Richard Roundtree as a superconfident black detective. Some critics used the term "blaxploitation" to describe these films. Rather than embodying the political messages associated with the Black Panther Party, the new heroes were loners, either criminals outside the law or detectives working on the margins of the criminal justice system. These films popularized new racial stereotypes even as they provided starring roles for black male actors, including former football stars Jim Brown and O. J. Simpson.

Diverging Directions of Black Politics

While some black filmmakers tried to remake the rebelliousness of the 1960s into the popular culture of the 1970s, Jesse Jackson transformed the militancy he had displayed in southern civil rights demonstrations into a successful political style as electoral politics supplanted black radicalism. One of the youngest members of SCLC's staff, Jackson became more prominent as SCLC declined following King's assassination. Some of his former colleagues resented Jackson's ambition, claiming he had once misled reporters by suggesting that King had died in his arms. But no one questioned his dedication. "He was willing to commit himself to the struggle with few if any reservations," SCLC administrator Andrew Young remembered.

Jackson's drive had been evident during his formative years in Greenville, South Carolina, where as the son of an unwed mother he had overcome class as well as racial barriers. He excelled as a student and an athlete in high school and became student body president at North Carolina A&T, where he also led protests in the early 1960s. In 1965 he left Chicago Theological Seminary to take part in the Montgomery March, impressing SCLC officials with his fiery speeches. The following year King recruited Jackson to run SCLC's Operation Breadbasket in Chicago. Following King's death, Jackson left SCLC and transformed Operation Breadbasket into an independent group called Operation People United to Save (later changed to Serve) Humanity (PUSH). By the early 1970s, Jackson's PUSH associates sensed he would become a major national leader. "I thought he was perhaps the most intense person that I had ever met," recalled Jackson advisor Richard Hatcher, black mayor of Gary, Indiana, in 1967. Weekly PUSH rallies attracted large, enthusiastic crowds.

The National Black Political Convention

The 3,000 delegates and 5,000 observers who came to Gary in March 1972 for the National Black Political Convention reflected the political diversity within black communities. Planners included not only Hatcher and Michigan congressman Charles C. Diggs but also Newark's Amiri Baraka. The conference aimed to bring together black leaders at the national and local levels, elected officials, and grassroots activists. The overall theme, the planners announced, would be "unity without uniformity." In addition to Diggs, several members of the Congressional Black Caucus were on the three-day program of speakers, including Ronald V. Dellums and Yvonne Braithwaite of California, Barbara Jordan of Texas, and Walter E. Fauntroy of Washington, DC. Delegates represented many black nationalist groups and community organizations formed during the 1960s, such as Baraka's Congress of African Peoples and Karenga's US organization.

Although Bobby Seale was there on behalf of the Black Panther Party and some veterans of the now defunct SNCC attended, the gathering was dominated by black activists who had moved away from black power radicalism. Yet the planners took pains to welcome various viewpoints, as evidenced by the presence of Coretta Scott King and Betty Shabazz, widows of the two men who had led opposing ideological camps during the 1960s. Hatcher noted that the delegates included some in "colorful dashikis," while others wore "three-piece suits." It was "an incredible sight to behold," he recalled.

Notably missing, however, was New York Democratic congresswoman Shirley Chisholm, who had announced earlier in the year that she would become the first black woman to run for president. The daughter of Barbadian immigrants, Chisholm had begun her career as a schoolteacher, but she soon understood that the schools would not change until teachers like her got involved in politics. "Our country needs women's idealism and determination, perhaps more in politics than anywhere else," she wrote in her combative political autobiography *Unbought and Unbossed* (1970). After defeating former CORE leader James Farmer to become the first black woman in the U.S. House of Representatives, she found that many of her House colleagues treated her "with a deference that was patronizing." Claiming that "being female put many more obstacles in my path than being black," she was a founding member of the National Women's Political Caucus in 1971. Her presidential campaign attracted little support from black power advocates or even from most black politicians. When the Congressional Black Caucus conferred on the 1972 presidential election, only Dellums agreed to support her.

The leader who best expressed the mood of the Gary convention was Jesse Jackson. His views were a blend of the militancy he displayed during sit-ins and voting rights demonstrations in the 1960s and the more pragmatic

PUSH strategy of using the threat of boycotts to prod concessions from major corporations. In a stirring speech Jackson expressed urgency while suggesting that reform of the existing political system was possible. "No more bowing and scraping!" he proclaimed. "We are twenty-five million strong. Cut us in or cut us out!" Jackson then began a chant, "What time is it?" The crowd responded, "Nation Time!"

Although the presence of Jackson and black elected officials such as Diggs and Hatcher ensured that the "Nation Time" rhetoric would be tempered by political pragmatism, differences at Gary were hard to overcome. Representatives of black community groups formed during the late 1960s were far more willing to take controversial political stands than were black elected officials and union representatives, including the large Detroit delegation from the United Automobile Workers. Some delegates called for "dismantling" the state of Israel, but others strongly objected. When delegates voted to denounce school desegregation as "racist" and "suicidal," citing the thousands of black teachers and school administrators it had put out of work, the NAACP and several other groups walked out. Detroit mayor Coleman Young and other Michigan union members withdrew after delegates condemned racial discrimination in the AFL-CIO and called for new all-black unions.

Despite these disagreements, however, the "Action Agenda for Black People" that emerged from the Gary convention set forth broad themes that united most delegates. Highly critical of the white-dominated political system, the fifty-five-page document charted a new political direction with statements on issues that remained unaddressed by the civil rights reforms of the 1960s. These included a call for proportional congressional representation for black communities (African Americans constituted 11 percent of the nation's population but only 3 percent of the House of Representatives and only 1 percent of the Senate). Delegates also proposed a guaranteed annual income for all Americans, a reduction of the military budget, reparations to compensate for past discrimination, and increased federal spending to control drug trafficking.

In the months after the convention it became clear that the unity the delegates sought was fleeting. While some black nationalists left Gary with dreams of building a national black political party, most black politicians reaffirmed ties to the Democratic Party. At the Democratic National Convention the next summer, Chisholm pleaded with the 452 black delegates to vote for her on the first ballot, but most delegates were already committed to other candidates, including the eventual nominee, liberal North Dakota senator George McGovern.

Although McGovern won overwhelming support from black voters in the November election, Nixon was reelected in a landside. For some black leaders, this election result simply confirmed the futility of involvement in either of the two major parties. But others remained determined to work within the Democratic Party to achieve limited reforms. When the second National Black Political Convention was held in Little Rock, Arkansas, in March 1974, attendance and enthusiasm were down. A discouraged Baraka insisted that the black revolution had been betrayed by middle-class black politicians. But the disagreements evident at the Gary meeting also exposed divisions that could not be readily bridged.

By the mid-1970s black nationalist political militancy receded. The Nation of Islam continued to attract support after Malcolm X's assassination, but after Elijah Muhammad's death in 1975, his son and successor, Wallace Muhammad, continued the organization's apolitical stance while abandoning the policy of excluding white "devils." He changed the organization's name to the World Community of Islam in the West (later the American Muslim Mission). Although Malcolm X's former protégé and then antagonist Louis Farrakhan (formerly Louis X) later reconstituted the Nation of Islam, the tone of black nationalism now emphasized cultural and psychological rather than political transformation. This inward focus was also evident in black poetry during the early 1970s, especially in the work of women writers like Nikki Giovanni, June Jordan, Sonia Sanchez, and Audre Lord.

Thus, even as black political militancy receded, the cultural and intellectual aspects of the black power movement were institutionalized. Among its lasting results was the formation of black community institutions, especially independent schools and educational centers, bookstores, art galleries, and drama groups, which survived for decades. The annual Kwanzaa celebration initiated by Maulana Karenga became increasingly popular. Similarly enduring were the African American academic programs established at hundreds of colleges and universities that gave black intellectuals a chance to teach and engage in research at the nation's wealthiest institutions. Pauli Murray accepted an offer from Brandeis University. Harold Cruse, author of the influential *Crisis of the Negro Intellectual* (1967), helped develop the University of Michigan's Black Studies program.

As the numbers of black elected officials grew during the 1970s, the Congressional Black Caucus became increasingly important in guiding African American politics at the national level. Some former civil rights activists like Andrew Young and Walter Fauntroy of SCLC were able to transform themselves into successful politicians, while others like Ralph Abernathy were not. In 1973, Black Panther Party founder Bobby Seale ran a strong but unsuccessful race for mayor of Oakland, but two decades later Bobby Rush, a former Black Panther leader in Illinois, won a congressional seat. Yet, though black power militancy no longer had much political influence, Carmichael's speeches and the Black Panther Party's programs had expressed an urgency and commitment that was felt by black politicians and their constituents. Compelled to tone down their speeches in order to get elected, these politicians were generally moderates instead of militants, but nonetheless were more militant than most white politicians. The Congressional Black Caucus continued to push many of the objectives initially put forward by King and groups such as SNCC and the Black Panther Party.

The Supreme Court's *Bakke* Decision

In 1967, when President Johnson appointed Thurgood Marshall as the first African American to serve on the Supreme Court, most Americans expected this former head of the NAACP's legal arm to be a strong advocate for civil rights. Marshall did not disappoint them, becoming a consistent voice not only for civil rights but also in opposition to the death penalty. But by the late 1970s he found himself increasingly out of step with the court's conservative direction. In 1974, Marshall was in the minority when the Court ruled in *Milliken* v. *Bradley* that courts could not order the busing of children between urban and suburban school districts. The ruling scaled back the legal meaning of desegregation to conform to American racial and political realities, as the busing of large numbers of urban black children to suburban schools had lost popular support, even among some African Americans.

Four years later, Marshall was again in the minority when the Court ruled in *University of California Regents* v. *Bakke* that affirmative action policies that put aside a set number of places for black students constituted reverse discrimination against white students. Although the Court allowed admissions policies promoting racial diversity, Marshall saw the *Bakke* decision as a major setback. In his dissenting opinion, he insisted, "The dream of America as the great melting pot has not been realized for the Negro; because of his skin color he never even made it into the pot."

The Carter Presidency and the Transformation of Black Leadership

"I felt somehow for many years that George Washington and Alexander Hamilton just left me out by mistake," Texas congresswoman Barbara Jordan admitted in 1973. "But through the process of amendment, interpretation, and court decision I have finally been included in 'We, the people.'" Jordan's statement was delivered as she and other members of the Judiciary Committee of the House of Representatives began hearings to investigate President Richard Nixon's role in a burglary of the Democratic Party's headquarters in Washington's Watergate complex. The burglary had taken place during Nixon's 1972 reelection campaign, but the resulting scandal had roots in the expanded FBI repression of black power militancy and antiwar dissent during the 1970s. When the *Washington Post* and other newspapers discovered that Nixon used similar illegal tactics against his Democratic opponents, Democratic Party leaders called for his impeachment. Jordan noted the irony of a black woman's passing judgment on a president. "My faith in the Constitution is whole," Jordan announced to millions watching the hearings on television. In July 1974, after months of testimony, the Judiciary Committee voted to impeach Nixon on charges of obstructing the investigation of the Watergate burglary. Facing almost certain conviction by the Senate, Nixon resigned on August 8, and Vice President Gerald Ford assumed the presidency.

Jordan's articulate and passionate statements during the Watergate hearings made her one of the nation's most prominent black elected officials. In 1976, she became the first African American to deliver the keynote address at the Democratic National Convention. Speaking again to a national audience, she called on Americans "to shape a common future." Jordan acknowledged that forming "a national community" would be difficult, "but a spirit of harmony will survive in America only if each of us remembers that we share a common destiny."

By the presidential election in 1976, much had changed since H. Rap Brown delivered his black power speech in Cambridge, Maryland, in 1967. Now going by the name Jamil Abdullah Al-Amin, Brown had completed his sentence at New York's Attica Prison and was living quietly in Atlanta. His one-time antagonist Spiro Agnew had also dropped from public view after being forced to resign the vice presidency in 1973 due to revelations that he had taken bribes even while advocating law and order. In the aftermath of the Watergate scandal, Congress investigated the political repression that led to Watergate and exposed the earlier illegal actions of the FBI's COINTELPRO against black organizations and leaders, including King. New laws were passed to prevent such abuses of law enforcement and cover-ups by public officials. These came too late to help those targeted by the program, and the racial divisions of the 1960s were still far from bridged. Nixon's Southern Strategy had transformed national politics, as most southern whites shifted their allegiance from the Democrats to an increasingly conservative Republican Party. Massive antibusing protests by whites in Boston that began in 1974 evidenced deep racial divisions in the North as well as the South. As black students attending South Boston High School faced violence and intimidation that compared to the experiences of the Little Rock Nine in the 1950s, the federal government retreated from the ideal of racial integration. Once the Supreme Court ruled in the *Milliken* case that busing to achieve desegregation could take place only within school districts, northern public schools with few black students remained that way.

Yet there were unmistakable signs of black progress and increasing racial tolerance. Just a year before the antibusing riots in Boston, a majority of Massachusetts voters had supported the reelection campaign of the Senate's only black member, Edward Brooke. During the same year, most white voters in Los Angeles joined an overwhelming majority of black voters in supporting the election of Thomas Bradley as the city's first black mayor. In the South, few whites supported black candidates, but Maynard Jackson's election in 1973 as Atlanta's mayor would be followed in 1979 by the election of Richard Arrington, Jr., as mayor of Birmingham. Elsewhere in the Deep South, hundreds of black candidates won local offices. Charles Evers, the brother of slain NAACP leader Medgar Evers, was elected mayor of Fayette, Mississippi. Even formerly segregationist politicians began to accept the pragmatism of racial reform. In 1972, Alabama Governor George Wallace, who had once proclaimed "segregation forever," reached out for black support in his 1972 reelection campaign by granting a full pardon to Willie Norris, the last surviving Scottsboro defendant.

The election of Georgian Jimmy Carter as President also indicated the new racial politics of the 1970s. Twenty years earlier, the segregationist policies of the South had isolated the region from the rest of the nation. Other than Lyndon Johnson, who initially became president after the assassination of Kennedy, no southerner had been elected president since the Civil War. But Johnson had shown that a southern politician could support civil rights. When, as governor of Georgia, Carter announced that he would run for president in 1976, few observers gave him much of a chance. But Carter was able to campaign as a pro–civil rights Southerner, attracting black support while still retaining the support of a substantial minority of white Democrats. He won endorsements from Congressman Andrew Young and Martin Luther King, Sr., Running against President Gerald Ford, a Michigan Republican weakened by his decision to pardon Nixon for his Watergate crimes, Carter won with overwhelming support from black voters.

As president, Carter appointed a number of prominent African Americans to high positions. Andrew Young became ambassador to the United Nations, while Patricia Roberts Harris, former dean of Howard University's law school, became secretary of the Department of Housing and Urban Development and the first black woman to serve as a cabinet member. Eleanor Holmes Norton, a former SNCC worker and one of the founders of the National Black Feminist Organization, became chair of the Equal Employment Opportunity Commission, the agency charged with enforcing civil rights policies. Former SNCC chair John Lewis also joined the Carter administration as associate director of Action, the federal volunteer agency. Lewis had spent the early 1970s directing the Voter Education Project, and the slogan of that organization provided a theme for the decade following voting rights reforms: "Hands That Pick Cotton Now Can Pick Our Elected Officials."

The "Roots" Phenomenon

During the first year of Carter's presidency, the phenomenal success of the "Roots" television series increased popular awareness of African American history and drew attention to the brutalities of past racial oppression. In some respects, "Roots" served as a corrective to earlier violence-filled blaxploitation films. Such films had provided roles for black actors, mostly as action heroes, but they were rarely well crafted and did not offer positive depictions of African American women. "Roots," based on Alex Haley's Pulitzer Prize–winning family saga, broadened the depiction of African Americans and provided positive roles for women.

Among the women featured in "Roots" was Cicely Tyson, the daughter of strictly religious Caribbean immigrants in New York who turned to acting after first working as a secretary. Gaining critical acclaim in Jean Genet's avant-garde play, *The Blacks,* which also starred James Earl Jones, Maya Angelou, and Roscoe Jones, Tyson continued to seek roles that "had to do with educating as well as entertaining." Her performance as a Louisiana sharecropper in the 1972 film *Sounder* boosted her career. Playing the wife of a man imprisoned for stealing food for his family, she displayed a quiet strength and dignity that earned her an Academy Award nomination and prompted one leading film critic to proclaim her "the first great black heroine on the screen." Soon after the success of *Sounder*, Tyson starred in *The Autobiography of Miss Jane Pittman* (1974), an adaptation of Ernest Gaines's novel about a black woman who survives from the Civil War to the era of civil rights protests. *Jane Pittman*

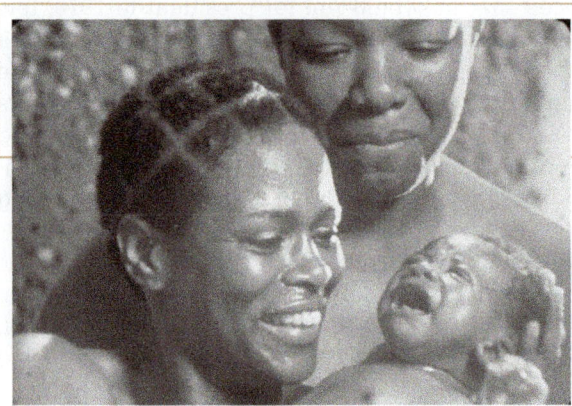

Actors Cicely Tyson (left) and Maya Angelou look lovingly at Kunta Kinte in a scene from the 1977 television miniseries "Roots."

attracted high ratings, won Tyson a best actress Emmy, and encouraged Hollywood to produce "Roots."

In "Roots," Tyson played the mother of an African youth, Kunta Kinte, who is enslaved and brought to America. Although she had only a supporting role, she received acclaim for her contribution to what became a historic event. "Roots" became television's most widely viewed drama, attracting some 130 million viewers. For many Americans of all races, the series became a source of education as well as entertainment. Its depiction of the capture and enslavement of Kunta Kinte (played by LeVar Burton) allowed viewers to gain a sense of the horrors of the Middle Passage on slave ships and the cruelty of the slave system. For African Americans, Haley's somewhat fictionalized account of his family history, based on twelve years of research, became a substitute for unknown aspects of their own history. By debunking the myth that it was impossible for black people to trace their family roots, Haley encouraged an explosion of genealogical research. The book *Roots: The Saga of an American Family* sold more than 8 million copies, and Haley's lectures, which recounted the story of his research, drew large crowds. Haley gained the enviable reputation of having produced two of the era's most influential books: *Roots* and *The Autobiography of Malcolm X.*

Conclusion

In the decade after H. Rap Brown attracted national attention as a black power proponent, there had been many changes in African American political life. The nation's racial divisions became visible as never before as black militants confronted white authorities in cities, on college campuses, and even in prisons. The violence of urban racial conflict and of warfare in Vietnam fueled calls for racial separatism and revolution. Although black power militancy encouraged racial pride and expressed resentment of long-standing racial injustices, racial unity and power remained elusive goals. The revolutionary objectives sought by Brown and other black power advocates were not achieved and the special problems confronting black women were generally ignored by black militants. But a new generation of black elected officials rejected black power rhetoric in favor of working with increasing effectiveness within the American political system to protect previous civil rights gains. Many African Americans found much to hope for in the election of Democrat Jimmy Carter in 1976, and their votes helped put him in office. But the racial gains were balanced against setbacks, as white resistance to affirmative action and school busing remained widespread. Thus, at the end of the 1970s, African American politics faced new challenges within an increasingly conservative political climate.

Questions for Review and Reflection

1. What accounts for the movement of many African Americans from King's "beloved community" ideal to "black power" slogan popularized by Stokely Carmichael and H. Rap Brown?

2. How was the national debate over the Vietnam War related to trends within the African American freedom struggle? What was the impact of the Vietnam war controversy on the civil rights movement?

3. Did the increasing militancy of the black struggle enhance or detract from its political effectiveness?

4. What was the relationship between the trends in African American politics and African American arts and culture during the late 1960s and early 1970s?

5. To what extent was Jesse Jackson's emergence as a nationally prominent political figure a reflection of broader trends in African American politics?

The Search for New Directions during a Conservative Era, 1979–1991

Michele Wallace on the Discontents of Black Women

"I went from obscurity to celebrity to notoriety overnight," said Michele Wallace, recalling the response to her *Black Macho and the Myth of the Superwoman* (1979). "At twenty-six I had written the book from hell and my life would change forever."

Although surprised by the intensity of the attacks against her, Wallace knew *Black Macho* would spark controversy. Even though still a teenager during the heyday of the black power movement, she had formed strong opinions about black militant leaders, and now she was ready to express them publicly. A self-described "black American princess" who grew up in Harlem and attended the private New Lincoln School, she had sympathized with the civil rights movement and initially admired Stokely Carmichael and other black power advocates. However, by the time she entered Howard University in the late 1960s, her attitudes had been transformed by the emerging women's liberation movement. She soon left Howard—"between the fraternities and the Black Power antics, misogyny ran amuck on a daily basis down there"—to enroll at New York's City College. Along with her

1979	U.N. Ambassador Andrew J. Young is forced to resign after meeting with Palestinians.
1980	Republican Ronald Reagan is elected president.
1983	Alice Walker's *The Color Purple* wins the Pulitzer Prize.
	Harold Washington is elected Chicago's first black mayor.
1984	Presidential hopeful Jesse Jackson garners considerable support in Democratic primaries.
	With less than 10 percent of the black vote, Republican President Ronald Reagan wins reelection.
	The Free South Africa campaign seeks to overturn the apartheid regime.
1986	The nation celebrates the first national holiday in honor of Martin Luther King, Jr.
1987	August Wilson's *Fences* receives Broadway acclaim.
1988	Toni Morrison's novel *Beloved* wins the Pulitzer Prize.
	Jesse Jackson runs another strong presidential race.
1989	Colin L. Powell becomes chair of the U.S. Joint Chiefs of Staff.
1990	Douglas Wilder of Virginia becomes the nation's first elected African American governor.
	In response to international protests, South African antiapartheid leader Nelson Mandela is released from prison.
1991	Despite sexual harassment charges by Anita Hill, Clarence Thomas wins Senate confirmation as Supreme Court justice.

artist mother, Faith Ringgold, she joined a small group of black women, many of them civil rights and antiwar activists, who identified with the new women's liberation movement.

No longer content with the agenda of the National Organization for Women (NOW), founded in 1966 to campaign to enforce the sex antidiscrimination provisions of the 1964 Civil Rights Act, Wallace and other black feminists of the early 1970s favored greater militancy for women's rights. They also believed both black power leaders and white feminists gave insufficient attention to the concerns of black women. Wallace felt there was "a basic communication gap" between black women and white women on some issues: "When the middle-class white woman said 'I want to work,' in her head was a desk in the executive suite, while the black woman saw a bin of dirty clothes, someone else's dirty clothes." In 1973, believing black women should entrust their liberation neither to black men nor to white women, Wallace became one of the founders of the National Black Feminist Organization (NBFO).

At this time only a small minority of black women identified themselves as feminists, but Wallace was convinced her views reflected the submerged discontents of many black women. In *Black Macho,* she insisted that black power leaders had not only failed to achieve racial unity but had increased tensions between black men and black women. Black power militancy had been tragic rather than heroic—an opportunity missed due to the "growing distrust, even hatred, between black men and black women." Wallace blamed the "narcissistic macho" of black male militants "blinded by their resentment of black women, their envy of white men, and their irresistible urge to bring white women down a peg."

Wallace argued that Richard Wright's *Native Son* (1940) had been "the starting point of the black writer's love affair with Black Macho," since the Bigger Thomas character "could only come to life in the act of punishing the white man." During the 1960s, the black macho theme was vividly expressed, according to Wallace, in Eldridge Cleaver's *Soul on Ice,* in which the Black Panther leader admitted "practicing" on black women before raping white women as "an insurrectionary act" of revenge against white men. She claimed Cleaver and other black power spokesmen equated black liberation with the violent assertion of black manhood. The Black Power movement, she asserted, had become "black men looting and rioting in the streets, taking over the country by brute force, arrogant lawlessness and an unquestionable sexual authority granted them as the victims of four hundred years of racism and abuse."

Although white feminists, such as *Ms.* magazine founder Gloria Steinem, applauded Wallace as a major black voice, some black activists saw her as a tool of white feminists or even a racial traitor who exaggerated the sexism of black power figures. Wallace's public appearances attracted hecklers. She opened herself to criticism from other feminists by alleging that black women activists wanted "to be models of fragile Victorian womanhood" and "were not allowed to do anything important in the Black Movement." This certainly did not apply to women such as Ella Baker, Diane Nash Bevel, and Ruby Doris Robinson of SNCC or Kathleen Cleaver, Erika Huggins, and Elaine Brown of the Black Panther Party.

Former civil rights worker and writer Alice Walker offered a qualified defense of *Black Macho* for providing "many good things that (though not as original as she thinks) can be very helpful to us, if we will *hear* them." But she criticized Wallace's assertion that black women accepted stereotypical roles as unfeminine "Mother Earth" types or as "superwomen." Walker insisted, "I've been hacking away at that stereotype for years, and so have a good many other black writers." Wallace herself later conceded that her incendiary polemic was "destined to be misread and misunderstood in its own time."

The controversy over *Black Macho* exposed the conflicts among African Americans that erupted as the ambitious hopes and expectations of the 1960s gave way to new racial realities. Black feminist writers did not have much immediate impact on black politics, but during the 1980s they reached a growing audience of receptive readers. A new generation of articulate, college-educated black women—many of them beneficiaries of Title VII of the 1964

Civil Rights Act, which outlawed employment discrimination based on race, color, religion, sex, and national origin—began to express their frustrations with male leaders who ignored their special concerns as women. Black women also began to play more prominent roles in African American intellectual life. An outpouring of innovative visual art, music, dance, drama, and literature by black women illuminated their distinctive experiences while challenging the emphasis on black manhood that had pervaded the Black Arts movement. Maya Angelou, Toni Morrison, Alice Walker, and many others produced insightful, sometimes caustic, portrayals of male-female relationships among black people. During a decade in which depictions of African Americans in the nation's mass media were still often distorted and demeaning, black women artists and intellectuals in many fields contributed in new and important ways to the continuing struggle of African Americans to create positive and realistic self-images.

The emergence of black feminism coincided with the growing prominence of black elected officials, including a considerable number of women, who rejected black power militancy in favor of more conventional leadership styles. These officials focused on achieving reform rather than revolution and on protecting rather than extending previous civil rights gains. Under the Republican administrations of Ronald Reagan and his successor, George H. W. Bush, no new civil rights legislation was enacted, but the NAACP and the Congressional Black Caucus fought effective defensive battles to preserve affirmative action programs. In addition, African Americans mobilized successful campaigns for a holiday celebrating the birthday of Martin Luther King, Jr., and for economic sanctions against the South African government's apartheid policies.

Yet little was achieved during this period to address the problems of economically hard-pressed black Americans who did not benefit from previous civil rights reforms. Despite increasingly visible black affluence, poverty remained endemic in black communities, especially among growing numbers of single women raising children by themselves. Indications of black progress contrasted sharply with highly visible signs of social deterioration, especially urban drug abuse and violent crime. The tensions dividing African Americans were suggested by the simultaneous popularity in the late 1980s of male-dominated gangsta rap and of black feminist writings. During the early 1990s, class, gender, and ideological conflicts among African Americans captured the nation's attention as black lawyer Anita Hill made sexual harassment accusations against her former boss, Clarence Thomas, the conservative black federal appeals judge nominated to replace retiring Supreme Court Justice Thurgood Marshall.

Finding a Place in the Political System

In the summer of 1979, Andrew Young became involved in a controversy that threatened his position as the U.S. ambassador to the United Nations. When reporters learned of his informal meeting with the U.N. representative of the

Palestinian Liberation Organization (PLO), Jewish-American leaders voiced strong objections. The highest-ranking black appointee in President Jimmy Carter's administration, Young placed his job in jeopardy by contacting a group his own government labeled as terrorist. Ironically, Young's rapid rise was due to his ability to display not only the cautiousness needed to thrive in electoral politics but also the commitment required to win respect in the civil rights movement.

An ordained minister of the United Church of Christ, Young had worked with the National Council of Churches before accepting the invitation of Martin Luther King, Jr., to become executive director of the Southern Christian Leadership Conference (SCLC). Rather than engaging in civil disobedience, he became a self-described "organizational man, the non-image staff person" within SCLC. Following King's assassination, he won a congressional seat representing a predominantly white district in Atlanta. Along with Barbara Jordan of Texas, he was among the first African Americans since Reconstruction to represent a southern state in Congress. In 1976, he was one of the first black elected officials to support the presidential campaign of Georgia governor Jimmy Carter. After Young's efforts to rally black voters helped elect Carter, he was rewarded with the U.N. post.

In this position, Young's civil rights perspectives put him at odds with his government's foreign policies, and he underestimated the negative response to his PLO meeting. As the controversy escalated, he decided to resign rather than threaten Carter's chances for reelection, but he continued to defend his actions. "It's absolutely necessary for the United States of America to be able to talk with anybody, on any occasion, anywhere," he later insisted.

Although Carter defused the controversy over the "Andrew Young affair," he failed in his reelection bid. Beleaguered by his inability to free Americans held hostage by Islamic militants inside the United States embassy in Tehran, Iran, he was soundly defeated by the conservative Republican candidate, former California Governor Ronald Reagan. Carter retained his overwhelming support among black voters, but Young's resignation sowed seeds of distrust in relations between African Americans and the Democratic Party. For many African Americans, the episode demonstrated that long-standing black loyalty to the party was not enough to save Young's job. But the White House was now occupied by an even less responsive president.

A New Conservative Era

When Reagan announced early in his presidency that the "era of big government" was over, black civil rights leaders feared he would target agencies established to enforce civil rights legislation and the remnants of Lyndon Johnson's antipoverty programs. In fact, Reagan exploited widespread antitax sentiment and white resentment of black "welfare mothers" even as he preserved programs such as Social Security and Medicare that benefited middle-class Americans. Unlike former vice president Spiro Agnew and former

Alabama governor George Wallace, who had linked conservatism with explicit attacks against black militants, Reagan rarely commented on racial issues, but he indicated an insensitivity to black concerns when he began his campaign by appearing with former Dixiecrat leader Strom Thurmond at a states' rights rally held in Philadelphia, Mississippi, the site of the 1964 murders of three civil rights workers. As Reagan's first term began in 1981, black leaders were forced to find ways to influence a conservative president who had gained office with little black support.

A Black Alternatives Conference held in San Francisco soon after the 1980 presidential election revealed that not all African Americans opposed Reagan's conservative views. Although the participants represented a variety of viewpoints, most believed the time had come for a departure from the Democratic liberalism that had shaped black electoral politics since the New Deal era. Many described themselves as neoconservatives to indicate they had been drawn to conservatism only after becoming disillusioned with governmental programs such as affirmative action that had been developed to implement civil rights reforms. The participants were outside the black political mainstream, but some saw themselves as linked to the tradition of black self-help efforts of Marcus Garvey and Booker T. Washington. Tony Brown, host of a popular television talk show, was the best known of the black participants. Less known at the time was Clarence Thomas, a Yale-educated lawyer who soon joined the Reagan administration.

Perhaps the most influential was one of the conference's organizers, the economist Thomas Sowell, whose writings had already had an impact on other black conservatives. For Sowell, the gathering in San Francisco marked a new stage in African American intellectual development: "It brought together blacks who debated their differing viewpoints in an atmosphere wholly free of rancor, of attempts to be blacker-than-thou, and without any charges of 'selling out' or the like."

Sowell had not always been a conservative. During the mid-1950s, as an undergraduate at Howard and then at Harvard University, he had been drawn to Marxian economics, the topic of his senior honors thesis. As a graduate student in economics at the University of Chicago, however, Sowell rejected Marxism, advocating instead minimal government involvement in the economy. Although he welcomed the dismantling of the old Jim Crow laws, he questioned whether removing racial barriers would bring economic gains for African Americans. In the late 1960s, as a professor at Cornell University, he spoke out against the "academic paternalism" of college administrators who gave in to black militant demands. He also criticized Cornell's affirmative action policies, arguing that civil rights policies should aim not to redress the consequences of past discrimination but only to remove current racial barriers to individual advancement. In *Race and Economics* (1975) he claimed that government action to combat discrimination was less effective than simply allowing economic forces to work.

The conservative views of Sowell and others provided an interpretive framework for explaining why all African Americans had not benefited from civil rights reforms. As the black sociologist William Julius Wilson observed in *The Declining Significance of Race* (1978), the problems of the black poor had not been ameliorated by civil rights laws or affirmative action programs. Instead, he claimed, these programs had created a gulf between the black middle class, which *had* benefited from reforms, and the black "underclass," which was "in a hopeless state of stagnation, falling further and further behind the rest of society." Although Wilson himself supported governmental programs focused on economic rather than racial problems, conservative analysts insisted that governmental welfare programs had produced a debilitating "culture of poverty" passed down through generations of welfare recipients. While liberals decried the funding cuts that had undermined antipoverty programs, conservatives called for still further cuts and for even harsher policies forcing welfare recipients to work and punishing the criminal behavior they associated with the black underclass. Scholars continued to question whether the "underclass" concept accurately described the black poor, but Sowell's writings signaled a shift away from the liberal assumptions underlying the social policies of Franklin Roosevelt and Lyndon Johnson.

From the time he took office in 1981, Reagan downgraded civil rights concerns. His early appointees to the federal courts and the Justice Department included conservatives who questioned the need for school busing and affirmative action. Sowell was mentioned as a possible Reagan appointment, but he accepted a post at the Hoover Institution, a think tank at Stanford University that gave him the time and resources to write articles and books popularizing his conservative views. Despite Sowell's decision to remain an academic, however, the Reagan administration's new direction on racial policies was clearly indicated when Clarence Thomas became Assistant Secretary for Civil Rights in the Department of Education.

Like Sowell, Thomas came late to conservatism. As a Holy Cross student during the late 1960s, he had identified with Bigger Thomas's anger and admired Malcolm X. As a Yale law student, he had voted for Democratic liberal George McGovern for president in 1972. But Thomas was deeply affected by Sowell's *Race and Economics,* and by the time of his appointment to be in charge of enforcing school desegregation policies, he was known as a critic of busing and affirmative action. Reagan soon promoted Thomas to an even more visible position as head of the Equal Employment Opportunity Commission (EEOC), replacing Eleanor Holmes Norton, a participant in SNCC's Mississippi voting rights campaign during the 1960s and the first woman to chair EEOC. Thomas quickly angered civil rights leaders by abandoning requirements that employers meet timetables and numerical goals in hiring minority workers. EEOC's budget and staff declined during Thomas's tenure, reducing its ability to investigate discrimination complaints from minorities and women. The time required for processing complaints grew to ten months as 40,000 cases awaited action.

Reagan's appointees to the Justice Department's Civil Rights Division were similarly critical of government efforts to implement civil rights legislation. Justice Department officials suggested that the racial policies of private all-white educational institutions, such as South Carolina's Bob Jones University, might not violate federal law. Furthermore, the department gave only qualified support for legislation to renew the Voting Rights Act of 1965. In this case, however, Reagan was not able to overcome voting rights supporters who mobilized in 1982 to pass a strengthened bill with enough votes to ensure that a presidential veto would be overridden.

The Civil Rights Commission, established to investigate civil rights violations, became a battleground due to a well-publicized clash between Reagan and a Carter appointee he hoped to replace: historian and civil rights activist Mary Frances Berry. Although Berry overturned her firing through a court challenge, Reagan conservatives soon came to dominate the commission.

In addition to downplaying civil rights, the Reagan administration reduced funding for domestic welfare programs. Consistent with the philosophy that American society was overgoverned but also responding to the white backlash that put him in office, Reagan promoted tax cuts that disproportionately benefited wealthy individuals. Although he said that these benefits would eventually "trickle down" to those less fortunate, Reagan's critics were unconvinced. Black unemployment increased from 11 percent in 1982 to 16 percent in 1984 even as the Reagan administration cut back programs assisting the poor, such as job training, food stamps, aid to low-income students, federal grants for the redevelopment of inner cities, and health services. At the end of Reagan's first term, 36 percent of African American families had an annual income below the federal government's stated poverty line.

Although civil rights proponents faced many setbacks during Reagan's first term, the campaign for a national holiday honoring Martin Luther King, Jr., was successful. The proposal was introduced in Congress by Michigan congressman John Conyers soon after King's assassination, and the Congressional Black Caucus backed the idea throughout the 1970s. But it did not garner much political support until Coretta Scott King spearheaded the effort in the 1980s. King's widow had emerged as a national leader in her own right in the years since her husband's assassination, establishing the King Center in Atlanta to carry on the legacy of nonviolent struggle. Skillfully attracting the endorsement of political figures as well as singer Stevie Wonder, who wrote a popular "Happy Birthday" song honoring King, she built support for the holiday legislation. In 1983 Congress approved the bill, and Reagan, despite voicing reservations, signed it. The annual observance of the holiday began in 1986.

Jesse Jackson's 1984 Presidential Campaign

"Mr. Reagan cuts energy assistance to the poor, cuts job training, cuts breakfast and lunch programs for children—and then says to an empty table, 'Let us pray.'" Jesse Jackson's sardonic remark aroused black audiences in 1983, especially when he added, "Apparently Mr. Reagan is not familiar with the structure of prayer. You thank the Lord for the food you are about to *receive,* not the food that has just *left.* I think we should pray, but not pray for the food that's left. Pray for the man that took the food . . . to leave." Jackson's forceful criticisms of Reagan contributed to his emergence as the nation's most influential black political figure. But he was also a critic of Carter, whom he saw as capitulating to Jewish leaders in the Andrew Young affair. Jackson's skepticism about both major political parties derived from his background as a civil rights activist in the 1960s. His passionate rhetorical style displayed elements of the Black Power era.

Jackson had been Young's colleague on the SCLC staff during the 1960s, but their leadership styles diverged in the years after King's death. Young had been raised in middle-class comfort by college-educated parents in New Orleans. Jackson, born to an unwed mother in South Carolina, had to overcome class as well as racial barriers. While Young served as SCLC's chief administrator, Jackson had been one of its brash young firebrands, his oratorical skills honed as he led civil rights demonstrations at North Carolina A&T College in Greensboro. During the 1970s, Young became a Democratic Party insider while Jackson remained an outsider, even suggesting that African Americans ought to form an independent political party. Jackson broke away from King's SCLC to form his own independent Chicago group called Operation People United to Serve Humanity (PUSH), which used boycotts to expand black economic opportunities. While Young returned to Atlanta after his forced resignation from the U.N. post and eventually became mayor, Jackson built on the anger caused by what happened to Young.

Jackson attracted considerable publicity by quickly arranging a trip to the Middle East. It was a bold gambit meant to demonstrate that black leaders no longer feared the castigation heaped on W. E. B. Du Bois and Paul Robeson for questioning the nation's foreign policies in the early Cold War years, and on King during the Vietnam War. Although Jackson indicated he would hear from both Israelis and Palestinians, his visit heightened Jewish fears that black leaders backed the Palestinian side. Black-Jewish relations deteriorated further when newspaper photographs showed Jackson visiting a Palestinian refugee camp and hugging Palestinian leader Yasser Arafat. Yet Jackson's mission demonstrated that leaders of other nations received him with respect, and he was increasingly perceived as the preeminent African American leader.

In the United States, Jackson developed extensive contacts not only through Operation PUSH but also through his prominent role in the 1972 Gary Convention. By 1980 he was resolving to increase black influence within the Democratic Party by mobilizing black voters. He knew the number of black registered voters had almost doubled since passage of the 1965 Voting Rights Act. But 7 million black adults—more than Reagan's margin of victory—were still not registered in 1980. If these potential voters were registered, Jackson believed, black voters could change the outcome of national and local elections and could also force future Democratic presidents to be more responsive to their concerns.

Jesse Jackson was more successful than any previous black presidential candidate in attracting white support and identifying with the plight of poor people of all races.

The Harold Washington Campaign

Jackson had a chance to test his strategy when Harold Washington announced his 1983 run to become Chicago's first black mayor. Washington had begun his political career as a loyalist to the Democratic machine that, under Mayor Richard J. Daley, had long dominated Chicago politics, but he had broken with the machine over issues such as police brutality. Now he believed he had a chance to win in the Democratic primary, even over the former mayor's son. Although he was not personally close to Jackson, Washington knew Jackson's ability to arouse black audiences would make him an indispensable ally. Jackson, for his part, recognized that helping elect Washington would demonstrate his own political clout in the nation's second largest city, where black residents constituted about 40 percent of the city's population. The election gained national significance when well-known Democratic leaders, including Senator Edward Kennedy and former Vice President Walter Mondale, gave their support to Washington's white opponents. Their intervention enraged Jackson and other Washington supporters, who saw them as abandoning Washington just as Carter had abandoned Young. While Washington ran a skillful campaign, doing well in debates with the other candidates, Jackson mobilized black voters. He even overcame the apolitical stance of the Nation of

Islam, convincing the group's leader, Louis Farrakhan, to encourage his followers to register.

Washington won the closely fought primary with the support of black voters: he received only 6 percent of the white vote and 13 percent of the Latino vote. Although the Chicago mayor's race was usually decided in the Democratic primary, Washington's election was in question until he prevailed over his Republican opponent. In the general election he increased his white support to about 19 percent while retaining his overwhelming support in black neighborhoods.

Washington's victory in Chicago encouraged black leaders seeking to respond to Reagan's election. Within weeks, some were suggesting replicating the Chicago voter registration campaign elsewhere in the nation, and Jackson proposed that a black presidential candidate would stimulate this effort. Even if the black candidate did not win, newly registered black voters might succeed in electing black candidates to Congress or to local offices. Few people who knew Jackson doubted he would offer himself as the best available black presidential candidate.

Run, Jesse, Run

Yet when Jackson called a meeting of black leaders to discuss a black presidential candidacy, not all of those invited thought it a good idea. Coretta Scott King and Andrew Young argued privately that Jackson would damage the prospects of a liberal white candidate with a better chance to defeat Reagan. Leading black mayors, including Detroit's Coleman Young, Birmingham's Richard Arrington, and Los Angeles's Tom Bradley, hesitated to back someone who had never run for political office. Yet Jackson received sufficient encouragement to continue his effort, especially after an ABC television poll of black opinion named him as the most important black leader by a wide margin over runner-up Andrew Young.

Jackson's supporters insisted his candidacy would enable African Americans to gain enough power within the Democratic Party to force it to support progressive policies. With the departure of southern whites for the Republican Party, black voters had an increased chance for a say in the Democratic Party's direction. Formally announcing his candidacy late in 1983, Jackson proved an effective campaigner, surprising his critics and even many of his supporters. He distinguished himself from other candidates by his strong support for civil rights, labor unions, women's rights, and environmental causes. Acknowledging that his campaign grew out of the "black perspective," Jackson nonetheless insisted, "This candidacy is not for blacks only." He claimed he could identify with the plight of poor white people in Appalachia "because I have known poverty. I know the pain of anti-Semitism because I have felt the humiliation of discrimination. I know firsthand the shame of bread lines and the horror of hopelessness and despair because my life has been dedicated to empowering the world's rejected to become respected." Addressing increasingly enthusiastic crowds, he used his background to express his empathy: "I *do* understand. I was born out of wedlock to a teen-age mother, who was born to a teen-age mother. How do I understand? I never slept in the house with my natural father one night in my life. I *understand.*"

In January 1984, Jackson's campaign received a boost when he flew to Syria to secure the release of a black Navy pilot, Lieutenant Robert O. Goodman, Jr., whose plane had been shot down over Syrian positions in eastern Lebanon. Although State Department officials had failed to gain Goodman's freedom, Jackson was able to capitalize on contacts from his 1979 trip to the Middle East. His unexpected diplomatic success prompted many voters to take him more seriously as a presidential candidate. Early in 1984, he won several state Democratic primaries and ran close races in others. Suddenly journalists covering the campaign began to consider the possibility that Jackson would win the nomination.

But Jackson's campaign experienced a major setback when a black reporter quoted him referring to New York City as "Hymie-town," a derogatory reference to its large Jewish population. Nation of Islam leader Louis Farrakhan, who had urged his followers to support Jackson and provided the candidate with a security force, made things worse for Jackson by urging the black community to ostracize the reporter, adding that one day "traitors" like him would be killed. Jewish leaders, already critical of Jackson for his embrace of PLO leader Arafat, saw his ties to Farrakhan as confirming an underlying anti-Semitism. Although Jackson denied the charge and denounced Farrakhan's comments, his campaign lost momentum. On the defensive for the rest of the primaries, Jackson still received about 3.5 million votes overall and arrived at the Democratic National Convention in San Francisco with 300 delegates committed to him.

By this time Jackson realized he could not win the nomination, but he had won far more support than Shirley Chisholm had attracted twelve years earlier. He had demonstrated that a black candidate could not only mobilize black voters but a substantial minority of all Democratic voters. Although Mondale won the Democratic nomination, Jackson's speech to the convention moved the delegates. He acknowledged his flaws: "If, in my low moments, in word, deed or attitude, through some error of temper, taste, or tone, I have caused anyone discomfort, created pain, or revived someone's fears, that was not my truest self." Describing himself as "not a perfect servant," he asked for patience: "God is not through with me yet." He presented his vision of a "rainbow" nation capable of overcoming its differences:

America is not like a blanket—one piece of unbroken cloth, the same color, the same texture, the same size. America is more like a quilt: many patches, many pieces, many colors, many sizes, all woven and held together by a common thread. The white, the Hispanic, the black, the Arab, the Jew, the woman, the native American, the small farmer, the businessperson, the environmentalist, the peace activist, the young, the old, the lesbian, the gay, and the disabled make up the American quilt.

Despite Reagan's landslide victory over Mondale in the 1984 election, Jackson was able to keep his newly formed "Rainbow Coalition" together, and his second run for the presidency in 1988 proved even more successful.

The Free South Africa Campaign

"The Reagan policy of 'constructive engagement' amounts to little more than letting the South African government go and do what it feels like doing," Eleanor Holmes Norton told reporters outside the South African embassy in Washington, DC, just weeks after the 1984 election. She announced that, along with two other black leaders, she intended to remain inside the embassy until the South African government released its political prisoners, including African National Congress leader Nelson Mandela, and ended its apartheid policies, which denied basic civil rights to black residents. Many African Americans had become dissatisfied with the Reagan administration's failure to enforce U.N. economic sanctions against South Africa. The Congressional Black Caucus had repeatedly called for sanctions, but the president refused to pressure an anti-communist Cold War ally on its racial policies. "We felt we had to do something," Norton explained.

A law professor at Georgetown University, Norton had attracted attention when Reagan fired her as head of the Equal Employment Opportunity Commission due to her sharp attacks on his civil rights policies. She was accompanied to the South African embassy by Mary Frances Berry, another civil rights advocate targeted by Reagan, and Walter Fauntroy, a leader of SCLC before becoming the congressional representative of Washington, DC. The embassy protest was organized by Randall Robinson, head of the anti-apartheid lobby group Trans-Africa, which sought to mobilize American support for the South African freedom movement. When the three leaders inside the embassy announced their intentions, the South African ambassador abruptly left, while his aide pleaded, "Is there anything we can do to work this out?" Berry replied bluntly, "You can comply with the demands."

The three protesters were arrested and charged with a misdemeanor for unlawful entry of an embassy. Quickly released on bail, they held a press conference to announce the founding of the Free South Africa Movement. During the next year, daily protests, including civil disobedience, were staged at the embassy as other black leaders and civil rights proponents joined the movement. Rosa Parks, Stevie Wonder, and Coretta Scott King, with several of her children, were among the many prominent figures who were jailed in the campaign. More than 6,000 protesters were eventually arrested at the embassy and at South African consulates around the country. South African Episcopal Bishop Desmond Tutu, winner of the 1984 Nobel Peace Prize, strengthened the campaign with his antiapartheid speeches in the United States. Student protests on a scale not seen since the early 1970s resulted in universities such as Columbia and Stanford withdrawing endowment investments from companies that did business in South Africa. Many cities, states, and pension funds took similar action, putting pressure on large corporations.

These events marked the first time since the 1960s that African Americans had spearheaded a national campaign of nonviolent direct action. Extensive news coverage of black uprisings throughout South Africa in 1985 added impetus to the American protests. The immediate goal of the Free South Africa Movement was to prod Congress to mandate economic sanctions and thereby force the South African government to change its racial policies. When California congressman Ronald Dellums introduced the Comprehensive Anti-Apartheid Act of 1986, few observers thought the bill could pass. But the spreading protests convinced many politicians, including some Republicans, to back the sanctions. Congress passed the bill, but Reagan vetoed it. His veto could be overturned only by a two-thirds vote in both houses.

In September 1986, the Democrat-controlled House voted overwhelmingly against the president. In October, Randall Robinson sat in the Senate chamber

The Free South Africa movement marked the first time since the 1960s that black Americans launched a major national campaign of nonviolent direct action.

TABLE 20.1 POLITICAL AND CIVIL RIGHTS ORGANIZATIONS

Congressional Black Caucus Formed in 1971 by black representatives to develop legislative strategies to deal with the concerns of African Americans.

Free South Africa Movement This offshoot of Randall Robinson's lobbying group Trans-Africa spearheaded the protest campaign to enact U.S. sanctions against South Africa's apartheid regime.

Nation of Islam Following the death of Elijah Muhammad in 1975, Louis Farrakhan reconstituted this religious group under his leadership.

National Rainbow Coalition Formed in 1985, the Rainbow Coalition carried on the political effort begun the previous year in Jesse Jackson's initial presidential campaign.

between Coretta Scott King and Jesse Jackson as the Senate also overrode the veto. "We had won. We had turned the course of the most powerful country on earth," Robinson jubilantly recalled. During the next few years, worldwide enforcement of economic sanctions as well as continued protests within South Africa finally led to the dismantling of apartheid laws and, in 1990, the release of Mandela from prison.

The Popularization of Modern Black Feminism

Alice Walker was among several black writers who participated in the Free South Africa Movement, but she attracted far more attention with her Pulitzer Prize-winning novel, *The Color Purple* (1982), and the film based on the book. There were sharp differences of opinion among African Americans regarding Walker's views of relations between black men and black women. Just as Michele Wallace had endured fierce criticism for *Black Macho and the Myth of the Superwoman,* so Walker became the target of attacks for her book. Yet, while the influence of Wallace's book had been largely restricted to black feminists, Walker's best-selling novel reached a vast audience, and the film was one Hollywood's most popular dramas. "The attacks, many of them personal and painful, continued for many years, right alongside the praise, the prizes, the Oscar award nominations," Walker recalled.

The Color Purple Controversy

The Color Purple was a work of fiction rather than a political statement, but it expressed views increasingly popular among black women. Walker was a founder of the National Black Feminist Organization, but she preferred the term *womanist* to describe the qualities—"outrageous, audacious, courageous, or *willful* behavior"—she thought should unite black women. Growing

Alice Walker, author of the Pulitzer Prize-winning novel *The Color Purple* (1983). Many criticized Walker for portraying black men too harshly.

up in a sharecropper family in rural Georgia, Walker had withdrawn into the world of books after being temporarily blinded and scarred by a pellet from her brother's BB gun. After surgery removed the scar, she excelled in school, becoming class valedictorian. At Spelman College in the early 1960s, she participated in civil rights protests, ignoring college officials who thought protest inappropriate for women college students. Transferring to New York's Sarah Lawrence College and graduating in 1965, she went to Mississippi to register black voters.

Late in the 1960s, Walker decided to pursue a career as a writer. While teaching at Jackson State University, she was inspired by fellow instructor Margaret Walker, author of the poetry collection *For My People* (1942) and the epic slave narrative *Jubilee* (1966). Walker learned about her older colleague's difficult relationship with Richard Wright, author of *Native Son* (1940). She also learned about Zora Neale Hurston, who had broken new ground during the 1930s in her depictions of black women. As Walker pursued her own writing career, she revived interest in Hurston by publishing a reader of her works. Walker later remarked that "a people [should] not throw away their geniuses. . . . [I]t is our duty as artists and as witnesses for the future to collect them."

Like Hurston, Walker created female characters in the context of their relationships within black families and black communities, not of external black–white relations. In *The Color Purple,* her narrator, an uneducated southern black woman named Celie, is oppressed less by white racists than by her stepfather, who rapes her and takes away her children, and by her abusive husband, whom she calls, simply, Mister. As Celie internalizes the scorn inflicted on her by men, she finds solace in nurturing relationships with black women. Her sister-in-law Sophia sets an example by refusing to be dominated by her husband. Shug, Mister's free-spirited girlfriend, introduces Celie to the pleasures of sex. *The Color Purple* reveals the brutality of gender oppression and the indomitable spirit of a woman who endures and ultimately prevails. "If and when Celie rises to her rightful, earned place in society across the planet, the world will be a different place," Walker asserted after the publication of her novel.

Walker's career built on a foundation established by earlier black women writers, especially Hurston, and she benefited from a growing interest in books by African Americans. Even as black studies programs stimulated sales of books expressing black power militancy, the emergence of black women scholars and women's studies programs drew attention to black feminist writings. Maya Angelou's best-selling memoir *I Know Why the Caged Bird Sings* (1970), the story of her struggle to find her voice (she became mute upon being raped as a child) was widely studied as a metaphor for the struggle of all women to liberate themselves. While an editor at Random House, Toni Morrison encouraged black activists such as Angela Davis and Muhammad Ali to write accounts of their lives. Morrison then launched her own distinguished literary career with *The Bluest Eye* (1970), the poignant story of a black girl who seeks love and acceptance by desiring to be blond and blue-eyed. Morrison later produced other critically applauded and widely read works, including *Song of Solomon* (1975) and her masterpiece, *Beloved* (1987), a historical novel about a black woman who kills her children rather than allow them to be returned to slavery. Gloria Naylor's *Women of Brewster Place* (1982) depicted the experiences of seven diverse black women living in decaying rented houses on a walled-off street of an urban neighborhood. Ntozake Shange introduced black feminist ideas to Broadway audiences in her hit play *For Colored Girls Who Have Considered Suicide When the Rainbow Is Enuf* (1975). Poets Audre Lorde, Sonia Sanchez, and June Jordan also blended militant feminist advocacy with black women's perspectives on male–female relations.

Like Walker, many of these black women writers had participated in the black struggles of the 1960s. Angelou was the northern coordinator of SCLC. Lorde taught at Mississippi's Tougaloo College during the Black Power era. Sanchez's early works, such as *We a BaddDDD People* (1970), reflected the influence of Malcolm X and the Black Arts movement. Despite their activism, their criticisms of the sexism of black males made them vulnerable to charges of racial disloyalty. In the late 1970s a more radical perspective was expressed by black lesbian feminists in the Combahee River Collective: "We realize that the liberation of all oppressed peoples necessitates the destruction of the political-economic systems of capitalism and imperialism as well as patriarchy."

Because of her prominence as an author and political activist, Walker bore the brunt of antifeminist attacks. Her decision to allow Steven Spielberg, a white director, to bring her book to the screen even prevented some from seeing the film as a Hollywood breakthrough in the depiction of African Americans. Since the early 1970s, blaxploitation films had portrayed black men as action figures in revenge fantasies, and comedies had also been built on stereotypes. In contrast, black actors in *The Color Purple* were able to display a full range of talents. Stand-up comic Whoopi Goldberg won acclaim for her lead role, as did Margaret Avery (Shug), Oprah Winfrey (Sophia), and Danny Glover (Mister). But despite eleven Academy Award nominations—a record for a picture with a mainly black cast—*The Color Purple* won no Academy Awards.

Race and Popular Culture

Walker attracted controversy because she was washing dirty linen in public—that is, making white people aware of conflicts among African Americans. Her dilemma was like that of earlier black writers: how to depict African Americans accurately but also positively so as to refute rather than inflame white racial prejudices. Langston Hughes, Zora Neale Hurston, Richard Wright, and James Baldwin had each addressed this dilemma as they examined previously ignored facets of black life. Even though *The Color Purple* reached a large multiracial audience and Walker's feminist or "womanist" views gained increasing acceptance, its influence seemed limited.

Most popular television shows and films of the 1980s, for example, showed little evidence of sensitivity in their treatment of black themes. Instead, racial issues were treated only lightly, with humor, if at all. On television, *The Jeffersons*, a spin-off of the earlier hit *All in the Family*, explored the comic possibilities of placing black people in a white-dominated racial environment. Variations of this genre included *Diff'rent Strokes* and *Webster* (black orphans adopted by white families), *Benson* (black butler of a white family), and *White Shadow* (black basketball players and their white coach). *The Cosby Show*, the television hit starring and produced by Bill Cosby, departed from this genre by featuring a black family, though the upper middle-class milieu of the Huxtables was enjoyed by only a tiny proportion of African Americans. Cosby, who had earned a doctorate studying the impact of mass media on racial attitudes, became an influential critic of racial stereotyping.

Hollywood films similarly featured formulaic black characters who lacked ties to black communities and adjusted uneasily (and often comically) to life among white people. After *The Color Purple*, Whoopi Goldberg went on to a successful film career playing black characters in largely white settings, winning a supporting actor Oscar for her role in *Ghost* (1990). In a variation of this theme, veteran actor Morgan Freeman's career received a boost when he played a longtime chauffeur who becomes friends with the rich white woman he drives around. *Driving Miss Daisy* (1989) won the Oscar for best picture, and Freeman, who also played a featured role in *Glory*, was able to move from supporting roles to major roles paired with leading white actors. He would later receive an Oscar for his supporting role in *Million Dollar Baby* (2004).

By far the most popular black film star of the 1980s was comic Eddie Murphy, who capitalized on the black–white cultural clash formula in *Trading Places* (1983) and two enormously profitable *Beverly Hills Cop* films (1984,

1987). In these action-comedies, Murphy played a stereotypically hip black man interacting with and gradually winning the friendship of unhip white characters. Like other black actors who achieved stardom in this period, Murphy demonstrated that a black film star could appeal to white audiences while also remaining distinctively black, so long as he remained humorous rather than threatening. "I'm not angry," Murphy told a reporter. "If somebody white called me 'nigger' on the street, I just laughed." Murphy's stardom prompted other films pairing black actors with white counterparts. After *The Color Purple,* Danny Glover starred in a series of highly popular *Lethal Weapon* movies with white actor Mel Gibson.

A few films did make serious attempts to illuminate African American life and history, most made on smaller budgets than action films and benefiting from the eagerness of black actors to take meaningful roles. These included *A Soldier's Story* (1984), based on Charles Fuller's Pulitzer Prize-winning World War II drama; *Cry Freedom* (1987), based on the life of South African freedom fighter Steve Bantu Biko; and *Glory* (1989), depicting the heroism of black soldiers in the Civil War battle at Fort Wagner. Denzel Washington, who appeared in these films and won an Academy Award for his supporting role in *Glory,* emerged as the highest-paid black film star since Sidney Poitier's heyday in the 1960s. Like Poitier, Washington appealed to white as well as black filmgoers, usually playing characters who kept a tight rein on their anger and sexuality while succeeding through diplomacy and discipline.

While most black actors made do with the limited range of Hollywood roles, film director Spike Lee demonstrated the possibilities for significant African American films outside the studio system. Lee confronted important issues in his early feature films: feminism in *She's Got to Have It* (1986), color prejudices among African Americans in *School Daze* (1988), urban racial violence in *Do the Right Thing* (1989), the declining popularity of jazz in *Mo' Better Blues* (1990), and interracial sex in *Jungle Fever* (1991). When Lee directed an epic film biography of Malcolm X, he overcame the reluctance of Hollywood producers to provide an adequate budget by appealing to wealthy black entertainers such as Bill Cosby, Oprah Winfrey, Tracy Chapman, and Janet Jackson as well as sports stars Magic Johnson and Michael Jordan. Starring Denzel Washington, *Malcolm X* (1991) was a sympathetic portrait that built on the revival of popular interest in the once controversial black nationalist leader.

While Lee broke new ground in filmmaking, August Wilson's plays captured the attention of audiences as had no black dramatist since Lorraine Hansberry's *Raisin in the Sun* (1958). Wilson's *Fences* (1987), set during the 1950s in the Pittsburgh ghetto known as The Hill, where Wilson had grown up, was widely applauded for its sensitive portrayal of African American family relationships and its accurate rendering of black dialogue. The play, which won the Pulitzer Prize, was one of a series of dramas by Wilson that depicted African American life in each decade of the twentieth century. His *Piano Lesson* (1989) also won the Pulitzer Prize.

Hip Hop and Gangsta Rap

Alice Walker's views contrasted sharply with the sometimes degrading images of women conveyed in the lyrics of rap or hip hop music, another emerging black cultural trend of the 1980s. While black feminist writings found an audience primarily among middle-class women, hip hop gained enormous popularity among poor and working-class African Americans in large cities. The roots of hip hop could be traced to several sources: the Black Power era's Gil Scott-Heron and the Last Poets, funk musicians of the 1970s, urban disc jockeys who developed techniques of mixing records on two turntables, and self-taught poets able to produce rhymes to accompany musical elements sampled from previous recordings. In contrast to the commercialized disco music of the 1970s, hip hop music (often referred to as rap), did not require elaborate instrumentation or formal music training. Rather than romantic ballads, the new style featured brashly aggressive expressions of male desire—only a few female rappers, such as Salt-N-Pepa and Sista Souljah, achieved success during the 1980s. Rap lyrics, which included frequent use of obscenities, reflected the growing isolation and alienation of poor black inner-city residents.

Since the emergence of rock 'n' roll in the 1950s, music styles popular among young people had faced criticism from worried parents. Thus, it was hardly surprising that rap music became highly popular as well as controversial. While some political leaders suggested that rap lyrics should be censored so they would not corrupt young people, many fans of the music valued its blunt honesty and willingness to address social and political issues. The group Public Enemy epitomized this political style of rap in its album *It Takes a Nation of Millions to Hold Us Back* (1988), which included the song "Fight the Power," featured in Spike Lee's *Do the Right Thing*. Proclaiming the importance of rap in black American culture, Public Enemy's lead singer, Chuck D., referred to it as the African American CNN (Cable News Network).

Alongside the rise of political rap came gangsta rap, which attempted to depict an outlaw lifestyle of sex, drugs, and violence in inner-city America. In 1988, the first major album of gangsta rap—*Straight Outta Compton* by N.W.A. (Niggaz With Attitude)—generated intense controversy for its violent imagery, drawing protests from several organizations and a probe by the FBI. But attempts to censor gangsta rap only served to publicize the music and make it more attractive to both black and white youths.

Racial Progress and Internal Tensions

Jesse Jackson's second presidential campaign was more successful than his first, yet it also exposed growing divisions among African Americans. While Jackson continued to encourage African Americans to register to vote, he also faced criticism of his "rainbow strategy," designed to build a multiracial coalition. In 1988 Jackson won seven primaries and attracted twice as many voters as he had in 1984, but when he arrived at the Democratic National Convention in Atlanta he found that party leaders believed the party had to distance itself from him to win the election. Although Jackson delivered a powerful speech that drew as much attention as Michael Dukakis's acceptance address, he was still somewhat of an outsider. He dutifully agreed to campaign on behalf of Dukakis, though the Massachusetts governor exhibited no passion for the social justice issues that were the foundation of Jackson's appeal. Rather than seeking to mobilize the discontented Jackson voters, Dukakis aimed to attract Reagan Democrats—former Democrats who had deserted to the Republicans.

As in 1984, the Democratic candidate failed to offer tangible concessions in return for Jackson's support, and that failure undermined black support for Jackson. Events outside the convention hall demonstrated how difficult it would be for Jackson to remain both a militant spokesman for the discontented and a loyal party supporter. At a rally in Atlanta, for example, Nation of Islam Minister Louis Farrakhan claimed that the hopes of black people were being "dashed with the disrespect toward Reverend Jackson by the leaders of the Democratic Party."

In the November election Republican George Bush, Reagan's vice president, soundly defeated Dukakis, in part by successfully labeling Dukakis as a tax-and-spend liberal who was also soft on criminals. A key element of Bush's campaign was a television ad featuring Willie Horton, a black convicted murderer in Massachusetts who had committed another murder and raped a woman while released on a furlough from prison. Although Dukakis had not created Massachusetts's prison furlough program, he had defended it as a way of preparing prisoners for eventual parole. The Horton ad, which ran repeatedly on television in closely contested states, disturbed many African Americans for its apparent incitement of white racial prejudice—reminiscent of the attacks against black militancy that had been part of Richard Nixon's Southern Strategy two decades earlier.

Jackson emerged from the election with his future in doubt. He had initially seen his candidacy as a means of gaining concessions on racial issues— "respect," he sometimes put it—from the Democratic Party, but now party leaders believed that concessions to Jackson would weaken the party's ability to attract white support. Concluding that Dukakis's defeat resulted from his liberal reputation, they determined that the party should veer away from the Lyndon Johnson tradition of civil rights reform. After the Democrats' third consecutive presidential defeat, many African Americans were starting to look for alternative ways to achieve racial goals.

Black neoconservatives of the 1980s argued that affirmative action and other racial preference programs were no longer necessary. In fact, black Americans continued to enter the middle class in large numbers. Whereas in 1940 hardly more than one in twenty black men and women held middle-class occupations, by 1990 nearly one in three black men and nearly three of every five black women worked in white-collar jobs. But poverty remained the lot of many undereducated African Americans, the percentage of black children with unmarried mothers jumped significantly, and the chance of a black child to be raised in a household without a father was three times as great as in white families. These facts indicated that the nation was still plagued by racial problems. The conservative politics of the Reagan and Bush administrations did little to address these problems, and some Great Society programs continued to be dismantled.

But even as conservative policies chipped away at antipoverty programs, individual African Americans continued to excel. Douglas Wilder of Virginia became the nation's first elected African American governor. Only months after Nelson Mandela's release from prison, President Bush appointed Colin Powell head of the Joint Chiefs of Staff, the first African American to occupy the highest military office in the armed services. Eighteen months later Powell played a pivotal role in overseeing Operation Desert Storm, the Persian Gulf War precipitated by an Iraqi invasion of Kuwait. Even though Jesse Jackson traveled to Iraq to negotiate the release of hundreds of hostages, Colin Powell, seen nightly on television, emerged from the Gulf War as the preeminent African American figure on the national political scene.

Anita Hill versus Clarence Thomas

"For years I had spent considerable time and effort convincing myself that what happened to me no longer mattered," Anita Hill remembered thinking when she heard in 1991 that Bush had nominated her former boss, Clarence Thomas, to the Supreme Court. Thomas's nomination to the seat once held by Justice Thurgood Marshall had already drawn criticism from many civil rights and feminist groups, who strongly disagreed with the nominee's conservative views on affirmative action. But Hill, a law professor at the University of Oklahoma, had more personal reasons for questioning Thomas's suitability. Having worked for Thomas a decade earlier when both served in the Reagan administration, she had become disturbed by Thomas's sexual banter, which included, according to later testimony, vivid descriptions of pornography. Hill never lodged a sexual harassment complaint against Thomas during the three years she worked with him; as she noted, "I do not believe that in the early 1980s I lived and worked in a society, either in Washington or in Tulsa, that would have supported my right to raise a claim of harassment against the head of the EEOC." But the prospect of Thomas on the Supreme Court convinced Hill to speak up. "For the first time I was forced to consider that it *did* matter—that the behavior was not only an offense to me but unfitting for someone who would sit on the Supreme Court," she later wrote.

Hill's decision to testify against Thomas set off a contentious national debate that touched on issues of gender and race. For several weeks in the fall of 1991, the nationally televised Thomas confirmation hearings captured the nation's attention. Hill's claim of sexual harassment forced African Americans to take sides in a dispute between a black man and a black woman, with a seat on the Supreme Court at stake. Hill did not consider herself a black feminist, but her testimony directed the glare of publicity on issues that had long concerned feminists, such as inequality and sexual

Anita Hill's testimony did not prevent Clarence Thomas's appointment to the U.S. Supreme Court, but it did spark an increase in political activity among women.

harassment in the workplace. Yet most Americans did not, at the time, think of sexual harassment in the workplace as a major social problem, particularly for professional women such as Hill. Even the term *sexual harassment* did not enter common usage until the 1980s. So Hill realized that testifying against Thomas would make her a target of harsh criticism, even from African Americans who saw her as damaging the reputation of a successful black man. While feminists and others rallied to her defense, she faced a storm of controversy. No member of the Senate Judiciary Committee publicly supported her. Thomas denied her charges, insisting he was a victim of a "high-tech lynching." He was confirmed by a vote of 52–48.

The Hill-Thomas hearings marked the convergence of cultural and political trends in the early 1990s. Two decades earlier, black feminism had been a small-scale movement with little political impact that spread its ideas largely through the writings of black women authors such as Alice Walker and Michele Wallace. Black male leaders such as Andrew Young and Jesse Jackson still dominated African American politics, although the emergence of female political leaders like Shirley Chisholm and Barbara Jordan revealed an accelerating trend. By the early 1990s, although some feminist ideas had been accepted, even commonplace, the controversy over *The Color Purple* and the Hill-Thomas hearing demonstrated the volatility of male–female relations among African Americans.

Though Anita Hill's testimony did not prevent Thomas's appointment to the Supreme Court, it did stimulate broader awareness of the problem of sexual harassment. It also helped mobilize women activists on behalf of political candidates who responded to feminist concerns. Eleanor Holmes Norton, a pioneering black feminist who was the District of Columbia's nonvoting representative in Congress, later argued that Hill, though not a politician, had "affected the political process." She credited Hill for the upsurge in political activity among women that helped elect a record number of women to national office in 1992, often called the "year of the woman" in American politics.

Conclusion

The transition from the activism of the 1960s to the conservatism of the Reagan-Bush era was challenging for many African Americans. The culmination of the long effort to pass civil rights legislation had been followed by a period of debate over the future direction of African American politics. Black neoconservatives argued that these reforms offered a sufficient basis for African American individual advancement, but Jesse Jackson succeeded in mobilizing widespread support for his 1984 and 1988 presidential campaigns by insisting that more government action was needed to ensure that the equal opportunity ideal became a reality. Although Reagan's conservatism prevailed in national politics during the 1980s, African Americans who disagreed with this trend were able to protect previous civil rights gains and even achieve significant victories. The King birthday legislation recognized the historical importance of the civil rights leader as the principal symbol of the modern African American freedom struggle. The Free South Africa Campaign marked the culmination of long-standing efforts by African Americans and Africans to aid one another's freedom struggles. The emergence of influential black writers and a black feminist (or womanist) movement helped black women gain the full benefit of previous civil rights struggles.

To be sure, even as some African Americans achieved breakthroughs in the 1980s, many others experienced new hardships as a result of widespread poverty and the deterioration of urban centers—problems that became the focus of subsequent black struggles. At the beginning of the 1990s, young black Americans born after the era of civil rights reforms began to take responsibility for ensuring that an earlier generation's racial advances were protected and perhaps even extended in new directions.

Questions for Review and Reflection

1. How did the African American freedom struggle affect subsequent controversies about general differences among African Americans? What was the relationship between black feminism/womanism and the white feminist movement?

2. How did the transition from the activism of the 1960s to the conservatism of the Reagan-Bush era affect African American politicians?

3. Compare and contrast tactics used in the Free South Africa movement with the African American Freedom struggle.

4. In what ways do trends in American popular culture reflect and affect trends in African American life?

5. What was the significance of the Hill-Thomas hearings?

CHAPTER 21

Continuing Struggles over Rights and Identity, 1992–2004

Oprah Winfrey and Social Healing

On May 4, 1992, just days after a major Los Angeles riot, Oprah Winfrey took her Chicago-based nationally syndicated television program to Los Angeles for a discussion of the riot and its causes. Following on the acquittal of policemen who had beaten black motorist Rodney King, the violence had taken more than fifty lives and resulted in more than $1 billion in property damage. "Over the last week I have, just like many of you, felt a sense of shock . . . of outrage and some tears, as people died," Winfrey explained to the Los Angeles residents invited to participate in the first of two telecasts. "What will be written into history books for our children and our grandchildren to read, the beating of Rodney King, came into our living rooms and smacked us in the face, and now we must, we *must,* listen to each other."

News coverage of the Los Angeles riot was extensive, but Winfrey's decision to address the issue reflected her confidence that she would be taken seriously and have a social impact. She had often been underestimated—seen simply as an engaging television personality able to connect emotionally with audiences and interviewees. A former teen beauty pageant winner, Winfrey had graduated from Tennessee State University with a major in speech and drama. When she entered the field of broadcast news in the mid-1970s, there

1992	An all-white jury acquits police officers involved in the beating of motorist Rodney King, sparking a three-day uprising in Los Angeles that results in more than fifty deaths.
	With overwhelming support from black voters, Bill Clinton is elected president.
	Illinois Democrat Carol Moseley Braun becomes the first African American woman elected to the U.S. Senate.
	Spike Lee's epic motion picture biography *Malcolm X* opens nationwide.
1993	In *Shaw* v. *Reno* the Supreme Court rules against a North Carolina redistricting plan that resulted in majority black congressional districts.
	Toni Morrison, author of *Beloved* and other acclaimed novels, wins the Nobel Prize for literature.
1994	The white supremacist Byron de la Beckwith receives life sentence for the 1963 murder of NAACP official Medgar Evers.
	Nelson Mandela becomes South Africa's first black president.
1995	Not guilty verdict in O. J. Simpson trial exposes continuing black–white divisions.
	The Million Man March, initiated by Louis Farrakhan, is held in Washington, DC.
1996	President Clinton signs a major welfare reform act calling for work requirements and time limits for recipients of government assistance.
1997	Clinton establishes Commission on Race Relations, chaired by the historian John Hope Franklin.
	The Haitian immigrant Abner Louima is tortured by a Brooklyn police officer, who is subsequently convicted of assault.
	Lee P. Brown is elected the first African American mayor of Houston.
1998	James Byrd, Jr., a black resident of Jasper, Texas, is dragged to death behind a pickup truck driven by white men.
2000	In a disputed election ultimately decided by a 5–4 Supreme Court decision, Republican George W. Bush prevails, though more than 90 percent of black voters supported Democrat Al Gore.
2001	Former military Chief of Staff Colin Powell is confirmed as secretary of state, and former Stanford provost Condoleezza Rice becomes President Bush's national security advisor.
2003	Supreme Court rulings in two Michigan affirmative action cases confirm racial diversity as a goal but invalidate point systems as the means.
2004	Illinois Democrat Barak Obama wins election to the U.S. Senate.

were few African American television reporters. She became Nashville's first black anchor, hosted a morning talk show in Baltimore, and then in the mid-1980s attracted a national audience as host of a Chicago talk show. She won many awards, including multiple Emmys, and became the youngest person ever selected as Broadcaster of the Year by the International Radio and Television Society.

Reading Alice Walker's *The Color Purple* provided inspiration for Winfrey's career choices. A victim of childhood sexual abuse, she identified with Celie's struggle to overcome oppression. She wept after finishing the book. "Oh, my God, this is my story!" she recalled. "Somebody knows how I felt." She auditioned for a part in the film based on Walker's book, despite lacking experience as a professional actor. Her vivid portrayal of Sophie won her an Academy Award nomination for best performance in a supporting role. Winfrey also decided to gain control over her television show by establishing her own company, Harpo Productions. As executive producer of the "Oprah Winfrey Show," she soon became an enormously wealthy and influential figure in the entertainment industry. She expanded her audience through involvement in serious films and television dramas. After gaining acclaim in *The Color Purple,* she accepted a challenging role in a film version of Richard Wright's *Native Son* (1986) and then produced and starred in a television miniseries, "The Women of Brewster Place" (1989), based on Gloria Naylor's novel. She would later produce and star in the feature film *Beloved* (1998), based on Toni Morrison's prize-winning novel, and would produce a Broadway musical version of *The Color Purple,* which opened in 2005.

But even these accomplishments did not begin to suggest the extent of Winfrey's influence. Although she usually avoided partisan involvement with political parties or candidates, viewers of her show learned to expect enlightenment about social issues as well as entertainment. Known to millions simply as Oprah, she set herself apart from other talk show hosts by moving beyond banter about weight loss and fashions to deeper discussions about major social problems, including racial conflict and child abuse. When civil rights advocates staged marches into Georgia's all-white Forsythe County in the 1980s, Winfrey took her show there to interview residents as well as protesters. Her moving congressional testimony on behalf of the National Child Protection Act of 1993 led some to call it "the Oprah bill." Her readiness to risk her own money and reputation on controversial African American films such as *Beloved* won her wide respect, as did her willingness to devote a portion of her wealth to philanthropic causes. Her influence expanded even more as a result of the phenomenally successful Oprah's Book Club, a feature of her television program that transformed her literary selections into immediate best sellers.

Winfrey's two television shows discussing the Los Angeles riot reflected her long-standing desire to use her exceptional success as an entertainer and producer to achieve broader goals. She conceded that a television program could not solve racial problems but insisted that conversation was a crucial step toward social healing: "People who had never talked to each other for years came together . . . and did what should have been done a long time ago. They listened to each other." In less sure hands, the Los Angeles broadcasts might have exacerbated resentment, but Winfrey's interviewing skills encouraged residents to understand the perspectives of others. After one audience member explained how pent-up resentment led him to join in looting, a black business owner pointed out that he had to lay off employees of his looted restaurant. Winfrey was able to draw attention to long-standing grievances, such as the killing of a fifteen-year-old black youngster by a Korean shop owner and the subsequent decision of a judge to release the convicted killer on probation. But she also encouraged a Korean immigrant to explain the dangers of operating a business in a poor black neighborhood. A black Vietnam veteran described being shot by another black person while trying to stop looting of a Korean-owned store.

Through it all, Winfrey managed to keep the discussion civil without suppressing emotions. She empathized with audience members without taking sides. "I don't pretend to know a whole lot about the world," she reflected at the end of the discussion. "I do know that 'ye shall know the truth and the truth shall set you free.' And I'm hoping that everything that's been said here today . . . we will take into our hearts and be willing in our own selves to make a difference." Afterward, she was convinced she had made a difference. "It was what television should do," Winfrey said. "It was utilizing the power of media for the good. You can't do better than that, I think."

Oprah Winfrey's enormous wealth and influence made her exceptional among black Americans at the end of the twentieth century. Her example nonetheless reveals the growing diversity of African American life following the civil rights struggles of the 1960s and the rise of black feminism in the 1970s and 1980s. While Winfrey's success was indicative of new opportunities available to African Americans by the 1990s, the Los Angeles riot was a chastening reminder that serious racial and economic problems remained unsolved. The gulf between Winfrey and the Los Angeles rioters, some of whom were Latino rather than black, was brought home during the telecast. "Listen, Oprah, when you leave your show, you go to a lavish home," an audience member told her. "We go home to empty refrigerators, you know, crying kids, no diapers, no jobs." Black icons of success such as Winfrey, basketball superstar and product endorser Michael Jordan, and military leader and future Secretary of State Colin Powell provided highly visible indications that long-standing racial barriers had been overcome. But other highly publicized black icons—police brutality victim Rodney King, Nation of Islam leader Louis Farrakhan, rap artist and actor Tupac Shakur—symbolized class divisions among African Americans and the persistence of racial antagonism.

African American voters elected ever-increasing numbers of black public officials, including Carol Moseley Braun as the first African American woman elected to the U.S. Senate, and continued to favor Democratic candidates, providing Bill Clinton's margin of victory in the 1992 presidential race. But the widespread support for Farrakhan's call for a Million Man March in 1995 revealed considerable disenchantment with conventional electoral politics and established civil rights leaders. Centuries of collective struggle against slavery and racial discrimination had produced distinctive African American institutions, forged a common racial identity, and provided inspiration for other freedom struggles throughout the world. But the gains of struggle were unevenly shared, and racial resentment remained evident in many black communities.

Having united to overcome slavery and the Jim Crow system, African Americans faced the challenge of determining whether they had a common destiny in the era following the major civil rights reforms of the 1960s. By the early twenty-first century, earlier African American freedom struggles were consigned to history—implanted in memories, recorded in history books, studied in college classes, celebrated in memorials and documentaries. To be sure, some black Americans still protested against racial injustices and on behalf of civil rights, but the issues were no longer as clearly framed as in the days when racism was openly expressed and backed by the brutal force of police dogs and fire hoses. African Americans still faced "glass ceilings" limiting occupational opportunities and "driving-while-black" encounters with police, but these indications of the continuing significance of race also reflected the growing importance of class, gender, and ethnicity as determinants of American racial relations. As civil rights progress produced new racial dilemmas, African Americans turned to each other to discuss enduring questions: How do we define ourselves? What experiences and history do we share? What is our place in a changing nation and world?

A New Day for African Americans?

During the inauguration ceremony of President William Jefferson Clinton on January 20, 1993, Maya Angelou stepped to the microphone to read a poem she had written. Angelou had achieved much in the sixty-four years since she was born in the black ghetto of St. Louis. Her autobiographical *I Know Why the Caged Bird Sings* (1970) told of her struggle to overcome the trauma of being raped at age seven. By the late 1950s, she had achieved success as a singer, dancer, actor, and writer. She accepted the invitation of Martin Luther King, Jr., to head the Southern Christian Leader Conference's northern fund-raising operations, then left to become a journalist in Egypt and Ghana. On returning to the United States, she published poetry and gained renown as a teacher (with a lifetime appointment at Wake Forest University) and actor (in the "Roots" television series). She was a mentor and an inspiration for Oprah Winfrey. But her spirited reading of "On the Pulse of the Morning" at Clinton's inauguration greatly expanded her fame and influence. Her poem, later published as a bestselling book, was both patriotic and provocative, referring to the "wretched pain" of American history for the diverse racial and cultural groups that "arrived on a nightmare praying for a dream." But Angelou also expressed optimism that the nation could bravely confront its past and then move beyond

Maya Angelou read the poem "On the Pulse of the Morning" during Bill Clinton's presidential inauguration.

it: "Lift up your eyes upon/This day break for you/Give birth again to the dream."

Racial Dilemmas of the Clinton Presidency

Clinton's decision to invite a black poet to speak at his inauguration was unprecedented and a reflection of his desire to reach out to African Americans. He was the first Democrat to hold the office since Jimmy Carter. Like Carter, he received the support of only a minority of white voters, and his margin of victory was due to his overwhelming black support. Yet, also like Carter and other Democratic presidents since Franklin D. Roosevelt, Clinton struggled to balance his appeal for black support against the risk of losing white support. As a youngster in Arkansas during the 1950s, he had been dismayed by the rioting against black students seeking to attend Little Rock's Central High School (as president, Clinton would present the Little Rock Nine with Congressional Gold Medals). He had opposed the Vietnam War and, after attending Yale Law School, campaigned for liberal Democrat George McGovern in 1972. When launching his own political career, however, he moderated his views and was sufficiently pragmatic to be elected to six terms as governor of Arkansas. By the early 1990s, he became the favored presidential candidate of Democratic Party leaders who believed the party had to break with the liberalism of Lyndon Johnson to defeat George Bush in 1992. Campaigning for president as a New Democrat, Clinton made a point of speaking to Jesse Jackson's Rainbow Coalition, but he used the occasion to publicly chastise rap singer Sista Souljah for suggesting that "blacks take a week and kill white people" in retaliation for racist attacks by whites. Although Clinton promised his administration would "look like America," he refused to support racial quotas.

Thus, from the start of his presidency, Clinton was sympathetic to black concerns yet reluctant to take controversial stands on racial issues. During his two terms in office, he became the first president to appoint African Americans as secretaries of commerce (Ron Brown), agriculture (Mike Espy), energy (Hazel O'Leary), veterans' affairs (Jesse Brown), labor (Alexis Herman), and transportation (Rodney Slater). He also appointed the black endocrinologist Jocelyn Elders surgeon general and chose the historian Mary Frances Berry to resume her role as chair of the Civil Rights Commission. Overall, Clinton appointed more African Americans to high-level posts than any other president. Of symbolic importance, he signed the 1994 King Holiday and Service Act—legislation cosponsored by Atlanta congressional representative John Lewis—designed to make the King Holiday a national day for public service. At a personal level, he appeared comfortable in predominantly black settings such as black churches. Clinton also scored points when he played saxophone on a popular late-night television show hosted by black entertainer Arsenio Hall. Morrison later jested that Clinton was the nation's first black president. He seemed to reflect a prevailing national consensus that black–white relations were no longer as contentious as they had been.

Yet, if the civil rights *movement* seemed to be part of history, civil rights *issues* had not gone away. For every indication of racial progress, a contrasting sign showed that racism remained strong. The Rodney King beating and the Los Angeles riot of 1992 were recent memories when Clinton took office. Affirmative action programs remained controversial, a continuing source of division in American politics. Even many relatively affluent African Americans felt civil rights gains were not secure. *The Rage of a Privileged Class* (1993) by the black journalist Ellis Cose revealed new kinds of frustrations and racial resentments that came with expanding job opportunities. Similarly, Cornel West's best-selling *Race Matters* (1993) decried "the widespread mistreatment of black people, especially black men, by law enforcement agencies." West recalled being ignored by taxi drivers on the streets of New York. He acknowledged that the racial slights middle-class blacks faced were "dwarfed by those like Rodney King's beating or the abuse of black targets of the FBI's COINTELPRO efforts in the 1960s and 1970s," but nonetheless, "the memories cut like a merciless knife at my soul as I waited on that godforsaken corner."

As African Americans anxiously looked for indications of Clinton's racial policies, they also sought answers to broader questions: What did African Americans want from Clinton and the federal government? Beyond protecting previous civil rights goals, what was the black agenda at the end of the twentieth century? To what extent did race still matter in American society?

The Lani Guinier Affair

Clinton's failure to name someone with strong civil rights credentials as attorney general prompted criticism by civil rights leaders, but the first major racial controversy of his administration came from his selection of his Yale law school classmate Lani Guinier to head the Justice Department's Civil Rights Division. A black University of Pennsylvania law professor, Guinier was a noted scholar and activist in the field of civil rights law. In the 1980s, she headed the NAACP's voting rights program. As a law professor, she wrote that democratic ideals were often subverted by winner-take-all election systems that allowed majorities to exclude the views of minorities. She seemed poised to become the first black woman to head the civil rights division until conservative critics labeled her a "quota queen." They claimed she favored allotting political representation according to race, ignoring her broader intention, which was to achieve the ideal of representative government. As Guinier realized, American political innovations had often helped guarantee minority representation—such as the Senate, in which each state had two seats, regardless of population. She urged Clinton to let her explain her views in confirmation hearings, but he refused to let the nomination go forward, fearing a major Senate fight early in his administration.

Many African Americans criticized Clinton's capitulation, which contrasted with President George Bush's staunch support for controversial Supreme Court nominee Clarence Thomas. As pro-Guinier demonstrators marched outside the White House, Maryland representative Kweisi Mfume, chair of the Congressional Black Caucus, predicted that Clinton's action would cost him black support. Clinton's failure to defend Guinier revealed that he, like previous Democratic presidents, was reluctant to take political risks to reward black voters' support. Guinier saw Clinton's capitulation as "an unfortunate metaphor for the way race and racism are viewed in this society. We are being defined, we are being characterized, are being misrepresented by other people."

The importance of the issues Guinier raised became apparent soon after her nomination was withdrawn, when the Supreme Court announced an important ruling affecting black representation in Congress. In *Shaw* v. *Reno*, the Court invalidated an effort by North Carolina's Democratic-controlled legislature to redraw congressional district lines so one district would have a majority of black voters. In other states, redrawing of congressional districts after the 1990 census had resulted in the election of thirty-nine black congressional representatives as compared to only twenty-four two years earlier. Proponents of the redistricting argued that American political parties often redrew districts for partisan purposes following the census. But, in a 5–4 decision, the Supreme Court ruled in 1993 that the North Carolina plan was unconstitutional because it was guided by racial considerations. Contention over redistricting continued during the 1990s and was only partly resolved when the Supreme Court ruled in 2001, in *Easley* v. *Cromartie*, that race could be considered in districting as long as it was not the "dominant and controlling" consideration.

The redistricting controversy revealed the complexity of questions facing African Americans as they exercised their hard-won civil rights. Were they better off when black voters were concentrated in congressional districts rather than dispersed in predominantly white districts? Most civil rights leaders and black elected officials believed black-majority districts were necessary as long as most white voters were reluctant to vote for black candidates or even for white candidates with substantial black support. As former SNCC leader and Georgia congressional representative John Lewis noted, the civil rights movement's goal was "to move beyond race," but, he added, "We are not there yet."

Ending Welfare and Continuing Poverty

"We should be ashamed we haven't made more progress in this economy," complained Marion Wright Edelman, head of the Children's Defense Fund. "It is totally unacceptable that with this much prosperity we have millions of uninsured children." The persistence of widespread poverty among African Americans indicated that the civil rights reforms of the 1960s had benefited some African Americans but not others. A Census Bureau report showed that the poverty rate for African Americans was 33 percent in 1993, yet the Democratic Party under Clinton was no longer committed to Lyndon Johnson's ambitious War on Poverty and even middle-class African Americans showed little concern about the issue that had once spurred King's Poor People's Campaign. Amid the rapid economic growth of the 1980s and 1990s, Edelman, the former Atlanta sit-in protester and civil rights lawyer who founded the Children's Defense Fund, was among the few leaders to draw attention to the increasing numbers of black children being raised in poverty.

During his first term as president, after his ambitious universal health care initiative failed to gain congressional support, Clinton concentrated on ending deficit spending by the federal government rather than launching new domestic reforms. Trying to reverse conservative gains in the 1994 midterm elections that left Republicans in control of both houses of Congress, his strategy was to show that Democrats were actually more fiscally responsible than Republicans. He also tried to follow through on his campaign promise to "end welfare as we know it." Republicans had long exploited widespread resentment of "welfare mothers" by depicting them as irresponsible, unwed black women raising their children at taxpayer expense. But Clinton preempted their efforts to force drastic cuts in welfare spending with a compromise proposal. The Personal Responsibility and Work Opportunity Reconciliation Act, passed in 1996, required states to revise their programs so that adult welfare recipients would have to find work within two years; after five years, even if they had not found work, government assistance would end.

In the short term, the consequences of this welfare reform act were neither as dire as critics predicted nor as positive as proponents hoped. Many welfare recipients were able to find work because the job market expanded during the late 1990s. During Clinton's presidency, the economy grew significantly; unemployment dropped from 7.2 percent to 5.5 percent; and American businesses established 10 million new jobs. Clinton was also able to mitigate some of the harsher aspects of the law by securing health care coverage for children of poor people and wage supplements for many low-wage workers.

A Census Bureau report showed that the poverty rate for African Americans had fallen by 2000 to an all-time low of 22 percent, from 33 percent in 1993 (although by 2004 the rate had risen back to 25 percent). The poverty rate for black children, however, was higher than for African Americans as a whole. In March 1999, the Secretary of Health and Human Services warned that though many welfare recipients had found work, their earnings typically remained below the poverty line and "most families exiting welfare continue to be poor."

Despite criticism from black leaders for his Guinier retreat and for his welfare reductions, Clinton maintained the support of most African Americans. Although he did not advocate new racial reforms, he also did not reverse the civil rights progress that had been made. He welcomed the transition to black-majority rule in South Africa, supporting the decision by the white government to hold free elections in 1994. His acceptance of the prospect that Nelson Mandela would be elected president of South Africa marked a clear reversal from Reagan's policy of "constructive engagement" with the apartheid regime. Clinton received the support of more than 90 percent of black voters when he won reelection in 1996.

Race and the Criminal Justice System

Although Rodney King never saw himself as a racial spokesperson, his video-taped beating by police in 1991 became a symbol of the troubled relationship between African Americans, especially those living in the nation's inner cities, and predominantly white police forces. Filmmaker Spike Lee included the

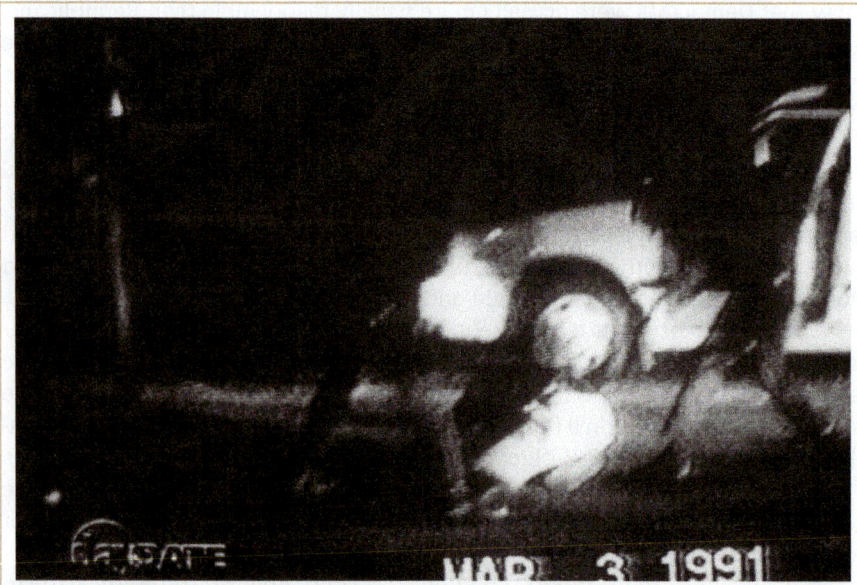

The beating of motorist Rodney King by Los Angeles police and the subsequent acquittal of several officers sparked riots across the city.

footage in the opening titles of his film *Malcolm X* (1992) and invited King to attend a premier screening. But Lee's linkage of Rodney King with Malcolm's political legacy obscured the complexities of the problems affecting urban black communities in the years since Malcolm's death. Although King was clearly a victim of police brutality, he had self-destructively contributed to the legal problems that marked his life. Twenty-five years old at the time of the beating, he had been arrested for assaulting his estranged wife and had served a prison term for robbery. Excessive drinking contributed to his occasional quick temper and obstinacy, and his run-ins with police and the legal system would continue in subsequent years. Still, the outrage among African Americans following King's assault was strengthened by the belief that it reflected a pattern of racial bias on the part of police and the criminal justice system in general. A jury later awarded King $3.8 million in compensatory damages for his injuries.

The O. J. Simpson Case

In the days after the beating, King's family contacted Johnnie Cochran, a lawyer with a reputation for winning cases against police accused of misconduct. A mix-up in Cochran's office prevented him from taking the case, but in 1994, he became the leader of the defense team in the most widely publicized trial of the century: the murder trial of former football star Orenthal James (widely known as O. J. or "the Juice") Simpson.

Even before Cochran agreed to represent Simpson, the case had drawn enormous public interest. Charged with murdering his ex-wife and her male friend, both of them white, Simpson had been a celebrity before becoming the nation's most famous criminal defendant. He had won the Heisman Trophy as the best college football player while attending the University of Southern California and set numerous records as a star running back in the National Football League. He had acquired still more wealth as a moderately successful actor (with a minor role in "Roots") and as spokesman for a rental car company. More than any other black athlete of his generation, he became a familiar, friendly face to Americans of all races. Because he had protected his public image by avoiding racial issues, Simpson's arrest was a shocking turn in a career that seemed to symbolize the ability of some African Americans to transcend racial barriers. Reporters from around the world covered the trial, and American television viewers saw live coverage of almost nine months of testimony—Simpson's was the longest criminal trial in California history.

Yet it was not Simpson's fame, nor even his guilt or innocence, that accounted for the historical importance of his trial. Instead, Cochran and other defense lawyers transformed the proceedings from a murder case involving a black celebrity into a public indictment of racist law enforcement. Cochran's background had prepared him both to provide effective legal advice and to put the case in a broader racial context. At the beginning of his career in the mid-1960s, he expressed admiration for Thurgood Marshall and often quoted King's statement that "injustice anywhere is a threat to justice everywhere." But he made his reputation as a no-holds-barred defense attorney. During the 1980s, in a series of highly publicized cases involving police misconduct, he won a settlement for the family of a black former college football star whose death in police custody was made to look like a suicide, and he won the highest jury award in the history of the city of Los Angeles when he represented a thirteen-year-old Latina who had been molested by a police officer. Cochran also got former Black Panther Geronimo ji Jaga Pratt released from a long prison term by exposing a key prosecution witness as a paid police informant.

These and similar cases convinced many black residents of Los Angeles of a pattern of police misconduct. A 1985 investigation of police abuse had concluded that "the issue of equitable law enforcement continues to be one of the contentious and serious problems for residents of South Central Los Angeles." In 1988, an erroneous tip prompted a police raid that terrorized residents of several apartment buildings and resulted in extensive property damage.

Despite this backdrop of police abuse and overzealous law enforcement, Cochran faced an uphill struggle in the Simpson case. Although there were no witnesses to the killings, prosecutors presented testimony that Simpson's ex-wife had previously called police to stop him from assaulting her. Police evidence also included a bloody glove found near Simpson's home. Cochran believed from experience, however, that Los Angeles police could not be relied upon to conduct an unbiased investigation involving a black man, and he suggested that physical evidence implicating Simpson could have been contaminated or planted by prejudiced police. He undermined the testimony of a white officer who had found the bloody glove by refuting his claim to have never used the term "nigger." The trial's most dramatic point came when Cochran asked Simpson to try on the glove. When Simpson had difficulty fitting his hand into the glove, Cochran planted doubt in jurors' minds: "If the glove don't fit, you must acquit," he said. The jury found Simpson not guilty. Later polls revealed that most African Americans agreed with the verdict, while most white Americans saw it as a miscarriage of justice. (A subsequent civil trial brought by the families of the victims resulted in a verdict against Simpson, who was assessed large monetary damages.)

The Simpson case raised large questions: Why did African Americans differ from other Americans in their reaction to the testimony? Did the verdict indicate that the predominantly black female jury sympathized more with the black male defendant than the white female victim? More generally, would the case matter in the long term? The Simpson trial had less effect on African Americans than had the Scottsboro cases of the 1930s, which produced important Supreme Court decisions: *Powell* v. *Alabama* (which ruled the Scottsboro defendants were denied legal counsel) and *Norris* v. *Alabama* (which ruled that black jurors could not be systematically excluded). Indeed, the Simpson trial reflected the changes that had occurred in the years since the Scottsboro trials. Rather than illiterate hobos being saved from execution (but not from prison) by a Communist-led legal effort and protest campaign, a black millionaire had been set free due to the efforts of a highly paid defense team led by a black attorney. Had class, therefore, become more important than race in determining how an African American defendant was treated by the criminal justice system?

The Prison System of Racial Control

"Mass incarceration is not a solution to unemployment, nor is it a solution to the vast array of social problems that are hidden away in a rapidly growing network of prisons and jail," Angela Davis insisted during the 1990s. Davis had herself been imprisoned during the 1970s, before she was acquitted on charges of aiding a failed attempt to free radical inmates. Though she returned to academic life, teaching at San Francisco State and the University of California, Santa Cruz, she never abandoned her concern about the injustices of the criminal justice system. "Most people commit crimes," she once remarked. "Some people are under much greater surveillance than others." Unlike Cochran's cases defending individual victims of police and prosecutorial misconduct, Davis raised a broader question: Why were African Americans and poor people in general more likely to be in prison? What should be done about the large number of African Americans and Latinos already incarcerated? While law-and-order advocates saw prisons as a way of reducing crime, Davis saw mass imprisonment as a substitute for dealing with social injustices. "Colored bodies constitute the main human raw material in this vast experiment to disappear the major social problems of our time," she insisted.

Davis's campaign against "the prison industrial complex" reflected both how much and how little had changed since the era of the Scottsboro cases. While the Simpson case demonstrated that a wealthy black man could put police and prosecutors on the defensive by forcing them to deny charges of racial bias in law enforcement, most black defendants did not have the advantage of Simpson's high-priced legal team. The publicity surrounding his trial had obscured less visible indications of racial bias in the criminal justice system. Studies conducted in the 1990s indicated that more than one in four black males in their twenties were in jail, on parole, or under some form of legal supervision. In some states, felons were barred from voting for the rest of their lives. Thus, more than a century after the end of slavery, a substantial proportion of African Americans were still not truly citizens nor legally free.

Moreover, since the late 1960s, law-and-order politicians had strengthened the hands of police, prompting increasing arrest and conviction rates in poor, predominantly black neighborhoods. Crackdowns on black militancy had sent another message: black rebelliousness would be harshly punished. The persistence of black poverty and gang turf wars associated with the explosion of drug usage (especially relatively cheap crack cocaine) also contributed to a rapid increase in the prison population. National political leaders responded to rising urban violence by calling for ever more forceful policing and longer prison sentences for crimes involving drugs or violence. Many states began imposing life terms for multiple convictions (often called "three strikes" laws), and federal laws imposed stiffer sentences for possession or use of crack cocaine, preferred by poor drug users, than for equivalent quantities of powdered cocaine, preferred by more affluent drug users.

Thus, despite civil rights gains, black Americans were still more likely than white Americans to be mistreated or treated more sternly by police, by prosecutors, and by the entire criminal justice system. Studies in the 1980s and 1990s revealed they were more likely to be stopped by police or arrested when stopped. While defenders of police pointed to the high incidence of criminal activity in poverty-stricken black communities, the practice of racial profiling was a concern to African Americans of every background. Even affluent black suburbanites who were uninvolved in criminal activity feared being stopped for "driving while black" by overzealous police officers.

The increased police surveillance of African Americans also increased the likelihood that African Americans engaged in criminal activity would be arrested and thereafter burdened with police records. Statistics indicated that black Americans charged with crimes were much more likely to be convicted. A study of nearly 700,000 California criminal cases during the 1980s revealed that white defendants were more likely to have their cases dismissed and charges dropped or to receive lighter sentences than were black defendants. In part because of their police records, black defendants convicted of crimes were more likely to serve long sentences or suffer the death penalty when convicted of capital crimes. Nationwide, capital punishment, which had been used with declining frequency during the 1960s in the United States and other advanced industrial nations, regained its popularity after the Supreme Court upheld its constitutionality in 1976. Critics of the death penalty pointed out that poor murder defendants unable to afford a lawyer were more likely to be executed than were more affluent defendants charged with similar crimes.

When Davis was imprisoned in the early 1970s, she was one of about 200,000 inmates held in local, state, and federal prisons. By 1990, the number of prisoners had grown to more than a million; by the early twenty-first century, there were more than two million inmates, according to Justice Department statistics. The total prison population of the United States was disproportionately large compared to that of other nations, and African Americans, especially young black men, were far more likely than other groups to be incarcerated.

In debates over the causes of these problems, conservatives held that strict law enforcement and harsh sentencing would reduce crime, while liberals were more likely to argue that social conditions contributed to criminal behavior and that rehabilitation, not retribution, should be the goal of incarceration. Not all African Americans agreed on which alternative was preferable. Most believed the criminal justice system was not just, but there was widespread awareness in black communities that black-on-black crime was extremely destructive. "To talk about the depressing statistics of unemployment, infant mortality, incarceration, teenage pregnancy, and violent crime is one thing," Cornel West argued in *Race Matters*. "But to face up to the monumental eclipse of hope, the unprecedented collapse of meaning, the incredible disregard for human (especially black) life and property in much of black America is something else." Back in 1968 the National Advisory Commission on Civil Disorders had warned that the United States was moving increasingly "toward two societies, one white, one black—separate and unequal." Although civil rights reforms eliminated many racial barriers and opened the way for many African Americans to enter the mainstream of the nation's economic and social life, at the beginning of the twenty-first century many were still left behind in economically depressed, highly segregated urban areas as well as in the rural South. The U.S. prison system seemed an emblem of the racial divide.

The Million Man March and Racial Atonement

"I can't say that I approved, and I really didn't disapprove," Louis Farrakhan recalled when a journalist asked about the assassination of Malcolm X. As interest in Malcolm increased during the 1990s due to politicized hip-hop lyrics and Spike Lee's 1991 film biography, Farrakhan also emerged as a somewhat unlikely inheritor of Malcolm's legacy. The two men had once been close. During the early 1950s, Malcolm had recruited Farrakhan, then known as Louis Eugene Walcott. The former calypso singer from a middle-class Boston family possessed exceptional skills as an orator and propagandist that enabled him to quickly rise to a leadership post in the Nation of Islam. As Louis X, he recorded a popular anthem, "The White Man's Heaven Is the Black Man's Hell." He remained loyal to Elijah Muhammad when the Nation of Islam leader suspended Malcolm for his remarks on the assassination of President John Kennedy. As the war of words escalated between Malcolm and his former comrades, Louis X denounced Malcolm as a "traitor" who was "worthy of death." After Malcolm's assassination, he took over the now-vacant post of the Nation of Islam's National Representative and later changed his named to Farrakhan.

After Muhammad died in 1975 and his son and successor Wallace Muhammad decided to create a new organization based on orthodox Islamic beliefs, Farrakhan responded by reestablishing the Nation of Islam, while retaining its antiwhite tenets. Farrahkan had first become nationally known in 1984 when his ties to Jesse Jackson drew press attention to his anti-Jewish statements. Although Jackson's campaign suffered, Farrakhan benefited from the considerable media attention he received. For many disaffected African Americans, his controversial statements contributed to his growing reputation as a militant black leader willing to express their anger and frustration. In October 1995, he provided the inspiration for the Million Man March, the largest gathering of African Americans in the nation's history.

Although some observers disputed whether march organizers reached their numerical goal, there was little doubt that the crowd was immense, far larger than the crowd at the 1963 March on Washington. Unlike that event, the 1995 march was neither a protest against racial discrimination nor a demand for civil rights legislation. Instead, organizers called it an opportunity for black men

Louis Farrakhan's 1995 Million Man March was an opportunity for black men to commit themselves to their families and communities.

to atone for past misdeeds and to commit themselves to take responsibility for their families and communities.

Those attending the march heard numerous speakers representing the wide range of supporting organizations. An indication of how much had changed over the previous decade was that Jesse Jackson was reduced to delivering a preliminary speech, while Farrakhan gave the feature address, thereby demonstrating his ability to arouse black audiences. Yet his message was hardly radical: "Every one of you must go back home and join some church, synagogue, temple, or mosque, and join organizations that are working to uplift black people."

Alice Walker watched the march on television, expecting that "whatever happened would be exciting, instructive, hopeful, and *different*." She reacted ambivalently to Farrakhan. "I was moved by him," she later wrote, "and underneath all the trappings of Islam, which I personally find frightening, I glimpsed a man of humor, a persuasive teacher, and someone unafraid to speak truth to power, a virtue that makes it easier to be patient as he struggles to subdue his flaws." She was pleased to see black male leaders braving criticisms in order to work with Farrakhan, even while excluding black women. "I think it is absolutely necessary that black men regroup as black men; until they can talk to each other, cry with each other, hug and kiss each other, they will never know how to do those things with me."

Rethinking the Meaning of Race

President Clinton paid little attention to the Million Man March, but in June 1997 he called on John Hope Franklin to lead the nation in a "great and unprecedented conversation about race." Eighty-two years old and professor emeritus at Duke University, Franklin was well prepared to head a new board charged with advising the president on ways to improve the nation's race relations. After graduating from Fisk University and receiving his doctorate from Harvard, Franklin had gained distinction as a pioneer in the fields of African American and southern history. In 1947, he published *From Slavery to Freedom,* which became the most widely read and influential survey of African American history. Author of numerous major historical studies, Franklin had the respect of scholars and was the first African American to serve as president of leading professional organizations, but he also spoke out on the contemporary implications of his scholarship. Franklin's own family had suffered in the 1921 Tulsa race riot, and his career options had been limited by racial barriers. The same Duke University that honored him with an endowed chair had once barred him from using its research facilities when he taught at nearby all-black North Carolina Central.

Franklin contributed to the NAACP's brief in *Brown* v. *Board of Education,* and, during the 1976 celebration of the two hundredth anniversary of the United States, he publicly questioned the widespread idolization of the Founding Fathers, whom he saw as less concerned with democratic ideals than with "protecting the inviolability of property and maintaining a stable social order." During the 1990s, Franklin responded to the argument that race was becoming less significant by updating a prediction W. E. B. Du Bois had made a century before: "I venture to state categorically that the problem of the twenty-first century will be the problem of the color line."

A Difficult "Conversation on Race"

Franklin's challenge was enormous, given the racial controversies that burst into public view during the 1990s. Underlying the contention over affirmative action, the ideas of Lani Guinier, and racial bias in the criminal justice system was the issue of the significance of race in American life at the end of the twentieth century. Had the nation moved beyond the days when racial discrimination severely limited the opportunities of African Americans? Early in the 1990s, several influential books by black intellectuals, notably Shelby Steele's *The Content of Our Character* (1990), had questioned the need for continued racial solidarity and civil rights agitation among African Americans. Steele and other conservatives even quoted King's 1963 "I Have a Dream" address to support their view that black Americans should not receive preferential treatment based on the "color of their skin" but should instead be judged by "the content of their character." Nevertheless, the decade also saw an outpouring of scholarly works, documentary films, and historical dramas that illuminated the extent to which racial oppression affected not only the past but the present. While Steele complained about the deleterious effects of "victim-focused black identity," other black intellectuals insisted that racial prejudices and discrimination still shaped the lives and identities of African Americans. Cornel West's best-selling *Race Matters* was one of many books that depicted white racism and prejudice as a continuing problem that affected black people of all classes.

Yet even intellectuals such as West, who believed that race still mattered, recognized that its significance was always changing. It became commonplace in the 1990s for thoughtful writers to point out that race was a social construct rather than a rigid biological category, even as they debated how American society was reconstructing the meaning of race. Following the publication of Derrick Bell's pioneering work *Race, Racism, and American Law* (1981), legal scholars contributed to this discussion by developing the field of critical race theory to explore the often subtle ways in which African Americans and other people of color were subordinated within the nation's supposedly egalitarian legal and political system.

Even as Franklin's panel began deliberations, a disturbing incident of police brutality impeded prospects for greater racial understanding. Abner Louima, a black Haitian immigrant, was brutally assaulted by white New York policemen after he was arrested in the mistaken belief that he had struck one of the officers. Louima was taken to the men's room at the police station. There, Justin Volpe, the officer he was accused of hitting, took the lead in torturing Louima by shoving a wooden plunger handle into his rectum, puncturing his bladder and severely damaging his colon. The police officer then forced the handle into Louima's mouth. All of this occurred while police yelled threats and racial epithets. Press reports of the assault and demands for an investigation led to Volpe's arrest and eventual sentencing to a 30-year prison term. A policeman who witnessed the assault received a five-year sentence for perjury. Louima was later awarded a multimillion-dollar settlement from the city of New York. A year after the Louima beating, James Byrd, Jr., a black man in Jasper, Texas, was dragged to death behind a pickup truck. Authorities convicted three white men with ties to white supremacists groups of the killing.

Although in both the Louima and Byrd incidents the racially motivated violence did not go unpunished, as did earlier southern lynchings, that they happened at all was a reminder that the struggle against racism was not over. But what conclusions could African Americans draw from these events? Were they indications of larger racial problems affecting all African Americans or exceptional acts of lawlessness unlikely to be repeated? Given that police brutality and murder were already illegal, what, if any, new racial policies or laws were required to deal with racist violence? Indeed, during the 1990s and the early twenty-first century, southern and federal authorities reopened investigations of a number of racially motivated murders of the 1960s. These included the 1963 murder of four black children in a Birmingham church and the 1964 killings of civil rights workers in Mississippi.

Members of Franklin's panel realized the nation's most pressing racial problems no longer involved overt acts of violence. Instead, their main concern was with the far more subtle, everyday practices that kept African Americans and other racial minorities in subordinate economic positions despite civil rights laws. As panel members listened to testimony from numerous experts on race relations, they assembled considerable evidence of racial inequality but found it hard to frame solutions. The panel successfully called for the appointment of a presidential assistant on racial and ethnic matters and an increase in the budget of the Equal Employment Opportunity Commission, charged with enforcing antidiscrimination laws. Overall, however, it accomplished little beyond contributing to the ongoing national conversation about race. Moreover, the nation's attention was soon diverted by a scandal stemming from Clinton's sexual relationship with a White House intern. Faced with the threat of impeachment for lying about this relationship, Clinton was unable to offer leadership on racial matters.

Affirmative Action and Reparations

Among the challenges Franklin's panel faced was how to deal with the contemporary consequences of past racial oppression. Although white Americans had come to agree that the overt racism and blatant discrimination of the Jim Crow era were wrong, they were divided over what, if anything, should be done to remedy the wrongs. Thus it was hardly surprising that the panel failed to resolve the ongoing debate over affirmative action, a legal strategy meant to compensate women, African Americans, and other minorities for discrimination against these groups in the past. As memories of slavery and the southern Jim Crow system faded, fewer Americans, black as well as white, felt personally connected to that history. Even Americans who were aware of past racial oppression did not always agree on an appropriate remedy for acts of injustice that occurred many years ago.

A year before Franklin's panel began deliberations, a federal appeals court ruled against the University of Texas Law School's affirmative action program, ordering the university not to use race as a factor in admissions. *Hopwood* v. *University of Texas Law School* seemed to indicate that programs designed to increase minority enrollment might not survive court challenges. Since the Supreme Court's 1978 *Bakke* decision, many colleges and universities had assumed such programs were legal as long as they did not use racial quotas and took race into account as only one of many factors considered in achieving a diverse student population.

People on both sides of the affirmative action issue paid close attention to cases involving the University of Michigan's programs to increase minority enrollment. White students who were denied admission sued the university, arguing that these policies were violations of the Fourteenth Amendment's guarantee of "equal protection of the laws." Among the amicus briefs filed to support the university's policies was one signed by twenty-nine retired military and civilian leaders who insisted the experiences of American troops in Vietnam showed that military effectiveness required special policies that created a racially diverse officer corps. In *Grutter* v. *Bollinger* (2003), the Court ruled, 5–4, that the University of Michigan Law School had a "compelling interest" in enrolling a racially and ethnically diverse student body because of the educational benefits of diversity. But in the related case of *Gratz* v. *Bollinger*, the Court ruled that admission to the University of Michigan through a system of points violated the Constitution's Equal Protection Clause and Title VI of the 1964 Civil Rights Act (which prohibits discrimination by public or private institutions that receive public funds).

As the debate over affirmative action continued, a related battle over racial reparations gathered momentum. The demand for payments to compensate African Americans for past racial oppression had been put forward as early as 1867, when Pennsylvania congressman Thaddeus Stevens introduced a bill to give former slaves 40 acres of land. Congress passed the measure, but President Andrew Johnson vetoed it. More than a century later Representative John Conyers of Michigan submitted legislation that would establish a commission to investigate the need for reparations to compensate for slavery and subsequent racial discrimination.

Although the national movement for racial reparations made little headway, the idea was not unprecedented. In the 1980s, efforts to compensate the survivors of the Japanese internment during World War II had been successful. In the 1990s, black residents of the town of Rosewood, Florida, obtained a $2.1 million settlement (but no official apology) from the Florida legislature for property losses suffered in 1923, when white people invaded the town to retaliate for an alleged sexual assault. In 2001, an Oklahoma commission recommended compensation for survivors of the 1921 Tulsa race riot. Although the legislature turned down the idea, it approved funds for redeveloping the riot area, establishing a memorial, and creating a scholarship funded by private donations. In 1999, black farmers won a billion-dollar settlement to compensate for discriminatory policies by the U.S. Department of Agriculture. Clinton hinted that a national apology for slavery might be appropriate, only to retreat when his suggestion came under attack, even from some black leaders.

Redefining *Black*

Black filmmaker Marlon Riggs died of AIDS before Franklin's panel was established, but his films on neglected aspects of African American history also contributed to the national racial dialogue of the 1990s. His first major documentary, the Emmy award-winning *Ethnic Notions* (1987), traced the evolution of the racial stereotypes he saw as deeply implanted in the psyche of Americans. *Color Adjustment* (1991) examined the depiction of African Americans on national television, from *Amos 'n' Andy* in the 1950s to *The Cosby Show* of the 1980s. But it was Riggs's *Tongues Untied* (1989) that focused national attention on his work and made him the target of criticism. The film was a moving, highly personal documentary that provided a wide-ranging discussion of the black gay experience. Though acclaimed by critics and awarded Best Documentary at Berlin and other film festivals, some viewers saw it as obscene because of its frank depiction of black homosexuals.

Even as Riggs confronted death, he was determined to finish another film arguing that the concept of blackness should capture the full diversity of

African American life. His *Black Is . . . Black Ain't* (1995), completed by his associates, was a challenge to black people "to get over the notion that you can only be unified as a people as long as everybody agrees. You know we don't achieve freedom by those means." Riggs saw his last film as initiating a much-needed conversation among African Americans: "There is a cure for what ails us as a people, and that is for us to talk to each other. We have got to start talking about the ways in which we hurt each other; and the ways in which we hurt each other is also through silence."

Riggs was one of many black intellectuals and artists who sought to understand and explain the diversity and complexity of African American lives. Riggs's final film reflected a trend in African American thought toward greater recognition of the extent to which racial identity was not permanent but constantly changing, not a single set of characteristics but a broad range of possibilities. For much of African American history, enslavement and racial oppression imposed a damaging black identity on the Africans brought to the New World, and that system of oppression had also given Europeans a positive new identity as white people. Yet, although black racial identity was initially forced on all Americans with African ancestry, that identity was later voluntarily chosen by African Americans who came to see themselves as a group not only oppressed but also struggling collectively against oppression. Riggs's films suggested that the African American identity was becoming increasingly varied in the era following the major civil rights reforms of the 1960s. As did the black feminist writers of the 1980s, Riggs attacked narrow definitions of blackness that either excluded many African Americans or forced them to conform to the expectations of others.

Among the themes of late-twentieth-century popular culture was that of individuals crossing cultural boundaries. Increasing cultural interaction throughout the United States—and indeed throughout the world—had led to ever greater transfers of cultural knowledge. Through the mass communications media, African American culture had been marketed to the world, and African Americans had consumed aspects of the cultures of other groups. White Americans and people in other nations had become more African American in their cultural outlook, while African Americans had become more like other Americans as well as more European, more Asian, more Latin, and more African.

At the beginning of the twentieth century, Du Bois had analyzed the "double-consciousness" of African Americans—"an American, a Negro; two souls, two thoughts, two unreconciled strivings"—but at the end of the century, African American identity had become even more conflicted. A steady stream of recent writings had shown that African Americans were increasingly differentiated along lines of class, color, religion, gender, sexuality, and even race. These writings revealed the variety of individual experiences that constituted the African American experience. Black identity was no longer imposed by a Jim Crow system, but African Americans could now choose to identify themselves with their rich history of struggles against racial barriers.

2000 Census Documents a Multiracial Nation

Increasing awareness among Americans that racial identity is socially deter-mined rather than based on biological or genetic factors led to disputes regarding how to conduct the 2000 census. Given that Americans are required to partici-pate in the census count, conducted every ten years to allocate seats in Congress and distribute federal expenditures, it is hardly surprising that Census Bureau policies and procedures have often been the subject of controversy. Since the first census in 1790, African Americans had had little control over how they were classified and recorded by census takers, who often assigned people to racial cat-egories by observing skin color and other appearance factors. After 1960, respon-dents were able to identify themselves racially, although mixed-race people were still forced to choose only one category. With respect to African Americans, this policy reinforced the so-called one-drop rule, as anyone with recognizable African ancestry tended to identify as black or Negro. By 2000, increased criti-cism caused government officials to greatly expand the list of racial categories and to create a new category called Hispanic Origin. For the first time, multiracial and multiethnic people were able to choose more than one category to identify their ancestry.

As a result of these changes, the 2000 census showed that the nation had changed rapidly over the preceding decade and reshaped the way many Americans saw their own nation. White Americans recognized that they were still a majority group, but, whereas in 1960, white people constituted 89 percent of the total population, by 2000 only 75 percent of Americans described them-selves as white (another 2 percent described themselves as partly white). The 2000 census revealed that African Americans had increased in numbers at a faster rate than white Americans, but that other minority groups had grown at an even faster rate. The number of Latinos (some of whom were African

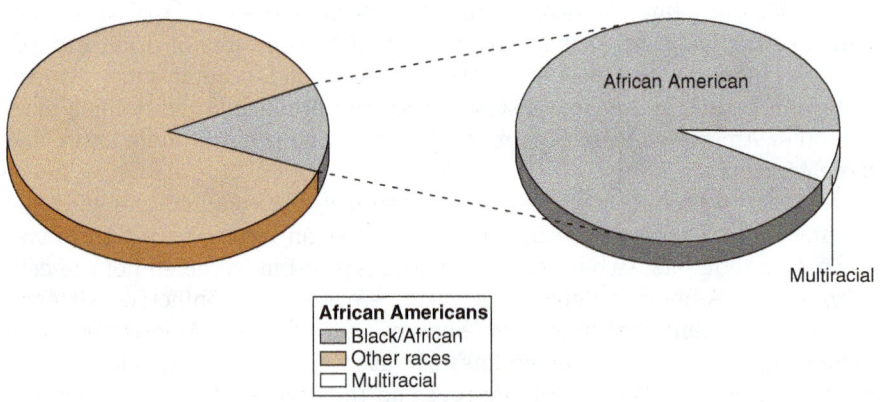

African Americans
- Black/African
- Other races
- Multiracial

FIGURE 21.1 African Americans in the U.S. Population, 2000

Taking advantage of new census policies, millions of Americans identified themselves as multiracial in the 2000 United States Census. Racial identity is increasingly recognized as being socially determined rather than biologically determined.

American) was now almost equal to the number of African Americans (some of whom were Latinos), and the former group was growing more rapidly than the latter. The number of Americans who identified themselves as having Asian ancestry had similarly increased at a faster rate than did those who identified themselves as black. Pacific Islanders were also rapidly expanding their numbers. The 2000 census also revealed that many Americans of African ancestry took advantage of the new census policies by identifying themselves as multiracial (see Figure 21.1). The black–white relationship that had been such an important factor in American history had evolved into a more complex multiracial society.

But the controversy over racial categories in the 2000 census touched on deeper issues. If racial identity was becoming a matter of voluntary choice rather than determined by genes, imposed by white domination, or forged in collective freedom struggles, would African Americans eventually lose their sense of common identity? Such a possibility would have seemed unlikely at the beginning of the twentieth century, when race was generally assumed to be a biological category, when ideas of white supremacy were evident throughout the world, and when black freedom struggles required a strong sense of solidarity. At the beginning of the twenty-first century, the meaning of race was widely debated, colonialism and Jim Crow had been overthrown, and the struggles to overcome these systems had become part of history. Perhaps for this reason, African American historical memory had become more essential to the maintenance of African American identity. Rather than being rooted in African ancestry or in the experience of resisting racial oppression, African American identity was increasingly rooted in understanding African American history.

Democracy and the Legacy of Race

Martin Luther King III understood the importance of historical understanding when he reacted to the disputed presidential election of 2000. Although Republican George W. Bush ultimately prevailed over the Democratic candidate, Vice President Al Gore, King was among those who charged that the election was a distortion of democracy. Speaking as president of the Southern Christian Leadership Conference, the group once led by his father, he claimed the election uncovered the ways in which, more than three decades after passage of the Voting Rights Act of 1965, African Americans continued to be disadvantaged in the American political system. In particular, he pointed to the removal of more than 94,000 Florida residents from the voter registration rolls in the months before the election. Although Florida officials, including Governor Jeb Bush, the new president's brother, claimed the purge was necessary to remove convicted felons, King countered that this computerized process had removed many voters "whose name, birth date and gender loosely matched that of a felon anywhere in America." He added, "The legacy of slavery—commonalities of black names—aided the racial bias of the 'scrub list.'" Recalling his father's protests against racial barriers to the vote, he lamented that the struggle had taken a new form. "Four decades ago, the opposition to the civil rights to vote was easy to identify—night riders wearing white sheets and burning crosses," he remarked. "Today, the threat comes from partisan politicians wearing pinstripe suits and clutching laptops."

The Disputed 2000 Election

King's complaint about the erroneous disqualification of voters was only one way the 2000 election served as a reminder of the complex and continuing relationship between African American history and American democracy. The nation's founders created not only a nation in which African Americans were oppressed but also an undemocratic political system that in most places enfranchised only white male property owners. Two hundred years of African American civil rights struggles had moved the nation closer to democratic ideals but had not achieved universal adult suffrage. Many voters of all races and a disproportionate number of black voters faced barriers to participation in the 2000 election: long residency requirements, burdensome registration procedures, disfranchisement of felons, and the scheduling of elections on a normal workday. Moreover, the Electoral College, intended to serve as a check on majority rule, distorted the electoral process. In most elections, the large numbers of Americans who do not vote is little noticed, and the Electoral College generally reflects the popular vote. But the 2000 election dramatically revealed the undemocratic aspects of the American political system.

Gore won about a half-million more votes than Bush, and 90 percent of African American votes. Bush's support, however, was concentrated in less populated states that carried the same weight in the Electoral College as the more densely populated states won by Gore. Thus, Bush's victories in the six sparsely populated western states, with a combined population of less than 5 million, gave him 16 electoral votes, while Gore's victory in New Jersey, with a population of more than 8 million, produced only 15 electoral votes. Despite this disparity, Bush still did not have a majority in the Electoral College without the disputed Florida vote.

Thus, the election demonstrated the importance of the issue raised by King as well as Lani Guinier: the need for an electoral system that accurately reflects the votes of all adult citizens. Voters who supported Bush could dismiss challenges as whining, but African American history provides ample evidence of the importance of enabling ever larger numbers of citizens to be represented and heard in the political system.

African Americans in an Interdependent World

President George W. Bush was elected with minimal black support, and four years later he attracted only slightly greater black support in his successful re-election bid. Most black voters remained suspicious of the Republican Party's generalized opposition to the expansion of federal social programs, and some still remembered its strategy of appealing to southern white voters who resented black civil rights gains. Despite his failure to attract the support of most black voters, Bush achieved an important racial breakthrough when he

named former military leader Colin Powell as his secretary of state and Condoleeza Rice as White House national security advisor; they became the first African Americans to hold these positions. Both had been shaped by their experiences as African Americans even as they embraced their new roles as government leaders shaping the future of the nation and, indeed, the world. In his Senate confirmation hearings, Powell affirmed Thomas Jefferson's dream of "popular government" but also acknowledged that "there is still so much that needs to be done here at home and around the world to bring that universal Jeffersonian dream to the whole world." He pledged that the guiding principle of American foreign policy would be "to help any country that wishes to join the democratic world—any country that puts the rule of law in place and begins to live by that rule, any country that seeks peace and prosperity and a place in the sun."

The terrorist attacks on September 11, 2001 against New York City's World Trade Center and the Pentagon focused considerable attention on the roles played by Rice and Powell in guiding the nation's foreign policy. But their prominence in the Bush administration also indicated the increasing diversity of African American experiences and attitudes in the twenty-first century. On the one hand, thousands of black soldiers had volunteered to serve in the U.S. military forces that responded to the terrorist attacks by invading Afghanistan and Iraq. Yet many African Americans opposed the war to overthrow Iraqi leader Saddam Hussein. Powell could look to his background as confirmation of his decision to join a Republican administration and to support the controversial war in Iraq. But Representative Barbara Lee, a California Democrat whose entry into politics had been inspired by Shirley Chisholm's presidential campaign, could also look to her background to justify her decision to cast the only vote in Congress against giving President Bush a free hand to wage war to overthrow Hussein.

While African American participation in the war effort continued a long tradition of fighting in all the nation's wars, Lee's action also continued a tradition of black antiwar dissent traceable back to King during the Vietnam War or A. Philip Randolph during World War I or Frederick Douglass during the Mexican American War. Although there was no single African American position on the nation's foreign policies, an April 2003 Gallup Poll revealed that only 29 percent of black respondents supported the Bush administration's decision to invade Iraq, compared to 78 percent of white respondents. This split in attitude was also evident in the critical stand taken by the Congressional Black Caucus, which, even before the war began in March 2003, objected to "the unilateral first strike action by the United States without a clearly demonstrated and imminent threat of attack on the United States" and warned that "any post-strike plan for maintaining stability in the region would be costly and would require a long-term commitment." Earlier black critics of American foreign policy such as Du Bois and King had identified with colonized nations in Africa and Asia, but few black opponents of the Iraq war had much sympathy for Saddam Hussein. Instead, their antiwar sentiment was likely rooted in distinctive experiences that had made them aware of the struggles and sacrifices required to achieve freedom and democracy at home, much less abroad.

Conclusion

As the twenty-first century began, African Americans could celebrate a long struggle for freedom that had been memorialized in the Martin Luther King, Jr., holiday and Black History Month. Much had changed since W. E. B. Du Bois attended the first Pan-African Conference in 1900. Then, most Africans were colonial subjects of European nations, and people of African descent in the United States lacked basic political rights. A century later, Africans had overcome colonialism, and African Americans had overcome the Jim Crow system of white supremacy. Five centuries after slave ships brought the first African slaves to the Americas, their descendants possessed the power to influence American policies toward Africa. Some African Americans had achieved exceptional wealth, celebrity, and influence. But racial progress was uneven. Many black communities suffered from broken families, failing public schools, and widespread crime. Increasingly, the criminal justice system controlled the lives of millions of incarcerated black Americans even more completely than did the Jim Crow system of white supremacy. Even African Americans who gained new opportunities as a result of civil rights reforms often experienced new anxieties owing to isolated incidents of brutal racism, subtle forms of racial profiling, and glass ceilings in professional occupations.

As African Americans freed themselves from the racial constraints of the past, they also faced new concerns and new questions. The Million Man March revealed a growing tendency of African Americans to assume collective responsibility for their destiny. But there were also indications that racial unity was lessening due to the increasing diversity in the experiences and attitudes of African Americans. Historical circumstances had once transformed Africans into black slaves; perhaps new historical circumstances were once again transforming the identities of the descendants of slaves. Even as they looked ahead to a new century, African Americans could look back with pride at the ways in which their struggles for freedom had shaped the nation and the world.

Questions for Review and Reflection

1. What does the persistence of poverty and the success of exceptional individuals such as Oprah Winfrey tells us about the long-term impact of the civil rights reforms of the 1960s?

2. Did the policies and actions of President Clinton justify the overwhelming support he received from black voters? Did President Bush's appointment of African Americans to high foreign policy positions indicate that both major political parties were equally committed to eliminating racial barriers?

3. How did the O. J. Simpson trial illuminate trends in American racial relations as well as the changing relationship between class and race identity?

4. Discuss the pros and cons of affirmative action and reparations as solutions to the problem of institutionalized racism? To what extent did affirmative action resolve these issues?

5. In what ways are American racial problems made more challenging as a result of the growing number of Americans who are neither black nor white?

Barack Obama and the Promise of Change, 2005–Present

Barack Obama's Call for a New Direction

As he waited anxiously to deliver his keynote speech at the 2004 Democratic Convention in Boston, Barack Obama realized that he had been given an opportunity that could shape his political future. The 43 year-old Illinois State Senator had already experienced a swift rise to national prominence. Just four years earlier, he was not even a delegate to the 2000 Democratic Convention. He was then mired in an unsuccessful campaign to unseat Democratic Congressman Bobby Rush, the former Black Panther Party member who had represented Chicago's South Side since 1993. Obama's crushing defeat left him broke and discouraged—"I began to harbor doubts about the path I had chosen," he recalled. After a period of reflection, however, he convinced his wife Michelle to support "one last shot to test out my ideas" before settling for "a calmer, more stable, and better-paying existence." Confident that he could learn from his mistakes in the campaign against Rush, he surprised many of his friends by announcing that he would run for a bigger prize: a seat in the United States Senate. Obama gradually built a strong campaign organization and began raising the millions of dollars needed for a statewide campaign based on the theme "Yes, we can." He attracted liberal support by boldly denouncing Bush's decision to invade Iraq. "A dumb war," he called it, warning of a military occupation

2005	Illinois Democrat Barack Obama becomes the second African American to represent Illinois in the U. S. Senate.
	Jamie Foxx wins the best actor Oscar for his portrayal of singer Ray Charles.
	After Hurricane Katrina strikes Gulf Coast, widespread flooding devastates much of New Orleans.
2006	The Congressional Black Caucus leads the successful effort to pass the Fannie Lou Hamer, Rosa Parks, Coretta Scott King Voting Rights Act extending provisions of the 1965 legislation.
2007	The Congressional Black Caucus includes 43 members.
2008	Senator Barack Obama elected President.
2009	Obama becomes the first African American president.
2010	Despite united Republican opposition, major health care legislation enacted.

of "undetermined length, at undetermined cost, with undetermined consequences." Increasingly effective in speeches before predominantly white as well as black audiences, he easily won the Democratic primary. His Republican opponent unexpectedly withdrew to avoid making public details about his divorce. While Republican leaders scrambled to find a replacement, the Democratic Party's expected presidential candidate, Senator John Kerry, invited Obama, the party's rising new African American political star, to open the national convention.

While realizing that much was riding on his speech, Obama had reason to be confident. He had already displayed exceptional talent as an orator. He was skilled at writing his own speeches, and his literary skills were also evident in his 1995 memoir, *Dreams from My Father: A Story of Race and Inheritance.* Readers were drawn to Obama's vivid account of his search for his Kenyan father, who had married a white student from Kansas while both attended the University of Hawaii and then had abandoned his wife and son. Growing up with his mother in Indonesia and then with his grandparents in Hawaii, Barack Obama struggled to come to terms with his biracial background. Rebellious and indifferent about school, he experimented with drugs during his teenage years. As a student at Occidental College in Los Angeles, he participated in the campaign against South African apartheid. But he also found it difficult to fit in socially, feeling a "constant, crippling fear that I didn't belong somehow, that unless I dodged and hid and pretended to be something I wasn't I would forever remain an outsider, with the rest of the world, black and white, always standing in judgment."

After transferring to Columbia University in New York, Obama became more studious but remained an outsider as he explored a city divided along class and racial lines. Thinking deeply about what he would do after graduation, he decided to become a grassroots organizer, recalling his mother's tales of SNCC workers "standing on a porch in some Mississippi backwater trying to convince a family of sharecroppers to register to vote." He accepted a job paying $10,000 for the first year working in the Roseland and West Pullman neighborhoods of Chicago. For the first time in his life, Obama immersed himself in a black social world, listening to residents reveal their "dashed hopes and powers of endurance, of ugliness and strife, subtlety and laughter." During his three years struggling to improve residents' lives, he achieved some gains and forged enduring relationships, but he was also disappointed by his limited accomplishments as an organizer. He decided to leave to attend Harvard Law School, hoping to learn "things that would help me bring about real change."

Before enrolling, however, he traveled to Kenya to discover more about his father and thereby fill the emptiness he still felt inside. Eventually learning that his father had died an embittered alcoholic after squandering his early promise, Obama's search for identity increased his appreciation for the lessons that his recently deceased mother had taught him about heroic figures such as King. "To be black was to be the beneficiary of a great inheritance, a special destiny," he concluded. Obama excelled at Harvard, becoming the first African American president of the *Harvard Law Review*. After earning his law degree, he turned down high-paying law firm jobs to return to Chicago, convinced that the law could be more than "a matter of applying narrow rules and arcane procedure." Instead, he would use his training to participate in "a long-running conversation, a nation arguing with its conscience." He recognized that the Declaration of Independence expressed not only the spirit of Jefferson but also of black leaders such as Douglass and Delany as well as "the struggles of Martin and Malcolm and unheralded marchers to bring these words to life."

By the time of his convention speech, Obama was no longer an outsider. Now married to Chicago native Michelle Robinson, like him a Harvard Law graduate, he was also a promising politician heavily favored to win a Senate seat in a predominantly white state. Having found his personal solution to the "double consciousness" problem that W. E. B. Du Bois had identified a century earlier, he saw himself as a new kind of leader able to bridge the nation's political divisions. Convinced "that politics could be different and that the voters wanted something different, that they were tired of distortion, name-calling, and sound-bite solutions to complicated problems," he prepared a speech that would express the hopes and values shared by Americans of all races. "Just don't screw it up, buddy!" Michelle advised her husband as they waited backstage. Walking past a reporter on the way to the podium, Obama joked, "I'm LeBron, baby," referring to the NBA basketball star. "I can play on this level. I got some game."

He began his speech by recounting the story of his biracial upbringing. "My parents shared not only an improbable love, they shared an abiding faith in the possibilities of this nation," he explained. "I stand here knowing that my story is part of the larger American story, that I owe a debt to all of those who came before me, and that, in no other country on earth, is my story even possible." Obama stirred his audience by stressing the nation's traditional values, while calling attention to the divisive partisanship that had infected the nation's politics since the late 1960s. He warned against "the spin masters, the negative ad peddlers who embrace the politics of 'anything goes.'" Obama then came to the heart of his message: "Well, I say to them tonight, there is not a liberal America and a conservative America—there is the United States of America. There is not a Black America and a White America and Latino America and Asian America—there's the United States of America." Rather than believe that nothing worthwhile could be achieved through politics, he urged Americans to join forces to seek a better future. He recalled a phrase from a sermon he had heard his pastor, Jeremiah Wright, deliver at Chicago's Trinity United Church of Christ:

> *The audacity of hope! In the end, that is God's greatest gift to us, the bedrock of this nation. A belief in things not seen. A belief that there are better days ahead. I believe that we can give our middle class relief and provide working families with a road to opportunity. I believe we can provide jobs to the jobless, homes to the homeless, and reclaim young people in cities across America from violence and despair. I believe that we have a righteous wind at our backs and that as we stand on the cross-roads of history, we can make the right choices, and meet the challenges that face us.*

Although Obama's oratory received an enthusiastic response, Kerry was unable to defeat President Bush in the 2004 presidential election. While the vast majority of black voters backed the Democratic candidate—as had been the case in every election since Lyndon Johnson identified the Democratic Party with the civil rights cause—Republicans continued to attract the support of most white voters and especially strong support from white southerners. Obama's win in his Senate race over a little-known black Republican meant that once again there would be one African American in the Senate, but his election did little to threaten Republican dominance of national politics. Even with his arrival, there were only forty-one members of the Congressional Black Caucus, about the same as the number a decade earlier. Disgruntled over the lack of access to Bush, the Caucus had little hope of influencing legislation, since all were Democrats in the Republican-controlled House and Senate. The news media paid little attention to Ohio voting-rights activists who complained that Bush would have lost the election if Republican election officials and faulty voting machines had not prevented several hundred thousand prospective voters in Democratic-leaning and predominantly black areas from expressing their preferences.

The Uncertain War against Terrorism

Despite Bush's reelection, there were indications early in his second term that popular support for the Iraq war was waning. No "weapons of mass destruction" had been found in Iraq, undermining Bush's principal reason for invading the country in 2003 and overthrowing its President Saddam Hussein. Most Democrats had joined with Republicans in approving war funding and giving the Bush administration unprecedented executive authority through the Patriot

Act of 2001, but American military forces had been unable to prevent increasing attacks from Iraqi insurgents. Moreover, al-Qaeda leader Osama bin Laden, who had inspired the plot against New York's World Trade Center towers, continued to elude capture by American troops searching for him in Afghanistan's mountainous area bordering Pakistan. Bush was forced to find new ways of justifying a war that had become unexpectedly costly in terms of lives and funding. He explained in his second inaugural speech that his overall policy was to support "the growth of democratic movements and institutions in every nation and culture, with the ultimate goal of ending tyranny in our world." Facing setbacks in achieving his ambitious foreign agenda, the president would also confront unexpected domestic challenges during his second term that would call into question his insistence on lower taxes and less government. Obama, Barbara Lee, John Conyers, and other members of the Congressional Black Caucus strongly criticized the Bush administration's belated response to Hurricane Katrina, which devastated New Orleans late in the summer of 2005. The natural disaster tested the Bush administration's ability to anticipate and respond effectively to major crises. A more severe test came in the fall of 2008, when the unregulated sales of securities backed by housing mortgages nearly resulted in the collapse of the American financial system. These foreign and domestic failures, combined with a growing budget deficit exacerbated by Bush's massive tax cuts for wealthy Americans, would open the door for Obama's historic campaign to change the nation's direction. More than any election since the start of the Great Depression, the 2008 contest would force Americans to reexamine long-held assumptions about their political values as well as their racial attitudes.

The resignation of Secretary of State Colin Powell shortly after the 2004 election drew public attention to Powell's conflicts with Vice President Dick Cheney and Defense Secretary Donald Rumsfeld, both of whom emphasized military force over diplomacy in the war against terror. When Bush named National Security Advisor Condoleezza Rice as Powell's successor, he insured that the State Department would be headed by a loyal confidant. But Rice, who became the first African American woman to serve as secretary of state, faced difficulties of her own in asserting herself against the forceful voices of Cheney and Rumsfeld when she argued against reliance on military threats to stop Iran from acquiring nuclear weapons. Rumsfeld's influence was weakened, however, when news articles appeared revealing that Iraqi prisoners had been tortured and severely abused by American soldiers at Abu Ghraib Prison in Baghdad. A subsequent investigation resulted in the demotions of officers and the prosecution of a few soldiers, but many observers blamed Rumsfeld and Bush himself for justifying so-called "enhanced interrogation techniques" on the grounds that captured suspected terrorists were "unlawful combatants" and thus not entitled to be treated according to the Geneva Convention's rules regarding prisoners of war. The Congressional Black Caucus joined a growing number of political leaders calling for Rumsfeld to resign. Although Rice supported the Iraq war, she privately questioned Rumsfeld's decision to hold suspected terrorists at Guantánamo prison in Cuba and at secret prisons elsewhere in the world. When Rumsfeld initially offered to resign early in 2005,

Bush asked him to stay on, but controversy continued over lack of progress in the war and more revelations about prisoner abuse.

Bush's foreign policies overshadowed his domestic agenda, which included making permanent the massive tax cuts, mostly benefiting wealthy Americans, that had been enacted in his first term. In his second inaugural address, Bush insisted that Republican conservatism could deal with social problems without increasing the size of government. He announced that his main domestic initiative would be to give all Americans "a stake in the promise and future of the country" by bringing "the highest standards to our schools" and building "an ownership society." Bush's "No Child Left Behind" legislation that passed with Democratic support early in his first term was the most ambitious federal educational legislation enacted since Lyndon Johnson's Great Society programs. States had responded to the law by setting higher graduation standards and educational goals as measured by standardized skills tests. But such reforms did not always result in more funding for schools and did little to improve the quality of teachers or schools, especially for black and Latino students living in poor urban areas. The Bush administration expanded Clinton's policy of encouraging minority home ownership by relaxing federal regulation of the mortgage loan industry. Many first-time homebuyers with low incomes were able to obtain affordable loans—often at adjustable interest rates rather than the fixed rates that had been common in this industry. Some mortgages allowed homeowners to pay only a small down payment and low interest costs during the initial years of the loan, leaving them with little or no actual equity in a home when the interest rates were adjusted upward. Although the negative consequence of these mortgage policies would only gradually become evident, Bush faced immediate opposition to his proposal to allow Americans to invest some of their social security contributions. Congress rejected the plan after critics argued that it would involve risking the retirement incomes of many Americans. Bush's declining political influence was also evident in his failure to attract sufficient Republican backing for major immigration legislation that would reduce illegal immigration while providing new ways for undocumented immigrants to obtain citizenship.

Hurricane Katrina's Challenge to Conservative Government

Although Lt. General Russel L. Honoré's main assignment as commander of the First U. S. Army was preparing troops for assignments in Iraq and Afghanistan, he unexpectedly became a central figure in the controversial federal response to the powerful hurricane that hit New Orleans in September 2005. The hurricane's eye hit southwest Mississippi rather than New Orleans, but poorly-constructed levees built by the Army Corps of Engineers failed, causing widespread flooding in the city. When the disaster overwhelmed local, state, and even federal emergency officials, Honoré found himself thrust into the role of leading the military response. He was familiar with the New Orleans area, having graduated in 1971 from historically black Southern University and A&M

College, located near the Louisiana farm where he grew up. During the first Persian Gulf War of the early 1990s, he served in Operation Desert Storm and later led American forces in Korea. As commander of military forces in the Eastern United States, he was the Army's highest ranking African American (he described himself as an African American creole, reflecting his mixed racial ancestry), but he was little known outside the military—that is until reporters noticed how quickly his firm leadership brought some order amidst the chaos that followed the hurricane.

Storms are a common occurrence in the Caribbean region, but Hurricane Katrina was measured at the highest intensity—category five. Although the hurricane hit the Gulf Coast on August 29, 2005, the greatest destruction came later when rising water levels caused catastrophic flooding of New Orleans. After a storm surge from Lake Pontchartrain broke through the levees, waters began rising in most parts of New Orleans. A shipping canal built by the Corps of Engineers also broke down. Damage was worst in the city's low-lying areas (some below sea level) where poor, black residents were concentrated. Although evacuation warnings were issued, many of the poorest and oldest residents lacked transportation. Some veterans of previous storms simply tried to ride it out. Thousands of residents, especially in the Lower Ninth Ward, were trapped in their homes as floodwaters rushed inside. Many others followed instructions to seek shelter at the New Orleans Superdome or gathered around the Convention Center expecting to be rescued. Help did not arrive for several days, however, even as journalists at the scene reported the increasingly desperate pleas of those waiting.

Hurricane Katrina victims

As rising floodwaters took over most of the city, aspiring 24-year-old hip hop artist and Ninth Ward resident Kimberly Rivers Roberts began recording the destruction around her with her new video camera. She and her husband Scott described themselves as street hustlers, but they unexpectedly became reporters. "It's going to be a day to remember," Kim declared as she began to realize the extent of the disaster. Their amateur footage—later included in the award-winning film *Trouble the Water* (2007)—included shots from their attic as the lower floor filled with water. While producing a film record of the horrific events of the following days, the couple joined with many others to rescue threatened neighbors, bringing some flood victims to their attic, which remained above flood level. After moving to a Red Cross shelter, they encountered two documentary filmmakers from Brooklyn who convinced them to join forces to record the story of the hurricane and the social injustices it exposed.

Veteran filmmaker Spike Lee also documented the aftermath of Katrina in his Emmy-winning *When the Levees Broke* (2006). He divided his documentary into four "acts" to make clear that the Katrina tragedy did not begin when the hurricane hit and did not end when the floodwaters receded. Like many books and articles that appeared afterward, Lee pointed out that government officials had ample warning about the city's vulnerability to massive flooding, but responded slowly even as live television news programs reported the dire situation of the thousands needing food, water, and medical help at the Superdome and Civic Center.

Both *Trouble the Water* and *When the Levees Broke* conveyed the confusion and sense of abandonment felt by residents as hurricane winds subsided and flooding began. Some longtime residents believed that the levees were allowed to flood to save affluent neighborhoods, just as the Great Mississippi Flood of 1927 had been diverted from New Orleans into the rural Delta area to the east. Although such a conspiracy was never proven in the investigations that followed the Katrina hurricane, many experts blamed the Army engineers for designing and building inadequate levees. Also responsible were local, state, and federal officials who argued among themselves about how to respond as residents waited to be rescued. Some New Orleans police abandoned their responsibilities, and those who remained were overwhelmed by calls for help and unable to stop looting. "It's too doggone late," Mayor Ray Nagin complained to a reporter. "Now get off your asses and do something, and let's fix the biggest goddamn crisis in the history of this country."

As local, state, and federal officials struggled to coordinate their responses to the emergency, Lt. General Honoré arrived to take charge of the military forces that finally came to assist New Orleans' exhausted and demoralized police. Honoré's gruff, no-nonsense manner soon became a visible contrast to the lackluster performance of political leaders and government institutions. His six-foot-two stature gave added authority to the commands he barked to soldiers patrolling the streets of New Orleans. Mayor Nagin was impressed, calling Honoré "one John Wayne dude," referring to the movie actor who had often portrayed soldiers. Yet, although his troops succeeded in evacuating thousands of flood victims and brought some order to the chaos, Honoré could do little to relieve the plight of the city's poorest residents.

The fact that most of those pleading for help were black served as a reminder that race continued to affect the opportunities of Americans. For Lee, the racial dimension of this inadequate governmental response provided a theme for his second act, which focused attention on the mixture of political bungling and racial hostility that transformed a natural disaster into an enduring human tragedy. Michael Brown, the inexperienced and inept head of the Federal Emergency Management Administration (FEMA), was soon forced to step down, but Lee's footage indicted all levels of government, from the president down to Nagin, who did not supplement his emotional pleas for state and federal help with strong leadership. Both documentaries also exposed the racial emotion that surfaced after the flooding. Exaggerated reports of violence by armed black men fueled these racial tensions. Honoré felt compelled to order police and soldiers to help victims rather than pointing their weapons at them. A predominantly black group walking into a white neighborhood that had not been flooded were confronted and turned back by armed lawmen. Some observers noted that whites shown in news photos taking items from markets were described as searching for provisions, while black flood victims doing the same thing were described as looters.

The documented toll of the flooding was enormous – more than 1800 deaths, at least $100 billion in property damage, and more than a million residents forced to leave their homes. But, as Lee made clear in his third and fourth acts (as well as in his 2010 documentary, "If God is Willing and da Creek Don't Rise"), the disaster's impact would continue to be felt in subsequent years. Without resources to relocate elsewhere, many residents forced to leave New Orleans came to be seen as refugees in their own nation. Kimberly Rivers Roberts and many of those Lee interviewed were evacuated to communities far from New Orleans, splitting up extended families and uprooting children at the beginning of a school year. FEMA eventually provided temporary housing for some of those displaced, but in the months after the hurricane thousands of former residents remained unsure about when or if they could return. Before Katrina, 37 percent of the city's residents were identified as black, according to Census Bureau statistics; a year after the disaster, blacks comprised only 22 percent of New Orleans residents. More affluent residents generally lived in higher areas that were less affected by the hurricane or, if affected, were soon rebuilt, while poorer residents had to relocate elsewhere as officials debated whether to rebuild their communities. Although Mayor Nagin would later spark controversy when he used the occasion of the King Holiday in January 2006 to urge the rebuilding of a new "chocolate New Orleans," there were many indications that the hurricane was used as an opportunity for a lasting change in the racial and class composition of a major American city.

Obama and the Longest Presidential Campaign

Even in his first year in the Senate, Barack Obama was often sought by reporters interested in his views on the New Orleans disaster, as well as other national and international issues. The new Senator was reluctant to provoke controversy, however, as he tried to deflect suggestions that he was already thinking about running for president. He realized that he would have to prove himself to Illinois voters by learning how to accomplish anything in Washington. Obama also wanted to demonstrate that he could avoid the excessive partisanship he had condemned. He had refused to support the Ohio activists who wanted to challenge Bush's election and refused to join Democrats opposing Condoleezza Rice's confirmation as Secretary of State. Yet he was also reliably liberal in his Senate votes. He denounced Bush's idea of an "ownership society" as "every man or woman for him or herself," describing this as "social Darwinism." He insisted that, while free markets had enabled the nation's economy to grow, America's "unrivaled political stability" also "depended on our sense of mutual regard for each other, the idea that everybody has a stake in the country, that we're all in it together and everybody's got a shot at opportunity." As other black leaders denounced the federal response to Katrina as racist—Jesse Jackson likened the abandoned flood victims in the Superdome to passengers in the "hull of a slave ship" and rapper Kanye West bluntly charged that "George Bush doesn't care about black people"—Obama was more restrained. In one of his few nationally televised interviews during 2005, he described federal incompetence as "color-blind," yet "so detached from the realities of inner city life . . . that they couldn't conceive of the notion that somebody couldn't load up their SUV, put one hundred dollars' worth of gas in there . . . and drive off to a hotel and check in with a credit card."

While deflecting questions about his presidential ambitions, Obama attracted special press attention as a result of his 2004 keynote speech and his sudden emergence as the nation's most famous black elected official. Adjusting to his lowly position as 99th on the Senate's seniority list, he took advantage of opportunities for foreign trips designed to broaden his understanding of issues such as the Sudanese government's genocidal policies in its Darfur region. His travels included a triumphal return to Kenya, where large crowds turned out to greet him. During the fall of 2006, his second book, *The Audacity of Hope: Thoughts on Reclaiming the American Dream*, was published and quickly became a best seller. His growing reputation also dramatically boosted sales of his earlier memoir. Although realizing that he was still a newcomer on the national political scene, Obama could not ignore the growing calls for him to enter the presidential race.

The 2006 election demonstrated that the nation's political climate was changing in Obama's direction. With his popularity steadily declining, Bush could do little to help Republican Senators and Representatives seeking reelection, and the party experienced a resounding setback. Democrats won control of both houses of Congress, although the party secured only a one-vote margin in the Senate. Soon after the election, Defense Secretary Rumsfeld announced that he would resign. Bush soon shifted military strategy in Iraq, sending more troops to combat the growing insurgency and agreeing to arm and finance Iraqi militias willing to cooperate with American forces. In the aftermath of the Katrina disaster and the revelations of torture in Iraq, the election returns indicated a major shift in public sentiment regarding Bush's presidency. Democrats were encouraged to believe that they could win the presidency in 2008, if only they chose the right candidate. New York Senator Hillary Clinton, the former First Lady, was the best known among the growing numbers of Democrats who indicated after the mid-term election that they were considering running.

Primaries

Early in 2007, Obama decided that, despite his relative inexperience, the following year's election might be his best opportunity to win. He was encouraged by the reception he received at speeches he delivered to Democratic audiences in New Hampshire and Iowa, sites of the earliest Democratic primaries. He scheduled an announcement in front of the Old State Capitol in Springfield, Illinois, where Abraham Lincoln had delivered his famous "House Divided" speech in 1858. "Because men and women of every race, from every walk of life, continued to march for freedom long after Lincoln was laid to rest," Obama told a crowd of supporters, "today we have the chance to face the challenges of this millennium together, as one people —as Americans."

Obama understood the historical significance of becoming the first black president, but he also knew that the campaign would be uphill. When Shirley Chisholm ran in 1972, her campaign had not even attracted much support from delegates to the National Black Political Convention held that year in Gary, Indiana. The Jesse Jackson campaigns of the 1980s demonstrated that a black candidate could actually win a few state Democratic primaries; yet Colin Powell was widely viewed in 1996 as the first African American with a serious chance to win a major party nomination (he declined to run). Would Democrats risk

Obama on the campaign trail

losing an opportunity to take back the White House by nominating a black candidate who was still a first-term Senator?

The presidential campaign attracted a large field of contenders, and Senator Clinton opened a clear lead in the polls over other Democrats, with less than 20 percent of likely voters indicating that they intended to vote for Obama in the upcoming state primaries. Even most black voters and older black leaders initially leaned toward Clinton, many of them expressing loyalty to the administration of her husband. Congressman John Lewis, a former leader of SNCC, threw his support to Clinton, while Andrew Young insisted that Bill Clinton was "every bit as black" as Obama, who, he added, might be ready for the presidency in 2016. Jesse Jackson, whose presidential campaigns in the 1980s had broken new ground for a black candidate, also publicly criticized Obama, questioning Obama's avoidance of racial controversy and his seeming eagerness to separate himself from an earlier generation of black protest leaders. He noted that Obama had failed to protest the imprisonment of the Jena Six—Louisiana teenagers who were arrested on dubious charges that grew out of racial conflicts at a high school. Conservative black scholar Shelby Steele's skepticism about Obama's presidential prospects was evident in the title of his 2008 book, *A Bound Man: Why We Are Excited about Obama and Why He Can't Win.*

But some black leaders, especially those who were too young to have taken part in the civil rights campaigns of the 1960s, thought that Obama could win. Journalist Gwen Ifill noted the generational divide that separated black civil rights leaders who had experienced legal segregation—"they marched, they preached, and they protested"—and Obama's generation, who "lived in a world shaped by access instead of denial." Ifill observed that younger, highly educated black politicians such as Massachusetts governor Deval Patrick, Newark mayor Cory Booker, and Alabama congressman Artur Davis, all early Obama supporters, were more aware than older black leaders of how much American racial attitudes had changed since the 1960s and appreciated Obama's emphasis on interracial coalitions instead of confrontations over civil rights issues.

When Obama delivered a King Holiday sermon in January 2008 at King's Ebenezer Baptist Church in Atlanta, he made clear that his goal was not to mobilize mass black protests or to forge racial unity. Rather than identifying himself with the "Moses Generation" of civil rights leaders, Obama saw himself as part of the "Joshua Generation" that would actually reach the Promised Land of equal opportunity. He urged the Ebenezer congregation to transcend racial differences, adding,

> if we are honest with ourselves, we must admit that none of our hands are entirely clean. If we're honest with ourselves, we'll acknowledge that our own community has not always been true to King's vision of a beloved community. We have scorned our gay brothers and sisters instead of embracing them. The scourge of anti-Semitism has, at times, revealed itself in our community. For too long, some of us have seen immigrants as competitors for jobs instead of companions in the fight for opportunity.

The enthusiastic response Obama received from the mostly black Ebenezer congregation reflected his success in gradually drawing black support away from Clinton, and Obama's stunning victory in the Iowa Democratic caucuses late in January 2008 demonstrated that he could win in a predominately white state. No longer a long shot, Obama suddenly became the front-runner. Even as several candidates dropped out of the race, however, Hilary Clinton rebounded by winning the New Hampshire primary, demonstrating that her campaign was far from over. As the first woman to make a strong race for a major party nomination, Clinton was a formidable candidate with the strong backing of her still influential husband. Clinton's television ads stressed that her experience in Washington made her "ready on day one" to handle a foreign crisis. She dismissed Obama as simply a good orator. But Obama exhibited his own strengths – most notably his able campaign organization, which made effective use of the Internet to attract support from young voters and to raise more campaign funds than any previous candidate. Moreover, after Obama won other primaries following his Iowa success, he also solidified his African American support. In southern states in particular, black voters supplied his margin of victory in Democratic primaries. After Obama's strong showing in the Georgia primary, Atlanta congressman Lewis switched his support to Obama.

In March, however, Obama's presidential prospects were seriously threatened by reports that his Chicago pastor, Jeremiah Wright, had delivered sermons that seemed to blame the terrorist attacks of September 2001 on American policies—"God damn America for as long as she acts like she is God." Repeated broadcast of recorded excerpts from Wright's sermons heightened white voters' fears that Obama shared his pastor's militant views (at the same time rumors spread that Obama was secretly a Muslim). Obama had previously avoided racial controversies, but he was now faced with the difficult task of explaining his ties to the pastor who had supplied the title for his second book and who had officiated at his wedding. Rejecting the cautions of some of his key advisors, Obama decided to deliver a major speech about race at Philadelphia's historic Constitution Center. He defended Wright as part of a black church tradition concerned with pressing social issues—"housing the homeless, ministering to the needy, providing day care services and scholarships and prison ministries, and reaching out to those suffering from HIV/AIDS." Suggesting that Wright's occasional angry outbursts were understandable in the context of the nation's long struggle to overcome racism, Obama explained, "I can no more disown him than I can my white grandmother— a woman who helped raise me, a woman who sacrificed again and again for me, a woman who loves me as much as she loves anything in this world, but a woman who once confessed her fear of black men who passed by her on the street, and who on more than one occasion has uttered racial or ethnic stereotypes that made me cringe."

Although Wright's later controversial statements led Obama to break off his ties with Trinity church, the thoughtful speech in Philadelphia saved his campaign. By early June, he had won enough delegates to force Clinton to concede, although some Clinton supporters continued unsuccessfully to press Obama to make Clinton his vice presidential running mate. When Obama accepted the Democratic nomination on August 28, he spent most of his speech defining the differences between the politics he proposed to implement and those of Republican nominee, Arizona Senator John McCain. Only as he reached his conclusion did he link his own appeal for national unity with King's earlier effort to bridge racial divisions. Recalling the crowd who had gathered to "hear a young preacher from Georgia speak of his dream," Obama observed that we "could've heard words of anger and discord" or "been told to succumb to the fear and frustration of so many dreams deferred." Instead, he asserted, "people of every creed and color, from every walk of life" heard "that in America, our destiny is inextricably linked. That together, our dreams can be one."

The General Election

The November election pitted the oldest candidate ever to run for the presidency against the youngest candidate since John F. Kennedy in 1960. After Obama passed over Clinton to choose veteran Delaware Senator Joe Biden as his vice presidential running mate, McCain made the surprising choice of Alaska governor Sarah Palin as his running mate. The first woman to run on a major party ticket, Palin was even less experienced in national politics than Obama, but her acceptance speech aroused the right wing of the Republican Party, which included many who questioned McCain's commitment to conservative principles. Palin later directed spirited attacks against Obama, claiming that he supported higher taxes and linking him to a white activist who had engaged in violence during the 1960s. Although Obama performed well in debates with McCain, he was often forced to defend himself. Even as Palin faltered when questioned by reporters about her knowledge of foreign issues, McCain was able to pull even with Obama in the polls by stressing his political and military experience (he had been a prisoner of war in Vietnam) and promising voters, "I will follow Bin Laden to the gates of hell and I will get him."

The presidential race took an unexpected turn, however, when a downturn in the stock market signaled a major crisis in the American financial system. After months of indications that a recession was near, the sudden collapse of Lehman Brothers financial firm sent shock waves throughout the international world of high finance. On September 24, President Bush proposed that the federal government undertake an unprecedented bailout of major banks. He explained that the crisis resulted from the widespread popularity of mortgage-backed securities, which had enabled investors to profit from the rapidly growing desire of Americans to own homes or take out home equity loans. Legislation passed late in the Clinton presidency had freed banks to issue these securities without federal regulation, and Bush administration officials ignored warnings that these seemingly safe investments were threatened by the widespread practice of offering mortgages to people unlikely to repay the loan. A growing wave of home foreclosures threatened to bring down all home values and thereby endanger many banks and investment firms. Even the retirement funds of ordinary Americans faced major losses due to a severe decline in the stock market. Bush warned that the amount required to stabilize the major banks would exceed $700 billion—about $5,000 per taxpayer—and because he already faced a large budget deficit, the bailout would require even more borrowing.

Bush's stunning announcement shifted the focus of the presidential campaign from foreign affairs, where many saw McCain as having an advantage, to domestic policies, which was Obama's strength. Obama was quick to remind McCain of his earlier statement that "the fundamentals of the economy are sound," but also telephoned his opponent to suggest that they develop a joint response to Bush's plan. McCain instead announced to reporters that he would suspend his campaign in order to provide leadership in Washington but backed down when Obama refused to postpone a scheduled debate. "It is going to be part of the president's job to deal with more than one thing at once," Obama explained. When the candidates debated late in September, Obama scored points by blaming the crisis on Bush's policies "supported by Senator McCain, that essentially said that we should strip away regulations, consumer protections, let the market run wild, and prosperity would rain down on all of us." Although both candidates agreed that some action was necessary to prevent a collapse of the financial system, a majority of House Republicans refused to follow McCain's lead and voted down Bush's bailout plan, while Obama convinced skeptical members of the Congressional Black Caucus to go along with the bailout.

After once again tying McCain to Bush's policies in the third and final presidential debate—"I am not President Bush," McCain countered—Obama maintained a modest but significant lead in the polls, and led in enough states to ensure a victory in the electoral college. Obama's calm response to the economic crisis contrasted with the increasing desperation of McCain and Palin, who continued to paint Obama as a radical who would raise taxes even while he promised to reduce them for Americans making under $250,000. Obama was also helped by the endorsement of former Secretary of State Collin Powell. Surprising his fellow Republicans and fellow military veteran McCain, Powell explained that the nation needed "a transformational figure" who represented "generational change." Despite Powell's bombshell announcement and Obama's apparent lead, there were concerns among his supporters that white voters unwilling to vote for a black candidate might not give honest answers to pollsters. There were also unanswered questions about Obama's bases of support. Would African American voters and young people of all races turn out in large numbers? Would Clinton's support in the primaries shift to Obama? Would problems with voter registration procedures and voting machines once again damage Democratic chances in closely contested states?

A Historic Election

Soon after the polls closed in West Coast states on November 4, major networks announced the history-making news: Obama and Biden had received almost 53 percent of the vote. Obama's victory in the electoral college was even more substantial: 365 votes to 173 for McCain. As numerous commentators noted the racial significance of the event, even McCain's concession speech acknowledged the "special significance" of Obama's victory, noting that just a

Washington Post headlines on Obama's victory

century earlier President Theodore Roosevelt had prompted white outrage when he had merely invited Booker T. Washington to dine at the White House. Crowds in numerous cities shouted with joy at the election news, and similarly joyous newspaper headlines appeared in many countries. "YES HE DID!" the *Huntsville Times* proclaimed. "A NEW ERA" announced the *Oakland Tribune*. The *Irish Independent* called the election a "WAVE OF CHANGE."

Eight years after tasting defeat in a Chicago congressional race, Obama delivered his victory speech to a racially diverse crowd jammed into Chicago's Grant Park—once a staging area of protests aimed at the 1968 Democratic convention. As news cameras recorded the tears of joy on the faces of Jesse Jackson and Oprah Winfrey, the president-elect acknowledged the uniqueness of the moment. "If there is anyone out there who still doubts that America is a place where all things are possible, who still wonders if the dream of our founders is alive in our time, who still questions the power of our democracy, tonight is your answer," he began. He reminded listeners of the challenges that lay ahead, and called for "a new spirit of sacrifice." Without mentioning King by name, Obama drew inspiration from the civil rights leader's final "promised land" oration in 1968, but, unlike King, he spoke now as the chosen leader of all Americans. "The road ahead will be long; our climb will be steep," he remarked. "We may not get there in one year or even in one term. But, America, I have never been more hopeful than I am tonight that we will get there. I promise you, we as a people will get there."

TABLE 22.1

OBAMA SUPPORT BY GROUP	PERCENT OF THE TOTAL PRESIDENTIAL VOTE
African Americans in states covered by 1965 Voting Rights Act because of previous history of racial discrimination (Alaska, Arizona)	97%
Whites in states covered by 1965 Voting Rights Act because of previous history of racial discrimination	26%
Whites in Mississippi	11%
Whites in Alabama	10%

How did Obama achieve his victory? Certainly Bush's unpopularity and the sudden economic collapse increased popular support for Obama's call for change, and the 2008 election was unusual in that no incumbent president or vice president was running. However, Obama won not only because of unusual circumstances, but also because his skilled campaign organization mobilized a record number of voters who were attracted to Obama's ideas and leadership. Some observers saw the election as evidence of the changing racial attitudes of white Americans, pointing to the fact that Obama received the support of 43 percent of white voters as compared to the 41 percent who had voted for John Kerry in 2004.

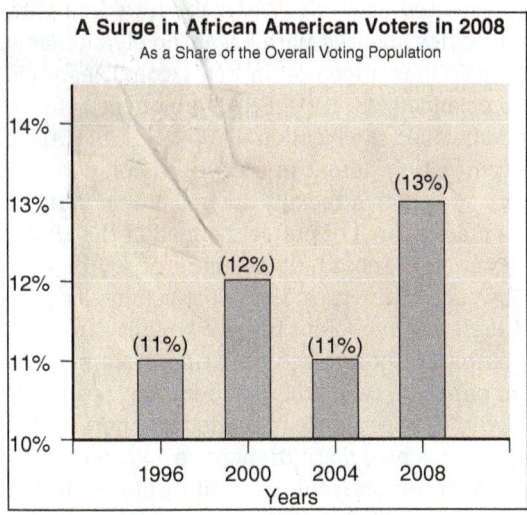

FIGURE 22.1   Surge in African American Voters 2008

Source: Figure 7.1 African-American voter turnout. Primary Source: CNN National Exit Poll for 1996, 2000, 2004 and 2008 General Elections, Pew Hispanic Center, US. Election Atlas, Secretaries of State. http://www.nonprofitvote.org/voterturnout2008#minorities <http://www.nonprofitvote.org/voterturnout2008>

Like previous Democratic presidential candidates in the years since Lyndon Johnson's landslide 1964 victory, Obama relied on the support of a substantial minority of white voters, but he also won the votes of record numbers of non-white and young voters. Although in the southern states, where there was intense opposition to civil rights reform, Obama received even less white support than did Kerry—10 percent in Alabama and 11 percent in Mississippi—strong black support enabled him to win in the two southern states, Virginia and North Carolina. Overall he received the votes of 95 percent of African Americans, 67 percent of Latinos, and 62 percent of Asians. Moreover, 66 percent of all voters under the age of thirty and 69 percent of first-time voters backed Obama. And these pro-Obama groups voted in unprecedented numbers. Thus, Obama's victory resulted from gradual changes in white racial attitudes but even more from a dramatic change in the racial composition of the American electorate.

The Obama Presidency and African Americans

Among the record two million Americans who gathered for Barack Obama's inauguration on January 20, 2009, African Americans were a conspicuous presence. Their numbers may have exceeded the attendance at the 1995 Million Man March. The event had special meaning for African Americans who had

Barack and Michelle Obama at inauguration

once experienced exclusion from politics, and many parents brought their children to witness history being made. In August 1963, several hundred thousand civil rights supporters had come to the Washington Mall to join the March on Washington and listened to speakers at the Lincoln Memorial demand action from political leaders at the Capitol on the other end of the Mall. At that time there had been only five black Representatives among the 535 congressmen and senators who would decide the fate of pending civil rights legislation. Forty-five years later, however, many of those who had been protesters in 1963 were back on the Mall to watch the inauguration of an African American president. Former Freedom Rider and SNCC chair John Lewis, who had bluntly asked, "Which side is the federal government on?" when he was the youngest speaker at the 1963 March, now had a reserved seat at the Capitol where he was a veteran House member. Obama had often expressed his indebtedness to the African American freedom struggle, but he was nonetheless determined to move beyond the role of racial leader. He relied on his visible presence and that of Michelle Obama, as the nation's new First Lady, to give substance to King's dream of a nation capable of judging people on the basis of character rather than skin color. The benediction of 87-year-old Joseph Lowery, former leader of the Southern Christian Leadership Conference, provided the most direct link to past struggles, with its sardonic prayer for "that day when black will not be asked to get back, when brown can stick around, when yellow will be mellow, when the red man can get ahead, man, and when white will embrace what is right."

Obama's inaugural speech reiterated his campaign theme of national unity. He praised Americans for choosing "hope over fear, unity of purpose over conflict and discord" and proclaimed "an end to the petty grievances and false promises, the recriminations and worn-out dogmas, that for far too long have strangled our politics." Obama stressed the seriousness of the nation's challenges—economic decline at home and continuing war abroad—while also recalling that previous generations of Americans had "faced down fascism and communism not just with missiles and tanks, but with sturdy alliances and enduring convictions." He described America's religious and cultural diversity as its "strength, not a weakness" and appealed for a new "spirit of service": "It is the kindness to take in a stranger when the levees break, the selflessness of workers who would rather cut their hours than see a friend lose their job which sees us through our darkest hours. It is the firefighter's courage to storm a stairway filled with smoke, but also a parent's willingness to nurture a child, that finally decides our fate." Although he had run as an advocate of change, he emphasized traditional values:

> . . . hard work and honesty, courage and fair play, tolerance and curiosity, loyalty and patriotism—these things are old. These things are true. They have been the quiet force of progress throughout our history. What is demanded then is a return to these truths. What is required of us now is a new era of responsibility—a recognition, on the part of every American, that we have duties to ourselves, our nation and the world; duties that we do not grudgingly accept but rather seize gladly, firm in the knowledge

that there is nothing so satisfying to the spirit, so defining of our charac-
ter, than giving our all to a difficult task.

A New Political Era?

Few presidents had confronted the range of pressing concerns facing President Obama when he became the 44th president. Could he deal effectively with the nation's severe recession—the sharpest decline in economic output in more than a half-century? Could he find a way to end the long war in Iraq and to combat the threat of violent Islamic terrorism in Afghanistan and Pakistan? Could he expand the availability of decent health care services to Americans without health insurance? Could he confront the threat of major global climate change? Could he deliver on his promise to reduce the destructive partisanship that had prevented politicians from solving the nation's major problems? In his inaugural Obama acknowledged the nation's challenges—"they are serious and they are many"—but he also promised, "They will be met." African Americans also wondered how Obama's success or failures would affect black communities suffering from increasing unemployment and home foreclosures. Would he protect previous civil rights gains? Obama did not promise any major civil rights initiatives, but he did appoint Eric Holder as the first African American Attorney General to head the department responsible for federal civil rights enforcement. Obama's former Democratic rival Hillary Clinton agreed to become his administration's Secretary of State, replacing Condoleezza Rice.

Although Democrats controlled both houses of Congress, Obama could not count on overriding the opposition of Republicans and conservative Democrats. This was especially true in the Senate where forty Senators could stop legislation through the threat of a filibuster, a practice that had once been used to stop civil rights legislation. Democrats would have to secure all the remaining sixty votes to end debate and force a vote on controversial legislation. Within the first few days after taking office, Obama issued an executive order intended to close the Guantanamo prison holding suspected terrorists and an order prohibiting the use of torture or other illegal techniques during interrogations of suspected terrorists. Obama also quickly signed legislation extending government-financed health care to millions of lower-income children, a bill that President George W. Bush twice vetoed, and signed another measure making it easier for workers to sue their employers for alleged job discrimination, effectively overturning a ruling by the Supreme Court's conservative majority.

When Obama outlined his legislative agenda in his State of the Union message, he set forth ambitious proposals that included funding increases to the major areas that he had emphasized during his campaign: economic recovery, health care, environmental protection, and education. He left unspoken the likelihood that black Americans would especially benefit from federal assistance in refinancing their mortgages, obtaining adequate health care, and paying for college education. Although Obama's proposals included unprecedented federal spending for job creation and social services, he faced a difficult challenge in transforming proposals into effective programs. Republicans generally opposed him, arguing that his spending proposals would further increase the deficits left behind by the Bush administration. Republicans also resisted Obama's proposals on the grounds that they would greatly expand the role of the federal government. With almost no Republican support, Congress passed his massive $787 billion economic stimulus package in February. Although funding for this legislation increased the nation's budget deficit, the stimulus included tax cuts that were intended to reverse the economic decline by encouraging Americans to spend more of their wages for goods and services. It also funded projects that provided jobs for workers who would otherwise have been unemployed. The Obama administration directed much of the stimulus spending to programs that reflected its priorities—especially public education, mass transit, new technologies for medical care, and "green" jobs that protected the environment.

Obama's initiatives were not specifically intended to help black Americans, and they did little to reduce black–white economic inequality. The overall unemployment rate would reach 10 percent by the end of 2009, and for black Americans the rate was about 15 percent. The median income for a black household was about $34,000, but for white households it was more than $55,000. Marc Morial, president of the National Urban League, called upon Obama to "hold mayors, governors and local school districts accountable for the stimulus dollars to ensure that African Americans are included in its benefits." NAACP President Benjamin Jealous criticized Obama's emphasis on middle-class concerns at the expense of the poor. "A large number of Americans live on Main Street," he explained, "however a large number of African Americans live on Back Street, and the President must continue to offer hope to those aspiring to be in the middle class." Obama's election represented both an opportunity and a new challenge for black leaders who had previously measured their success by their ability to communicate the needs and desires of black Americans to white leaders. For the first time, black leaders faced the reality that an African American had become the nation's most powerful politician.

Obama indicated that he would push for major energy and immigration legislation, but his reform agenda became stalled when Republicans sharply attacked his proposal to reform the nation's health care system. Addressing Congress on health care, Obama noted that previous presidents going back to Theodore Roosevelt had sought to make medical care more available. Presidents Clinton and Nixon had attempted to bring the United States closer to the kind of government-funded universal health care systems that existed in Europe, Canada, and other nations. "I am not the first President to take up this cause, but I am determined to be the last," he announced. But opponents argued that such "socialized medicine" was inferior to the American medical care system, in which workers typically acquired medical insurance through their employers and self-employed doctors charged fees for their services. Rather than proposing a completely new health care system, Obama negotiated with drug and insurance companies, hospitals, and organizations of doctors and then pushed Congress to draft legislation that left much of the existing system intact. But he insisted that insurance companies be prohibited from denying coverage to applicants with "pre-existing conditions" such as diabetes or from canceling coverage once a policyholder became sick. In return for these concessions, insurance companies were promised that most uninsured Americans would be required to purchase insurance (those with low incomes would receive government subsidies). To help pay for expanding insurance coverage to more than 30 million uninsured people, supporters of the legislation called for cost-saving changes in the Medicare program for elderly Americans.

These reforms fell far short of more radical proposals, such as a government-funded "single payer" system or making Medicare available for all, but Republicans and other highly vocal opponents including "Tea Party" activists insisted that Obama's plan would result in higher taxes and a federal government "takeover" of medical care. Obama countered that comprehensive reform was needed to contain rapidly rising health care costs—which amounted to more than one-sixth of the nation's output of goods and services. Health care reform backers pointed out that the United States spent more on medical care than any other nation, even though 40 million Americans lacked health insurance. "We are the only democracy—the only advanced democracy on Earth—the only wealthy nation—that allows such hardship for millions of its people," Obama noted. With unanimous support from the Congressional Black Caucus, the House passed its version of the legislation in November 2009, and the Senate passed another version late in December. No Republican in either body voted in favor, and early in 2010, Democrats lost their 60-vote majority in the Senate when a Republican unexpectedly won the Massachusetts seat left vacant when staunch reform supporter Edward Kennedy died. Fearing that the legislation was doomed, some Democrats advised Obama to abandon the comprehensive reform in favor of piecemeal changes that could garner some Republican support. Facing the toughest test yet of his presidential leadership, Obama instead urged House Democrats to approve the already-passed Senate bill and then to adopt separate legislation changing some of the bill's provisions. The latter "reconciliation" legislation required only a majority vote in the Senate. Obama was able to win the most important victory of his presidency, but Republicans were outraged that Obama had snatched victory from apparent defeat and promised to continue their opposition in the fall 2010 election campaigns.

Although Obama's initial accomplishments were substantial, his election had generated high expectations that were difficult for him to meet. In passing the health care bill, he had succeeded where previous presidents had failed, but his victory left Congress more bitterly divided than before. Obama hoped that racial issues would not affect his ability to govern, but, in the midst of the health care debate, he became briefly involved in a racial controversy when he criticized police who arrested his friend, Harvard Professor Henry Louis Gates, at Gate's home after a white neighbor suspected that the black scholar was a burglar. Later in the year, Obama had a more pleasant distraction when he became the surprise winner of the 2009 Nobel Peace Prize, becoming the third African American recipient after Ralph Bunche and Martin Luther King, Jr. Obama agreed with many of his critics that he had not accomplished enough to deserve the award, and he acknowledged that he was likely to commit even more troops to fight an inconclusive war in Afghanistan. His Nobel acceptance speech expressed the challenge he faced as "someone who stands here as a direct result of Dr. King's life's work." While conceding that "there is nothing weak, nothing passive, nothing naïve in the creed and lives of Gandhi and King," Obama argued that as president he could not "be guided by their examples alone. I face the world as it is, and cannot stand idle in the face of threats to the American people." Implying that Gandhi and King provided no meaningful answer to the evil of Hitler or of al-Qaeda terrorists, he insisted that "force is sometimes necessary."

As Obama faced the mid-term elections of 2010, it was apparent that he had not achieved his goal of reducing partisanship in American politics. Two years after taking office with high approval ratings, his support had declined, especially among white independents, and he faced fierce opposition from the staunch conservatives who dominated the Republican Party. The enthusiasm that had mobilized African Americans and young voters to support Obama's campaign had become less evident than the determination displayed by Obama's harsh critics in the new Tea Party movement. Despite the fact that the recession he inherited from President Bush ended, Obama was blamed for the fact that his stimulus program had increased the national debt without producing the overall economic recovery and job growth he had promised. With the unemployment rate approaching about 10 percent of the workforce (and even higher for African Americans), Obama made the difficult argument that conditions would have been worse without the stimulus and his controversial decision to extend government loans to automobile companies facing bankruptcy. Passage of a major health care legislation was a historic victory for the president, but this too provoked sharp attacks from Republicans and the Tea Party movement. When Obama carried out his campaign promise to remove combat troops from Iraq, his critics remained hostile, and some Democrats were disturbed by the continued American military presence there and by Obama's decision to send more troops to Afghanistan. Even while some of Obama's supporters pressed him to close the Guantanamo prison and end discrimination against gays in the military, his critics denounced him for trying to do so.

Conclusion

The long African American struggle for freedom made possible Barack Obama's presidency, but his election raised questions about the continued need for the civil rights struggles that had shaped African American history. A half century after Martin Luther King, Jr., delivered his "I Have a Dream" address, had the United States finally become a place where black Americans could be judged by the content of their character rather than the color of their skin? To what extent did racial factors continue to shape American politics and other aspects of life? Had the long struggle to expand the scope of civil rights come to an end or had it merely reached a new stage? Although Obama himself was inspired by King and earlier generations of black leaders who had sought to realize the ideals of the Declaration of Independence, he also tried to provide a new model of transracial leadership. The health care legislation could not have passed without strong support from black members of Congress; it would affect the lives of almost all African Americans, but it did not explicitly deal with race or racial discrimination. The African American freedom struggle had often focused on appeals to the federal government and white political leaders, but the freedom struggle had also relied on grassroots black leaders and black-controlled institutions and organizations to address racial problems that government could not or would not address. More than any other African American leader, Obama would shape the lives of African Americans, but he could not be expected unlikely to solve the persistent problems that plague black communities. Perhaps the most important lesson to be drawn from the election of a black president was that Obama's victory was a product of but not the central goal of the long struggle of African Americans to advance their common interests and to realize democratic ideals.

Questions for Review and Reflection

1. Discuss the extent to which the destruction following Hurricane Katrina was caused by human mistakes rather than natural forces.

2. Discuss the relative importance of racial and class factors in determining the nation's response to the Katrina disaster.

3. To what extent did the Bush presidency pave the way for Obama's election?

4. Did the election of Barack Obama indicate that the United States has entered a new era of race relations?

5. What twenty-first-century events support or refute the notion that American political life is becoming less partisan?

Appendix

The Declaration of Independence

In Congress, July 4, 1776

The Unanimous Declaration of the Thirteen United States of America

When, in the course of human events, it becomes necessary for one people to dissolve the political bonds which have connected them with another, and to assume, among the powers of the earth, the separate and equal station to which the laws of nature and of nature's God entitle them, a decent respect to the opinions of mankind requires that they should declare the causes which impel them to the separation.

We hold these truths to be self-evident: That all men are created equal; that they are endowed by their Creator with certain unalienable rights; that among these are life, liberty, and the pursuit of happiness; that, to secure these rights, governments are instituted among men, deriving their just powers from the consent of the governed; that whenever any form of government becomes destructive of these ends, it is the right of the people to alter or to abolish it, and to institute a new government, laying its foundation on such principles, and organizing its powers in such form, as to them shall seem most likely to effect their safety and happiness. Prudence, indeed, will dictate that governments long established should not be changed for light and transient causes; and accordingly all experience hath shown that mankind are more disposed to suffer, while evils are sufferable, than to right themselves by abolishing the forms to which they are accustomed. But when a long train of abuses and usurpations, pursuing invariably the same object, evinces a design to reduce them under absolute despotism, it is their right, it is their duty, to throw off such government, and to provide new guards for their future security. Such has been the patient sufferance of these colonies; and such is now the necessity which constrains them to alter their former systems of government. The history of the present King of Great Britain is a history of repeated injuries and usurpations, all having in direct object the establishment of an absolute tyranny over these states. To prove this, let facts be submitted to a candid world.

He has refused his assent to laws, the most wholesome and necessary for the public good.

He has forbidden his governors to pass laws of immediate and pressing importance, unless suspended in their operation till his assent should be obtained; and, when so suspended, he has utterly neglected to attend to them.

He has refused to pass other laws for the accommodation of large districts of people, unless those people would relinquish the right of representation in the legislature, a right inestimable to them, and formidable to tyrants only.

He has called together legislative bodies at places unusual, uncomfortable, and distant from the depository of their public records, for the sole purpose of fatiguing them into compliance with his measures.

He has dissolved representative houses repeatedly, for opposing, with manly firmness, his invasions on the rights of the people.

He has refused for a long time, after such dissolutions, to cause others to be elected; whereby the legislative powers, incapable of annihilation, have returned to the people at large for their exercise; the state remaining, in the mean time, exposed to all the dangers of invasions from without and convulsions within.

He has endeavored to prevent the population of these states; for that purpose obstructing the laws for naturalization of foreigners; refusing to pass others to encourage their migration hither, and raising the conditions of new appropriations of lands.

He has obstructed the administration of justice, by refusing his assent to laws for establishing judiciary powers.

He has made judges dependent on his will alone, for the tenure of their offices, and the amount and payment of their salaries.

He has erected a multitude of new offices, and sent hither swarms of officers to harass our people and eat out their substance.

He has kept among us, in times of peace, standing armies, without the consent of our legislatures.

He has affected to render the military independent of, and superior to, the civil power.

He has combined with others to subject us to a jurisdiction foreign to our constitution, and unacknowledged by our laws, giving his assent to their acts of pretended legislation:

For quartering large bodies of armed troops among us;

For protecting them, by a mock trial, from punishment for any murder which they should commit on the inhabitants of these states;

For cutting off our trade with all parts of the world;

For imposing taxes on us without our consent;

For depriving us, in many cases, of the benefits of trial by jury;

For transporting us beyond seas, to be tried for pretended offenses;

For abolishing the free system of English laws in a neighboring province, establishing therein an arbitrary government, and enlarging its boundaries, so as to render it at once an example and fit instrument for introducing the same absolute rule into these colonies;

For taking away our charters, abolishing our most valuable laws, and altering fundamentally the forms of our governments;

For suspending our own legislatures, and declaring themselves invested with power to legislate for us in all cases whatsoever.

He has abdicated government here, by declaring us out of his protection and waging war against us.

He has plundered our seas, ravaged our coasts, burned our towns, and destroyed the lives of our people.

He is at this time transporting large armies of foreign mercenaries to complete the works of death, desolation, and tyranny already begun with circumstances of cruelty and perfidy scarcely paralleled in the most barbarous ages, and totally unworthy the head of a civilized nation.

He has constrained our fellow-citizens, taken captive on the high seas, to bear arms against their country, to become the executioners of their friends and brethren, or to fall themselves by their hands.

He has excited domestic insurrection among us, and has endeavored to bring on the inhabitants of our frontiers the merciless Indian savages, whose known rule of warfare is an undistinguished destruction of all ages, sexes, and conditions.

In every stage of these oppressions we have petitioned for redress in the most humble terms; our repeated petitions have been answered only by repeated injury. A prince, whose character is thus marked by every act which may define a tyrant, is unfit to be the ruler of a free people.

Nor have we been wanting in our attentions to our British brethren. We have warned them, from time to time, of attempts by their legislature to extend an unwarrantable jurisdiction over us. We have reminded them of the circumstances of our emigration and settlement here. We have appealed to their native justice and magnanimity; and we have conjured them, by the ties of our common kindred, to disavow these usurpations, which would inevitably interrupt our connections and correspondence. They, too, have been deaf to the voice of justice and of consanguinity. We must, therefore, acquiesce in the necessity which denounces our separation, and hold them, as we hold the rest of mankind, enemies in war, in peace friends.

We, therefore, the representatives of the United States of America, in General Congress assembled, appealing to the Supreme Judge of the world for the rectitude of our intentions, do, in the name and by the authority of the good people of these colonies, solemnly publish and declare, that these United Colonies are, and of right ought to be, FREE AND INDEPENDENT STATES; that they are absolved from all allegiance to the British crown, and that all political connection between them and the state of Great Britain is, and ought to be, totally dissolved; and that, as free and independent states, they have full power to levy war, conclude peace, contract alliances, establish commerce, and do all other acts and things which independent states may of right do. And for the support of this declaration, with a firm reliance on the protection of Divine Providence, we mutually pledge to each other our lives, our fortunes, and our sacred honor.

John Hancock	Joseph Hewes	Arthur Middleton
Button Gwinnett	John Penn	Samuel Chase
Lyman Hall	Edward Rutledge	Wm. Paca
Geo. Walton	Thos. Heyward, Junr.	Thos. Stone
Wm. Hooper	Thomas Lynch, Junr.	Charles Carroll of Carrollton

George Wythe	James Wilson	Josiah Bartlett
Richard Henry Lee	Geo. Ross	Wm. Whipple
Th. Jefferson	Caesar Rodney	Saml. Adams
Benj. Harrison	Geo. Read	John Adams
Thos. Nelson, Jr.	Tho. M'kean	Robt. Treat Paine
Francis Lightfoot Lee	Wm. Floyd	Elbridge Gerry
Carter Braxton	Phil. Livingston	Step. Hopkins
Robt. Morris	Frans. Lewis	William Ellery
Benjamin Rush	Lewis Morris	Roger Sherman
Benja. Franklin	Richd. Stockton	Sam'el Huntington
John Morton	Jno. Witherspoon	Wm. Williams
Geo. Clymer	Fras. Hopkinson	Oliver Wolcott
Jas. Smith	John Hart	Matthew Thornton
Geo. Taylor	Abra. Clark	

The Constitution of the United States of America

We the people of the United States, in order to form a more perfect union, establish justice, insure domestic tranquillity, provide for the common defense, promote the general welfare, and secure the blessings of liberty to ourselves and our posterity, do ordain and establish this Constitution for the United States of America.

Article I

Section 1

All legislative powers herein granted shall be vested in a Congress of the United States, which shall consist of a Senate and House of Representatives.

Section 2

1. The House of Representatives shall be composed of members chosen every second year by the people of the several States, and the electors in each State shall have the qualifications requisite for electors of the most numerous branch of the State legislature.
2. No person shall be a representative who shall not have attained to the age of twenty-five years, and been seven years a citizen of the United States, and who shall not, when elected, be an inhabitant of that State in which he shall be chosen.
3. Representatives and direct taxes[1] shall be apportioned among the several States which may be included within this Union, according to their respective numbers, which shall be determined by adding to the whole number of free persons, including those bound to service for a term of years, and excluding

---

[1]See the Sixteenth Amendment.

Indians not taxed, three fifths of all other persons.[2] The actual enumeration shall be made within three years after the first meeting of the Congress of the United States, and within every subsequent term of ten years, in such manner as they shall by law direct. The number of representatives shall not exceed one for every thirty thousand, but each State shall have at least one representative; and until such enumeration shall be made, the State of New Hampshire shall be entitled to choose three, Massachusetts eight, Rhode Island and Providence Plantations one, Connecticut five, New York six, New Jersey four, Pennsylvania eight, Delaware one, Maryland six, Virginia ten, North Carolina five, South Carolina five, and Georgia three.

4. When vacancies happen in the representation from any State, the executive authority thereof shall issue writs of election to fill such vacancies.
5. The House of Representatives shall choose their speaker and other officers; and shall have the sole power of impeachment.

Section 3

1. The Senate of the United States shall be composed of two senators from each State, chosen by the legislature thereof,[3] for six years; and each senator shall have one vote.
2. Immediately after they shall be assembled in consequence of the first election, they shall be divided as equally as may be into three classes. The seats of the senators of the first class shall be vacated at the expiration of the second year, of the second class at the expiration of the fourth year, and of the third class at the expiration of the sixth year, so that one third may be chosen every second year; and if vacancies happen by resignation, or otherwise, during the recess of the legislature of any State, the executive thereof may make temporary appointments until the next meeting of the legislature, which shall then fill such vacancies.[4]
3. No person shall be a senator who shall not have attained to the age of thirty years, and been nine years a citizen of the United States, and who shall not, when elected, be an inhabitant of that State for which he shall be chosen.
4. The Vice President of the United States shall be President of the Senate, but shall have no vote, unless they be equally divided.
5. The Senate shall choose their other officers, and also a president pro tempore, in the absence of the Vice President, or when he shall exercise the office of the President of the United States.
6. The Senate shall have the sole power to try all impeachments. When sitting for that purpose, they shall be on oath or affirmation. When the President of the United States is tried, the chief justice shall preside: and no person shall be convicted without the concurrence of two thirds of the members present.
7. Judgment in cases of impeachment shall not extend further than to removal from office, and disqualification to hold and enjoy any office of honor, trust or profit under the United States: but the party convicted shall

---

[2]See the Fourteenth Amendment.
[3]See the Seventeenth Amendment.
[4]See the Seventeenth Amendment.

nevertheless be liable and subject to indictment, trial, judgment and punishment, according to law.

Section 4

1. The times, places, and manner of holding elections for senators and representatives, shall be prescribed in each State by the legislature thereof; but the Congress may at any time by law make or alter such regulations, except as to the places of choosing senators.
2. The Congress shall assemble at least once in every year, and such meeting shall be on the first Monday in December, unless they shall by law appoint a different day.

Section 5

1. Each House shall be the judge of the elections, returns and qualifications of its own members, and a majority of each shall constitute a quorum to do business; but a smaller number may adjourn from day to day, and may be authorized to compel the attendance of absent members, in such manner, and under such penalties as each House may provide.
2. Each House may determine the rules of its proceedings, punish its members for disorderly behavior, and, with the concurrence of two thirds, expel a member.
3. Each House shall keep a journal of its proceedings, and from time to time publish the same, excepting such parts as may in their judgment require secrecy; and the yeas and nays of the members of either House on any question shall, at the desire of one fifth of those present, be entered on the journal.
4. Neither House, during the session of Congress, shall, without the consent of the other, adjourn for more than three days, nor to any other place than that in which the two Houses shall be sitting.

Section 6

1. The senators and representatives shall receive a compensation for their services, to be ascertained by law, and paid out of the Treasury of the United States. They shall in all cases, except treason, felony, and breach of the peace, be privileged from arrest during their attendance at the session of their respective Houses, and in going to and returning from the same; and for any speech or debate in either House, they shall not be questioned in any other place.
2. No senator or representative shall, during the time for which he was elected, be appointed to any civil office under the authority of the United States, which shall have been created, or the emoluments whereof shall have been increased, during such time; and no person holding any office under the United States shall be a member of either House during his continuance in office.

Section 7

1. All bills for raising revenue shall originate in the House of Representatives; but the Senate may propose or concur with amendments as on other bills.
2. Every bill which shall have passed the House of Representatives and the Senate, shall, before it become a law, be presented to the President of the

United States; If he approves he shall sign it, but if not he shall return it, with his objections, to that House in which it shall have originated, who shall enter the objections at large on their journal, and proceed to reconsider it. If after such reconsideration two thirds of that House shall agree to pass the bill, it shall be sent, together with the objections, to the other House, by which it shall likewise be reconsidered, and if approved by two thirds of that House, it shall become a law. But in all such cases the votes of both Houses shall be determined by yeas and nays, and the names of the persons voting for and against the bill shall be entered on the journal of each House respectively. If any bill shall not be returned by the President within ten days (Sundays excepted) after it shall have been presented to him, the same shall be a law, in like manner as if he had signed it, unless the Congress by their adjournment prevent its return, in which case it shall not be a law.

3. Every order, resolution, or vote to which the concurrence of the Senate and the House of Repre-sentatives may be necessary (except on a question of adjournment) shall be presented to the President of the United States; and before the same shall take effect, shall be approved by him, or being disapproved by him, shall be repassed by two thirds of the Senate and House of Representatives, according to the rules and limitations prescribed in the case of a bill.

Section 8

1. The Congress shall have the power to lay and collect taxes, duties, imposts, and excises, to pay the debts and provide for the common defense and general welfare of the United States; but all duties, imposts, and excises shall be uniform throughout the United States.
2. To borrow money on the credit of the United States;
3. To regulate commerce with foreign nations, and among the several States, and with the Indian tribes;
4. To establish a uniform rule of naturalization, and uniform laws on the subject of bankruptcies throughout the United States;
5. To coin money, regulate the value thereof, and of foreign coin, and fix the standard of weights and measures;
6. To provide for the punishment of counterfeiting the securities and current coin of the United States;
7. To establish post offices and post roads;
8. To promote the progress of science and useful arts, by securing for limited times to authors and inventors the exclusive right to their respective writings and discoveries;
9. To constitute tribunals inferior to the Supreme Court;
10. To define and punish piracies and felonies committed on the high seas, and offenses against the law of nations;
11. To declare war, grant letters of marque and reprisal, and make rules concerning captures on land and water;
12. To raise and support armies, but no appropriation of money to that use shall be for a longer term than two years;

13. To provide and maintain a navy;

14. To make rules for the government and regulation of the land and naval forces;

15. To provide for calling forth the militia to execute the laws of the Union, suppress insurrections and repel invasions;

16. To provide for organizing, arming, and disciplining the militia, and for governing such part of them as may be employed in the service of the United States, reserving to the States respectively, the appointment of the officers, and the authority of training the militia according to the discipline prescribed by Congress;

17. To exercise exclusive legislation in all cases whatsoever, over such district (not exceeding ten miles square) as may, by cession of particular States, and the acceptance of Congress, become the seat of the government of the United States, and to exercise like authority over all places purchased by the consent of the legislature of the State in which the same shall be, for the erection of forts, magazines, arsenals, dockyards, and other needful buildings; and

18. To make all laws which shall be necessary and proper for carrying into execution the foregoing powers, and all other powers vested by this Constitution in the government of the United States, or any department or officer thereof.

Section 9

1. The migration or importation of such persons as any of the States now existing shall think proper to admit, shall not be prohibited by the Congress prior to the year one thousand eight hundred and eight, but a tax or duty may be imposed on such importation, not exceeding ten dollars for each person.

2. The privilege of the writ of habeas corpus shall not be suspended, unless when in cases of rebellion or invasion the public safety may require it.

3. No bill of attainder or ex post facto law shall be passed.

4. No capitation, or other direct, tax shall be laid, unless in proportion to the census or enumeration herein-before directed to be taken.[5]

5. No tax or duty shall be laid on articles exported from any State.

6. No preference shall be given by any regulation of commerce or revenue to the ports of one State over those of another: nor shall vessels bound to, or from, one State be obliged to enter, clear, or pay duties in another.

7. No money shall be drawn from the treasury, but in consequence of appropriations made by law; and a regular statement and account of the receipts and expenditures of all public money shall be published from time to time.

8. No title of nobility shall be granted by the United States: and no person holding any office of profit or trust under them, shall, without the consent of the Congress, accept of any present, emolument, office, or title, of any kind whatever, from any king, prince, or foreign State.

---

[5]See the Sixteenth Amendment.

Section 10

1. No State shall enter into any treaty, alliance, or confederation; grant letters of marque and reprisal; coin money; emit bills of credit; make any thing but gold and silver coin a tender in payment of debts; pass any bill of attainder, ex post facto law, or law impairing the obligation of contracts, or grant, any title of nobility.

2. No State shall, without the consent of the Congress, lay any imposts or duties on imports or exports, except what may be absolutely necessary for executing its inspection laws: and the net produce of all duties and imposts laid by any State on imports or exports, shall be for the use of the treasury of the United States; and all such laws shall be subject to the revision and control of the Congress.

3. No State shall, without the consent of the Congress, lay any duty of tonnage, keep troops, or ships of war in time of peace, enter into any agreement or compact with another State, or with a foreign power, or engage in war, unless actually invaded, or in such imminent danger as will not admit of delay.

Article II

Section 1

1. The executive power shall be vested in a President of the United States of America. He shall hold his office during the term of four years, and, together with the Vice President, chosen for the same term, be elected, as follows:

2. Each State shall appoint, in such manner as the legislature thereof may direct, a number of electors, equal to the whole number of senators and representatives to which the State may be entitled in the Congress: but no senator or representative, or person holding any office of trust or profit under the United States, shall be appointed an elector.

The electors shall meet in their respective States, and vote by ballot for two persons, of whom one at least shall not be an inhabitant of the same State with themselves. And they shall make a list of all the persons voted for, and of the number of votes for each; which list they shall sign and certify, and transmit sealed to the seat of the government of the United States, directed to the president of the Senate. The president of the Senate shall, in the presence of the Senate and House of Representatives, open all the certificates, and the votes shall then be counted. The person having the greatest number of votes shall be the President, if such number be a majority of the whole number of electors appointed; and if there be more than one who have such majority, and have an equal number of votes, then the House of Representatives shall immediately choose by ballot one of them for President; and if no person have a majority, then from the five highest on the list the said House shall in like manner choose the President. But in choosing the President, the votes shall be taken by States, the representation from each State having one vote; a quorum for this purpose shall consist of a member or members from two thirds of the States, and a majority of all the States shall be necessary to a choice. In every case after the choice of the President, the person having the greatest number of votes of the electors shall be the Vice President. But if there should remain two or more who have equal votes, the Senate shall choose from them by ballot the Vice President.[6]

3. The Congress may determine the time of choosing the electors, and the day on which they shall give their votes; which day shall be the same throughout the United States.

4. No person except a natural born citizen, or a citizen of the United States, at the time of the adoption of this Constitution, shall be eligible to the office of President; neither shall any person be eligible to the office who shall not have attained to the age of thirty-five years, and been fourteen years a resident within the United States.

5. In case of the removal of the President from office, or of his death, resignation, or inability to discharge the powers and duties of the said office, the same shall devolve on the Vice President, and the congress may by law provide for the case of removal, death, resignation or inability, both of the President and Vice President, declaring what officer shall then act as President, and such officer shall act accordingly until the disability be removed, or a President shall be elected.

6. The President shall, at stated times, receive for his services a compensation which shall neither be increased nor diminished during the period for which he shall have been elected, and he shall not receive within that period any other emolument from the United States, or any of them.

7. Before he enter on the execution of his office, he shall take the following oath or affirmation:—"I do solemnly swear (or affirm) that I will faithfully execute the office of President of the United States, and will to the best of my ability, preserve, protect and defend the Constitution of the United States."

Section 2

1. The President shall be commander in chief of the army and navy of the United States, and of the militia of the several States, when called into the actual service of the United States; he may require the opinion in writing, of the principal officer in each of the executive departments, upon any subject relating to the duties of their respective offices, and he shall have power to grant reprieves and pardons for offenses against the United States, except in cases of impeachment.

2. He shall have power, by and with the advice and consent of the Senate, to make treaties, provided two thirds of the senators present concur; and he shall nominate, and by and with the advice and consent of the Senate, shall appoint ambassadors, other public ministers and consuls, judges of the Supreme Court, and all other officers of the United States, whose appointments are not herein otherwise provided for, and which shall be established

---

[6]Superseded by the Twelfth Amendment.

by law; but the Congress may by law vest the appointment of such inferior officers, as they think proper, in the President alone, in the courts of laws, or in the heads of departments.

3. The President shall have power to fill up all vacancies that may happen during the recess of the Senate, by granting commissions which shall expire at the end of their next session.

Section 3

He shall from time to time give to the Congress information of the state of the Union, and recommend to their consideration such measures as he shall judge necessary and expedient; he may, on extraordinary occasions, convene both Houses, or either of them, and in case of disagreement between them with respect to the time of adjournment, he may adjourn them to such time as he shall think proper; he shall receive ambassadors and other public ministers; he shall take care that the laws be faithfully executed, and shall commission all the officers of the United States.

Section 4

The President, Vice President, and all civil officers of the United States, shall be removed from office on impeachment for, and conviction of, treason, bribery, or other high crimes and misdemeanors.

Article III

Section 1

The judicial power of the United States shall be vested in one Supreme Court, and in such inferior courts as the Congress may from time to time ordain and establish. The judges, both of the Supreme and inferior courts, shall hold their offices during good behavior, and shall, at stated times, receive for their services, a compensation, which shall not be diminished during their continuance in office.

Section 2

1. The judicial power shall extend to all cases, in law and equity, arising under this Constitution, the laws of the United States, and treaties made, or which shall be made, under their authority;—to all cases of admiralty and maritime jurisdiction;—to controversies to which the United States shall be a party;[7]—to controversies between two or more States;—between a State and citizens of another State;—between citizens of different States;—between citizens of the same State claiming lands under grants of different States, and between a State, or the citizens thereof, and foreign States, citizens or subjects.

2. In all cases affecting ambassadors, other public ministers and consuls, and those in which a State shall be party, the Supreme Court shall have original jurisdiction. In all the other cases before mentioned, the Supreme Court shall have appellate jurisdiction, both as to law and fact, with such exceptions, and under such regulations as the Congress shall make.

A-11

[7]See the Eleventh Amendment.

3. The trial of all crimes, except in cases of impeachment, shall be by jury; and such trial shall be held in the State where the said crimes shall have been committed; but when not committed within any State, the trial shall be such place or places as the congress may by law have directed.

Section 3

1. Treason against the United States shall consist only in levying war against them, or in adhering to their enemies, giving them aid and comfort. No person shall be convicted of treason unless on the testimony of two witnesses to the same overt act, or on confession in open court.
2. The Congress shall have power to declare the punishment of treason, but no attainder of treason shall work corruption of blood, or forfeiture except during the life of the person attained.

Article IV

Section 1

Full faith and credit shall be given in each State to the public acts, records, and judicial proceedings of every other State. And the Congress may by general laws prescribe the manner in which such acts, records and proceedings shall be proved, and the effect thereof.

Section 2

1. The citizens of each State shall be entitled to all privileges and immunities of citizens in the several States.[8]
2. A person charged in any State with treason, felony, or other crime, who shall flee from justice, and be found in another State, shall on demand of the executive authority of the State from which he fled, be delivered up to be removed to the State having jurisdiction of the crime.
3. No person held to service or labor in one State under the laws thereof, escaping into another, shall, in consequence of any law or regulation therein, be discharged from such service or labor, but shall be delivered up on claim of the party to whom such service or labor may be due.[9]

Section 3

1. New States may be admitted by the Congress into this Union; but no new State shall be formed or erected within the jurisdiction of any other State, nor any State be formed by the junction of two or more States, or parts of States, without the consent of the legislatures of the States concerned as well as of the Congress.
2. The Congress shall have power to dispose of and make all needful rules and regulations respecting the territory or other property belonging to the United States; and nothing in this Constitution shall be so construed as to prejudice any claims of the United States, or of any particular State.

---

[8]See the Fourteenth Amendment, Sec. 1.
[9]See the Thirteenth Amendment.

Section 4

The United States shall guarantee to every State in this Union a republican form of government, and shall protect each of them against invasion; and on application of the legislature, or of the executive (when the legislature cannot be convened) against domestic violence.

Article V

The Congress, whenever two thirds of both Houses shall deem it necessary, shall propose amendments to this Constitution, or, on the application of the legislatures of two thirds of the several States, shall call a convention for proposing amendments, which in either case shall be valid to all intents and purposes, as part of this Constitution, when ratified by the legislatures of three fourths of the several States, or by conventions in three fourths thereof, as the one or the other mode of ratification may be proposed by the Congress; Provided that no amendment which may be made prior to the year one thousand eight hundred and eight shall in any manner affect the first and fourth clauses in the ninth section of the first article; and that no State, without its consent, shall be deprived of its equal suffrage in the Senate.

Article VI

1. All debts contracted and engagements entered into, before the adoption of this Constitution, shall be as valid against the United States under this Constitution, as under the Confederation.[10]
2. This Constitution, and the laws of the United States which shall be made in pursuance thereof; and all treaties made, or which shall be made, under the authority of the United States, shall be the supreme law of the land; and the judges in every State shall be bound thereby, any thing in the Constitution or laws of any State to the contrary notwithstanding.
3. The senators and representatives before mentioned, and the members of the several State legislatures, and all executive and judicial officers, both of the United States and of the several States, shall be bound by oath or affirmation to support this Constitution; but no religious test shall ever be required as a qualification to any office or public trust under the United States.

Article VII

The ratification of the conventions of nine States shall be sufficient for the establishment of this Constitution between the States so ratifying the same.

Done in Convention by the unanimous consent of the States present the seventeenth day of September in the year of our Lord one thousand seven hundred and eighty-seven, and of the independence of the United States of America the twelfth. In witness whereof we have hereunto subscribed our names.

---

[10]See the Fourteenth Amendment, Sec. 4.

[Signatories' names omitted]

Articles in addition to, and amendment of, the Constitution of the United States of America, proposed by Congress, and ratified by the legislatures of the several States, pursuant to the fifth article of the original Constitution.

Amendment I

[First ten amendments ratified December 15, 1791]

Congress shall make no law respecting an establishment of religion, or prohibiting the free exercise thereof; or abridging the freedom of speech, or of the press; or the right of the people peaceably to assemble, and to petition the government for a redress of grievances.

Amendment II

A well-regulated militia, being necessary to the security of a free State, the right of the people to keep and bear arms, shall not be infringed.

Amendment III

No soldier shall, in time of peace be quartered in any house, without the consent of the owner, nor in time of war, but in a manner to be prescribed by law.

Amendment IV

The right of the people to be secure in their persons, houses, papers, and effects, against unreasonable searches and seizures, shall not be violated, and no warrants shall issue, but upon probable cause, supported by oath or affirmation, and particularly describing the place to be searched, and the persons or things to be seized.

Amendment V

No person shall be held to answer for a capital or otherwise infamous crime, unless on a presentment or indictment of a grand jury, except in cases arising in the land or naval forces, or in the militia, when in actual service in time of war or public danger; nor shall any person be subject for the same offense to be twice put in jeopardy of life or limb; nor shall be compelled in any criminal case to be a witness against himself, nor be deprived of life, liberty, or property, without due process of law; nor shall private property be taken for public use, without just compensation.

Amendment VI

In all criminal prosecutions, the accused shall enjoy the right to a speedy and public trial, by an impartial jury of the State and district wherein the crime shall have been committed, which district shall have been previously ascertained by law, and to be informed of the nature and cause of the accusation; to be confronted with the witnesses against him; to have compulsory process for obtaining witnesses in his favor, and to have the assistance of counsel for his defense.

Amendment VII

In suits at common law, where the value in controversy shall exceed twenty dollars, the right of trial by jury shall be preserved, and no fact tried by a jury shall be otherwise reexamined in any court of the United States, than according to the rules of the common law.

Amendment VIII

Excessive bail shall not be required, nor excessive fines imposed, nor cruel and unusual punishments inflicted.

Amendment IX

The enumeration in the Constitution of certain rights shall not be construed to deny or disparage others retained by the people.

Amendment X

The powers not delegated to the United States by the Constitution, nor prohibited by it to the States, are reserved to the States respectively, or to the people.

Amendment XI [January 8, 1798]

The judicial power of the United States shall not be construed to extend to any suit in law or equity, commended or prosecuted against one of the United States by citizens of another State, or by citizens or subjects of any foreign State.

Amendment XII [September 25, 1804]

The electors shall meet in their respective States, and vote by ballot for President and Vice President, one of whom, at least, shall not be an inhabitant of the same State with themselves; they shall name in their ballots the person voted for as President, and in distinct ballots, the person voted for as Vice President, and they shall make distinct lists of all persons voted for as President and of all persons voted for as Vice President, and of the number of votes for each, which lists they shall sign and certify, and transmit sealed to the seat of the government of the United States, directed to the President of the Senate— The President of the Senate shall, in the presence of the Senate and House of Representatives, open all the certificates and the votes shall then be counted—The person having the greatest number of votes for President, shall be the President, if such number be a majority of the whole number of electors appointed; and if no person have such majority, then from the persons having the highest numbers not exceeding three on the list of those voted for as President, the House of Representatives shall choose immediately, by ballot, the President. But in choosing the President, the votes shall be taken by States, the representation from each State having one vote; a quorum for this purpose shall consist of a member or members from two thirds of the States, and a majority of all the States shall be necessary to a choice. And if the House of

Representatives shall not choose a President whenever the right of choice shall devolve upon them, before the fourth day of March next following, then the Vice President shall act as President, as in the case of the death or other constitutional disability of the President. The person having the greatest number of votes as Vice President shall be the Vice President, if such number be a majority of the whole number of electors appointed, and if no person have a majority, then from the two highest numbers on the list, the Senate shall choose the Vice President; a quorum for the purpose shall consist of two thirds of the whole number of Senators, and a majority of the whole number shall be necessary to a choice. But no person constitutionally ineligible to the office of President shall be eligible to that of Vice President of the United States.

Amendment XIII [December 18, 1865]

Section 1

Neither slavery nor involuntary servitude, except as a punishment for crime whereof the party shall have been duly convicted, shall exist within the United States, or any place subject to their jurisdiction.

Section 2

Congress shall have power to enforce this article by appropriate legislation.

Amendment XIV [July 28, 1868]

Section 1

All persons born or naturalized in the United States, and subject to the jurisdiction thereof, are citizens of the United States and of the State wherein they reside. No State shall make or enforce any law which shall abridge the privileges or immunities of citizens of the United States; nor shall any State deprive any person of life, liberty, or property, without due process of law; nor deny to any person within its jurisdiction the equal protection of the laws.

Section 2

Representatives shall be apportioned among the several States according to their respective numbers, counting the whole number of persons in each State, excluding Indians not taxed. But when the right to vote at any election for the choice of electors for President and Vice President of the United States, representatives in Congress, the executive and judicial officers of a State, or the members of the legislature thereof, is denied to any of the male inhabitants of such State, being twenty-one years of age, and citizens of the United States, or in any way abridged, except for participating in rebellion, or other crime, the basis of representation there shall be reduced in the proportion which the number of such male citizens shall bear to the whole number of male citizens twenty-one years of age in such State.

Section 3

No person shall be a senator or representative in Congress, or elector of President and Vice President, or hold any office, civil or military, under the

United States, or under any State, who having previously taken an oath, as a member of Congress, or as an officer of the United States, or as a member of any State legislature, or as an executive or judicial officer of any State, to support the Constitution of the United States, shall have engaged in insurrection or rebellion against the same, or given aid or comfort to the enemies thereof. But Congress may by a vote of two thirds of each House, remove such disability.

Section 4

The validity of the public debt of the United States, authorized by law, including debts incurred for payment of pensions and bounties for services in suppressing insurrection or rebellion; shall not be questioned. But neither the United States nor any State shall assume or pay any debt or obligation incurred in aid of insurrection or rebellion against the United States, or any claim for the loss or emancipation of any slave; but all such debts, obligations, and claims shall be held illegal and void.

Section 5

The Congress shall have the power to enforce, by appropriate legislation, the provisions of this article.

Amendment XV [March 30, 1870]

Section 1

The right of citizens of the United States to vote shall not be denied or abridged by the United States or by any State on account of race, color, or previous condition of servitude.

Section 2

The Congress shall have power to enforce this article by appropriate legislation.

Amendment XVI [February 25, 1913]

The Congress shall have power to lay and collect taxes on incomes, from whatever source derived, without apportionment among the several States, and without regard to any census or enumeration.

Amendment XVII [May 31, 1913]

The Senate of the United States shall be composed of two senators from each State, elected by the people thereof, for six years; and each senator shall have one vote. The electors in each State shall have the qualifications requisite for electors of the most numerous branch of the State legislature.

When vacancies happen in the representation of any State in the Senate, the executive authority of such State shall issue writs of election to fill such vacancies: Provided, That the legislature of any State may empower the executive thereof to make temporary appointments until the people fill the vacancies by election as the legislature may direct.

This amendment shall not be so construed as to affect the election or term of any senator chosen before it becomes valid as part of the Constitution.

Amendment XVIII[11] [January 29, 1919]

After one year from the ratification of this article, the manufacture, sale, or transportation of intoxicating liquors within, the importation thereof into, or the exportation thereof from the United States and all territory subject to the jurisdiction thereof for beverage purposes is thereby prohibited.

The Congress and the several States shall have concurrent power to enforce this article by appropriate legislation.

This article shall be inoperative unless it shall have been ratified as an amendment to the Constitution by the legislatures of the several States, as provided in the constitution, within seven years from the date of the submission hereof to the States by Congress.

Amendment XIX [August 26, 1920]

The right of citizens of the United States to vote shall not be denied or abridged by the United States or by any State on account of sex.

Congress shall have the power to enforce this article by appropriate legislation.

Amendment XX [January 23, 1933]

Section 1

The terms of the President and Vice President shall end at noon on the 20th day of January and the terms of Senators and Representatives at noon on the 3d day of January, of the years in which such terms would have ended if this article had not been ratified; and the terms of their successors shall then begin.

Section 2

The Congress shall assemble at least once in every year, and such meeting shall begin at noon on the 3d day of January, unless they shall by law appoint a different day.

Section 3

If, at the time fixed for the beginning of the term of President, the President-elect shall have died, the Vice President-elect shall become President. If a President shall not have been chosen before the time fixed for the beginning of his term, or if the President-elect shall have failed to qualify, then the Vice President-elect shall act as President until a President shall have qualified; and the Congress may by law provide for the case wherein neither a President-elect nor a Vice President-elect shall have qualified, declaring who shall then act as President, or the manner in which one who is to act shall be selected, and such person shall act accordingly until a President or Vice President shall have qualified.

---

[11]Repealed by the Twenty-first Amendment.

Section 4

The Congress may by law provide for the case of the death of any of the persons from whom, the House of Representatives may choose a President whenever the right of choice shall have devolved upon them, and for the case of the death of any of the persons from whom the Senate may choose a Vice President whenever the right of choice shall have devolved upon them.

Section 5

Sections 1 and 2 shall take effect on the 15th day of October following the ratification of this article.

Section 6

This article shall be inoperative unless it shall have been ratified as an amendment to the Constitution by the legislatures of three-fourths of the several States within seven years from the date of its submission.

Amendment XXI [December 5, 1933]

Section 1

The Eighteenth Article of amendment to the Constitution of the United States is hereby repealed.

Section 2

The transportation or importation into any State, Territory, or possession of the United States for delivery or use therein of intoxicating liquors in violation of the laws thereof, is hereby prohibited.

Section 3

This article shall be inoperative unless it shall have been ratified as an amendment to the Constitution by conventions in the several States, as provided in the Constitution, within seven years from the date of the submission thereof to the States by the Congress.

Amendment XXII [March 1, 1951]

No person shall be elected to the office of the President more than twice, and no person who has held the office of President, or acted as President, for more than two years of a term to which some other person was elected President shall be elected to the office of the President more than once.

But this article shall not apply to any person holding the office of President when this article was proposed by the Congress, and shall not prevent any person who may be holding the office of President, or acting as President, during the term within which this article becomes operative from holding the office of President or acting as President during the remainder of such term.

This article shall be inoperative unless it shall have been ratified as an amendment to the Constitution by the legislatures of three-fourths of the several States within seven years from the date of its submission to the States by the Congress.

Amendment XXIII [March 29, 1961]

Section 1

The District constituting the seat of Government of the United States shall appoint in such manner as the Congress may direct.

A number of electors of President and Vice President equal to the whole number of Senators and Representa-tives in Congress to which the District would be entitled if it were a State, but in no event more than the least populous State; they shall be in addition to those appointed by the States, but they shall be considered, for the purposes of the election of President and Vice President, to be electors appointed by a State; and they shall meet in the District and perform such duties as provided by the twelfth article of amendment.

Section 2

The Congress shall have power to enforce this article by appropriate legislation.

Amendment XXIV [January 23, 1964]

Section 1

The right of citizens of the United States to vote in any primary or other election for President or Vice President, for electors for President or Vice President, or for Senator or Representative in Congress, shall not be denied or abridged by the United States or any State by reason of failure to pay any poll tax or other tax.

Section 2

The Congress shall have power to enforce this article by appropriate legislation.

Amendment XXV [February 10, 1967]

Section 1

In case of the removal of the President from office or of his death or resignation, the Vice President shall become President.

Section 2

Whenever there is a vacancy in the office of the Vice President, the President shall nominate a Vice President who shall take office upon confirmation by a majority of both Houses of Congress.

Section 3

Whenever the President transmits to the President pro tempore of the Senate and the Speaker of the House of Representatives his written declaration that he is unable to discharge the powers and duties of his office, and until he transmits to them a written declaration to the contrary, such powers and duties shall be discharged by the Vice President as Acting President.

Section 4

Whenever the Vice President and a majority of either the principal officers of the executive departments or of such other body as Congress may by law provide, transmit to the President pro tempore of the Senate and the Speaker of the House of Representatives their written declaration that the President is unable to discharge the powers and duties of his office, the Vice President shall immediately assume the powers and duties of the office as Acting President.

Thereafter, when the President transmits to the President pro tempore of the Senate and the Speaker of the House of Representatives his written declaration that no inability exists, he shall resume the powers and duties of his office unless the Vice President and a majority of either the principal officers of the executive departments or of such other body as Congress may by law provide, transmit within four days to the President pro tempore of the Senate and the Speaker of the House of Representatives their written declaration that the President is unable to discharge the powers and duties of his office. Thereupon Congress shall decide the issue, assembling within forty-eight hours for that purpose if not in session. If the Congress, within twenty-one days after receipt of the latter written declaration, or, if Congress is not in session, within twenty-one days after Congress is required to assemble, determines by two-thirds vote of both Houses that the President is unable to discharge the powers and duties of his office, the Vice President shall continue to discharge the same as Acting President; otherwise, the President shall resume the powers and duties of his office.

Amendment XXVI [June 30, 1971]

Section 1

The right of citizens of the United States who are eighteen years of age or older to vote shall not be denied or abridged by the United States or by any State on account of age.

Section 2

The Congress shall have power to enforce this article by appropriate legislation.

Amendment XXVII[12] [May 7, 1992]

No law, varying the compensation for services of the Senators and Representatives, shall take effect until an election of Representatives shall have intervened.

---

[12]James Madison proposed this amendment in 1789 together with the ten amendments that were adopted as the Bill of Rights, but it failed to win ratification at the time. Congress, however, had set no deadline for its ratification, and over the years—particularly in the 1980s and 1990s—many states voted to add it to the Constitution. With the ratification of Michigan in 1992, it passed the threshold of 3/4ths of the states required for adoption, but because the process took more than 200 years, its validity remains in doubt.

Credits

CHAPTER 12   296 Library of Congress, Washington D.C., USA/The Bridgeman Art Library; 297 Courtesy of the Library of Congress; 309 Chicago Historical Society; 313 Courtesy of the Library of Congress.

CHAPTER 13   322 Courtesy of the Library of Congress; 325 The Ohio Historical Society; 330 Getty Images Inc. - Hulton Archive Photos; 336 Courtesy of the Library of Congress; 339 National Archives of Canada.

CHAPTER 14   352 Author's Private Collection; 355 Author's Private Collection; 361 © Donna Mussenden VanDerZee; 369 © Donna Mussenden VanDerZee.

CHAPTER 15   384 Brown Brothers; 389 CORBIS- NY; 393 (c) Carl Van Vechten/Courtesy of the Library of Congress; 400 CORBIS- NY; 401 © Bradley Smith/CORBIS.

CHAPTER 16   409 Courtesy of the Library of Congress; 414 U.S. Air Force; 416 Courtesy of the Library of Congress; 423 CORBIS; 430 Getty Images.

CHAPTER 17   438 © Bettmann/CORBIS All Rights Reserved; 442 AP Wide World Photos; 445 Eddie Adams\AP Wide World Photos; 452 CORBIS- NY; 456 Bruce Roberts\Photo Researchers, Inc.

CHAPTER 18   470 © Bettmann/CORBIS All Rights Reserved; 473 Carl van Vechten/Library of Congress; 478 AP Wide World Photos; 480 CORBIS- NY; 486 Creative Eye/Mira.com

CHAPTER 19   495 Historical Museum of Southern Florida, USA/The Bridgeman Art Library; 497 AP Wide World Photos; 503 CORBIS- NY; 506 AP Wide World Photos; 516 Getty Images Inc. RF.

CHAPTER 20   527 CORBIS- NY; 531 Tito Avilei/AP Wide World Photos; 533 Getty Images Inc. - Hulton Archive Photos; 540 Mark L./CORBIS- NY.

CHAPTER 21   548 Leif Skoogfors/CORBIS- NY; 552 Newscom; 558 Larry Downing/CORBIS- NY; 567 Agence France Presse/Getty Images.

CHAPTER 22   576 JOHN MCCUSKER/Landov Media;580 Gary Miller/Getty Images - WireImage.com; 585 The Mitchell Archives; 587 © Jim Young/Reuters/CORBIS All Rights Reserved.

Index

Page numbers followed by *f* indicate figure; those followed by *m* indicate map; and followed by *t* indicate table.

post-Civil War, 300
in Progressive era, 335, 336–338
"race music," 428
ragtime, 335, 336, 351
rap (hip hop), 527
rhythm and blues, 428–429
rock-and-roll, 451
slave life and, 92, 92f, 94,
    168–169, 168f
sorrow songs, 90
swing era, 400–402
musicians, in African culture, 22
Muslim Arab traders, 18
Muslim Berber warriors, 12
Muslim culture, slavery in, 31–32
Muslims, 8–9. *See also* Islam
African slaves as, 91
beliefs of, 9
in Egypt, 9
scholars and artisans in
    Timbuktu, 13
slave traders, 31
Myrdal, Gunnar, 420–421
The Mystery, 197–198
Myth of the Superwoman, 518

N

NAACP. *See* National Association for
    the Advancement of Colored
    People (NAACP)
NACW. *See* National Association of
    Colored Women (NACW)
Nagin, Ray, 577, 578
Name/naming
for African American identity,
    146–148
of children, slaves, 164, 168
Narrative of the Life and Adventures
    of Henry Bibb, 223
A Narrative of the Proceedings of
    the Black People, During the
    Late Awful Calamity in
    Philadelphia, 139
Nash, Diane, 455, 457, 465, 467
Natchez Indians, African slaves
    and, 86
National Advisory Commission on Civil
    Disorders, 500, 557
National Association for the
    Advancement of Colored People
    (NAACP), 323, 342t–343t, 420t,
    444t, 484t
affirmative action and, 521
Alabama outlawing of, 450
Amenia Conference, 347
Bethune and, 395

black militancy and, 387–390
Briggs v. Elliott, 440
civil rights activism, 418–419, 422,
    423, 424, 436–437, 454, 457
COFO, 467
dominance of, 426–427
establishment of, 334
Harlem and, 340
Hastie and, 412
legal assault, 346
Legal Defense and Education
    Fund, 438
membership, 363–364
Montgomery bus boycott and,
    445, 449
Niagara Movement and, 334–335
Plessy v. Ferguson, 438
Scottsboro campaign and, 381,
    382, 385
Spingarn Medal, 402, 412
and Urban League, 341, 363–364
World War I and, 323
National Association of Colored Women
    (NACW), 320, 322–323, 342t,
    371–372, 394
National Black Feminist Organization
    (NBFO), 519, 532
National Black Political Convention,
    510–512
National Child Protection Act
    of 1993, 545
National Colored Men's Labor
    Convention, 281
National Conference on Black
    Power, 499
National Council of Churches, 522
National Equal Rights League,
    258, 259
National Labor Relations Act. *See*
    Wagner Act
National Negro Committee
    Conference, 334
National Organization for Women
    (NOW), 519
National Rainbow Coalition, 530, 532t
National Recovery Administration
    (NRA), 387
National Security Advisor, 574
National Urban League, 343t, 360
Harlem and, 340–341
NAACP, 363–364
newspaper, 363, 395
National Woman Suffrage
    Association, 269
National Youth Administration (NYA),
    392–393

W